Cite This Volume:

10 USCS §—

★ ★ ★ ★ **UNITED STATES CODE SERVICE** ★ ★ ★

Lawyers Edition

All federal laws of a general and permanent nature arranged in accordance with the section numbering of the United States Code and the supplements thereto.

10 USCS

Armed Forces

§§ 8001 – End; Index

1998

LEXIS® LAW PUBLISHING

701 East Water Street
Charlottesville, VA 22902

Library of Congress Catalog Card Number 72-76254

ISBN 0-327-06352-1

PUBLICATION EDITOR:
Derrick R. Wilborn, J.D.

CONSULTING EDITOR:
Martin M. Heit, J.D.

CONTRIBUTING EDITORS:
Michele D. Ferrara, J.D.
Gary Knapp, J.D.

TECHNICAL EDITOR:
Kathryn D. Lindfors

TECHNICAL SUPPORT STAFF:
Sheri Ashton
Mary Carey
Annapurna Kurup
Julie Lisciandro
Dolores Marlowe
Jennifer Nealon

ABBREVIATIONS

Reporters, Texts, Etc.

A	Atlantic Reporter
A2d	Atlantic Reporter, Second Series
ACMR	Army Court of Military Review
AD	Appellate Division Reports (NY)
AD2d	Appellate Division Reports, Second Series (NY)
AdL2d	Pike and Fischer Administrative Law, Second Series
ADVA	Administrator's Decisions, Veterans' Administration
AFCMR	Air Force Court of Military Review
AFTR	American Federal Tax Reports
AFTR2d	American Federal Tax Reports, Second Series
AGBCA	Department of Agriculture Board of Contract Appeals
Ag Dec	Agriculture Decisions
ALAB	NRC Atomic Safety and Licensing Appeal Board
ALR	American Law Reports
ALR2d	American Law Reports, Second Series
ALR3d	American Law Reports, Third Series
ALR4th	American Law Reports, Fourth Series
ALR5th	American Law Reports, Fifth Series
ALR Fed	American Law Reports, Federal
Am Bankr NS	American Bankruptcy, New Series
ADD	Americans With Disabilities Decisions
AMC	American Maritime Cases
Am Disab	Americans With Disabilities: Practice and Compliance Manual
Am Jur 2d	American Jurisprudence, Second Edition
Am Jur Legal Forms 2d	American Jurisprudence Legal Forms, Second Edition
Am Jur Pl & Pr Forms (Rev ed)	American Jurisprudence Pleading and Practice Forms, Revised Edition
Am Jur Proof of Facts	American Jurisprudence Proof of Facts
Am Jur Proof of Facts 2d	American Jurisprudence Proof of Facts, Second Series

Am Jur Proof of Facts 3d	American Jurisprudence Proof of Facts, Third Series
Am Jur Trials	American Jurisprudence Trials
Am Law Prod Liab 3d	American Law of Products Liability, Third Edition
App DC	United States Court of Appeals for the District of Columbia
Appx	Appendix
ASBCA	Armed Services Board of Contract Appeals
ATF Qtrly Bull	Quarterly Bulletin, Alcohol, Tobacco and Firearms Bureau, U.S. Dept. Treas.
ATR Rul	Ruling of Alcohol, Tobacco and Firearms Bureau, U.S. Dept. Treas.
BAMSL	Bankruptcy Reporter of the Bar Association of Metropolitan St. Louis
BCA	Board of Contract Appeals
BCD	Bankruptcy Court Decisions
Bd Imm App	Board of Immigration Appeals
BIA	Board of Immigration Appeals
Bkr L Ed	Bankruptcy Service, Lawyers Edition
BLR	BRBS Black Lung Reporter
BNA EBC	Employee Benefits Cases
BNA FEP Cas	Fair Employment Practices Cases
BNA IER Cas	Individual Employment Rights Cases
BNA LRRM	Labor Relations Reference Manual
BNA OSHC	Occupational Safety and Health Cases
BNA WH Cas	Wage and Hour Cases
BR	Bankruptcy Reporter
BRBS	Benefits Review Board Service
BTA	Board of Tax Appeals
BTA Mem	Board of Tax Appeals Memorandum Decisions
CA	United States Court of Appeals
CAB Adv Dig	Civil Aeronautics Board Advance Digest
CAD	Customs Appeals Decisions
Cal Rptr	California Reporter
CB	Cumulative Bulletin of the Internal Revenue Service
CBC	Collier Bankruptcy Cases
CBD	Customs Bulletin and Decisions, Customs Service, Department of the Treasury
CCG	Consumer Credit Guide
CCH Bankr L Rptr	Bankruptcy Law Reporter
CCH BCA Dec	Board of Contract Appeals Decisions
CCH CCG	Consumer Credit Guide
CCH Comm Fut L Rep	Commodity Futures Law Reporter
CCH EEOC Dec	Decisions of the Equal Employment Opportunity Commission
CCH EPD	Employment Practice Decisions
CCH Fed Secur L Rep	Federal Securities Law Reporter

Abbreviations

CCH FERC	Federal Energy Regulatory Commission Reports
CCH Lab Cas	Labor Cases
CCH LC	Labor Cases
CCH NLRB	National Labor Relations Board Decisions
CCH OSHD	Occupational Safety and Health Decisions
CCH TCM	Tax Court Memorandum Decisions
CCH Trade Cas	Trade Cases
CCH Trade Reg Rep	Trade Regulation Reports
CCH Unemployment Ins Rep	Unemployment Insurance Reporter
CCPA	Court of Customs and Patent Appeals
CD	Customs Decisions
CDOS	California Daily Opinion Service
CFR	Code of Federal Regulations
CFTC	Commodity Futures Trading Commission
CGCMR	Coast Guard Court of Military Review
CGLB	Coast Guard Law Bulletin
CIT	Court of International Trade
CLI	Commission Licensing Issuance
CMA	Court of Military Appeals
CMR	Court-Martial Reports
COGSA	Carriage of Goods by Sea Act
Comm Fut L Rep	Commodity Futures Law Reporter
Comp Gen	Decisions of the U.S. Comptroller General
Comp Gen Unpub Dec	Unpublished decisions of the U.S. Comptroller General
Comr Pat	Commissioner of Patents and Trademarks
CPD	Customs Penalty Decisions
CPSC Advisory Op No	Consumer Product Safety Commission Advisory Opinion Number
CRD	Customs Rules Decisions
CR L	Criminal Law Reporter
CSD	Customs Service Decisions
Ct Cl	Court of Claims
Cust Bull	Customs Bulletin and Decisions, US Department of Treasury
Cust Ct	Customs Court
Cust & Pat App (Cust)	U.S. Court of Customs and Patent Appeals (Customs)
Cust & Pat App (Pat)	U.S. Court of Customs and Patent Appeals (Patents)
DC	United States District Court
DCAB	Department of Commerce Contract Appeals Board
DCO	Department of Commerce Orders
Dist Col App	District of Columbia Court of Appeals
DOA	Department of Agriculture
DOC	Department of Commerce

DOE	Department of Energy
DOHA	Department of Defense Office of Hearings and Appeals
DOT CAB	Department of Transportation Contract Appeals Board
DPRM	Denial of Petition for Rulemaking, NRC Decision
EBC	Employee Benefits Cases
EBCA	Department of Energy Board of Contract Appeals
ECAB	Employees' Compensation Appeals Board, U.S. Department of Labor
EEOC DEC	Equal Employment Opportunity Commission Decisions
ELR	Environmental Law Reporter
Em Ct App	Emergency Court of Appeals
EMP COORD	Employment Coordinator
ENG BCA	Corps of Engineers Board of Contract Appeals
EPD	Employment Practices Decisions
ERA	Economic Regulatory Administration
ERC	Environmental Reporter Cases
ERISA Op Letters	Employee Retirement Income Security Act Opinion Letters
Ex Or	Executive Order
F	Federal Reporter
F2d	Federal Reporter, Second Series
F3d	Federal Reporter, Third Series
F Cas	Federal Cases
FCC	Federal Communications Commission
FCC2d	Federal Communications Commission Reports, Second Series
FCSC	Foreign Claims Settlement Commission
FCSC 1981 Ann Rpt	FCSC Annual Report for 1981
FCSC Dec & Anno (1968)	FCSC Decisions and Annotations, 1968 edition
FDA	Food and Drug Administration
FDA Dec	Food and Drug Administration Decisions
FEA	Federal Energy Administration
Fed Cl.	Court of Federal Claims Reporter
Fed Evid Rep	Federal Rules of Evidence Service
Fed Proc, L Ed	Federal Procedure, Lawyers Edition
Fed Procedural Forms, L Ed	Federal Procedure Forms, Lawyers Edition
Fed Reg	Federal Register
Fed Rules Evid Serv	Federal Rules of Evidence Service
Fed Rules Serv.	Federal Rules Service
Fed Rules Serv 2d	Federal Rules Service, Second Series
FEP Case	Fair Employment Practice Cases (BNA)
FEPC	Fair Employment Practice Cases
FERC	Federal Energy Regulatory Commission Reports
Fed Secur L Rep	Federal Securities Law Reporter

FHLBB	Federal Home Loan Bank Board
FLRA	Federal Labor Relations Authority
FLRA GCO	Federal Labor Relations Authority, General Counsel Opinions
FLRC	Federal Labor Relations Council
FMC	Federal Maritime Commission
FMSHRC	Federal Mine Safety and Health Review Commission
FOIA	Freedom of Information Act
FPC	Federal Power Commission
FR	Federal Register
FRB	Federal Reserve Bulletin
FRCP	Federal Rules of Civil Procedure
FRCrP	Federal Rules of Criminal Procedure
FRD	Federal Rules Decisions
FRE	Federal Rules of Evidence
FRS	Federal Reserve System
FSIP	Federal Service Impasses Panel
F Supp	Federal Supplement
F Supp 2d	Federal Supplement, Second Series
FTC	Federal Trade Commission
GAO	General Accounting Office
GSBCA	General Services Administration Board of Contract Appeals
HEW	Department of Health, Education and Welfare
HHS	Department of Health and Human Services
HUD	Department of Housing and Urban Development
HUD BCA	Department of Housing and Urban Development Board of Contract Appeals
IBCA	Interior Department Board of Contract Appeals
IBIA	Interior Board of Indian Appeals (Dept. of the Interior)
ICC	Interstate Commerce Commission
ID	Decisions of the Department of the Interior
I & N Dec	Immigration and Naturalization Service Decisions
ILS	Immigration Law Service
INS	Immigration and Naturalization Service
IRB	Internal Revenue Bulletin
IRS	Internal Revenue Service
ITRD	Internal Trade Reporter Decisions
JAG	Judge Advocate General
Jud Pan Mult Lit	Rulings of the Judicial Panel on Multidistrict Litigation
LBCA	Department of Labor Board of Contract Appeals
LC	Labor Cases
LD	Land Decisions
L Ed	Lawyers Edition U.S. Supreme Court Reports

L Ed 2d .... Lawyers Edition U.S. Supreme Court Reports, Second Series
LRRM..................... Labor Relations Reference Manual
MA....................... Maritime Administration
MCC...................... Motor Carrier Cases (decided by ICC)
Mich .... Michigan Reports
Mich App .... Michigan Appeals Reports
Misc .... Miscellaneous Reports (NY)
Misc 2d................... Miscellaneous Reports, Second Series (NY)
MJ........................ Military Justice Reporter
MSB .... Maritime Subsidy Board
MSPB..................... Merit Systems Protection Board
MSPR..................... United States Merit Systems Protection Board Reporter
Mun Ct App Dist Col ...... Municipal Court of Appeals for District of Columbia
NASA BCA .... National Aeronautics and Space Administration Board of Contract Appeals
NCMR.................... Navy Court of Military Review
NE....................... North Eastern Reporter
NE2d..................... North Eastern Reporter, Second Series
NLRB .... Decisions and Orders of the National Labor Relations Board
NLRB Advice Mem Case No .... National Labor Relations Board Advice Memorandum Case Number
NMCMR.................. U.S. Navy—Marine Corps Court of Military Review
NOAA.................... National Oceanic and Atmospheric Administration
NRC .... Nuclear Regulatory Commission
NTSB .... National Transportation Safety Board
NW .... North Western Reporter
NW2d .... North Western Reporter, Second Series
NY....................... New York Reports
NY2d..................... New York Reports, Second Series
NYS .... New York Supplement
NYS2d .... New York Supplement, Second Series
nt........................ note
nts....................... notes
OAG .... Opinions of the Attorney General
OCSLA................... Outer Continental Shelf Lands Act
OFCCP................... Office of Federal Contract Compliance Programs
Op Atty Gen .... Opinions of Attorney General
Op Comp Gen .... Opinions of Comptroller General
ORW..................... Ocean Resources and Wildlife Reporter
OSAHRC .... Occupational Safety and Health Review Commission (Official Reports)
OSHRC .... Occupational Safety and Health Review Commission

P	Pacific Reporter
P2d	Pacific Reporter, Second Series
PBGC Op No	Pension Benefit Guaranty Corporation Opinion Number
PRD	Protest Review Decisions
Proc	Proclamation
PSBCA	Postal Service Board of Contract Appeals
PS Docket	Postal Service Docket
PTE	Prohibited Transaction Exemption Decisions of The Office of Pension and Welfare Benefit Programs, Department of Labor
PUR3d	Public Utilities Reports, Third Series
PUR4th	Public Utilities Reports, Fourth Series
RD	Reappraisement Decision, U. S. Customs Court
RESPA	Real Estate Settlement Procedures Act
Rev Proc	Revenue Procedure
Rev Rul	Revenue Ruling
RIA	Research Institute of America.
RIA Corp Capital Trans Coord	RIA Corporate Capital Transaction Coordinator
RIA Employee Ben Comp Coord	RIA Employee Benefits Compliance Coordinator
RIA Employment Coord	RIA Employee Coordinator
RIA Employ Discrim Coord.	RIA Employment Discrimination Coordinator
RIA Estate Plan & Tax Coord	RIA Estate Planning & Taxation Coordinator
RIA Exec Comp & Tax Coord	RIA Executive Compensation & Taxation Coordinator
RIA Fed Tax Coord 2d	RIA Federal Tax Coordinator 2d
RIA Partnership & S Corp Coord	RIA Partnership & S Corporation Coordinator
RIA Pension Coord	RIA Pension Coordinator
RIA Real Estate Coord	RIA Real Estate Coordinator
RIA Tax Action Coord	RIA Tax Action Coordinator
RIA TC Memo	Tax Court Memorandum Decisions
RICO	RICO Business Disputes Guide
RRRA	Regional Rail Reorganization Act
R.S.	Revised Statutes
RUSCC	Rules of United States Claims Court
S Ct	United States Supreme Court Reporter
SE	South Eastern Reporter
SE2d	South Eastern Reporter, Second Series
SEC	Securities and Exchange Commission, also SEC Docket
So	Southern Reporter
So 2d	Southern Reporter, Second Series
Soc Sec LP	Social Security Law and Practice

Soc Sec & Unemployment Ins Rep.	Social Security and Unemployment Insurance Reporter
Sp Ct RRRA	Special Court, Regional Rail Reorganization Act
SSA	Social Security Administration
SSR	Social Security Rulings
Stat	Statutes at Large
SW	South Western Reporter
SW2d	South Western Reporter, Second Series
TC	United States Tax Court Reports
TCM	Tax Court Memorandum
T Ct	United States Tax Court
TD	Treasury Decisions
TD ATF	Treasury Decisions concerning matters of Alcohol, Tobacco and Firearms Bureau
TIAS	Treaties and International Agreements Series
TMT & App Bd	Trademark Trial and Appeal Board
TNT	Tax Notes Today
UCCRS	Uniform Commercial Code Reporting Service
US	United States Reports
USC	United States Code
USCMA	United States Court of Military Appeals
USCS	United States Code Service
USEPA GCO	United States Environmental Protection Agency, General Counsel Opinions
USEPA RCO	United States Environmental Protection Agency, Regional Counsel Opinions
USEPA NPDES	United States Environmental Protection Agency, National Pollutant Discharge Elimination System
USLW	United States Law Week
USPQ	United States Patents Quarterly
USSG	United States Sentencing Guidelines
UST	United States Treaties and Other International Agreements
USTC	United States Tax Cases
VA CAB	Veterans Administration Contract Appeals Board
VA GCO	Veterans Administration, General Counsel Opinions
Vet Apps	Court of Veterans Appeals Reporter
Vet App R	Rules of Veterans Appeals
WAB	Wage Appeals Board Decision, Dept. of Labor
WGL	Warren Gorham Lamont
WGL Employee Ben Comp Coord	WGL Employee Benefits Compliance Coordinator
WGL Employment Coord	WGL Employee Coordinator
WGL Employ Discrim Coord	WGL Employment Discrimination Coordinator

WH Cases	Wage and Hour Cases
WH2d	Wage and Hour Cases, Second Series
WH Op Letter	Wage and Hour Opinion Letter

Legal Periodicals

ABA J	American Bar Association Journal
AFL Rev	Air Force Law Review
Adelphia LJ	Adelphia Law Journal
Admin LJ	Administrative Law Journal
Admin LJ Am U	Administrative Law Journal of American University
Admin L Rev	Administrative Law Review
Advoc Q	Advocates' Quarterly
AILPA QJ	AILPA Quarterly Journal
Akron L Rev	Akron Law Review
Akron Tax J	Akron Tax Journal
Ala L Rev	Alabama Law Review
Alaska L Rev	Alaska Law Review
Alb L Rev	Albany Law Review
Am Bankr Inst L Rev	American Bankruptcy Institute Law Review
Am Bankr LJ	American Bankruptcy Law Journal
Am Bus LJ	American Business Law Journal
Am Crim L Rev	American Criminal Law Review
Am Indian L Rev	American Indian Law Review
Am J Comp L	American Journal of Comparative Law
Am J Crim L	American Journal of Criminal Law
Am J Fam L	American Journal of Family Law
Am J Int'l L	American Journal of International Law
Am JL & Med	American Journal of Law and Medicine
Am J Tax Pol'y	American Journal of Tax Policy
Am J Trial Advoc	American Journal of Trial Advocacy
Am Soc'y Int'l L Proc	American Society of International Law Proceedings
Am UJ Int'l L & Pol'y	American University Journal of International Law and Policy
Am U L Rev	American University Law Review
Ann Rev Banking L	Annual Review of Banking Law
Antitrust Bull	Antitrust Bulletin
Antitrust LJ	Antitrust Law Journal
Arb J	Arbitration Journal
Ariz J Int'l & Comp L	Arizona Journal of International and Comparative Law
Ariz L Rev	Arizona Law Review
Ariz St LJ	Arizona State Law Journal
Ark L Rev	Arkansas Law Review
Army Law	Army Lawyer
BC Envtl Aff L Rev	Boston College Environmental Affairs Law Review

BC Int'l & Comp L Rev	Boston College International and Comparative Law Review
BC L Rev	Boston College Law Review
BU Int'l LJ	Boston University International Law Journal
BU L Rev	Boston University Law Review
BYU J Pub L	Brigham Young University Journal of Public Law
BYU L Rev	Brigham Young University Law Review
Banking LJ	Banking Law Journal
Banking L Rev	Banking Law Review
Baylor L Rev	Baylor Law Review
Benefits LJ	Benefits Law Journal
Bridgeport L Rev	Bridgeport Law Review
Brook J Int'l L	Brooklyn Journal of International Law
Brook L Rev	Brooklyn Law Review
Buff Envtl LJ	Buffalo Environmental Law Journal
Buff L Rev	Buffalo Law Review
Bus Law	Business Lawyer
Cal Bankr J	California Bankruptcy Journal
Cal Intl Prac	California International Practitioner
Cal L Rev	California Law Review
Cal W Int'l LJ	California Western International Law Journal
Cap U L Rev	Capital University Law Review
Cardozo Arts & Ent LJ	Cardozo Arts and Entertainment Law Journal
Cardozo L Rev	Cardozo Law Review
Case W Res J Int'l L	Case Western Reserve Journal of International Law
Case W Res L Rev	Case Western Reserve Law Review
Cath U L Rev	Catholic University Law Review
Chi-Kent L Rev	Chicago-Kent Law Review
Clearinghouse Rev	Clearinghouse Review
Clev St L Rev	Cleveland State Law Review
Colo J Int'l Envtl L & Pol'y	Colorado Journal of Environmental Law and Policy
Colum Bus L Rev	Columbia Business Law Review
Colum J Envtl L	Columbia Journal of Environmental Law
Colum JL & Soc Probs	Columbia Journal of Law and Social Problems
Colum J Transnat'l L	Columbia Journal of Transnational Law
Colum L Rev	Columbia Law Review
Colum-VLA JL & Arts	Columbia-VLA Journal of Law and the Arts
Com LJ	Commercial Law Journal
Comm & L	Communications and the Law
Comp Lab LJ	Comparative Labor Law Journal
Computer LJ	Computer Law Journal
Computer Law	Computer Lawyer
Conn J Int'l L	Connecticut Journal of International Law
Conn L Rev	Connecticut Law Review
Copyright L Symp	Copyright Law Symposium

Copyright World	Copyright World
Cornell Int'l LJ	Cornell International Law Journal
Cornell JL & Pub Pol'y	Cornell Journal of Law and Public Policy
Cornell L Rev	Cornell Law Review
Corp & Bus LJ	Corporate and Business Law Journal
Creighton L Rev	Creighton Law Review
Crim Just J	Criminal Justice Journal
Crim L Bull	Criminal Law Bulletin
Crim LJ	Criminal Law Journal
Crim LQ	Criminal Law Quarterly
Crim L Rev	Criminal Law Review
Cumb L Rev	Cumberland Law Review
Current Legal Probs	Current Legal Problems
Def Couns J	Defense Counsel Journal
Denning LJ	Denning Law Journal
Denver J Int'l L & Pol'y	Denver Journal of International Law and Policy
Denv U L Rev	Denver University Law Review
DePaul Bus LJ	DePaul Business Law Journal
DePaul L Rev	DePaul Law Review
Det CL Rev	Detroit College of Law Review
Dick J Int'l L	Dickinson Journal of International Law
Dick L Rev	Dickinson Law Review
Drake L Rev	Drake Law Review
Duke J Comp & Int'l L	Duke Journal of Comparative and International Law
Duq L Rev	Duquesne Law Review
Emory Int'l L Rev	Emory International Law Review
Emory LJ	Emory Law Journal
Empl Rel LJ	Employee Relations Law Journal
Envtl & Plan LJ	Environmental and Planning Law Journal
Envtl Claims J	Environmental Claims Journal
Envtl L	Environmental Law
Fed B News & J	Federal Bar News and Journal
Fed Comm LJ	Federal Communications Law Journal
Fla J Int'l L	Florida Journal of International Law
Fla L Rev	Florida Law Review
Fla St L Rev	Florida State University Law Review
Food Drug LJ	Food and Drug Law Journal
Fordham Intell Prop Media & Ent LJ	Fordham Intellectual Property, Media & Entertainment Law Journal
Fordham Int'l LJ	Fordham International Law Journal
Fordham L Rev	Fordham Law Review
Ga J Int & Comp L	Georgia Journal of International and Comparative Law
Ga L Rev	Georgia Law Review
Ga St U L Rev	Georgia State University Law Review
Geo Immigr LJ	Georgetown Immigration Law Journal

Geo LJ	Georgetown Law Journal
Geo Mason U L Rev	George Mason University Law Review
Geo Wash L Rev	George Washington Law Review
Glendale L Rev	Glendale Law Review
Golden Gate U L Rev	Golden Gate University Law Review
Gonz L Rev	Gonzaga Law Review
Hamline J Pub L & Pol'y	Hamline Journal of Law and Public Policy
Hamline L Rev	Hamline Law Review
Harv CR-CL L Rev	Harvard Civil Rights and Civil Liberties Law Review
Harv Envtl L Rev	Harvard Environmental Law Review
Harv Int'l LJ	Harvard International Law Journal
Harv JL & Pub Pol'y	Harvard Journal of Law and Public Policy
Harv JL & Tech	Harvard Journal of Law and Technology
Harv J Legis	Harvard Journal on Legislation
Harv L Rev	Harvard Law Review
Hastings Comm & Ent LJ	Hastings Communications and Entertainment Law Journal
Hastings Const LQ	Hastings Constitutional Law Quarterly
Hastings Int'l & Comp L Rev	Hastings International and Comparative Law Review
Hastings LJ	Hastings Law Journal
High Tech LJ	High Technology Law Journal
Hofstra L Rev	Hofstra Law Review
Hofstra Lab LJ	Hofstra Labor Law Journal
Hous J Int'l L	Houston Journal of International Law
Hous L Rev	Houston Law Review
How LJ	Howard Law Journal
Idaho L Rev	Idaho Law Review
ILSA J Int'l L	ILSA Journal of International Law
Ind Int'l & Comp L Rev	Indiana International and Comparative Law Review
Ind L Rev	Indiana Law Review
Ind Rel LJ	Industrial Relations Law Journal
Int'l & Comp LQ	International and Comparative Law Quarterly
Int'l Law	International Lawyer
Iowa L Rev	Iowa Law Review
J Bankr L & Prac	Journal of Bankruptcy Law and Practice
J Copyright Soc'y USA	Journal of the Copyright Society of the USA
J Corp Law	Journal of Corporate Law
J Corp Tax'n	Journal of Corporate Taxation
J Energy & Nat Resources L	Journal of Energy and Natural Resources Law
J Energy Nat Resources and Envtl L	Journal of Energy, Natural Resources and Environmental Law
J Envtl L	Journal of Environmental Law
J Envtl L & Litig	Journal of Environmental Law and Litigation

J Health & Hosp L	Journal of Hospital and Health Law
JL & Com	Journal of Law and Commerce
J Mar L & Com	Journal of Maritime Law and Commerce
J Nat Resources & Envtl L	Journal of Natural Resources and Environmental Law
J Pat & Trademark Off Soc'y	Journal of Patent and Trademark Office Society
J Real Est Tax'n	Journal of Real Estate Taxation
J S Corp Tax'n	Journal of S Corporation Taxation
J Tax'n	Journal of Taxation
J Transp L Logist & Pol'y	Journal of Transportation Law, Logistics and Policy
La L Rev	Louisiana Law Review
Lab LJ	Labor Law Journal
Lab Law	Labor Lawyer
Land & Water L Rev	Land and Water Law Review
Law & Contemp Probs	Law and Contemporary Problems
Litig	Litigation
Loy LA Ent LJ	Loyola of Los Angeles Entertainment Law Journal
Loy LA Int'l & Comp LJ	Loyola of Los Angeles International and Comparative Law Journal
Loy LA L Rev	Loyola of Los Angeles Law Review
Loy L Rev	Loyola Law Review
Lo U Chi LJ	Loyola University Chicago Law Journal
Marq L Rev	Marquette Law Review
Mass L Rev	Massachusetts Law Review
Mass LQ	Massachusetts Law Quarterly
Md J Int'l L & Trade	Maryland Journal of International Law and Trade
Md L Rev	Maryland Law Review
Me L Rev	Maine Law Review
Mem St U L Rev	Memphis State University Law review
Mercer L Rev	Mercer Law Review
Mich J Int'l L	Michigan Journal of International Law
Mich L Rev	Michigan Law Review
Mil L Rev	Military Law Review
Minn L Rev	Minnesota Law Review
Miss C L Rev	Mississippi College Law Review
Mo L Rev	Missouri Law Review
Mont L Rev	Montana Law Review
NC Cent LJ	North Carolina Central Law Journal
NC J Int'l L & Com Reg	North Carolina Journal of International Law and Commercial Regulation
NC L Rev	North Carolina Law Review
ND L Rev	North Dakota Law Review
N Ill U L Rev	Northern Illinois University Law Review
N Ky L Rev	Northern Kentucky Law Review

NM L Rev	New Mexico Law Review
NY Int'l L Rev	New York International Law Review
NYL Sch J Int'l & Comp L	New York Law School Journal of International and Comparative Law
NYL Sch L Rev	New York Law School Law Review
NYU Envtl LJ	New York University Environmental Law Journal
NYU J Int'l L & Pol	New York University Journal of International Law and Politics
NYU L Rev	New York University Law Review
Nat Resources & Envt	Natural Resources and Environment
Nat Resources J	Natural Resources Journal
Nav L Rev	Naval Law Review
Neb L Rev	Nebraska Law Review
New Eng L Rev	New England Law Review
Notre Dame L Rev	Notre Dame Law Review
Nova L Rev	Nova Law Review
Nw J Int'l L & Bus	Northwestern Journal of International Law and Business
Nw U L Rev	Northwestern University Law Review
Ohio NU L Rev	Ohio Northern University Law Review
Ohio St LJ	Ohio State Law Journal
Oil & Gas Tax Q	Oil and Gas Tax Quarterly
Okla City U L Rev	Oklahoma City University Law Review
Okla L Rev	Oklahoma Law Review
Or L Rev	Oregon Law Review
Pac LJ	Pacific Law Journal
Pace Envtl L Rev	Pace Environmental Law Review
Pace Int'l L Rev	Pace International Law Review
Pace L Rev	Pace Law Review
Pat World	Patent World
Pepp L Rev	Pepperdine Law Review
Prac Law	Practical Lawyer
Prac Litig	Practical Litigator
Prac Real Est Law	Practical Real Estate Lawyer
Prac Tax Law	Practical Tax Lawyer
Pub Cont LJ	Public Contract Law Journal
Pub Land L Rev	Public Land Law Review
Real Prop Prob & Tr J	Real Property, Probate and Trust Journal
Rev Litig	Review of Litigation
Rutgers Computer & Tech LJ	Rutgers Computer and Technology Law Journal
Rutgers LJ	Rutgers Law Journal
Rutgers L Rev	Rutgers Law Review
SC L Rev	South Carolina Law Review
S Cal L Rev	Southern California Law Review
SD L Rev	South Dakota Law Review
S Ill U L Rev	Southern Illinois University Law Review
S Tex L Rev	South Texas Law Review

SU L Rev	Southern University Law Review
San Diego L Rev	San Diego Law Review
Santa Clara Computer & High Tech LJ	Santa Clara Computer and High Technology Law Journal
Santa Clara L Rev	Santa Clara Law Review
Sec Reg LJ	Securities Regulation Law Journal
Seton Hall Const LJ	Seton Hall Constitutional Law Journal
Seton Hall L Rev	Seton Hall Law Review
SMU L Rev	SMU Law Review
Software LJ	Software Law Journal
St John's L Rev	St John's Law Review
St Louis U LJ	Saint Louis University Law Journal
St Mary's LJ	St Mary's Law Journal
St Thomas L Rev	St Thomas Law Review
Stan Envtl LJ	Stanford Environmental Law Journal
Stan J Int'l L	Stanford Journal of International Law
Stan L Rev	Stanford Law Review
Stetson L Rev	Stetson Law Review
Suffolk Transnat'l LJ	Suffolk Transnational Law Journal
Suffolk U L Rev	Suffolk University Law Review
Sw U L Rev	Southwestern University Law Review
Syracuse J Int'l L & Com	Syracuse Journal of International Law and Commerce
Syracuse L Rev	Syracuse Law Review
Tax L Rev	Tax Law Review
Temple Envtl L & Tech J	Temple Environmental Law and Technology Journal
Temple L Rev	Temple Law Review
Tenn L Rev	Tennessee Law Review
Tex Intell Prop LJ	Texas Intellectual Property Law Journal
Tex Int'l LJ	Texas International Law Journal
Tex L Rev	Texas Law Review
Tex Tech L Rev	Texas Tech Law Review
Thomas M Cooley L Rev	Thomas M Cooley Law Review
Tort & Ins LJ	Torts and Insurance Law Journal
Touro L Rev	Touro Law Review
Trademark Rep	Trademark Reporter
Trademark World	Trademark World
Transp LJ	Transportation Law Journal
Trans Prac J	Transportation Practitioners Journal
Tul Envtl LJ	Tulane Environmental Law Journal
Tul L Rev	Tulane Law Review
Tul Mar LJ	Tulane Maritime Law Journal
Tulsa LJ	Tulsa Law Journal
U Ark LJ	University of Arkansas Law Journal
U Balt J Envtl L	University of Baltimore Journal of Environmental Law

U Balt L Rev	University of Baltimore Law Review
UC Davis L Rev	UC Davis Law Review
U Chi L Rev	University of Chicago Law Review
U Cin L Rev	University of Cincinnati Law Review
U Colo L Rev	University of Colorado Law Review
U Dayton L Rev	University of Dayton Law Review
U Det Mercy L Rev	University of Detroit Mercy Law Review
U Fla JL & Pub Pol'y	University of Florida Journal of Law and Public Policy
U Haw L Rev	University of Hawaii Law Review
U Ill L Rev	University of Illinois Law Review
U Kan L Rev	University of Kansas Law Review
U Miami L Rev	University of Miami Law Review
U Pa L Rev	University of Pennsylvania Law Review
U Pitt L Rev.	University of Pittsburgh Law Review
U Puget Sound L Rev	University of Puget Sound Law Review
U Rich L Rev	University of Richmond Law Review
USF L Rev.	University of San Francisco Law Review
USF Mar LJ.	University of San Francisco Maritime Law Journal
US-Mex LJ.	United States-Mexico Law Journal
U Tol L Rev	University of Toledo Law Review
U West LA L Rev	University of West Los Angeles Law Review
UCLA J Envtl L & Pol'y	UCLA Journal of Environmental Law and Policy
UCLA L Rev	UCLA Law Review
UCLA Pac Basin LJ	UCLA Pacific Basin Law Journal
Utah L Rev	Utah Law Review
Va Envtl LJ	Virginia Environmental Law Journal
Va J Int'l L	Virginia Journal of International Law
Va L Rev	Virginia Law Review
Va Tax Rev	Virginia Tax Review
Val U L Rev.	Valparaiso University Law Review
Vand J Transnat'l L	Vanderbilt Journal of Transnational Law
Vand L Rev	Vanderbilt Law Review
Vill Envtl LJ	Villanova Environmental Law Journal
Vill L Rev	Villanova Law Review
Vt L Rev.	Vermont Law Review
W New Eng L Rev	Western New England Law Review
W St U L Rev	Western State University Law Review
W Va L Rev.	West Virginia Law Review
Wake Forest L Rev	Wake Forest Law Review
Wash & Lee L Rev.	Washington and Lee Law Review
Wash L Rev.	Washington Law Review
Wash U LQ	Washington University Law Quarterly
Washburn LJ.	Washburn Law Journal
Wayne L Rev	Wayne Law Review
Whittier L Rev	Whittier Law Review
Widener J Pub L	Widener Journal of Public Law

Wis Int'l LJ	Wisconsin International Law Journal
Wis L Rev	Wisconsin Law Review
Wm & Mary L Rev	William & Mary Law Review
Wm Mitchell L Rev	William Mitchell Law Review
Yale J Int'l L	Yale Journal of International Law
Yale Law & Pol'y Rev	Yale Law and Policy Review
Yale LJ	Yale Law Journal

Auto-Cite®: Cases and annotations referred to herein can be further researched through the Auto-Cite® computer-assisted research service. Use Auto-Cite to check citations for form, parallel references, prior and later history, and annotation references.

TABLE OF CONTENTS

TITLE 10-ARMED FORCES

[Chapters 801 through 1805 are contained in this volume.]

SUBTITLE I-GENERAL MILITARY LAW

Part I-Organization and General Military Powers

Part II-Personnel

PART III-Training and Education

Table of Contents

SUBTITLE B-ARMY

PART I-Organization

PART II-Personnel

PART III-Training

PART IV-Service, Supply, and Procurement

SUBTITLE C-NAVY AND MARINE CORPS

PART I-Organization

PART II-Personnel

PART III-Training

PART IV-Service, Supply, and Procurement

Table of Contents

SUBTITLE E-RESERVE COMPONENTS

PART I-Organization and Administration

PART II-Personnel Generally

PART III-Promotion and Retention of Officers on the Reserve Active-status List

PART IV-Training for Reserve Components and Educational Assistance Programs

TABLE OF CONTENTS

PART V-Service, Supply, and Procurement

THE CODE OF THE LAWS

OF THE

UNITED STATES OF AMERICA

TITLE 10 — ARMED FORCES

SUBTITLE D. AIR FORCE

PART I. ORGANIZATION

PART II. PERSONNEL

PART III. TRAINING

PART IV. SERVICE, SUPPLY, AND PROCUREMENT

HISTORY; ANCILLARY LAWS AND DIRECTIVES

Amendments:

1958. Act Sept. 2, 1958, P. L. 85-861, § 1(93), 72 Stat. 1538, amended the analysis of this subtitle in Chapter 863, by substituting ''8841'' for ''[No present sections]''.

1960. Act July 12, 1960, P. L. 86-616, §§ 7(b), 8(b), 74 Stat. 393, 395, amended the analysis of this subtitle in Chapter 859 by substituting ''Substandard Performance of Duty'' for ''Failure to Meet Standards''; and added Chapter 860.

1964. Act Oct. 13, 1964, P. L. 88-647, Title III, § 301(27), 78 Stat. 1073, amended the analysis of this subtitle by deleting Chapter 905, which read: ''905. Air Force Reserve Officers' Training Corps . . . . . 9381''.

1968. Act Jan. 2, 1968, P. L. 90-235, § 8(6), 81 Stat. 764, amended the analysis of this subtitle by deleting Chapter 847, which read: ''847. The Uniform . . . . . 8611''.

Act July 5, 1968, P. L. 90-377, § 5, 82 Stat. 288, amended the analysis of this subtitle by deleting Chapter 851, which read: ''851. United States Disciplinary Barracks . . . . . 8662''.

1980. Act Dec. 12, 1980, P.L. 96-513, Title V, Part B, § 514(1), 94 Stat. 2935 (effective upon enactment on 12/12/80, as provided by § 701(b)(3) of such Act, which appears as 10 USCS § 101 note), amended the analysis of this Subtitle in Chapter 803 by substituting ''8010'' for ''8011''.

Act Dec. 12, 1980, P.L. 96-513, Title V, Part A, § 504(1), 94 Stat. 2915 (effective 9/15/81, as provided by § 701(a) of such Act, which appears as 10 USCS § 101 note), amended the analysis of this subtitle by deleting chapters 859, 860, and 865, which read: ''859. Separation from Regular Air

Force for Substandard Performance of Duty . . . . . 8781'', ''860. Separation from Regular Air Force for Moral or Professional Dereliction or in Interests of National Security . . . . . 8791'', and ''865. Retirement for Age . . . . . 8881''.

1987. Act April 21, 1987, P. L. 100-26, § 7(j)(10)(B), 101 Stat. 283, in the item relating to chapter 803, substituted ''8011'' for ''8010''.

1993. Act Nov. 30, 1993, P. L. 103-160, Div A, Title VIII, Subtitle C, § 828(c)(8)(B) 107 Stat. 1715, amended the analysis of this subtitle by substituting item 931 for one which read: ''931. Industrial Mobilization, Research, and Development . . . . . 9511''.

Act Nov. 30, 1993, P. L. 103-160, Div A, Title XI, Subtitle H, § 1178(c), 107 Stat. 1769, amended the analysis of this subtitle by adding item 905.

1994. Act Oct. 5, 1994, P. L. 103-337, Div A, Title XVI, Subtitle D, § 1674(a), 108 Stat. 3016 (effective 10/1/96, pursuant to § 1501(f)(2) of Act Feb. 10, 1996, P. L. 104-106, which appears as 10 USCS § 10001 note), amended the analysis of this subtitle by deleting items 837 and 863, which read: ''837. Appointments as Reserve Officers . . . . . 8351'' and ''863. Separation or Transfer to Retired Reserve . . . . . 8841''.

1996. Act Feb. 10, 1996, P. L. 104-106, Div A, Title XV, § 1503(b)(6), 110 Stat. 513, amended the analysis of this subtitle by inserting a comma after ''SUPPLY' in the Part IV heading.

PART I. ORGANIZATION

HISTORY; ANCILLARY LAWS AND DIRECTIVES

Explanatory notes:

Act Sept. 7, 1962, P. L. 87-651, Title II, § 213, 76 Stat. 524, added 10 USCS § 8010 and amended the analysis of Chapter 803 without a corresponding amendment of the analysis of this part.

Amendments:

1980. Act Dec. 12, 1980, P.L. 96-513, Title V, Part B, § 514(1), 94 Stat. 2935 (effective upon enactment on 12/12/80, as provided by § 701(b)(3) of such Act, which appears as 10 USCS § 101 note), amended the analysis of this part in item 803 by substituting ''8010'' for ''8011''.

1987. Act April 21, 1987, P. L. 100-26, § 7(j)(10)(B), 101 Stat. 283, in the item relating to chapter 803, substituted ''8011'' for ''8010''.

CHAPTER 801. DEFINITIONS

[No present sections]

[§§ 8001–8009. Reserved]

HISTORY; ANCILLARY LAWS AND DIRECTIVES

Explanatory notes:

No laws are presently classified to these sections which are editorially designated as ''Reserved'' for future legislation. For laws which may be classified to these sections in the future, see the Supplement.

CHAPTER 803. DEPARTMENT OF THE AIR FORCE

HISTORY; ANCILLARY LAWS AND DIRECTIVES

Amendments:

1958. Act Sept. 2, 1958, P. L. 85-861, § 1(154)(B), 72 Stat. 1513, amended the analysis of this chapter by adding item 8018.

1962. Act Sept. 7, 1962, P. L. 87-651, Title II, § 213(b), 76 Stat. 524, amended the analysis of this chapter by adding item 8010.

1964. Act Aug. 14, 1964, P.L. 88-426, Title III, §§ 305(40)(B), 306(j)(8), 78 Stat. 427, 432, amended the analysis of this chapter by deleting ''; compensation'' from item 8012, and by deleting item 8018, which read ''8018. Compensation of General Counsel''.

1967. Act Dec. 1, 1967, P. L. 90-168, § 2(20), 81 Stat. 525, amended the analysis of this chapter by adding item 8019.

1986. Act Oct. 1, 1986, P. L. 99-433, Title V, Part C, § 521(b), 100 Stat. 1060, substituted this analysis for one which read:

''8010. Organization
''8011. Department of the Air Force: seal
''8012. Secretary of the Air Force: powers and duties; delegation by
''8013. Under Secretary of the Air Force; Assistant Secretaries of the Air Force
''8014. Comptroller of the Air Force: appointment; functions
''8017. Secretary of the Air Force: successors to duties
''8019. Office of Air Force Reserve: appointment of Chief''.

1988. Act Sept. 29, 1988, P. L. 100-456, Div A, Title VII, Part A, § 702(c)(3), 102 Stat. 1996, effective July 1, 1989, or earlier, but not before Jan. 21, 1989, as may be prescribed by the President in advance by Executive Order, as provided by § 702(e)(2), which appears as 10 USCS § 8016 note, amended the analysis of this chapter by adding item 8022.

[§ 8010. Transferred]

HISTORY; ANCILLARY LAWS AND DIRECTIVES

This section (Act Sept. 7, 1962, P. L. 87-651, Title II, § 213(a), 76 Stat.

524) was transferred by Act Oct. 1, 1986, P. L. 99-433, Title V, Part C, § 521(a)(1) in part, 100 Stat. 1055 and appears as 10 USCS § 8011.

§ 8011. Organization

The Department of the Air Force is separately organized under the Secretary of the Air Force. It operates under the authority, direction, and control of the Secretary of Defense.

(Added Sept. 7, 1962, P. L. 87-651, Title II, § 213(a), 76 Stat. 524; Oct. 1, 1986, P. L. 99-433, Title V, Part C, § 521(a)(1) in part, 100 Stat. 1055.)

HISTORY; ANCILLARY LAWS AND DIRECTIVES

Prior law and revision:

Revised Section	Source (USCS)	Source (Statutes at Large)
8010	5:171a(c)(7) (1st sentence, as applicable to Department of Air Force).	July 26, 1947, ch 343, § 202(c)(7) (1st sentence as applicable to Department of Air Force); added Aug. 6, 1958, Pub. L. 85-599, § 3(a) (1st sentence of 8th para., as applicable to Department of Air Force), 72 Stat. 516.

The word "operates" is substituted for the words "shall function".

Explanatory notes:

A prior §§ 8011 (Act Aug. 10, 1956, ch 1041, § 1, 70A Stat. 488) was transferred by Act Oct. 1, 1986, P. L. 99-433, Title V, Part C, § 521(a)(1) in part, 100 Stat. 1055 to appear as 10 USCS § 8012.

Amendments:

1986. Act Oct. 1, 1986 redesignated this section, formerly 10 USCS § 8010, as 10 USCS § 8011.

RESEARCH GUIDE

Am Jur:

53 Am Jur 2d, Military, and Civil Defense § 21.

§ 8012. Department of the Air Force: seal

The Secretary of the Air Force shall have a seal for the Department of the Air Force. The design of the seal must be approved by the President. Judicial notice shall be taken of the seal.

(Aug. 10, 1956, ch 1041, § 1, 70A Stat. 488; Oct. 1, 1986, P. L. 99-433, Title V, Part C, § 521(a)(1) in part, 100 Stat. 1055.)

HISTORY; ANCILLARY LAWS AND DIRECTIVES

Prior law and revision:

Revised Section	Source (USCS)	Source (Statutes at Large)
8011	5:626(g).	July 26, 1947, ch 343, § 207(g), 61 Stat. 503.

The words ''of office'' are omitted as surplusage. The words ''a design'' are substituted for the words ''such device''.

Explanatory notes:

A prior § 8012 (Act Aug. 10, 1956, ch 1041, § 1, 70A Stat. 488; Sept. 2, 1958, P. L. 85-861, § 1(152), 72 Stat. 1513; Sept. 7, 1962, P. L. 87-651, Title II, § 211, 76 Stat. 524; Aug. 14, 1964, P. L. 88-426, Title III, §§ 305(7), 306(j)(7), 78 Stat. 423, 432) was transferred by Act Oct. 1, 1986, P. L. 99-433, Title V, Part C, § 521(a)(1) in part, 100 Stat. 1055 to appear as 10 USCS § 8013 and repealed.

Amendments:

1986. Act Oct. 1, 1986 redesignated this section, formerly 10 USCS § 8011, as 10 USCS § 8012.

Other provisions:

Seal for the Department of the Air Force. Ex. Or. No. 9902 of Nov. 1, 1947, 12 Fed. Reg. 7153, provided:

''Whereas section 207 (g) of the National Security Act of 1947, approved July 26, 1947 (Public Law 253, 80th Congress 1st Session [former 5 USC § 626(g)]) provides, in part, that the Secretary of the Air Force shall cause a seal of office to be made for the Department of the Air Force of such device as the President shall approve; and

''Whereas the Secretary of the Air Force has caused to be made and has recommended that I approve a seal the design of which accompanies and is hereby made a part of this order, and which is described in heraldic terms as follows:

''Shield: Per fess nebuly abased azure and argent, in chief a thunderbolt or inflamed proper.

''Crest: On a wreath argent and azure an American bald eagle, wings displayed and partially elevated proper in front of a cloud argent.

''Encircling the shield and crest an arc of thirteen stars and below the shield the inscription 'MCMXLVII'.

''On a band encircling the whole the inscriptions 'Department of the Air Force' and 'United States of America.'

''When illustrating the seal in color the background shall be ultramarine blue, the shield a light blue and white, and the thunderbolt in gold with flames in natural color. The twists of the wreath shall be alternated white and blue, and the eagle shall be in natural color in front of a white cloud. The thirteen stars shall be white, and the Roman numerals shall be gold. The encircling band shall be white edged in gold with black letters.

''And whereas it appears that such seal is of suitable design and is appropriate for establishment as the official seal of the Department of the Air Force:

"Now, therefore, by virtue of and pursuant to the authority vested in me by the said section 207(g) of the National Security Act of 1947 [former 5 USC § 626(g)], I hereby approve such seal as the official seal of the Department of the Air Force.".

CODE OF FEDERAL REGULATIONS

Department of the Air Force—Enforcement of order at Air Force installations, control of civil disturbances, support of disaster relief operations, and special consideration for overseas areas, 32 CFR Part 809a.

Department of the Air Force—Procedures for reporting on defense related employment, 32 CFR Part 809d.

Department of the Air Force—User charges, 32 CFR Part 812.

Department of the Air Force—Licensing government-owned inventions in the custody of the Department of the Air Force, 32 CFR Part 841.

Department of the Air Force—Counsel fees and other expenses in foreign tribunals, 32 CFR Part 845.

Department of the Air Force—Personnel Review Boards, 32 CFR Part 865.

Department of the Air Force—Organizational and representational activities of military personnel, 32 CFR Part 888g.

Department of the Air Force—Appointment to the United States Air Force Academy, 32 CFR Part 901.

Department of the Air Force—Air Force Academy Preparatory School, 32 CFR Part 903.

RESEARCH GUIDE

Federal Procedure:
12 Fed Proc L Ed, Evidence § 33:69.

§ 8013. Secretary of the Air Force

(a)(1) There is a Secretary of the Air Force, appointed from civilian life by the President, by and with the advice and consent of the Senate. The Secretary is the head of the Department of the Air Force.

(2) A person may not be appointed as Secretary of the Air Force within five years after relief from active duty as a commissioned officer of a regular component of an armed force.

(b) Subject to the authority, direction, and control of the Secretary of Defense and subject to the provisions of chapter 6 of this title [10 USCS §§ 161 et seq.], the Secretary of the Air Force is responsible for, and has the authority necessary to conduct, all affairs of the Department of the Air Force, including the following functions:

(1) Recruiting.
(2) Organizing.
(3) Supplying.
(4) Equipping (including research and development).
(5) Training.
(6) Servicing.

(7) Mobilizing.
(8) Demobilizing.
(9) Administering (including the morale and welfare of personnel).
(10) Maintaining.
(11) The construction, outfitting, and repair of military equipment.
(12) The construction, maintenance, and repair of buildings, structures, and utilities and the acquisition of real property and interests in real property necessary to carry out the responsibilities specified in this section.

(c) Subject to the authority, direction, and control of the Secretary of Defense, the Secretary of the Air Force is also responsible to the Secretary of Defense for—

(1) the functioning and efficiency of the Department of the Air Force;
(2) the formulation of policies and programs by the Department of the Air Force that are fully consistent with national security objectives and policies established by the President or the Secretary of Defense;
(3) the effective and timely implementation of policy, program, and budget decisions and instructions of the President or the Secretary of Defense relating to the functions of the Department of the Air Force;
(4) carrying out the functions of the Department of the Air Force so as to fulfill (to the maximum extent practicable) the current and future operational requirements of the unified and specified combatant commands;
(5) effective cooperation and coordination between the Department of the Air Force and the other military departments and agencies of the Department of Defense to provide for more effective, efficient, and economical administration and to eliminate duplication;
(6) the presentation and justification of the positions of the Department of the Air Force on the plans, programs, and policies of the Department of Defense; and
(7) the effective supervision and control of the intelligence activities of the Department of the Air Force.

(d) The Secretary of the Air Force is also responsible for such other activities as may be prescribed by law or by the President or Secretary of Defense.

(e) After first informing the Secretary of Defense, the Secretary of the Air Force may make such recommendations to Congress relating to the Department of Defense as he considers appropriate.

(f) The Secretary of the Air Force may assign such of his functions, powers, and duties as he considers appropriate to the Under Secretary of the Air Force and to the Assistant Secretaries of the Air Force. Officers of the Air Force shall, as directed by the Secretary, report on any matter to the Secretary, the Under Secretary, or any Assistant Secretary.

(g) The Secretary of the Air Force may—

(1) assign, detail, and prescribe the duties of members of the Air Force and civilian personnel of the Department of the Air Force;
(2) change the title of any officer or activity of the Department of the Air Force not prescribed by law; and

(3) prescribe regulations to carry out his functions, powers, and duties under this title [10 USCS §§ 101 et seq.].

(Added Oct. 1, 1986, P. L. 99-433, Title V, Part C, § 521(a)(3), 100 Stat. 1055; Nov. 14, 1986, P. L. 99-661, Div A, Title V, Part C, § 534, 100 Stat. 3873.)

HISTORY; ANCILLARY LAWS AND DIRECTIVES

Explanatory notes:

A prior § 8013 (Act Aug. 10, 1956, ch 1041, § 1, 70A Stat. 489; Aug. 6, 1958, P. L. 85-599, § 8(c), 72 Stat. 520; Sept. 2, 1958, P. L. 85-861, § 1(153), 72 Stat. 1513; Aug. 14, 1964, P. L. 88-426, Title III, § 305(8), 78 Stat. 423; Dec. 1, 1967, P. L. 90-168, § 2(15), 81 Stat. 523; Nov. 9, 1979, P. L. 96-107, Title VIII, § 820(d), 93 Stat. 819) was transferred by Act Oct. 1, 1986, P. L. 99-433, Title V, Part C, § 521(a)(1) in part, 100 Stat. 1055 to appear as 10 USCS § 8014 and was repealed.

A further prior § 8013, formerly § 8012 (Act Aug. 10, 1956, ch 1041, § 1, 70A Stat. 488; Sept. 2, 1958, P. L. 85-861, § 1(152), 72 Stat. 1513; Sept. 7, 1962, P. L. 87-651, Title II, § 211, 76 Stat. 524, Aug. 14, 1964, P. L. 88-426, Title III, §§ 305(7), 306(j)(7), 78 Stat. 423, 432; Oct. 1, 1986, P. L. 99-433, Title V, Part C, § 521(a)(1), 100 Stat. 1055) was repealed by Act Oct. 1, 1986, P. L. 99-433, Title V, Part C, § 521(a)(3) 100 Stat. 1055. Such section related to the Secretary of the Air Force, powers and duties, and delegation.

Amendments:

1986. Act Nov. 14, 1986, in subsec. (a), in para. (2), substituted "five years" for "10 years".

Other provisions:

Order of succession of Secretary of Defense. For order of succession in event of death, permanent disability, or resignation of Secretary of Defense, see Ex. Or. 13000 of April 24, 1996, 61 Fed. Reg. 18483, which appears as 5 USCS § 12787 note.

Order of succession of Secretary of Air Force. For order of succession in event of death, permanent disability, or resignation of Secretary of the Air Force, see Ex. Or. No. 12909 of April 22, 1994, 59 Fed. Reg. 21909, which appears as 5 USCS § 3347 note.

CODE OF FEDERAL REGULATIONS

Department of the Air Force—Sale to the public, 32 CFR Part 807.

Department of the Air Force—Release , dissemination, and sale of visual information materials, 32 CFR Part 811.

Department of the Air Force—Visual information documentation (VIDOC) program, 32 CFR Part 811a.

Department of the Air Force—Personal financial responsibility, 32 CFR Part 818.

Department of the Air Force—Administrative claims, 32 CFR Part 842.

Department of the Air Force—Department of Defense commercial air carrier quality and safety review program, 32 CFR Part 861.

Department of the Air Force—Making military personnel, employees, and dependents available to civilian authorities for trial, 32 CFR Part 884.

Department of the Air Force—Environmental Impact Analysis Process (EIAP), 32 CFR Part 898.

CROSS REFERENCES

Compensation of Secretary, 5 USCS § 5313.

Armed Forces Policy Council, member of, 10 USCS § 171.

Establishment of advisory committees and panels for research and development activities, 10 USCS § 174.

Courts-martial, authority to convene, 10 USCS §§ 822—824.

Chief of Staff, duties, 10 USCS § 8033.

This section is referred to in 10 USCS §§ 162, 8033, 10174.

RESEARCH GUIDE

Am Jur:

53 Am Jur 2d, Military, and Civil Defense § 22.

INTERPRETIVE NOTES AND DECISIONS

Under predecessor of 10 USCS § 8013, Secretary of Defense was granted power to direct transfer of functions and personnel from Department of Army to Department of Air Force. Updegraff v Pace (1951) 88 US App DC 202, 188 F2d 646.

§ 8014. Office of the Secretary of the Air Force

(a) There is in the Department of the Air Force an Office of the Secretary of the Air Force. The function of the Office is to assist the Secretary of the Air Force in carrying out his responsibilities.

(b) The Office of the Secretary of the Air Force is composed of the following:

(1) The Under Secretary of the Air Force.

(2) The Assistant Secretaries of the Air Force.

(3) The General Counsel of the Department of the Air Force.

(4) The Inspector General of the Air Force.

(5) The Air Reserve Forces Policy Committee.

(6) Such other offices and officials as may be established by law or as the Secretary of the Air Force may establish or designate.

(c)(1) The Office of the Secretary of the Air Force shall have sole responsibility within the Office of the Secretary and the Air Staff for the following functions:

(A) Acquisition.

(B) Auditing.

(C) Comptroller (including financial management).

(D) Information management.

(E) Inspector General.

(F) Legislative affairs.

(G) Public affairs.

(2) The Secretary of the Air Force shall establish or designate a single office or other entity within the Office of the Secretary of the Air Force to conduct each function specified in paragraph (1). No office or other entity may be established or designated within the Air Staff to conduct any of the functions specified in paragraph (1).

(3) The Secretary shall prescribe the relationship of each office or other entity established or designated under paragraph (2) to the Chief of Staff and to the Air Staff and shall ensure that each such office or entity provides the Chief of Staff such staff support as the Chief of Staff considers necessary to perform his duties and responsibilities.

(4) The vesting in the Office of the Secretary of the Air Force of the responsibility for the conduct of a function specified in paragraph (1) does not preclude other elements of the executive part of the Department of the Air Force (including the Air Staff) from providing advice or assistance to the Chief of Staff or otherwise participating in that function within the executive part of the Department under the direction of the office assigned responsibility for that function in the Office of the Secretary of the Air Force.

(5) The head of the office or other entity established or designated by the Secretary to conduct the auditing function shall have at least five years of professional experience in accounting or auditing. The position shall be considered to be a career reserved position as defined in section 3132(a)(8) of title 5.

(d)(1) Subject to paragraph (2), the Office of the Secretary of the Air Force shall have sole responsibility within the Office of the Secretary and the Air Staff for the function of research and development.

(2) The Secretary of the Air Force may assign to the Air Staff responsibility for those aspects of the function of research and development that relate to military requirements and test and evaluation.

(3) The Secretary shall establish or designate a single office or other entity within the Office of the Secretary of the Air Force to conduct the function specified in paragraph (1).

(4) The Secretary shall prescribe the relationship of the office or other entity established or designated under paragraph (3) to the Chief of Staff of the Air Force and to the Air Staff and shall ensure that each such office or entity provides the Chief of Staff such staff support as the Chief of Staff considers necessary to perform his duties and responsibilities.

(e) The Secretary of the Air Force shall ensure that the Office of the Secretary of the Air Force and the Air Staff do not duplicate specific functions for which the Secretary has assigned responsibility to the other.

(f)(1) The total number of members of the armed forces and civilian employees of the Department of the Air Force assigned or detailed to permanent duty in the Office of the Secretary of the Air Force and on the Air Staff may not exceed 2,639.

(2) Not more than 1,585 officers of the Air Force on the active-duty list may be assigned or detailed to permanent duty in the Office of the Secretary of the Air Force and on the Air Staff.

(3) The total number of general officers assigned or detailed to permanent duty in the Office of the Secretary of the Air Force and on the Air Staff may not exceed the number equal to 85 percent of the number of general officers assigned or detailed to such duty on the date of the enactment of this subsection [enacted Oct. 1, 1986].

(4) The limitations in paragraph (1), (2), and (3) do not apply in time of war or during a national emergency declared by the President or Congress. The limitation in paragraph (2) does not apply whenever the President determines that it is in the national interest to increase the number of officers assigned or detailed to permanent duty in the Office of the Secretary of the Air Force or on the Air Staff.

(Added Oct. 1, 1986, P. L. 99-433, Title V, Part C, § 521(a)(3), 100 Stat. 1057; Dec. 4, 1987, P. L. 100-180, Div A, Title XIII, Part B, § 131(b)(7), 101 Stat. 1175; Sept. 29, 1988, P. L. 100-456, Div A, Title III, Part C, § 325(c), 102 Stat. 1955; Nov. 29, 1989, P. L. 101-189, Div A, Title VI, Part F, § 652(a)(4), 103 Stat. 1461.)

HISTORY; ANCILLARY LAWS AND DIRECTIVES

Explanatory notes:

A prior § 8014 (Act Aug. 10, 1956, ch 1041, § 1, 70A Stat. 489) was transferred by Act Oct. 1, 1986, P. L. 99-433, Title V, Part C, § 521(a)(1) in part, 100 Stat. 1055 to appear as 10 USCS § 8015 and was repealed.

Another prior § 8014, formerly § 8013 (Aug. 10, 1956, ch 1041, § 1, 70A Stat. 489; Aug. 6, 1958, P. L. 85-599, § 8(c), 72 Stat. 520; Sept. 2, 1958, P. L. 85-861, § 1(153), 72 Stat. 1513; Aug. 14, 1964, P. L. 88-426, Title III, § 305(8), 78 Stat. 423; Dec. 1, 1967, P. L. 90-168, § 2(15), 81 Stat. 523; Nov. 9, 1979, P. L. 96-107, Title VIII, § 820(d), 93 Stat. 819; Oct. 1, 1986, P. L. 99-433, Title V, Part C, § 521(a)(1), 100 Stat. 1055) was repealed by Act Oct. 1, 1986, P. L. 99-433, Title V, Part C, § 521(a)(3) 100 Stat. 1055. Such section related to the Under Secretary and Assistant Secretaries of the Air Force, appointment, and duties.

Amendments:

1987. Act Dec. 4, 1987, in subsec. (f)(4), inserted "the President or".

1988. Act Sept. 29, 1988 (applicable as provided by § 325(d)(1) of such Act, which appears as 10 USCS § 5014 note), in subsec. (c), added para. (5).

1989. Act Nov. 29, 1989, in subsec. (f), deleted para. (5), which read: "The limitations in paragraphs (1), (2), and (3) do not apply before October 1, 1988.".

Other provisions:

Implementation of subsecs. (c) and (d). Act Oct. 1, 1986, P. L. 99-433, Title V, Part D, § 532(a), 100 Stat. 1063, which appears as 10 USCS § 3014 note, provides that the provisions of subsecs. (c) and (d) of this section shall be implemented not later than 180 days after enactment on Oct. 1, 1986.

CROSS REFERENCES

This section is referred to in 10 USCS § 8032.

RESEARCH GUIDE

Am Jur:

53 Am Jur 2d, Military, and Civil Defense § 22.

§ 8015. Under Secretary of the Air Force

(a) There is an Under Secretary of the Air Force, appointed from civilian life by the President, by and with the advice and consent of the Senate.

(b) The Under Secretary shall perform such duties and exercise such powers as the Secretary of the Air Force may prescribe.

(Added Oct. 1, 1986, P. L. 99-433, Title V, Part C, § 521(a)(3), 100 Stat. 1058.)

HISTORY; ANCILLARY LAWS AND DIRECTIVES

Explanatory notes:

A prior section 8015, formerly § 8014 (Act Aug. 10, 1958, ch 1041, 70A Stat. 489; Oct. 1, 1986, P. L. 99-433, Title V, Part C, § 521(a)(1), 100 Stat. 1055), was repealed by Act Oct. 1, 1986, P. L. 99-433, Title V, Part C, § 521(a)(3), 100 Stat. 1055. Such section provided for A Comptroller and Deputy Comptroller of the Air Force, powers, duties and appointments, and similar provisions were contained in former 10 USCS § 1013 before enactment of Act Aug. 10, 1958.

Other provisions:

Order of succession of Secretary of Defense. For order of succession in event of death, permanent disability, or resignation of Secretary of Defense, see Ex. Or. 13000 of April 24, 1996, 61 Fed. Reg. 18483, which appears as 5 USCS § 12787 note.

Order of succession of Secretary of Air Force. For oder of succession in event of death, permanent disability, or resignation of Secretary of the Air Force, see Ex. Or. No. 12909 of April 22, 1994, 59 Fed. Reg. 21909, which appears as 5 USCS § 3347 note.

CROSS REFERENCES

Compensation of Under Secretary, 5 USCS § 5315.

§ 8016. Assistant Secretaries of the Air Force

(a) There are four Assistant Secretaries of the Air Force. They shall be appointed from civilian life by the President, by and with the advice and consent of the Senate.

(b)(1) The Assistant Secretaries shall perform such duties and exercise such powers as the Secretary of the Air Force may prescribe.

(2) One of the Assistant Secretaries shall be the Assistant Secretary of the Air Force for Manpower and Reserve Affairs. He shall have as his principal duty the overall supervision of manpower and reserve component affairs of the Department of the Air Force.

(3) One of the Assistant Secretaries shall be the Assistant Secretary of the Air Force for Financial Management. The Assistant Secretary shall have as his principal responsibility the exercise of the comptroller functions of the Department of the Air Force, including financial management functions. The Assistant Secretary shall be responsible for all financial management activities and operations of the Department of the Air Force and shall advise the Secretary of the Air Force on financial management.

(Added Oct. 1, 1986, P. L. 99-433, Title V, Part C, § 521(a)(3) in part, 100 Stat. 1058; Sept. 29, 1988, P. L. 100-456, Div A, Title VII, Part A, §§ 702(c) [(1)], (d), 102 Stat. 1995, 1996.)

HISTORY; ANCILLARY LAWS AND DIRECTIVES

Explanatory notes:

The bracketed ''(1)'' is inserted in the credits citation for § 702(c) of Act Sept. 29, 1988 as the probable intention of Congress because subsec. (c) of such § 702 contains paras. (2) and (3).

Amendments:

1988. Act Sept. 29, 1988 (effective as provided by § 702(e)(2) of such Act, which appears as a note to this section), in subsec. (a), substituted ''four'' for ''three'' and added subsec. (b)(3).

Other provisions:

Effective date of amendments made by § 702(c), (d) of Act Sept. 29, 1988. Act Sept. 29, 1988, P. L. 100-456, Div A, Title VII, Part A, § 702(e)(2), 102 Stat. 1996, provides: ''(2) The amendments made by subsections (c) and (d) [adding 10 USCS § 8022 and item prec. 8011 and amending this section] shall take effect on July 1, 1989, except that such amendments shall take effect on such earlier date, but not before January 21, 1989, as may be prescribed by the President in advance by Executive order.''.

CROSS REFERENCES

Compensation of Assistant Secretaries, 5 USCS § 5315.

§ 8017. Secretary of the Air Force: successors to duties

If the Secretary of the Air Force dies, resigns, is removed from office, is absent, or is disabled, the person who is highest on the following list, and who is not absent or disabled, shall perform the duties of the Secretary until the President, under section 3347 of title 5, directs another person to perform those duties or until the absence or disability ceases:

(1) The Under Secretary of the Air Force.

(2) The Assistant Secretaries of the Air Force, in the order prescribed by the Secretary of the Air Force and approved by the Secretary of Defense.

(3) The General Counsel of the Department of the Air Force.

(4) The Chief of Staff.

(Aug. 10, 1956, ch 1041, § 1, 70A Stat. 489; Nov. 2, 1966, P. L. 89-718, § 23, 80 Stat. 1118; Jan. 2, 1968, P. L. 90-235, § 4(a)(9), 81 Stat. 760; Oct. 1, 1986, P. L. 99-433, Title V, Part C, § 521(a)(4), 100 Stat. 1058; Oct. 5, 1994, P. L. 103-337, Div A, Title IX, Subtitle A, § 902(c), 108 Stat. 2823.)

HISTORY; ANCILLARY LAWS AND DIRECTIVES

Prior law and revision:

Revised Section	Source (USCS)	Source (Statutes at Large)
8017(a)	5:626-1(b).	Sept. 19, 1951, ch 407, § 102 (less (a)), 65 Stat. 327.
8017(b)	5:626-1(c).	

In subsection (a), the word "person" is substituted for the words "officer of the United States". The words "until a successor is appointed" are omitted as surplusage.

Subsection (b) is substituted for 5:626-1(c) and states the effect of section 8544(b) of this title.

Amendments:

1966. Act Nov. 2, 1966, in subsec (a), in the preliminary matter, and in subsec. (b), substituted "3447" for "6".

1968. Act Jan. 2, 1968, in subsec. (b), substituted "973(b)" for "8544(b)".

1986. Act Oct. 1, 1986 deleted the subsec. designator "(a)" preceding "If the Secretary", substituted para. (2) for one which read: "The Assistant Secretaries of the Air Force in order of their length of service as such.", and deleted subsec. (b), which read: "Performance of the duties of the Secretary by the Chief of Staff or any officer of the Air Force designated under section 3347 of title 5 shall not be considered as the holding of a civil office within the meaning of section 973(b) of this title.".

1994. Act Oct. 5, 1994 redesignated para. (3) as para. (4), and added new para. (3).

Other provisions:

Order of succession of Secretary of Defense. For order of succession in event of death, permanent disability, or resignation of Secretary of Defense, see Ex. Or. 13000 of April 24, 1996, 61 Fed. Reg. 18483, which appears as 5 USCS § 12787 note.

Order of succession of Secretary of Air Force. For oder of succession in event of death, permanent disability, or resignation of Secretary of the Air Force, see Ex. Or. No. 12909 of April 22, 1994, 59 Fed. Reg. 21909, which appears as 5 USCS § 3347 note.

§ 8018. Administrative Assistant

The Secretary of the Air Force may appoint an Administrative Assistant in the Office of the Secretary of the Air Force. The Administrative Assistant shall perform such duties as the Secretary may prescribe.

(Added Oct. 1, 1986, P. L. 99-433, Title V, Part C, § 521(a)(5) in part, 100 Stat. 1059.)

HISTORY; ANCILLARY LAWS AND DIRECTIVES

Explanatory notes:

A prior § 8018 (Act Sept. 2, 1958, P. L. 85-861, § 1(154)(A), 72 Stat. 1513) was repealed by Act Aug. 14, 1964, P. L. 88-426, Title III, § 305(40)(A), 78 Stat. 427, effective on the first day of the first pay period which begins on or after July 1, 1964, as provided by § 501 of such Act. It prescribed the compensation of the General Counsel of the Department of the Air Force. For similar provisions see 5 USCS § 5316.

§ 8019. General Counsel

(a) There is a General Counsel of the Department of the Air Force, appointed from civilian life by the President, by and with the advice and consent of the Senate.

(b) The General Counsel shall perform such functions as the Secretary of the Air Force may prescribe.

(Added Oct. 1, 1986, P. L. 99-433, Title V, Part C, § 521(a)(5) in part, 100 Stat. 1059; Sept. 29, 1988, P. L. 100-456, Div A, Title VII, Part A, § 703(a), 102 Stat. 1996.)

HISTORY; ANCILLARY LAWS AND DIRECTIVES

Explanatory notes:

A prior § 8019 (Act Dec. 1, 1967, P. L. 90-168, § 2(19), 81 Stat. 524) was transferred by Act Oct. 1, 1986, P. L. 99-433, Title V, Part C, § 821(a)(2), 100 Stat. 1055 to appear as 10 USCS § 8038.

Amendments:

1988. Act Sept. 29, 1988 (applicable to appointments made under this section on and after enactment, as provided by § 703(c) of such Act, which appears as 10 USCS § 3019 note), in subsec. (a), inserted ", by and with the advice and consent of the Senate".

CROSS REFERENCES

Compensation of General Counsel of Department of the Air Force, 5 USCS § 5316.

§ 8020. Inspector General

(a) There is an Inspector General of the Air Force who shall be detailed to such position by the Secretary of the Air Force from the general officers of the Air Force. An officer may not be detailed to such position for a tour of duty of more than four years, except that the Secretary may extend such a tour of duty if he makes a special finding that the extension is necessary in the public interest.

(b) When directed by the Secretary or the Chief of Staff, the Inspector General shall—

(1) inquire into and report upon the discipline, efficiency, and economy of the Air Force; and

(2) perform any other duties prescribed by the Secretary or the Chief of Staff.

(c) The Inspector General shall periodically propose programs of inspections to the Secretary of the Air Force and shall recommend additional inspections and investigations as may appear appropriate.

(d) The Inspector General shall cooperate fully with the Inspector General of the Department of Defense in connection with the performance of any duty or function by the Inspector General of the Department of Defense under the Inspector General Act of 1978 (5 U.S.C. App. 3) regarding the Department of the Air Force.

(e) The Inspector General shall have such deputies and assistants as the Secretary of the Air Force may prescribe. Each such deputy and assistant shall be an officer detailed by the Secretary to that position from the officers of the Air Force for a tour of duty of not more than four years, under a procedure prescribed by the Secretary.

(Added Oct. 1, 1986, P. L. 99-433, Title V, Part C, § 521(a)(5) in part, 100 Stat. 1059.)

HISTORY; ANCILLARY LAWS AND DIRECTIVES

References in text:

"The Inspector General Act of 1978 (5 U.S.C.App. 3)", referred to in this section, is Act Oct. 12, 1978, P. L. 95-452, 92 Stat. 1101, which appears generally as 5 USCS Appx. For full classification of such Act, consult USCS Tables volumes.

CROSS REFERENCES

Inspector General—Army, 10 USCS § 3020.

Inspector General—Navy, 10 USCS § 5020.

§ 8021. Air Force Reserve Forces Policy Committee

There is in the Office of the Secretary of the Air Force an Air Force Reserve Forces Policy Committee. The functions, membership, and organization of that committee are set forth in section 10305 of this title.

(Added Oct. 5, 1994, P. L. 103-337, Div A, Title XVI, Subtitle C, § 1661(b)(4)(B), 108 Stat. 2982.)

HISTORY; ANCILLARY LAWS AND DIRECTIVES

Explanatory notes:

A prior § 8021 was redesignated as 10 USCS § 10305 and transferred to Chapter 1009 by Act Oct. 5, 1994, P. L. 103-337, Div A, Title XVI, Subtitle C, § 1661(b)(2)(B), 108 Stat. 2981, effective Dec. 1, 1994, as provided by § 1691 of such Act, which appears as 10 USCS § 10001 note.

Effective date of section:

This section took effect on Dec. 1, 1994, pursuant to Act Oct. 5, 1994, P. L. 103-337, Div A, Title XVI, Subtitle F, § 1691, 108 Stat. 3026, which appears as 10 USCS 10001 note.

§ 8022. Financial management

(a) The Secretary of the Air Force shall provide that the Assistant Secretary of the Air Force for Financial Management shall direct and manage financial management activities and operations of the Department of the Air Force, including ensuring that financial management systems of the Department of the Air Force comply with subsection (b). The authority of the Assistant Secretary for such direction and management shall include the authority to—

(1) supervise and direct the preparation of budget estimates of the Department of the Air Force and otherwise carry out, with respect to the Department of the Air Force, the functions specified for the Under Secretary of Defense (Comptroller) in section 135(c) of this title;

(2) approve and supervise any project to design or enhance a financial management system for the Department of the Air Force; and

(3) approve the establishment and supervise the operation of any asset management system of the Department of the Air Force, including—

(A) systems for cash management, credit management, and debt collection; and

(B) systems for the accounting for the quantity, location, and cost of property and inventory.

(b)(1) Financial management systems of the Department of the Air Force (including accounting systems, internal control systems, and financial reporting systems) shall be established and maintained in conformance with—

(A) the accounting and financial reporting principles, standards, and requirements established by the Comptroller General under section 3511 of title 31; and

(B) the internal control standards established by the Comptroller General under section 3512 of title 31.

(2) Such systems shall provide for—

(A) complete, reliable, consistent, and timely information which is prepared on a uniform basis and which is responsive to the financial information needs of department management;

(B) the development and reporting of cost information;

(C) the integration of accounting and budgeting information; and

(D) the systematic measurement of performance.

(c) The Assistant Secretary shall maintain a five-year plan describing the activities the Department of the Air Force proposes to conduct over the next five fiscal years to improve financial management. Such plan shall be revised annually.

(d) The Assistant Secretary of the Air Force for Financial Management shall transmit to the Secretary of the Air Force a report each year on the activities of the Assistant Secretary during the preceding year. Each such report shall include a description and analysis of the status of Department of the Air Force financial management.

(Added Sept. 29, 1988, P. L. 100-456, Div A, Title VII, Part A, § 702(c)(2), 102 Stat. 1995; Oct. 5, 1994, P. L. 103-337, Div A, Title X, Subtitle G, § 1070(a)(15), 108 Stat. 2856; Feb. 10, 1996, P. L. 104-106, Div A, Title XV, § 1503(b)(1), 110 Stat. 512.)

HISTORY; ANCILLARY LAWS AND DIRECTIVES

Effective date of section:

Act Sept. 29, 1988, P. L. 100-456, Div A, Title VII, Part A, § 702(e)(2), 102 Stat. 1996, which appears as 10 USCS § 8016 note, provides that this section is effective on July 1, 1989, except that such section shall take effect on such earlier date, but not before Jan. 21, 1989, as may be prescribed by the President in advance by Executive Order.

Amendments:

1994. Act Oct. 5, 1994, in subsec. (a)(1), substituted ''section 135(c)'' for ''section 137(c)''.

1996. Act Feb. 10, 1996, in subsec. (a)(1), substituted ''Under Secretary of Defense (Comptroller)'' for ''Comptroller of the Department of Defense''.

CHAPTER 805. THE AIR STAFF

HISTORY; ANCILLARY LAWS AND DIRECTIVES

Amendments:

1965. Act Oct. 22, 1965, P. L. 89-288, § 5(b), 79 Stat. 1050, amended the analysis of this chapter by adding item 8036.

1986. Act Oct. 1, 1986, P. L. 99-433, Title V, Part C, § 522(g)(1), 100 Stat. 1063, substituted this analysis for one which read:

''8031. Composition: assignment and detail of members of Air Force and civilians

''8032. General duties

''8033. Reserve components of Air Force; policies and regulations for government of: functions of National Guard Bureau with respect to Air National Guard

''8034. Chief of Staff: appointment; duties

''8035. Vice Chief of Staff; Deputy Chiefs of Staff: succession to duties of Chief of Staff and Vice Chief of Staff

''8036. Surgeon General: appointment, grade''.

§ 8031. The Air Staff: function; composition

(a) There is in the executive part of the Department of the Air Force an Air Staff. The function of the Air Staff is to assist the Secretary of the Air Force in carrying out his responsibilities.

(b) The Air Staff is composed of the following:

(1) The Chief of Staff.

(2) The Vice Chief of Staff.

(3) The Deputy Chiefs of Staff.

(4) The Assistant Chiefs of Staff.

(5) The Surgeon General of the Air Force.

(6) The Judge Advocate General of the Air Force.

(7) The Chief of the Air Force Reserve.

(8) Other members of the Air Force assigned or detailed to the Air Staff.

(9) Civilian employees in the Department of the Air Force assigned or detailed to the Air Staff.

(c) Except as otherwise specifically prescribed by law, the Air Staff shall be organized in such manner, and its members shall perform such duties and have such titles, as the Secretary may prescribe.

(Aug. 10, 1956, ch 1041, § 1, 70A Stat. 490; Nov. 2, 1966, P. L. 89-718, § 45, 80 Stat. 1121; Jan 2, 1975, P. L. 93-608, § 1(5), 88 Stat. 1968; Oct. 19, 1984, P. L. 98-525, Title V, Part B, § 515 in part, 98 Stat. 2522; Oct. 1, 1986, P. L. 99-433, Title V, Part C, § 522(a), 100 Stat. 1060.)

HISTORY; ANCILLARY LAWS AND DIRECTIVES

Prior law and revision:

Revised Section	Source (USCS)	Source (Statutes at Large)
8031(a)	10:1811(a).	Sept. 19, 1951, ch 407, § 201, 65 Stat. 327.
8031(b)	10:1811(b).	
8031(c)	10:1811(c).	
8031(d)	10:1811(d).	

In subsection (a), the words "an Air Staff consisting of—" are substituted for the words "a staff, which shall be known as the Air Staff, and which shall consist of—". The words "under regulations prescribed by the Secretary of the Air Force" are omitted, since the Secretary has inherent authority to issue regulations appropriate to exercising his statutory functions.

In subsection (b), 10:1811(b) (proviso) is omitted as superseded by section 264(c) of this title.

In subsection (c), the third sentence is substituted for 10:1811(c) (1st 13 words and 1st proviso). The words "officers and employees . . . or under the jurisdiction of" are omitted as surplusage.

In subsections (c) and (d), the word "hereafter" is omitted, since all wars and emergencies declared by Congress before September 19, 1951, have been terminated.

In subsections (d), the words "now or hereafter" are omitted as surplusage and as executed. The second sentence is substituted for 10:1811(d) (last 31 words of 1st sentence). The third sentence is substituted for 10:1811(d) (2d sentence). 10:1811(d) (1st 13 words of last sentence) is omitted as executed. The words "This subsection does not apply" are substituted for the words "and shall be inapplicable".

Amendments:

1966. Act Nov. 2, 1966, in subsec. (c), substituted "annually" for "quarterly".

1975. Act Jan 2, 1975, in subsec. (c), after the sentence beginning "However. . . .", deleted one which read: "The Secretary shall report annually to Congress the number of officers in the executive part of the Department of the Air Force and the justification therefor.".

1984. Act Oct. 19, 1984 (effective 10/1/84, as provided by § 515 in part of such Act) deleted subsec. (d) which read: "No commissioned officer who is assigned or detailed to duty in the executive part of the Department of the Air Force may serve for a tour of duty of more than four years.

However, the Secretary may extend such a tour of duty if he makes a special finding that the extension is necessary in the public interest. No officer may be assigned or detailed to duty in the executive part of the Department of the Air Force within two years after relief from that duty, except upon a special finding by the Secretary that the assignment or detail is necessary in the public interest. This subsection does not apply in time of war, or of national emergency declared by Congress.''.

1986. Act Oct. 1, 1986 substituted this section and catchline for ones which read:

''§ 8031. Composition: assignment and detail of members of Air Force and civilians

''(a) There is in the executive part of the Department of the Air Force an Air Staff consisting of—

''(1) the Chief of Staff;

''(2) the Vice Chief of Staff;

''(3) not more than five Deputy Chiefs of Staff;

''(4) other members of the Air Force assigned or detailed to the Air Staff; and

''(5) civilians in the Department of the Air Force assigned or detailed to the Air Staff.

''(b) The Air Staff shall be organized in such manner, and its members shall perform such duties and have such titles, as the Secretary may prescribe.

''(c) Not more than 2,800 officers of the Air Force may be assigned or detailed to permanent duty in the executive part of the Department of the Air Force. However, this limitation does not apply in time of war, or of national emergency declared by Congress, or whenever the President finds that it is in the national interest to increase the number of officers in the executive part of the Department.

''No commissioned officer who is assigned or detailed to duty in the executive part of the Department of the Air Force may serve for a tour of duty of more than four years. However, the Secretary may extend such a tour of duty if he makes a special finding that the extension is necessary in the public interest. No officer may be assigned or detailed to duty in the executive part of the Department of the Air Force within two years after relief from that duty, except upon a special finding by the Secretary that the assignment or detail is necessary in the public interest. This subsection does not apply in time of war, or of national emergency declared by Congress.''

§ 8032. The Air Staff: general duties

(a) The Air Staff shall furnish professional assistance to the Secretary, the Under Secretary, and the Assistant Secretaries of the Air Force, and the Chief of Staff of the Air Force.

(b) Under the authority, direction, and control of the Secretary of the Air Force, the Air Staff shall—

(1) subject to subsections (c) and (d) of section 8014 of this title [10 USCS § 8014(c), (d)], prepare for such employment of the Air Force, and for such recruiting, organizing, supplying, equipping (including those aspects of

research and development assigned by the Secretary of the Air Force), training, servicing, mobilizing, demobilizing, administering, and maintaining of the Air Force, as will assist in the execution of any power, duty, or function of the Secretary or the Chief of Staff;

(2) investigate and report upon the efficiency of the Air Force and its preparation to support military operations by combatant commands;

(3) prepare detailed instructions for the execution of approved plans and supervise the execution of those plans and instructions;

(4) as directed by the Secretary or the Chief of Staff, coordinate the action of organizations of the Air Force; and

(5) perform such other duties, not otherwise assigned by law, as may be prescribed by the Secretary.

(Aug. 10, 1956, ch 1041, § 1, 70A Stat. 490; Aug. 6, 1958, P. L. 85-599, § 4(h), 72 Stat. 517; Oct. 1, 1986, P. L. 99-433, Title V, Part C, § 522(b), 100 Stat. 1060.)

HISTORY; ANCILLARY LAWS AND DIRECTIVES

Prior law and revision:

Revised Section	Source (USCS)	Source (Statutes at Large)
8032(a)	10:1815(a).	Sept. 19, 1951, ch 407,
8032(b)	10:1815(b).	§ 205, 65 Stat. 329.

In subsection (a), the word "furnish" is substituted for the word "render".
In subsection (b)(1), the words "power, duty, or function of" are substituted for the words "power vested in, duty imposed upon, or function assigned to".
In subsection (b)(2), the words "all questions affecting" and "state of" are omitted as surplusage.

Amendments:

1958. Act Aug. 6, 1958 substituted subsec. (b)(1) for one which read: "prepare such plans for the national security, for employment of the Air Force for that purpose, both separately and in conjunction with the land and naval forces, and for recruiting, organizing, supplying, equipping, training, serving, mobilizing, and demobilizing the Air Force, as will assist in the execution of any power, duty, or function of the Secretary or the Chief of Staff;".

1986. Act Oct. 1, 1986 substituted this catchline for one which read: "§ 8032. General duties"; in subsec. (a), inserted "of the Air Force" following "Chief of Staff"; in subsec. (b), in the introductory matter, substituted "Under the authority, direction, and control of the Secretary of the Air Force, the Air Staff" for "The Air Staff", in para. (1), inserted "subject to subjections (c) and (d) of section 8014 of this title," and substituted "(including those aspects of research and development assigned by the Secretary of the Air Force), training, servicing, mobilizing, demobilizing, administering, and maintaining" for ", training, serving, mobilizing, and demobilizing", in para. (2), substituted "to support military operations by combatant commands'' for ''for military operations'', and substituted para. (4) for one which read: ''act as agent of the Secretary and the Chief of Staff in coordinating the action of all organizations of the Department of the Air Force; and''.

§ 8033. Chief of Staff

(a)(1) There is a Chief of Staff of the Air Force, appointed for a period of four years by the President, by and with the advice and consent of the Senate, from the general officers of the Air Force. He serves at the pleasure of the President. In time of war or during a national emergency declared by Congress, he may be reappointed for a term of not more than four years.

(2) The President may appoint an officer as Chief of Staff only if—

(A) the officer has had significant experience in joint duty assignments; and

(B) such experience includes at least one full tour of duty in a joint duty assignment (as defined in section 664(f) of this title) as a general officer.

(3) The President may waive paragraph (2) in the case of an officer if the President determines such action is necessary in the national interest.

(b) The Chief of Staff, while so serving, has the grade of general without vacating his permanent grade.

(c) Except as otherwise prescribed by law and subject to section 8013(f) of this title [10 USCS § 8013(f)], the Chief of Staff performs his duties under the authority, direction, and control of the Secretary of the Air Force and is directly responsible to the Secretary.

(d) Subject to the authority, direction, and control of the Secretary of the Air Force, the Chief of Staff shall—

(1) preside over the Air Staff;

(2) transmit the plans and recommendations of the Air Staff to the Secretary and advise the Secretary with regard to such plans and recommendations;

(3) after approval of the plans or recommendations of the Air Staff by the Secretary, act as the agent of the Secretary in carrying them into effect;

(4) exercise supervision, consistent with the authority assigned to commanders of unified or specified combatant commands under chapter 6 of this title [10 USCS §§ 161 et seq.], over such of the members and organizations of the Air Force as the Secretary determines;

(5) perform the duties prescribed for him by section 171 of this title [10 USCS § 171] and other provisions of law; and

(6) perform such other military duties, not otherwise assigned by law, as are assigned to him by the President, the Secretary of Defense, or the Secretary of the Air Force.

(e)(1) The Chief of Staff shall also perform the duties prescribed for him as a member of the Joint Chiefs of Staff under section 151 of this title [10 USCS § 151].

(2) To the extent that such action does not impair the independence of the

Chief of Staff in the performance of his duties as a member of the Joint Chiefs of Staff, the Chief of Staff shall inform the Secretary regarding military advice rendered by members of the Joint Chiefs of Staff on matters affecting the Department of the Air Force.

(3) Subject to the authority, direction, and control of the Secretary of Defense, the Chief of Staff shall keep the Secretary of the Air Force fully informed of significant military operations affecting the duties and responsibilities of the Secretary.

(Aug. 10, 1956, ch 1041, § 1, 70A Stat. 492; Aug. 6, 1958, P. L. 85-599, § 4(d), (e), 72 Stat. 517; Sept. 7, 1962, P. L. 87-651, Title I, § 114, 76 Stat. 513; June 5, 1967, P. L. 90-22, Title IV, § 403, 81 Stat. 53; Dec. 12, 1980, P.L. 96-513, Title V, Part A, § 504(2), 94 Stat. 2915; July 10, 1981, P. L. 97-22, § 10(b)(9), 95 Stat. 137; Oct. 1, 1986, P. L. 99-433, Title V, Part C, § 522(c), 100 Stat. 1061; Sept. 29, 1988, P. L. 100-456, Div A, Title V, Part B, § 519(a)(3), 102 Stat. 1972.)

HISTORY; ANCILLARY LAWS AND DIRECTIVES

Prior law and revision:

1956 ACT

Revised Section	Source (USCS)	Source (Statutes at Large)
8034(a)	10:1812 (1st sentence).	Sept. 19, 1951, ch 407, §§ 202, 204, 65 Stat. 328.
8034(b)	10:1812 (less 1st sentence).	
8034(c)	10:1814(a) (1st 10 words). 10:1814(b) (2d sentence). 10:1814(c).	June 3, 1916, ch 134, § 5 (last para.); added June 15, 1933, ch 87, § 2 (last para.), 48 Stat. 154.
8034(d)	10:38 (last para.). 10:1814(a) (less 1st 10 words). 10:1814(b) (less 2d sentence).	

In subsection (a), the words "not for" are substituted for the words "no person shall serve as Chief of Staff for a term of".

In subsection (b), the words "so serving" are substituted for the words "holding office as such". The words "regular or reserve" are substituted for the word "permanent", since there are no other "permanent" grades in the Air Force. The words "in the Air Force" are omitted as surplusage. The words "and shall take rank as prescribed by law" are omitted as superseded by section 743 of this title. The words "He shall receive the compensation prescribed by law" are omitted as covered by the Career Compensation Act of 1949, 63 Stat. 802 (37 U.S.C. 231 et seq.).

In subsection (c), the provisions of 10:1814 relating to the direction of the Secretary of the Air Force over the Chief of Staff are combined. The words "and subsection (c) of this section" and "state of" are omitted as surplusage.

In subsection (d), 10:38 (last para.) is omitted as covered by 10:1814(a). The words "and other provisions of law" are substituted for the words "and by other laws".

1962 ACT

The changes correct references to section 202(j) of the National Security Act of 1947, which is now set out as section 124 of title 10.

Explanatory notes:

A prior § 8033 (Act Aug. 10, 1956, ch 1041, § 1, 70A Stat. 491; Sept. 2, 1958, P. L. 85-861, § 33(a)(17), 72 Stat. 1565; Dec. 1, 1967, P. L. 90-168, § 2(21), 81 Stat. 525) was transferred by Act Oct. 1, 1986, P. L. 99-433, Title V, Part C, § 521(a)(6), 100 Stat. 1059 and appears as 10 USCS § 8021.

Amendments:

1958. Act Aug. 6, 1958, in subsec. (d), deleted para. (4), which read: "exercise command over the air defense command, the strategic air command, the tactical air command, and such other major commands as may be established under section 8074(c) of this title;"; redesignated para. (5) as para. (4) and substituted para. (4) as so redesignated for one which read: "supervise all other members and organizations of the Air Force;"; and redesignated paras. (6) and (7) as paras. (5) and (6), respectively.

1962. Act Sept. 7, 1962, in subsec. (d)(4), substituted "under section 124 of this title" for "pursuant to section 202(j) of the National Security Act of 1947, as amended".

1967. Act June 5, 1967 (effective 1/1/69, as provided by § 405 of such Act, which appears as 10 USCS § 3034 note), substituted subsec. (a) for one which read: "The Chief of Staff shall be appointed by the President, by and with the advice and consent of the Senate, from the general officers of the Air Force. He serves during the pleasure of the President, but not for more than four years unless reappointed by the President, by and with the advice and consent of the Senate.".

1980. Act Dec. 12, 1980 (effective 9/15/81, as provided by § 701(a) of such Act, which appears as 10 USCS § 101 note), in subsec. (b), deleted "and is counted as one of the officers authorized to serve in a grade above lieutenant general under section 8066 of this title" after "or reserve grade,".

1981. Act July 10, 1981 (effective 9/15/81, as provided by § 10(b)(1) in part), in subsec. (b), deleted the comma following "grade".

1986. Act Oct. 1, 1986 redesignated this section, formerly 10 USCS § 8034, as 10 USCS § 8033, and substituted this section and catchline for the redesignated ones which read:

"§ 8034. Chief of staff: appointment; duties

"(a) The Chief of Staff shall be appointed for a period of four years by the President, by and with the advice and consent of the Senate, from the general officers of the Air Force. He serves during the pleasure of the President. In time of war or national emergency declared by the Congress after December 31, 1968, he may be reappointed for a term of not more than four years.

"(b) The Chief of Staff, while so serving, has the grade of general without vacating his regular or reserve grade.

"(c) Except as otherwise prescribed by law and subject to section 8012(c) and (d) of this title, the Chief of Staff performs his duties under the direction of the Secretary of the Air Force, and is directly responsible to the Secretary for the efficiency of the Air Force, its preparedness for military operations, and plans therefor.

''(d) The Chief of Staff shall—

''(1) preside over the Air Staff;

''(2) send the plans and recommendations of the Air Staff to the Secretary and advise him with regard thereto;

''(3) after approval of the plans or recommendations of the Air Staff by the Secretary, act as the agent of the Secretary in carrying them into effect;

''(4) exercise supervision over such of the members and organizations of the Air Force as the Secretary of the Air Force determines. Such supervision shall be exercised in a manner consistent with the full operational command vested in unified or specified combatant commanders under section 124 of this title.

''(5) perform the duties prescribed for him by sections 141 and 171 of this title and other provisions of law; and

''(6) perform such other military duties, not otherwise assigned by law, as are assigned to him by the President.''.

1988. Act Sept. 29, 1988, in subsec. (a)(2)(B), substituted ''full tour of duty in a joint duty assignment (as defined in section 664(f) of this title)'' for ''joint duty assignment''.

CROSS REFERENCES

Armed Forces Policy Council, member of, 10 USCS § 171.

Personal money allowance, 10 USCS § 414.

Rank, 10 USCS § 743.

Higher retired grade for service in special position, 10 USCS § 8962.

Air National Guard in Federal service, 10 USCS § 12502.

§ 8034. Vice Chief of Staff

(a) There is a Vice Chief of Staff of the Air Force, appointed by the President, by and with the advice and consent of the Senate, from the general officers of the Air Force.

(b) The Vice Chief of Staff of the Air Force, while so serving, has the grade of general without vacating his permanent grade.

(c) The Vice Chief of Staff has such authority and duties with respect to the Department of the Air Force as the Chief of Staff, with the approval of the Secretary of the Air Force, may delegate to or prescribe for him. Orders issued by the Vice Chief of Staff in performing such duties have the same effect as those issued by the Chief of Staff.

(d) When there is a vacancy in the office of Chief of Staff or during the absence or disability of the Chief of Staff—

(1) the Vice Chief of Staff shall perform the duties of the Chief of Staff until a successor is appointed or the absence or disability ceases; or

(2) if there is a vacancy in the office of the Vice Chief of Staff or the Vice Chief of Staff is absent or disabled, unless the President directs otherwise, the most senior officer of the Air Force in the Air Staff who is not absent or disabled and who is not restricted in performance of duty shall perform the duties of the Chief of Staff until a successor to the Chief of Staff or the Vice Chief of Staff is appointed or until the absence or disability of the Chief of Staff or Vice Chief of Staff ceases, whichever occurs first.

(Aug. 10, 1956, ch 1041, § 1, 70A Stat. 492; Aug. 6, 1958, P. L. 85-599, § 6(d), 72 Stat. 519; Oct. 1, 1986, P. L. 99-433, Title V, Part C, § 522(d), 100 Stat. 1062.)

HISTORY; ANCILLARY LAWS AND DIRECTIVES

Prior law and revision:

Revised Section	Source (USCS)	Source (Statutes at Large)
8035(a)	10:1813(a) (1st sentence).	Sept. 19, 1951, ch 407, § 203, 65 Stat. 328.
8035(b)	10:1813(a) (less 1st sentence).	
8035(c)	10:1813(b).	

In subsection (a), the words "of the Air Force" are omitted as surplusage.

In subsection (b), the words "if the Chief of Staff is absent or disabled or if that office is vacant" are substituted for 10:1813(a) (1st 18 words of last sentence). The words "the officer who is highest on the following list and" are inserted for clarity. The words "until his successor is appointed" are omitted as surplusage.

In subsection (c), the words "If the Vice Chief of Staff is absent or disabled or if that office is vacant" are substituted for 10:1813(b) (1st 19 words).

Explanatory notes:

A prior § 8034 (Act Aug. 10, 1956, ch 1041, § 1, 70A Stat. 492; Aug. 6, 1958, P. L. 85-599, § 4(d), (e), 72 Stat. 517; Sept. 7, 1962, P. L. 87-651, Title I, § 114, 76 Stat. 513; June 5, 1967, P. L. 90-22, Title IV, § 403, 81 Stat. 53; Dec. 12, 1980, P.L. 96-513, Title V, Part A, § 504(2), 94 Stat. 2915; July 10, 1981, P. L. 97-22, § 10(b)(9), 95 Stat. 137) was transferred by Act Oct. 1, 1986, P. L. 99-433, Title V, Part C, § 522(c), 100 Stat. 1061 and appears as 10 USCS § 8033.

Amendments:

1958. Act Aug. 6, 1958, added subsec. (d).

1986. Act Oct. 1, 1986 redesignated this section, formerly 10 USCS § 8035, as 10 USCS § 8034, and in this section as redesignated, substituted the catchline and subsecs. (a) and (b) for ones which read:

"§ 8035. Vice Chief of Staff; Deputy Chiefs of Staff: succession to duties of Chief of Staff and Vice Chief of Staff

"(a) The Vice Chief of Staff and the Deputy Chiefs of Staff shall be general officers detailed to those positions.

"(b) If the Chief of Staff is absent or disabled or if that office is vacant, the officer who is highest on the following list and who is not absent or disabled shall, unless otherwise directed by the President, perform the duties of the Chief of Staff until a successor is appointed or the absence or disability ceases:

"(1) The Vice Chief of Staff.

"(2) The Deputy Chiefs of Staff in order of seniority.".

Such Act further deleted subsec. (c), which read:

"If the Vice Chief of Staff is absent or disabled or if that office is vacant, the senior Deputy Chief of Staff who is not absent or disabled shall, unless otherwise directed by the Secretary of the Air Force, perform the duties of the Vice Chief of Staff until a successor is designated or the absence or disability ceases."; redesignated subsec. (d) as subsec. (c); and added a new subsec. (d).

§ 8035. Deputy Chiefs of Staff and Assistant Chiefs of Staff

(a) The Deputy Chiefs of Staff and the Assistant Chiefs of Staff shall be general officers detailed to those positions.

(b) The number of Deputy Chiefs of Staff and Assistant Chiefs of Staff shall be prescribed by the Secretary, except that—

(1) there may not be more than five Deputy Chiefs of Staff; and

(2) there may not be more than three Assistant Chiefs of Staff.

(Added Oct. 1, 1986, P. L. 99-433, Title V, Part C, § 522(e), 100 Stat. 1062.)

HISTORY; ANCILLARY LAWS AND DIRECTIVES

Explanatory notes:

A prior § 8035 (Act Aug. 10, 1956, ch 1041, § 1, 70A Stat. 492; Aug. 6, 1958, P. L. 85-599, § 6(d), 72 Stat. 519) was transferred by Act Oct. 1, 1986, P. L. 99-433, Title V, Part C, § 522(d), 100 Stat. 1062 and appears as 10 USCS § 8034.

§ 8036. Surgeon General: appointment; grade

There is a Surgeon General of the Air Force who is appointed by the President by and with the advice and consent of the Senate from officers of the Air Force who are in the Air Force medical department. The Surgeon General, while so serving, has the grade of lieutenant general.

(Added Oct. 22, 1965, P. L. 89-288, § 5(a), 79 Stat. 1050; Oct. 1, 1986, P. L. 99-433, Title V, Part C, § 522(g)(2), 100 Stat. 1063; Feb. 10, 1996, P. L. 104-106, Div A, Title V, Subtitle A, § 506(c), 110 Stat. 296.)

HISTORY; ANCILLARY LAWS AND DIRECTIVES

Amendments:

1986. Act Oct. 1, 1986, in the catchline, substituted a semicolon for a comma.

1996. Act Feb. 10, 1996 substituted "in the Air Force medical department" for "designated as medical officers under section 8067(a) of this title".

§ 8037. Judge Advocate General, Deputy Judge Advocate General: appointment; duties

(a) There is a Judge Advocate General in the Air Force, who is appointed by the President, by and with the advice and consent of the Senate, from officers of the Air Force. The term of office is four years, but may be sooner terminated or extended by the President. An appointee who holds a lower regular grade shall be appointed in the regular grade of major general.

(b) The Judge Advocate General of the Air Force shall be appointed from those officers who at the time of appointment are members of the bar of a Federal court or the highest court of a State or Territory, and who have had at least eight years of experience in legal duties as commissioned officers.

(c) The Judge Advocate General shall, in addition to other duties prescribed by law—

(1) receive, revise, and have recorded the proceedings of courts of inquiry and military commissions; and

(2) perform such other legal duties as may be directed by the Secretary of the Air Force.

(d)(1) There is a Deputy Judge Advocate General in the Air Force, who is appointed by the President, by and with the advice and consent of the Senate, from officers of the Air Force who have the qualifications prescribed in subsection (b) for the Judge Advocate General. The term of office of the Deputy Judge Advocate General is four years, but may be sooner terminated or extended by the President. An officer appointed as Deputy Judge Advocate General who holds a lower regular grade shall be appointed in the regular grade of major general.

(2) When there is a vacancy in the office of the Judge Advocate General, or during the absence or disability of the Judge Advocate General, the Deputy Judge Advocate General shall perform the duties of the Judge Advocate General until a successor is appointed or the absence or disability ceases.

(3) When paragraph (2) cannot be complied with because of the absence or disability of the Deputy Judge Advocate General, the heads of the major divisions of the Office of the Judge Advocate General, in the order directed by the Secretary of the Air Force, shall perform the duties of the Judge Advocate General, unless otherwise directed by the President.

(e) Under regulations prescribed by the Secretary of Defense, the Secretary of the Air Force, in selecting an officer for recommendation to the President under subsection (a) for appointment as the Judge Advocate General or under subsection (d) for appointment as the Deputy Judge Advocate General, shall ensure that the officer selected is recommended by a board of officers that, insofar as practicable, is subject to the procedures applicable to selection boards convened under chapter 36 of this title [10 USCS §§ 611 et seq.].

(Aug. 10, 1956, ch 1041, § 1, 70A Stat. 495; Sept. 8, 1980, P.L. 96-343, § 12(a), (b)(1), 94 Stat. 1130, 1131; Oct. 1, 1986, P. L. 99-433, Title V, Part C, § 522(f), 100 Stat. 1063; Oct. 5, 1994, P. L. 103-337, Div A, Title V, Subtitle A, § 504(c), 108 Stat. 2751; Feb. 10, 1996, P. L. 104-106, Div A, Title V, Subtitle A, § 507(a), 110 Stat. 296.)

HISTORY; ANCILLARY LAWS AND DIRECTIVES

Prior law and revision:

Revised Section	Source (USCS)	Source (Statutes at Large)
8072(a)	10:1840(a).	Sept. 19, 1951, ch 407, § 310(a), (b) (less 1st sentence), 65 Stat. 332.
8072(b)	50:741.	May 5, 1950, ch 169, § 13 (as applicable to Air Force), 64 Stat. 147.
8072(c)	10:62, 10:1840(b) (last sentence).	R.S. 1199. June 23, 1874, ch 458, § 2, 18 Stat. 244.

In subsection (a), the words ''subject to the provisions of section 741 of Title 50'' are omitted as surplusage. The words ''but may be sooner terminated, or extended, by the President'' are substituted for 10:1840(a) (last 11 words of 1st sentence, and 2d sentence). 10:1840(a) (1st 46 words of 3d sentence) is omitted as surplusage. 10:1840(a) (last sentence) is omitted as executed. The words ''by the President, by and with the advice and consent of the Senate'', as they relate to the appointment as a major general in the Regular Air Force, are omitted as covered by section 8284 of this title.

In subsection (b), the words ''Hereafter'' and ''exclusive of the present incumbents'' are omitted as surplusage. The words ''at least'' are substituted for the words ''not less than a total''.

In subsection (c), the Act of June 23, 1874, ch 458, § 2 (words before semicolon of 1st sentence, and last sentence), 18 Stat. 244, are not contained in 10:62. They are also omitted from the revised section, since the Air Force does not have organic corps created by statute.

Amendments:

1980. Act Sept. 8, 1980 substituted the catchline for one which read: ''§ 8072. Judge Advocate General: appointment; duties''; and added subsec. (d).

1986. Act Oct. 1, 1986 redesignated this section, formerly 10 USCS § 8072, as 10 USCS § 8037.

1994. Act Oct. 5, 1994 added subsec. (e).

1996. Act Feb. 10, 1996 (applicable as provided by § 507(b) of such Act, which appears as a note to this section), in subsec. (d)(1), substituted ''four years'' for ''two years'' and substituted ''An officer appointed as Deputy Judge Advocate General who holds a lower regular grade shall be appointed in the regular grade of major general.'' for ''An officer appointed as Deputy Judge Advocate General shall be appointed in a regular grade to be determined by the Secretary of Defense.''.

Other provisions:

Application of Feb. 10, 1996 amendments. Act Feb. 10, 1996, P. L. 104-106, Div A, Title V, Subtitle A, § 507(b), 110 Stat. 296, provides: ''The amendments made by subsection (a) [amending subsec. (d)(1) of this section] apply to any appointment to the position of Deputy Judge Advocate General of the Air Force that is made after the date of the enactment of this Act.''.

CROSS REFERENCES

Army, appointment and duties of Judge Advocate General, 10 USCS § 3037.
Marine Corps, Staff Judge Advocate to Commandant, 10 USCS § 5046.
Navy, appointment, term, emoluments and duties of Judge Advocate General, 10 USCS § 5148.

§ 8038. Office of Air Force Reserve: appointment of Chief

(a) There is in the executive part of the Department of the Air Force an Office of Air Force Reserve which is headed by a chief who is the adviser to the Chief of Staff on Air Force Reserve matters.

(b) The President, by and with the advice and consent of the Senate, shall appoint the Chief of Air Force Reserve from officers of the Air Force Reserve not on active duty, or on active duty under section 10211 of this title, who—

(1) have had at least 10 years of commissioned service in the Air Force;

(2) are in grade of brigadier general and above; and

(3) have been recommended by the Secretary of the Air Force.

(c) The Chief of Air Force Reserve holds office for four years, but may be removed for cause at any time. He is eligible to succeed himself. If he holds a lower reserve grade, he shall be appointed in the grade of major general for service in the Air Force Reserve.

(d) Budget. The Chief of Air Force Reserve is the official within the executive part of the Department of the Air Force who, subject to the authority, direction, and control of the Secretary of the Air Force and the Chief of Staff, is responsible for preparation, justification, and execution of the personnel, operation and maintenance, and construction budgets for the Air Force Reserve. As such, the Chief of Air Force Reserve is the director and functional manager of appropriations made for the Air Force Reserve in those areas.

(e) Full Time Support Program. The Chief of Air Force Reserve manages, with respect to the Air Force Reserve, the personnel program of the Department of Defense known as the Full Time Support Program.

(f) Annual report. (1) The Chief of Air Force Reserve shall submit to the Secretary of Defense, through the Secretary of the Air Force, an annual report on the state of the Air Force Reserve and the ability of the Air Force Reserve to meet its missions. The report shall be prepared in conjunction with the Chief of Staff of the Air Force and may be submitted in classified and unclassified versions.

(2) The Secretary of Defense shall transmit the annual report of the Chief of Air Force Reserve under paragraph (1) to Congress, together with such comments on the report as the Secretary considers appropriate. The report shall be transmitted at the same time each year that the annual report of the Secretary under section 113 of this title is submitted to Congress.

(Added Dec. 1, 1967, P. L. 90-168, § 2(19), 81 Stat. 524; Oct. 1, 1986, P. L.

99-433, Title V, Part C, §§ 521(a)(2), 522(g)(3), 100 Stat. 1055, 1063; Oct. 5, 1994, P. L. 103-337, Div A, Title XVI, Subtitle D, § 1674(c)(1), 108 Stat. 3016; Sept. 23, 1996, P. L. 104-201, Div A, Title XII, Subtitle A, § 1212(d), 110 Stat. 2693; Nov. 18, 1997, P. L. 105-85, Div A, Title X, Subtitle G, § 1073(a)(65), 111 Stat. 1904.)

HISTORY; ANCILLARY LAWS AND DIRECTIVES

Effective date of section:

Act Dec. 1, 1967, P. L. 90-168, § 7, 81 Stat. 526, which appears as 10 USCS § 138 note, provided that this section shall become effective on the first day of the first calendar month following the date of enactment.

Amendments:

1986. Act Oct. 1, 1986 redesignated this section, formerly 10 USCS § 8019, as 10 USCS § 8038 and in this section as redesignated, in subsec. (a), deleted a comma following "Chief of Staff".

1994. Act Oct. 5, 1994 (effective 12/1/94 as provided by § 1691 of such Act, which appears as 10 USCS § 10001 note), in subsec. (b), substituted "section 10211" for "section 265".

1996. Act Sept. 23, 1996 added subsecs. (d)–(f).

1997. Act Nov. 18, 1997 (applicable as provided by § 1073(i) of such Act, which appears as 10 USCS § 101 note), in subsec. (e), deleted "(1)" following the subsection heading.

CROSS REFERENCES

This section is referred to in 10 USCS § 641.

CHAPTER 807. THE AIR FORCE

HISTORY; ANCILLARY LAWS AND DIRECTIVES

Amendments:

1960. Act July 7, 1960, P. L. 86-603, § 1(3)(B), 74 Stat. 358, amended the analysis of this chapter by adding item 8080.

1967. Act Nov. 8, 1967, P. L. 90-130, § 1(25), 81 Stat. 382, amended the analysis of this chapter by deleting item 8071, which read: ''8071. Temporary grade of colonel in the Air Force: appointment of women''.

1978. Act Oct. 20, 1978, P. L. 95-485, Title VIII, § 805(c)(2), 92 Stat. 1622, amended the analysis of this chapter by adding item 8081.

1980. Act Sept. 8, 1980, P. L. 96-343, § 12(b)(2), 94 Stat. 1131, amended the analysis of this chapter by substituting item 8072 for one which read: ''8072. Judge Advocate General: appointment; duties''.

Act Dec. 12, 1980, P. L. 96-513, Title V, Part A, § 504(3), 94 Stat. 2915, amended the analysis of this chapter by deleting item 8066 which read: ''8066. Generals and lieutenant generals''.

1986. Act Oct. 1, 1986, P. L. 99-433, Title V, Part C, § 522(g)(4), 100 Stat. 1063, amended the analysis of this chapter by deleting item 8072, which read: ''8072. Judge Advocate General, Deputy Judge Advocate General: appointment; duties''.

1994. Act Oct. 5, 1994, P. L. 103-337, Div A, Title XVI, Subtitle D, § 1674(b)(1), 108 Stat. 3016, amended the analysis of this chapter by deleting items 8076–8080, which read: ''8076. Air Force Reserve: composition'', ''8077. Air National Guard of United States: composition'', ''8078. Air National Guard: when a component of Air Force'', ''8079. Air National Guard of United States: status when not in Federal service'', and ''8080. Air National Guard of the United States: authority of officers with respect to Federal status''.

1996. Act Sept. 23, 1996, P. L. 104-201, Div A, Title V, Subtitle A, § 502(c)(2), 110 Stat. 2511, amended the analysis of this chapter by adding item 8069.

1997. Act Nov. 18, 1997, P. L. 105-85, Div A, Title X, Subtitle G, § 1073(a)(66), 111 Stat. 1904, amended the analysis of this chapter by substituting ''nurses'' for ''Nurse Corps'' in item 8609.

§ 8061. Regulations

The President may prescribe regulations for the government of the Air Force.
(Aug. 10, 1956, ch 1041, § 1, 70A Stat. 493.)

HISTORY; ANCILLARY LAWS AND DIRECTIVES

Prior law and revision:

Revised Section	Source (USCS)	Source (Statutes at Large)
8061	10:16.	July 15, 1870, ch 294, § 20, 16 Stat. 319; Mar. 1, 1875, ch 115, 18 Stat. 337.

The word ''prescribe'' is substituted for the words ''make and publish''. 10:16 (last 35 words) is omitted as surplusage.

CROSS REFERENCES

General regulatory powers of President, 10 USCS § 121.

§ 8062. Policy; composition; aircraft authorization

(a) It is the intent of Congress to provide an Air Force that is capable, in conjunction with the other armed forces, of—

(1) preserving the peace and security, and providing for the defense, of the United States, the Territories, Commonwealths, and possessions, and any areas occupied by the United States;

(2) supporting the national policies;

(3) implementing the national objectives; and

(4) overcoming any nations responsible for aggressive acts that imperil the peace and security of the United States.

(b) There is a United States Air Force within the Department of the Air Force.

(c) In general, the Air Force includes aviation forces both combat and service not otherwise assigned. It shall be organized, trained, and equipped primarily for prompt and sustained offensive and defensive air operations. It is responsible for the preparation of the air forces necessary for the effective prosecution of war except as otherwise assigned and, in accordance with integrated joint mobilization plans, for the expansion of the peacetime components of the Air Force to meet the needs of war.

(d) The Air Force consists of—

(1) the Regular Air Force, the Air National Guard of the United States, the Air National Guard while in the service of the United States, and the Air Force Reserve;

(2) all persons appointed or enlisted in, or conscripted into, the Air Force without component; and

(3) all Air Force units and other Air Force organizations, with their installations and supporting and auxiliary combat, training, administrative, and logistic elements; and all members of the Air Force, including those not assigned to units; necessary to form the basis for a complete and immediate mobilization for the national defense in the event of a national emergency.

(e) Subject to subsection (f) of this section, chapter 831 of this title [10 USCS §§ 8201 et seq.], and the strength authorized by law pursuant to section 115 of this title, the authorized strength of the Air Force is 70 Regular Air Force groups and such separate Regular Air Force squadrons, reserve groups, and supporting and auxiliary regular and reserve units as required.

(f) There are authorized for the Air Force 24,000 serviceable aircraft or 225,000 airframe tons of serviceable aircraft, whichever the Secretary of the Air Force considers appropriate to carry out this section. This subsection does not apply to guided missiles.

(Aug. 10, 1956, ch 1041, § 1, 70A Stat. 493; Dec. 12, 1980, P.L. 96-513, Title V, Part A, § 504(4), 94 Stat. 2916; Oct. 1, 1986, P. L. 99-433, Title V, Part C, § 110(g)(10), 100 Stat. 1004; April 21, 1987, P. L. 100-26, § 7(g)(3), 101 Stat. 282; Dec. 4, 1987, P. L. 100-180, Div A, Title XIII, Part B, § 1314(b)(9), 101 Stat. 1176.)

HISTORY; ANCILLARY LAWS AND DIRECTIVES

Prior law and revision:

Revised Section	Source (USCS)	Source (Statutes at Large)
8062(a)	10:20.	July 26, 1947, ch 343, § 208(a), (f), 61 Stat. 503;
8062(b)	5:626c(a).	Aug. 10, 1949, ch 412, § 12(d), 63 Stat. 591.
8062(c)	5:626c(f).	July 10, 1950, ch 454, §§ 2, 201, 203, 64 Stat. 321, 323, 324.
8062(d)	10:20r(a).	Sept. 19, 1951, ch 407, § 301, 65 Stat. 329.
	10:1831.	July 9, 1952, ch 608, § 601, 66 Stat. 501.
	50:1091.	
8062(e)	10:20r(b).	
8062(f)	10:20t.	

In subsection (a), 10:20 (1st 19 words) is omitted as surplusage. The words "any areas occupied by the United States" are substituted for the words "occupied areas wherever located".

Subsection (b) is substituted for 5:626c(a) (1st sentence). 5:626c(a) (last sentence) is omitted as executed.

In subsection (d), the words "consists of" are substituted for the word "includes".

In subsection (d)(1), 10:20r(a) is omitted as superseded by 10:1831. The words "all persons serving in the Air Force under call or. . . under any provision of law, including members of the Air National Guard of the several States, Territories, and the District of Columbia when in the service of the United States pursuant to call as provided by law" are omitted as covered by the words "the Air National Guard while in the service of the United States". 50:1091 (last sentence) is omitted, since the components listed include their members.

In subsection (d)(2), the words "or inducted" are omitted as covered by the word "conscripted".

In subsection (e), the words "Effective on July 10, 1950" are omitted as executed. The words "the limitations imposed by" are omitted as surplusage. The words "not to exceed" are omitted as surplusage, since the revised section states the authorized number and any number over that would not be authorized. The words "and chapter 31 of this title" are substituted for the reference to 10:20s to make it clear that the authority for a 70 group Air Force is subject to all provisions which prescribe the authorized personnel strength of the Air Force.

In subsection (f), the word "considers" is substituted for the words "may determine is more". The words "aggregate" and "amount" are omitted as surplusage. The words "carry out this section" are substituted for the words "fulfill the requirements of the Air Force of the United States for aircraft necessary to carry out the purposes of this chapter, section 481 of this title, and sections 235, 235a, 628, and 628a of title 5", since the purposes to which the reference is made are stated in the revised section. The last sentence is substituted for 10:20t (proviso).

Amendments:

1980. Act Dec. 12, 1980 (effective 9/15/81, as provided by § 701(a) of such Act, which appears as 10 USCS § 101 note), in subsec. (e), substituted ", chapter 831 of this title, and the strength authorized by law pursuant to section 138" for "and chapter 831".

1986. Act Oct. 1, 1986, in subsec. (e), substituted "section 114" for "section 138".

1987. Act April 21, 1987, in subsec. (e), substituted "section 115" for "section 114".

Act Dec. 4, 1987, in subsec. (e), purported to substitute "section 115" for "section 114", but such amendment could not be executed because the substitution had already been effectuated in accordance with Act April 21, 1987.

CROSS REFERENCES

Transfer, reassignment, consolidation or abolition of functions, powers and duties, 10 USCS § 125.

This section is referred to in 10 USCS § 125.

[§ 8066. Repealed]

HISTORY; ANCILLARY LAWS AND DIRECTIVES

This section (Act Aug. 10, 1956, ch 1041, § 1, 70A Stat. 494; Sept. 2, 1958, P. L. 85-861, § 33(a)(36), 72 Stat. 1566) was repealed by Act Dec. 12, 1980, P.L. 96-513, Title II, Part A, § 201, 94 Stat. 2878, effective Sept. 15, 1981, as provided by § 701(a) of such Act, which appears as 10 USCS § 101 note. It provided for the appointment of generals and lieutenant generals. For similar provisions, see 10 USCS § 601.

§ 8067. Designation: officers to perform certain professional functions

(a) Medical functions in the Air Force shall be performed by commissioned officers of the Air Force who are qualified under regulations prescribed by the Secretary of the Air Force and who are designated as medical officers.

(b) Dental functions in the Air Force shall be performed by commissioned officers of the Air Force who are qualified under regulations prescribed by the Secretary and who are designated as dental officers.

(c) Veterinary functions in the Air Force shall be performed by commissioned officers of the Air Force who are qualified under regulations prescribed by the Secretary, and who are designated as veterinary officers.

(d) Medical service functions in the Air Force shall be performed by commissioned officers of the Air Force who are qualified under regulations prescribed by the Secretary, and who are designated as medical service officers.

(e) Nursing functions in the Air Force shall be performed by commissioned officers of the Air Force who are qualified under regulations prescribed by the Secretary and who are designated as Air Force nurses.

(f) Biomedical science functions, including physician assistant functions and chiropractic functions, in the Air Force shall be performed by commissioned officers of the Air Force who are qualified under regulations prescribed by the Secretary, and who are designated as biomedical science officers.

(g) Judge advocate functions in the Air Force shall be performed by commissioned officers of the Air Force who are qualified under regulations prescribed by the Secretary, and who are designated as judge advocates.

(h) Chaplain functions in the Air Force shall be performed by commissioned officers of the Air Force who are qualified under regulations prescribed by the Secretary and who are designated as chaplains.

(i) Other functions in the Air Force requiring special training or experience shall be performed by members of the Air Force who are qualified under regulations prescribed by the Secretary, and who are designated as being in named categories.

(Aug. 10, 1956, ch 1041, § 1, 70A Stat. 494; Sept. 2, 1958, P. L. 85-861, § 1(156), 72 Stat. 1513; Dec. 12, 1980, P.L. 96-513, Title V, Part A, § 504(5), 94 Stat. 2916; Dec. 1, 1981, P. L. 97-86, Title IV, § 403, 95 Stat. 1105; Oct. 23, 1992, P. L. 102-484, Div A, Title V, Subtitle A, § 505(c), 106 Stat. 2404.)

HISTORY; ANCILLARY LAWS AND DIRECTIVES

Prior law and revision:

1956 ACT

Revised Section	Source (USCS)	Source (Statutes at Large)
8067(a)	10:1837(a) (as applicable to medical officers).	Sept. 19, 1951, ch 407, § 307(less (d)), 65 Stat. 330.

Revised Section	Source (USCS)	Source (Statutes at Large)
8067(b)	10:1837(a) (as applicable to dental officers).	June 24, 1952, ch 457 (less 1st and last provisos), 66 Stat. 156.
8067(c)	10:1837(a) (as applicable to veterinary officers).	
8067(d)	10:1837(a) (as applicable to medical service officers).	
8067(e)	10:1837(a) (as applicable to nurses).	
8067(f)	10:1837(a) (as applicable to women medical specialists).	
8067(g)	10:1837(a) (as applicable to judge advocates).	
8067(h)	10:1837(a) (as applicable to chaplins).	
8067(i)	10:1837(a) (less categories covered by subsecs. (a)-(h)).	
	10:1837(b), (c).	
	10:81-2 (less 1st and last provisos).	

The references in cls. (4), (6), and (7) of 10:1837(a) are omitted, since the laws to which reference is made deal with qualifications for appointment as commissioned officers and do not specify professional qualifications prerequisite to designation to duties requiring special training or experience. The reference in cl. (8) is omitted as executed.

10:1837(b) and (c) are omitted, since, except in the case of a reference to a law not presently in effect, their substance is covered by including the laws referred to in various revised sections of this title (see the distribution tables). 10:81-2 (less 1st and last provisos) is omitted as unnecessary.

In subsecstions (a)–(d), (g), and (h), the words ''commissioned officers'' are substituted for the word ''members'', in 10:1837(a), since, under the laws to which reference is made, only commissioned officers may be designated to perform these functions.

In subsections), the words ''female commissioned officers'' are substituted for the word ''members'', in 10:1837(a), since, under the laws to which reference is made, only female commissioned officers may be designated to perform these functions.

1958 ACT

Revised Section	Source (USCS)	Source (Statutes at Large)
8067(e), (f)	10 App.:166b-3.	Aug. 9, 1955, ch 654, §§ 1, 3(b), 69 Stat. 579.

The section is amended to reflect the authority contained in the source statute to appoint male reserve officers with a view to designation as Air Force nurses or medical specialists.

Amendments:

1958. Act Sept. 2, 1958, in subsec. (e), deleted "female" preceding "commissioned"; and, in subsec. (f), deleted "female" preceding "commissioned", and deleted "women" after "designated as".

1980. Act Dec. 12, 1980 (effective 9/15/81, as provided by § 701(a) of such Act, which appears as 10 USCS § 101 note), in subsec. (a), deleted "in conformity with section 8289 or 8294 of this title," before "and who are"; in subsec. (b), deleted "in conformity with section 8294 of this title," before "and who are"; in subsec. (e), deleted "in conformity with section 8291 of this title," before "and who are"; in subsec. (f), substituted "Biomedical science functions" for "Medical specialist functions" and substituted "biomedical science officers" for "medical specialists"; and, in subsec. (h), deleted "in conformity with section 8293 of this title," before "and who are".

1981. Act Dec. 1, 1981, in subsec. (f), inserted ", including physician assistant functions,".

1992. Act Oct. 23, 1992, in subsec. (f), inserted "and chiropractic functions".

CROSS REFERENCES

This section is referred to in 10 USCS §§ 8036, 8081, 8579, 8848, 16201.

§ 8069. Air Force nurses: Chief and assistant chief; appointment; grade

(a) Positions of Chief and assistant chief. There are a Chief and assistant chief of the Air Force Nurse Corps.

(b) Chief. The Secretary of the Air Force shall appoint the Chief from the officers of the Regular Air Force designated as Air Force nurses whose regular grade is above lieutenant colonel and who are recommended by the Surgeon General. An appointee who holds a lower regular grade shall be appointed in the regular grade of brigadier general. The Chief serves during the pleasure of the Secretary, but not for more than three years, and may not be reappointed to the same position.

(c) Assistant chief. The Surgeon General shall appoint the assistant chief from the officers of the Regular Air Force designated as Air Force nurses whose regular grade is above lieutenant colonel.

(Added Sept. 23, 1996, P. L. 104-201, Div A, Title V, Subtitle A, § 502(b), 110 Stat. 2511.)

[§ 8071. Repealed]

HISTORY; ANCILLARY LAWS AND DIRECTIVES

This section (Act Aug. 10, 1956, ch 1041, § 1, 70A Stat. 495) was repealed by Act Nov. 8, 1967, P. L. 90-130, § 1(25), 81 Stat. 382. It provided for the appointment of a female Air Force officer in the temporary grade of colonel.

[§ 8072. Transferred]

HISTORY; ANCILLARY LAWS AND DIRECTIVES

This section (Act Aug. 10, 1956, ch 1041, § 1, 70A Stat. 495; Sept 8, 1980, P. L. 96-343, § 12(a), (b)(1), 94 Stat. 1130, 1131) was transferred by Act Oct. 1, 1986, P. L. 99-433, Title V, Part C, § 522(f), 100 Stat. 1063 and appears as 10 USCS § 8037.

§ 8074. Commands: territorial organization

(a) Except as otherwise prescribed by law or by the Secretary of Defense, the Air Force shall be divided into such organizations as the Secretary of the Air Force may prescribe.

(b) For Air Force purposes, the United States, its Territories, its possessions, and other places in which the Air Force is stationed or is operating, may be divided into such areas as directed by the Secretary. Officers of the Air Force may be assigned to command Air Force activities, installations, and personnel in those areas. In the discharge of the Air Force functions or other functions authorized by law, officers so assigned have the duties and powers prescribed by the Secretary.

(c) The Military Air Transport Service is redesignated as the Military Airlift Command.

(Aug. 10, 1956, ch 1041, § 1, 70A Stat. 495; Aug. 6, 1958, P. L. 85-599, § 4(f), 72 Stat. 517; June 11, 1965, P. L. 89-37, Title III, § 306(a), 79 Stat. 129; Oct. 1, 1986, P. L. 99-433, Title V, Part C, § 523, 100 Stat. 1063.)

HISTORY; ANCILLARY LAWS AND DIRECTIVES

Prior law and revision:

Revised Section	Source (USCS)	Source (Statutes at Large)
8074(a)	10:1838(a)(1).	Sept. 19, 1951, ch. 407, §§ 308, 309, 65 Stat. 332.
8074(b)	10:1838(a)(2).	
8074(c)	10:1838(b).	
8074(d)	10:1839.	

In subsection, the words ''from time to time'' are omitted as surplusage.

In subsection, the words ''have the duties and powers'' are substituted for the words ''shall perform such duties and exercise such powers''. The words ''of America'', ''elements of'', ''other provisions of'', and ''so assigned'' are omitted as surplusage.

Amendments:

1958. Act Aug. 6, 1958, substituted subsec. (a) for one which read: ''There are in the Air Force the following major commands:

''(1) An air defense command.

"(2) A strategic air command.

"(3) A tactical air command.";

Such Act further deleted former subsecs. (b) and (c) which read:

"(b) The Secretary of the Air Force may establish additional commands and organizations in the interest of efficiency and economy of operation.

"(c) For the duration of any war or any national emergency declared by Congress or the President, the Secretary may establish new major commands in place of the major commands named in subsection (a), or he may consolidate or discontinue those major commands.";

And, such Act further redesignated subsec. (d) as subsec. (b).

1965. Act June 11, 1965 (effective 1/1/66, as provided by § 306(b) of such Act), added subsec. (c).

1986. Act Oct. 1, 1986, in subsec. (a), substituted "Except as otherwise prescribed by law or by the Secretary of Defense, the" for "The".

§ 8075. Regular Air Force: composition

(a) The Regular Air Force is the component of the Air Force that consists of persons whose continuous service on active duty in both peace and war is contemplated by law, and of retired members of the Regular Air Force.

(b) The Regular Air Force includes—

(1) the officers and enlisted members of the Regular Air Force;

(2) the professors, registrar, and cadets at the United States Air Force Academy; and

(3) the retired officers and enlisted members of the Regular Air Force.

(Aug. 10, 1956, ch 1041, § 1, 70A Stat. 496; Aug. 6, 1958, P. L. 85-600, § 1(13), 72 Stat. 523.)

HISTORY; ANCILLARY LAWS AND DIRECTIVES

Prior law and revision:

Revised Section	Source (USCS)	Source (Statutes at Large)
8075(a)	10:1832(a).	Sept. 19, 1951, ch. 407, § 302, 65 Stat. 329; Apr. 1, 1954, ch. 127, § 7, 68 Stat. 48.
8075(b)	10:1832 (less (a)).	

In subsection, the words "holding appointments or enlisted in the Regular Air Force as now or hereafter provided by law", "and such other persons as are now or may hereafter be specified by law", and "commissioned . . . warrant officers" are omitted as surplusage, since the revised section lists all persons in the Regular Air Force. 10:1832(b) (last sentence) is omitted as executed.

Amendments:

1958. Act Aug. 6, 1958, in subsec. (b)(2) inserted ", registrar,".

INTERPRETIVE NOTES AND DECISIONS

1. Legal status of cadet

Cadet at United States Air Force Academy, as "member" of Regular Air Force within terms of 10 USCS § 8075, is as much part of Armed Forces as commissioned officer already assigned to permanent duty station, and as such, is emancipated insofar as his legal status is concerned. Dingley v Dingley (1981) 121 NH 670, 433 A2d 1281.

[§§ 8076–8079. Repealed]

HISTORY; ANCILLARY LAWS AND DIRECTIVES

These sections (Act Aug. 10, 1956, ch 1041, § 1, 70A Stat. 496) were repealed by Act Oct. 5, 1994, P. L. 103-337, Div A, Title XVI, Subtitle C, § 1661(a)(3)(A), 108 Stat. 2980 (effective Dec. 1, 1994, as provided by § 1691 of such Act, which appears as 10 USCS § 10001 note). Section 8076 provided for composition of the Air Force Reserve; § 8077 provided for composition of the Air National Guard; § 8078 provided for when the Air National Guard is a component of the Air Force; § 8079 provided for status of the Air National Guard when not in Federal service. For similar provisions, see 10 USCS §§ 10110–10113.

[§ 8080. Repealed]

HISTORY; ANCILLARY LAWS AND DIRECTIVES

This section (Act July 7, 1960, P. L. 86-603, § 1, 74 Stat. 357) was repealed by Act Oct. 5, 1994, P. L. 103-337, Div A, Title XVI, Subtitle C, § 1661(a)(3)(A), 108 Stat. 2980 (effective Dec. 1, 1994, as provided by § 1691 of such Act, which appears as 10 USCS § 10001 note). This section provided for authority of officers of the Air National Guard with respect to Federal status. For similar provisions, see 10 USCS § 10215.

§ 8081. Assistant Surgeon General for Dental Services.

There is an Assistant Surgeon General for Dental Services in the Air Force who is appointed by the Secretary of the Air Force upon the recommendation of the Surgeon General from officers of the Air Force above the grade of major who are designated as dental officers under section 8067(b) of this title [10 USCS § 8067(b)]. The term of office of the Assistant Surgeon General for Dental Services is four years but may be increased or decreased by the Secretary of the Air Force.

(Added Oct. 20, 1978, P. L. 95-485, Title VIII, § 805(c)(1), 92 Stat. 1622.)

PART II. PERSONNEL

HISTORY; ANCILLARY LAWS AND DIRECTIVES

Amendments:

1958. Act Sept. 2, 1958, P. L. 85-861, § 1(193), 72 Stat. 1538, amended the chapter analysis of this part by substituting Chapter 863 for one which read "Separation or Transfer to Retired Reserve. [No present sections]".

1960. Act July 12, 1960, P. L. 86-616, §§ 7(b), 8(b), 74 Stat. 393, 395, amended the chapter analysis of this part by substituting Chapter 859 for one which read "Separation from Regular Air Force for Failure to Meet Standards"; and by adding Chapter 860.

1968. Act Jan. 2, 1968, P. L. 90-235, § 8(6), 81 Stat. 764, amended the analysis of this part by deleting Chapter 847, which read: "847. The Uniform".

Act July 5, 1968, P. L. 90-377, § 5, 82 Stat. 288, amended the analysis of this part by deleting Chapter 851, which read: "851. United States Disciplinary Barracks".

1980. Act Dec. 12, 1980, P.L. 96-513, Title V, Part A, § 504(1), 94 Stat. 2915 (effective 9/15/81, as provided by § 701(a) of such Act, which appears as 10 USCS § 101 note), amended the analysis of this part by deleting chapters 859, 860, and 865, which read: "859. Separation from Regular Air Force for Substandard Performance of Duty . . . . . 8781", "860. Separation from Regular Air Force for Moral or Professional Dereliction or in Interests of National Security . . . . . 8791", and "865. Retirement for Age . . . . . 8881".

1994. Act Oct. 5, 1994, P. L. 103-337, Div A, Title XVI, Subtitle D, § 1674(a), 108 Stat. 3016 (effective 10/1/96, pursuant to § 1501(f)(2) of Act Feb. 10, 1996, P. L. 104-106, which appears as 10 USCS § 10001 note), amended the analysis of this part by deleting items 837 and 863, which read: ''837. Appointments as Reserve Officers . . . . . 8351'' and ''863. Separation or Transfer to Retired Reserve . . . . . 8841''.

CHAPTER 831. STRENGTH

Section
[8201–8209. Repealed]
8210. Regular Air Force: strength in grade; general officers
[8211–8215. Repealed]
[8217–8219. Repealed]
[8221–8225. Repealed]
[8230. Repealed]

HISTORY; ANCILLARY LAWS AND DIRECTIVES

Amendments:

1958. Act Sept. 2, 1958, P. L. 85-861, § 1(165), 72 Stat. 1516, amended the analysis of this chapter in item 8207 by substituting ''Air Force medical specialists'' for ''women medical specialists''; in item 8212 by inserting ''; Air Force Reserve; Air National Guard of United States''; and by adding items 8217, 8218, 8219 and 8230.

1967. Act Nov. 8, 1967, P. L. 90-130, § 1(26)(F), 81 Stat. 382, amended the analysis of this chapter in item 8215 by deleting ''; female enlisted members on active duty'' after ''active list''.

1980. Act Dec. 12, 1980, P.L. 96-513, Title V, Part A, § 504(6), 94 Stat. 2916 (effective 9/15/81, as provided by § 701(a) of such Act, which appears as 10 USCS § 101 note), amended the analysis of this chapter by deleting item 8201 which read: ''8201. Air Force: members on active duty''; by substituting item 8202 for one which read: ''8202. Air Force: officers in certain commissioned grades''; by deleting items 8203–8209, and 8211 which read: ''8203. Regular Air Force: members on active duty'', ''8204. Regular Air Force: commissioned officers on active list'', ''8205. Regular Air Force: commissioned officers on active list, exclusive of certain categories'', ''8206. Regular Air Force: commissioned officers on active list; Air Force nurses'', ''8207. Regular Air Force: commissioned officers on active list; Air Force medical specialists'', ''8208. Regular Air Force: commissioned officers on active list; female commissioned officers, other than those designated under section 8067 of this title to perform professional functions'', ''8209. Regular Air Force: commissioned officers on active list; special categories'', and ''8211. Regular Air Force: strength in grade; promotion-list officers''; by substituting item 8212 for one which read: ''8212. Regular Air Force; Air Force Reserve; Air National Guard of United States: strength in grade; temporary increases''; and by deleting items 8213–8215 and 8230 which read: ''8213. Regular Air Force: warrant officers on active list'', ''8214. Regular Air Force: enlisted members on active duty'', ''8215. Regular Air Force: female warrant officers on active list'', and ''8230. Personnel detailed outside Department of Defense''.

1985. Act Nov. 8, 1985, P. L. 99-145, Title XIII, § 1303(a)(26), 99 Stat. 740, amended the analysis of this chapter by substituting item 8202 for one which read: "Air Force: strength in grade".

1990. Act Nov. 5, 1990, P. L. 101-510, Div A, Title IV, Part A, § 403(b)(3)(B), 104 Stat. 1545, amended the analysis of this chapter by deleting item 8202, which read: "8202, Air Force; strength in grade; general officers".

1994. Act Oct. 5, 1994, P. L. 103-337, Div A, Title XVI, Subtitle D, § 1674(b)(2), 108 Stat. 3016 (effective 12/1/94 as provided by § 1691 of such Act, which appears as 10 USCS § 10001 note), amended the analysis of this chapter by deleting items 8212 and 8217–8225, which read: "8212. Air Reserve; Air National Guard of the United States: strength in grade; temporary increases", "8217. Reserves: commissioned officers in an active status", "8218. Reserves: strength in grade; general officers in an active status", "8219. Reserves: strength in grade; commissioned officers in grades below brigadier general in an active status", "8221. Air Force Reserve", "8222. Air Force Reserve, exclusive of members on active duty", "8223. Air Force Reserve: warrant officers", "8224. Air National Guard of United States", and "8225. Air National Guard and Air National Guard of United States, exclusive of members on active duty".

[§ 8201. Repealed]

HISTORY; ANCILLARY LAWS AND DIRECTIVES

This section (Act Aug. 10, 1956, ch 1041, § 1, 70A Stat. 497; Sept. 2, 1958, P. L. 85-861, § 1(157), 72 Stat. 1513; Oct. 13, 1964, P. L. 88-647, Title III, § 301(20), 78 Stat. 1073) was repealed by Act Dec. 12, 1980, P.L. 96-513, Title II, Part A, § 202, 94 Stat. 2878, effective Sept. 15, 1981, as provided by § 701(a) of such Act, which appears as 10 USCS § 101 note. It provided for the authorized strength of the Air Force in members on active duty.

[§ 8202. Repealed]

HISTORY; ANCILLARY LAWS AND DIRECTIVES

This section (Act Aug. 10, 1956, ch 1041, § 1, 70A Stat. 498; Sept. 2, 1958, P. L. 85-861, § 1(158), 72 Stat. 1514; Dec. 28, 1967, P. L. 90-228, § 1(4), (5), 81 Stat. 745; Dec. 12, 1980, P. L. 96-513, Title II, Part A, § 203(b), 94 Stat. 2879) was repealed by Act Nov. 5, 1990, P. L. 101-510, Div A, Title IV, Part A, § 403(b)(3)(A), 104 Stat. 1545. This section provided for strength of the Air Force in general officers on active duty. For similar provisions see 10 USCS § 526.

[§§ 8203–8209. Repealed]

HISTORY; ANCILLARY LAWS AND DIRECTIVES

These sections (§ 8203—Act Aug. 10, 1956, ch 1041, § 1, 70A Stat. 498; Sept. 2, 1958, P. L. 85-861, § 1(159), 72 Stat. 1514; § 8204—Act Aug. 10, 1956, ch 1041, § 1, 70A Stat. 499; Aug. 6, 1958, P. L. 85-600, § 1(14), 72 Stat. 523; § 8205—Act Aug. 10, 1956, ch 1041, § 1, 70A Stat. 499; Aug.

6, 1958, P. L. 85-600, § 1(15), 72 Stat. 523; Sept. 2, 1958, P. L. 85-861, § 1(160), 72 Stat. 1514; §§ 8206, 8207—Act Aug. 10, 1956, ch 1041, § 1, 70A Stat. 499; Aug. 21, 1957, P. L. 85-155, Title III, § 301(1), (2), 71 Stat. 386; Nov. 8, 1967, P. L. 90-130, § 1(26)(A), (B), 81 Stat. 382; § 8208—Act Aug. 10, 1956, ch 1041, § 1, 70A Stat. 499; Nov. 8, 1967, P. L. 90-130, § 1(26)(C), 81 Stat. 382; § 8209—Act Aug. 10, 1956, ch 1041, § 1, 70A Stat. 500; Sept. 2, 1958, P. L. 85-861, § 1 (156), 72 Stat. 1513; Nov. 8, 1967, P. L. 90-130, § 1(26)(D), 81 Stat. 382) were repealed by Act Dec. 12, 1980, P.L. 96-513, Title II, Part A, § 202, 94 Stat. 2878, effective Sept. 15, 1981, as provided by § 701(a) of such Act, which appears as 10 USCS § 101 note. Section 8203 provided for the authorized strength of the Regular Air Force in members on active duty; § 8204 provided for the computation of the authorized strength of the Regular Air Force in commissioned officers on the active list; § 8205 provided for the numerical authorized strength of Regular Air Force in commissioned officers on the active list; § 8206 provided for the authorized strength in Air Force nurses on the active list; § 8207 provided for the authorized strength in Air Force medical specialists on the active list; § 8208 provided for the authorized strength in female commissioned officers on the active list; and § 8209 provided for the authorized strength of the Regular Air Force in commissioned officers on the active list in special categories. For similar provisions, see 10 USCS § 522.

§ 8210. Regular Air Force: strength in grade; general officers

(a) Subject to section 526 of this title, the authorized strength of the Regular Air Force in general officers on the active-duty list is 75/10,000 of the authorized strength of the Regular Air Force in commissioned officers on the active-duty list. Of this authorized strength, not more than one-half may be in a regular grade above brigadier general.

(b) When the application of subsection (a) results in a fraction, of one-half or more is counted as one, and a fraction of less than one-half is disregarded.

(c) General officers on the active-duty list of the Regular Air Force who are specifically authorized by law to hold a civil office under the United States, or an instrumentality thereof, are not counted in determining authorized strength under this section.

(Aug. 10, 1956, ch 1041, § 1, 70A Stat. 500; Sept. 2, 1958, P. L. 85-861, § 1(161), 72 Stat. 1514; Dec. 12, 1980, P.L. 96-513, Title V, Part A, § 504(7), 94 Stat. 2916; Dec. 5, 1991, P. L. 102-190, Div A, Title X, Part E, § 1061(a)(23)(A), 105 Stat. 1473.)

HISTORY; ANCILLARY LAWS AND DIRECTIVES

Prior law and revision:

1956 ACT

Revised Section	Source (USCS)	Source (Statutes at Large)
8210(a)	10:506a(a) (words before 1st semicolon).	Aug. 7, 1947, ch. 512, § 503(a), 61 Stat. 885.
8210(b)	10:506a(a) (less words before 1st semicolon, and less provisos).	
8210(c)	10:506a(a) (1st, 2d, and 3d provisos).	
8210(d)	10:506a(a) (4th proviso).	
8210(e)	10:506a(a) (last proviso).	

As enacted, section 503(a) of the Officer Personnel Act of 1947 (10:506a(a)) provided, subject to certain percentage limitations, for the following authorized strength of the Regular Army in general officers on the active list:

Medical Corps	16
Dental Corps	4
Veterinary Corps	1
The Chaplains	2
Army, exclusive of the above	334
Total	357

Under section 208(e) of the National Security Act of 1947 (5 U.S.C. 626c(e)), allocations of those authorized strengths were made between the Army and the Air Force as follows:

	Army	Air Force
Medical Corps	12	4
Dental Corps	3	1
Veterinary Corps	1	0
The Chaplains	1	1
Army and Air Force, exclusive of the above	184	150
Total	201	156

After the enactment of the Officer Personnel Act of 1947, section 308 of the Army Organization Act of 1950 (10:61-1) provided for an Assistant Judge Advocate General and three brigadier generals in the Judge Advocate General's Corps of the Army. The creation of these four general officer spaces served to increase the mentioned authorized strength figure from 357 to 361, and the figure 201 to 205. The opinion of the Judge Advocate General of the Army (JAGA 1948/5806, 2 Sept. 1948) is in accord with that conclusion.

The revised section reflects the authorized strength of the Regular Air Force in general officers on the active list resulting from the mentioned allocation to the Air Force.

That allocation, and those mentioned in the explanation of subsec. (c) below, have had the force of law since July 26, 1950, when the period for transfers, including the administrative authority to change these allocations, expired.

The word ''regular'' is substituted for the word ''permanent'' throughout the revised subsection.

In subsection (c), 10:506a(a) (1st proviso) is omitted, since there is no authority to appoint to a regular grade above major general. 10:506a(a) (last 65 words of 2d proviso) is omitted as executed by the declaration of a national emergency on December 16, 1950.

In subsection (c)(1), the figures ''4'' and ''2'' result from the allocation of the original figures ''16'' and ''8''.

In subsection (c)(2), the figure ''1'' results from the allocation of the original figures ''4'' and ''2''.

In subsection (c)(3), the figure ''1'' results from the allocation of the original figures ''2'' and ''1''. (The major general was allocated to the Army, the brigadier general to the Air Force.)

In subsection (c)(4), the figures ''150'' and ''75'' result from the allocation of the original figures ''334'' and ''167''. That allocation corresponds to the allotment made by the Secretary of War between the Air Corps and the Army exclusive of the Air Corps, the Medical Department, and the Chaplains, under 10: 506a(a) (3d proviso). That proviso is omitted as executed.

In subsection (e), the words ''by law to hold any civil office under the United States'' are substituted for the words ''by Acts of Congress to hold appointments in the Diplomatic or Consular Service of the Government or to hold any civil office under the Government''.

1958 ACT

Revised Section	Source (USCS)	Source (Statutes at Large)
8210(a)	10 App.:506a(a)(2) (less 4th and last sentences).	July 20, 1956, ch. 646, § 302 (less 1st par.), 70 Stat. 587.
8210(b)	10 App.:506a(a)(2) (4th sentence).	
8210(c)	10 App.:506a(a)(2) (last sentence).	

In subsection (a), the words ''Subject to section 8202(a) of this title'' are substituted for 10 App.:506a(a)(2) (3d sentence).

Amendments:

1958. Act Sept. 2, 1958, substituted this section, subject to subsequent amendment, for one which read:

''(a) The authorized strength of the Regular Air Force in general officers on the active list, exclusive of the number authorized for the categories named in subsection (b), is 75/10,000 of the authorized strength of the Regular Air Force in commissioned officers on the active list, exclusive of the number of commissioned officers on the active list authorized in each of the categories named in subsection (b) and exclusive of medical service officers. Of this authorized strength, not more than one-half may be in a regular grade above brigadier general.

"(b) The authorized strength of each of the following categories—

"(1) medical officers;

"(2) dental officers;

"(3) veterinary officers; and

"(4) chaplains;

in general officers on the active list of the Regular Air Force is 5/1,000 of the authorized strength of the category concerned in commissioned officers on the active list of the Regular Air Force. Not more than one-half of the authorized strength in general officers in such a category may be in a regular grade above brigadier general.

"(c) The number of general officers authorized for the active list of the Regular Air Force by subsections (a) and (b) may not be more than 156. Of this total there may not be more than—

"(1) 4 medical officers, of whom not more than 2 may be in a regular grade above brigadier general;

"(2) 1 dental officer, in the regular grade of brigadier general;

"(3) 1 chaplain, in the regular grade of brigadier general;

"(4) 150 on the active list of the Regular Air Force, exclusive of those authorized under clauses (1)-(3) of this subsection, of whom not more than 75 may be in a regular grade above brigadier general.

"(d) When the application of the percentages and ratios specified in this section results in a fraction, a fraction of one-half or more is counted as one, and a fraction of less than one-half is disregarded.

"(e) General officers on the active list of the Regular Air Force who are specifically authorized by law to hold any civil office under the United States, or any instrumentality thereof, are not counted in determining authorized strength under this section.".

1980. Act Dec. 12, 1980 (effective 9/15/81, as provided by § 701(a) of such Act, which appears as 10 USCS § 101 note), in subsec. (a), in two places, and in subsec. (c), substituted "active-duty list" for "active list".

1991. Act Dec. 5, 1991, in subsec. (a), substituted "section 526" for "section 8202(a)".

[§ 8211. Repealed]

HISTORY; ANCILLARY LAWS AND DIRECTIVES

This section (Act Aug. 10, 1956, ch. 1041, § 1, 70A Stat. 501; Sept. 2, 1958, P. L. 85-861, § 1(162), 72 Stat. 1514) was repealed by Act Dec. 12, 1980, P.L. 96-513, Title II, Part A, § 202, 94 Stat. 2878, effective Sept. 15, 1981, as provided by § 701(a) of such Act, which appears as 10 USCS § 101 note. It provided for the strength in grade of the Regular Air Force in promotion-list officers. For similar provisions, see 10 USCS §§ 521 et seq.

[§ 8212. Repealed]

HISTORY; ANCILLARY LAWS AND DIRECTIVES

This section (Act Aug. 10, 1956, ch 1041, § 1, 70A Stat. 501; Aug. 21,

1597. P. L. 85-155, Title III, § 301(3), 71 Stat. 386; Sept. 2, 1958, P. L. 85-861, § 1(163), 72 Stat. 1515; June 30, 1960, P. L. 86-559, § 1(48), 74 Stat. 275; Dec. 12, 1980, P.L. 96-513, Title V, Part A, § 504(8), 94 Stat. 2916) was repealed by Act Oct. 5, 1994, P. L. 103-337, Div A, Title XVI, Subtitle C, § 1662(a)(3), 108 Stat. 2988 (effective Dec. 1, 1994, as provided by § 1691 of such Act, which appears as 10 USCS § 10001 note). This section provided for strength in grade and temporary increases with respect to the Air National Guard of the United States. For similar provisions, see 10 USCS § 12009.

[§§ 8213–8215. Repealed]

HISTORY; ANCILLARY LAWS AND DIRECTIVES

These sections (§ 8213—Act Aug. 10, 1956, ch 1041, § 1, 70A Stat. 501; § 8214—Act Aug. 10, 1956, ch 1041, § 1, 70A Stat. 501; Sept. 2, 1958, P. L. 85-861, § 1(159), 72 Stat. 1514; § 8215—Act Aug. 10, 1956, ch 1041, § 1, 70A Stat. 502; Nov. 8, 1967, P. L. 90-130, § 1(26)(E), (F), 81 Stat. 382) were repealed by Act Dec. 12, 1980, P.L. 96-513, Title II, Part A, § 202, 94 Stat. 2878, effective Sept. 15, 1981, as provided by § 701(a) of such Act, which appears as 10 USCS § 101 note. Section 8213 provided for the authorized strength of the Regular Air Force in warrant officers on the active list; § 8214 provided for the authorized strength of the Regular Air Force in enlisted members on active duty; and § 8215 provided for the authorized strength of the Regular Air Force in female warrant officers on the active list.

[§§ 8217–8219. Repealed]

HISTORY; ANCILLARY LAWS AND DIRECTIVES

These sections (§ 8217–Act Sept. 2, 1958, P. L. 85-861, § 1(164)(A), 72 Stat. 1515; § 8218–Act Sept. 2, 1958, P. L. 85-861, § 1(164)(A), 72 Stat. 1515; Nov. 9, 1979, P. L. 96-107, Title III, § 302(d), 93 Stat. 806; Sept. 29, 1988, P. L. 100-456, Div A, Title XII, Part D, § 1234(a)(1), 102 Stat. 2059; Dec. 5, 1991, P. L. 102-190, Div A, Title X, Part E, § 1061(a)(23)(B), 105 Stat. 1473; § 8219–Act Sept. 2, 1958, P. L. 85-861, § 1(164)(A), 72 Stat. 1515) were repealed by Act Oct. 5, 1994, P. L. 103-337, Div A, Title XVI, Subtitle C, § 1662(a)(3), 108 Stat. 2988 (effective Dec. 1, 1994, as provided by § 1691 of such Act, which appears as 10 USCS § 10001 note). Section 8217 provided for commissioned officers in an active status in the Reserves; § 8218 provided strength in grade of general officers in an active status; § 8219 provided for strength in grade of commissioned officers in grades below brigadier general in an active status. For similar provisions, see 10 USCS §§ 12003–12005.

[§§ 8221–8225. Repealed]

HISTORY; ANCILLARY LAWS AND DIRECTIVES

These sections (§ 8221–Act Aug. 10, 1956, ch 1041, § 1, 70A Stat. 502; § 8222–Act Aug. 10, 1956, ch 1041, § 1, 70A Stat. 502; Dec. 12, 1980, P.L. 96-513, Title V, Part A, § 504(a), 94 Stat. 2916; § 8223–Act Aug. 10,

1956, ch 1041, § 1, 70A Stat. 502; § 8224–Act Aug. 10, 1956, ch 1041, § 1, 70A Stat. 502; § 8225–Act Aug. 10, 1956, ch 1041, § 1, 70A Stat. 503) were repealed by Act Oct. 5, 1994, P. L. 103-337, Div A, Title XVI, Subtitle C, § 1662(a)(3), 108 Stat. 2988 (effective Dec. 1, 1994, as provided by § 1691 of such Act, which appears as 10 USCS § 10001 note). Section 8221 related to the authorized strength of the Air Force Reserve; § 8222 related to the authorized strength of the Air Force Reserve, exclusive of members on active duty; § 8223 related to the authorized strength of the Air Force Reserve in warrant officers; § 8224 related to the authorized strength of the Air National Guard of United States; § 8225 related to the authorized strength of the Air National Guard and the Air National Guard of United States, exclusive of members on active duty. For similar provisions, see 10 USCS §§ 12001, 12002, 12008.

[§ 8230. Repealed]

HISTORY; ANCILLARY LAWS AND DIRECTIVES

This section (Act Sept. 2, 1958, P.L. 85-861, § 1(164)(B), 72 Stat. 1515) was repealed by Act Dec. 12, 1980, P.L. 96-513, Title II, Part B, § 232, 94 Stat. 2886, effective Sept. 15, 1981, as provided by § 701(a) of such Act, which appears as 10 USCS § 101 note. It provided that personnel detailed outside the Department of Defense were not to be counted in computing strengths.

CHAPTER 833. ENLISTMENTS

HISTORY; ANCILLARY LAWS AND DIRECTIVES

Amendments:

1958. Act Sept. 2, 1958, P. L. 85-861, § 1(166)(C), (D), 72 Stat. 1516, amended the analysis of this chapter by substituting item 8261 for one which read ''Air National Guard of United States: enlistment''; and by adding item 8263.

1968. Act Jan. 2, 1968, P. L. 90-235, § 2(a)(4)(C), 81 Stat. 756, amended the analysis of this chapter by deleting items 8252, 8254, 8255, 8256, 8262, and 8263, which read: ''8252. Temporary enlistments''; ''8254. Air Force: during war or emergency''; ''8255. Regular Air Force: recruiting campaigns''; ''8256. Regular Air Force: qualifications, term, grade''; ''8262. Extension of enlistment for members needing medical care or hospitalization''; and ''8263. Voluntary extension of enlistment''.

1988. Act Sept. 29, 1988, P. L. 100-456, Div A, Title V, Part C, § 522(a)(2), 102 Stat. 1973, amended the analysis of this chapter by adding item 8252.

1994. Act Oct. 5, 1994, P. L. 103-337, Div A, Title XVI, Subtitle D, § 1674(b)(3), 108 Stat. 3016 (effective 12/1/94 as provided by § 1691 of such Act, which appears as 10 USCS § 10001 note), amended the analysis of this chapter by deleting items 8259–8261, which read: ''8259. Air Force Reserve: transfer from Air National Guard of United States'', ''8260. Air Force Reserve: transfer to upon withdrawal as member of Air National Guard'', and ''8261. Air National Guard of United States''.

§ 8251. Definition

In this chapter [10 USCS §§ 8251 et seq.], the term ''enlistment'' means original enlistment or reenlistment.

(Aug. 10, 1956, ch 1041, § 1, 70A Stat. 503; Dec. 4, 1987, P. L. 100-180, Div A, Title XII, Part D, § 1231(19)(A), 101 Stat. 1161.)

HISTORY; ANCILLARY LAWS AND DIRECTIVES

Prior law and revision:

Revised Section	Source (USCS)	Source (Statutes at Large)
8251	[No source].	[No source].

The revised section is inserted for clarity.

Amendments:

1987. Act Dec. 4, 1987 inserted ", the term".

Other provisions:

Repeal of provision relating to women in the Air Force. Act Oct. 19, 1984, P. L. 98-525, Title V, Part E, § 551(a), 98 Stat. 2530; Nov. 14, 1986, P. L. 99-661, Div A, Title V, Part A, § 504, 100 Stat. 3864; Dec. 4, 1987, P. L. 100-180, Div A, Title V, § 506, 101 Stat. 1086, which formerly appeared as a note to this section, was repealed by Sept. 29, 1988, P. L. 100-456, Div A, Title V, Part C, § 522(d), 102 Stat. 1974. Section 551(a) of Act Oct. 19, 1984 provided that the Secretary of the Air Force was to provide that of all persons originally enlisting in the Regular Air Force during fiscal year 1989, not less than 22 percent shall be women.

§ 8252. Regular Air Force: gender-free basis for acceptance of original enlistments

In accepting persons for original enlistment in the Regular Air Force, the Secretary of the Air Force may not—

(1) set a minimum or maximum percentage of persons who may be accepted for such an enlistment according to gender for skill categories or jobs; or

(2) in any other way base the acceptance of a person for such an enlistment on gender.

(Added Sept. 29, 1988, P. L. 100-456, Div A, Title V, Part C, § 522(a)(1), 102 Stat. 1973; Oct. 23, 1992, P. L. 102-484, Div A, Title X, Subtitle F, § 1052(40), 106 Stat. 2501.)

HISTORY; ANCILLARY LAWS AND DIRECTIVES

Explanatory notes:

A prior § 8252 (Act Aug. 10, 1956, ch 1041, § 1, 70A Stat. 503) was repealed by Act Jan. 2, 1968, P. L. 90-235, § 2(a)(4)(B), 81 Stat. 756. It provided that temporary enlistments could be made only in the Air Force without specification of component.

Amendments:

1992. Act Oct. 23, 1992 (applicable as if enacted immediately before the other provisions of such Act, as provided by § 1055 of such Act, which appears as 10 USCS § 101 note), substituted "In" for "(a) Except as provided in subsection (b), in"; and deleted subsec. (b), which read: "(b) Subsection (a) shall not apply with respect to an enlistment specified as being for training leading to designation in a skill category involving duty assignments to which, under section 8549 of this title, female members of the Air Force may not be assigned.".

Other provisions:

Implementation of section. Act Sept. 29, 1988, P. L. 100-456, Div A, Title V, Part C, § 522(b), 102 Stat. 1973, provides: "The Secretary of the Air Force shall develop a methodology for implementing section 8252 of title 10, United States Code, as added by subsection (a), not later than October 1, 1989.".

Applicability of section. Act Sept. 29, 1988, P. L. 100-456, Div A, Title V, Part C, § 522(c), 102 Stat. 1974, provides: "Such section [this section] shall apply with respect to persons accepted for original enlistment in the Regular Air Force after September 30, 1989.".

§ 8253. Air Force: persons not qualified

In time of peace, no person may be accepted for original enlistment in the Air Force unless he is a citizen of the United States or has been lawfully admitted to the United States for permanent residence under the applicable provisions of the Immigration and Nationality Act (8 U.S.C. 1101 et seq.).

(Aug. 10, 1956, ch 1041, § 1, 70A Stat. 503; Aug. 17, 1961, P. L. 87-143, § 1(2), 75 Stat. 364; Jan. 2, 1968, P. L. 90-235, § 2(a)(4)(A), 81 Stat. 756; Dec. 12, 1980, P. L. 96-513, Title V, Part B, § 514(2), 94 Stat. 2935.)

HISTORY; ANCILLARY LAWS AND DIRECTIVES

Prior law and revision:

Revised Section	Source (USCS)	Source (Statutes at Large)
8253(a)	10:622.	R.S. 1118: Feb 27, 1877, ch. 69, (17th par.), 19 Stat. 242; July 29, 1941, ch. 325, 55 Stat. 606.
8253(b)	10:623.	R.S. 1998; restated Aug. 22, 1912, ch. 336, § 1, 37 Stat. 356; Oct. 14, 1940, ch. 876, § 504 (9th clause), 54 Stat. 1172.
	10:624.	Aug. 1, 1894, ch. 179, § 2, 28 Stat. 216; June 14, 1920, ch. 286, 41 Stat. 1077.
8253(c)	10:625.	

In subsection (a), the words "an armed force" are substituted for the words "the military service of the United States". The words "and no person" are omitted as surplusage. The last sentence is substituted for 10:622 (proviso). The words "by regulations or otherwise" are omitted, since the Secretary has inherent authority to issue regulations appropriate to exercising his statutory functions. Since the authority to enlist deserters "in meritorious cases", granted to the Secretary by 10:622 is equivalent to or broader than his authority to do so under 10:624, the applicability of 10:624 to 10:622 is omitted as surplusage.

In subsection (b), the word "soldier", in 10:623, is omitted as covered by the word "person". The last sentence is substituted for 10:624.

In subsection (b) and (c), the first 15 words and the proviso of section 2 of the Act of August 1, 1894, ch 179, 28 Stat. 216, are not contained in 10:623 or 625. They are also omitted from the revised section, since the first 15 words are superseded by 8256(a) of this title, and the proviso is executed. In subsection (c), the words "(except an Indian)", in section 2 of the Act of August 1, 1894, ch. 179, 28 Stat. 216, are not contained in 10:625. They are also omitted from the revised section, since section 201(b) of the Act of October 14, 1940, ch 876, 54 Stat. 1138 (8 U.S.C. 601), provides that Indians are citizens and nationals of the United States. The words "may be accepted for original" are substituted for the words "shall be enlisted for the first".

Amendments:

1961. Act Aug. 17, 1961, in subsec. (c), deleted ", or has made a legal declaration of intention to become," preceding "a citizen" and inserted "or has been lawfully admitted to the United States for permanent residence under the applicable provisions of chapter 12 of title 8".

1968. Act Jan. 2, 1968, substituted this section, subject to subsequent amendment, for one which read:

"(a) No person who is insane, intoxicated, or a deserter from an armed force, or who has been convicted of a felony, may be enlisted or mustered into the Air Force. However, the Secretary of the Air Force may authorize exceptions, in meritorious cases, for the enlistment or muster into the Air Force of deserters and persons convicted of felonies.

"(b) No person whose service during his last term of enlistment was not honest and faithful may be reenlisted in the Air Force. However, the Secretary may authorize the reenlistment or muster into the Air Force of such a person if his conduct after that service has been good.

"(c) In time of peace, no person may be accepted for original enlistment in the Air Force unless he is a citizen of the United States or has been lawfully admitted to the United States for permanent residence under the applicable provisions of chapter 12 of title 8.".

1980. Act Dec. 12, 1980 (effective upon enactment on 12/12/80, as provided by § 701(b)(3) of such Act, which appears as 10 USCS § 101 note), substituted "the Immigration and Nationality Act (8 U.S.C. 1101 et seq.)" for "chapter 12 of title 8".

Other provisions:

Enlistment of citizens of Northern Mariana Islands in U. S. Armed Forces. For authorization, notwithstanding 10 USCS §§ 3235, 8235, of a citizen of the Northern Mariana Islands to enlist in the Armed Forces of the United States upon meeting certain requirements and for termination of the enlistment period, see Act Sept. 15, 1980, P. L. 96-351, 94 Stat. 1161, which appears as 10 USCS § 3253 note.

RESEARCH GUIDE

Am Jur:

3A Am Jur 2d, Aliens and Citizens § 2109.

Annotations:

Enlistment or re-enlistment in branches of United States Armed Forces as protected by Federal Constitution or by federal statutes. 64 ALR Fed 489.

INTERPRETIVE NOTES AND DECISIONS

1. Nature of unlawful enlistments
2. Persons not qualified; insane or intoxicated persons
3. —Deserters
4. —Persons not rendering honest and faithful service
5. —Aliens

1. Nature of unlawful enlistments

Under predecessor of 10 USCS § 8253, enlistments contrary to law were not void, but voidable. In re Cosenow (1889, CCD Mich) 37 F 668.

2. Persons not qualified; insane or intoxicated persons

Congress has right to determine that no insane person may be enlisted in armed forces of United States; Congress, in its use of words ''insane person'' in predecessor of 10 USCS § 8253, did not intend to employ term which would vary in definition from state to state and term as used by Congress was meant to apply uniformly in all states and under all conditions; presumption that insanity continued after initial adjudication of incompetency is disputable and it is for court to determine whether presumption of insanity at time of enlistment has been outweighed by other evidence; individual seeking to obtain discharge from Air Force has burden of proof to establish insanity upon date of enlistment. In re Petition of Judge (1956, DC Cal) 148 F Supp 80.

Under predecessor of 10 USCS § 8253, where individual was insane or intoxicated at time of enlistment, such enlistment was voidable and individual could obtain his own discharge upon those grounds. In re Cosenow (1889, CCD Mich) 37 F 668.

3. —Deserters

Deserter who enlists, and afterwards again deserts, cannot, on being brought to trial for second offense, defend on ground that his enlistment was void and that he, therefore, is not amenable to trial. In re McVey (1885, DC Cal) 11 Sawy 25, 23 F 878.

Presidential pardon for convicted deserter will restore individual's rights of citizenship for purposes of predecessor of 10 USCS § 8253. (1898) 22 Op Atty Gen 36.

4. —Persons not rendering honest and faithful service

Individual whose prior service in armed forces could not be described as ''honest and faithful'' might be rejected as candidate for enlistment, despite his having been pardoned for offenses. (1898) 22 Op Atty Gen 36.

5. —Aliens

Limitation upon enlistment of aliens in predecessor of 10 USCS § 8253 applied only in times of peace, not in time of war. Ex parte Dostal (1917, ND Ohio) 243 F 664, 15 Ohiolr 365.

Even in time of peace, alien duly enlisted cannot obtain his discharge by writ of habeas corpus from military service and escape liability for offenses against military law by invoking provisions of predecessor of 10 USCS § 8253; United States alone is allowed to plead his disability to avoid his enlistment contract. Ex parte Beaver (1921, DC Ohio) 271 F 493.

[§§ 8254–8256. Repealed]

HISTORY; ANCILLARY LAWS AND DIRECTIVES

These sections (Act Aug. 10, 1956, ch 1041, § 1, 70A Stat. 503, 504) were repealed by Act Jan. 2, 1968, P. L. 90-235, § 2(a)(4)(B), 81 Stat. 756. Section 8254 provided for temporary enlistments in the Air Force during war or emergency; § 8255 provided for recruiting campaigns to obtain enlistments in the Regular Air Force; § 8256 set forth the qualifications for and term of enlistments in the Regular Air Force and the grade in which such enlistments were made.

Other provisions:

Members of Army and Air Force serving under enlistments for unspecified periods on Jan. 2, 1968; continuance in status; discharge. Act Jan. 2, 1968, P. L. 90-235, § 3(c), 81 Stat. 758, provided: ''Members of the Army or the Air Force who, on the effective date of this Act [enacted Jan. 2, 1968], are serving under enlistments for unspecified periods under sections 3256(b) and 8256(b) of title 10, United States Code [10 USCS §§ 3256(b), 8256(b)], shall continue in that status and shall be discharged therefrom in accordance with laws applicable to such discharges on the day before the effective date of this Act [enacted Jan. 2, 1968].''

§ 8257. Regular Air Force: aviation cadets; qualifications, grade, limitations

(a) The grade of aviation cadet is a special enlisted grade in the Regular Air Force.

(b) Any citizen of the United States may be enlisted as an aviation cadet, if he is otherwise qualified.

(c) Any enlisted member of the Regular Air Force who is otherwise qualified may be designated, with his consent, as an aviation cadet by the Secretary of the Air Force.

(d) Except in time of war or of emergency declared by Congress, at least 20 percent of the aviation cadets designated in each fiscal year shall be selected from members of the Regular Air Force or the Regular Army who are eligible and qualified. No person may be enlisted or designated as an aviation cadet unless—

(1) he agrees in writing that, upon his successful completion of the course of training as an aviation cadet, he will accept a commission as second lieutenant in the Air Force Reserve, and will serve on active duty as such for a period of three years, unless sooner released; and

(2) if under 21 years of age, he has the consent of his parent or guardian to his agreement.

(e) While on active duty, an aviation cadet is entitled to uniforms, clothing, and equipment at the expense of the United States.

(Aug. 10, 1956, ch 1041, § 1, 70A Stat. 504; Sept. 2, 1958, P. L. 85-861, § 33(a)(37), 72 Stat. 1566; Dec. 12, 1980, P.L. 96-513, Title II, Part B, § 237, 94 Stat. 2887.)

HISTORY; ANCILLARY LAWS AND DIRECTIVES

Prior law and revision:

1956 ACT

Revised Section	Source (USCS)	Source (Statutes at Large)
8257(a)	10:297a.	June 3, 1941, ch. 165, §§ 1, 3 (1st and 2d sentences), 55 Stat. 239.
8257(b)	10:299 (1st sentence, less last 19 words).	
8257(c)	10:291f-2 (less 1st 55 words of 1st proviso).	June 13, 1949, ch. 199, § 3, 63 Stat 175.
8257(d)	10:291f-2 (1st 55 words of 1t proviso). 10:299 (2d sentence).	

In subsection (b), the words ''Under such regulations as the Secretary of the Army may prescribe'' are omitted, since the Secretary has inherent authority to issue regulations appropriate to exercising his statutory functions.

In subsection (c), the words ''who is otherwise qualified'' and ''with his consent'' are substituted for 10:291f-2 (less 1st 55 words of 1st proviso).

In subsection (d), the first sentence is substituted for 10:291f-2 (proviso). The words ''after June 13, 1940'' (the date of enactment of the source statute) are substituted for the word ''hereafter'', in 10:291f-2. The words ''after June 13, 1949'', in 10:291f-2, are omitted as executed. The first 17 words of the last sentence are substituted for 10:299 (1st 20 words of 2d sentence). Clause (2) is substituted for 10:299 (proviso of 2d sentence).

1958 ACT

The new subsection (e) is necessary to reflect the last 11 words of the second sentence of section 4 of the Army Aviation Cadet Act (formerly 10 U.S.C. 304), which were omitted from the original military codification act, the Act of August 10, 1956, chapter 1041, as part of the source law for section 20(b) of that Act (70A Stat. 627). See Senate Report No. 2484, 84th Congress, 2d Session, page 738. Since the source law did not permit the payment of a money allowance to an aviation cadet in place of the issuance of uniforms, clothing, and equipment, as may be done for enlisted members generally, it is necessary to restate this provision separately. See Opinion of the Deputy General Counsel, Department of Defense, May 29, 1957.

Amendments:

1958. Act Sept. 2, 1958 (effective as provided by § 33(g) of such Act, which appears as 10 USCS § 101 note) added subsec. (e).

1980. Act Dec. 12, 1980 (effective 9/15/81, as provided by § 701(a) of such Act, which appears as 10 USCS § 101 note), in subsecs. (b) and (c), deleted ''male'' after ''Any''.

§ 8258. Regular Air Force: reenlistment after service as an officer

(a) Any former enlisted member of the Regular Air Force who has served on active duty as a reserve officer of the Air Force, or who was discharged as an enlisted member to accept a temporary appointment as an officer of the Air Force, is entitled to be reenlisted in the Regular Air Force in the enlisted grade that he held before his service as an officer, without loss of seniority or credit for service, regardless of the existence of a vacancy in his grade or of a physical disability incurred or having its inception in line of duty, if (1) his service as an officer is terminated by an honorable discharge or he is relieved from active duty for a purpose other than to await appellate review of a sentence that includes dismissal or dishonorable discharge, and (2) he applies for reenlistment within six months (or such other period as the Secretary of the Air Force prescribes for exceptional circumstances) after termination of that service.

(b) A person is not entitled to be reenlisted under this section if—

(1) the person was discharged or released from active duty as a Reserve officer on the basis of a determination of—

(A) misconduct;

(B) moral or professional dereliction;

(C) duty performance below prescribed standards for the grade held; or

(D) retention being inconsistent with the interests of national security; or

(2) the person's former enlisted status and grade was based solely on the participation by that person in a precommissioning program that resulted in the Reserve commission held by that person during the active duty from which the person was released or discharged.

(Aug. 10, 1956, ch 1041, § 1, 70A Stat. 505; Aug. 8, 1958, P. L. 85-603, § 1(3), 72 Stat. 526; Oct. 23, 1992, P. L. 102-484, Div A, Title V, Subtitle B, § 520(b), 106 Stat. 2409.)

HISTORY; ANCILLARY LAWS AND DIRECTIVES

Prior law and revision:

Revised Section	Source (USCS)	Source (Statutes at Large)
8258	10:631a (less last proviso).	July 14, 1939, ch. 267, § 1 (less last proviso); restated May 29, 1954, ch. 249, § 19(b) (less last proviso), 68 Stat. 166.

The words ''former'' and ''as an enlisted member'' are inserted for clarity. The words ''credit for service'' are substituted for the words ''of service''. The words ''in his grade'' are substituted for the words ''in the appropriate enlisted grade''. The words ''he applies'' are substituted for the words ''application . . . shall be made''. The words ''Hereafter'' and ''while on active duty'' are omitted as surplusage.

Amendments:

1958. Act Aug. 8, 1958, substituted this section, subject to subsequent amendment, for one which read: ''Any former enlisted member of the Regular Air Force who has served on active duty as a reserve officer of the Air Force, or who was discharged as an enlisted member to accept a temporary appointment in the Air Force, is entitled to be reenlisted in the Regular Air Force in the enlisted grade that he held before his service as an officer, without loss of seniority or credit for service, if his service as an officer terminated honorably and he applies for reenlistment within six months or such other period as the Secretary of the Air Force prescribes for exceptional circumstances, after the termination of that service, regardless of the existence of a vacancy in his grade or of a physical disability incurred or having its inception in line of duty.''.

1992. Act Oct. 23, 1992 (applicable as provided by § 520(c) of such Act, which appears as 10 USCS § 3258 note), designated the existing provisions as subsec. (a), in subsec. (a) as so designated, deleted ''However, if his service as an officer terminated by a general discharge, he may, under regulations to be prescribed by the Secretary of the Air Force, be so reenlisted.'' following ''termination of that service.''; and added subsec. (b).

CROSS REFERENCES

Service by enlisted member as an officer counted as enlisted service, 10 USCS § 8684.

RESEARCH GUIDE

Annotations:

Enlistment or re-enlistment in branches of United States Armed Forces as protected by Federal Constitution or by federal statutes. 64 ALR Fed 489.

INTERPRETIVE NOTES AND DECISIONS

Section 8258 does not grant re-enlistment rights to person who was former enlisted member of Regular Air Force who served on active duty as officer in Air Force Reserves but then was given commission and served on active duty as officer in Regular Air Force. Marcotte v Secretary of Defense (1985, DC Kan) 618 F Supp 756.

Statute does not grant any Air Force Reserve officer, who has at any point in his life served as enlisted person, statutory right to reenlist, rather term ''former enlisted members'' includes only those enlisted members discharged from active duty immediately before their entry into active duty as commissioned officers. Zavislak v United States (1993) 29 Fed Cl 525.

[§§ 8259–8261. Repealed]

HISTORY; ANCILLARY LAWS AND DIRECTIVES

These sections (§ 8259–Act Aug. 10, 1956, ch 1041, § 1, 70A Stat. 505; Sept. 29, 1988, P. L. 100-456, Div A, Title XII, Part D, § 1234(a)(1), 102 Stat. 2059; § 8260–Act Aug. 10, 1956, ch 1041, § 1, 70A Stat. 50; § 8261–Act Aug. 10, 1956, ch 1041, § 1, 70A Stat. 505; Oct. 4, 1961, P. L. 87-378, § 4, 75 Stat. 808) were repealed by Act Oct. 5, 1994, P. L. 103-337, Div A, Title XVI, Subtitle C, § 1662(c)(3), 108 Stat. 2990 (effective Dec. 1, 1994, as provided by § 1691 of such Act, which appears as 10 USCS § 10001 note). Section 8259 provided for transfer to the Air Force Reserve from Air National Guard of United States; § 8260 provided for transfer to the Air Force Reserve upon withdrawal as member of Air National Guard; § 8261 provided for enlistment in the Air National Guard of United States. For similar provisions, see 10 USCS §§ 12105–12107.

[§§ 8262, 8263. Repealed]

HISTORY; ANCILLARY LAWS AND DIRECTIVES

These sections (§ 8262—Act Aug. 10, 1956, ch 1041, § 1, 70A Stat. 506; Sept. 2, 1958, P. L. 85-861, § 1(166)(A), 72 Stat. 1516; § 8263—Act Sept. 2, 1958, P. L. 85-861, § 1(166)(B), 72 Stat. 1516; Sept. 7, 1962, P. L. 87-649, § 14(c)(53), 76 Stat. 501) were repealed by Act Jan. 2, 1968, P. L. 90-235, § 2(a)(4)(B), 81 Stat. 756. Section 8262 provided for extension of enlistment of members of the Air Force needing medical care or hospitalization; § 8263 provided for voluntary extension of enlistments in the Air Force.

CHAPTER 835. APPOINTMENTS IN THE REGULAR AIR FORCE

HISTORY; ANCILLARY LAWS AND DIRECTIVES

Amendments:

1957. Act Aug. 21, 1957, P. L. 85-155, Title III, § 301(15), 71 Stat. 388, amended the analysis of this chapter by deleting items 8291 and 8304, which read: ''8291. Commissioned officers; Air Force nurses and women medical specialists: original appointment; additional qualifications, grade'' and ''8304. Commissioned officers; Air Force nurses and women medical specialists: promotion to first lieutenant, captain, major, lieutenant colonel, or colonel''.

1958. Act Sept. 2, 1958, P. L. 85-861, §§ 1(177)(B), 33(a)(38), 72 Stat. 1520, 1566, amended the analysis of this chapter by adding item 8314 and by substituting item 8309 for one which read ''Commissioned Officers: physical examination for promotion''.

1980. Act Dec. 12, 1980, P.L. 96-513, Title V, Part A, § 504(10), 94 Stat. 2916 (effective 9/15/81, as provided by § 701(a), which appears as 10 USCS § 101 note), amended the analysis of this chapter by deleting items 8284, 8285, 8286, 8287, 8288, 8289, 8293, 8294, 8295, 8296, 8297, 8298, 8299, 8300, 8301, 8302, 8303, 8305, 8306, 8307, 8308, 8309, 8312, 8313, and 8314, which read ''8284. Commissioned officers: appointment, how made.'', ''8285. Commissioned officers: original appointment; qualifications.'', ''8286. Commissioned officers: original appointment; age limitations.'', ''8287. Commissioned officers: original appointment; service credit.'', ''8288. Commissioned officers: original appointment; determination of grade.'', ''8289. Commissioned officers; medical officers; original appointment; professional examination.'', ''8293. Commissioned officers; chaplains: original appointment; examination.'', ''8294. Commissioned officers; medical and dental officers: original appointment; additional method authorized as exception to general procedure.'', ''8295. Commissioned officers: original appointment; determination of place on promotion list.'', ''8296. Promotion lists: promotion-list officer defined; determination of place upon transfer or promotion.'', ''8297. Selection boards.'', ''8298. Commissioned officers: promotion to first lieutenant; effect of failure of promotion.'', ''8299. Commissioned officers: promotion to captain, major, or lieutenant colonel.'', ''8300. Commissioned officers: promotion to captain, major, or lieutenant colonel; selection board procedure.'', ''8301. Commissioned officers: promotion to captain, major, or lieutenant colonel; officers with special qualifications.'', ''8302. Commissioned officers; medical, dental, and veterinary officers: promotion to captain, major, or lieutenant colonel; professional examination.'', ''8303. Commissioned officers: effect of failure of promotion to captain, major, or lieutenant colonel.'', ''8305. Commissioned officers: promotion to colonel.'', ''8306. Commissioned officers: promotion to brigadier general.'', ''8307. Commissioned officers: promotion to major general.'', ''8308. Commissioned officers: effect of removal from recommended list by President or failure of confirmation by Senate.'', ''8309. Commissioned officers: physical examination for promotion.'', ''8312. Officers: acceptance of promotion.'', ''8313. Suspension of laws for promotion or mandatory retirement or separation during war or emergency.'', and ''8314. Commissioned officers: promotion not to be delayed by another appointment.''.

§ 8281. Commissioned officer grades

The commissioned grades in the Regular Air Force are:

(1) Major general.
(2) Brigadier general.
(3) Colonel.
(4) Lieutenant colonel.
(5) Major.
(6) Captain.
(7) First lieutenant.
(8) Second lieutenant.

(Aug. 10, 1956, ch 1041, § 1, 70A Stat. 507.)

HISTORY; ANCILLARY LAWS AND DIRECTIVES

Prior law and revision:

Revised Section	Source (USCS)	Source (Statutes at Large)
8281	10:506(a) (last 24 words).	Aug. 7, 1947, ch. 512, § 502(a) (last 24 words), 61 Stat. 884.

CROSS REFERENCES

Rank, 10 USCS § 741.

[§§ 8284–8289. Repealed]

HISTORY; ANCILLARY LAWS AND DIRECTIVES

These sections (§ 8284—Act Aug. 10, 1956, ch 1041, § 1, 70A Stat. 507; §§ 8285, 8286—Act Aug. 10, 1956, ch 1041, § 1, 70A Stat. 507; Aug. 21, 1957, P. L. 85-155, Title III, § 301(4), (5), 71 Stat. 386; Sept. 2, 1958, P. L. 85-861, § 1(167), (168), 72 Stat. 1516, 1517; § 8287—Act Aug. 10, 1956, ch 1041, § 1, 70A Stat. 508; Aug. 21, 1957, P. L. 85-155, Title III, § 301(6), 71 Stat. 386; Sept. 2, 1958, P. L. 85-861, § 1(169), 72 Stat. 1517; Sept. 30, 1966, P. L. 89-609, § 1(28), 80 Stat. 854; § 8288—(Act Aug. 10, 1956, ch 1041, § 1, 70A Stat. 508; Aug. 21, 1957, P. L. 85-155, Title III,

§ 301(7), 71 Stat. 387; Sept. 2, 1958, P. L. 85-861, § 1(170), 72 Stat. 1518; § 8289—Act Aug. 10, 1956, ch 1041, § 1, 70A Stat. 509) were repealed by Act Dec. 12, 1980, P.L. 96-513, Title II, Part A, § 204, 94 Stat. 2880, effective Sept. 15, 1981, as provided by § 701(a) of such Act, which appears as 10 USCS § 101 note. Section 8284 provided that appointments in commissioned grades in the Regular Air Force were to be made by the President, by and with the advice and consent of the Senate; § 8285 related to qualifications of commissioned officers; § 8286 related to age limitations of commissioned officers; § 8287 related to service credit for commissioned officers; § 8288 related to determination of the grade of commissioned officers; and § 8289 related to professional examinations for medical officers. For similar provisions, see 10 USCS §§ 531–533.

[§ 8291. Repealed]

HISTORY; ANCILLARY LAWS AND DIRECTIVES

This section (Act Aug. 10, 1956, ch 1041, § 1, 70A Stat. 509) was repealed by Act Aug. 21, 1957, P. L. 85-155, Title IV, § 401(1), 71 Stat. 390. It related to original appointments in the Regular Air Force of nurses or woman medical specialists, and prescribed qualifications for appointment as a nurse.

[§§ 8293–8303. Repealed]

HISTORY; ANCILLARY LAWS AND DIRECTIVES

These sections (§ 8293—Act Aug. 10, 1956, ch 1041, § 1, 70A Stat. 509; §§ 8294, 8295—Act Aug. 10, 1956, ch 1041, § 1, 70A Stat. 509, 510; Sept. 2, 1958, P. L. 85-861, § 1(173), (174), 72 Stat. 1518, 1519; § 8296—Act Aug. 10, 1956, ch 1041, § 1, 70A Stat. 510; Aug. 6, 1958, P. L. 85-600, § 1(16), 72 Stat. 523; Sept. 2, 1958, P. L. 85-861, § 1(156), (175), 72 Stat. 1513, 1519); § 8297—Act Aug. 10, 1956, ch 1041, § 1, 70A Stat. 510; Aug. 21, 1957, P. L. 85-155, Title III, § 301(8), 71 Stat. 387; July 12, 1960, P. L. 86-616, § 6(1), 74 Stat. 391; § 8298—Act Aug. 10, 1956, ch 1041, § 1, 70A Stat. 511; Aug. 21, 1957, P. L. 85-155, Title III, § 301(9), Title IV, § 401(1), 71 Stat. 387, 390; § 8299—Act Aug. 10, 1956, ch 1041, § 1, 70A Stat. 511; Aug. 21, 1957, P. L. 85-155, Title III, § 301(10), Title IV, § 401(1), 71 Stat. 387, 390; Sept. 2, 1958, P. L. 85-861, § 33(a)(21), 72 Stat. 1565; Sept. 30, 1966, P. L. 89-609, § 1(29), 80 Stat. 854; Nov. 8, 1967, P. L. 90-130, § 1(27)(A), 81 Stat. 382; § 8300—Act Aug. 10, 1956, ch 1041, § 1, 70A Stat. 512; Aug. 21, 1957, P. L. 85-155, Title III, § 301(11), 71 Stat. 388; July 12, 1960, P. L. 86-616, § 6(2), 74 Stat. 391; Nov. 8, 1967, P. L. 90-130, § 1(27)(B), 81 Stat. 382; § 8301—Act Aug. 10, 1956, ch 1041, § 1, 70A Stat. 513; Aug. 21, 1957, P. L. 85-155, Title III, § 301(12), 71 Stat. 388; Nov. 8, 1967, P. L. 90-130, § 1(27)(C), 81 Stat. 382; § 8302—Act Aug. 10, 1956, ch 1041, § 1, 70A Stat. 513; § 8303—Act Aug. 10, 1956, ch 1041, § 1, 70A Stat. 514; Aug. 21, 1957, P. L. 85-155, Title III, § 301(13), 71 Stat. 388; July 12, 1960, P. L. 86-616, § 6(3), 74 Stat. 391; June 28, 1962, P. L. 87-509, § 4(a), 76 Stat. 121; Nov. 8, 1967, P. L. 90-130, § 1(27)(D), 81 Stat. 382) were repealed by Act Dec. 12, 1980, P.L. 96-513, Title II, Part A, § 204, 94 Stat. 2880, effective Sept. 15, 1981, as provided by § 701(a) of such Act, which appears as 10 USCS § 101 note. Section 8293 related to a moral, mental, and physical examinations for chaplains; § 8294 related to medical and dental officers; § 8295 related to determination of place on the promotion list; § 8296 defined promotion-list officer and related to determination of place upon transfer or promotion; § 8297 related to selection boards; § 8298 related to promotion to first lieutenant and the effect of failure of promotion; § 8299 related to promotion to captain, major, or lieutenant colonel; § 8300 related to selection board procedure upon promotion to captain, major, or lieutenant colonel; § 8301 related to consideration of officers with special qualifications for promotion to captain, major, or lieutenant colonel; § 8302 related to professional examinations of medical, dental, and veterinary officers before promotion to captain, major, or lieutenant colonel; and § 8303 related to failure of promotion to captain, major, or lieutenant colonel. For similar provisions, see 10 USCS §§ 532, 611 et seq., 624, 630–632.

[§ 8304. Repealed]

HISTORY; ANCILLARY LAWS AND DIRECTIVES

This section (Act Aug. 10, 1956, ch 1041, § 1, 70A Stat. 515) was repealed by Act Aug. 21, 1957, P. L. 85-155, Title IV, § 401(1), 71 Stat. 390. It related to promotion of Air Force nurses or women medical specialists to grades of first lieutenant, captain, major, lieutenant colonel, or colonel.

[§§ 8305–8309. Repealed]

HISTORY; ANCILLARY LAWS AND DIRECTIVES

These sections (§ 8305 Act Aug. 10, 1956, ch 1041, § 1, 70A Stat. 516; Aug. 21, 1957, P. L. 85-155, Title III, § 301(14), 71 Stat. 388; Nov. 8, 1967, P. L. 90-130, § 1(27)(E), 81 Stat. 382; §§ 8306–8309—Act Aug. 10, 1956, ch 1041, § 1, 70A Stat. 516–518) were repealed by Act Dec. 12, 1980, P.L. 96-513, Title II, Part A, § 204, 94 Stat. 2880, effective Sept. 15, 1981, as provided by § 701(a) of such Act, which appears as 10 USCS § 101 note. Section 8305 related to promotion to colonel; § 8306 related to promotion to brigadier general; § 8307 related to promotion to major general; § 8308 related to the effect of removal from the recommended list by the President or failure of confirmation by the Senate; and § 8309 related to physical examinations for promotion. For similar provisions, see 10 USCS §§ 619 et seq.

§ 8310. Warrant officers: original appointment; qualifications

Original appointments as warrant officers in the Regular Air Force shall be made from persons who have served on active duty at least one year in the Air Force.

(Aug. 10, 1956, ch 1041, § 1, 70A Stat. 518.)

HISTORY; ANCILLARY LAWS AND DIRECTIVES

Prior law and revision:

Revised Section	Source (USCS)	Source (Statutes at Large)
8310	10:591. [Uncodified: June 3, 1916, ch. 134, § 4a (less 3d and last sentences); added June 4, 1920, ch. 227, subch. I, § 4 (3d par., less 3d and last sentences), 41 Stat. 761].	June 3, 1916, ch. 134, § 4a (less 3d and last sentences); added June 4, 1920, ch. 227, subch. I, § 4 (3d par., less 3d and last sentences), 41 Stat. 761. Aug. 21, 1941, ch. 384, § 2; restated May 29, 1954, ch. 249, § 19(c), 68 Stat. 166.

The first sentence of section 4a of the Act of June 3, 1916, cited above, is omitted as superseded by 10 USCS § 8213. The second sentence, less first nine words, of section 4a of that act, is omitted as superseded by 10:591.

[§§ 8312–8314. Repealed]

HISTORY; ANCILLARY LAWS AND DIRECTIVES

These sections (§§ 8312, 8313—Act Aug. 10, 1956, ch 1041, § 1, 70A Stat. 519; § 8314—Act Sept. 2, 1958, P. L. 85-861, § 1(177)(A), 72 Stat. 1519) were repealed by Act Dec. 12, 1980, P.L. 96-513, Title II, Part A, § 204, 94 Stat. 2880, effective Sept. 15, 1981, as provided by § 701(a) of such Act, which appears as 10 USCS § 101 note. Section 8312 related to acceptance of promotion; § 8313 related to suspension of the laws for promotion or mandatory retirement or separation during war or emergency; and § 8314 provided that a promotion was not to be delayed by another appointment. For similar provisions, see 10 USCS §§ 624, 626, 644.

CHAPTER 837. APPOINTMENTS AS RESERVE OFFICERS [TRANSFERRED OR REPEALED]

HISTORY; ANCILLARY LAWS AND DIRECTIVES

This chapter (other than sections 8351 and 8352) was repealed by Act Oct. 5, 1994, P. L. 103-337, Div A, Title XVI, Subtitle A, Part II, § 1629(c)(1), 108 Stat. 2963 (effective Oct. 1, 1996, as provided by § 1691(b)(1) of such Act, which appears as 10 USCS § 10001 note). Sections 8351 and 8352 were transferred to 10 USCS §§ 12212 and 12214, respectively.

[§§ 8351, 8352. Transferred]

HISTORY; ANCILLARY LAWS AND DIRECTIVES

These sections were transferred to Chapter 1205 and redesignated as 10 USCS §§ 12212, 12214, respectively, by Act Oct. 5, 1994, P. L. 103-337, Div A, Title XVI, Subtitle C, § 1662(c)(3), 108 Stat. 2990 (effective Dec. 1, 1994, as provided by § 1691 of such Act, which appears as 10 USCS § 10001 note).

[§ 8353. Repealed]

HISTORY; ANCILLARY LAWS AND DIRECTIVES

This section (Act Sept. 2, 1958, P. L. 85-861, § 1(178)(A), 72 Stat. 1520; June 30, 1960, P. L. 86-559, § 1(49), 74 Stat. 275; Dec. 12, 1980, P.L. 96-513, Title II, Part A, § 205(b), 94 Stat. 2882; July 10, 1981, P. L. 97-22, § 7, 95 Stat. 131; Sept. 24, 1983, P. L. 98-94, Title X, Part A, § 1007(c)(5), 97 Stat. 662; Dec. 4, 1987, P. L. 100-180, Div A, Title VII, Part A, § 714(d), 101 Stat. 1113; Nov. 30, 1993, P. L. 103-160, Div A, Title V, Subtitle A, § 509(d), 107 Stat. 1648) was repealed by Act Oct. 5, 1994, P. L. 103-337, Div A, Title XVI, Subtitle A, Part II, § 1629(c)(1), 108 Stat. 2963 (effective Oct. 1, 1996, as provided by § 1691(b)(1) of such Act, which appears as 10 USCS § 10001 note). It provided for service credit upon original appointment of reserve commissioned officers. For similar provisions, see 10 USCS § 12207.

[§ 8354. Repealed]

HISTORY; ANCILLARY LAWS AND DIRECTIVES

This section (Act Aug. 10, 1956, ch 1041, § 1, 70A Stat. 520; Sept. 2, 1958, P. L. 85-861, § 1(178)(B), 72 Stat. 1520) was repealed by Act Oct. 5, 1994, P. L. 103-337, Div A, Title XVI, Subtitle A, Part II, § 1629(c)(1), 108 Stat. 2963 (effective Oct. 1, 1996, as provided by § 1691(b)(1) of such Act, which appears as 10 USCS § 10001 note). It provided for appointment and status of warrant officers and enlisted members of Air National Guard.

[§ 8355. Repealed]

HISTORY; ANCILLARY LAWS AND DIRECTIVES

This section (Act Aug. 10, 1956, ch 1041, § 1, 70A Stat. 520; Sept. 2, 1958, P. L. 85-861, § 33(a)(22), 72 Stat. 1565) was repealed by Act Oct. 13, 1964, P. L. 88-647, Title III, § 301(21), 78 Stat. 1073. It related to the appointment of graduates of the junior or senior division of the Air Force Reserve Officers' Training Corps as reserve commissioned officers.

[§ 8356. Repealed]

HISTORY; ANCILLARY LAWS AND DIRECTIVES

This section (Act Aug. 10, 1956, ch 1041, § 1, 70A Stat. 520) was repealed by Act Oct. 5, 1994, P. L. 103-337, Div A, Title XVI, Subtitle A, Part II, § 1629(c)(1), Subtitle B, Part I, § 1636(b), 108 Stat. 2963, 2698 (effective Oct. 1, 1996, as provided by § 1691(b)(1) of such Act, which appears as 10 USCS § 10001 note). It provided for appointment and qualifications of aviation cadets as Reserve officers.

[§§ 8358–8363. Repealed]

HISTORY; ANCILLARY LAWS AND DIRECTIVES

These sections (§ 8358–Added Act Sept. 2, 1958, § 1(178)(C), 72 Stat. 1520; § 8359–Act Sept. 2, 1958, P. L. 85-861, § 1(178)(C), 72 Stat. 1521; Sept. 24, 1983, P. L. 98-94, Title X, Part B, § 1014(b), 97 Stat. 666; Oct. 19, 1984, P. L. 98-525, Title V, Part C, § 521(b), 98 Stat. 2522; Nov. 8, 1985, P. L. 99-145, Title V, Part C, § 521(a), 99 Stat. 631; Dec. 4, 1987, P. L. 100-180, Div A, Title V, § 502(a), 101 Stat. 1085; Nov. 29, 1989, P. L. 101-189, Div A, Title V, Part A, § 503(a), 103 Stat. 1437; Oct. 23, 1992, P. L. 102-484, Div A, Title V, Subtitle B, § 519(a), 106 Stat. 2408; Nov. 30, 1993, P. L. 103-160, Div A, Title V, Subtitle B, § 514(a), 107 Stat. 1649; Feb. 10, 1996, P. L. 104-106, Div A, Title V, Subtitle B, § 511(a), 110 Stat. 298; § 8360–Act Sept. 2, 1958, P. L. 85-861, § 1(178)(C), 72 Stat. 1521; Sept. 29, 1988, P. L. 100-456, Div A, Title XII, Part D, § 1234(a)(1), 102 Stat. 2059; Feb. 10, 1996, P. L. 104-106, Div A, Title XV, § 1501(c)(30), 110 Stat. 500; § 8361–Act Sept. 2, 1958, P. L. 85-861, § 1(178)(c), 72 Stat. 1522; June 30, 1960, P. L. 86-559, § 1(50), 74 Stat. 275; § 8362–Act Sept. 2, 1958, P. L. 85-861, § 1(178)(C), 72 Stat. 1522; June 30, 1960, P. L. 86-559, § 1(51), 74 Stat. 275; § 8363–Act Sept. 2, 1958, P. L. 85-861, § 1(178)(C), 72 Stat. 1522; June 30, 1960, P. L. 86-559, § 1(52), 74 Stat. 275; Sept. 29, 1988, P. L. 100-456, Div A, Title XII, Part D, § 1234(a)(1), 102 Stat. 2059) were repealed by Act Oct. 5, 1994, P. L. 103-337, Div A, Title XVI, Subtitle A, Part II, § 1629(c)(1), 108 Stat. 2963 (effective Oct. 1, 1996, as provided by § 1691(b)(1) of such Act, which appears as 10 USCS § 10001 note). Section 8358 provided for original appointment and service credit for purpose of determining seniority in reserve grade and eligibility for promotion; § 8359 provided for determination of grade in original appointment; § 8360 provided for promotion service for commissioned officers; § 8361 provided for seniority for promotion purposes; § 8362 provided for selection boards; and § 8363 provided for general procedure for selection boards. For similar provisions, see 10 USCS §§ 12201 et seq., 14001 et seq., 14301 et seq.

[§§ 8365–8368. Repealed]

HISTORY; ANCILLARY LAWS AND DIRECTIVES

These sections (§ 8365–Act Sept. 2, 1958, P. L. 85-861, § 1(178)(C), 72 Stat. 1523; § 8366–Act Sept. 2, 1958, P. L. 85-861, § 1(178)(C), 72 Stat. 1523; June 30, 1960, P. L. 86-559, § 1(53), 74 Stat. 275; Nov. 8, 1967, P. L. 90-130, § 1(28)(A), 81 Stat. 382; § 8367–Act Sept. 2, 1958, P. L. 85-861, § 1(178)(C), 72 Stat. 1525; June 30, 1960, P. L. 86-559, § 1(54), (55), 74 Stat. 276; § 8368–Act Sept. 2, 1958, P. L. 85-861, § 1(178)(C), 72 Stat. 1525; June 30, 1960, P. L. 86-559, § 1(54), (55), 74 Stat. 276; Nov. 8, 1967, P. L. 90-130, § 1(28)(B), 81 Stat. 382; Dec. 4, 1987, P. L. 100-180, Div A, Title XII, Part D, § 1231(19)(B), 101 Stat. 1161) were repealed by Act Oct. 5, 1994, P. L. 103-337, Div A, Title XVI, Subtitle A, Part II, § 1629(c)(1), 108 Stat. 2963 (effective Oct. 1, 1996, as provided by § 1691(b)(1) of such Act, which appears as 10 USCS § 10001 note). Section 8365 provided for promotion to first lieutenant; § 8366 provided for promotion to captain, major, or lieutenant colonel; § 8367 provided selection board procedure for promotion to captain, major, or lieutenant colonel; and § 8368 provided for effect of failure of promotion to captain, major, or lieutenant colonel. For similar provisions, see 10 USCS §§ 14001 et seq., 14301 et seq.

[§ 8370. Repealed]

HISTORY; ANCILLARY LAWS AND DIRECTIVES

This section (Act Sept. 2, 1958, P. L. 85-861, § 1(178)(C), 72 Stat. 1526; June 30, 1960, P. L. 86-559, § 1(56), 74 Stat. 276) was repealed by Act Nov. 8, 1967, P. L. 90-130, § 1(28)(C), 81 Stat. 382. It placed restrictions on promotion consideration of Air Force nurses, medical specialists, and female officers being considered for promotion to the Reserve grades of lieutenant colonel and colonel.

[§§ 8371–8379. Repealed]

HISTORY; ANCILLARY LAWS AND DIRECTIVES

These sections (§ 8371–Act Sept. 2, 1958, P. L. 85-861, § 1(178)(C), 72 Stat. 1527; § 8372–Act Sept. 2, 1958, P. L. 85-861, § 1(178)(C), 72 Stat. 1527; June 30, 1960, P. L. 86-559, § 1(57), 74 Stat. 276; § 8373–Act Sept. 8, 1965, P. L. 89-172, § 1, 79 Stat. 662; § 8374–Act Sept. 2, 1958, P. L. 85-861, § 1(178)(C), 72 Stat. 1528; § 8375–Act Sept. 2, 1958, P. L. 85-861, § 1(178)(C), 72 Stat. 1528; June 30, 1960, P. L. 86-559, § 1(59), 74 Stat. 277; Dec. 12, 1980, P. L. 96-513, Title V, Part B, § 514(3), 94 Stat. 2935; § 8376–Act Sept. 2, 1958, P. L. 85-861, § 1 (178)(C), 72 Stat. 1528; June 30, 1960, P. L. 86-559, § 1(60), 74 Stat. 277; § 8377–Act Sept. 2, 1958, P. L. 85-861, § 1(178)(C), 72 Stat. 1529; June 30, 1960, P. L. 86-559, § 1(61), 74 Stat. 277; § 8378–Act Sept. 2, 1958, P. L. 85-861, § 1(178)(C), 72 Stat. 1530; § 8379–Act Sept. 2, 1958, P. L. 85-861, § 1(178)(C), 72 Stat. 1530) were repealed by Act Oct. 5, 1994, P. L. 103-337, Div A, Title XVI, Subtitle A, Part II, § 1629(c)(1), 108 Stat. 2963 (effective Oct. 1, 1996, as provided by § 1691(b)(1) of such Act, which appears as 10 USCS § 10001 note). Section 8371 provided for promotion to colonel in the Air Force Reserve; § 8372 provided for promotion of officers with special qualifications; § 8373 provided for promotion to brigadier general and major general; § 8374 provided that promotion was effective as of the date of Federal recognition; § 8375 provided for procedure on reassignment of brigadier general or major general; § 8376 provided for promotion when serving in temporary grade higher than reserve grade; § 8377 provided for effect of removal from recommended list by the President; § 8378 provided for promotion of officers removed from active status; and § 8379 provided that appointment of commissioned officers in Air National Guard was function of governor. For similar provisions, see 10 USCS §§ 14301 et seq.

A prior § 8373 (Act Sept. 2, 1958, P. L. 85-861, § 1(178)(C), 72 Stat. 1528; June 30, 1960, P. L. 86-559, § 1(58), 74 Stat. 277), containing similar subject matter, expired by its own terms on June 30, 1964.

[§ 8380. Repealed]

HISTORY; ANCILLARY LAWS AND DIRECTIVES

This section (Act Sept. 2, 1958, P. L. 85-861, § 1(178)(C), 72 Stat. 1530; June 30, 1960, P. L. 86-559, § 1(62), 74 Stat. 277; Sept. 24, 1983, P. L. 98-94, Title X, Part B, § 1015(b)(1), 97 Stat. 667; Nov. 8, 1985, P. L. 99-145, Title V, Part C, § 521(b) in part, 99 Stat. 631; Dec. 4, 1987, P. L. 100-180, Div A Title V, § 502(b)(1), 101 Stat. 1085; Nov. 29, 1989, P. L. 101-189, Div A, Title V, Part A, § 503(b)(1), 103 Stat. 1437; Oct. 23, 1992, P. L. 102-484, Div A, Title V, Subtitle B, § 519(b), 106 Stat. 2408; Nov. 30, 1993, P. L. 103-160, Div A, Title V, Subtitle B, § 514(b), 107 Stat. 1649; Feb. 10, 1996, P. L. 104-106, Div A, Title V, Subtitle B, § 511(b), Title XV, § 1501(c)(31), 110 Stat. 298, 500) was repealed by Act Oct. 5, 1994, P. L. 103-337, Div A, Title XVI, Subtitle A, Part II, § 1629(c)(1), 108 Stat. 2963 (effective Oct. 1, 1996, as provided by § 1691(b)(1) of such Act, which appears as 10 USCS § 10001 note). It provided for promotion of reserve commissioned officers on active duty and not on active duty list. For similar provisions, see 10 USCS § 14311(e).

[§ 8381. Repealed]

HISTORY; ANCILLARY LAWS AND DIRECTIVES

This section (Act Sept. 2, 1958, P. L. 85-861, § 1(178)(C), 72 Stat. 1531; Sept. 29, 1988, P. L. 100-456, Div A, Title XII, Part D, § 1234(a)(1), 102 Stat. 2059) was repealed by Act Oct. 5, 1994, P. L. 103-337, Div A, Title XVI, Subtitle A, Part II, § 1629(c)(1), 108 Stat. 2963 (effective Oct. 1, 1996, as provided by § 1691(b)(1) of such Act, which appears as 10 USCS § 10001 note). It provided for effect of adjutants general and assistant adjutants general ceasing to occupy position. For similar provisions, see 10 USCS § 14314(b), (c).

[§§ 8392–8396. Repealed]

HISTORY; ANCILLARY LAWS AND DIRECTIVES

These sections (§ 8392–Act Sept. 2, 1958, P. L. 85-861, § 1(178)(C), 72

Stat. 1531; Sept. 29, 1988, P. L. 100-456, Div A, Title XII, Part D, § 1234(a)(1), 102 Stat. 2059; § 8393–Act Sept. 2, 1958, P. L. 85-861, § 1(178)(C), 72 Stat. 1531; § 8394–Act Aug. 10, 1956, ch 1041, § 1, 70A Stat. 521; § 8395–Act Aug. 10, 1956, ch 1041, § 1, 70A Stat. 521; § 8396–Act Dec. 12, 1980, P. L. 96-513, Title II, Part A, § 206(b), 94 Stat. 2884) were repealed by Act Oct. 5, 1994, P. L. 103-337, Div A, Title XVI, Subtitle A, Part II, § 1629(c)(1), 108 Stat. 2963 (effective Oct. 1, 1996, as provided by § 1691(b)(1) of such Act, which appears as 10 USCS § 10001 note). Section 8392 provided for reserve grade of adjutants general and assistant adjutants general; § 8393 provided that sea or foreign service was not required for promotion; 8394 provided for acceptance of promotion; § 8395 provided for appointments in time of war; and § 8396 provided for exclusion of officers on active-duty list. For provisions similar to § 8392, see 10 USCS § 12215(b); for provisions similar to § 8394, see 10 USCS § 14309; for provisions similar to § 8395, see 10 USCS § 14317(e).

CHAPTER 839. TEMPORARY APPOINTMENTS

HISTORY; ANCILLARY LAWS AND DIRECTIVES

Amendments:

1958. Act Sept. 2, 1958, P. L. 85-861, § 1(180)(F), (G), 72 Stat. 1532, amended the analysis of this chapter by deleting item 8443, which read: ''8443. Commissioned officers; Reserves: appointment in higher or lower grade.''; and by adding item 8452.

1968. Act Jan. 2, 1968, P. L. 90-235, § 3(b)(6), 81 Stat. 758, amended the analysis of this chapter by deleting item 8450, which read: ''8450. Warrant officers: suspension of laws for promotion or mandatory retirement or separation during war or emergency.''.

1980. Act Dec. 12, 1980, P.L. 96-513, Title V, Part A, § 504(12), 94 Stat. 2917 (effective 9/15/81, as provided by § 701(a) of such Act, which appears as 10 USCS § 101 note), amended the analysis of this chapter by deleting items 8441, 8442, 8444, 8445, 8447, 8448, 8449, 8451, and 8452, which read: ''8441. General rule.'', ''8442. Commissioned officers; regular and reserve components: appointment in higher grade.'', ''8444. Commissioned officers: during war or emergency.'',''8445. Officers: additional appointments during war or emergency.'', ''8447. Appointments in commissioned grade: how made; how terminated.'', ''8448. Warrant officers: grades; appointment.'', ''8449. Warrant officers: promotion.'', ''8451. Officers: acceptance of appointment in higher grade.'', and ''8452. Medical and dental officers: temporary promotion to captain.''.

[§§ 8441, 8442. Repealed]

HISTORY; ANCILLARY LAWS AND DIRECTIVES

These sections (Act Aug. 10, 1956, ch 1041, § 1, 70A Stat. 521; § 8442—Act Aug. 10, 1956, ch 1041, § 1, 70A Stat. 522; Sept. 2, 1958, P. L. 85-861, § 1(180)(A), 72 Stat. 1532) were repealed by Act Dec. 12, 1980, P.L. 96-513, Title II, Part A, § 207, 94 Stat. 2884, effective Sept. 15, 1981, as provided by § 701(a) of such Act, which appears as 10 USCS § 101 note. Section 8441 provided that temporary appointments could be made only in the Air Force without specification of component; and § 8442 related to temporary appointments in higher grades. For provisions similar to § 8442, see 10 USCS § 601.

[§ 8443. Repealed]

HISTORY; ANCILLARY LAWS AND DIRECTIVES

This section (Act Aug. 10, 1956, ch 1041, § 1, 70A Stat. 522) was repealed by Act Sept. 2, 1958, P. L. 85-861, § 36(B)(25), 72 Stat. 1571. It related to grade of reserve commissioned officers ordered to active duty or serving on active duty.

[§§ 8444, 8445. Repealed]

HISTORY; ANCILLARY LAWS AND DIRECTIVES

These sections (Act Aug. 10, 1956, ch 1041, § 1, 70A Stat. 522; Sept. 2, 1958, P. L. 85-861, § 1(180)(A), (B), 72 Stat. 1532) were repealed by Act Dec. 12, 1980, P.L. 96-513, Title II, Part A, § 207, 94 Stat. 2884, effective Sept. 15, 1981, as provided by § 701(a) of such Act, which appears as 10 USCS § 101 note. Section 8444 provided for temporary appointments during war or emergency; and § 8445 related to additional temporary appointments during was or emergency. For similar provisions, see 10 USCS § 603.

§ 8446. Retention on active duty

The President may retain on active duty a disabled officer until—

(1) the physical condition of the officer is such that the officer will not be further benefited by retention in a military hospital or a medical facility of the Department of Veterans Affairs; or

(2) the officer is processed for physical disability benefits provided by law.

(Aug. 10, 1956, ch 1041, § 1, 70A Stat. 522; Sept. 2, 1958, P. L. 85-861, § 1(180)(C), 72 Stat. 1532; Nov. 29, 1989, P. L. 101-189, Div A, Title XVI, Part C, § 1621(a)(10), 103 Stat. 1603; April 6, 1991, P. L. 102-25, Title VII, § 701(j)(6), 105 Stat. 116.)

HISTORY; ANCILLARY LAWS AND DIRECTIVES

Prior law and revision:

1956 ACT

Revised Section	Source (USCS)	Source (Statutes at Large)
8446	10:499.	June 19, 1948, ch. 511, 62 Stat. 489.

The word "Shall" is substituted for the words "authorized and directed". The words "on active duty" are substituted for the words "in service". The words "warrant officers, and flight officers" are omitted, since the definition of "officer" in 10 USCS § 101(14) covers commissioned, warrant, and flight officers. The words "who has only a temporary appointment" are substituted for the words "of the Air Force . . . of the United States". The words "his physical condition is such that he" are substituted for the words "their treatment for physical reconstruction has reached a point where they". The words "in the Air Force" are substituted for the words "in the military service".

1958 ACT

Revised Section	Source (USCS)	Source (Statutes at Large)
8446	10 App.:499.	June 15, 1956, ch. 388, 70 Stat. 282.

The words ''commissioned officers and warrant'' are omitted as covered by the definition of the word ''officer'' in 10 USCS § 101(14). The words ''condition is such that'' are substituted for the words ''reconstruction has reached a point where''.

Amendments:

1958. Act Sept. 2, 1958, substituted ''may'' for ''shall'', deleted ''who has only a temporary appointment'' following ''officer'', inserted ''or Veterans' Administration'', and substituted ''until he is processed for physical disability benefits provided by law'' for ''in the Air Force''.

1989. Act Nov. 29, 1989 substituted this section for one which read: ''Notwithstanding any other provision of law, the President may retain on active duty any disabled officer until his physical condition is such that he will not be further benefited by retention in a military or Veterans' Administration hospital or until he is processed for physical disability benefits provided by law.''.

1991. Act April 6, 1991, in para. (2), deleted ''as'' before ''provided by law''.

[§ 8447. Repealed]

HISTORY; ANCILLARY LAWS AND DIRECTIVES

This section (Act Aug. 10, 1956, ch 1041, § 1, 70A Stat. 523; Sept. 2, 1958, P. L. 85-861, § 1(180)(D), 72 Stat. 1532; Sept. 28, 1971, P. L. 92-129, Title VI, § 60, 85 Stat. 362) was repealed by Act Dec. 12, 1980, P.L. 96-513, Title II, Part A, §§ 207, 208, 94 Stat. 2884, effective Sept. 15, 1981, as provided by § 701(a) of such Act, which appears as 10 USCS § 101 note. Such section provided for the making and termination of temporary appointments in commissioned grades. For similar provisions, see 10 USCS § 601.

§§ 8448, 8449. [Repealed]

HISTORY; ANCILLARY LAWS AND DIRECTIVES

These sections (§ 8448—Act Aug. 10, 1956, ch 1041, § 1, 70A Stat. 523; Aug. 8, 1958, P. L. 85-603, § 1(4), 72 Stat. 526; Sept. 2, 1958, P. L. 85-861, § 33(a)(39), 72 Stat. 1566; § 8449—Act Aug. 10, 1956, ch 1041, § 1, 70A Stat. 523) were repealed by Act Dec. 12, 1980, P.L. 96-513, Title II, Part A, §§ 207, 208, 94 Stat. 2884, effective Sept. 15, 1981, as provided by § 701(a) of such Act, which appears as 10 USCS § 101 note. Section 8448 provided for temporary warrant officers; and § 8449 related to temporary promotions in warrant officer grades. For similar provisions, see 10 USCS § 602.

[§ 8450. Repealed]

HISTORY; ANCILLARY LAWS AND DIRECTIVES

This section (Act Aug. 10, 1956, ch 1041, § 1, 70A Stat. 523) was repealed by Act Jan. 2, 1968, P. L. 90-235, § 3(b)(1), 81 Stat. 758. It provided for the suspension of laws for promotion or mandatory retirement or separation during war or emergency of temporary warrant officers of the Air Force.

[§§ 8451, 8452. Repealed]

HISTORY; ANCILLARY LAWS AND DIRECTIVES

These sections (§ 8451—Act Aug. 10, 1956, ch 1041, § 1, 70A Stat. 524; § 8452—Act Sept. 2, 1958, P. L. 85-861, § 1(180)(E), 72 Stat. 1532) were repealed by Act Dec. 12, 1980, P.L. 96-513, Title II, Part A, § 207, 94 Stat. 2884, effective Sept. 15, 1981, as provided by § 701(a) of such Act, which appears as 10 USCS § 101 note. Section 8451 related to acceptance of an appointment in a higher grade; and § 8452 related to temporary promotions of medical and dental officers to captain.

CHAPTER 841. ACTIVE DUTY

HISTORY; ANCILLARY LAWS AND DIRECTIVES

Amendments:

1958. Act Sept. 2, 1958, P. L. 85-861, § 1(181)(B), 72 Stat. 1533, amended the analysis of this chapter by adding item 8494.

1967. Act Nov. 8, 1967, P. L. 90-130, § 1(29)(B), 81 Stat. 382, amended the analysis of this chapter in item 8504 by deleting '': limitations; grade'' after ''members''.

1968. Act Jan. 2, 1968, P. L. 90-235, § 1(a)(4), 81 Stat. 753, amended the analysis of this chapter by deleting item 8492, which read: ''8492. Members: service extension during war''.

1980. Act Dec. 12, 1980, P.L. 96-513, Title V, Part A, § 504(13), 94 Stat. 2917 (effective 9/15/81, as provided by § 701(a) of such Act, which appears as 10 USCS § 101 note), amended the analysis of this chapter by deleting items 8494 and 8504, which read: ''8494. Commissioned officers: grade in which ordered to active duty'', and ''8504. Retired members''.

1994. Act Oct. 5, 1994, P. L. 103-337, Div A, Title XVI, Subtitle D, § 1674(b)(4), 108 Stat. 3016, amended the analysis of this chapter by deleting items 8495–8502, which read: ''8495. Air National Guard of United States: status'', ''8496. Air National Guard of United States: commissioned officers; duty in National Guard Bureau'', ''8497. Air National Guard of United States: members; status in which ordered into Federal service'', ''8498. Air National Guard of United States: mobilization; maintenance of organization'', ''8499. Air National Guard in Federal service: status'', ''8500. Air National Guard in Federal service: call'', ''8501. Air National Guard in Federal service: period of service; apportionment'', and ''8502. Air National Guard in Federal service: physical examination''.

§ 8491. Non-regular officers; status

A commissioned officer of the Air Force, other than of the Regular Air Force, who is on active duty in any commissioned grade has the rights and privileges, and is entitled to the benefits, provided by law for a commissioned officer of the Air Force Reserve—

(1) whose reserve grade is that in which the officer not of the Regular Air Force is serving;

(2) who has the same length of service as the officer not of the Regular Air Force; and

(3) who is on active duty in his reserve grade.

(Aug. 10, 1956, ch 1041, § 1, 70A Stat. 524.)

HISTORY; ANCILLARY LAWS AND DIRECTIVES

Prior law and revision:

Revised Section	Source (USCS)	Source (Statutes at Large)
8491	10:506d(h).	Aug. 7, 1947, ch. 512, § 515(h), 61 Stat. 908.

The first 12 words are substituted for 10:506d(h) (1st 11 words). The words "has the rights and privileges, and is entitled to the benefits" are substituted for the words "shall be entitled . . . to the same rights, privileges, and benefits". Clause (1) is substituted for the words "in a grade the same as such 'active-duty grade'". The words "as the officer not of the Regular Air Force" are substituted for the words "holding appointment in the Army Reserve". The words "his reserve grade" are substituted for the words "the grade held in the Army".

INTERPRETIVE NOTES AND DECISIONS

Call of Air Force reserve officer to active duty under voluntary program should be reviewed by civilian courts under test to determine whether such call was arbitrary and irrational. Karlan v Reed (1978, CA10 Colo) 584 F2d 365.

[§ 8492. Repealed]

HISTORY; ANCILLARY LAWS AND DIRECTIVES

This section (Act Aug. 10, 1956, ch 1041, § 1, 70A Stat. 524) was repealed by Act Jan. 2, 1968, P. L. 90-235, § 1(a)(2), 81 Stat. 753. It provided for extension of active service of Air Force members during war. For similar provisions, see 10 USCS § 671a.

[§ 8494. Repealed]

HISTORY; ANCILLARY LAWS AND DIRECTIVES

This section (Act Sept. 2, 1958, P. L. 85-861, § 1(181)(A), 72 Stat. 1532; June 30, 1960, P. L. 86-559, § 1(63), 74 Stat. 278) was repealed by Act Dec. 12, 1980, P.L. 96-513, Title II, Part A, § 209, 94 Stat. 2884, effective Sept. 15, 1981, as provided by § 701(a) of such Act, which appears as 10 USCS § 101 note. It related to the grade in which commissioned officers were ordered to active duty. For similar provisions, see 10 USCS § 12320.

[§§ 8495–8502. Repealed]

HISTORY; ANCILLARY LAWS AND DIRECTIVES

These sections (§§ 8495–8499–Act Aug. 10, 1956, ch 1041, § 1, 70A Stat. 524; §§ 8500, 8501–Act Aug. 10, 1956, ch 1041, § 1, 70A Stat. 525; Sept. 29, 1988, P. L. 100-456, Div A, Title XII, Part D, § 1234(a)(1), (3), 102 Stat. 2059; § 8502–Act Aug. 10, 1956, ch 1041, § 1, 70A Stat. 526) were repealed by Act Oct. 5, 1994, P. L. 103-337, Div A, Title XVI, Subtitle C, § 1662(f)(2), 108 Stat. 2994 (effective Dec. 1, 1994, as provided by § 1691 of such Act, which appears as 10 USCS § 10001 note). Section 8495 provided for status of members of the Air National Guard of the United States; § 8496 provided for duty of commissioned officers of the Air National Guard of the United States in the National Guard Bureau; § 8497 provided status of members of the Air National Guard of the United States when ordered into Federal service; § 8498 provided for maintenance of the organization of a unit of the Air National Guard of the United States during initial mobilization; § 8499 provided for the status of members of the Air National Guard called into Federal service; § 8500 provided for calling members of the Air National Guard into Federal service; § 8501 provided for periods of service and apportionment among jurisdictions when the Air National Guard is called into Federal service; and § 8502 provided for physical examinations of members of the Air National Guard called into Federal service. For similar provisions, see 10 USCS §§ 12401–12408.

§ 8503. Retired commissioned officers: status

A retired commissioned officer of the Air Force who is on active duty is considered, for all purposes except promotion, to be an officer of the organization to which he is assigned.
(Aug. 10, 1956, ch 1041, § 1, 70A Stat. 526.)

HISTORY; ANCILLARY LAWS AND DIRECTIVES

Prior law and revision:

Revised Section	Source (USCS)	Source (Statutes at Large)
8503	10:999.	July 9, 1918, ch. 143, subch. XX, (2d par.), 40 Stat. 893.

The words ''and shall be an extra number therein'' are omitted, since, in the opinion of the Judge Advocate General of the Army (JAG 210.85, Feb. 21, 1923), they were repealed by the Act of July 31, 1935, ch 422, 49 Stat. 505. The words ''in the discretion of the President, employed . . . assigned to duty'' are omitted as surplusage. The words ''arms, corps, department'' are omitted, since the Air Force does not have organic corps created by statute.

INTERPRETIVE NOTES AND DECISIONS

10 USCS § 593, dealing with promotion by President of commissioned officers in Reserves in grades below general, should be read together with former 10 USCS §§ 8380, former 8360(a), 8503, and former 8848, which deal with eligibility requirements for promotion. Jamerson v United States (1968) 185 Ct Cl 471, 401 F2d 808.

[§ 8504. Repealed]

HISTORY; ANCILLARY LAWS AND DIRECTIVES

This section (Act Aug. 10, 1956, ch 1041, § 1, 70A Stat. 526; Nov. 8, 1967, P. L. 90-130, § 1(29), 81 Stat. 382) was repealed by Act Dec. 12, 1980, P.L. 96-513, Title II, Part A, § 210, 94 Stat. 2884, effective Sept. 15, 1981, as provided by § 701(a) of such Act, which appears as 10 USCS § 101 note. It provided that the President could order any retired member of the Regular Air Force to active duty. For similar provisions, see 10 USCS § 688.

CHAPTER 843. SPECIAL APPOINTMENTS, ASSIGNMENTS, DETAILS, AND DUTIES

HISTORY; ANCILLARY LAWS AND DIRECTIVES

Amendments:

1958. Act Sept. 2, 1958, P. L. 85-861, § 1(182), 72 Stat. 1533, amended the analysis of this chapter by deleting item 8546, which read: "8546. Duties: medical officers, contract surgeons; attendance on families of members".

1964. Act Oct. 13, 1964, P. L. 88-647, Title III, § 301(24), 78 Stat. 1073, amended the analysis of this chapter by deleting item 8540, which read: "8540. Educational institutions: detail of members of regular or reserve components as professors and instructors in air science and tactics".

1968. Act Jan. 2, 1968, P. L. 90-235, § 4(a)(11), (b)(4), 81 Stat. 760, amended the analysis of this chapter by deleting items 8537, 8544, and 8545, which read: "8537. Department of Commerce: detail in aid of civil aviation"; "8544. Duties: regular officers; performance of civil functions restricted"; and "8545. Duties: officers; superintendence of cooking for enlisted members".

1980. Act Dec. 12, 1980, P.L. 96-513, Title V, Part A, § 504(14), 94 Stat. 2917 (effective 9/15/81, as provided by § 701(a) of such Act, which appears as 10 USCS § 101 note), amended the analysis of this chapter by deleting item 8531, which read: "8531. Chief of Staff to President: appointment".

1991. Act Dec. 5, 1991, P. L. 102-190, Div A, Title V, Part D, Subpart 1, § 531(a)(2), 105 Stat. 1365, amended the analysis of this chapter by deleting item 8549 which read: "8549. Duties; female members; limitations".

1994. Act Oct. 5, 1994, P. L. 103-337, Div A, Title XVI, Subtitle D, § 1674(b)(5), 108 Stat. 3016 (effective 12/1/94 as provided by § 1691 of such Act, which appears as 10 USCS § 10001 note), amended the analysis of this chapter by deleting items 8541 and 8542, which read: "8541. National Guard Bureau: assignment of officers of regular or reserve components" and "8542. Chief and assistant chief of staff of wings of Air National Guard in Federal service: detail".

[§ 8531. Repealed]

HISTORY; ANCILLARY LAWS AND DIRECTIVES

This section (Act Aug. 10, 1956, ch 1041, § 1, 70A Stat. 526) was repealed

by Act Dec. 12, 1980, P.L. 96-513, Title II, Part B, § 233(b), 94 Stat. 2881, effective Sept. 15, 1981, as provided by § 701(a) of such Act, which appears as 10 USCS § 101 note. It provided for the appointment of an Air Force general as the Chief of Staff to the President.

[§ 8537. Repealed]

HISTORY; ANCILLARY LAWS AND DIRECTIVES

This section (Act Aug. 10, 1956, ch 1041, § 1, 70A Stat. 526) was repealed by Act Jan. 2, 1968, P. L. 90-235, § 4(b)(1), 81 Stat. 760. It provided for the detail of Air Force officers to duty under the Secretary of Commerce in connection with the promotion of civil aviation.

[§ 8540. Repealed]

HISTORY; ANCILLARY LAWS AND DIRECTIVES

This section (Act Aug. 10, 1956, ch 1041, § 1, 70A Stat. 527) was repealed by Act Oct. 13, 1964, P. L. 88-647, Title III, § 301(23), 78 Stat. 1073. It related to the detail of members of regular or reserve components as professors and instructors in air science and tactics. For similar provisions, see 10 USCS § 2111.

[§ 8541. Repealed]

HISTORY; ANCILLARY LAWS AND DIRECTIVES

This section (Act Aug. 10, 1956, ch 1041, § 1, 70A Stat. 527) was repealed by Act Oct. 5, 1994, P. L. 103-337, Div A, Title XVI, Subtitle C, § 1661(c)(2), 108 Stat. 2982 (effective Dec. 1, 1994, as provided by § 1691 of such Act, which appears as 10 USCS § 10001 note). This section provided for assignment of officers of regular or reserve components to the National Guard Bureau. For similar provisions, see 10 USCS § 10507.

[§ 8542. Repealed]

HISTORY; ANCILLARY LAWS AND DIRECTIVES

This section (Act Aug. 10, 1956, ch 1041, § 1, 70A Stat. 527) was repealed by Act Oct. 5, 1994, P. L. 103-337, Div A, Title XVI, Subtitle C, § 1662(g)(2), 108 Stat. 2995 (effective Dec. 1, 1994, as provided by § 1691 of such Act, which appears as 10 USCS § 10001 note). This section provided for detail of chief and assistant chief of staff of wings of Air National Guard in Federal service. For similar provisions, see 10 USCS § 12502.

§ 8543. Aides: detail; number authorized

(a) Each major general of the Air Force is entitled to three aides selected by him from commissioned officers of the Air Force in any grade below major.

(b) Each brigadier general of the Air Force is entitled to two aides selected by him from commissioned officers of the Air Force in any grade below captain.
(Aug. 10, 1956, ch 1041, § 1, 70A Stat. 527.)

HISTORY; ANCILLARY LAWS AND DIRECTIVES

Prior law and revision:

Revised Section	Source (USCS)	Source (Statutes at Large)
8543(a)	10:498 (1st 20 words).	R.S. 1098.
8543(b)	10:498 (less 1st 20 words).	

In subsection (a), the words ''commissioned officers . . . in any grade below major'' are substituted for the words ''captains or lieutenants''.

In subsections (a) and (b), the words ''is entitled to'' are substituted for the words ''shall have''.

In subsection (b), the words ''commissioned officers in any grade below captain'' are substituted for the word ''lieutenants''.

[§§ 8544, 8545. Repealed]

HISTORY; ANCILLARY LAWS AND DIRECTIVES

These sections (Act Aug. 10, 1956, ch 1041, § 1, 70A Stat. 527, 528) were repealed by Act Jan. 2, 1968, P. L. 90-235, § 4(a)(6), (b)(1), 81 Stat. 759, 760. Section 8544 restricted the performance of civil functions by commissioned officers of the Regular Air Force; and § 8545 provided that cooking for enlisted members of the Air Force should be superintended by the officers of the organizations to which the members belonged. For provisions similar to § 8544, se 10 USCS § 973.

[§ 8546. Repealed]

HISTORY; ANCILLARY LAWS AND DIRECTIVES

This section (Act Aug. 10, 1956, ch 1041, § 1, 70A Stat. 528) was repealed by Act Sept. 2, 1958, P. L. 85-861, § 36B(26), 72 Stat. 1571. It required medical officers and contract surgeons to attend families of members of the Air Force.

§ 8547. Duties: chaplains; assistance required of commanding officers

(a) Each chaplain shall, when practicable, hold appropriate religious services at least once on each Sunday for the command to which he is assigned, and shall perform appropriate religious burial services for members of the Air Force who die while in that command.

(b) Each commanding officer shall furnish facilities, including necessary transportation, to any chaplain assigned to his command, to assist the chaplain in performing his duties.

(Aug. 10, 1956, ch 1041, § 1, 70A Stat. 528.)

HISTORY; ANCILLARY LAWS AND DIRECTIVES

Prior law and revision:

Revised Section	Source (USCS)	Source (Statutes at Large)
8547(a)	10:238.	R.S. 1125.
8547(b)	10:239.	R.S. 1127.
	[Uncodified: feb. 2, 1901, ch. 192, § 12 (last sentence), 31 Stat. 750].	Feb. 2, 1901, ch. 192, § 12 (last sentence), 31 Stat. 750.

In subsection (a), the words ''members of the Air Force'' are substituted for the words ''officers and soldiers''.

In subsection (b), the words ''regiments, hospitals, and posts'', in 10:239, are omitted, since at the time of the enactment of section 1127 of the Revised Statutes, chaplains were authorized only for regiments, hospitals, and posts. The revised section preserves the broad coverage of the original statute. The words ''each commanding officer shall'' are substituted for the words ''It shall be the duty of commanders'', in 10:239. The word ''furnish'' is substituted for the words ''to afford'', in 10:239. The words ''including necessary transportation'' are substituted for the last sentence of section 12 of the Act of February 2, 1901, ch 192, 31 Stat. 750. The words ''his command'' are substituted for the words ''the same'', in 10:239. The words ''to assist'' are substituted for the words ''as may aid them'', in 10:239.

§ 8548. Duties: warrant officers; limitations

Under regulations prescribed by the President, a warrant officer may be assigned to perform duties that necessarily include those normally performed by a commissioned officer.

(Aug. 10, 1956, ch 1041, § 1, 70A Stat. 528.)

HISTORY; ANCILLARY LAWS AND DIRECTIVES

Prior law and revision:

Revised Section	Source (USCS)	Source (Statutes at Large)
8548	10:593 (1st sentence).	Aug. 21, 1941, ch. 384, § 4, (1st sentence), 55 Stat. 653.

10:593 (1st sentence, less provisos) is omitted as superseded by 10 USCS § 8012(e). 10:593 (last proviso) is omitted as covered by 10 USCS § 936(a)(4) (Article 136(a)(4) of the Uniform Code of Military Justice). The words ''may be assigned'' are substituted for the words ''shall be vested with power to''.

[§ 8549. Repealed]

HISTORY; ANCILLARY LAWS AND DIRECTIVES

This section (Aug. 10, 1956, ch 1041, § 1, 70A Stat. 528) was repealed by

Act Dec. 5, 1991, P. L. 102-190, Div A, Title V, Part D, Subpart 1, § 531(a)(1), 105 Stat. 1365. This section prohibited assignment of female Air Force members, except for those designated under 10 USCS § 8067 or appointed with a view to such designation, to duty in aircraft engaged in combat missions.

CHAPTER 845. RANK AND COMMAND

HISTORY; ANCILLARY LAWS AND DIRECTIVES

Amendments:

1967. Act Nov. 8, 1967, P. L. 90-130, § 1(30), 81 Stat. 382, amended the analysis of this chapter by deleting item 8580, which read: ''8580. Command: female members of Air Force.''.

1968. Act Jan. 2, 1968, P. L. 90-235, § 5(a)(5), 81 Stat. 761, amended the analysis of this chapter by deleting items 8576 and 8578, which read: ''8576. Command: when different commands of Air Force and Marine Corps join.'' and ''8578. Command: commissioned officers of Air Force in same grade on duty at same place.''.

1974. Act Dec. 18, 1974, P. L. 93-525, 88 Stat. 1695, amended the analysis of this chapter by deleting item 8577, which read: ''8577. Command: flying units.''.

1980. Act Dec. 12, 1980, P.L. 96-513, Title V, Part A, § 504(15), 94 Stat. 2917, amended the analysis of this chapter by deleting items 8571, 8573, 8574, and 8582, which read: ''8571. Rank: commissioned officers on active duty.'', ''8573. Rank: commissioned officers in regular grades of brigadier general and major general; seniority list.'', ''8574. Rank: commissioned officers in regular grades below brigadier general.'', and ''8582. Command: retired officers.''.

1997. Act Nov. 18, 1997, P. L. 105-85, Div A, Title V, Subtitle A, § 507(b)(2), 111 Stat. 1727, amended the analysis of this chapter by adding item 8583.

[§ 8571. Repealed]

HISTORY; ANCILLARY LAWS AND DIRECTIVES

This section (Act Aug. 10, 1956, ch 1041, § 1, 70A Stat. 528; Sept. 2, 1958, P. L. 85-861, §§ 1(183), 33(a)(41), 72 Stat. 1533, 1566; June 30, 1960, P. L. 86-559, § 1(64), 74 Stat. 278) was repealed by Act Dec. 12, 1980, P.L. 96-513, Title II, Part A, § 211, 94 Stat. 2885, effective Sept. 15, 1981, as provided by § 701(a) of such Act, which appears as 10 USCS

§ 101 note. It related to the rank of commissioned officers on active duty. For similar provisions, see 10 USCS § 741.

§ 8572. Rank: commissioned officers serving under temporary appointments

The President may, in accordance with the needs of the Air Force, adjust dates of rank of commissioned officers of the Air Force serving in temporary grades.
(Aug. 10, 1956, ch 1041, § 1, 70A Stat. 529.)

HISTORY; ANCILLARY LAWS AND DIRECTIVES

Prior law and revision:

Revised Section	Source (USCS)	Source (Statutes at Large)
8572	10:506d(c) (last sentence).	Aug. 7, 1947, ch. 512, § 515(c) (last sentence), 61 Stat. 907.

The word "commissioned" is inserted for clarity, since the source statute related only to commissioned officers. The words "in his discretion, from time to time" are omitted as surplusage.

CROSS REFERENCES

Temporary appointments, 10 USCS § 601.

[§§ 8573, 8574. Repealed]

HISTORY; ANCILLARY LAWS AND DIRECTIVES

These sections (§ 8573—Act Aug. 10, 1956, ch 1041, § 1, 70A Stat. 529; § 8574—Act Aug. 10, 1956, ch 1041, § 1, 70A Stat. 530; Sept. 2, 1958, P. L. 85-861, §§ 1(184) 33(a)(24), 72 Stat. 1533, 1565) were repealed by Act Dec. 12, 1980, P.L. 96-513, Title II, Part A, § 211, 94 Stat. 2885, effective Sept. 15, 1981, as provided by § 701(a) of such Act, which appears as 10 USCS § 101 note. Section 8573 related to the date of rank of commissioned officers in the regular grades of brigadier general and major general; and § 8574 related to the rank of commissioned officers in regular grades below brigadier general. For similar provisions, see 10 USCS § 741.

§ 8575. Rank: warrant officers

Warrant officers rank next below second lieutenants and rank among themselves within each warrant officer grade under regulations to be prescribed by the Secretary of the Air Force.
(Aug. 10, 1956, ch 1041, § 1, 70A Stat. 530.)

HISTORY; ANCILLARY LAWS AND DIRECTIVES

Prior law and revision:

Revised Section	Source (USCS)	Source (Statutes at Large)
8575	10:593 (less 1st sentence).	Aug. 21, 1941, ch. 384, § 4 (less 1st sentence), 55 Stat. 653; May 29, 1954, ch. 249, § 19(e), 68 Stat. 167.

10:593 (2d sentence) is omitted as executed. The words ''within each warrant officer grade'' are inserted for clarity, since 10 USCS § 745 covers rank between warrant officers in different warrant officer grades. The words ''they shall take precedence'' are omitted as surplusage.

CROSS REFERENCES

Rank of warrant officers, general military law provisions, 10 USCS § 742.

[§ 8576. Repealed]

HISTORY; ANCILLARY LAWS AND DIRECTIVES

This section (Act Aug. 10, 1956, ch 1041, § 1, 70A Stat. 530) was repealed by Act Jan. 2, 1968, P. L. 90-235, § 5(a)(2), 81 Stat. 761. It provided for command when different commands of the Air Force and Marine Corps joined or served together. For similar provisions, see 10 USCS § 747.

[§ 8577. Repealed]

HISTORY; ANCILLARY LAWS AND DIRECTIVES

This section (Act Aug. 10, 1956, ch 1041, § 1, 70A Stat. 530) was repealed by Act Dec. 18, 1974, P. L. 93-525, 88 Stat. 1695. It provided for the command of flying units by commissioned officers of the Air Force who had received aeronautical ratings as pilots of service types of aircraft.

[§ 8578. Repealed]

HISTORY; ANCILLARY LAWS AND DIRECTIVES

This section (Act Aug. 10, 1956, ch 1041, § 1, 70A Stat. 530) was repealed by Act Jan. 2, 1968, P. L. 90-235, § 5(a)(2), 81 Stat. 761. It provided for command when two or more commissioned officers of the Air Force in the same grade were on duty at the same place. For similar provisions, see 10 USCS § 749.

§ 8579. Command: commissioned officers in certain designated categories

An officer designated as a medical, dental, veterinary, medical service, or biomedical sciences officer or as a nurse is not entitled to exercise command because of rank, except within the categories prescribed in subsection (a), (b),

(c), (d), (e), (f), or (i) of section 8067 of this title [10 USCS §§ 8067(a)–(f), (i)], or over persons placed under his charge.
(Aug. 10, 1956, ch 1041, § 1, 70A Stat. 531; Sept. 2, 1958, P. L. 85-861, § 1(156), (185), 72 Stat. 1513, 1533; Dec. 12, 1980, P.L. 96-513, Title II, Part A, § 212(b), 94 Stat. 2885.)

HISTORY; ANCILLARY LAWS AND DIRECTIVES

Prior law and revision:

1956 ACT

Revised Section	Source (USCS)	Source (Statutes at Large)
8579(a)	10:82.	R.S. 1169.
8579(b)	10:166e (less 1st sentence).	Apr. 16, 1947, ch. 38, § 106 (less 1st sentence), 61 Stat. 44.

In subsection (a), the words "Except as provided in section 94 of this title", not contained in section 1169 of the Revised Statutes, but contained in the United States Code, are omitted as surplusage, since 10:94 deals exclusively with assignments. The words "except within the categories prescribed in section 8067(a)–(d) of this title" are substituted for the words "in the line or in other staff corps". Air Force nurses and women medical specialists are not covered by subsection (a), since their command authority is specifically stated in subsection (b).
In subsection (b), the words "may exercise command only" are substituted for the words "shall not be entitled . . . to command except". The words "by virtue of their rank" and "by competent authority" are omitted as surplusage. 10:166(e) (last 22 words of last sentence) is omitted as superseded by section 8012(e) of this title.

1958 ACT

Revised Section	Source (USCS)	Source (Statutes at Large)
8579(b)	10 App.:166b-3.	Aug. 9, 1955, ch. 654, § 1, 69 Stat. 579.

This amendment reflects the authority contained in section 8067(e) and (f) of this title to appoint male reserve officers with a view to designation as Air Force nurses or medical specialists.

Amendments:

1958. Act Sept. 2, 1958, in subsec. (b), deleted "women" preceding "medical" and substituted "his" for "her" in two places.
1980. Act Dec. 12, 1980 (effective 9/15/81, as provided by § 701(a) of such Act, which appears as 10 USCS § 101 note), substituted this section for one which read:
"(a) An officer designated as a medical, dental, veterinary, or medical service officer is not entitled to exercise command because of his rank, except within the categories prescribed in section 8067(a)–(d) of this title.

"(b) An Air Force nurse or medical specialist may exercise command only within his category, or over persons placed under his charge.".

[§ 8580. Repealed]

HISTORY; ANCILLARY LAWS AND DIRECTIVES

This section (Act Aug. 10, 1956, ch 1041, § 1, 70A Stat. 531) was repealed by Act Nov. 8, 1967, P. L. 90-130, § 1(30), 81 Stat. 382. It provided that the Secretary of the Air Force should prescribe the military authority that female members of the Air Force, except those designated under 10 USCS § 8067 to perform professional functions, might exercise.

§ 8581. Command: chaplains

An officer designated as a chaplain has rank without command.
(Aug. 10, 1956, ch 1041, § 1, 70A Stat. 531.)

HISTORY; ANCILLARY LAWS AND DIRECTIVES

Prior law and revision:

Revised Section	Source (USCS)	Source (Statutes at Large)
8581	10:235.	R.S. 1122.

The words "and shall be on the same footing with other officers of the Army, as to tenure of office, retirement, and pensions" are omitted as obsolete, since there is no distinction between the status of a chaplain as an officer and the status of other officers of the Air Force.

[§ 8582. Repealed]

HISTORY; ANCILLARY LAWS AND DIRECTIVES

This section (Act Aug. 10, 1956, ch 1041, § 1, 70A Stat. 531) was repealed by Act Dec. 12, 1980, P.L. 96-513, Title II, Part A, § 211, 94 Stat. 2885, effective Sept. 15, 1981, as provided by § 701(a) of such Act, which appears as 10 USCS § 101 note. It provided that a retired officer has no right to command except when on active duty. For similar provisions, see 10 USCS § 750.

§ 8583. Requirement of exemplary conduct

All commanding officers and others in authority in the Air Force are required—

(1) to show in themselves a good example of virtue, honor, patriotism, and subordination;

(2) to be vigilant in inspecting the conduct of all persons who are placed under their command;

(3) to guard against and suppress all dissolute and immoral practices, and to correct, according to the laws and regulations of the Air Force, all persons who are guilty of them; and

(4) to take all necessary and proper measures, under the laws, regulations, and customs of the Air Force, to promote and safeguard the morale, the physical well-being, and the general welfare of the officers and enlisted persons under their command or charge.

(Added Nov. 18, 1997, P. L. 105-85, Div A, Title V, Subtitle A, § 507(b)(1), 111 Stat. 1727.)

CHAPTER 847. THE UNIFORM [REPEALED]

HISTORY; ANCILLARY LAWS AND DIRECTIVES

This chapter was repealed by Act Jan. 2, 1968, P. L. 90-235, § 8(2), 81 Stat. 764.

§ 8611, 8612. [Repealed]

HISTORY; ANCILLARY LAWS AND DIRECTIVES

These sections (Act Aug. 10, 1956, ch 1041, § 1, 70A Stat. 531) were repealed by Act Jan. 2, 1968, P. L. 90-235, § 8(2), 81 Stat. 764. Section 8611 provided that the President could prescribe the uniform of the Air Force; and § 8612 provided for the disposition of uniforms of enlisted members of the Air Force who were discharged and for the disposition of uniforms of and issuance of civilian clothing to enlisted members of the Air Force who were discharged otherwise than honorably.

CHAPTER 849. MISCELLANEOUS PROHIBITIONS AND PENALTIES

HISTORY; ANCILLARY LAWS AND DIRECTIVES

Amendments:

1958. Act Sept. 2, 1958, P. L. 85-861, §§ 1(186), 33(a)(40), 72 Stat. 1533, 1566, amended the analysis of this chapter by deleting item 8638 which read: ''8638. Enlisted members: required to make up time lost.''; and by correcting item numbered 8362 to be 8632.

1968. Act Jan. 2, 1968, P. L. 90-235, §§ 6(a)(10), 7(b)(5), 81 Stat. 762, 763, amended the analysis of this chapter by deleting items 8631, 8635, and 8637, which read: ''8631. Dealing in quartermaster supplies prohibited.''; ''8635. Enlisted members: restriction on civilian employment.''; and ''8637. Enlisted members: forfeiture of right to pension by deserters.''.

1980. Act Dec. 12, 1980, P.L. 96-513, Title V, Part B, § 514(4), 94 Stat. 2935 (effective upon enactment on 12/12/80, as provided by § 701(b)(3) of such Act, which appears as 10 USCS § 101 note), amended the analysis of this chapter by deleting item 8632 which read: ''8632. Members of Air Force: forfeiture of pay during absence from duty due to disease from intemperate use of alcohol and drugs.''; item 8633 which read: ''8633. Commissioned officers: forfeiture of pay when dropped from rolls.''; and item 8636 which read: ''8636. Enlisted members: pay and allowances not to accrue during suspended sentence of dishonorable discharge.''.

[§ 8631. Repealed]

HISTORY; ANCILLARY LAWS AND DIRECTIVES

This section (Act Aug. 10, 1956, ch 1041, § 1, 70A Stat. 532) was repealed by Act Jan. 2, 1968, P. L. 90-235, § 7(b)(1), 81 Stat. 763. It prohibited any officer of the Air Force who was engaged in the procurement or sale of quartermaster supplies from dealing in said supplies.

[§§ 8632, 8633. Repealed]

HISTORY; ANCILLARY LAWS AND DIRECTIVES

These sections (Act Aug. 10, 1956, ch 1041, § 1, 70A Stat. 532) were repealed by Act Sept. 7, 1962, P. L. 87-649, § 14(c)(54), (55), 76 Stat. 501, 502, effective as provided by § 15 of such Act, which appears as 37 USCS prec § 101 note. Section 8632 provided for forfeiture of pay during absence from duty due to disease from intemperate use of alcohol or drugs; and § 8633 provided for forfeiture when dropped from rolls. For similar provisions, see 37 USCS §§ 802 and 803.

§ 8634. Air Force band: may not be paid for performance outside air base

(a) Prohibition. Except as provided in subsection (b), no Air Force band or member thereof may receive remuneration for furnishing music outside the limits of an air base in competition with local civilian musicians.

(b) Recordings. (1) Any Air Force band designated as a special band may produce recordings for commercial sale.

(2) Amounts received as proceeds from the sale of any such recordings may be credited to applicable appropriations of the Department of the Air Force for expenses of Air Force bands.

(3) The Secretary of the Air Force shall prescribe regulations governing the accounting of such proceeds.

(Aug. 10, 1956, ch 1041, § 1, 70A Stat. 532; Nov. 5, 1990, P. L. 101-510, Div A, Title III, Part C, § 327(c), 104 Stat. 1532.)

HISTORY; ANCILLARY LAWS AND DIRECTIVES

Prior law and revision:

Revised Section	Source (USCS)	Source (Statutes at Large)
8634	10:905.	May 11, 1908, ch. 163, 35 Stat. 110.

The last six words are substituted for 10:905 (last 14 words).

Amendments:

1990. Act Nov. 5, 1990 designated the existing provisions as subsec. (a) and in such subsec., added the caption and substituted ''Except as provided in subsection (b), no'' for ''No''; and added subsec. (b).

Other provisions:

American Revolution Bicentennial; Recordings for Commercial Sale. For authorization for the Air Force Band to participate in the production of a collection of recordings for commercial sale in connection with the American Revolution Bicentennial, and for Secretary of Defense to enter into contracts for the production and sale of the collection of recordings, see Act Dec. 31, 1974, P. L. 93-571, 88 Stat. 1868, which appears as a note to 10 USCS § 3634.

CROSS REFERENCES

This section is referred to in 10 USCS § 974.

[§ 8635. Repealed]

HISTORY; ANCILLARY LAWS AND DIRECTIVES

This section (Act Aug. 10, 1956, ch 1041, § 1, 70A Stat. 532) was repealed

by Act Jan. 2, 1968, P. L. 90-235, § 6(a)(7), 81 Stat. 762. It set forth restrictions on civilian employment for enlisted members of the Air Force on active duty. For similar provisions, see 10 USCS § 974.

[§ 8636. Repealed]

HISTORY; ANCILLARY LAWS AND DIRECTIVES

This section (Act Aug. 10, 1956, ch 1041, § 1, 70A Stat. 533) was repealed by Act Sept. 7, 1962, P. L. 87-649, § 14(c)(56), 76 Stat. 502, effective as provided by § 15 of such Act, which appears as 37 USCS prec § 101 note. It provided that pay and allowances do not accrue to an enlisted member of the Air Force who is in confinement under sentence of dishonorable discharge, while the execution of the sentence to discharge is suspended. For similar provisions, see 37 USCS § 804.

[§ 8637. Repealed]

HISTORY; ANCILLARY LAWS AND DIRECTIVES

This section (Act Aug. 10, 1956, ch 1041, § 1, 70A Stat. 533) was repealed by Act Jan. 2, 1968, P. L. 90-235, § 7(b)(1), 81 Stat. 763. It provided that an enlisted member of the Air Force who deserted forfeited all rights to a pension.

[§ 8638. Repealed]

HISTORY; ANCILLARY LAWS AND DIRECTIVES

This section (Act Aug. 10, 1956, ch 1041, § 1, 70A Stat. 533) was repealed by Act Sept. 2, 1958, P. L. 85-861, § 36(B)(27), 72 Stat. 1571. It required enlisted members to make up time lost. For similar provisions, see 10 USCS § 972.

§ 8639. Enlisted members: officers not to use as servants

No officer of the Air Force may use an enlisted member of the Air Force as a servant.

(Aug. 10, 1956, ch 1041, § 1, 70A Stat. 533.)

HISTORY; ANCILLARY LAWS AND DIRECTIVES

Prior law and revision:

Revised Section	Source (USCS)	Source (Statutes at Large)
8639	10:608.	R.S. 1232.

The words ''in any case whatever'' are omitted as surplusage.

CHAPTER 851. UNITED STATES DISCIPLINARY BARRACKS [REPEALED]

Section
[8662, 8663. Repealed]

HISTORY; ANCILLARY LAWS AND DIRECTIVES

This chapter was repealed by Act July 5, 1968, P. L. 90-377, § 6(3), 82 Stat. 288.

[§§ 8662, 8663. Repealed]

HISTORY; ANCILLARY LAWS AND DIRECTIVES

These sections (Act Aug. 10, 1956, ch 1041, § 1, 70A Stat. 533) were repealed by Act July 5, 1968, P. L. 90-377, § 6(3), 82 Stat. 288. Section 8662 provided for the military training, organization, and equipping of prisoners who have been sent to the United States Disciplinary Barracks; and § 8663 authorized the Secretary of the Air Force to parole or remit the sentence and restore to duty offenders who are confined in the United States Disciplinary Barracks.

CHAPTER 853. MISCELLANEOUS RIGHTS AND BENEFITS

HISTORY; ANCILLARY LAWS AND DIRECTIVES

Amendments:

1958. Act Sept. 2, 1958, P. L. 85-861, § 1(189), 72 Stat. 1534, amended the analysis of this chapter by deleting items 8681 and 8688, which read: ''8681. Air Force Register: Regular Air Force officers; service to be listed''; and ''8688. Death gratuity''.

1968. Act Jan. 2, 1968, P. L. 90-235, §§ 6(a)(5), 7(a)(6), 81 Stat. 762, 763, amended the analysis of this chapter by deleting items 8682, 8685, 8690 and 8693, which read: ''8682. Service credit: officers; service as cadet not counted''; ''8685. Regular Air Force; Air Force Reserve: female members; definition of 'dependents'''; ''8690. Exemption from arrest for debt: enlisted members''; and ''8693. Replacement of certificates of discharge''.

1971. Act Nov. 24, 1971, P. L. 92-168, § 3(2), 85 Stat. 489, amended the analysis of this chapter by deleting item 8692, which read: ''8692. Pilot rating in time of peace: qualifications''.

1980. Act Dec. 12, 1980, P.L. 96-513, Title V, Part B, § 514(5), 94 Stat. 2935 (effective upon enactment on 12/12/80, as provided by § 701(b)(3) of such Act, which appears as 10 USCS § 101 note), amended the analysis of this chapter by deleting item 8689 which read: ''8689. Assignments and allotments of pay''.

1985. Act Nov. 8, 1985, P. L. 99-145, Title XIII, § 1301(d)(1)(B), 99 Stat. 736, amended the analysis of this chapter by deleting item 8683 which read: ''Service credit: certain service as a nurse, woman medical specialist, or civilian employee of Army Medical Department to be counted''.

1986. Act Nov. 14, 1986, P. L. 99-661, Div A, Title VI, Part A, § 604(f)(1)(B)(iv), 100 Stat. 3877 (applicable as provided by § 604(g) of such Act, which appears as 10 USCS § 1074a note), amended the analysis of this chapter by deleting item 8687 which read: ''8687. Compensation: members of Air Force other than of Regular Air Force; when same as that provided for members of Regular Air Force''.

1994. Act Oct. 5, 1994, P. L. 103-337, Div A, Title XVI, Subtitle D, § 1674(b)(6), 108 Stat. 3016 (effective 12/1/94 as provided by § 1691 of such Act, which appears as 10 USCS § 10001 note), amended the analysis of this chapter by deleting item 8686, which read: ''8686. Members of Air National Guard of United States: credit for service as members of Air National Guard''.

[§ 8681. Repealed]

HISTORY; ANCILLARY LAWS AND DIRECTIVES

This section (Act Aug. 10, 1956, ch 1041, § 1, 70A Stat. 534) was repealed

by Act Sept. 2, 1958, P. L. 85-861, § 36(B)(28), 72 Stat. 1571. It prescribed the service to be listed in the official Air Force Register.

[§ 8682. Repealed]

HISTORY; ANCILLARY LAWS AND DIRECTIVES

This section (Act Aug. 10, 1956, ch 1041, § 1, 70A Stat. 535) was repealed by Act Jan. 2, 1968, P. L. 90-235, § 6(a)(2), 81 Stat. 761. It provided that in computing length of service, no commissioned officer of the Air Force could be credited with service as a cadet at the Military Academy or the Air Force Academy, or as a midshipman at the Naval Academy, if he was appointed as a cadet or midshipman after Aug. 24, 1912. For similar provisions, see 10 USCS § 971.

[§ 8683. Repealed]

HISTORY; ANCILLARY LAWS AND DIRECTIVES

This section (Act Aug. 10, 1956, ch 1041, § 1, 70A Stat. 535; Sept. 2, 1958, P. L. 85-861, § 1(156), 72 Stat. 1513; Aug. 25, 1959, P. L. 86-197, § 1(7), 73 Stat. 426) was repealed by Act Nov. 8, 1985, P. L. 99-145, Title XIII, § 1301(d)(1)(A), 99 Stat. 736. It provided for service credit: certain service as a nurse, woman medical specialist, or civilian employee of Army Medical Department to be counted.

Other provisions:

Application of repeal of section. Act Nov. 8, 1985, P. L. 99-145, Title XIII, § 1301(d)(1)(C), 99 Stat. 736, provides: "The repeal made by subparagraph (A) [repealing this section] shall not apply in the case of a person who performed active service described in section 8683 of title 10, United States Code [formerly this section], as such section was in effect on the day before the date of the enactment of this Act [enacted Nov. 8, 1985].".

§ 8684. Service credit: regular enlisted members; service as an officer to be counted as enlisted service

An enlisted member of the Regular Air Force is entitled to count active service as an officer in the Air Force, and in the Army, as enlisted service for all purposes.

(Aug. 10, 1956, ch 1041, § 1, 70A Stat. 535.)

HISTORY; ANCILLARY LAWS AND DIRECTIVES

Prior law and revision:

Revised Section	Source (USCS)	Source (Statutes at Large)
8684	10:631a (last proviso).	July 14, 1939, ch. 267, § 1 (last proviso); restated May 29, 1954, ch. 249, § 19(b) (last proviso), 68 Stat. 166.

CROSS REFERENCES

Reenlistment after service as officer, 10 USCS § 8258.

[§ 8685. Repealed]

HISTORY; ANCILLARY LAWS AND DIRECTIVES

This section (Act Aug. 10, 1956, ch 1041, § 1, 70A Stat. 535; Sept. 2, 1958, P. L. 85-861, § 1(187), 72 Stat. 1534) was repealed by Act Jan. 2, 1968, P. L. 90-235, § 7(a)(3), 81 Stat. 763. It set forth restrictions on the consideration of a husband or child as the dependent of a female member of the Regular Air Force, Air National Guard of the United States or Air Force Reserve.

[§ 8686. Repealed]

HISTORY; ANCILLARY LAWS AND DIRECTIVES

This section (Act Aug. 10, 1956, ch 1041, § 1, 70A Stat. 536; Sept. 24, 1980, P. L. 96-357, § 5(a) in part, 94 Stat. 1182; Oct. 19, 1984, P. L. 98-525, Title IV, Part B, § 414(a)(7)(B), 98 Stat. 2519) was repealed by Oct. 5, 1994, P. L. 103-337, Div A, Title XVI, Subtitle C, § 1662(g)(2), 108 Stat. 2995 (effective Dec. 1, 1994, as provided by § 1691 of such Act, which appears as 10 USCS § 10001 note). This section provided for credit for service in the Air National Guard. For similar provisions, see 10 USCS § 12602.

[§ 8687. Repealed]

HISTORY; ANCILLARY LAWS AND DIRECTIVES

This section (Act Aug. 10, 1956, ch 1041, § 1, 70A Stat. 536; Sept. 2, 1958, P. L. 85-861, § 1(188), 72 Stat. 1534; Sept. 7, 1962, P. L. 87-649, § 6(d), 76 Stat. 494) was repealed by Act Nov. 14, 1986, P. L. 99-661, Div A, Title VI, Part A, § 604(f)(1)(A), 100 Stat. 3877, applicable as provided by § 604(g) of such Act, which appears as 10 USCS § 1074a note. It provided for compensation for members of the Air Force, other than members of the Regular Air Force.

[§ 8688. Repealed]

HISTORY; ANCILLARY LAWS AND DIRECTIVES

This section (Act Aug. 10, 1956, ch 1041, § 1, 70A Stat. 536) was repealed

by Act Sept. 2, 1958, P. L. 85-861, § 36B(29), 72 Stat. 1571. It related to the death gratuity payable to survivors of members of the Air Force. For similar provisions, see 10 USCS §§ 1475–1480.

[§ 8689. Repealed]

HISTORY; ANCILLARY LAWS AND DIRECTIVES

This section (Act Aug. 10, 1956, ch 1041, § 1, 70A Stat. 537; Sept. 26, 1961, P. L. 87-304, § 9(d), 75 Stat. 665) was repealed by Act Sept. 7, 1962, P. L. 87-649, § 14(c)(57), 76 Stat. 502, effective 11/1/62, as provided by § 15 of such Act, which appears as 37 USCS prec § 101 note. Similar provisions were re-enacted as 37 USCS § 701.

[§ 8690. Repealed]

HISTORY; ANCILLARY LAWS AND DIRECTIVES

This section (Act Aug. 10, 1956, ch 1041, § 1, 70A Stat. 538) was repealed by Act Jan. 2, 1968, P. L. 90-235, § 7(b)(1), 81 Stat. 763. It exempted enlisted members of the Air Force, while on active duty, from arrest for any debt, unless it was contracted before enlistment and amounted to at least $20 when first contracted.

§ 8691. Flying officer rating: qualifications

Only officers of the Air Force in the following categories may be rated as flying officers:

(1) Officers who have aeronautical ratings as pilots of service types of aircraft or as aircraft observers.

(2) Flight surgeons.

(3) Officers undergoing flight training.

(4) Officers who are members of combat crews, other than pilots of service types of aircraft, aircraft observers, and observers.

(5) In time of war, officers who have aeronautical ratings as observers.

(Aug. 10, 1956, ch 1041, § 1, 70A Stat. 538.)

HISTORY; ANCILLARY LAWS AND DIRECTIVES

Prior law and revision:

Revised Section	Source (USCS)	Source (Statutes at Large)
8691	10:291c. 10:291c-1.	June 3, 1916, ch. 134, § 13a (8th, 9th, and 11th provi-

Revised Section	Source (USCS)	Source (Statutes at Large)
	10:291e.	sos); added July 2, 1926, ch. 721, § 2 (4th sentence, less 2d proviso), 44 Stat. 781; June 16, 1936, ch. 587, § 3, 49 Stat. 1524; Oct. 4, 1940, ch. 742 (last proviso), 54 Stat. 963. June 24, 1948, ch. 632 (2d proviso under ''Finance Department''), 62 Stat. 650.

10:291c (proviso) and the words ''after June 30, 1948'', in 10:291c-1, are omitted as executed. The definition of the term ''flying officer'', in 10:291c, originally was a definition of the term ''flying officer in time of peace'' as provided by section 2 of the Act of July 2, 1926, ch 721, 44 Stat. 781. Section 1 of the Act of October 4, 1940, ch 742, 54 Stat. 963, eliminated the words ''in time of peace''. As a consequence of that amendment, 10:291e (1st 26 words) is omitted as surplusage. Cl. (2) is substituted for 10:291c-1 (less last 10 words). The words ''commissioned officers or warrant'', in 10:291c-1, are omitted as surplusage. In cl. (4), the last 19 words are substituted for the words ''any other''.

[§ 8692. Repealed]

HISTORY; ANCILLARY LAWS AND DIRECTIVES

This section (Act Aug. 10, 1956, ch 1041, § 1, 70A Stat. 538), was repealed by Act Nov. 24, 1971, P. L. 92-168, § 3(1), 85 Stat. 489. It provided qualifications to receive a rating of pilot in time of peace. For similar provisions, see 10 USCS § 2003.

[§ 8693. Repealed]

HISTORY; ANCILLARY LAWS AND DIRECTIVES

This section (Act Aug. 10, 1956, ch 1041, § 1, 70A Stat. 538) was repealed by Act Jan. 2, 1968, P. L. 90-235, § 7(a)(3), 81 Stat. 763. It provided for the replacement of a lost or destroyed certificate of discharge from the Air Force. For similar provisions, see 10 USCS § 1040.

CHAPTER 855. HOSPITALIZATION

HISTORY; ANCILLARY LAWS AND DIRECTIVES

Amendments:

1958. Act Sept. 2, 1958, P. L. 85-861, § 1(190)(D), 72 Stat. 1534, amended the analysis of this chapter by substituting item 8722 for one which read "Members of A. F. R. O. T. C. and C. A. T. C.; members of Air Force not covered by section 8721 of this title.".

1986. Act Nov. 14, 1986, P. L. 99-661, Div A, Title VI, Part A, § 604(f)(1)(B)(v), 100 Stat. 3877 (applicable as provided by § 604(g) of such Act, which appears as 10 USCS § 1074a note), amended the analysis of this chapter by deleting items 8721 and 8722 which read: "8721. Members of Air Force, other than of Regular Air Force.", and "8722. Members of C.A.T.C.; members of Air Force not covered by section 8721 of this title.".

[§§ 8721, 8722. Repealed]

HISTORY; ANCILLARY LAWS AND DIRECTIVES

These sections (Act Aug. 10, 1956, ch 1041, § 1, 70A Stat. 538; Sept. 2, 1958, P. L. 85-861, § 1(190)(A)–(C), 72 Stat. 1534) were repealed by Act Nov. 14, 1986, P. L. 99-661, Div A, Title VI, Part A, § 604(f)(1)(A), 100 Stat. 3877, applicable as provided by § 604(g) of such Act, which appears as 10 USCS § 1074a note. Section 8721 provided hospital benefits for members of the Air Force, other than members of the Regular Air Force; and § 8722 provided hospital benefits for members attending Citizens' Air Training Camps not covered by § 8721.

§ 8723. When Secretary may require

The Secretary of the Air Force may order the hospitalization, medical and surgical treatment, and domiciliary care for as long as necessary, of any member of the Air Force on active duty, and may incur obligations with respect thereto, whether or not the member incurred an injury, illness, or disease in line of duty, except in the case of a member treated in a private hospital, or by a civilian physician, while on leave of absence for more than 24 hours.

(Aug. 10, 1956, ch 1041, § 1, 70A Stat. 539; Nov. 14, 1986, P. L. 99-661, Div A, Title VI, Part A, § 604(f)(1)(D), 100 Stat. 3878; April 21, 1987, P. L. 100-26, § 7(j)(11) in part, 101 Stat. 283.)

HISTORY; ANCILLARY LAWS AND DIRECTIVES

Prior law and revision:

Revised Section	Source (USCS)	Source (Statutes at Large)
8723	10:455e. 32:164.	July 15, 1939, ch. 282; re-stated Oct. 14, 1940, ch. 875, § 5, 54 Stat. 1137.

The words ''under such regulations as he may prescribe'', in 10:455e and 32:164d, are omitted, since the Secretary has inherent authority to issue regulations appropriate to exercising his statutory functions. The references to 10:455a–455d and 32:164a–164c, and the words ''nor any other law of the United States shall be construed as limiting the power and authority'', are omitted, since the revised section makes explicit the authority of the Secretary to require the prescribed hospitalization and care. The words ''or in training, under the provision of section 62—'' are omitted as covered by the words ''active duty''. The words ''so long as any or all are necessary'' and ''in the active military service'' are omitted as surplusage. With the exception of 32:62 (4th proviso of last sentence), the references to 32:62–65, 144–146, 183, and 186, in 10:455e and 32:164d, do not refer to members of the Air National Guard of the United States and are therefore omitted from the revised section. 10:455e (1st proviso) and 32:164d (1st proviso) are omitted, since they apply only to the National Guard and are covered by section 320 of title 32.

Amendments:

1986. Act Nov. 14, 1986 (applicable as provided by § 604(g) of such Act, which appears as 10 USCS § 1074a note), substituted ''incurred an injury, illness, or disease,'' for ''was injured, or contracted a disease,''.

1987. Act April 21, 1987 deleted a comma following ''disease''.

CHAPTER 857. DECORATIONS AND AWARDS

HISTORY; ANCILLARY LAWS AND DIRECTIVES

Amendments:

1960. Act July 6, 1960, P. L. 86-593, § 1(7), 74 Stat. 332, amended the analysis of this chapter in items 8742, 8744, and 8745 by substituting ''Air Force cross'' for ''distinguished-service cross''; in items 8747 and 8748 by inserting ''; Air Force cross''; in item 8750 by substituting ''Airman's Medal'' for ''Soldier's Medal''.

Other provisions:

Extension of time for award of decoration. For an extension of time for award of decoration, or device in lieu of decoration, for an act or service performed while on active duty in military or naval forces, or while serving with such forces, between June 27, 1950, and July 27, 1953, see Act Aug. 2, 1956, ch. 877, 70 Stat. 933, which appears as a note preceding 10 USCS § 3741

For an extension of time for the award of decorations, or devices in lieu of decorations, for acts or services performed in direct support of military operations in Southeast Asia between July 1, 1958, and March 28, 1973, see Act Oct. 24, 1974, P. L. 93-469, 88 Stat. 1422, which appears as a note preceding 10 USCS § 3741.

Meritorious Service Medal. For the establishment of the Meritorious Service Medal, see Ex. Or. No. 11448 of Jan. 22, 1969, 34 Fed. Reg. 915, which appears as a note preceding 10 USCS § 1121.

§ 8741. Medal of honor: award

The President may award, and present in the name of Congress, a medal of honor of appropriate design, with ribbons and appurtenances, to a person who, while a member of the Air Force, distinguishes himself conspicuously by gallantry and intrepidity at the risk of his life above and beyond the call of duty—

(1) while engaged in an action against an enemy of the United States;

(2) while engaged in military operations involving conflict with an opposing foreign force; or

(3) while serving with friendly foreign forces engaged in an armed conflict against an opposing armed force in which the United States is not a belligerent party.

(Aug. 10, 1956, ch 1041, § 1, 70A Stat. 540; July 25, 1963, P. L. 88-77, § 3(1), 77 Stat. 94.)

HISTORY; ANCILLARY LAWS AND DIRECTIVES

Prior law and revision:

Revised Section	Source (USCS)	Source (Statutes at Large)
8741	10:1403.	July 9, 1918, ch. 143, (8th par. under Ordnance Department''), 40 Stat. 870.

The words ''That the provisions of existing law relating to the award of medals of honor to officers, noncommissioned officers, and privates of the Army be, and they hereby are, amended so that'', in the Act of July 9, 1918, ch 143, (8th para. under ''Ordnance Department''), 40 Stat. 870, are not contained in 10:1403. They are also omitted from the revised section as surplusage. The word ''member'' is substituted for the words ''officer or enlisted man''. The word ''only'' is omitted as surplusage. The word ''award'' is inserted for clarity, since the President determines the recipient of the medal in addition to presenting it.

Amendments:

1963. Act July 25, 1963, in the preliminary matter, inserted ''of appropriate design, with ribbons and appurtenances,''; deleted ''and in action involving actual conflict with an enemy'' after ''Air Force''; inserted the dash; and added paras. (1)–(3).

CROSS REFERENCES

Award of Medal of Honor to members of Army and Navy, 10 USCS §§ 3741, 6241.

This section is referred to in 10 USCS § 8748; 18 USCS § 704.

§ 8742. Air Force cross: award

The President may award an Air Force cross of appropriate design, with ribbons and appurtenances, to a person who, while serving in any capacity with the Air Force, distinguishes himself by extraordinary heroism not justifying the award of a medal of honor—

(1) while engaged in an action against an enemy of the United States;

(2) while engaged in military operations involving conflict with an opposing foreign force; or

(3) while serving with friendly foreign forces engaged in an armed conflict

against an opposing armed force in which the United States is not a belligerent party.

(Aug. 10, 1956, ch 1041, § 1, 70A Stat. 540; July 6, 1960, P. L. 86-593, § 1(1), 74 Stat. 331; July 25, 1963, P. L. 88-77, § 3(2), 77 Stat. 94.)

HISTORY; ANCILLARY LAWS AND DIRECTIVES

Prior law and revision:

Revised Section	Source (USCS)	Source (Statutes at Large)
8742	10:1406.	July 9, 1918, ch. 143 (9th par. under Ordnance Department''), 40 Stat. 870.

The words ''but not in the name of Congress'' are omitted as surplusage, since a medal is presented in the name of Congress only if the law so directs. The words ''since the 6th day of April, 1917'' are omitted as executed. The word ''award'' is substituted for the word ''present'' to cover the determination of the recipients as well as the actual presentation of the medal, and to conform to other sections of this chapter [10 USCS §§ 8741 et seq.]. The words ''or herself'' are omitted, since, under section 1 of title 1, words importing the masculine gender include the feminine. The words ''or who shall hereafter distinguish'' are omitted as surplusage.

Amendments:

1960. Act July 6, 1960, in the catchline, substituted ''Air Force cross'' for ''Distinguished-service cross''; and substituted ''an Air Force cross'' for ''a distinguished-service cross''.

1963. Act July 25, 1963, in the preliminary matter, substituted '', with ribbons and appurtenances'' for ''and a ribbon, together with a rosette or other device to be worn in place thereof''; substituted ''not justifying the award of a medal of honor'' for ''in connection with military operations against an armed enemy''; inserted the dash; and added paras. (1)–(3).

Other provisions:

References to Distinguished-Service Cross and Soldier's Medal considered made to Air Force Cross and Airman's Medal. Act July 6, 1960, P. L. 86-593, § 3, 74 Stat. 332, provided: ''References that other laws, regulations, and orders make, with respect to the Air Force, to the distinguished-service cross and the Soldier's Medal shall be considered to be made to the Air Force cross and the Airman's Medal, respectively.''.

CROSS REFERENCES

This section is referred to in 10 USCS § 8748.

§ 8743. Distinguished-service medal: award

The President may award a distinguished-service medal of appropriate design and a ribbon, together with a rosette or other device to be worn in place thereof, to a person who, while serving in any capacity with the Air Force, distinguishes himself by exceptionally meritorious service to the United States in a duty of great responsibility.

(Aug. 10, 1956, ch 1041, § 1, 70A Stat. 540.)

HISTORY; ANCILLARY LAWS AND DIRECTIVES

Prior law and revision:

Revised Section	Source (USCS)	Source (Statutes at Large)
8743	10:1407.	July 9, 1918, ch. 143 (10th par., less words after 1st semicolon, under "Ordnance Department"), 40 Stat 870.

The words "but not in the name of Congress" are omitted as surplusage, since a medal is presented in the name of Congress only if the law so directs. The words "since the 6th day of April, 1917" are omitted as executed. The word "award" is substituted for the word "present" to cover the determination of the recipients as well as the actual presentation of the medal, and to conform to other sections of this chapter [10 USCS §§ 8741 et seq.]. The words "or herself" are omitted, since, under section 1 of title 1, words importing the masculine gender include the feminine. The words "or who shall distinguish" are omitted as surplusage.

CROSS REFERENCES

Award of distinguished-service medal to members of Army and Navy, 10 USCS §§ 3743 and 6243.

This section is referred to in 10 USCS § 8748.

§ 8744. Medal of honor; Air Force cross; distinguished-service medal: limitations on award

(a) No more than one medal of honor, Air Force cross, or distinguished-service medal may be awarded to a person. However, for each succeeding act that would otherwise justify the award of such a medal or cross, the President may award a suitable bar or other device to be worn as he directs.

(b) Except as provided in subsection (d), no medal of honor, Air Force cross, distinguished-service medal, or device in place thereof, may be awarded to a person unless—

(1) the award is made within three years after the date of the act justifying the award;

(2) a statement setting forth the distinguished service and recommending official recognition of it was made within two years after the distinguished service; and

(3) it appears from records of the Department of the Air Force that the person is entitled to the award.

(c) No medal of honor, Air Force cross, distinguished-service medal, or device in place thereof, may be awarded or presented to a person whose service after he distinguished himself has not been honorable.

(d) If the Secretary of the Air Force determines that—

(1) a statement setting forth the distinguished service and recommending official recognition of it was made and supported by sufficient evidence within two years after the distinguished service; and

(2) no award was made, because the statement was lost or through inadvertence the recommendation was not acted on;

a medal of honor, Air Force cross, distinguished-service medal, or device in place thereof, as the case may be, may be awarded to the person concerned within two years after the date of that determination.

(Aug. 10, 1956, ch 1041, § 1, 70A Stat. 540; July 5, 1960, P. L. 86-582, § 1(3), 74 Stat. 320; July 6, 1960, P. L. 86-593, § 1(2), 74 Stat. 331.)

HISTORY; ANCILLARY LAWS AND DIRECTIVES

Prior law and revision:

Revised Section	Source (USCS)	Source (Statutes at Large)
8744(a)	10:1411.	July 9, 1918, ch. 143 (12th par., less words after 2d semicolon, under "Ordnance Department"); restated Jan. 24, 1920, ch. 55, § 1 (less last sentence), 41 Stat. 398.
8744(b)	10:1409 (words before 1st semicolon).	
8744(c)	10:1409 (words after 2d semicolon).	July 9, 1918, ch. 143 (less words between 1st and 2d semicolons of 15th par. under "Ordnance Department"), 40 Stat. 871.

In subsection (a), the words "may be awarded to a person" are substituted for the words "shall be issued to any one person" to conform to the other subsections of the revised section.

In subsection (b), the word "thereof" is substituted for the words "of either of said medal or of said cross". The words "Except as otherwise prescribed in this section", "at the time of", "specific", "official", and "has so distinguished himself as" are omitted as surplusage.

In subsection (c), 10:1409 (words after 3d semicolon) is omitted as executed. The words "hereinbefore authorized" are omitted as surplusage.

Amendments:

1960. Act July 5, 1960, in subsec. (b), in the preliminary matter, substituted "Except as provided in subsec. (d), no" for "No"; and added subsec. (d).

Act July 6, 1960, in the catchline, in subsec. (a), in subsec. (b) in the preliminary matter, in subsec. (c), and in subsec. (d) in the concluding matter, substituted "Air Force cross" for "distinguished-service cross".

Other provisions:

Persons awarded Distinguished-Service Cross or Soldier's Medal Before July 6, 1960. Act July 6, 1960, P. L. 86-593, § 2, 74 Stat. 332, provided: "For the purposes of sections 8744(a) and 8750(b) of title 10, United States Code [subsec. (a) of this section and 10 USCS § 8750(b)], a person who was awarded a distinguished-service cross or Soldier's Medal before the date of enactment of this Act [enacted July 6, 1960] shall be treated as if he had not been awarded an Air Force cross or Airman's Medal, as the case may be.".

CROSS REFERENCES

This section is referred to in 10 USCS § 8748.

INTERPRETIVE NOTES AND DECISIONS

Claim for medal of honor presented 28 years after occurrence of relevant acts and unaccompanied by any official evidence of statements setting forth distinguished service in question would not be entertained. (1892) 20 Op Atty Gen 421.

President may present medal of honor to individual who rendered distinguished service as long as individual was in service when recommendation for award was made, even though individual had been discharged by time case reached President for consideration. (1903) 24 Op Atty Gen 580.

§ 8745. Medal of honor; Air Force cross; distinguished-service medal: delegation of power to award

The President may delegate his authority to award the medal of honor, Air Force cross, and distinguished-service medal, to a commanding general of a separate air force or higher unit in the field.

(Aug. 10, 1956, ch 1041, § 1, 70A Stat. 541; July 6, 1960, P. L. 86-593, § 1(3), 74 Stat. 332.)

HISTORY; ANCILLARY LAWS AND DIRECTIVES

Prior law and revision:

Revised Section	Source (USCS)	Source (Statutes at Large)
8745	10:1410.	July 9, 1918, ch. 143 (16th par., less words after semicolon, under "Ordnance Department"), 40 Stat. 872.

The words "under such conditions, regulations, and limitations as he shall prescribe" are omitted as surplusage. The words "his authority" are substituted for the words "the power conferred upon him by sections 1403, 1406–1408, 1409–1412, 1416, 1420, 1422, 1423, and 1424 of this title".

Amendments:

1960. Act July 6, 1960, in the catchline and text, substituted "Air Force cross" for "distinguished-service cross".

CROSS REFERENCES

Delegation of functions, 3 USCS § 301.

§ 8746. Silver star: award

The President may award a silver star of appropriate design, with ribbons and appurtenances, to a person who, while serving in any capacity with the Air Force, is cited for gallantry in action that does not warrant a medal of honor or Air Force cross—

(1) while engaged in an action against an enemy of the United States;

(2) while engaged in military operations involving conflict with an opposing foreign force; or

(3) while serving with friendly foreign forces engaged in an armed conflict against an opposing armed force in which the United States is not a belligerent party.

(Aug. 10, 1956, ch 1041, § 1, 70A Stat. 541; July 25, 1963, P. L. 88-77, § 3(3), 77 Stat. 95.)

HISTORY; ANCILLARY LAWS AND DIRECTIVES

Prior law and revision:

Revised Section	Source (USCS)	Source (Statutes at Large)
8746	10:1412.	July 9, 1918, ch. 143 (words after 2d semicolon of 12th par., under ''Ordnance Department''); restated Jan. 24, 1920, ch. 55, § 1 (last sentence); restated Dec. 15, 1942, ch. 736, 56 Stat. 1052.

The words ''may award'' are inserted to conform to other sections of this chapter. The words ''if the person earned'' are inserted for clarity. The words ''commanded by'' are omitted as surplusage.

Amendments:

1963. Act July 25, 1963, this section, subject to subsequent amendment, for one which read: ''The President may award a silver star, three-sixteenths of an inch in diameter, for each citation for gallantry in action that does not warrant a medal of honor or distinguished-service cross, if the person earned the citation while serving in any capacity with the Air Force and it has been published in orders issued from the headquarters of a force that is the appropriate command of a general officer. The silver star shall be worn as the President directs.''.

CROSS REFERENCES

Award of silver star to members of Army and Navy, 10 USCS §§ 3746, 6244.

This section is referred to in 10 USCS § 8748.

§ 8747. Medal of honor; Air Force cross; distinguished-service cross; distinguished-service medal; silver star: replacement

Any medal of honor, Air Force cross, distinguished-service cross, distinguished-service medal, or silver star, or any bar, ribbon, rosette, or other device issued for wear with or in place of any of them, that is lost or destroyed,

or becomes unfit for use, without fault or neglect of the person to whom it was awarded, shall be replaced without charge.
(Aug. 10, 1956, ch 1041, § 1, 70A Stat. 541; July 6, 1960, P. L. 86-593, § 1(4), 74 Stat. 332.)

HISTORY; ANCILLARY LAWS AND DIRECTIVES

Prior law and revision:

Revised Section	Source (USCS)	Source (Statutes at Large)
8747	10:1416.	July 9, 1918, ch. 143 (14th par. under "Ordnance Department"), 40 Stat. 871.

The words "issued for wear with or in place of any of them" are inserted for clarity. The words "presented under the provisions of this title" and "such medal, cross, bar, ribbon, rosette, or device" are omitted as surplusage.

Amendments:

1960 Act July 6, 1960, in the catchline inserted "; Air Force cross"; and, in the text, inserted "Air Force cross,".

CROSS REFERENCES

This section is referred to in 10 USCS § 8748.

§ 8748. Medal of honor; Air Force cross; distinguished-service cross; distinguished-service medal; silver star: availability of appropriations

The Secretary of the Air Force may spend, from any appropriation for contingent expenses of the Department of the Air Force, amounts necessary to provide medals and devices under sections 8741, 8742, 8743, 8744, 8746, 8747, and 8752 of this title [10 USCS §§ 8741–8744, 8746, 8747, 8752].
(Aug. 10, 1956, ch 1041, § 1, 70A Stat. 541; July 6, 1960, P. L. 86-593, § 1(5), 74 Stat. 332.)

HISTORY; ANCILLARY LAWS AND DIRECTIVES

Prior law and revision:

Revised Section	Source (USCS)	Source (Statutes at Large)
8748	10:1424.	July 9, 1918, ch. 143 (13th par. under "Ordnance Department"), 40 Stat 871.

The word "amounts" is substituted for the words "so much as may be". The word "provides" is substituted for the words "defray the cost of".

The words "medals and devices under" are substituted for the words "medals of honor, distinguished-service crosses, distinguished-service medals, bars, rosettes, and other devices provided for in". The words "from time to time" are omitted as surplusage.

Amendments:

1960. Act July 6, 1960, in the catchline, inserted "Air Force cross;".

§ 8749. Distinguished flying cross: award; limitations

(a) The President may award a distinguished flying cross of appropriate design with accompanying ribbon to any person who, while serving in any capacity with the Air Force, distinguishes himself by heroism or extraordinary achievement while participating in an aerial flight.

(b) Not more than one distinguished flying cross may be awarded to a person. However, for each succeeding act that would otherwise justify the award of such a cross, the President may award a suitable bar or other device to be worn as he directs.

(c) No distinguished flying cross, or device in place thereof, may be awarded or presented to a person whose service after he distinguished himself has not been honorable.

(Aug. 10, 1956, ch 1041, § 1, 70A Stat. 541.)

HISTORY; ANCILLARY LAWS AND DIRECTIVES

Prior law and revision:

Revised Section	Source (USCS)	Source (Statutes at Large)
8749(a)	10:1429 (less 2d and last sentences).	July 2, 1926, ch. 721, § 12 (less 1st 49 words of last sentence), 44 Stat. 789;
8749(b)	10:1429 (2d sentence).	July 30, 1937, ch. 545, § 4, 50 Stat. 549.
8749(c)	10:1429 (last sentence, less 1st 49 words).	

In subsection (a), the words "under such rules and regulations as he may prescribe" are omitted, since the President has inherent authority to issue regulations appropriate to exercising his functions. The words "but not in the name of Congress" are omitted as surplusage, since a medal is presented in the name of Congress only if the law so directs. The word "award" is substituted for the word "present" to cover the determination of the recipients as well as the actual presentation of the medal. The words "since the 6th day of April, 1917, has distinguished, or who, after July 2, 1926" and 10:1429 (proviso of 1st sentence) are omitted as executed.

CROSS REFERENCES

Award of distinguished flying cross to members of Army and Navy, 10 USCS §§ 3749, 6245.

§ 8750. Airman's Medal: award; limitations

(a)(1) The President may award a decoration called the "Airman's Medal," of appropriate design with accompanying ribbon, to any person who, while serving in any capacity with the Air Force, distinguishes himself by heroism not involving actual conflict with an enemy.

(2) The authority in paragraph (1) includes authority to award the medal to a member of the Ready Reserve who was not in a duty status defined in section 101(d) of this title when the member distinguished himself by heroism.

(b) Not more than one Airman's Medal may be awarded to a person. However, for each succeeding act that would otherwise justify the award of such a medal, the President may award a suitable bar or other device to be worn as he directs.

(Aug. 10, 1956, ch 1041, § 1, 70A Stat. 542; July 6, 1960, P. L. 86-593, § 1(6), 74 Stat. 332; Nov. 18, 1997, P. L. 105-85, Div A, Title V, Subtitle G, § 574(c), 111 Stat. 1758.)

HISTORY; ANCILLARY LAWS AND DIRECTIVES

Prior law and revision:

Revised Section	Source (USCS)	Source (Statutes at Large)
8750(a)	10:1428 (less last sentence).	July 2, 1926, ch. 721, § 11, 44 Stat. 789.
8750(b)	10:1428 (last sentence).	

The words "Under such rules and regulations as he may prescribe" are omitted, since the President has inherent authority to issue regulations appropriate to exercising his functions. The words "but not in the name of Congress" are omitted as surplusage, since a medal is presented in the name of Congress only if the law so directs. The word "award" is substituted for the word "present" to cover the determination of the recipients as well as the actual presentation of the medal. The words "a decoration called" are substituted for the words "a medal to be known as". The words "including the National Guard and the Organized Reserves" are omitted as surplusage. The words "or herself" are omitted, since, under section 1 of title 1, words importing the masculine gender include the feminine. The words "after July 2, 1926" are omitted as executed.

In subsection (b), the words "that would otherwise justify" are substituted for the words "sufficient to".

Amendments:

1960. Act July 6, 1960, in the catchline and in subsecs. (a) and (b), substituted "Airman's Medal" for "Soldier's Medal".

1997. Act Nov. 18, 1997, in subsec. (a), designated the existing provisions as para. (1), and added para. (2).

CROSS REFERENCES

Award of Soldier's Medal to member of Army, 10 USCS § 3750.

§ 8751. Service medals: issue; replacement; availability of appropriations

(a) The Secretary of the Air Force shall procure, and issue without charge to any person entitled thereto, any service medal authorized for members of the Air Force after September 26, 1947, and any ribbon, clasp, star, or similar device prescribed as a part of that medal.

(b) Under such regulations as the Secretary may prescribe, any medal or other device issued under subsection (a) that is lost, destroyed, or becomes unfit for use without fault or neglect of the owner, may be replaced at cost. However, if the owner is a member of the Air Force, the medal or device may be replaced without charge.

(c) The Secretary may spend, from any appropriation for the support of the Air Force, amounts necessary to provide medals and devices under this section.

(Aug. 10, 1956, ch 1041, § 1, 70A Stat. 542.)

HISTORY; ANCILLARY LAWS AND DIRECTIVES

Prior law and revision:

Revised Section	Source (USCS)	Source (Statutes at Large)
8751(a)	10:1415a (less 21st through 30th words, and less clauses (a) through (n)).	May 12, 1928, ch. 528, §§ 1 (less 25th through 34th words, and less clauses (a) through (n)), 2 (less applicability to § 1 (clauses (a) through (n))), 3 (less applicability to § 1 (clauses (a) through (n))), 45 Stat. 500.
8751(b)	10:1415b (less applicability to 10:1415a (clauses (a) through (n))).	
8751(c)	10:1415c (less applicability to 10:1415a (clauses (a) through (n))).	

In subsection (a), the words "authorized for members of the Air Force after September 26, 1947" are substituted for the words "hereafter authorized", since, under Transfer Order 1, that date was the effective date of the transfer of personnel from the Army to the Air Force under section 208(e) of the National Security Act of 1947, as amended (5 U.S.C. 626c(e)). 10:1415a (proviso) is omitted as surplusage, since the revised section is not limited to persons who are members of the Air Force at the time of the issue.

In subsection (b), the words "member of the Air Force" are substituted for the words "persons in the military service of the United States".

In subsection (c), the last 16 words are substituted for 10:1415c (last 16 words).

CROSS REFERENCES

This section is referred to in 10 USCS § 8752.

RESEARCH GUIDE

Am Jur:

77 Am Jur 2d, Veterans and Veterans' Laws § 4.

§ 8752. Medals: posthumous award and presentation

(a) If a person dies before the award of a medal of honor, distinguished-service cross, distinguished-service medal, distinguished flying cross, or device in place thereof, to which he is entitled, the award may be made and the medal or device presented to his representative, as designated by the President.

(b) If a person dies before an authorized service medal or device prescribed as a part thereof is presented to him under section 8751 of this title [10 USCS § 8751], it shall be presented to his family.

(Aug. 10, 1956, ch 1041, § 1, 70A Stat. 542; Sept. 2, 1958, P. L. 85-861, § 33(a)(23), 72 Stat. 1565.)

HISTORY; ANCILLARY LAWS AND DIRECTIVES

Prior law and revision:

1956 ACT

Revised Section	Source (USCS)	Source (Statutes at Large)
8752(a)	10:1409 (words between 1st and 2d semicolons). 10:1429 (1st 49 words of last sentence).	July 9, 1918, ch. 143 (words between 1st and 2d semicolons of 15th par. under ''Ordnance Department''), 40 Stat. 871.
8752(b)	10:1415a (21st through 30th words, less applicability to clauses (a) through (n)).	July 2, 1926, ch, 721, § 12 (1st 49 words of last sentence), 44 Stat. 789; July 30, 1937, ch. 545, § 4, 50 Stat. 549. May 12, 1928, ch. 528, § 1 (25th through 34th words, less applicability to clauses (a) through (n)), 45 Stat. 500.

In subsection (a), the words ''If a person'' are substituted for the words ''In case an individual . . . dies'', in 10:1409, and ''In case an individual . . . shall have died'', in 10:1429. The words ''within three years from the date'', in 10:1409, are omitted as covered by section 8744 of this title. The words ''who shall distinguish himself'', in 10:1409, and ''who distinguishes himself'', in 10:1429, are omitted as covered by the words ''the award . . . to which he is entitled''.

1958 ACT

The change reflects the fact that the source statute for these sections (sec. 1 of the Act of May 12, 1928, ch. 528, 45 Stat. 500) was mandatory and not merely permissive.

Amendments:

1958. Act Sept. 2, 1958, (effective 8/10/56, as provided by § 33(g) of such Act, which appears as 10 USCS § 101 note) in subsec (b), substituted "shall" for "may".

CROSS REFERENCES

This section is referred to in 10 USCS § 8748.

CHAPTER 859. SEPARATION FROM REGULAR AIR FORCE FOR SUBSTANDARD PERFORMANCE OF DUTY [REPEALED]

HISTORY; ANCILLARY LAWS AND DIRECTIVES

This chapter was repealed by Act Dec. 12, 1980, P.L. 96-513, Title II, Part A, § 213, 94 Stat. 2885, effective Sept. 15, 1981, as provided by § 701(a) of such Act, which appears as 10 USCS § 101 note.

[§§ 8781–8787. Repealed]

HISTORY; ANCILLARY LAWS AND DIRECTIVES

These sections (§§ 8781–8786—Act Aug. 10, 1956, ch 1041, § 1, 70A Stat. 542–544; July 12, 1960, P.L. 86-616, § 7(a), 74 Stat. 391, 392; § 8787—Act July 12, 1960, P.L. 86-616, § 7(a), 74 Stat. 392) were repealed by Act Dec. 12, 1980, P.L. 96-513, Title II, Part A, § 213, 94 Stat. 2885, effective Sept. 15, 1981, as provided by § 701(a) of such Act, which appears as 10 USCS § 101 note. Section 8781 related to the composition and duties of selection boards; § 8782 related to the composition and duties of boards of inquiry; § 8783 related to the composition and duties of boards of review; § 8784 related to the removal of officers by the Secretary of the Air Force; § 8785 related to rights and procedures; § 8786 related to the voluntary retirement or honorable discharge of an officer being considered for removal; and § 8787 related to the eligibility of officers to serve on boards under this chapter. For similar provisions, see 10 USCS §§ 1181–1187.

CHAPTER 860. SEPARATION FROM REGULAR AIR FORCE FOR MORAL OR PROFESSIONAL DERELICTION OR IN INTERESTS OF NATIONAL SECURITY [REPEALED]

HISTORY; ANCILLARY LAWS AND DIRECTIVES

Explanatory notes:
This chapter was repealed by Act Dec. 12, 1980, P.L. 96-513, Title II, Part A, § 213, 94 Stat. 2885, effective Sept. 15, 1981, as provided by § 701(a) of such Act, which appears as 10 USCS § 101 note.

Amendments:
1960. Act July 12, 1960, P. L. 86-616, § 8(a), 74 Stat. 393, added this chapter.

[§§ 8791–8797. Repealed]

HISTORY; ANCILLARY LAWS AND DIRECTIVES

These sections (Act July 12, 1960, P.L. 86-616, § 8(a), 74 Stat. 393, 394) were repealed by Act Dec. 12, 1980, P.L. 95-513, Title II, Part A, § 213, 94 Stat. 2885, effective Sept. 15, 1981, as provided by § 701(a) of such Act, which appears as 10 USCS § 101 note. Section 8791 related to the composition and duties of selection boards; § 8792 related to the composition and duties of boards of inquiry; § 8793 related to the composition and duties of boards of review; § 8794 related to the removal of an officer by the Secretary of the Air Force; § 8795 related to rights and procedures; § 8796 related to the retirement or discharge of an officer being considered for removal; and § 8797 related to the eligibility of officers to serve on boards under this chapter. For similar provisions, see 10 USCS §§ 1181–1187.

CHAPTER 861. SEPARATION FOR VARIOUS REASONS

HISTORY; ANCILLARY LAWS AND DIRECTIVES

Amendments:

1958. Act Sept. 2, 1958, P. L. 85-861, § 1(191)(B), 72 Stat. 1534, amended the analysis of this chapter by adding item 8819.

1968. Act Jan. 2, 1968, P. L. 90-235, § 3(a)(5), (b)(7), 81 Stat. 758, amended the analysis of this chapter by deleting items 8811–8813, 8815, and 8816, which read: ''8811. Air Force enlisted members: discharge certificate; limitations on discharge''; ''8812. Air Force enlisted members: during war or emergency; discharge''; ''8813. Air Force enlisted members: dependency discharge''; ''8815. Regular enlisted members: resignation of members enlisted on career basis; limitations''; and ''8816. Regular enlisted members: minority discharge''.

1980. Act Dec. 12, 1980, P.L. 96-513, Title V, Part A, § 504(16), 94 Stat. 2917 (effective 9/15/81, as provided by § 701(a) of such Act, which appears as 10 USCS § 101 note), amended the analysis of this chapter by deleting items 8814 and 8818, which read: ''8814. Regular commissioned officers: discharge during three-year probationary period'', and ''8818. Regular female members: termination of appointment or enlistment''.

1994. Act Oct. 5, 1994, P. L. 103-337, Div A, Title XVI, Subtitle D, § 1674(b)(7), 108 Stat. 3016 (effective 10/1/96, pursuant to § 1501(f)(2) of Act Feb. 10, 1996, P. L. 104-106, which appears as 10 USCS § 10001 note), amended the analysis of this chapter by deleting items 8819 and 8820, which read: ''8819. Reserve officers: discharge for failure of promotion to first lieutenant'' and ''8820. Air National Guard of United States officers: discharge''.

[§§ 8811–8813. Repealed]

HISTORY; ANCILLARY LAWS AND DIRECTIVES

These sections (Act Aug. 10, 1956, ch 1041, § 1, 70A Stat. 544) were repealed by Act Jan. 2, 1968, P. L. 90-235, § 3(a)(2), (b)(1), 81 Stat. 757, 758. Section 8811 provided for the discharge of enlisted members of the Air Force and limitations thereon, and for the issuance of discharge certificates; § 8812 provided for the discharge of members of the Air Force enlisted during war or emergency; and § 8813 provided for dependency discharges for enlisted members of the Air Force. For provisions similar to § 8811, see 10 USCS § 1169; for provisions similar to § 8812, see 10 USCS § 1172.

[§ 8814. Repealed]

HISTORY; ANCILLARY LAWS AND DIRECTIVES

This section (Act Aug. 10, 1956, ch 1041, § 1, 70A Stat. 545) was repealed

by Act Dec. 12, 1980, P.L. 96-513, Title II, Part A, § 214, 94 Stat. 2885, effective Sept. 15, 1981, as provided by § 701(a) of such Act, which appears as 10 USCS § 101 note. It provided for discharge of regular commissioned officers during the 3-year probationary period. For similar provisions, see 10 USCS § 630.

[§§ 8815, 8816. Repealed]

HISTORY; ANCILLARY LAWS AND DIRECTIVES

These sections (Act Aug. 10, 1956, c. 1041, § 1, 70A Stat. 545) were repealed by Act Jan. 2, 1968, P. L. 90-235, § 3(a)(2), (b)(1), 81 Stat. 757, 758. Section 8815 provided for the resignation of regular enlisted members of the Air Force enlisted on a career basis and limitations thereon; section 8816 provided for minority discharges for regular enlisted members of the Air Force. Similar provisions appear as 10 USCS § 1170.

§ 8817. Aviation cadets: discharge

The Secretary of the Air Force may discharge an aviation cadet at any time.
(Aug. 10, 1956, ch 1041, § 1, 70A Stat. 545.)

HISTORY; ANCILLARY LAWS AND DIRECTIVES

Prior law and revision:

Revised Section	Source (USCS)	Source (Statutes at Large)
8817	10:299 (last sentence).	June 3, 1941, ch. 165, § 3 (last sentence), 55 Stat. 239.

10:299 (last sentence, less 1st 14 words) is omitted as superseded by section 681 of this title.

[§ 8818. Repealed]

HISTORY; ANCILLARY LAWS AND DIRECTIVES

This section (Act Aug. 10, 1956, ch 1041, § 1, 70A Stat. 545) was repealed by Act Dec. 12, 1980, P.L. 96-513, Title II, Part B, § 236, 94 Stat. 2887, effective Sept. 15, 1981, as provided by § 701(a) of such Act, which appears as 10 USCS § 101 note. It provided for termination of appointments and enlistments of female members.

[§§ 8819, 8820. Repealed]

HISTORY; ANCILLARY LAWS AND DIRECTIVES

These sections (§ 8819–Act Sept. 2, 1958, P. L. 85-861, § 1(191)(A), 72 Stat. 1534; June 30, 1960, P. L. 86-559, § 1(65), 74 Stat. 278; Oct. 19, 1984, P. L. 98-525, Title V, Part C, § 528(d), 98 Stat. 2526; Feb. 10, 1996, P. L. 104-106, Div A, Title XV, § 1501(c)(32), (33), 110 Stat. 500; § 8820–Act Aug. 10, 1956, ch 1041, § 1, 70A Stat. 546) were repealed by Act Oct.

5, 1994, P. L. 103-337, Div A, Title XVI, Subtitle A, Part II, § 1629(c)(2), 108 Stat. 2963 (effective Oct. 1, 1996, as provided by § 1691(b)(1) of such Act, which appears as 10 USCS § 10001 note). Section 8819 provided for discharge for failure of promotion to first lieutenant; and § 8820 provided for discharge of Air National Guard officers. For provisions similar to § 8819, see 10 USCS § 14503; for provisions similar to § 8820, see 10 USCS § 14907.

CHAPTER 863. SEPARATION OR TRANSFER TO RETIRED RESERVE [REPEALED]

HISTORY; ANCILLARY LAWS AND DIRECTIVES

This chapter was repealed by Act Oct. 5, 1994, P. L. 103-337, Div A, Title XVI, Subtitle A, Part II, § 1629(c)(3), 108 Stat. 2963 (effective Oct. 1, 1996, as provided by § 1691(b)(1), which appears as 10 USCS § 10001 note).

[§§ 8841, 8842. Repealed]

HISTORY; ANCILLARY LAWS AND DIRECTIVES

These sections (Act Sept. 2, 1958, P. L. 85-861, § 1(192), 72 Stat. 1535) were repealed by Act June 30, 1960, P. L. 86-559, § 1 (66), 74 Stat. 278. They related to the separation or transfer to Retired Reserve of female reserve nurses and medical specialists at age 50 if in a Reserve grade below major and at age 55 if in a Reserve grade above captain.

[§§ 8843–8846. Repealed]

HISTORY; ANCILLARY LAWS AND DIRECTIVES

These sections (§ 8843–Act Sept. 2, 1958, P. L. 85-861, § 1(192), 72 Stat. 1535; June 30, 1960, P. L. 86-559, § 1(67), (68), (69) 74 Stat. 278; § 8844–Act Sept. 2, 1958, P. L. 85-861, § 1(192), 72 Stat. 1535; June 30, 1960, P. L. 86-559, § 1(67), (68), (69) 74 Stat. 279; § 8845–Act Sept. 2, 1958, P. L. 85-861, § 1(192), 72 Stat. 1535; June 30, 1960, P. L. 86-559, § 1(67), (68), (69) 74 Stat. 279; Sept. 29, 1988, P. L. 100-456, Div A, Title XII, Part D, § 1234(a)(1), 102 Stat. 2059; § 8846–Act Sept. 2, 1958, P. L. 85-861, § 1(192), 72 Stat. 1536; Feb. 10, 1996, P. L. 104-106, Div A, Title XV, § 1501(c)(32), 110 Stat. 500) were repealed by Act Oct. 5, 1994, P. L. 103-337, Div A, Title XVI, Subtitle A, Part II, § 1629(c)(3), 108 Stat. 2963 (effective Oct. 1, 1996, as provided by § 1691(b)(1) of such Act, which appears as 10 USCS § 10001 note). Section 8843 provided for reserve officers below major general, except those covered by former § 8845; § 8844 provided for reserve major generals, except those covered by former § 8845; § 8845 provided for the Chief of the National Guard Bureau or adjutants general; and § 8846 provided for deferred officers. For provisions similar to § 8843, see 10 USCS § 14510; for provisions similar to § 8844, see 10 USCS § 14511; for provisions similar to § 8845, see 10 USCS § 14512(a).

[§ 8846. Repealed]

HISTORY; ANCILLARY LAWS AND DIRECTIVES

This section (Act Sept. 2, 1958, P. L. 85-861, § 1(192), 72 Stat. 1536; Feb.

10, 1996, P. L. 104-106, Div A, Title XV, § 1501(c)(32), 110 Stat. 500) was repealed by Act Oct. 5, 1994, P. L. 103-337, Div A, Title XVI, Subtitle A, Part II, § 1629(c)(3), 108 Stat. 2963 (effective Oct. 1, 1996, as provided by § 1691(b)(1) of such Act, which appears as 10 USCS § 10001 note). It provided for deferred officers.

[§ 8847. Repealed]

HISTORY; ANCILLARY LAWS AND DIRECTIVES

This section (Act Sept. 2, 1958, P. L. 85-861, § 1(192), 72 Stat. 1536; June 30, 1960, P. L. 86-559, § 1(70), 74 Stat. 279) was repealed by Act Nov. 8, 1967, P. L. 90-130, § 1(31)(A), 81 Stat. 382. It provided for the mandatory retirement of female commissioned officers, Air Force nurses, and medical specialists on active duty in a Reserve grade below lieutenant colonel after the completion of 25 years of service computed under 10 USCS § 8853.

[§ 8848. Repealed]

HISTORY; ANCILLARY LAWS AND DIRECTIVES

This section (Act Sept. 2, 1958, P. L. 85-861, § 1(192), 72 Stat. 1536; June 30, 1960, P. L. 86-559, § 1(71), 74 Stat. 279; Nov. 8, 1967, P. L. 90-130, § 1(31)(B), 81 Stat. 382; Aug. 13, 1968, P. L. 90-486, § 9(2), 82 Stat. 760; Dec. 12, 1980, P. L. 96-513, Title V, Part B, § 514(7), 94 Stat. 2935; Nov. 8, 1985, P. L. 99-145, Title V, Part C, § 522(b)(1), Title XIII, § 1303(a)(27)(A), 99 Stat. 632, 740) was repealed by Act Oct. 5, 1994, P. L. 103-337, Div A, Title XVI, Subtitle A, Part II, § 1629(c)(3), 108 Stat. 2963 (effective Oct. 1, 1996, as provided by § 1691(b)(1) of such Act, which appears as 10 USCS § 10001 note). It provided for effect of completion twenty-eight years' service by reserve first lieutenants, captains, majors, and lieutenant colonels. For similar provisions, see 10 USCS § 14501 et seq.

[§ 8849. Repealed]

HISTORY; ANCILLARY LAWS AND DIRECTIVES

This section (Act Sept. 2, 1958, P. L. 85-861, § 1(192), 72 Stat. 1536) was repealed by Act June 30, 1960, P. L. 86-559, § 1(72), 74 Stat. 279. It related to the separation or transfer to the Retired Reserve of female reserve lieutenant colonels, except those designated under 10 USCS § 8067, upon completion of 28 years of service.

[§§ 8850–8853. Repealed]

HISTORY; ANCILLARY LAWS AND DIRECTIVES

These sections (§ 8850–Act Sept. 2, 1958, P. L. 85-861, § 1(192), 72 Stat. 1537; Dec. 1, 1967, P. L. 90-168, § 2(22), 81 Stat. 525; Feb. 10, 1996, P. L. 104-106, Div A, Title XV, § 1501(c)(25), 110 Stat. 499; § 8851–Act Sept. 2, 1958, P. L. 85-861, § 1 (192), 72 Stat. 1537; June 30, 1960, P. L. 86-559, § 1(73), 74 Stat. 280; Sept. 11, 1967, P. L. 90-83, § 3(6), 81 Stat.

220; Aug. 13, 1968, P. L. 90-486, § 9(2), 82 Stat. 760; Dec. 12, 1980, P.L. 96-513, Title V, Part B, § 514(7), 94 Stat. 2935; Oct. 19, 1984, P. L. 98-525, Title XIV, § 1405(55), 98 Stat. 2626; Nov. 8, 1985, P. L. 99-134, Title V, Part C, § 522(b)(2), Title XIII, § 1303(a)(27)(B) in part, 99 Stat. 632, 740; Sept. 29, 1988, P. L. 100-456, Div A, Title XII, Part D, § 1234(a)(1), 102 Stat. 2059; § 8852–Act Sept. 2, 1958, P. L. 85-861, § 1(192), 72 Stat. 1537; June 30, 1960, P. L. 86-559, § 1(74), 74 Stat. 280; Nov. 8, 1985, P. L. 99-145, Title XIII, § 1303(a)(27)(B) in part, 99 Stat. 740; Sept. 29, 1988, P. L. 100-456, Div A, Title XII, Part D, § 1234(a)(1), 102 Stat. 2059; § 8853–Act Sept. 2, 1958, P. L. 85-861, § 1(192), 72 Stat. 1538; June 30, 1960, P. L. 86-559, § 1(75), 74 Stat. 280; Sept. 24, 1983, P. L. 98-94, Title X, Part B, § 1016(c), 97 Stat. 668) were repealed by Act Oct. 5, 1994, P. L. 103-337, Div A, Title XVI, Subtitle A, Part II, § 1629(c)(3), 108 Stat. 2963 (effective Oct. 1, 1996, as provided by § 1691(b)(1) of such Act, which appears as 10 USCS § 10001 note). Section 8850 provided for reserve commissioned officers with thirty or more years of service; § 8851 provided for Reserve colonels and brigadier generals with thirty years or five years in grade service; § 8852 provided for Reserve major generals with thirty-five years or five years in grade; and § 8853 provided for computation of years of service. For provisions similar to § 8850, see 10 USCS §§ 14514, 14704; for provisions similar to § 8851, see 10 USCS § 14508(a), (c); for provisions similar to § 8852, see 10 USCS § 14508; for provisions similar to § 8853, see 10 USCS § 14706.

[§ 8855. Repealed]

HISTORY; ANCILLARY LAWS AND DIRECTIVES

This section (Act June 30, 1960, P. L. 86-559, § 1(76), 74 Stat. 280; Nov. 9, 1979, P. L. 96-107, Title IV, § 403(b), 93 Stat. 808; Dec. 12, 1980, P.L. 96-513, Title II, Part A, § 215(b), 94 Stat. 2885; Dec. 4, 1987, P. L. 100-180, Div A, Title VII, Part A, § 717(c), (d)(2)(A), 101 Stat. 1114; Sept. 29, 1988, P. L. 100-456, Div A, Title XI, Part D, § 1233(l)(2), 102 Stat. 2058; Nov. 29, 1989, P. L. 101-189, Div A, Title VII, Part A, § 710(c), 103 Stat. 1477; Oct. 5, 1994, P. L. 103-337, Div A, Title XVI, Subtitle A, Part II, § 1629(c)(3), 108 Stat. 2963) was repealed by Act Oct. 5, 1994, P. L. 103-337, Div A, Title XVI, Subtitle A, Part II, § 1629(c)(3), 108 Stat. 2963 (effective Oct. 1, 1996, as provided by § 1691(b)(1) of such Act, which appears as 10 USCS § 10001 note). It provided for retention in active status of certain officers. For similar provisions, see 10 USCS § 14703(a)(3), (b).

CHAPTER 865. RETIREMENT FOR AGE [REPEALED]

HISTORY; ANCILLARY LAWS AND DIRECTIVES

Explanatory notes:

This chapter was repealed by Act Dec. 12, 1980, P. L. 96-513, Title II, Part A, § 216, 94 Stat. 2886, effective Sept. 15, 1981, as provided by § 701(a) of such Act, which appears as 10 USCS § 101 note.

[§§ 8881, 8882. Repealed]

HISTORY; ANCILLARY LAWS AND DIRECTIVES

These sections (Act Aug. 10, 1956, ch 1041, § 1, 70A Stat. 546) were repealed by Act Aug. 21, 1957, P. L. 85-155, Title IV, § 401(1), 71 Stat. 390. Section 8881 authorized the Secretary of the Air Force to retire Air Force nurses and woman medical specialists whose regular grade is below major; and § 8882 authorized the Secretary of the Air Force to retire Air Force nurses or woman medical specialists whose regular grade is above captain.

[§§ 8883–8886. Repealed]

HISTORY; ANCILLARY LAWS AND DIRECTIVES

These sections (§ 8883—Act Aug. 10, 1956, ch 1041, § 1, 70A Stat. 546; Aug. 6, 1958, P. L. 85-600, § 1(17), 72 Stat. 523; Nov. 2, 1966, P. L. 89-718, § 3, 80 Stat. 1115; § 8884—Act Aug. 10, 1956, ch 1041, § 1, 70A Stat. 547; Nov. 2, 1966, P. L. 89-718, § 3, 80 Stat. 1115; § 8885—Act Aug. 10, 1956, ch 1041, § 1, 70A Stat. 547; Sept. 2, 1958, P. L. 85-861, § 33(a)(42), 72 Stat. 1567; Nov. 2, 1966, P. L. 89-718, § 3, 80 Stat. 1115; § 8886—Act Aug. 10, 1956, ch 1041, § 1, 70A Stat. 547; Aug. 6, 1958, P. L. 85-600, § 1(18), 72 Stat. 523; Nov. 2, 1966, P. L. 89-718, § 3, 80 Stat. 1115), were repealed by Act Dec. 12, 1980, P. L. 96-513, Title II, Part A, § 216, 94 Stat. 2886, effective Sept. 15, 1981, as provided by § 701(a) of such Act, which appears as 10 USCS § 101 note. Section 8883 related to the retirement of regular commissioned officers below the grade of major general at age 60; § 8884 related to the retirement at age 60 of regular major generals whose retirement had been deferred; § 8885 related to the retirement of regular major generals at age 62; and § 8886 related to the retirement at age 64 of regular major generals whose retirement had been deferred. For similar provisions, see 10 USCS § 1251.

[§ 8887. Repealed]

HISTORY; ANCILLARY LAWS AND DIRECTIVES

This section (Act Aug. 10, 1956, ch 1041, § 1, 70A Stat. 547) was repealed

by Act Aug. 21, 1957, P. L. 85-155, Title IV, § 401(1), 71 Stat. 390. It related to computation of years of service of Air Force nurses or woman medical specialists for the purposes of retirement under former 10 USCS §§ 8881 or 8882 or retirement pay under 10 USCS § 8991.

[§§ 8888, 8889. Repealed]

HISTORY; ANCILLARY LAWS AND DIRECTIVES

These sections (§ 8888—Act Aug. 10, 1956, ch 1041, § 1, 70A Stat. 547; Aug. 21, 1957, P. L. 85-155, Title III, § 301(16), 71 Stat. 388; May 20, 1958, P. L. 85-422, § 11(a)(7), 72 Stat. 131; Sept. 2, 1958, P. L. 85-861, § 1(194), 72 Stat. 1538; Sept. 30, 1966, P. L. 89-609, § 1(30), 80 Stat. 854; § 8889—Act Aug. 10, 1956, ch 1041, § 1, 70A Stat. 548) were repealed by Act Dec. 12, 1980, P.L. 96-513, Title II, Part A, § 216, 94 Stat. 2886, effective Sept. 15, 1981, as provided by § 701(a) of such Act, which appears as 10 USCS § 101 note. Section 8888 related to the computation of the years of service of an officer retired under 10 USCS §§ 8883–8886; and § 8889 related to the computation of retired pay. For provisions similar to § 8888, see 10 USCS § 1405.

CHAPTER 867. RETIREMENT FOR LENGTH OF SERVICE

HISTORY; ANCILLARY LAWS AND DIRECTIVES

Amendments:

1957. Act Aug. 21, 1957, P. L. 85-155, Title III, § 301(21), 71 Stat. 389, amended the analysis of this chapter by deleting items 8912 which read: ''8912. Twenty years or more: Regular Air Force nurses and women medical specialists.''; by substituting item 8915 for one which read: ''Twenty-five years: female majors except those designated under section 8067 of this title.''; and by deleting item 8928, which read: ''8928. Computation of years of service: voluntary retirement; Regular Air Force nurses and women medical specialists.''.

1966. Act Sept. 30, 1966, P. L. 89-609, § 1(32), 80 Stat. 854, amended the analysis of this chapter by substituting item 8915 for one which read ''8915. Twenty-five years: female majors except those designated under section 8067(a)–(d) or (g)–(i) of this title.''.

1967. Act Nov. 8, 1967, P. L. 90-130, § 1(32)(C), 81 Stat. 383, amended the analysis of this chapter by substituting a new item 8915 for one which read: ''8915. Twenty-five years: female majors except those designated under section 8067(a)–(d) or (g)–(i) of this title; male majors designated under section 8067(e) or (f) of this title.''.

1980. Act Sept. 8, 1980, P.L. 96-343, § 9(b)(3), 94 Stat. 1129 (effective as provided by § 9(c) of such Act, which appears as 10 USCS § 3914 note), amended the analysis of this chapter in item 8914 by deleting ''regular'' preceding ''enlisted''; and in item 8925 by deleting ''regular'' preceding ''enlisted''.

Act Dec. 12, 1980, P.L. 96-513, Title V, Part A, § 504(17), 94 Stat. 2917 (effective 9/15/81, as provided by § 701(a) of such Act, which appears as

10 USCS § 101 note), amended the analysis of this chapter by deleting items 8913, 8915, 8916, 8919, 8921, 8922, 8923, and 8927, which read: ''8913. Twenty years or more: deferred officers not recommended for promotion.'', ''8915. Twenty-eight years: deferred retirement of nurses and medical specialists in regular grade of major.'', ''8916. Twenty-eight years: promotion-list lieutenant colonels.'', ''8919. Thirty years or more: regular commissioned officers; excessive number.'', ''8921. Thirty years or five years in grade: promotion-list colonels.'', ''8922. Thirty years or five years in grade: regular brigadier generals. 8923. Thirty-five years or five years in grade: regular major generals.'', and ''8927. Computation of years of service: mandatory retirement; regular commissioned officers.''.

1996. Act Feb. 10, 1996, P. L. 104-106, Div A, Title V, Subtitle A, § 509(b)(2), 110 Stat. 298, amended the analysis of this chapter by substituting item 8920 for one which read: ''8920. More than thirty years: professors of the United States Air Force Academy''.

§ 8911. Twenty years or more: regular or reserve commissioned officers

(a) The Secretary of the Air Force may, upon the officer's request, retire a regular or reserve commissioned officer of the Air Force who has at least 20 years of service computed under section 8926 of this title, at least 10 years of which have been active service as a commissioned officer.

(b) The Secretary of Defense may authorize the Secretary of the Air Force, during the nine-year period beginning on October 1, 1990, to reduce the requirement under subsection (a) for at least 10 years of active service as a commissioned officer to a period (determined by the Secretary of the Air Force) of not less than eight years.

(Aug. 10, 1956, ch 1041, § 1, 70A Stat. 549; Nov. 5, 1990, P. L. 101-510, Div A, Title V, Part B, § 523(c), 104 Stat. 1562; Nov. 30, 1993, P. L. 103-160, Div A, Title V, Subtitle F, § 561(c), 107 Stat. 1667.)

HISTORY; ANCILLARY LAWS AND DIRECTIVES

Prior law and revision:

Revised Section	Source (USCS)	Source (Statutes at Large)
8911	10:943a. 10:971b (1st 100 words).	July 31, ch. 422, § 5 (1st 101 words); restated June 13, 1940, ch. 344, § 3 (1st 45 words), 54 Stat. 380; June 29, 1948, ch. 708, § 202 (1st 105 words), 62 Stat. 1084; July 16, 1953, ch. 203, 67 Stat. 175.

The words ''a regular or reserve commissioned officer of the Air Force'' are substituted for the words ''any officer on the active list of the . . . Regular Air Force . . . or any officer of the reserve components of the . . .

Air Force of the United States''. The words ''Philippine Scouts'' are omitted as obsolete. The words ''has at least 20'' are substituted for the words ''shall have completed not less than twenty''. The words ''upon his request'' are substituted for the words ''upon his own application''. The words ''service computed under section 8926 of this title'' are substituted for the words ''active Federal service in the armed forces of the United States'', since that revised section makes explicit the service covered.

Amendments:

1990. Act Nov. 5, 1990 designated the existing provisions as subsec. (a); and added subsec. (b).

1993. Act Nov. 30, 1993, in subsec. (b), substituted ''nine-year period'' for ''five-year period''.

Other provisions:

Applicability of section during period of active force drawdown. For applicability of the provisions of this section during period of active force drawdown to individuals with at least 15 but less than 20 years of service, see Act Oct. 23, 1992, P. L. 102-484, Div D, Title XLIV, Subtitle A, § 4403, 106 Stat. 2702, which appears as 10 USCS § 1293 note.

CROSS REFERENCES

This section is referred to in 10 USCS §§ 631, 632, 637, 638, 638a, 688, 1370, 1406, 8926, 10154, 12646.

INTERPRETIVE NOTES AND DECISIONS

1. Entitlement to benefits
2. Miscellaneous

1. Entitlement to benefits

Air Force Reserve officer retired under 10 USCS § 8911 loses entitlement to retirement pay upon becoming citizen of foreign country, such citizenship being inconsistent with oath taken to defend Constitution of United States since officer is no longer subject to recall in time of war or national emergency. (1962) 41 Op Comp Gen 715.

Children of deceased Air Force Reserve officer killed while on active duty for training after having elected coverage for his children under Survivor Benefit Plan (10 USCS §§ 1447 et seq.) and subsequently qualifying for retirement under § 8911, are entitled to annuity payments under Survivor Benefit Plan, where officer was not actually retired and entitled to retired pay under § 8911, since merely qualifying for retirement under another statute does not void election to participate in Survivor Benefit Plan where election was valid when made. (1982) 61 Op Comp Gen 441.

Retired officer who was entitled to retirement benefits under 10 USCS § 8911 was not entitled to retirement benefits under 10 USCS § 1331; latter statute clearly precludes its application to those entitled to retirement benefits under any other provision of law, not merely those actually receiving other retirement benefits. Flurett v United States (1993) 28 Fed Cl 153.

2. Miscellaneous

Air Force officer retired under 10 USCS § 8911, and subsequently missing since civilian plane which he was flying as employee of defense contractor disappeared in Southeast Asia is not entitled to retired pay for any period after last date officer was known to be alive; retirement account is to be placed in suspense status until member returns or until information is received or judicial action is taken to establish death and date of death. (1983) 62 Op Comp Gen 211.

[§ 8912. Repealed]

HISTORY; ANCILLARY LAWS AND DIRECTIVES

This section (Act Aug. 10, 1956, ch 1041, § 1, 70A Stat. 549) was repealed by Act Aug. 21, 1957, P. L. 85-155, Title IV, § 401(1), 71 Stat. 390. It permitted the Secretary of the Air Force, upon the officer's request, to retire an Air Force nurse, or a woman medical specialist, of the Regular Air

Force, who has at least 20 years of service computed under former 10 USCS § 8928.

[§ 8913. Repealed]

HISTORY; ANCILLARY LAWS AND DIRECTIVES

This section (Act Aug. 10, 1956, ch 1041, § 1, 70A Stat. 549; July 12, 1960, P. L. 86-616, § 9, 74 Stat. 395; Nov. 2, 1966, P. L. 89-718, § 3, 80 Stat. 1115) was repealed by Act Dec. 12, 1980, P.L. 96-513, Title II, Part A, § 217(a), 94 Stat. 2886, effective Sept. 15, 1981, as provided by § 701(a) of such Act, which appears as 10 USCS § 101 note. It provided for the retirement after at least 20 years of service of an officer not recommended for promotion. For similar provisions, see 10 USCS §§ 627 et seq.

§ 8914. Twenty to thirty years: enlisted members

Under regulations to be prescribed by the Secretary of the Air Force, an enlisted member of the Air Force who has at least 20, but less than 30, years of service computed under section 8925 of this title may, upon his request, be retired.

(Aug. 10, 1956, ch 1041, § 1, 70A Stat. 550; Sept. 8, 1980, P.L. 96-343, § 9(b)(1), 94 Stat. 1128; Oct. 5, 1994, P. L. 103-337, Div A, Title V, Subtitle B, § 515(b), 108 Stat. 2753.)

HISTORY; ANCILLARY LAWS AND DIRECTIVES

Prior law and revision:

Revised Section	Source (USCS)	Source (Statutes at Large)
8914	10:948 (1st sentence).	Oct. 6, 1945, ch. 393, § 4 (1st sentence); restated Aug. 10, 1946, ch. 952, § 6(a) (1st sentence), 60 Stat. 996.
		Aug. 10, 1946, ch. 952, § 7, 60 Stat. 996.

The words "now or hereafter", in 10:948a, are omitted as surplusage. The words "computed under section 8925 of this title" are substituted for the words "active Federal service", in 10:948, and "active Federal military service", in 10:948a, since that revised section makes explicit the service covered. The words "be retired from" are substituted for the words "will be placed on the retired list of", in 10:948. The words "completed a minimum", in 10:948; and "the period of", "be subject to", "period of", and "now or after August 10, 1946", in 10:948a; are omitted as surplusage.

Amendments:

1980. Act Sept. 8, 1980 (effective as provided by § 9(c) of such Act, which appears as 10 USCS § 3914 note) substituted this section and catchline for ones which read:

"§ 8914. Twenty to thirty years: regular enlisted members

"Under regulations to be prescribed by the Secretary of the Air Force, a regular enlisted member of the Air Force who has at least 20, but less than 30, years of service computed under section 8925 of this title may, upon his request, be retired. He then becomes a member of the Air Force Reserve, and shall perform such active duty as may be prescribed under law, until his service computed under section 8925 of this title, plus his inactive service as a member of the Air Force Reserve, equals 30 years."

1994. Act Oct. 5, 1994 deleted "A regular enlisted member then becomes a member of the Air Force Reserve. A member retired under this section shall perform such active duty as may be prescribed by law until his service computed under section 8925 of this title, plus his inactive service as a member of the Air Force Reserve, equals 30 years." following "retired.".

Other provisions:

Applicability of section during period of active force drawdown. For applicability of the provisions of this section during period of active force drawdown to individuals with at least 15 but less than 20 years of service, see Act Oct. 23, 1992, P. L. 102-484, Div D, Title XLIV, Subtitle A, § 4403, 106 Stat. 2702, which appears as 10 USCS § 1293 note.

CODE OF FEDERAL REGULATIONS

Office of the Secretary of Defense—Reserve Components Common Personnel Data System (RCCPDS), 32 CFR Part 114.

CROSS REFERENCES

This section is referred to in 10 USCS §§ 688, 1176, 1402, 1402a, 1406, 1407, 8925, 8963.

Auto-Cite®: Cases and annotations referred to herein can be further researched through the Auto-Cite® computer-assisted research service. Use Auto-Cite to check citations for form, parallel references, prior and later history, and annotation references.

INTERPRETIVE NOTES AND DECISIONS

1. Eligibility
2. Benefits
3. Judicial review
4. Recission of order
5. Miscellaneous

1. Eligibility

Claim for longevity retired pay and allowances under 10 USCS § 8914 accrues when all events required to fix government's liability for such pay have occurred; Air Force enlisted man who has failed to complete at least 20 years of qualifying service pursuant to 10 USCS § 8914 is not entitled to retirement benefits. Kirby v United States (1973) 201 Ct Cl 527, cert den (1974) 417 US 919, 41 L Ed 2d 224, 94 S Ct 2626.

Member of Air Force was not entitled to retirement benefits under Air Force's voluntary early retirement program (10 USCS §§ 8914 and 8925), where member had accumulated eighteen years of active duty service at time of his criminal conviction and incarceration, and at time of his discharge, more than two years later, more than twenty years had elapsed since member had entered Air Force, because period from member's initial incarceration through his eventual dishonorable discharge constituted lost time not creditable towards enlistment term or retirement eligibility (10 USCS § 972). Hare v United States (1996) 35 Fed Cl 353, affd (1997, CA FC) 1997 US App LEXIS 2390.

Service member has no guaranteed right of immediate retirement, and his entitlement to retirement pay is dependent upon approval of Secretary. Cedillo v United States (1997) 37 Fed Cl 128, affd without op (1997, CA FC) 1997 US App LEXIS 24843, reported in full (1997, CA FC) 1997 US App LEXIS 16956 and cert den (1998, US) 139 L Ed 2d 658,

118 S Ct 718, reh den (1998, US) 140 L Ed 2d 503, 118 S Ct 1343 and affd (1997, CA FC) 124 F3d 1266.

2. Benefits

Discharged state National Guard member was entitled to retirement pay from time of his application, even though he was eligible proximately 15 months earlier at time he was discharged, where he chose not to apply for voluntary retirement status at that time to avoid creating impression he consented to discharge, since statute's language requiring request is plain. Gant v United States (1990, CA) 918 F2d 168, cert den (1991) 498 US 1107, 112 L Ed 2d 1095, 111 S Ct 1013.

3. Judicial review

Retirement issues are not beyond judicial scrutiny merely because statute uses term "may" rather than "shall." Webb v United States (1988) 15 Cl Ct 23.

4. Recission of order

Court of Federal Claims did not err in finding that servicemember's arraignment on attempted murder, involuntary manslaughter, and evading law enforcement officials constituted substantial new evidence warranting rescission of retirement order and benefits prior to order's effective date. Cedillo v United States (1997, CA FC) 124 F3d 1266.

5. Miscellaneous

Predecessor to § 8914 conferred retirement benefits only upon regular Air Force enlisted personnel and did not apply to individual who, on date he was released from active duty, was commissioned officer of regular Air Force. Burke v United States (1985) 8 Cl Ct 75.

[§§ 8915, 8916. Repealed]

HISTORY; ANCILLARY LAWS AND DIRECTIVES

These sections (§ 8915—Act Aug. 10, 1956, ch 1041, § 1, 70A Stat. 550; Aug. 21, 1957, P. L. 85-155, Title III, § 301(18), 71 Stat. 389; Sept. 30, 1966, P. L. 89-609, § 1(31), 80 Stat. 854; Nov. 2, 1966, P. L. 89-718, § 3, 80 Stat. 1115; Nov. 8, 1967, P. L. 90-130, § 1(32)(A), 81 Stat. 382; § 8916—Act Aug. 10, 1956, ch 1041, § 1, 70A Stat. 550; Aug. 21, 1957, P. L. 85-155, Title III, § 301(19), 71 Stat. 389; Nov. 2, 1966, P. L. 89-718, § 3, 80 Stat. 1115; Nov. 8, 1967, P. L. 90-130, § 1(32)(B), 81 Stat. 383) were repealed by Act Dec. 12, 1980, P.L. 96-513, Title II, Part B, § 217(a), 94 Stat. 2886, effective Sept. 15, 1981, as provided by § 701(a) of such Act, which appears as 10 USCS § 101 note. Section 8915 related to deferment of the retirement of nurses and medical specialists until after 28 years of service; and § 8916 related to the retirement of promotion-list lieutenant colonels after 28 years of service. For similar provisions, see 10 USCS §§ 632, 633.

§ 8917. Thirty years or more: regular enlisted members

A regular enlisted member of the Air Force who has at least 30 years of service computed under section 8925 of this title [10 USCS § 8925] shall be retired upon his request.

(Aug. 10, 1956, ch 1041, § 1, 70A Stat. 550.)

HISTORY; ANCILLARY LAWS AND DIRECTIVES

Prior law and revision:

Revised Section	Source (USCS)	Source (Statutes at Large)
8917	10:947 (less proviso). 10:947a (less last 11 words).	Mar. 2, 1907, ch. 2515, § 1, (1st 35 words), 34 Stat. 1217.
		Feb. 14, 1885, ch. 67 (less 43d through 53d words); restated Sept. 30, 1890, ch. 1125 (less 43d through 53d words), 26 Stat. 504.

The word ''regular'' is inserted to conform to an opinion of the Judge Advocate General of the Army (JAGA 1953/2301, 23 March 1953). The words ''upon his request'' are substituted for the words ''upon making application to the President'', in 10:947, and ''by application to the President'', in 10:947a. The words ''either as a private or non-commissioned officer, or both'', in 10:947a, are omitted as surplusage. The words ''shall be retired'' are substituted for the words ''be placed upon the retired list'', in 10:947, and ''be placed on the retired list heretofore created'', in 10:947a. The words ''computed under section 8925 of this title'' are inserted for clarity. The 21 words before the proviso and the proviso of the Act of February 14, 1885, as restated, are not contained in 10:947a. They are also omitted from the revised section, since the proviso is executed and the 21 words before the proviso are omitted as covered by formula E of section 8991 of this title.

CROSS REFERENCES

This section is referred to in 10 USCS §§ 1406, 8925.

INTERPRETIVE NOTES AND DECISIONS

Provisions of predecessor of 10 USCS § 8917 were not in any respect ambiguous but were positive and direct; predecessors of 10 USCS § 8917 and § 8991 both related to matter of retirement of enlisted men but language of two acts, with reference to retirement and retirement pay, was not same and rights and privileges granted by predecessor of § 8991 must control whether they are more, or less, favorable to enlisted men. Hornblass v United States (1941) 93 Ct Cl 148.

§ 8918. Thirty years or more: regular commissioned officers

A regular commissioned officer of the Air Force who has at least 30 years of service computed under section 8926 of this title [10 USCS § 8926] may be retired upon his request, in the discretion of the President.

(Aug. 10, 1956, ch 1041, § 1, 70A Stat. 550.)

HISTORY; ANCILLARY LAWS AND DIRECTIVES

Prior law and revision:

Revised Section	Source (USCS)	Source (Statutes at Large)
8918	10:843.	R.S. 1243; Dec. 16, 1930, ch. 14, § 1 (as applicable to R.S. 1243), 46 Stat. 1028.

The word ''commissioned'' is inserted, since the retirement of warrant officers for length of service is covered by section 1293 of this title. The word ''regular'' is inserted, since 10:943 is applicable historically only to officers of a regular component. The words ''and placed on the retired list'' are omitted as surplusage. The words ''computed under section 8926 of this title'' are inserted for clarity.

Other provisions:

Delegation of functions. Ex. Or. 12396, Dec. 3, 1982, §§ 1(f), (3), 47 Fed. Reg. 55897, 55898, which appears as 3 USCS § 301 note, provides that the functions of President under this section to approve request of a regular commissioned officer of Air Force to retire after at least 30 years of service delegated to Secretary of Defense to perform, without approval, ratification, or other action by President, and with authority for Secretary to redelegate.

CROSS REFERENCES

This section is referred to in 10 USCS §§ 1406, 8926.

[§ 8919. Repealed]

HISTORY; ANCILLARY LAWS AND DIRECTIVES

This section (Act Aug. 10, 1956, ch 1041, § 1, 70A Stat. 551) was repealed by Act Dec. 12, 1980, P.L. 96-513, Title II, Part A, § 217(a), 94 Stat. 2886, effective Sept. 15, 1981, as provided by § 701(a) of such Act, which appears as 10 USCS § 101 note. It provided for the retirement of regular commissioned officers with at least 30 years of service whenever there are an excessive number.

§ 8920. More than thirty years: permanent professors and the Director of Admissions of the United States Air Force Academy

(a) The Secretary of the Air Force may retire an officer specified in subsection (b) who has more than 30 years of service as a commissioned officer.

(b) Subsection (a) applies in the case of the following officers:

(1) Any permanent professor of the United States Air Force Academy.

(2) The Director of Admissions of the United States Air Force Academy.

(Aug. 10, 1956, ch 1041, § 1, 70A Stat. 551; Feb. 10, 1996, P. L. 104-106, Div A, Title V, Subtitle A, § 509(b)(1), 110 Stat. 298.)

HISTORY; ANCILLARY LAWS AND DIRECTIVES

Prior law and revision:

Revised Section	Source (USCS)	Source (Statutes at Large)
8920	10:1079a(c) (proviso).	Aug. 7, 1947, ch. 512, § 520(c) (proviso), 61 Stat. 912.

The word ''retire'' is substituted for the words ''direct the retirement of''. The words ''as a commissioned officer'' are substituted for the word ''commissioned''.

Amendments:

1996. Act Feb. 10, 1996 substituted this section for one which read:

''§ 8920. More than thirty years: professors of the United States Air Force Academy

''The Secretary of the Air Force may retire any permanent professor of the United States Air Force Academy who has more than 30 years of service as a commissioned officer.''.

CROSS REFERENCES

This section is referred to in 10 USCS § 1406.

[§§ 8921–8923. Repealed]

HISTORY; ANCILLARY LAWS AND DIRECTIVES

These sections (Act Aug. 10, 1956, ch 1041, § 1, 70A Stat. 551, 552; Nov. 2, 1966, P. L. 89-718, § 3, 80 Stat. 1115) were repealed by Act Dec. 12, 1980, P.L. 96-513, Title II, Part A, § 217(a), 94 Stat. 2886, effective Sept. 15, 1981, as provided by § 701(a) of such Act, which appears as 10 USCS § 101 note. Section 8921 related to the retirement of promotion-list colonels after 30 years of service or 5 years in grade; § 8922 related to the retirement of regular brigadier generals after 30 years of service or 5 years in grade; and § 8923 related to the retirement of regular major generals after 35 years of service or 5 years in grade. For similar provisions, see 10 USCS §§ 634–636.

§ 8924. Forty years or more: Air Force officers

(a) Except as provided in section 1186 of this title [10 USCS § 1186], a commissioned officer of the Air Force who has at least 40 years of service computed under section 8926 of this title [10 USCS § 8926] shall be retired upon his request.

(b) Any warrant officer of the Air Force who has at least 40 years of service computed under section 8926(a) of this title [10 USCS § 8926(a)] shall be retired upon his request.

(Aug. 10, 1956, ch 1041, § 1, 70A Stat. 552; Dec. 12, 1980, P.L. 96-513, Title V, Part A, § 504(18), 94 Stat. 2917.)

HISTORY; ANCILLARY LAWS AND DIRECTIVES

Prior law and revision:

Revised Section	Source (USCS)	Source (Statutes at Large)
8924(a)	10:942 (as applicable to commissioned officers).	June 30, 1882, ch. 254 (last 21 words of 3d proviso under "Pay Department"), 22 Stat. 118.
8924(b)	10:942 (less applicability to commissioned officers).	

In subsection (a), the words "Except as provided in section 8786 of this title" are inserted, since, under that revised section, when board proceedings are pending against a commissioned officer, his right to retire under this revised section, which is otherwise absolute, is discretionary with the Secretary under that revised section.

In subsection (a) and (b), the words "or volunteer service, or both" are omitted as obsolete in accordance with an opinion of the Attorney General, 22 Ops. Atty. Gen. 199, Aug. 30, 1898, holding that such words refer to volunteer service in the Civil War. The words "upon his request" are substituted for the words "if he make application therefor to the President".

In subsection (b), the applicability of 10:942 to warrant officers is based on an opinion of the Judge Advocate General of the Army (JAGA 1950/6951, 4 Jan. 1951), which holds that 10:594 (less provisos) makes 10:942 applicable to warrant officers.

Amendments:

1980. Act Dec. 12, 1980 (effective 9/15/81, as provided by § 701(a) of such Act, which appears as 10 USCS § 101 note), in subsec. (a), substituted "1186" for "8786".

CROSS REFERENCES

This section is referred to in 10 USCS §§ 1406, 8926.

§ 8925. Computation of years of service: voluntary retirement; enlisted members

(a) For the purpose of determining whether an enlisted member of the Air Force may be retired under section 8914 or 8917 of this title, his years of service are computed by adding all active service in the armed forces.

(b) Time required to be made up under section 972(a) of this title may not be counted in computing years of service under subsection (a).

(Aug. 10, 1956, ch 1041, § 1, 70A Stat. 552; Sept. 2, 1958, P. L. 85-861, § 1(195), 72 Stat. 1540; Sept. 8, 1980, P.L. 96-343, § 9(a)(2), 94 Stat. 1129; July 1, 1986, P. L. 99-348, Title II, § 204(c), 100 Stat. 698; Nov. 29, 1989, P. L. 101-189, Div A, Title VI, Part F, § 652(a)(6), 103 Stat. 1461; Oct. 5, 1994, P. L. 103-337, Div A, Title VI, Subtitle D, § 635(c)(1), 108 Stat. 2789; Feb. 10, 1996, P. L. 104-106, Div A, Title V, Subtitle F, § 561(d)(4)(A), 110 Stat. 323.)

HISTORY; ANCILLARY LAWS AND DIRECTIVES

Prior law and revision:

1956 ACT

Revised Section	Source (USCS)	Source (Statutes at Large)
8925(a)	10:947 (proviso). 10:958.	Mar. 2, 1907, ch. 2515, § 1 (proviso), 34 Stat. 1218.
8925(b)	[No source].	Aug. 10, 1946, ch. 952, § 6(b), 60 Stat. 996.

In subsection (a), the words "active service" are substituted for the word "service", in 10:947, and "active Federal service performed", in 10:958, for uniformity. The words "service computed under section 8683 of this title" are inserted, since a person entitled to count service under that revised section might cease to be a nurse or woman medical specialist and thereafter become entitled to retire under one of the revised sections referred to in subsec. (a) of this revised section.

Subsection (b) is inserted because of section 8638 of this title and in accordance with long standing interpretation of the effect of 10:629 upon the computation of years of service for retirement.

1958 ACT

Revised Section	Source (USCS)	Source (Statutes at Large)
8925	[No source].	[No source].

The amendment reflects the repeal of section 8638 of this title and the enactment of a similar provision in section 972 of this title.

Amendments:

1958. Act Sept. 2, 1958, in subsec. (b), substituted "972" for "8638".

1980. Act Sept 8, 1980 (effective as provided by § 9(c) of such Act, which appears as 10 USCS § 3914 note), in the catchline, deleted "regular" following "retirement" and, in subsec. (a), substituted "an" for "a regular".

1986. Act July 1, 1986 added subsec. (c).

1989. Act Nov. 29, 1989, in subsec. (a), deleted "and service computed under section 8683 of this title" following "forces".

1994. Act Oct. 5, 1994 (applicable as provided by § 635(e) of such Act, which appears as 10 USCS § 1405 note), in subsec. (a), deleted "and of computing his retired pay under section 8991 of this title," preceding "his years"; and deleted subsec. (c), which read:

"(c) In determining a member's years of service under subsection (a) for the purpose of computing the member's retired pay under section 8991 of this title—

"(1) each full month of service that is in addition to the number of full years of service creditable to the member shall be credited as $1/12$ of a year; and

"(2) any remaining fractional part of a year shall be disregarded.".

1996. Act Feb. 10, 1996 (effective on enactment and applicable to any period of time covered by 10 USCS § 972 that occurs after that date, as provided by § 561(e) of such Act, which appears as 10 USCS § 972 note), in subsec. (b), substituted ''section 972(a)'' for ''section 972''.

CROSS REFERENCES

Active service as an officer to be counted as enlisted service for all purposes, 10 USCS § 8684.

This section is referred to in 10 USCS §§ 8914, 8917.

INTERPRETIVE NOTES AND DECISIONS

Member of Air Force was not entitled to retirement benefits under Air Force's voluntary early retirement program (10 USCS §§ 8914 and 8925), where member had accumulated eighteen years of active duty service at time of his criminal conviction and incarceration, and at time of his discharge, more than two years later, more than twenty years had elapsed since member had entered Air Force, because period from member's initial incarceration through his eventual dishonorable discharge constituted lost time not creditable towards enlistment term or retirement eligibility (10 USCS § 972). Hare v United States (1996) 35 Fed Cl 353, affd (1997, CA FC) 1997 US App LEXIS 2390.

§ 8926. Computation of years of service: voluntary retirement; regular and reserve commissioned officers

(a) For the purpose of determining whether an officer of the Air Force may be retired under section 8911, 8918, or 8924 of this title, his years of service are computed by adding—

(1) all active service performed as a member of the Army or the Air Force; and

(2) all service in the Navy or Marine Corps that may be included in determining the eligibility of an officer of the Navy or Marine Corps for retirement.

(b) For the purpose of determining whether a medical officer of the Regular Air Force may be retired under section 8911, 8918, or 8924 of this title, his years of service are computed by adding to his service under subsection (a) all service performed as a contract surgeon, acting assistant surgeon, or contract physician, under a contract to serve full time and to take and change station as ordered.

(c) For the purpose of determining whether a dental officer of the Regular Air Force may be retired under section 8911, 8918, or 8924 of this title, his years of service are computed by adding to his service under subsection (a) all service as a contract dental surgeon or acting dental surgeon.

(d) Section 972(b) of this title excludes from computation of an officer's years of service for purposes of this section any time identified with respect to that officer under that section.

(Aug. 10, 1956, ch 1041, § 1, 70A Stat. 552; Aug. 25, 1959, P. L. 86-197, § 1(8), 73 Stat. 426; Nov. 29, 1989, P. L. 101-189, Div A, Title VI, Part F, § 652(a)(7), 103 Stat. 1461; Feb. 10, 1996, P. L. 104-106, Div A, Title V, Subtitle F, § 561(d)(4)(B), 110 Stat. 323.)

HISTORY; ANCILLARY LAWS AND DIRECTIVES

Prior law and revision:

Revised Section	Source (USCS)	Source (Statutes at Large)
8926(a)	10:951 (less applicability to 10:166g(a)). 10:951a. 10:951b (less applicability to 10:168g(a)). [Uncodified June 18, 1878, ch. 263, § 7 (less applicability to 10:166g(a)), 20 Stat. 150.]	June 3, 1916, ch. 134, § 127a (6th para., less 1sr 13 words, and less appli cability to § 108(a) of the Act of Apr. 16, 1949, ch. 38, as amended); added June 4, 1920, ch. 227, subch. I, § 51 (6th para., less 1st 13 words, and less applicability to § 108(a) of the Act of Apr. 16, 1949, ch. 38, as amended); 41 Stat. 785. May 23, ch. 716, 45 Stat. 720. June 15, 1935, ch. 257, (less applicability to § 108(a) of the Act of Apr. 16, 1949, ch. 38, as amended), 49 Stat. 377. June 18, 1878 ch. 263, § 7 (less applicability to § 108(a) of the Act of Apr. 16, 1949, ch. 38, as amended), 20 Stat. 150. May 29, 1928, ch. 902, 45 Stat. 996; Jan. 29, 1938, ch. 12, § 2, 52 Stat. 8.
8926(b)	10:953a (1st sentence).	
8926(c)	10:953a (less 1st sentence).	

Subsection (a) consolidates the various service computation provisions applicable to voluntary retirement of commissioned officers. Cl. (1) is substituted for 10:951. Cl. (2) is substituted for 10:951b. The words "pay period and", in 10:951a, are omitted as superseded by section 202 of the Career Compensation Act of 1949, 63 Stat. 807 (37 U.S.C. 233). The words "longevity pay and", in section 7 of the Act of June 18, 1878, ch 263, 20 Stat. 150, are omitted for the same reason. The last sentence of section 7 of that Act is omitted, since the distinction between limited and unlimited retired lists was abolished by section 201 of the Act of June 29, 1948, ch 708, 62 Stat. 1084. Cl. (3) is inserted, since a person entitled to count service under section 8683 of this title might cease to be a nurse or woman medical specialist and thereafter become entitled to retire under one of the revised sections referred to in subsec. (a) of this revised section.

In subsection (b), the words "as a member of the Medical Reserve Corps", in 10:953a, are omitted as covered by subsec. (a)(1). The words "are computed by adding to his service under subsection (a)" are substituted for the words "shall be credited to the same extent as service under a Regular Army commission".

Subsection (c) is substituted for 10:953a (less 1st sentence).

Amendments:

1959. Act Aug. 25, 1959, added subsec. (d).

1989. Act Nov. 29, 1989, in subsec. (a), in para. (1), deleted "and" following "Force;", in para. (2), substituted a concluding period for a concluding semicolon, and deleted paras. (3) and (4), which read:

"(3) all service computed under section 8683 of this title; and

"(4) if an officer of the Regular Air Force, all active service performed as an officer of the Philippine Constabulary.";

and deleted subsec. (d), which read: "For the purpose of determining whether an Air Force nurse or medical specialist may be retired under section 8911 of this title, all service computed under section 8683 of this title shall be treated as if it were service as a commissioned officer.".

1996. Act Feb. 10, 1996 (effective on enactment and applicable to any period of time covered by 10 USCS § 972 that occurs after that date, as provided by § 561(e) of such Act, which appears as 10 USCS § 972 note) added subsec. (d).

CROSS REFERENCES

Service as cadet at Military or Air Force Academy not counted as service in determining length of service, 10 USCS § 971.

This section is referred to in 10 USCS §§ 8911, 8918, 8924, 8928.

[§ 8927. Repealed]

HISTORY; ANCILLARY LAWS AND DIRECTIVES

This section (Act Aug. 10, 1956, ch 1041, § 1, 70A Stat. 553; Aug. 21, 1957, P. L. 85-155, Title III, § 301(20), 71 Stat. 389; May 20, 1958, P. L. 85-422, § 11(a)(8), 72 Stat. 131; Sept. 2, 1958, P. L. 85-861, § 1(196), 72 Stat. 1540; Sept. 30, 1966, P. L. 89-609, § 1(33), 80 Stat. 854) was repealed by Act Dec. 12, 1980, P. L. 96-513, Title II, Part A, § 217(a), 94 Stat. 2886, effective Sept. 15, 1981, as provided by § 701(a) of such Act, which appears as 10 USCS § 101 note. It provided for the computation of years of service of regular commissioned officers for the purposes of retirement under this chapter. For similar provisions, see 10 USCS § 1405.

[§ 8928. Repealed]

HISTORY; ANCILLARY LAWS AND DIRECTIVES

This section (Act Aug. 10, 1956, ch 1041, § 1, 70A Stat. 554) was repealed by Act Aug. 21, 1957, P. L. 85-155, Title IV, § 401(1), 71 Stat. 390. It related to computation of years of service of Air Force Nurses or women medical specialists for the purposes of retirement under former 10 USCS § 8912, or retirement pay under 10 USCS § 8991.

§ 8929. Computation of retired pay: law applicable

A member of the Air Force retired under this chapter [10 USCS §§ 8911 et seq.] is entitled to retired pay computed under chapter 871 of this title [10 USCS §§ 8991 et seq.].

(Aug. 10, 1956, ch 1041, § 1, 70A Stat. 554.)

HISTORY; ANCILLARY LAWS AND DIRECTIVES

Prior law and revision:

Revised Section	Source (USCS)	Source (Statutes at Large)
8929	[No source].	[No source].

The revised section is based on the various retirement provisions in this chapter and is inserted to make explicit the entitlement to retired pay upon retirement.

INTERPRETIVE NOTES AND DECISIONS

State court decree in divorce action awarding wife divorce from Air Force officer and community property share of his prospective retirement pay is entitled to full faith and credit in federal court action by wife to enforce state judgment, where parties and facts are same, decree was final, and officer failed at trial or by appeal to contest state court's classification of retirement pay not then accrued as community property. Wilson v Wilson (1980, MD La) 532 F Supp 152, affd (1982, CA5 La) 667 F2d 497, 3 EBC 1859, cert den (1982) 458 US 1107, 73 L Ed 2d 1368, 102 S Ct 3485, 3 EBC 1861.

Military retirement benefits must be apportioned as community or separate property according to where the active service on which benefits are based took place prior to or after marriage. Ramsey v Ramsey (1975) 96 Idaho 672, 535 P2d 53.

CHAPTER 869. RETIRED GRADE

HISTORY; ANCILLARY LAWS AND DIRECTIVES

Amendments:

1980. Act Sept. 8, 1980, P.L. 96-343, § 13(b)(3), 94 Stat. 1131, amended the analysis of this chapter by substituting item 8962 for one which read: ''8962. Higher grade for service in special positions: regular commissioned officers.''.

1985. Act Nov. 8, 1985, P. L. 99-145, Title XIII, § 1301(d)(2)(B), 99 Stat. 736, amended the analysis of this chapter by deleting item 8963 which read: ''Higher grade for service during certain periods: regular and reserve commissioned officers.''.

1987. Act Dec. 4, 1987, P. L. 100-180, Div A, Title V, § 512(e)(3), 101 Stat. 1091, amended the analysis of this chapter by substituting item 8964 for one which read: ''8964. Higher grade after 30 years of service: Air Force warrant officers; regular enlisted members.''.

1988. Act Sept. 29, 1988, P. L. 100-456, Div A, Title XII, Part D, § 1233(i)(2)(B), 102 Stat. 2058, amended the analysis of this chapter by substituting item 8965 for one which read: ''8965. Restoration to former grade: Regular Air Force warrant officers and enlisted members.''.

1996. Act Sept. 23, 1996, P. L. 104-201, Div A, Title V, Subtitle D, § 532(c)(2), 110 Stat. 2520, amended the analysis of this chapter by adding item 8963.

§ 8961. General rule

(a) The retired grade of a regular commissioned officer of the Air Force who retires other than for physical disability, and the retired grade of a reserve commissioned officer of the Air Force who retires other than for physical disability or for nonregular service under chapter 1223 of this title [10 USCS §§ 12731 et seq.], is determined under section 1370 of this title.

(b) Unless entitled to a higher retired grade under some other provision of law, a Regular or Reserve of the Air Force not covered by subsection (a) who retires other than for physical disability retires in the regular or reserve grade that he holds on the date of his retirement.

(Aug. 10, 1956, ch 1041, § 1, 70A Stat. 554; Dec. 12, 1980, P.L. 96-513, Title

V, Part A, § 504(19), 94 Stat. 2917; Oct. 5, 1994, P. L. 103-337, Div A, Title XVI, Subtitle D, § 1674(c)(2), 108 Stat. 3016.)

HISTORY; ANCILLARY LAWS AND DIRECTIVES

Prior law and revision:

Revised Section	Source (USCS)	Source (Statutes at Large)
8961	10:941a(a)(3) (31st through 42d words; and proviso, as applicable to retired grade). 10:941a(e) (17th through 25th words of cl. (1); and 1st proviso of cl. (1), as applicable to retired grade). 10:947a (last 11 words). 10:1025.	Aug. 7, 1947, ch. 512, §§ 514 (a)(3) (31st through 42d words; and proviso, as applicable to retired grade), 514(e) (17th through 25th words of cl. (1); and 1st proviso of cl. (1), as applicable to retired grade), 61 Stat. 902, 905. Feb. 14, 1885, ch. 67 (43d through 53d words); restated Sept. 30, 1890, ch. 1125 (43d through 53d words), 26 Stat. 504.

The applicability of the rule stated in the revised section to situations not expressly covered by the laws named in the source credits above is necessarily implied from laws providing for retirement in higher grade in those situations.

Amendments:

1980. Act Dec. 12, 1980 (effective 9/15/81, as provided by § 701(a) of such Act, which appears as 10 USCS § 101 note), substituted this section for one which read: ''Unless entitled to a higher retired grade under some other provision of law, a Regular or Reserve of the Air Force who retires other than for physical disability retires in the regular or reserve grade that he holds on the date of his retirement.''.

1994. Act Oct. 5, 1994 (effective 12/1/94 as provided by § 1691 of such Act, which appears as 10 USCS § 10001 note), in subsec. (a), substituted ''chapter 1223'' for ''chapter 67''.

§ 8962. Higher grade for service in special positions

Upon retirement, any permanent professor of the United States Air Force Academy whose grade is below brigadier general, and whose service as such a professor has been long and distinguished, may, in the discretion of the President, be retired in the grade of brigadier general.

(Aug. 10, 1956, ch 1041, § 1, 70A Stat. 554; Sept. 2, 1958, P. L. 85-861, § 1(197), 72 Stat. 1541; Oct. 22, 1965, P. L. 89-288, § 6, 79 Stat. 1050; Sept. 8, 1980, P.L. 96-343, § 13(b)(1), (2), 94 Stat. 1131; Dec. 12, 1980, P.L. 96-513, Title V, Part A, § 504(20), 94 Stat. 2917; Feb. 10, 1996, P. L. 104-106, Div A, Title V, Subtitle A, § 502(c), (d)(1), 110 Stat. 293.)

HISTORY; ANCILLARY LAWS AND DIRECTIVES

Prior law and revision:

1956 ACT

Revised Section	Source (USCS)	Source (Statutes at Large)
8962(a)	10:506b(d) (less 1st and last provisos).	Aug. 7, 1947, ch. 512, §§ 504(d) (less 1st and last provisos), 520(b) (less proviso), 61 Stat. 888, 912.
8962(b)	5:627b(h) (1st 42 words of 3d proviso).	June 12, 1948, ch. 449, § 303(h) (1st 42 words of 3d proviso), 62 Stat. 372.
8962(c)	10:1097a(b) (less proviso).	

In subsection (a), the words "who has served (1) as Chief of Staff to the President, (2) as Chief of Staff of the Air Force, (3) as a senior member of the Military Staff Committee of the United Nations, or (4) in a position of importance and responsibility designated by the President to carry the grade of general or lieutenant general under section 8066 of this title" are substituted for the words "while serving in accordance with the provisions of subsection (b) or (c) of this section".

In subsection (b), the words "in that grade" are substituted for the words "in such higher temporary grade". The words "under section 8071 of this title" are inserted for clarity.

In subsection (c), the words "Upon retirement" are substituted for the words "When . . . is retired". The word "allowances" is omitted, since retired officers are not entitled to allowances. The words "grade is below brigadier general" are inserted, since any permanent professor who has the grade of brigadier general retires in that grade under section 9335 of this title.

1958 ACT

Revised Section	Source (USCS)	Source (Statutes at Large)
8962	[No source].	[No source].

The amendment reflects section 1 of the Act of May 31, 1956, ch 348 (70 Stat. 222), which in effect amended section 8963 of this title to cover regular and reserve officers covered by section 8962(b). As to temporary officers, section 8962(b) is obsolete. (See opinion of the Judge Advocate General of the Air Force, May 2, 1957.)

Amendments:

1958. Act Sept. 2, 1958, redesignated subsec. (c) as subsec. (b) and deleted former subsec. (b) which read: "Upon retirement, any woman Air Force officer who has served at least two and one-half years on active duty in the temporary grade of colonel in the Air Force under section 8071 of this title may, in the discretion of the President, be retired in that grade.".

1965. Act Oct. 22, 1965 substituted subsec. (a) for one which read: "Upon retirement, a commissioned officer of the Regular Air Force who has served (1) as Chief of Staff to the President, (2) as Chief of Staff of the Air Force, (3) as a senior member of the Military Staff Committee of the United Nations, or (4) in a position of importance and responsibility designated by the President to carry the grade of general or lieutenant general under section 8066 of this title may, in the discretion of the President, be retired, by and with the advice and consent of the Senate, in the highest grade held by him at any time on the active list.''

1980. Act Sept. 8, 1980 substituted the section heading for one which read: ''§ 8962. Higher grade for service in special positions: regular commissioned officers''; and, in subsec. (a), deleted ''Regular'' preceding ''Air Force who'', and substituted ''in which he served on active duty'' for ''held by him at any time on the active list''.

Act Dec. 12, 1980 (effective 9/15/81, as provided by § 701(a) of such Act, which appears as 10 USCS § 101 note), in subsec. (a), substituted ''or (4)'' for ''(4) in a position of importance and responsibility designated by the President to carry the grade of general or lieutenant general under section 8066 of this title, or (5)''.

1996. Act Feb. 10, 1996 repealed subsec. (a), which read: ''Upon retirement, a commissioned officer of the Air Force who has served (1) as Chief of Staff to the President, (2) as Chief of Staff of the Air Force, (3) as a senior member of the Military Staff Committee of the United Nations, or (4) as Surgeon General of the Air Force in the grade of lieutenant general may, in the discretion of the President, be retired, by and with the advice and consent of the Senate, in the highest grade in which he served on active duty.''; and deleted ''(b)'' preceding ''Upon''.

Other provisions:

Retired grade for certain general officers. For an extension of privilege granted by subsec. (a) of this section to officers, heretofore or hereafter retired, who served in the grade of general or lieutenant general after Dec. 7, 1941, and before July 1, 1946, see § 38 of Act Aug. 10, 1956, which appears as a note under 10 USCS § 3962.

Appointment by President of retired commissioned officer of reserve component to higher retired grade; recalculation of pay. For authority of the President to appoint a retired commissioned officer of a reserve component to a higher retired grade and for recalculation of pay, see Act Sept. 4, 1980, P. L. 96-343, § 13(c), 94 Stat. 1132, which appears as 10 USCS § 3962 note.

CROSS REFERENCES

Senior member of Military Staff Committee, 10 USCS § 711.

Chief of Staff, 10 USCS § 8033.

This section is referred to in 10 USCS § 1406.

§ 8963. Highest grade held satisfactorily: Reserve enlisted members reduced in grade not as a result of the member's misconduct

(a) A Reserve enlisted member of the Air Force described in subsection (b) who is retired under section 8914 of this title shall be retired in the highest enlisted grade in which the member served on active duty satisfactorily (or, in the case of a member of the National Guard, in which the member served on full-time National Guard duty satisfactorily), as determined by the Secretary of the Air Force.

(b) This section applies to a Reserve enlisted member who—

(1) at the time of retirement is serving on active duty (or, in the case of a member of the National Guard, on full-time National Guard duty) in a grade lower than the highest enlisted grade held by the member while on active duty (or full-time National Guard duty); and

(2) was previously administratively reduced in grade not as a result of the member's own misconduct, as determined by the Secretary of the Air Force.

(c) This section applies with respect to Reserve enlisted members who are retired under section 8914 of this title after September 30, 1996.

(Added Sept. 23, 1996, P. L. 104-201, Div A, Title V, Subtitle D, § 532(c)(1), 110 Stat. 2519.)

HISTORY; ANCILLARY LAWS AND DIRECTIVES

Explanatory notes:

A prior § 8963 (Act Aug. 10, 1956, ch 1041, § 1, 70A Stat. 535; Sept. 2, 1958, P. L. 85-861, § 1(156), (198), 72 Stat. 1513, 1541; Dec. 12, 1980, P. L. 96-513, Title V, Part A, § 504(21), 94 Stat. 2917) was repealed by Act Nov. 8, 1985, P. L. 99-145, Title XIII, § 1301(d)(2)(A), 99 Stat. 736. It provided for higher grade for service during certain periods: regular and reserve commissioned officers.

CROSS REFERENCES

This section is referred to in 10 USCS § 8991.

§ 8964. Higher grade after 30 years of service: warrant officers and enlisted members

(a) Each retired member of the Air Force covered by subsection (b) who is retired with less than 30 years of active service is entitled, when his active service plus his service on the retired list totals 30 years, to be advanced on the retired list to the highest grade in which he served on active duty satisfactorily (or, in the case of a member of the National Guard, in which he served on full-time duty satisfactorily), as determined by the Secretary of the Air Force.

(b) This section applies to—

(1) warrant officers of the Air Force;

(2) enlisted members of the Regular Air Force; and

(3) reserve enlisted members of the Air Force who, at the time of retirement, are serving on active duty (or, in the case of members of the National Guard, on full-time duty).

(Aug. 10, 1956, ch 1041, § 1, 70A Stat. 555; Sept. 2, 1958, P. L. 85-861, § 1(198A), 72 Stat. 1541; Oct. 19, 1984, P. L. 98-525, Title V, Part C, § 533(c) in part, 98 Stat. 2528; Dec. 4, 1987, P. L. 100-180, Div A, Title V, § 512(c), 101 Stat. 1090.)

HISTORY; ANCILLARY LAWS AND DIRECTIVES

Prior law and revision:

1956 Act

Revised Section	Source (USCS)	Source (Statutes at Large)
8964	10:594 (1st proviso, less last 39 words; and last proviso). 10:1004 (less 30 words before proviso).	Aug. 21, 1941, ch. 384, § 5 (1st proviso, less last 39 words; and last proviso); restated June 29, 1948, ch. 708, § 203(c) (1st proviso, less last 39 words; and last proviso), 62 Stat. 1085; May 29, 1954, ch. 249, § 19(f), 68 Stat. 167. June 29, 1948, ch. 708, § 203,(3) (less 30 words before proviso), 62 Stat. 1086.

The words "when his active service plus his service on the retired list totals 30 years" are substituted for the words "upon the completion of thirty years' [years of] service, to include the sum of his active service and his service on the retired list", in 10:594 and 1004. The words "under any provision of law", in 10:594 and 1004; "officer, flight officer, or warrant officer", in 10:594; and "commissioned, warrant, or enlisted", in 10:1004; are omitted as surplusage. 10:594 (last proviso) and 1004 (proviso) are omitted as superseded by section 1372 of this title.

1958 Act

Revised Section	Source (USCS)	Source (Statutes at Large)
8964	10 App.:1004.	May 31, 1956, ch. 348, § 1, 70 Stat. 222.

Amendments:

1958. Act Sept. 2, 1958, deleted ", after September 8, 1940, and before July 1, 1946" after "Secretary of the Air Force".

1984. Act Oct. 19, 1984 deleted "temporary" following "the highest".

1987. Act Dec. 4, 1987 (effective as provided by § 512(f) of such Act, which appears as 10 USCS § 3964 note) substituted this heading and section for ones which read:

"§ 8964. Higher grade after 30 years of service: Air Force warrant officers; regular enlisted members

"Each warrant officer of the Air Force, and each enlisted member of the Regular Air Force, who is retired before or after this title is enacted is entitled, when his active service plus his service on the enacted list totals 30 years, to be advanced on the retired list to the grade that is equal to the highest grade in which he served on active duty satisfactorily, as determined by the Secretary of the Air Force.".

CROSS REFERENCES

Restoration to former grade, 10 USCS § 8965.

Recomputation of retired pay to reflect advancement on retired list, 10 USCS § 8992.

This section is referred to in 10 USCS §§ 8965, 8992.

INTERPRETIVE NOTES AND DECISIONS

Determination of what constitutes satisfactory service in highest temporary officer grade required to be made by Secretary of Air Force involved before advancement on retired list to that rank can be made under predecessor of 10 USCS § 8964 is not required to be made on basis of any particular criteria; accordingly, directive by Secretary of Air Force that enlisted man promoted to commissioned rank must have served at least 6 months in such rank before his service will certified as ''satisfactory'' for purposes of advancement on retirement, is neither arbitrary nor illegal but is within Secretary's authority to promulgate regulations. Roberts v United States (1960) 151 Ct Cl 360.

§ 8965. Restoration to former grade: retired warrant officers and enlisted members

Each retired warrant officer or enlisted member of the Air Force who has been advanced on the retired list to a higher commissioned grade under section 8964 of this title, and who applies to the Secretary of the Air Force within three months after his advancement, shall, if the Secretary approves, be restored on the retired list to his former warrant-officer or enlisted status, as the case may be.

(Aug. 10, 1956, ch 1041, § 1, 70A Stat. 555; Dec. 4, 1987, P. L. 100-180, Div A, Title V, § 512(d)(3), 101 Stat. 1090; Sept. 29, 1988, P. L. 100-456, Div A, Title XII, Part D, § 1233(i)(2)(A), 102 Stat. 2058.)

HISTORY; ANCILLARY LAWS AND DIRECTIVES

Prior law and revision:

Revised Section	Source (USCS)	Source (Statutes at Large)
8965	10:1006.	June 29, 1948, ch. 708, § 204, 62 Stat. 1086.

The words ''hereafter'', ''rank or'', and ''shall thereafter be deemed to be enlisted or warrant officer personnel, as appropriate, for all purposes'' are omitted as surplusage. The words ''three months from June 29, 1948'' and ''whichever is later'' are omitted as executed.

Amendments:

1987. Act Dec. 4, 1987 deleted ''Regular'' following ''member of the''.

1988. Act Sept. 29, 1988 substituted this section heading for one which read: ''§ 8965. Restoration to former grade: Regular Air Force warrant officers and enlisted members''.

§ 8966. Retired lists

(a) The Secretary of the Air Force shall maintain a retired list containing the name of each retired commissioned officer of the Regular Air Force.

(b) The Secretary shall maintain a retired list containing the name of—

(1) each person entitled to retired pay under any law providing retired pay for commissioned officers of the Air Force, other than of the Regular Air Force; and

(2) each retired warrant officer or enlisted member of the Air Force who is advanced to a commissioned grade.

(c) The Secretary shall maintain a retired list containing the name of each retired warrant officer of the Air Force.

(d) The Secretary shall maintain a retired list containing the name of each retired enlisted member of the Regular Air Force.

(Aug. 10, 1956, ch 1041, § 1, 70A Stat. 556; Sept. 2, 1958, P. L. 85-861, § 1(199), 72 Stat. 1541; Dec. 4, 1987, P. L. 100-180, Div A, Title V, § 512(d)(3), 101 Stat. 1090.)

HISTORY; ANCILLARY LAWS AND DIRECTIVES

Prior law and revision:

1956 ACT

Revised Section	Source (USCS)	Source (Statutes at Large)
8966(a)	10:1001.	June 29, 1948, ch. 708, §§ 201, 301(a), 62 Stat. 1084, 1087.
8966(b)	10:1036.	
8966(c)	[No source].	
8966(d)	[No source].	

In subsections (a), (b), and (d), the word "maintain" is substituted for the word "establish", and in subsection (c) the word "maintain" is substituted for the word "established", since the lists have been established and are published annually.

In subsection (a), the words "Effective upon June 29, 1948" are omitted as executed. 10:1001 (last 12 words of 1st sentence, and last sentence) is omitted as no longer required, since, upon enactment of this Title, laws referring to the limited or unlimited retired list will be expressly repealed.

In subsection (b), the word "shall" is substituted for the word "may", since 10:1036 further requires that such a list be published annually in the Register. The requirement as to publication necessarily implies that the list must be maintained.

Subsection (b)(1) is substituted for the words "all commissioned officers and former commissioned officers . . . or the Air Force of the United States, as the case may be . . . or the Regular Air Force, heretofore or hereafter granted retirement pay under sections 456, 456a, and 1036a of this title, or any law hereafter enacted to provide retirement pay for commissioned officers . . . or the Regular Air Force".

In subsection (b)(2), the words "who is advanced to a commissioned grade" are substituted for the words "heretofore or hereafter retired under any provision of law who, by reason of service in temporary commissioned grades . . . or the Air Force of the United States, or in any of the respective components thereof, are entitled to be retired with commissioned rank or grade".

Subsection (c) and (d) are inserted, since sections 8964 and 8965 of this title refer to service on the retired list as a warrant officer or enlisted member.

1958 ACT

Revised Section	Source (USCS)	Source (Statutes at Large)
8966(a)	10 App.:1001.	July 24, 1056, ch. 677,
8966(b)	10 App.:1036	§ 2(f), (g), 70 Stat. 623.

Amendments:

1958. Act Sept. 2, 1958, in subsec. (a) and in the preliminary matter of subsec. (b) deleted ", to be published annually in the official Air Force Register," following "retired list".

1987. Act Dec. 4, 1987, in subsec. (b)(2), deleted "Regular" preceding "Air Force".

INTERPRETIVE NOTES AND DECISIONS

Under predecessor of 5 USCS § 5534, officers on retired list of Air Force reserve were entitled to retired pay under predecessor of 10 USCS § 8966 in addition to pay from civilian government employment, notwithstanding restrictions imposed by predecessor of 5 USCS § 5532. Tanner v United States (1954) 129 Ct Cl 792, 125 F Supp 240, cert den (1955) 350 US 842, 100 L Ed 751, 76 S Ct 83.

CHAPTER 871. COMPUTATION OF RETIRED PAY

§ 8991. Computation of retired pay

(a) Computation. (1) Formula. The monthly retired pay of a member entitled to such pay under this subtitle [10 USCS §§ 8011 et seq.] is computed by multiplying—

(A) the member's retired pay base (as computed under section 1406(e) or 1407 of this title), by

(B) the retired pay multiplier prescribed in section 1409 of this title for the number of years credited to the member under section 1405 of this title.

(2) Additional 10 percent for certain enlisted members credited with extraordinary heroism. If a member who is retired under section 8914 of this title has been credited by the Secretary of the Air Force with extraordinary heroism in the line of duty, the member's retired pay shall be increased by 10 percent of the amount determined under paragraph (1) (but to not more than 75 percent of the retired pay base upon which the computation of such retired pay is based). The Secretary's determination as to extraordinary heroism is conclusive for all purposes.

(b) General rules. (1) Use of most favorable formula. If a person would otherwise be entitled to retired pay computed under more than one formula in subsection (a) or the table in section 1401 of this title, he is entitled to be paid under the applicable formula that is most favorable to him.

(2) Rounding to next lower dollar. The amount computed under subsection (a), if not a multiple of $1, shall be rounded to the next lower multiple of $1.

(c) Special rule for retired Reserve enlisted members covered by section 8963. In the case of a Reserve enlisted member retired under section 8914 of this title whose retired grade is determined under section 8963 of this title and who first became a member of a uniformed service before September 8, 1980, the retired pay base of the member (notwithstanding section 1406(a)(1) of this title) is the amount of the monthly basic pay of the member's retired grade (determined based upon the rates of basic pay applicable on the date of the member's retirement), and that amount shall be used for the purposes of subsection (a)(1)(A) rather than the amount computed under section 1406(e) of this title.

(Aug. 10, 1956, ch 1041, § 1, 70A Stat. 556; Aug. 21, 1957, P. L. 85-155, Title III, § 301(22), 71 Stat. 389; May 20, 1958, P. L. 85-422, §§ 6(6), (8), 11(a)(9), 72 Stat. 129, 131; Sept. 2, 1958, P. L. 85-861, § 1(199A), 72 Stat. 1541; Sept.

7, 1962, P. L. 87-651, Title I, § 127, 76 Stat. 514; Oct. 2, 1963, P. L. 88-132, § 5(h)(2), 77 Stat. 214; Dec. 16, 1967, P. L. 90-207, § 3(5), 81 Stat. 654; Sept. 8, 1980, P. L. 96-342, Title VIII, § 813(e) in part, 94 Stat. 1109; Dec. 12, 1980, P.L. 96-513, Title V, Part A, § 504(22) Part B, § 514(8), 94 Stat. 2917, 2935; Sept. 24, 1983, P. L. 98-94, Title IX, Part B, §§ 922(a)(12), 923(a) in part, 97 Stat. 641, 642; July 1, 1986, P. L. 99-348, Title II, § 204(a), 100 Stat. 697; Oct. 5, 1994, P. L. 103-337, Div A, Title VI, Subtitle D, § 635(c)(2), 108 Stat. 2789; Sept. 23, 1996, P. L. 104-201, Div A, Title V, Subtitle D, § 532(d)(3), 110 Stat. 2520.)

HISTORY; ANCILLARY LAWS AND DIRECTIVES

Prior law and revision:

1956 Act

Revised Section	Source (USCS)	Source (Statutes at Large)
8991 Introductory paragraph	10:941a(a)(3) (proviso, less applicability to retired grade). 10:941a(e) (1st proviso of clause (1), less applicability to retired grade).	R.S. 1274. Mar. 2, 1907, ch. 2515, § 1 (less 1st 35 words, and less proviso), 34 Stat. 1217. July 31, 1935, ch. 422, § 5 (less 1st 101 words, and less 3d proviso); restated June 13, 1940, ch. 344, § 3 (less 1st 45 words, and less 2d proviso), 54 Stat. 380; Aug. 7, 1947, ch. 512, §§ 514(g), 521(a), 61 Stat. 906, 912; June 29, 1948, ch. 708, § 202 (less 1st 105 words), 62 Stat. 1084.
8991(A)	10:166g(a) (less 1st 49 words; less 1st proviso; and less 1st 84 words of last proviso).	
8991(B)	10:941a(a)(3) (less 31st through 42d words, and less proviso). 10:941a(e) (clause (1), less 1st 25, and 59th through 113th, words; and less 1st proviso).	
8991(C)	10:971. 10:971b (less 1st 100 words, and less 1st and 3d proviso).	Oct. 6, 1945, ch. 393, § 4 (less 1st sentence); restated Aug. 10, 1946, ch. 952, § 6(a) (less 1st sentence), 60 Stat. 996.
8991(D)	10:948 (less 1st sentence, and less 1st and last provisos of last sentence).	
8991(E)	10:980.	Aug. 10, 1946, ch. 952, § 6(c), 60 Stat. 996.
8991 Footnote 1.	10:50b(d) (1st proviso). 10:1079a(b)(proviso)	Apr. 16, 1947, ch. 38, § 108(a) (less 1st 49 words, and less 1st 84 words of last proviso), 61 Stat. 44.
8991 Footnote 2.	5:627b(h) (3d proviso, less 1st 42, and last 13, words. 10:1002 (34 words before proviso and proviso).	Aug. 7, 1947, ch. 512, §§ 504(d) (1st proviso), 514(a)(3) (less 31st

Revised Section	Source (USCS)	Source (Statutes at Large)
8991	10:1003 (last 40 words).	through 42d words; and
Footnote 3.	8991 [No source]. 10:166g(a) (1st proviso).	less proviso, less applicability to retired grade),
Footnote 4.	10:941a(e) (94th through 113th words of clause (1)). 10:948 (last proviso of last sentence). 10:971b (1st proviso). 37:272(d) (1st proviso).	514(e) (cl. (1), less 1st 25, and 59th through 93d words; and less 1st proviso, as applicable to retired grade), 520(b) (proviso), 61 Stat. 888, 902, 905, 912. June 12, 1948, ch. 449, § 303(h) (3d proviso, less 1st 42d and last 13, words), 62 Stat. 372.
8991 Footnote 5.	10:948 (1st proviso of last sentence).	June 29, 1948, ch. 708 §§ 203(a) (34 words before proviso, and proviso), 203(d) (last 40 words), 62 Stat. 1085.

In the introductory paragraph, the applicability of the rule stated in the third sentence to situations not expressly covered by the laws named in the source statutes above is a practical construction that the rule must be reciprocally applied in all cases.

In formula B, the words ''basic pay'' are substituted for the words ''base and longevity pay'' to conform to the terminology of the Career Compensation Act of 1949, 63 Stat. 802 (37 U.S.C. 231 et seq.). The words ''his retired grade'' are substituted for the words ''permanent grade held at time of retirement'' to reflect the right to higher retired grade when qualified under other provisions of law. 10:941a(e) (last proviso of cl. (1)), is omitted, since, under section 202 of the Career Compensation Act of 1949, 63 Stat. 807 (37 U.S.C. 233), the active duty pay of all members of the Air Force is based upon years of service.

In formula C, the computation is based on monthly pay instead of annual pay to conform to the other formulas of the revised section. The words ''basic pay'' are substituted for the words ''active duty base and longevity pay'', and the words ''in determining his basic pay'' are substituted for the words ''for longevity pay purposes'', to conform to the terminology of the Career Compensation Act of 1949, 63 Stat. 802 (37 U.S.C. 231 et seq.). The words ''Monthly basic pay of member's retired grade'' are substituted for the words ''the rank upon which they are retired'', in 10:971, and ''rank with which retired'', in 10:971b, to reflect their right to advancement on the retired list, 10:971 now applies only when the retiring officer has 30 or more years of service which may be credited in computing his retired pay. 10:971b (2d proviso) is omitted, since, under section 202 of the Career Compensation Act of 1949, 63 Stat. 807 (37 U.S.C. 233), the pay of all members is based upon cumulative years of service. 10:971b (4th proviso) is omitted as executed. 10:971b (last proviso) is omitted, since the distinction between limited and unlimited retired lists was abolished by section 201 of the Act of June 29, 1948, ch 708, 62 Stat. 1084. 10 USCS §§ 8918, 8920, and 8924 are included under this formula, since it achieves the same result as is reached on a basis of 30 years multiplied by 2$^1/_2$ percent, and simplifies the table.

In formulas D and E the words ''credited under section 8925'' are substituted for the words ''active Federal service'', since that revised section makes explicit the service covered. The Act of August 10, 1946, ch 952, § 6(c), 60 Stat. 996, is not contained in 10:948. It is also omitted from the revised section as executed. 10:980 now applies only when the retiring enlisted member has at least 30 years of service which may be credited in computing his retired pay. However, as noted above, 10:980 is the only provision of law applicable to cases in which the retiring member has at least 30 years of service. The Act of June 16, 1942, ch 413, § 19 (63d through 75th words of 2d para.), 56 Stat. 369, repealed so much of the Act of March 2, 1907, ch 2513, 34 Stat. 1217, as provided allowances for enlisted men on the retired list. The repeal of section 19 of the Act of June 16, 1942, by section 531(b)(34) of the Career Compensation Act of 1949, 63 Stat. 839, did not revive that portion of the Act of March 2, 1907, which had been repealed by the Act of June 16, 1942. Accordingly, the Act of March 2, 1907, as thus modified by the Act of June 16, 1942, is used as the basis for formula E.

Footnote 2 reflects the long-standing construction of those provisions dealing with computation of retired pay which do not specifically provide that the member is entitled to compute his retired pay on the basis of the monthly basic pay to which he would be entitled if he were on active duty in his retired grade. Except in cases covered by formula C, the pertinent basic computation provisions for such retirement either provide for computation of retired pay on the same basis as the provisions dealing with higher retired grade, or the basic retirement provisions were themselves enacted after the provisions authorizing higher retired grade. The provisos of 10:1002 and 1005 are omitted as surplusage, since no formula for the computation of retired pay includes inactive service on the retired list as a credit.

The words ''at rates applicable on date of retirement and adjust to reflect later changes in permanent rates'', in footnote 2; and all of footnote 4; are based on the source statutes incorporated in the formulas to which footnotes 2 and 4 apply.

In footnote 4, the words ''and disregard a part of a year that is less than six months'' are made applicable to formulas A–E, although this part of the rule is expressed only as to formula B, in 10:941a(4)(1). The legislative history of the Career Compensation Act of 1949 (Hearings before the Committee on Armed Services of the Senate on H.R. 5007, 81st Congress, first session, p. 313, July 6, 1949) indicates that the provisions, upon which formulas A and C–E are based, should be construed to require that a part of a year that is less than six months be disregarded.

1958 ACT

Revised Section	Source (USCS)	Source (Statutes at Large)
8991	[No source].	[No source].

The amendment reflects section 1(197) of the bill [amendment of section 8962 of title 10].

1962 ACT

The change corrects a cross-reference error.

Amendments:

1957. Act Aug. 21, 1957, struck out formula "A" of the table, which related to computation of retirement pay for persons retired under former 10 USCS §§ 8881, 8882, and 8912, and redesignated formulas "B," "C," "D," and "E" as "A," "B," "C," and "D," respectively.

1958. Act May 20, 1958 (effective 6/1/58, as provided by § 9 of such Act, and applicable as provided by § 6 of such Act, which appears as 10 USCS § 3991 note), in column 2 of Formula B, substituted "under section 1405 of this title" for "in determining basic pay"; in column 1 of Formula C, substituted "pay[3]" for "pay" and substituted "day before he retired" for "date when he applied for retirement"; in column 1 of Formula D, substituted "to which member was entitled on day before he retired" for "of member's retired grade"; in footnote 1, substituted "(c)" for "(a)" and inserted "and, for an officer who has served as Chief of Staff, compute at the the highest rates of basic pay applicable to him while he served in that office".

Act Sept. 2, 1958, in footnote 2, substituted "8963(a)" for "8962(a), 8963(a),".

1962. Act Sept. 7, 1962, in footnote 1, substituted "(b)" for "(c)".

1963. Act Oct. 2, 1963 (effective 10/1/63, as provided by § 14 of such Act, which appears as 37 USCS § 201 note) in column 1 of Formula A, substituted "Monthly basic pay[2] of member's retired grade[1]." for "Monthly basic pay to which member would be entitled if he were on active duty in his retired grade.[1]"; in footnote 2, deleted "and adjust to reflect later changes in applicable permanent rates. However, if member's retired grade is determined under section 8963(a) or 8963(b), use pay to which member would be entitled if he were on active duty in his retired grade", after "date of retirement".

1967. Act Dec. 16, 1967 (effective 10/1/67, as provided by § 7 of such Act, which appears as 37 USCS § 203 note), in footnote 3, inserted ", or if the member has served as chief master sergeant of the Air Force, compute at the highest basic pay applicable to him while he so served, if such basic pay is greater".

1980. Act Sept. 8, 1980, in the table headings, in column 1, substituted "For a person who first became a member of a uniformed service (as defined in section 1407(a)(2) of this title) on or after the date of the enactment of the Department of Defense Authorization Act, 1981, take the monthly retired pay base as computed under section 1407(e). For all others, take" for "Take".

Act Dec. 12, 1980 (effective upon enactment on 12/12/80, as provided by

§ 701(b)(3) of such Act, which appears as 10 USCS § 101 note), in the table heading for column 1, substituted ''after September 7, 1980'' for ''on or after the date of the enactment of the Department of Defense Authorization Act, 1981''.

Act Dec. 12, 1980 (effective 9/15/81, as provided by § 701(a) of such Act, which appears as 10 USCS § 101 note), in the tabular matter, deleted:

''A	8883 8884 8885 8886 8913 8915 8916 8919 8921 8922 8923	Monthly basic pay [2] of member's retired grade. [1]	2 1/2% of years of service credited to him under section 8888 or 8927(b) whichever is applicable. [4]	Amount necessary to increase product of columns 1 and 2 to 50% of pay upon which computation is based.	Excess over 75% of pay upon which computation is based.''.

Such Act further, under the column headed ''Formula'', redesignated the former designations B–D as A–C, respectively.

1983. Act Sept. 24, 1983, § 923(a) in part, (applicable as provided by § 923(g) of such Act, which appears as 10 USCS § 1174 note), substituted footnote 4 for one which read: ''Before applying percentage factor, credit a part of a year that is six months or more as a whole year, and disregard a part of a year that is less than six months.''.

Section 922(a)(13) (effective 10/1/83, as provided by § 922(e) of such Act, which appears as 10 USCS § 1401 note), in the introductory matter, added the sentence beginning ''The amount computed, . . .''.

1986. Act July 1, 1986 substituted this section for one which read:

''The monthly retired pay of a person entitled thereto under this subtitle is computed according to the following table. The amount computed, if not a multiple of $1, shall be rounded to the next lower multiple of $1. For each case covered by a section of this title named in the column headed 'For sections', retired pay is computed by taking, in order, the steps prescribed opposite it in columns 1, 2, 3, and 4, as modified by the applicable footnotes. However, if a person would otherwise be entitled to retired pay computed under more than one pay formula of this table or the table in section 1401 of this title, he is entitled to be paid under the applicable formula that is most favorable to him. Section references below are to sections of this title.

''Formula	For sections	Column 1	Column 2 Multiply by	Column 3 Add	Column 4 Subtract
		For a person who first became a member of a uniformed service (as defined in section 1407(a)(2) of this title) after September 7, 1980, take the monthly retired pay base as computed			

		under section 1407(e). For all others, take			
"A	8911 8918 8920 8924	Monthly basic pay [2] of member's retired grade. [1]	2 1/2% of years of service credited to him under section 1405 of this title. [4]		Excess over 75% of pay upon which computation is based.
"B	8914	Monthly basic pay to which member was entitled on the day before he retired.	2 1/2% of years of service credted to him under section 8925. [4]	10% of product of columns 1 and 2 for extraordinary heroism in line of duty. [5]	Excess over 75% of pay upon which computation is based.
"C	8917	Monthly basic pay [3] to which member was entitled on the day before he retired.	2 1/2% of years of service credited to him under section 8925. [4]		Excess over 75% of pay upon which computation is based.

[1] For the purposes of this section, determine member's retired grade as if section 8962(b) did not apply and, for an officer who has served as Chief of Staff, compute at the highest rates of basic pay applicable to him while he served in that office.

[2] Compute at rates applicable on date of retirement.

[3] Compute at rates applicable on date of retirement, or if the member has served as chief master sergeant of the Air Force, compute at the highest basic pay applicable to him while he so served, if such basic pay is greater.

[4] Before applying percentage factor, credit each full month of service that is in addition to the number of full years of service creditable to the member as one-twelfth of a year and disregard any remaining fractional part of a month.

[5] The Secretary of the Air Force's determination as to extraordinary heroism is conclusive for all purposes.".

1994. Act Oct. 5, 1994 (applicable as provided by § 635(e) of such Act, which appears as 10 USCS § 1405 note) substituted subsec. (a)(1) for one which read: "(1) In general. The monthly retired pay of a member entitled to such pay under this subtitle is computed according to the following table. For each case covered by a section of this title named in the column headed 'For sections', retired pay is computed by taking the steps prescribed opposite it in columns 1 and 2.

Formula	For sections	Column 1 Take	Column 2 Multiply by
A	8911 8918 8920 8924	Retired pay base as computed under section 1406(e) or 1407.	The retired pay multiplier prescribed in section 1409 for the years of services credited to him under section 1405.
B	8914 8917 8920 8924	Retired pay base as computed under section 1406(e) or 1407.	The retired pay multiplier prescribed in section 1409 for the years of services credited to him under section 8925.

and, in subsec. (b), in para. (1), deleted "of the table" following "one formula", and deleted para. (3), which read: "(3) References. Section references in the table in subsection (a) are to sections of this title.".

1996. Act Sept. 23, 1996 added subsec. (c).

CROSS REFERENCES

This section is referred to in 10 USCS § 1406.

INTERPRETIVE NOTES AND DECISIONS

1. Construction
2. Relation to other laws
3. Powers of President
4. Retiree's obligations
5. Retirement pay and divorce settlements

1. Construction

Provisions of predecessor of 10 USCS § 8991 were not in any respect ambiguous but were positive and direct. Hornblass v United States (1941) 93 Ct Cl 148.

2. Relation to other laws

Predecessors of 10 USCS § 8917 and § 8991 both related to matter of retirement of enlisted men but language of two acts, with reference to retirement and retirement pay, was not same and rights and privileges granted by predecessor of § 8991 must control whether they are more, or less, favorable to enlisted men. Hornblass v United States (1941) 93 Ct Cl 148.

3. Powers of President

President did not have authority to order retirement pay at rate different than that provided under predecessor of 10 USCS § 8991. (1878) 15 Op Atty Gen 442.

4. Retiree's obligations

Officer on retired list owes no service to government and his retired pay is honorary form of pension. Geddes v United States (1903) 38 Ct Cl 428.

5. Retirement pay and divorce settlements

Retirement pay received by retired Air Force personnel is community property with regard to issue of property settlements in California divorces; although portion of retirement payments were technically attributable to services rendered outside California, payments were properly divided without any allocation other than that reflected in number of years of marriage. In re Marriage of Karlin (1972, 4th Dist) 24 Cal App 3d 25, 101 Cal Rptr 240.

Divorce decree award of husband's community property retirement pay would be based on 17/20 ths of pay earned where husband was married for 17 of his 20 years of service, and wife was entitled to lump sum amounting to 40 per cent of present value of husband's retirement pay based on his life expectancy at time of decree, plus interest. Ramsey v Ramsey (1975) 96 Idaho 672, 535 P2d 53.

Portion of serviceman's military pension earned during months of coverture are contingent earnings of community and community asset subject to consideration along with other property in division of estate of parties to divorce action in Texas. Cearley v Cearley (1976, Tex) 544 SW2d 661 (ovrld in part by Trahan v Trahan (1981, Tex) 626 SW2d 485) and (superseded by statute as stated in Grier v Grier (1987, Tex) 30 Tex Sup Ct Jour 362).

§ 8992. Recomputation of retired pay to reflect advancement on retired list

(a) Entitlement to recomputation. An enlisted member or warrant officer of the Air Force who is advanced on the retired list under section 8964 of this title is entitled to recompute his retired pay in accordance with this section.

(b) Formula. The monthly retired pay of a member entitled to recompute that pay under this section is computed by multiplying—

(1) the member's retired pay base (as computed under section 1406(e) or 1407 of this title), by

(2) the retired pay multiplier prescribed in section 1409 of this title for the number of years credited to the member under section 1405 of this title.

(c) Rounding to next lower dollar. The amount computed under subsection (b), if not a multiple of $1, shall be rounded to the next lower multiple of $1.

(Aug. 10, 1956, ch 1041, § 1, 70A Stat. 557; Sept. 8, 1980, P.L. 96-342, Title

VIII, § 813(e) in part, 94 Stat. 1109; Dec. 12, 1980, P.L. 96-513, Title V, Part B, § 514(8), 94 Stat. 2935; Oct. 12, 1982, P. L. 97-295, § 1(52), 96 Stat. 1300; Sept. 24, 1983, P. L. 98-94, Title IX, Part B. §§ 922(a)(13), 923(a) in part, 97 Stat. 641, 642; July 1, 1986, P. L. 99-348, Title II, § 204(b), 100 Stat. 698; Oct. 5, 1994, P. L. 103-337, Div A, Title VI, Subtitle D, § 635(c)(3), 108 Stat. 2789.)

HISTORY; ANCILLARY LAWS AND DIRECTIVES

Prior law and revision:

1956 Act

Revised Section	Source (USCS)	Source (Statutes at Large)
8992	10:594 (last 39 words of 1st proviso). 10:1004 (30 words before proviso).	Aug. 21, 1941, ch. 384, § 5 (last 39 words of 1st pro viso); restated June 29, 1948, ch. 708, § 203(c) (last 39 words of 1st proviso), 62 Stat. 1085; May 29, 1954, ch. 249, § 19(f), 68 Stat. 167. June 29, 1948, ch. 708, § 203(e) (30 words before proviso), 62 Stat. 1086.

The words "basic pay . . . as the case may be" are inserted to conform to the terminology of the Career Compensation Act of 1949, 63 Stat. 802 (37 U.S.C. 231 et seq.). The words "at the rate prescribed by law for his length of service", in 10:1004, are omitted as covered by the words "base and longevity pay". The words "base and longevity pay" are retained to cover the cases of members retired before the enactment of the Career Compensation Act of 1949, and advanced on the retired list after the enactment of that Act. The words "and disregard a part of a year that is less than six months" are inserted to conform to footnote 4 of section 8991 of this title.

1982 Act

This amends 10:8992 to correct an inadvertent error in the codification of title 10 in 1956 relating to retirement pay of warrant officers advanced on the retired list. For further details, see the explanation for amendment of 10:1405 by section 1(17).

Amendments:

1980. Act Sept. 8, 1980, in the table heading, in column 1, substituted "For a person who first became a member of a uniformed service (as defined in section 1407(a)(2) of this title) on or after the date of the enactment of the Department of Defense Authorization Act, 1981, take the monthly retired pay base as computed under section 1407(e). For all others, take" for "Take".

Act Dec. 12, 1980 (effective upon enactment on 12/12/80, as provided by § 701(b)(3) of such Act, which appears as 10 USCS § 101 note), in the table heading for column 1, substituted "after September 7, 1980" for "on or after the date of the enactment of the Department of Defense Authorization Act, 1981".

1982. Act Oct. 12, 1982, substituted this section for one which read:

"A member of the Air Force who is advanced on the retired list under section 8964 of this title is entitled to recompute his retired pay as follows:

Column 1	Column 2 Multiply by	Column 3 Add	Column 4 Subtract
For a person who first became a member of a uniformed service (as defined in section 1407(a)(2) of this title) after September 7, 1980, take the monthly retired pay base as computed under section 1407(e). For all others, take Monthly basic pay or base and longevity pay, as the case may be, [1] of grade to which member is advanced on retired list.	2 1/2% of years of service credited to him under section 8925 of this title. [2]		Excess over 75% of pay upon which computation is based.

" [1] Compute at rates applicable on date of retirement.

" [2] Before applying percentage factor, credit a part of a year that is six months or more as a whole year, and disregard a part of a year that is less than six months."

1983. Act Sept. 24, 1983, § 923(a) in part (applicable as provided by § 923(g) of such Act, which appears as 10 USCS § 1174 note), substituted footnote 2 for one which read: "Before applying percentage factor, credit a part of a year that is six months or more as a whole year, and disregard a part of a year that is less than six months.".

Section 922(a)(13) of such Act further (effective 10/1/83, as provided by § 922(e) of such Act, which appears as 10 USCS § 1401 note), in the introductory matter, added the sentence beginning "The amount recomputed, . . .".

1986. Act July 1, 1986 substituted the tabular matter for one which read:

	Column 1	Column 2	Column 3	Column 4
"Formula	For a person who first became a member of a uniformed service (as defined in section 1407(a)(2) of this title) after September 7, 1980, take the monthly retired pay base as computed under section 1407(e). For all others, take	Multiply by	Add	Subtract
A	Monthly basic pay or base and longevity pay, as the case may be, [1] of grade to which member is advanced on retired list.	2 1/2% of years of service credited to him under section 8925 of this title. [2]		Excess over 75% of pay upon which computation is based.

B	Monthly basic pay or base and longevity pay, as the case may be, [1] of grade to which member is advanced on retired list.	2 1/2% of years of service credited to him under section 8925 of this title. [2]	Excess over 75% of pay upon which computation is based.

[1] Compute at rate applicable on date of retirement.
[2] Before applying percentage factor, credit each full month of service that is in addition to the number of full years of service creditable to the member as one-twelfth of a year and disregard any remaining fractional part of a month.''.

1994. Act Oct. 5, 1994 (applicable as provided by § 635(e) of such Act, which appears as 10 USCS § 1405 note) substituted the text of this section for text which read: ''An enlisted member of the Air Force who is advanced on the retired list under section 8964 of this title is entitled to recompute his retired pay under formula A of the following table, and a warrant officer of the Air Force so advanced is entitled to recompute his retired pay under formula B of that table. The amount recomputed, if not a multiple of $1, shall be rounded to the next lower multiple of $1.

Formula	Column 1 Take	Column 2 Multiply by
A	Retired pay base as computed under section 1406(e) or 1407 of this title.	The retired pay multiplier prescribed in section 1409 of this title for the number of years credited to him under section 8925 of this title. [1]
B	Retired pay base as computed under section 1406(e) or 1407 of this title.	The retired pay multiplier prescribed in section 1409 of this title for the number of years credited to him under section 1405 of this title.

[1] In determining retired pay multiplier, credit each full month of service that is in addition to the number of full years of service creditable to the member as 1/12 of a year and disregard any remaining fractional part of a month.

CROSS REFERENCES

This section is referred to in 10 USCS § 1406.

CHAPTER 873. CIVILIAN EMPLOYEES

HISTORY; ANCILLARY LAWS AND DIRECTIVES

Amendments:

1958. Act Sept. 2, 1958, P. L. 85-861, § 1(200), 72 Stat. 1541, amended the analysis of this chapter by deleting item 9021, which read: ''9021. Appointment: professional and scientific services.''.

1962. Act Sept. 7, 1962, P. L. 87-651, Title I, § 128(2), 76 Stat. 514, amended the analysis of this chapter by deleting item 9023 which read: ''9023. Service club and library services.''.

1983. Act Sept. 24, 1983, P. L. 98-94, Title IX, Part C, § 932(c)(2), 97 Stat. 650 (effective 10/1/83, as provided by § 932(f) of such Act, which appears as 10 USCS § 1091 note), amended the analysis of this chapter by deleting item 9022 which read: ''9022. Contract surgeons''.

1989. Act Nov. 29, 1989, P. L. 101-189, Div A, Title XI, Part C, § 1124(d)(2), 103 Stat. 1560, amended the analysis of this chapter by adding item 9021.

§ 9021. Air University: civilian faculty members

(a) Authority of Secretary. The Secretary of the Air Force may employ as many civilians as professors, instructors, and lecturers at a school of the Air University as the Secretary considers necessary.

(b) Compensation of faculty members. The compensation of persons employed under this section shall be as prescribed by the Secretary.

(c) Application to certain faculty members. (1) Except as provided in paragraph (2), this section shall apply with respect to persons who are selected by the Secretary for employment as professors, instructors, and lecturers at a school of the Air University after February 27, 1990.

(2) This section shall not apply with respect to professors, instructors, and lecturers employed at a school of the Air University if the duration of the principal course of instruction offered at that school is less than 10 months.

(Added Nov. 29, 1989, P. L. 101-189, Div A, Title XI, Part C, § 1124(d)(1), 103 Stat. 1559; Oct. 5, 1994, P. L. 103-337, Div A, Title X, Subtitle G, § 1070(a)(17), 108 Stat. 2856.)

HISTORY; ANCILLARY LAWS AND DIRECTIVES

Explanatory notes:

A prior § 9021 (Act Aug. 10, 1956, ch 1041, § 1, 70A Stat. 558) was repealed by Act Sept. 2, 1958, P. L. 85-861, § 36(b)(30), 72 Stat 1571. It related to appointments in the professional and scientific service. For similar provisions, see 10 USCS § 1581.

Amendments:

1994. Act Oct. 5, 1994, in subsec. (c)(1), substituted "after February 27, 1990" for "after the end of the 90-day period beginning on the date of the enactment of this section".

CROSS REFERENCES

This section is referred to in 5 USCS § 5102.

[§ 9022. Repealed]

HISTORY; ANCILLARY LAWS AND DIRECTIVES

This section (Act Aug. 10, 1956, ch 1042, § 1, 70A Stat. 558) was repealed by Act Sept. 24, 1983, P. L. 98-94, Title IX, Part C, § 932(c)(1), 97 Stat. 650, effective Oct. 1, 1983, as provided by § 932(f) of such Act, which appears as 10 USCS § 1091 note. It provided for contract surgeons.

[§ 9023. Repealed]

HISTORY; ANCILLARY LAWS AND DIRECTIVES

This section (Act Aug. 10, 1956, ch 1041, § 1, 70A Stat. 558) was repealed by Act Sept. 7, 1962, P. L. 87-651, Title I, § 128(1), 76 Stat. 514. It related to employment of civilians in service club and library services.

§ 9025. Production of supplies and munitions: hours and pay of laborers and mechanics

During a national emergency declared by the President, the regular working hours of laborers and mechanics of the Department of the Air Force producing military supplies or munitions are 8 hours a day or 40 hours a week. However, under regulations prescribed by the Secretary of the Air Force these hours may be exceeded. Each laborer or mechanic who works more than 40 hours in a workweek shall be paid at a rate not less than one and one-half times the regular hourly rate for each hour in excess of 40.

(Aug. 10, 1956, ch 1041, § 1, 70A Stat. 558.)

HISTORY; ANCILLARY LAWS AND DIRECTIVES

Prior law and revision:

Revised Section	Source (USCS)	Source (Statutes at Large)
9025	5:189a.	July 2, 1940, ch. 508, § 4(b), 54 Stat. 714.

The words "Notwithstanding the provisions of any other law" are omitted as surplusage. The word "producing" is substituted for the words "who are engaged in the manufacture or production". The last sentence is substituted for 5:189a (last 34 words).

CROSS REFERENCES

Hours of work of Government employees, 5 USCS §§ 6101 et seq.

INTERPRETIVE NOTES AND DECISIONS

Term "laborers and mechanics" within predecessor of 10 USCS § 9025 included employees of munitions plant operated by private contractor under contract with United States Government. Kennedy v Silas Mason Co. (1946, DC La) 68 F Supp 576, 11 CCH LC ¶ 63423, different results reached on other grounds on reh (1947, DC La) 70 F Supp 929, 12 CCH LC ¶ 63693 and affd (1947, CA5 La) 164 F2d 1016, 13 CCH LC ¶ 64170, vacated on other grounds (1948) 334 US 249, 92 L Ed 1347, 68 S Ct 1031, 14 CCH LC ¶ 51264.

PART III. TRAINING

HISTORY; ANCILLARY LAWS AND DIRECTIVES

Amendments:

1964. Act Oct. 13, 1964, P. L. 88-647, Title III, § 301(27), 78 Stat. 1073, amended the analysis of this part by deleting item 905, which read: ''Chapter 905. Air Force Reserve Officers' Training Corps . . . . . 9381''.

1993. Act Nov. 30, 1993, P. L. 103-160, Div A, Title XI, Subtitle H, § 1178(c), 107 Stat. 1769, amended the analysis of this part by adding item 905.

CHAPTER 901. TRAINING GENERALLY

HISTORY; ANCILLARY LAWS AND DIRECTIVES

Amendments:

1976. Act July 14, 1976, P. L. 94-361, Title VI, § 602, 90 Stat. 928, amended the analysis of this chapter by adding item 9315.

1985. Act Nov. 8, 1985, P. L. 99-145, Title V, Part A, § 504(a)(2)(B), 99 Stat. 622, substituted item 9314 for one which read: ''9314. United States Air Force Institute of Technology: degrees''.

1990. Act Nov. 5, 1990, P. L. 101-510, Div A, Title XIV, Part C, § 1439(d), 104 Stat. 1689, amended the analysis of this chapter by adding item 9316.

1991. Act Dec. 5, 1991, P. L. 102-190, Div A, Title X, Part E, § 1061(a)(25), 105 Stat. 1474, amended the analysis of this chapter by deleting a section symbol preceding item 9316.

1994. Act Oct. 5, 1994, P. L. 103-337, Div A, Title IX, Subtitle B, § 913(a)(2), 108 Stat. 2828, amended the analysis of this chapter by adding item 9317.

§ 9301. Members of Air Force: detail as students, observers, and investigators at educational institutions, industrial plants, and hospitals

(a) The Secretary of the Air Force may detail members of the Air Force as students at such technical, professional, and other civilian educational institutions, or as students, observers, or investigators at such industrial plants, hospitals, and other places, as are best suited to enable them to acquire knowledge or experience in the specialties in which it is considered necessary that they perfect themselves.

(b) An officer, other than one of the Regular Air Force on the active-duty list, who is detailed under subsection (a) shall be ordered to additional active duty immediately upon termination of the detail, for a period at least as long as the detail. However, if the detail is for 90 days or less, the officer may be ordered to that additional duty only with his consent and in the discretion of the Secretary.

(c) No Reserve of the Air Force may be detailed as a student, observer, or investigator, or ordered to active duty under this section, without his consent and, if a member of the Air National Guard of the United States, without the approval of the governor or other appropriate authority of the State or Territory, Puerto Rico, or the District of Columbia of whose Air National Guard he is a member.

(d) The Secretary may require, as a condition of a detail under subsection (a), that an enlisted member accept a discharge and be reenlisted in his component for at least three years.

(e) The total length of details of an enlisted member of the Air Force under subsection (a) during one enlistment period may not exceed 50 percent of that enlistment.

(f) At no time may more than 8 percent of the authorized strength in commissioned officers, 8 percent of the authorized strength in warrant officers, or 2 percent of the authorized strength in enlisted members, of the Regular Air Force, or more than 8 percent of the actual strength in commissioned officers, 8 percent of the actual strength in warrant officers, or 2 percent of the actual strength in enlisted members, of the total of reserve components of the Air Force, be detailed as students under subsection (a). For the purposes of this subsection, the actual strength of each category of Reserves includes both members on active duty and those not on active duty.

(g) Expenses incident to the detail of members under this section shall be paid from any funds appropriated for the Department of the Air Force.

(Aug. 10, 1956, ch 1041, § 1, 70A Stat. 559; Nov. 29, 1973, P. L. 93-169, § 1, 87 Stat. 689; Dec. 12, 1980, P.L. 96-513, Title V, Part A, § 504(23), 94 Stat. 2917; Sept. 29, 1988, P. L. 100-456, Div A, Title XII, Part D, § 1234(a)(1), 102 Stat. 2059.)

HISTORY; ANCILLARY LAWS AND DIRECTIVES

Prior law and revision:

Revised Section	Source (USCS)	Source (Statutes at Large)
9301(a)	5:626q (last 78 words).	June 3, 1916, ch. 134, § 127a (13th para.); added June 4, 1920, ch. 227, subch. 1, § 51 (13th para.); restated June 8, 1926, ch. 495; May 13, 1941, ch. 113; June 30, 1941, ch. 262 (4th proviso under Finance department''); restated June 19, 1948, ch. 501, §§ 1, 2, 3, 62 Stat. 477, 478.
9301(b)	5:626q (less 1st 78 words, and less provisos).	
9301(c)	5:626q (1st proviso).	
9301(d)	5:626q (words of 2d proviso before semicolon).	
9301(e)	5:626q (words of 2d proviso after semicolon).	
9301(f)	5:626q (last proviso).	
9301(g)	5:626r.	

In subsection (a), the words ''members of the Air Force'' are substituted for the words ''personnel of the Air Force of the United States, without regard to component''.

In subsection (b), the words ''is detailed under subsection (a)'' are substituted for the words ''receives such instruction''. The words ''as long as the detail'' are substituted for the words ''equal to the duration of his period of instruction''. The words ''However, if the detail is for'' are substituted for the words ''except that where the duration of such training is''. The words ''other than one of the Regular Air Force on the active list'' are inserted, since members of the Regular Air Force on the active list are on continuous active duty. The word ''additional'' is inserted, since the detail under this section is active duty. The words ''the officer may be ordered to that additional duty'' are substituted for the words ''such subsequent active duty may . . . the officer concerned''.

In subsection (c), the words ''of whose Air National Guard he is a member'' are substituted for the words ''whichever is concerned''.

In subsection (d), the words ''as a condition of a detail under subsection (a)'' are substituted for the words ''prior to his detail pursuant to the provisions of this paragraph''. The words ''accept the discharge'' are substituted for the words ''be discharged''.

In subsection (e), the words ''during an enlistment'' are inserted for clarity.

In subsection (f), the last sentence is substituted for 5:626q (words within parentheses of last proviso).

In subsection (g), the words ''under this section'' are substituted for 5:626r (9th through 41st words).

Amendments:

1973. Act Nov. 29, 1973, in subsec. (b) in the sentence beginning ''An officer . . .'' deleted ''but not longer than four years'' after ''as long as the detail''.

1980. Act Dec. 12, 1980 (effective 9/15/81, as provided by § 701(a) of such Act, which appears as 10 USCS § 101 note), in subsec. (b), substituted ''active-duty list'' for ''active list''.

1988. Act Sept. 29, 1988, in subsec. (c), deleted "the Canal Zone," following "Puerto Rico,".

§ 9302. Enlisted members of Air Force: schools

(a) So far as consistent with the requirements of military training and service, and under regulations to be prescribed by the Secretary of the Air Force with the approval of the President, enlisted members of the Air Force shall be permitted to study and receive instruction to increase their military efficiency and to enable them to return to civilian life better equipped for industrial, commercial, and business occupations. Part of this instruction may be vocational education in agriculture or the mechanic arts. Civilian teachers may be employed to aid Air Force officers in this instruction.

(b) Schools for the instruction of enlisted members of the Air Force in the common branches of education, including United States history, shall be maintained at all air bases at which members of the Air Force are stationed. The Secretary may detail members of the Air Force to carry out this subsection. The commander of each air base where schools are maintained under this subsection shall provide a suitable room or building for school and religious purposes.
(Aug. 10, 1956, ch 1041, § 1, 70A Stat. 560.)

HISTORY; ANCILLARY LAWS AND DIRECTIVES

Prior law and revision:

Revised Section	Source (USCS)	Source (Statutes at Large)
9302(a)	10:1176.	June 3, 1916, ch. 134, § 27 (last para.), 39 Stat. 186.
9302(b)	10:1172.	R.S. 1231.

In subsection (a), the first 12 words are substituted for 10:1176 (1st 5, and last 18, words). The words "and the Secretary of the Army shall have the power at all times to suspend, increase, or decrease the amount of such instruction offered" are omitted as surplusage.
In subsection (b), the words "garrisons, and permanent camps" are omitted as covered by the word "post". The word "including" is substituted for the words "and especially in". The word "members" is substituted for the words "officers and enlisted men". The words "as may be necessary", "It . . . be the duty", and "or garrison" are omitted as surplusage.

Other provisions:

Delegation of Presidential functions. Functions of the President under this section were delegated to the Secretary of Defense by Ex. Or. No. 11390 of Jan. 22, 1968, § 1(6), 33 Fed. Reg. 841, which appears as 3 USCS § 301 note.

§ 9303. Aviation cadets and aviation students: schools

The Secretary of the Air Force shall establish and maintain—

(1) one or more schools for the training and instruction of aviation cadets; and

(2) courses of instruction for aviation students at one or more established flying schools.

(Aug. 10, 1956, ch 1041, § 1, 70A Stat. 560.)

HISTORY; ANCILLARY LAWS AND DIRECTIVES

Prior law and revision:

Revised Section	Source (USCS)	Source (Statutes at Large)
9303	10:296. 10:296a.	July 11, 1919, ch. 8 (2d par. under "Air Service"), 41 Stat. 109. June 3, 1941, ch. 165, § 2, 55 Stat. 239.

CROSS REFERENCES

Discharge of aviation cadets at any time, 10 USCS § 8817.

Subsistence allowance, 37 USCS § 402.

§ 9304. Aviation students: detail of enlisted members of Air Force

The Secretary of the Air Force may detail enlisted Regulars of the Air Force, and enlisted Reserves of the Air Force who are on active duty, for training and instruction as aviation students in their respective grades at schools selected by him.

(Aug. 10, 1956, ch 1041, § 1, 70A Stat. 560.)

HISTORY; ANCILLARY LAWS AND DIRECTIVES

Prior law and revision:

Revised Section	Source (USCS)	Source (Statutes at Large)
9304	10:298a-1.	June 1941, ch. 167, 55 Stat. 241.

The words "under such regulations as he may prescribe" are omitted, since the Secretary has inherent authority to issue regulations appropriate to exercising his statutory functions. 10:298a-1 (1st proviso) is omitted as impliedly repealed by section 10 of the Insurance Act of 1951, ch 39, 65 Stat. 36. 10:298a-1 (last proviso) is omitted as surplusage. The words "active duty" are substituted for the words "active Federal service".

CROSS REFERENCES

Discharge of aviation cadets at any time, 10 USCS § 8817.

§ 9305. Civilian flying school instructors: instruction at Air Force training commands

(a) The Secretary of the Air Force may provide for the instruction and training, at Air Force training commands, of civilians selected from the instructional staffs of civilian flying schools that are accredited by the Department of the Air Force for the education and training of members of the Air Force.

(b) The training of civilians under subsection (a) shall be without cost to the United States, except for supplies necessary for training purposes.

(c) A civilian undergoing training under subsection (a) may be treated in a Government hospital if he becomes sick or is injured. However, that treatment shall be without cost to the United States except for services of Government medical personnel and the use of hospital equipment other than medicine or supplies.

(d) No civilian who sustains a personal injury, and no dependent of a civilian who dies of disease or injury, while undergoing training under subsection (a), is entitled to any compensation, pension, or gratuity for that injury or death.

(Aug. 10, 1956, ch 1041, § 1, 70A Stat. 560.)

HISTORY; ANCILLARY LAWS AND DIRECTIVES

Prior law and revision:

Revised Section	Source (USCS)	Source (Statutes at Large)
9305(a)	10:292c-1 (less provisos).	Apr. 3, 1939, ch. 35, § 3, 53 Stat. 556.
9305(b)	10:292c-1 (1st proviso).	
9305(c)	10:292c-1 (2d proviso).	
9305(d)	10:292c-1 (last proviso).	

In subsection (a), the words ''under such rules and regulations as he may prescribe'' are omitted, since the Secretary has inherent authority to issue regulations appropriate to exercising his statutory functions. The words ''Air Force training commands'' are substituted for the words ''the Air Corps Training Center'', since those commands now perform the functions formerly performed by the Air Corps Training Center. The words ''in his discretion'', ''experience'', and ''upon their own applications'' are omitted as surplusage. The words ''and may provide for the instruction and training'' are substituted for the words ''is authorized to enroll as students . . . for the pursuit of such courses of instruction as may be prescribed therefor''.

In subsection (b), the words ''the furnishing of such'' are omitted as surplusage. The words ''material, or equipment'' are omitted as covered by the word ''supplies'', as defined in section 101(26) of this title.

In subsection (c), the word ''Government'' is substituted for the words ''Medical Department'' to conform to the first sentence of the revised subsection.

§ 9306. Service schools: leaves of absence for instructors

The officer in charge of an Air Force service school may grant a leave of absence for the period of the suspension of the ordinary academic studies, without deduction of pay or allowances, to any officer on duty exclusively as an instructor at the school.

(Aug. 10, 1956, ch 1041, § 1, 70A Stat. 561.)

HISTORY; ANCILLARY LAWS AND DIRECTIVES

Prior law and revision:

Revised Section	Source (USCS)	Source (Statutes at Large)
9306	10:843.	Mar. 23, 1910, ch. 115, (proviso under "United States Service Schools"), 36 Stat. 244.

The words "The provisions of section 1144 of this title, authorizing leaves of absence to certain officers of the Military Academy . . . are hereby extended to include" are omitted as surplusage.

§ 9314. United States Air Force Institute of Technology

(a) When the United States Air Force Institute of Technology is accredited by a nationally recognized accreditation association or authority, the Commander of the Air University may, under such regulations as the Secretary of the Air Force may prescribe, confer appropriate degrees upon persons who meet the requirements for those degrees in the Resident College of that Institute.

(b)(1) The Secretary of the Air Force may employ as many civilian faculty members at the United States Air Force Institute of Technology as is consistent with the needs of the Air Force and with Department of Defense personnel limits.

(2) The Secretary shall prescribe regulations determining—

(A) titles and duties of civilian members of the faculty; and

(B) pay of civilian members of the faculty, notwithstanding chapter 53 of title 5 [5 USCS §§ 5301 et seq.], but subject to the limitation set out in section 5306(e) of title 5.

(Aug. 10, 1956, ch 1041, § 1, 70A Stat. 561; Nov. 8, 1985, P. L. 99-145, Title V, Part A, § 504(a)(1), (2)(A), 99 Stat. 622; Nov. 14, 1986, P. L. 99-661, Div A, Title V, Part A, § 510, 100 Stat. 3868; Nov. 5, 1990, P. L. 101-509, Title V, § 529 [Title I, § 101(b)(6)(C)], 104 Stat. 1440.)

HISTORY; ANCILLARY LAWS AND DIRECTIVES

Prior law and revision:

Revised Section	Source (USCS)	Source (Statutes at Large)
9314	[Uncodified]	Aug. 31, 1954, ch. 1151, 68 Stat. 1006.

Amendments:

1985. Act Nov. 8, 1985, in the catchline, deleted ": degrees" following "Technology"; designated the existing provisions as subsec. (a); and added subsec. (b).

1986. Act Nov. 14, 1986, in subsec. (b)(2)(B), deleted "rates of basic" preceding "pay of civilian".

1990. Act Nov. 5, 1990 (effective as provided by § 305 of such Act, which appears as 5 USCS § 5301 note), in subsec. (b)(2)(B), substituted "5306(e)" for "5308".

Other provisions:

Application of subsec. (b)(2) of this section. For provisions as to the application of subsec. (b)(2) of this section, see Act Nov. 8, 1985, P.L. 99-145, Title V, Part A, § 504(c), 99 Stat. 622, which appears as 5 USCS § 5102 note.

CROSS REFERENCES

This section is referred to in 5 USCS § 5102.

§ 9315. Community College of the Air Force: associate degrees

(a) Establishment and mission. There is in the Air Force a Community College of the Air Force. Such college, in cooperation with civilian colleges and universities, shall—

(1) prescribe programs of higher education for enlisted members described in subsection (b) designed to improve the technical, managerial, and related skills of such members and to prepare such members for military jobs which require the utilization of such skills; and

(2) monitor on a continuing basis the progress of members pursuing such programs.

(b) Members eligible for programs. Subject to such other eligibility requirements as the Secretary concerned may prescribe, the following members of the armed forces are eligible to participate in programs of higher education under subsection (a)(1):

(1) Enlisted members of the Air Force.

(2) Enlisted members of the armed forces other than the Air Force who are serving as instructors at Air Force training schools.

(c) Conferral of degrees. (1) Subject to paragraph (2), the commander of the Air Education and Training Command of the Air Force may confer an academic degree at the level of associate upon any enlisted member who has completed the program prescribed by the Community College of the Air Force.

(2) No degree may be conferred upon any enlisted member under this section unless (A) the Community College of the Air Force certifies to the commander of the Air Education and Training Command of the Air Force that such member has satisfied all the requirements prescribed for such degree, and (B) the Secretary of Education determines that the standards for the award of academic degrees in agencies of the United States have been met.

(Added July 14, 1976, P. L. 94-361, Title VI, § 602, 90 Stat. 928; Dec. 12,

1980, P. L. 96-513, Title V, Part B, § 514(9), 94 Stat. 2935; Nov. 30, 1993, P. L. 103-160, Div A, Title XI, Subtitle H, § 1182(a)(12), 107 Stat. 1772; Feb. 10, 1996, P. L. 104-106, Div A, Title X, Subtitle G, § 1078(a), 110 Stat. 451; Nov. 18, 1997, P. L. 105-85, Div A, Title V, Subtitle E, Part II, § 552(a), (b), 111 Stat. 1748.)

HISTORY; ANCILLARY LAWS AND DIRECTIVES

Amendments:

1980. Act Dec. 12, 1980 (effective upon enactment as provided by § 701(b)(3) of such Act, which appears as 10 USCS § 101 note), in subsec. (c), substituted ''Secretary of Education'' for ''Commissioner of Education of the Department of Health, Education, and Welfare''.

1993. Act Nov. 30, 1993, in subsec. (b), substituted ''Air Education and Training Command'' for ''Air Training Command''; and, in subsec. (c), substituted ''Air Education and Training Command of the Air Force'' for ''Air Force Training Command''.

1996. Act Feb. 10, 1996 (applicable as provided by § 1078(b) of such Act, which appears as a note to this section), in subsec. (a)(1), substituted ''for enlisted members of the Air Force'' for ''for enlisted members of the armed forces''.

1997. Act Nov. 18, 1997, in subsec. (a), inserted the heading and, in para. (1), substituted ''enlisted members described in subsection (b)'' for ''enlisted members of the Air Force''; redesignated subsecs. (b) and (c) as paras. (1) and (2) of new subsec. (c), respectively, and, in such subsection, inserted the heading, in para. (1), substituted ''Subject to paragraph (2),'' for ''Subject to subsection (c),'' and, in para. (2), redesignated former paras. (1) and (2) as subparas. (A) and (B), respectively.

Such Act further (applicable with respect to enrollments in the Community College of the Air Force after 3/31/96, as provided by § 552(c) of such Act, which appears as a note to this section) added new subsec. (b).

Other provisions:

Application of Feb. 10, 1996 amendment. Act Feb. 10, 1996, P. L. 104-106, Div A, Title X, Subtitle G, § 1078(b), 110 Stat.451, provides: "The amendment made by subsection (a) [amending subsec. (a)(1) of this section] shall apply with respect to enrollments in the Community College of the Air Force after March 31, 1996.''.

Application of subsection (b), as added Nov. 18, 1997. Act Nov. 18, 1997, P. L. 105-85, Div A, Title V, Subtitle E, Part II, § 552(c), 111 Stat. 1748, provides: ''Subsection (b) of section 9315 of such title, as added by subsection (a)(4), applies with respect to enrollments in the Community College of the Air Force after March 31, 1996.''.

§ 9316. Training and support for A-10 aircraft

The Secretary of the Air Force shall provide each military department with flight training, fleet support, and depot maintenance with respect to all A-10 aircraft assigned to each such department.

(Added Nov. 5, 1990, P. L. 101-510, Div A, Title XIV, Part C, § 1439(c), 104 Stat. 1689.)

§ 9317. Air University: master of airpower art and science

(a) Authority. Upon the recommendation of the faculty of the School of Advanced Airpower Studies of the Air University, the Commander of the university may confer the degree of master of airpower art and science upon graduates of the school who fulfill the requirements for the degree.

(b) Regulations. The authority provided by subsection (a) shall be exercised under regulations prescribed by the Secretary of the Air Force.

(Added Oct. 5, 1994, P. L. 103-337, Div A, Title IX, Subtitle B, § 913(a)(1), 108 Stat. 2828.)

HISTORY; ANCILLARY LAWS AND DIRECTIVES

Other provisions:

Authority; effective date. Act Oct. 5, 1994, P. L. 103-337, Div A, Title IX, Subtitle B, § 913(b), 108 Stat. 2828, provides: "The authority provided by section 9317(a) of title 10, United States Code, as added by subsection (a), shall become effective on the date on which the Secretary of Education determines that the requirements established by the School of Advanced Airpower Studies of the Air University for the degree of master of airpower art and science are in accordance with generally applicable requirements for a degree of master of arts or a degree of master of science.".

CHAPTER 903. UNITED STATES AIR FORCE ACADEMY

HISTORY; ANCILLARY LAWS AND DIRECTIVES

Amendments:

1958. Act Aug. 6, 1958, P. L. 85-600, § 1(23), 72 Stat. 524, amended the analysis of this chapter by substituting item 9336 for one which read ''Permanent professors.''

1981. Act Oct. 14, 1981, P.L. 97-60, Title II, § 203(c)(2)(B), 95 Stat. 1006 (effective as provided by § 203(d) of such Act, which appears as 10 USCS § 4341a note), amended the analysis of this chapter by adding item 9341a.

1983. Act Sept. 24, 1983, P. L. 98-94, Title X, Part A, § 1004(c)(3), 97 Stat. 660, amended the analysis to this chapter by substituting item 9344 for one which read: ''9344. Selection of persons from Canada and American Republics.''; and by deleting item 9345 which read: ''9345. Selection of Filipinos.''.

1989. Act Nov. 29, 1989, P. L. 101-189, Div A, Title V, Part B, § 515(b)(2), 103 Stat. 1441, amended the analysis of this chapter by substituting item 9336 for one which read: ''9336. Permanent professors: registrar.''.

1993. Act Nov. 30, 1993, P. L. 103-160, Div A, Title V, Subtitle C, § 533(b)(2), 107 Stat. 1658, amended the analysis of this chapter by adding item 9338.

1994. Act Oct. 5, 1994, P. L. 103-337, Div A, Title V, Subtitle E, § 556(c)(2), 108 Stat. 2775, amended the analysis of this chapter by adding item 9356.

1996. Act Feb. 10, 1996, P. L. 104-106, Div A, Title V, Subtitle D, Part I, § 533(c)(2), 110 Stat. 315, amended the analysis of this chapter by deleting item 9356, which read: "9356. Athletics program: athletic director; nonappropriated fund account.".

1997. Act Nov. 18, 1997, P. L. 105-85, Div A, Title V, Subtitle E, Part I, § 542(c)(2), 111 Stat. 1743, amended the analysis of this chapter by adding item 9345.

§ 9331. Establishment; Superintendent; faculty

(a) There is in the Department of the Air Force an Air Force Academy (hereinafter in this chapter [10 USCS §§ 9331 et seq.] referred to as the "Academy") for the instruction and preparation for military service of selected persons called "Air Force cadets". The organization of the Academy shall be prescribed by the Secretary of the Air Force.

(b) There shall be at the Academy the following:

(1) A Superintendent.

(2) A dean of the Faculty, who is a permanent professor.

(3) A Commandant of Cadets.

(4) 21 permanent professors.

(5) A chaplain.

(6) A director of admissions.

(Aug. 10, 1956, ch 1041, § 1, 70A Stat. 561; Aug. 6, 1958, P. L. 85-600, § 1(19), 72 Stat. 523; Dec. 12, 1980, P. L. 96-513, Title V, Part B, § 514(10), 94 Stat. 2935; Nov. 29, 1989, P. L. 101-189, Div A, Title V, Part B, § 515(a)(1), 103 Stat. 1441; Oct. 23, 1992, P. L. 102-484, Div A, Title V, Subtitle C, § 523(b), 106 Stat. 2410; Nov. 30, 1993, P. L. 103-160, Div A, Title V, Subtitle C, § 533(b)(3), 107 Stat. 1658.)

HISTORY; ANCILLARY LAWS AND DIRECTIVES

Prior law and revision:

Revised Section	Source (USCS)	Source (Statutes at Large)
9331(a)	10:1851. 10:1854.	R.S. 1309, Feb. 18, 1896, ch. 22 (less proviso), 29 Stat. 8.
9331(b)	10:1061. 10:1087. 10:1089 (1st 20 words).	June 26, 1946, ch. 495, §§ 1, 3 (1st 20 words), 60 Stat. 312. Apr. 1, 1954, ch. 127, §§ 2, 5, 68 Stat. 47, 48.

In subsection (b), reference to the senior instructors of artillery, cavalry, and infantry, and the master of the sword, in 10:1061, are omitted, as obsolete. The names of the other departments are omitted as inapplicable to the Air Force. The departmental names will be established under section 9332 of this title. The words "and one assistant professor", in 10:1061, are omitted as superseded by section 9333 of this title. 10:1061 (words before colon) is omitted as inapplicable to the Air Force. 10:1854 (less last sentence) is omitted as executed by the inclusion in this chapter of the laws applicable to the Air Force Academy. 10:1087 (proviso) is omitted as inapplicable to the Air Force.

Subsection (b)(3) is based on those laws establishing the various departments at the United States Military Academy (see revision note for 4331 of this title).

Amendments:

1958. Act Aug. 6, 1958, added subsec. (b)(6).

1980. Act Dec. 12, 1980 (effective upon enactment on 12/12/80, as provided by § 701(b)(3) of such Act, which appears as 10 USCS § 101 note), in subsec. (a), substituted "(hereinafter in this chapter referred to as the 'Academy')" for ", in this chapter called the 'Academy',".

1989. Act Nov. 29, 1989, in subsec. (b)(6), substituted "director of admissions" for "registrar".

1992. Act Oct. 23, 1992, added subsec. (c).

1993. Act Nov. 30, 1993, deleted subsec. (c), which read:

"(c)(1) The Secretary of the Air Force may employ as many civilians as professors, instructors, and lecturers at the Academy as the Secretary considers necessary.

"(2) The compensation of persons employed under this subsection shall be as prescribed by the Secretary.

"(3) The Secretary may delegate the authority conferred by this subsection to any person in the Department of the Air Force to the extent the Secretary considers proper. Such delegation may be made with or without the authority to make successive redelegations.".

Other provisions:

Temporary buildings and facilities. Act April 1, 1954, ch 127, § 4, 68 Stat. 47, provided: "For the purpose of providing temporary facilities and enabling early operation of the Academy, the Secretary of the Air Force is authorized to provide for the erection of the minimum additional number of temporary buildings and the modification of existing structures and facilities at an existing Air Force base and to provide for the proper functioning, equipping, maintaining, and repairing thereof; and to contract with civilian institutions for such operation or instruction as he may deem necessary.".

Appropriation for Air Force Academy. Act April 1, 1954, ch 127, § 9, 68 Stat. 49; Aug. 3, 1956, ch 939, Title IV, § 413(b), 70 Stat. 1018; Aug. 30, 1957, P. L. 85-241, Title V, § 508, 71 Stat. 559; Aug. 20, 1958, P. L. 85-685, Title III, § 309, 72 Stat. 659; June 27, 1961, P. L. 87-57, Title III, § 304, 75 Stat. 108; July 21, 1968, P. L. 90-408, Title III, § 304, 82 Stat. 385, provided: "There is hereby authorized to be appropriated not to exceed the sum of $141,978,000 to carry out the provisions of this Act [this note among other things; for classification, consult USCS Tables volumes], of which not to exceed $26,000,000 shall be appropriated for any period beginning prior to January 1, 1955. Of the amount so appropriated for any such period, not to exceed $1,858,000 may be utilized for the purpose of section 4 of this Act [note to this section].''.

Appropriations for the Air Force Academy after August 1, 1964; requirement of authorization in subsequent legislation; appropriations for advance planning and minor construction. Act Aug. 1, 1964, P. L. 88-390, Title VI, § 608, 78 Stat. 364, provided: ''Notwithstanding the provisions of section 9 of the Act of April 1, 1954 (Public Law 325) as amended [note to this section], no funds may be appropriated after the date of enactment of this Act for construction at the Air Force Academy unless appropriation of such funds has been authorized in this Act or any Act enacted after the date of enactment of this Act: Provided, That funds are authorized to be appropriated to accomplish advance planning and minor construction at the Air Force Academy in the same manner as for other projects under the Act of September 28, 1951, as amended (31 U. S. C. 723), and title 10, United States Code, section 2674, as amended.''.

CODE OF FEDERAL REGULATIONS

Department of the Air Force—Appointment to the United States Air Force Academy, 32 CFR Part 901.

CROSS REFERENCES

United States Military Academy, 10 USCS §§ 4331 et seq.

United States Naval Academy, 10 USCS §§ 6951 et seq.

§ 9332. Departments and professors: titles

The Secretary of the Air Force may prescribe the titles of each of the departments of instruction and the professors of the Academy. However, the change of the title of a department or officer does not affect the status, rank, or eligibility for promotion or retirement of, or otherwise prejudice, a professor at the Academy.

(Aug. 10, 1956, ch 1041, § 1, 70A Stat. 562.)

HISTORY; ANCILLARY LAWS AND DIRECTIVES

Prior law and revision:

Revised Section	Source (USCS)	Source (Statutes at Large)
9332	10:1061a.	DFec. 14, 1942, ch. 729, 56 Stat. 1049.

The words ''now or after December 14, 1942, established at'' are omitted as surplusage. The word ''precedence'' is omitted as covered by the word ''rank''. The words ''pay allowances'' are omitted, since they are determined by the grade held. The words ''from time to time'', ''shall be known'', and ''operate in any case or on any account'' are omitted as surplusage.

§ 9333. Superintendent; faculty: appointment and detail

(a) The Superintendent and the Commandant of Cadets of the Academy shall be detailed to those positions by the President from the officers of the Air Force.

(b) The permanent professors of the Academy shall be appointed by the President, by and with the advice and consent of the Senate.

(c) The director of admissions of the Academy shall be appointed by the President, by and with the advice and consent of the Senate, and shall perform such duties as the Superintendent of the Academy may prescribe with the approval of the Secretary of the Air Force.

(Aug. 10, 1956, ch 1041, § 1, 70A Stat. 562; Aug. 6, 1958, P. L. 85-600, § 1(20), 72 Stat. 523; Nov. 29, 1989, P. L. 101-189, Div A, Title V, Part B, § 515(a)(2), 103 Stat. 1441.)

HISTORY; ANCILLARY LAWS AND DIRECTIVES

Prior law and revision:

Revised Section	Source (USCS)	Source (Statutes at Large)
9333(a)	10:1062.	R.S. 1313.
9333(b)	10:1063.	R.S. 1314 (words before semicolon).

In subsection (a), the word "detailed" is substituted for the word "selected", since historically the offices of superintendent and commandant of cadets have been filled by detail. The words "the officers of the Air Force" are substituted for the words "any arm of the service", since the Air Force does not have statutory arms or corps. 10:1063 (1st sentence and 1st 26 words of last sentence) is omitted as covered by section 8012 of this title.

In subsection (b), the words "by and with the advice and consent of the Senate" are inserted, since many of the statutes establishing particular permanent professorships from time to time have so provided, and historically it has been the uniform practice to make these appointments in this manner. 10:1063 (last 14 words) is omitted as obsolete and as covered by section 9349(b) of this title.

Amendments:

1958. Act Aug. 6, 1958, added subsec. (c).

1989. Act Nov. 29, 1989, in subsec. (c), substituted "director of admissions" for "registrar".

§ 9334. Command and supervision

(a) The immediate government of the Academy is under the Superintendent, who is also the commanding officer of the Academy and of the military post.

(b) The permanent professors and the director of admissions exercise command only in the academic department of the Academy.

(Aug. 10, 1956, ch 1041, § 1, 70A Stat. 562; Aug. 6, 1958, P. L. 85-600, § 1(21), 72 Stat. 524; Nov. 29, 1989, P. L. 101-189, Div A, Title V, Part B, § 515(a)(3), 103 Stat. 1441.)

HISTORY; ANCILLARY LAWS AND DIRECTIVES

Prior law and revision:

Revised Section	Source (USCS)	Source (Statutes at Large)
9334(a)	10:1042.	R.S. 1311.
9334(b)	10:1079.	June 28, 1902, ch. 1300, (1st proviso under "Permanent Establishment"), 32 Stat. 409.

In subsection (a), the words "and, in his absence, the next in rank" are omitted as surplusage.

In subsection (b), reference to assimilated rank is omitted as superseded by section 9336 of this title. The words "and the associate professor" are omitted as obsolete.

Amendments:

1958. Act Aug. 6, 1958, in subsec. (b), inserted "and the registrar".

1989. Act Nov. 29, 1989, in subsec. (b), substituted "director of admissions" for "registrar".

§ 9335. Dean of the Faculty

The Dean of the Faculty shall be appointed as an additional permanent professor from the permanent professors who have served as heads of departments of instruction at the Academy.

(Aug. 10, 1956, ch 1041, § 1, 70A Stat. 562; Sept. 2, 1958, P. L. 85-861, § 33(a)(46)(A), 72 Stat. 1567; Nov. 14, 1986, P. L. 99-661, Div A, Title V, Part A, § 508(c), 100 Stat. 3867; Oct. 23, 1992, P. L. 102-484, Div A, Title V, Subtitle C, § 521(b), 106 Stat. 2409.)

HISTORY; ANCILLARY LAWS AND DIRECTIVES

Prior law and revision:

1956 ACT

Revised Section	Source (USCS)	Source (Statutes at Large)
9335(a)	10:1089 (2d sentence).	June 26, 1946, ch. 495, § 3 (less 1st 20 words), 60 Stat. 312.
9335(b)	10:1089 (less 1st 20 words, and less 2d sen tence).	

In subsection (b), the word "grade" is substituted to the word "rank". The words "pay, allowances" an omitted, since they are determined by the grade held. The words "retirement rights" are omitted as covered by the word "benefits". The words "There is authorized", "from time to time", and "statutory" are omitted as surplusage. So much of 10:1089 as relates to the duties of the Dean of the Faculty is omitted as covered by section 8012(e) of this title.

1958 ACT

The word "regular" is deleted [in sections 9335 and 9336 of this title] to make clear that a Dean or professor of the United States Air Force Academy holds only the office of "Dean" or "professor" and not the office of "brigadier general" or "colonel", as the case may be, even though he is entitled to the pay and allowances of that grade.

Amendments:

1958. Act Sept. 2, 1958 (effective 8/10/56, as provided by § 33(g) of such Act, which appears as 10 USCS § 101 note) in subsec. (b) deleted "regular" preceding "grade".

1986. Act Nov. 14, 1986 (applicable only with respect to appointments or details made on or after the date of enactment of this Act, as provided by § 508(f) of this Act, which appears as 10 USCS § 12210 note), substituted subsec. (b) for one which read: "The Dean has the grade of brigadier general while serving as such, with the benefits authorized for regular brigadier generals of the Air Force, except that his retirement age is that of a permanent professor of the Academy.".

1992. Act Oct. 23, 1992, deleted "(a)" preceding "The Dean of"; and deleted subsec. (b) which read: "(b) The Dean has the grade of brigadier general while serving in such position, with the benefits authorized for regular brigadier generals of the Air Force, if appointed to that grade by the President, by and with the advice and consent of the Senate. However, the retirement age of an officer so appointed is that of a permanent professor of the Academy.".

§ 9336. Permanent professors; director of admissions

(a) A permanent professor of the Academy, other than the Dean of the Faculty, who is the head of a department of instruction, or who has served as such a professor for more than six years, has the grade of colonel. However, a permanent professor appointed from the Regular Air Force has the grade of colonel after the date when he completes six years of service as a professor, or after the date on which he would have been promoted had he been selected for promotion from among officers in the promotion zone, whichever is earlier. All other permanent professors have the grade of lieutenant colonel.

(b) A person appointed as director of admissions of the Academy has the regular grade of lieutenant colonel, and, after he has served six years as director of admissions, has the regular grade of colonel. However, a person appointed from the Regular Air Force has the regular grade of colonel after the date when he completes six years of service as director of admissions, or after the date on which he would have been promoted had he been selected for promotion from among officers in the promotion zone, whichever is earlier.

(Aug. 10, 1956, ch 1041, § 1, 70A Stat. 562; Aug. 6, 1958, P. L. 85-600, § 1(22), 72 Stat. 524; Sept. 2, 1958, P. L. 85-861, § 33(a)(46)(B), 72 Stat. 1567; Dec. 12, 1980, P.L. 96-513, Title II, Part A, § 218(b), Title V, Part A, § 504(24), 94 Stat. 2886, 2917; Oct. 19, 1984, P. L. 98-525, Title V, Part C, § 533(d)(2), 98 Stat. 2528; Nov. 29, 1989, P. L. 101-189, Div A, Title V, Part B, § 515(a)(4), (b)(1), 103 Stat. 1441.)

HISTORY; ANCILLARY LAWS AND DIRECTIVES

Prior law and revision:

1956 ACT

Revised Section	Source (USCS)	Source (Statutes at Large)
9336	10:1079a(a).	Aug. 7, 1947, ch. 512, § 520(a), 61 Stat. 912.

The word ''grade'' is substituted for the word ''rank''. The words ''pay, and allowances'' are omitted, since they are determined by the grade held. 10:1079a(a) (last proviso), and the words ''Hereafter each of'', ''who have been or may hereafter be'', and ''and appointed in'' are omitted as surplusage.

1958 ACT

The word ''regular'' is deleted (in sections 9335 and 9336 of this title) to make clear that a Dean or professor of the United States Air Force Academy holds only the office of ''Dean'' or ''professor'' and not the office of ''brigadier general'' or ''colonel'', as the case may be, even though he is entitled to the pay and allowances of that grade.

Amendments:

1958. Act Aug. 6, 1958, in the catchline, inserted '': registrar''; designated existing provisions as subsec. (a); and added subsecs. (b) and (c).

Act Sept. 2, 1958 (effective 8/10/56, as provided by § 33(g) of such Act), in subsec. (a), in the sentences beginning ''A permanent professor. . . .'' and ''However . . . .'', deleted ''regular'' preceding ''grade of colonel'' and in the sentence beginning ''All other. . . .'', deleted ''regular'' preceding ''grade of lieutenant colonel''.

1980. Act Dec. 12, 1980, (effective as provided by § 701(b)(1) of such Act, which appears as 10 USCS § 101 note) deleted subsec. (c), which read: ''Unless he is serving in a higher grade, an officer detailed to perform the duties of registrar has, while performing those duties, the temporary grade of lieutenant colonel and, after performing those duties for a period of six years, has the temporary grade of colonel.''.

Such Act further (effective 9/15/81, as provided by § 701(a) of such Act, which appears as 10 USCS § 101 note), in subsecs. (a) and (b), substituted ''a regular officer'' for ''a promotion-list officer'' and inserted ''or active-duty list''.

1984. Act Oct. 19, 1984, in subsecs. (a) and (b), substituted ''on which he would have been promoted had he been selected for promotion from among officers in the promotion zone,'' for ''when a regular officer, junior to him on the promotion list, or active-duty list on which his name was carried before his appointment as a professor, is promoted to the regular grade of colonel,''.

1989. Act Nov. 29, 1989 substituted this section heading for one which read:

''§ 9336. Permanent professors: registrar''; and, in subsec. (b), substituted ''director of admissions'' for ''registrar''.

Other provisions:

Service performed as registrar prior to August 6, 1958. For a prohibition against the accrual of an increase in pay or allowances for service performed prior to Aug. 6, 1958, see 10 USCS § 4336 note.

CROSS REFERENCES

Retirement of permanent professors after more than 30 years of service as a commissioned officer, 10 USCS § 8920.

§ 9337. Chaplain

There shall be a chaplain at the Academy, who must be a clergyman, appointed by the President for a term of four years. The chaplain is entitled to the same allowances for public quarters as are allowed to a captain, and to fuel and light for quarters in kind. The chaplain may be reappointed.

(Aug. 10, 1956, ch 1041, § 1, 70A Stat. 562; Sept. 7, 1962, P. L. 87-651, Title I, § 117, 76 Stat. 513.)

HISTORY; ANCILLARY LAWS AND DIRECTIVES

Prior law and revision:

1956 ACT

Revised Section	Source (USCS)	Source (Statutes at Large)
9337	10:1083. 10:1137.	Feb. 18, 1896, ch. ch. 22 (proviso), 29 Stat. 8; May 16, 1928, ch. 579, 45 Stat. 573; June 2, 1945, ch. 172, 59 Stat. 230.

The words ''The chaplain may be reappointed'' are substituted for the words ''and said chaplain shall be eligible for reappointment for an additional term or terms''. The figures ''$5,482.80'' and ''$6,714'' are substituted for the figures ''$4,000'' and ''$5,000'' to reflect increases in the rates of salary of that office effected by Federal Employees Pay Act of 1945, 59 Stat. 295, the Federal Employees Pay Act of 1946, 60 Stat. 216, the Postal Rate Revision and Federal Employees Salary Act of 1948, 62 Stat. 1260, and the Classification Act of 1949, 63 Stat. 954.

1962 ACT

The change reflects the opinion of the Assistant General Counsel, Civil Service Commission (GC:JHF:fz, May 4, 1959), that those parts of 10 USCS §§ d4337 and 9337 that relate to the salaries of the chaplains at the United States Military Academy and the United States Air Force Academy were superseded by the Classification Act of 1949 (5 U.S.C. 1071 et seq.). While the positions of chaplain at those Academies are not specifically covered by the Act, the Act has been determined to apply to those positions in accordance with section 203 thereof (5 U.S.C. 1083).

Amendments:

1962 Act Sept. 7, 1962, in the sentence beginning ''The chaplain is entitled. . . .'', deleted ''a salary of $5,482.80 a year, and to'' preceding ''the same''; in the sentence beginning ''The chaplain may be. . . .'', deleted ''and, if reappointed, he is entitled to a salary of $6,714 a year and those allowances'' after ''reappointed''.

Other provisions:

Delegation of Presidential functions. Functions of the President under this section were delegated to the Secretary of Defense by Ex. Or. No. 11390 of Jan. 22, 1968, § 1(5), 33 Fed. Reg. 841, which appears as 3 USCS § 301 note.

§ 9338. Civilian faculty: number; compensation

(a) The Secretary of the Air Force may employ as many civilians as professors, instructors, and lecturers at the Academy as the Secretary considers necessary.

(b) The compensation of persons employed under this section is as prescribed by the Secretary.

(Added Nov. 30, 1993, P. L. 103-160, Div A, Title V, Subtitle C, § 533(b)(1), 107 Stat. 1658.)

CROSS REFERENCES

This section is referred to in 5 USCS § 5102.

§ 9341. Faculty and other officers: leaves of absence

The Superintendent of the Academy may grant a leave of absence for the period of the suspension of the ordinary academic studies, without deduction of pay or allowances, to a professor, assistant professor, instructor, or other officer of the Academy.

(Aug. 10, 1956, ch 1041, § 1, 70A Stat. 563.)

HISTORY; ANCILLARY LAWS AND DIRECTIVES

Prior law and revision:

Revised Section	Source (USCS)	Source (Statutes at Large)
9341	10:1144.	R.S. 1330.

The words ''under regulations prescribed by the Secretary of the Army'' are omitted, since the Secretary has inherent authority to issue regulations appropriate to exercising his statutory functions.

CROSS REFERENCES

Service schools, leaves of absence for instructors, 10 USCS § 9306.

Leave allowances, 37 USCS §§ 501 et seq.

§ 9341a. Cadets: appointment by the President

Cadets at the Academy shall be appointed by the President alone. An appointment is conditional until the cadet is admitted.

(Added Oct. 14, 1981, P. L. 97-60, Title II, § 203(c)(2)(A), 95 Stat. 1006.)

HISTORY; ANCILLARY LAWS AND DIRECTIVES

Other provisions:

Effective date and application of amendments made by Act Oct. 14, 1981. Act Oct. 14, 1981, P. L. 97-60, Title II, § 203(d), 95 Stat. 1007, which appears as 10 USCS § 4341a note, provided that the amendments made to this section by § 203(c)(2)(A) of such Act are effective with respect to nominations for appointment to the first class admitted to each Academy after the date of enactment on Oct. 14, 1981.

§ 9342. Cadets: appointment; numbers, territorial distribution

(a) The authorized strength of Air Force Cadets of the Academy is as follows:

(1) 65 cadets selected in order of merit as established by competitive examination from the children of members of the armed forces who were killed in action or died of, or have a service-connected disability rated at not less than 100 per centum resulting from wounds or injuries received or diseases contracted in, or preexisting injury or disease aggravated by, active service, children of members who are in a "missing status" as defined in section 551(2) of title 37, and children of civilian employees who are in "missing status" as defined in section 5561(5) of title 5. The determination of the Department of Veterans Affairs as to service connection of the cause of death or disability, and the percentage at which the disability is rated is binding upon the Secretary of the Air Force.

(2) Five cadets nominated at large by the Vice President or, if there is no Vice President, by the President pro tempore of the Senate.

(3) Ten cadets from each State, five of whom are nominated by each Senator from that State.

(4) Five cadets from each congressional district, nominated by the Representative from the district.

(5) Five cadets from the District of Columbia, nominated by the Delegate to the House of Representatives from the District of Columbia.

(6) Two cadets from the Virgin Islands, nominated by the Delegate in Congress from the Virgin Islands.

(7) Six cadets from Puerto Rico, five of whom are nominated by the Resident Commissioner from Puerto Rico and one who is a native of Puerto Rico nominated by the Governor of Puerto Rico.

(8) Two cadets from Guam, nominated by the Delegate in Congress from Guam.

(9) One cadet from American Samoa, nominated by the Delegate in Congress from American Samoa.

(10) One cadet from the Commonwealth of the Northern Mariana Islands, nominated by the resident representative from the commonwealth.

Each Senator, Representative, and Delegate in Congress, including the Resident Commissioner from Puerto Rico, is entitled to nominate 10 persons for each vacancy that is available to him under this section. Nominees may be submitted without ranking or with a principal candidate and 9 ranked or unranked alternates. Qualified nominees not selected for appointment under this subsection shall be considered qualified alternates for the purposes of selection under other provisions of this chapter [10 USCS §§ 9331 et seq.].

(b) In addition, there may be appointed each year at the Academy cadets as follows:

(1) one hundred selected by the President from the children of members of an armed force who—

(A) are on active duty (other than for training) and who have served continuously on active duty for at least eight years;

(B) are, or who died while they were, retired with pay or granted retired or retainer pay, other than those granted retired pay under section 12731 of this title (or under section 1331 of this title as in effect before the effective date of the Reserve Officer Personnel Management Act);

however, a person who is eligible for selection under clause (1) of subsection (a) may not be selected under this clause.

(2) 85 nominated by the Secretary of the Air Force from enlisted members of the Regular Air Force.

(3) 85 nominated by the Secretary of the Air Force from enlisted members of reserve components of the Air Force.

(4) 20 nominated by the Secretary of the Air Force, under regulations prescribed by him, from the honor graduates of schools designated as honor schools by the Department of the Army, the Department of the Navy, or the Department of the Air Force, and from members of the Air Force Reserve Officers' Training Corps.

(5) 150 selected by the Secretary of the Air Force in order of merit (prescribed pursuant to section 9343 of this title) from qualified alternates nominated by persons named in clauses (3) and (4) of subsection (a).

(c) The President may also appoint as cadets at the Academy children of persons who have been awarded the Medal of Honor for acts performed while in the armed forces.

(d) The Superintendent may nominate for appointment each year 50 persons from the country at large. Persons nominated under this paragraph may not displace any appointment authorized under clauses (2) through (9) of subsection (a) and may not cause the total strength of Air Force Cadets to exceed the authorized number.

(e) If the annual quota of cadets under subsection (b)(1), (2), or (3) is not filled, the Secretary may fill the vacancies by nominating for appointment other candidates from any of these sources who were found best qualified on examination for admission and not otherwise nominated.

(f) Each candidate for admission nominated under clauses (3) through (9) of subsection (a) must be domiciled in the State, or in the congressional district, from which he is nominated, or in the District of Columbia, Puerto Rico, American Samoa, Guam, or the Virgin Islands, if nominated from one of those places.

(g) The Secretary of the Air Force may limit the number of cadets authorized to be appointed under this section to the number that can be adequately accommodated at the Academy as determined by the Secretary after consulting with the Committee on Armed Services of the Senate and the Committee on National Security of the House of Representatives, subject to the following:

(1) Cadets chargeable to each nominating authority named in subsection (a)(3) or (4) may not be limited to less than four.

(2) If the Secretary limits the number of appointments under subsection (a)(3) or (4), appointments under subsection (b)(1)–(4) are limited as follows:

(A) 27 appointments under subsection (b)(1);

(B) 27 appointments under subsection (b)(2);

(C) 27 appointments under subsection (b)(3); and

(D) 13 appointments under subsection (b)(4).

(3) If the Secretary limits the number of appointments under subsection (b)(5), appointments under subsection (b)(2)–(4) are limited as follows:

(A) 27 appointments under subsection (b)(2);

(B) 27 appointments under subsection (b)(3); and

(C) 13 appointments under subsection (b)(4).

(4) The limitations provided for in this subsection do not affect the operation of subsection (e).

(h) The Secretary of the Air Force shall furnish to any Member of Congress, upon the written request of such Member, the name of the Congressman or other nominating authority responsible for the nomination of any named or identified person for appointment to the Academy.

(Aug. 10, 1956, ch 1041, § 1, 70A Stat. 563; Sept. 14, 1962, P. L. 87-663, § 1(5), (6), 76 Stat. 547; March 3, 1964, P. L. 88-276, § 4(1), 78 Stat. 151; Oct. 13, 1966, P. L. 89-650, § 1(1)–(3), (5), 80 Stat. 896; July 5, 1968, P. L. 90-374, 82 Stat. 283; Oct. 22, 1968, P. L. 90-623, § 2(8), 82 Stat. 1314; Sept. 22, 1970, P. L. 91-405, Title II, § 204(c), 84 Stat. 852; Aug. 7, 1972, P. L. 92-365, § 1(3), 86 Stat. 505; Nov. 29, 1973, P. L. 93-171, § 3(1)–(4), 87 Stat. 690; Oct. 7, 1975, P. L. 94-106, Title VIII, § 803(b)(1), 89 Stat. 538; Dec. 12, 1980, P. L. 96-513, Title V, Part B, § 514(11), 94 Stat. 2935; Dec. 4, 1980, P. L. 96-600, § 2(c), 94 Stat. 3493; Oct. 14, 1981, P. L. 97-60, Title II, § 203(c)(1), 95 Stat. 1006; Sept. 24, 1983, P. L. 98-94, Title X, Part A, § 1005(a)(3), (b)(3), 97 Stat. 660, 661; Nov. 29, 1989, P. L. 101-189, Div A, Title XVI, Part C, § 1621(a)(1), 103 Stat. 1602; Nov. 5, 1990, P. L. 101-510, Div A, Title V, Part C, § 532(c)(1), 104 Stat. 1563; Nov. 30, 1993, P. L. 103-160, Div A, Title V, Subtitle C, § 531, 107 Stat. 1657; Oct. 5, 1994, P. L. 103-337, Div A, Title XVI, Subtitle D, § 1674(c)(3), 108 Stat. 3017; Feb. 10, 1996, P. L. 104-106, Div A, Title V, Subtitle D, Part I, § 532(c), Title XV, § 1502(a)(1), 110 Stat. 315, 502; Nov. 18, 1997, P. L. 105-85, Div A, Title X, Subtitle G, § 1073(a)(62), 111 Stat. 1903.)

HISTORY; ANCILLARY LAWS AND DIRECTIVES

Prior law and revision:

Revised Section	Source (USCS)	Source (Statutes at Large)
9342(a)	10:1092a (1st par., less clauses (a) through (e)).	R.S. 1317.
	10:1092a (clause (a), less 14th through 52d words after 4th semicolon; and less last 32 words).	June 30, 1950, ch. 421, §§ 1, 2, (last proviso), 64 Stat. 303, 304; June 3, 1954, ch. 251, § 2, 68 Stat. 169.
	10:1092a (1st 13 words of clause (b)).	
	10:1092a (1st 26 words of clause (c)).	
	10:1092a (clause (d)).	
	10:1092a (clause (e)), less last 53 words).	
9342(b)	10:1092a (last par.).	
	10:1098.	
9342(c)	10:1092a (14th through 52d words after 4th semicolon of clause (a)).	
	10:1092b (last proviso).	
9342(d)	10:1092a (last 32 words of clause (a)).	
9342(e)	10:1092a (clause (b), less 1st 13 words, and less 1st proviso).	
9342(f)	10:1092a (1st proviso of clause (b)).	
9342(g)	10:1092a (clause (c), less 1st 26 words).	
9342(h)	10:1092a (last 53 words of clause (e)).	

In subsection (a), the words ''the authorized strength . . . is as follows—'' are substituted for the words ''shall be authorized and consist of the following''. The words ''at large'' and ''which totals two thousand four hundred and ninety-six'', and 10:1092a (clause (d)) are omitted as surplusage.

In subsection (b), the words ''from whatever source of admission'', in 10:1092a, are omitted as surplusage. 10:1098 (words before last semicolon) is omitted as obsolete.

In subsection (c), the first 15 words are substituted for the words ''all of which cadets shall be''. The words ''domiciled in'' are substituted for the words ''actual residents of'' to conform to opinions of the Judge Advocate General of the Army (R. 29, 83; J.A.G. 351.11, Feb. 10, 1925).

In subsection (e)(4), the words ''armed forces'' are substituted for the description of the land or naval forces. The date February 1, 1955, fixed by Proc. No. 3080 (Jan. 7, 1955; 20 Fed. Reg. 173), is substituted for the words ''such date as shall thereafter be determined by Presidential proclamation or concurrent resolution of the Congress under section 745 of title 38''. The words ''including male and female members of . . . and all components thereof'' are omitted as surplusage.

In subsection (f), the words ''whether a death is service-connected'' are substituted for the words ''as to the service connection of the cause of death''.

In subsection (g), the words ''(National Guard of the United States, the Air National Guard of the United States and Army Reserve, and the Air Force Reserve)'', ''Regular components'', ''by members of the National Guard of the United States, and the Air National Guard of the United States'', and ''established at the competitive entrance examination'' are omitted as surplusage. The word ''grades'' is substituted for the words ''proficiency averages''.

In subsection (h), the words ''or shall hereafter be'' are omitted as surplusage.

References in text:

For the ''effective date of the Reserve Officer Personnel Management Act'', which is Title XVI of Act Oct. 5, 1994, P. L. 103-337, see § 1691 of such Title, which appears as 10 USCS § 10001 note.

Amendments:

1962. Act Sept. 14, 1962, in subsec. (a), in para. (8), deleted ''and'' after the semicolon, in para. (9), substituted ''; and'' for a period, and added para. (10); and, in subsec. (c), inserted ''and (10)'' and substituted '', Puerto Rico, American Samoa, Guam, or the Virgin Islands'' for ''or Puerto Rico''.

1964. Act March 3, 1964, substituted the text of this section for text which read:

''(a) The authorized strength of Air Force Cadets of the Academy is as follows—

''(1) eight cadets from each State, four nominated by each Senator from the State;

''(2) four cadets from each congressional district, nominated by the Representative from the district;

''(3) four cadets from each Territory, nominated by the Delegate in Congress from the Territory;

''(4) four cadets from Puerto Rico, nominated by its Resident Commissioner;

''(5) six cadets from the District of Columbia, nominated by its Commissioners;

''(6) two cadets nominated by the Governor of the Canal Zone;

''(7) 172 cadets from the United States at large, selected or nominated under subsection (e);

''(8) 180 cadets from enlisted members of the Air Force, appointed under subsection (g);

''(9) in addition to the cadets authorized in clauses (1)-(8), any cadets appointed under subsection (h); and

"(10) one cadet from American Samoa, Guam, or the Virgin Islands nominated by the Secretary of the Air Force upon recommendations of their respective Governors."

"(b) All cadets are appointed by the President. An appointment is conditional until the cadet is admitted.

"(c) No person may be nominated under clauses (1)-(5) and (10) of subsection (a), unless he is domiciled in the State or Territory, or in the congressional district, from which he is nominated, or in the District of Columbia, Puerto Rico, American Samoa, Guam, or the Virgin Islands, if nominated from one of those places.

"(d) To be eligible for nomination by the Governor of the Canal Zone, a person must be the son of a civilian residing in the Canal Zone, or of a civilian officer or employee of the United States or the Panama Canal Company residing in the Republic of Panama.

"(e) Of the 172 cadets authorized to be appointed from the United States at large—

"(1) 89 may be personally selected by the President;

"(2) 3 may be nominated by the Vice President;

"(3) 40 shall be nominated under regulations prescribed by the Secretary of the Air Force, from honor graduates of the schools designated by the Department of the Army or the Department of the Air Force as honor military schools or by the Department of the Navy as honor naval schools; and

"(4) 40, otherwise qualified for admission, may be selected in order of merit as established by competitive examination, from the sons of members of the armed forces who were killed in action or died of wounds or injuries received or diseases contracted in, or preexisting injury or disease aggravated by, active service (A) during World War I or World War II, as defined by laws providing service-connected compensation or pension benefits for veterans of those wars and their dependents, or (B) after June 26, 1950, and before February 1, 1955.

"(f) For the purposes of subsection (e)(4), a determination by the Veterans' Administration whether a death is service-connected is binding upon the Secretary of the Air Force.

"(g) Of the 180 cadets authorized to be appointed from the enlisted members of the Army and the Air Force, 90 may be appointed from the Regular Army and the Regular Air Force, and 90 from the reserve components of the Army and the Air Force. For each vacancy to be filled from one of those categories, there may be selected to compete at an annual examination three candidates from that category who have served at least one year on active duty or in an active-duty training status, including training performed under sections 502, 503, 504, and 505 of title 32. Appointments to fill vacancies from those categories shall be made from candidates, in order of their merit, making the highest grades on the examination. The Secretary shall prescribe regulations for the selection of candidates under this subsection.

"(h) If he is otherwise qualified for admission, the son of a person to whom the Medal of Honor has been awarded for an act performed while in the armed forces may be appointed a cadet from the United States at large."

1966. Act Oct. 13, 1966, in subsec. (a), in para. (1), in the preliminary matter, inserted ", or have a service-connected disability rated at not less than 100 per centum resulting from,", substituted "active service." for "active service—

"(A) during World War I or World War II as defined by laws providing service-connected compensation or pension benefits for veterans of those wars and their dependents; or

"(B) after June 26, 1950, and before February 1, 1955.",

and, in the concluding matter, inserted "or disability, and the percentage at which the disability is rated,", and, in para. (2), inserted "or, if there is no Vice President, by the President pro tempore of the Senate"; and substituted subsec. (b)(3) for one which read: "85 nominated by the Secretary of the Air Force from enlisted members of the Regular Air Force.".

1968. Act July 5, 1968, in subsec. (a), in the concluding matter, substituted "nine" for "five".

Act Oct. 22, 1968 (effective as provided by § 6 of such Act, which appears as 5 USCS § 5334), in subsec. (a)(5), substituted "Commissioner" for "Commissioners".

1970. Act Sept. 22, 1970 (effective 9/22/70, as provided by § 206(b) of such Act, which appears as 2 USCS § 25a note), in subsec. (a)(5), substituted "by the Delegate to the House of Representatives from the District of Columbia" for "by the Commissioner of that District".

1972. Act Aug. 7, 1972, in subsec. (a)(1), substituted "65" for "40" and inserted ", sons of members who are in a 'missing status' as defined in section 551(2) of title 37, and sons of civilian employees who are in a 'missing status' as defined in section 5561(5) of title 5".

1973. Act Nov. 29, 1973 (effective beginning with the nominations for appointments to the service academies in the calendar year 1974, as provided by § 4 of such Act, which appears as 10 USCS § 4342 note), in subsec. (a), substituted para. (6) for one which read: "Five cadets from each Territory, nominated by the Delegate in Congress from that Territory.", substituted para. (9) for one which read: "One cadet from American Samoa, Guam, or the Virgin Islands nominated by the Secretary of the Air Force upon recommendations of their respective Governors.", and added para. (10); and, in subsec. (f), substituted ", (9) and (10)" for "and (9)", and deleted "or Territory" after "State".

1975. Act Oct. 7, 1975, in subsecs. (a)(1), in three places, (a)(8), in two places, (b)(1), in the preliminary matter, and (c), substituted "children" for "sons".

1980. Act Dec. 12, 1980 (effective upon enactment, as provided by § 701(b)(3) of such Act, which appears as 10 USCS § 101 note), in subsec. (h), substituted "The" for "Effective beginning with the nominations for appointment to the Academy in the calendar year 1964, the".

Act Dec. 24, 1980 (effective as provided by § 2(d) of such Act, which appears as 10 USCS § 4342 note), in subsec. (a), in clauses (6) and (9), substituted "Two cadets" for "One cadet".

1981. Act Oct. 14, 1981 (effective as provided by § 203(d) of such Act, which appears as 10 USCS § 4341a note), substituted subsec. (d) for one which read: "All cadets are appointed by the President. An appointment is conditional until the cadet is admitted.".

1983. Act Sept. 24, 1983, in subsec. (a), substituted cl. (8) for one which read: ''(8) One cadet nominated by the Governor of the Panama Canal from the children of civilians residing in the Canal Zone or the children of civilian personnel of the United States Government, or the Panama Canal Company, residing in the Republic of Panama.'' and substituted cl. (10) for one which read: ''(10) One cadet from American Samoa nominated by the Secretary of the Air Force upon recommendation of the Governor of American Samoa.''.

1989. Act Nov. 29, 1989, in subsec. (a)(1), substituted ''Department of Veterans Affairs'' for ''Veterans' Administration''.

1990. Act Nov. 5, 1990, in subsec. (a), deleted para. (8), which read: ''One cadet nominated by the Administrator of the Panama Canal Commission from the children of civilian personnel of the United States Government residing in the Republic of Panama who are citizens of the United States.'', redesignated former paras. (9) and (10) as paras. (8) and (9), respectively, in subsec. (d), substituted ''(2) through (9)'' for ''(2)–(7), (9), or (10)''; and, in subsec. (f), substituted ''(3) through (9)'' for ''(3)–(7), (9) and (10)''.

1993. Act Nov. 30, 1993, in subsec. (a), in the concluding matter, substituted ''10 persons'' for ''a principal candidate and nine alternates'' and added the sentences beginning ''Nominees may be submitted . . .'' and ''Qualified nominees not selected . . .''.

1994. Act Oct. 5, 1994 (effective 12/1/94 as provided by § 1691 of such Act, which appears as 10 USCS § 10001 note), in subsec. (b)(1)(B), substituted ''section 12731 of this title (or under section 1331 of this title as in effect before the effective date of the Reserve Officer Personnel Management Act)'' for ''section 1331 of this title''.

1996. Act Feb. 10, 1996, in subsec. (a), added para. (10); and, in subsec. (g), in the introductory matter, substituted ''Committee on Armed Services of the Senate and the Committee on National Security of the House of Representatives'' for ''Committees on Armed Services of the Senate and House of Representatives''.

1997. Act Nov. 18, 1997 (applicable as provided by § 1073(i) of such Act, which appears as 10 USCS § 101 note), in subsec. (a)(10), substituted ''Mariana'' for ''Marianas''.

Other provisions:

Effective date; interim system for appointment of cadets. Act Aug. 10, 1956, ch 1041, § 52(b), 70A Stat. 641; Aug. 28, 1957 P. L. 85-182, 71 Stat. 463, provided that subsec. (a) of this section would take effect four years after the entrance of the initial class at the United States Air Force Academy. However, for the four-year period beginning with the class of cadets entering in July 1959, not more than one quarter of the number of cadets authorized by clause (1), (2), (3), (4), (7), or (8) of that section could be appointed in any one academic year; two of the number of cadets authorized by clause (5) of that section could be appointed in the first and third years of that four-year period, and not more than one of the number authorized by it could be appointed in the second and fourth years of that period; and one cadet authorized by clause (6) of that section could be appointed in the first two years of that four-year period, and not more than one of the number authorized by it could be appointed in the second two years of that period. In addition, during that four-year period, the nominating authority named in clauses (1) to (6) of that section could select for each cadet allocated to him for the year concerned a principal candidate and not more than ten alternate candidates, or he could nominate as many candidates as the Secretary prescribed and authorize the Secretary to select the principal candidates in order of merit as determined by competitive examination. In carrying out this section during that four-year period, only qualified alternates who were nominated by the authorities named in clauses (1) to (4) of subsec. (a) could be nominated for appointment as cadets. Not more than one qualified alternate nominated by any one authority named in those classes could be appointed as a cadet, after nomination under this section, during each year of that four-year period.

Eligibility of female individuals for appointment and admission to service academies; uniform application of academic and other standards to male and female individuals. The secretary is required to take such action as may be necessary and appropriate to insure that (1) female individuals shall be eligible for appointment and admission to the United States Air Force Academy, beginning with appointments to such academy for the class beginning in calendar year 1976, and (2) the academic and other relevant standards required for appointment, admission, training, graduation, and commissioning of female individuals shall be the same as those required for male individuals, except for those minimum essential adjustments in such standards required because of physiological differences between male and female individuals, see § 803(a) of Act Oct. 7, 1975, which appears as a note under 10 USCS § 4342.

Secretary to implement policy of expeditious admission of women to the academy. The secretary is to continue to exercise the authority granted under this chapter and chapters 403 and 603 of this title (10 USCS §§ 4331 et seq., 6951 et seq.) but such authority to be exercised within a program providing for the orderly and expeditious admission of women to the Academy, consistent with the needs of the services, see § 803(c) of Act Oct. 7, 1975, which appears as a note under 10 USCS § 4342.

Limitation on number of cadets and midshipmen authorized to attend service academies. Act Dec. 5, 1991, P. L. 102-190, Div A, Title V, Part B, § 511(a)-(d), 105 Stat. 1359, which appears as 10 USCS § 4342 note, provides (a) that the authorized strength of the Corps of Cadets of the United States Military Academy, the Air Force Cadets of the United States Air Force Academy, and the brigade of midshipmen of the United States Naval Academy may not exceed 4,000 for each service academy for class years beginning after 1994, and (b) that any required reduction in the number of appointments to a class may not be achieved by reducing the number of appointments under 10 USCS § 4342(a), 6954(a), or 9342(a). Such section also requires a report by the Comptroller General of the United States concerning the percentage of service academy graduates among commissioned officers receiving original appointments in selected benchmark years.

CROSS REFERENCES

Effect upon enlisted status of acceptance of appointment as a cadet, 10 USCS § 516.

This section is referred to in 5 USCS §§ 9343, 9344.

§ 9343. Cadets: appointment; to bring to full strength

If it is determined that, upon the admission of a new class to the Academy, the

number of cadets at the Academy will be below the authorized number, the Secretary of the Air Force may fill the vacancies by nominating additional cadets from qualified candidates designated as alternates and from other qualified candidates who competed for nomination and are recommended and found qualified by the Academy Board. At least three-fourths of those nominated under this section shall be selected from qualified alternates nominated by the persons named in clauses (2) through (8) of section 9342(a) of this title, and the remainder from qualified candidates holding competitive nominations under any other provision of law. An appointment under this section is an additional appointment and is not in place of an appointment otherwise authorized by law.
(Aug. 10, 1956, ch 1041, § 1, 70A Stat. 564; March 3, 1964, P. L. 88-276, § 4(2), 78 Stat. 153; Nov. 2, 1966, P. L. 89-718, § 46, 80 Stat. 1121; Nov. 29, 1973, P. L. 93-171, § 3(5), 87 Stat. 691; Nov. 5, 1990, P. L. 101-510, Div A, Title V, Part C, § 532(a)(2), (c)(2), 104 Stat. 1563, 1564.)

HISTORY; ANCILLARY LAWS AND DIRECTIVES

Prior law and revision:

Revised Section	Source (USCS)	Source (Statutes at Large)
9343	10:1092d.	June 30, 1950, ch. 421, § 4, 64 Stat. 305.

The words "If it is determined" are substituted for the words "When upon determination". The words "within his discretion" are omitted as covered by the word "may". The words "within the capacity of the Academy", "from the remaining sources of admission authorized by law", and "to be admitted in such class" are omitted as surplusage. The words "by the persons named in clauses (1)–(6) of section 9342(a), and clause (2) of section 9342(e), of this title" are substituted for the words "by the Vice President, Members of the Senate and House of Representatives of the United States, Delegates and Resident Commissioners, the Commissioners of the District of Columbia, and the Governor of the Canal Zone". The words "under any other provision of law" are substituted for the words "from sources authorized by law other than those holding such alternate appointments".

Amendments:

1964. Act March 3, 1964, subject to subsequent amendment, substituted this section for one which read: "If it is determined that, upon the admission of a new class to the Academy, the number of cadets at the Academy will be below the authorized number, the Secretary of the Air Force may nominate as many qualified alternates and other qualified candidates who competed for nomination and are recommended and found qualified by the Faculty as are necessary to meet the needs of the Air Force, but not more than the authorized strength of Air Force cadets. At least two-thirds of those nominated under this section shall be selected from qualified alternates nominated by the persons named in clauses (1)–(6) of section 9342(a), and clause (2) of section 9342(e), of this title, and the remainder from qualified candidates holding competitive nominations under any other provision of law. An appointment under this section is an additional appointment and is not in place of an appointment otherwise authorized by law.".

1966. Act Nov. 2, 1966, in the sentence beginning ''If it is determined . . .'' substituted ''Academy Board'' for ''faculty''.

1973. Act Nov. 29, 1973 (effective as provided by § 4 of such Act, which appears as 10 USCS § 4342 note), in the sentence beginning ''At least . . .'' substituted ''(9)'' for ''(8)''.

1990. Act Nov. 5, 1990 substituted ''(2) through (8)'' for ''(2)–(9)''. Section 532(a)(2) of such Act purported to make the same amendment as § 532(c)(2).

Other provisions:

Number of alternate appointees from congressional sources not to be reduced because of additional presidential appointments. Act Oct. 13, 1966, P. L. 89-650, § 2, 80 Stat. 896, provided: ''Notwithstanding any other provision of law, none of the additional appointments authorized in sections 4342(b)(1), 6954(b)(1) and 9342(b)(1) [10 USCS §§ 4342(b)(1), 6954(b)(1), 9342(b)(1)] as provided by this Act shall serve to reduce or diminish the number of qualified alternates from congressional sources who would otherwise be appointed by the appropriate service Secretary under the authority contained in sections 4343, 6956, and 9343 of title 10, United States Code [10 USCS §§ 4343, 6956, 9343].''.

CROSS REFERENCES

This section is referred to in 10 USCS § 9342.

§ 9344. Selection of persons from foreign countries

(a)(1) The Secretary of the Air Force may permit not more than 40 persons at any one time from foreign countries to receive instruction at the Academy. Such persons shall be in addition to the authorized strength of the Air Force Cadets of the Academy under section 9342 of this title.

(2) The Secretary of the Air Force, upon approval by the Secretary of Defense, shall determine the countries from which persons may be selected for appointment under this section and the number of persons that may be selected from each country. The Secretary of the Air Force may establish entrance qualifications and methods of competition for selection among individual applicants under this section and shall select those persons who will be permitted to receive instruction at the Academy under this section.

(b)(1) A person receiving instruction under this section is entitled to the pay, allowances, and emoluments of a cadet appointed from the United States, and from the same appropriations.

(2) Each foreign country from which a cadet is permitted to receive instruction at the Academy under this section shall reimburse the United States for the cost of providing such instruction, including the cost of pay, allowances, and emoluments provided under paragraph (1) unless a written waiver of reimbursement is granted by the Secretary of Defense. The Secretary of the Air Force shall prescribe the rates for reimbursement under this paragraph, except that the reimbursement rates may not be less than the cost to the United States of providing such instruction, including pay, allowances, and emoluments, to a cadet appointed from the United States.

(3) The amount of reimbursement waived under paragraph (2) may not exceed 35 percent of the per-person reimbursement amount otherwise required to be paid by a foreign country under such paragraph, except in the case of not more than five persons receiving instruction at the Air Force Academy under this section at any one time.

(c)(1) Except as the Secretary of the Air Force determines, a person receiving instruction under this section is subject to the same regulations governing admission, attendance, discipline, resignation, discharge, dismissal, and graduation as a cadet at the Academy appointed from the United States. The Secretary may prescribe regulations with respect to access to classified information by a person receiving instruction under this section that differ from the regulations that apply to a cadet at the Academy appointed from the United States.

(2) A person receiving instruction under this section is not entitled to an appointment in an armed force of the United States by reason of graduation from the Academy.

(d) A person receiving instruction under this section is not subject to section 9346(d) of this title [10 USCS § 9346(d)].

(Aug. 10, 1956, ch 1041, § 1, 70A Stat. 564; Sept. 24, 1983, P. L. 98-94, Title X, Part A, § 1004(c)(1), 97 Stat. 659; Nov. 18, 1997, P. L. 105-85, Div A, Title V, Subtitle E, Part I, § 543(c), 111 Stat. 1744.)

HISTORY; ANCILLARY LAWS AND DIRECTIVES

Prior law and revision:

Revised Section	Source (USCS)	Source (Statutes at Large)
9344(a)	10:1093c (less 3d and last sentences).	June 26, 1946, ch. 493, § 1, 60 Stat. 311; June 1, 1948, ch. 357, § 2, 62 Stat. 280.
9344(b)	10:1093c (3d sentence).	
9344(c)	10:1093c (last sentence).	

In subsection (a), the words ''at West Point, New York'' are omitted as inapplicable to the Air Force.

In subsection (b), the words ''is entitled to'' are substituted for the words ''shall receive''. The words ''performed in proceeding'' are omitted as surplusage. The words ''continental limits'' are omitted, since section 101(1) of this title defines the United States to include only the States and the District of Columbia.

In subsection (c), the words ''to any office or position'' are omitted as surplusage; 10:1093c (proviso of last sentence) is omitted, since 10:1099 is inapplicable to the Air Force and section 1321 of the Revised Statutes, previously codified in 10:1101, was repealed by section 6(b) of the Act of June 30, 1950, ch. 421, 64 Stat. 305.

Amendments:

1983. Act Sept. 24, 1983 (effective one year after enactment on 9/24/83, as provided by § 1004(d)(2) of such Act, which appears as 10 USCS § 4344 note) substituted this section for one which read:

"§ 9344. Selection of persons from Canada and American Republics

"(a) Upon designation by the President, the Secretary of the Air Force may permit not more than 20 persons at any one time from Canada and the American Republics, other than the United States, to receive instruction at the Academy. However, not more than three persons from any one of those republics or from Canada may receive instruction under this section at any one time.

"(b) A person receiving instruction under this section is entitled to the pay, allowances, and emoluments of a cadet appointed from the United States, and from the same appropriations. However, the mileage allowance payable to that person for travel to the Academy for initial admission is not limited to mileage for travel within the United States.

"(c) Except as the Secretary determines, a person receiving instruction under this section is subject to the same regulations governing admission, attendance, discipline, resignation, discharge, dismissal, and graduation as a cadet at the Academy appointed from the United States. However, a person receiving instruction under this section is not entitled to appointment in the Air Force by reason of his graduation from the Academy.".

1997. Act Nov. 18, 1997 (applicable with respect to students from a foreign country entering the United States Air Force Academy on or after 5/1/98, as provided by § 543(d) of such Act, which appears as 10 USCS § 4344 note), in subsec. (b), in para. (2), inserted ", except that the reimbursement rates may not be less than the cost to the United States of providing such instruction, including pay, allowances, and emoluments, to a cadet appointed from the United States", and added para. (3).

Other provisions:

Persons from countries assisting U.S. in Vietnam; Air Force Academy instruction; benefits, limitations, restrictions, and regulations; oath of trainees. For Air Force Academy instruction of persons from countries assisting U.S. in Vietnam, numerical limitation, prohibition against appointment of graduates to the Armed Forces, exemption from oath, etc., see Act Nov. 9, 1966, P. L. 89-802, 80 Stat. 1518, which appears as a note under 10 USCS § 4344.

CROSS REFERENCES

This section is referred to in 20 USCS § 221a.

§ 9345. Exchange program with foreign military academies

(a) Exchange program authorized. The Secretary of the Air Force may permit a student enrolled at a military academy of a foreign country to receive instruction at the Air Force Academy in exchange for an Air Force cadet receiving instruction at that foreign military academy pursuant to an exchange agreement entered into between the Secretary and appropriate officials of the foreign country. Students receiving instruction at the Academy under the exchange program shall be in addition to persons receiving instruction at the Academy under section 9344 of this title.

(b) Limitations on number and duration of exchanges. An exchange agreement under this section between the Secretary and a foreign country shall provide for the exchange of students on a one-for-one basis each fiscal year. Not more than 10 Air Force cadets and a comparable number of students from all foreign military academies participating in the exchange program may be exchanged during any fiscal year. The duration of an exchange may not exceed the equivalent of one academic semester at the Air Force Academy.

(c) Costs and expenses. (1) A student from a military academy of a foreign country is not entitled to the pay, allowances, and emoluments of an Air Force cadet by reason of attendance at the Air Force Academy under the exchange program, and the Department of Defense may not incur any cost of international travel required for transportation of such a student to and from the sponsoring foreign country.

(2) The Secretary may provide a student from a foreign country under the exchange program, during the period of the exchange, with subsistence, transportation within the continental United States, clothing, health care, and other services to the same extent that the foreign country provides comparable support and services to the exchanged Air Force cadet in that foreign country.

(3) The Air Force Academy shall bear all costs of the exchange program from funds appropriated for the Academy. Expenditures in support of the exchange program may not exceed $50,000 during any fiscal year.

(d) Application of other laws. Subsections (c) and (d) of section 9344 of this title shall apply with respect to a student enrolled at a military academy of a foreign country while attending the Air Force Academy under the exchange program.

(e) Regulations. The Secretary shall prescribe regulations to implement this section. Such regulations may include qualification criteria and methods of selection for students of foreign military academies to participate in the exchange program.

(Added Nov. 18, 1997, P. L. 105-85, Div A, Title V, Subtitle E, Part I, § 542(c)(1), 111 Stat. 1742.)

HISTORY; ANCILLARY LAWS AND DIRECTIVES

Explanatory notes:

A prior § 9345 (Act Aug. 10, 1956, ch 1041, § 1, 70A Stat. 242) was repealed by Act Sept. 24, 1983, P. L. 98-94, Title X, Part A, § 1004(c)(2), 97 Stat. 660. Such section provided for admission of Filipinos to the United States Air Force Academy.

§ 9346. Cadets: requirements for admission

(a) To be eligible for admission to the Academy a candidate must be at least 17 years of age and must not have passed his twenty-third birthday on July 1 of the year in which he enters the Academy.

(b) To be admitted to the Academy, an appointee must show, by an examination held under regulations prescribed by the Secretary of the Air Force, that he is qualified in the subjects prescribed by the Secretary.

(c) A candidate designated as a principal or an alternate for appointment as a cadet shall appear for physical examination at a time and place designated by the Secretary.

(d) To be admitted to the Academy, an appointee must take and subscribe to an oath prescribed by the Secretary of the Air Force. If a candidate for admission refuses to take and subscribe to the prescribed oath, his appointment is terminated.

(Aug. 10, 1956, ch 1041, § 1, 70A Stat. 565; Nov. 2, 1966, P. L. 89-718, § 47, 80 Stat. 1121; Sept. 23, 1996, P. L. 104-201, Div A, Title V, Subtitle F, § 555(d), 110 Stat. 2527.)

HISTORY; ANCILLARY LAWS AND DIRECTIVES

Prior law and revision:

Revised Section	Source (USCS)	Source (Statutes at Large)
9346(a)	10:1092b (less provisos).	June 30, 1950, ch. 421, § 2 (less provisos), 64 Stat. 304.
9346(b)	10:1096.	R.S. 1319; restated Mar. 2, 1901, ch. 804 (1st proviso under ''Permanent Establishment''), 31 Stat. 911.
9346(c)	10:1095.	Aug. 9, 1912, ch. 275 (2d proviso under ''Permanent Establishment''), 37 Stat. 252.

In subsection (a), the words ''Effective January 1, 1951'' are omitted as executed. The word ''Calendar'' is omitted as surplusage. The words ''must not have passed his twenty-second birthday'' are substituted for the words ''not more than twenty-two years of age'', to make it clear that a person whose twenty-second birthday falls on July 1 of the year of admission is eligible (see opinion of the Judge Advocate General of the Army (JAGA 1952/7083, 2 Sept. 1952)).

In subsection (b), the words ''is qualified in'' are substituted for the words ''to be well versed in''. The words ''To be'' are substituted for the words ''before they shall be''. The words ''an appointee must show that he is qualified'' are substituted for the words ''shall be required to be well versed''. The words ''from time to time'' are omitted as surplusage.

In subsection (c), the word ''shall'' is substituted for the word ''may'', since the nominee is required to appear for the examination. The word ''appear'' is substituted for the words ''present himself''. The words ''at a place'' are substituted for the words ''at West Point, New York, or other prescribed places''.

Amendments:

1966. Act Nov. 2, 1966 added subsec. (d).

1996. Act Sept. 23, 1996, in subsec. (a), substituted ''twenty-third birthday'' for ''twenty-second birthday''.

Other provisions:

Waiver of maximum age limitation on admission to service academies for certain enlisted members who served during the Persian Gulf War. Act Dec. 5, 1991, P. L. 102-190, Div A, Title V, Part B, § 514, 105 Stat. 1361, which appears as 10 USCS § 4346 note, provides for waiver of the maximum age limitation with respect to enlisted members of the Armed Forces who (1) became 22 years of age while serving on active duty in the Persian Gulf area of operations in connection with Operation Desert Storm, or (2) were candidates for admission to a service academy in 1990, were prevented from being admitted during that year by reason of active duty service in the Persian Gulf area of operations in connection with Operation Desert Storm, and became 22 years of age after July 1, 1990, and before the end of such service.

CROSS REFERENCES

This section is referred to in 10 USCS § 9344.

§ 9347. Cadets; nominees: effect of redistricting of States

If as a result of redistricting a State the domicile of a cadet, or a nominee, nominated by a Representative falls within a congressional district other than that from which he was nominated, he is charged to the district in which his domicile so falls. For this purpose, the number of cadets otherwise authorized for that district is increased to include him. However, the number as so increased is reduced by one if he fails to become a cadet or when he is finally separated from the Academy.

(Aug. 10, 1956, ch 1041, § 1, 70A Stat. 565.)

HISTORY; ANCILLARY LAWS AND DIRECTIVES

Prior law and revision:

Revised Section	Source (USCS)	Source (Statutes at Large)
9347	10:1091-1.	July 7, 1943, ch. 193, 57 Stat. 383.

The word ''domicile'' is substituted for the words ''place of residence'' and ''residence'' to conform to opinions of the Judge Advocate General of the Army (R. 29, 83; J.A.G. 351, 11, Feb. 10, 1925). The words ''a . . . other than that from which he was nominated'' are substituted for the word ''another''. The words ''were appointed with respect to'', ''of the former district'', ''as additional numbers'', ''at such academy for the Representative'', ''temporarily'', and ''in attendance at such academy under an appointment from such former district'' are omitted as surplusage. The words ''the district in which his domicile so falls'' are substituted for the words ''of the latter district''. The words ''to include him'' are substituted for 10:1091-1 (18 words before proviso). The words ''but the number as so increased'' are substituted for 10:1091-1 (1st 13 words of proviso). The words ''if he fails to become a cadet'' are inserted for clarity.

§ 9348. Cadets: agreement to serve as officer

(a) Each cadet shall sign an agreement with respect to the cadet's length of service in the armed forces. The agreement shall provide that the cadet agrees to the following:

(1) That the cadet will complete the course of instruction at the Academy.

(2) That upon graduation from the Academy the cadet—

(A) will accept an appointment, if tendered, as a commissioned officer of the Regular Air Force; and

(B) will serve on active duty for at least five years immediately after such appointment.

(3) That if an appointment described in paragraph (2) is not tendered or if the cadet is permitted to resign as a regular officer before completion of the commissioned service obligation of the cadet, the cadet—

(A) will accept an appointment as a commissioned officer as a Reserve in the Air Force for service in the Air Force Reserve; and

(B) will remain in that reserve component until completion of the commissioned service obligation of the cadet.

(b)(1) The Secretary of the Air Force may transfer to the Air Force Reserve, and may order to active duty for such period of time as the Secretary prescribes (but not to exceed four years), a cadet who breaches an agreement under subsection (a). The period of time for which a cadet is ordered to active duty under this paragraph may be determined without regard to section 651(a) of this title.

(2) A cadet who is transferred to the Air Force Reserve under paragraph (1) shall be transferred in an appropriate enlisted grade or rating, as determined by the Secretary.

(3) For the purposes of paragraph (1), a cadet shall be considered to have breached an agreement under subsection (a) if the cadet is separated from the Academy under circumstances which the Secretary determines constitute a breach by the cadet of the cadet's agreement to complete the course of instruction at the Academy and accept an appointment as a commissioned officer upon graduation from the Academy.

(c) The Secretary of the Air Force shall prescribe regulations to carry out this section. Those regulations shall include—

(1) standards for determining what constitutes, for the purpose of subsection (b), a breach of an agreement under subsection (a);

(2) procedures for determining whether such a breach has occurred; and

(3) standards for determining the period of time for which a person may be ordered to serve on active duty under subsection (b).

(d) In this section, the term ''commissioned service obligation'', with respect to an officer who is a graduate of the Academy, means the period beginning on the date of the officer's appointment as a commissioned officer and ending on the sixth anniversary of such appointment or, at the discretion of the Secretary of Defense, any later date up to the eighth anniversary of such appointment.

(e)(1) This section does not apply to a cadet who is not a citizen or national of the United States.

(2) In the case of a cadet who is a minor and who has parents or a guardian, the cadet may sign the agreement required by subsection (a) only with the consent of a parent or guardian.

(Aug. 10, 1956, ch 1041, § 1, 70A Stat. 565; March 3, 1964, P. L. 88-276, § 5(a), 78 Stat. 153; Oct. 13, 1964, P. L. 88-647, Title III, § 301(25), 78 Stat. 1073; Oct. 19, 1984, P. L. 98-525, Title V, Part D, §§ 541(c), 542(d), 98 Stat. 2529; Nov. 8, 1985, P.L. 99-145, Title V, Part B, § 512(c), 99 Stat. 625; Nov. 29, 1989, P. L. 101-189, Div A, Title V, Part B, § 511(d), Title XVI, Part C, § 1622(e)(5), 103 Stat. 1439, 1605; Feb. 10, 1996, P. L. 104-106, Div A, Title V, Subtitle D, Part I, § 531(c), 110 Stat. 314.)

HISTORY; ANCILLARY LAWS AND DIRECTIVES

Prior law and revision:

Revised Section	Source (USCS)	Source (Statutes at Large)
9348	10:1092c.	June 30, 1950, ch. 421, § 3, 64 Stat. 304.

The word ''agreement'' is substituted for the word ''articles''. The words ''Hereafter'', ''appointed to the United States Military Academy'', ''engage'', and 10:1092c (1st 25 words of cl. (2) are omitted as surplusage. The word ''separated'' is substituted for the words ''discharged by competent authority''. The words ''if he is permitted to resign'' are substituted for the words ''in the event of the acceptance of his resignation'', since a resignation is effective only when accepted. The first 32 words of cl. (3) are substituted for 10:1092c (last 29 words of cl. (3)). The last sentence is substituted for the words ''with the consent of his parents or guardian if he be a minor, and if any he have''.

Amendments:

1964. Act March 3, 1964 (effective as provided by § 5(c) of such Act, which appears as 10 USCS § 4348 note), in para. (2), substituted ''five'' for ''three''.

Act Oct. 13, 1964, designated existing provisions as subsec. (a), and added subsec. (b).

1984. Act Oct. 19, 1984, § 541(c) (applicable as provided by § 541(d) of such Act, which appears as 10 USCS § 4348 note), in subsec. (a), in the introductory matter, deleted '', unless sooner separated,'' following ''an agreement that'', in para. (1), inserted ''unless sooner separated from the Academy,'', and in paras. (2) and (3), inserted '', unless sooner separated from the service,''.

Section 542(d) of such Act, in subsec. (a)(3), substituted ''at least the sixth anniversary and, at the direction of the Secretary of Defense, up to the eighth anniversary'' for ''the sixth anniversary''.

1985. Act Nov. 8, 1985 (effective as provided by § 512(e) of such Act, which appears as 10 USCS § 4348 note), substituted this section for one which read:

''(a) Each cadet who is a citizen or national of the United States shall sign an agreement that he will—

"(1) unless sooner separated from the Academy, complete the course of instruction at the Academy;

"(2) accept an appointment and, unless sooner separated from the service, serve as a commissioned officer of the Regular Air Force for at least five years immediately after graduation; and

"(3) accept an appointment as a commissioned officer as a Reserve for service in the Air Force Reserve and, unless sooner separated from the service, remain therein until at least the sixth anniversary and, at the direction of the Secretary of Defense, up to the eighth anniversary of his graduation, if an appointment in the Regular Air Force is not tendered to him, or if he is permitted to resign as a commissioned officer of that component before that anniversary.

"If the cadet is a minor and has parents or a guardian, he may sign the agreement only with the consent of the parents or guardian.

"(b) A cadet who does not fulfill his agreement under subsection (a) may be transferred by the Secretary of the Air Force to the Air Force Reserve in an appropriate enlisted grade and, notwithstanding section 651 of this title, may be ordered to active duty to serve in that grade for such period of time as the Secretary prescribes but not for more than four years.".

1989. Act Nov. 29, 1989, in subsec. (d) inserted "the term".

Such Act further (applicable as provided by § 511(e) of such Act, which appears as 10 USCS § 2114), in subsec. (a)(2)(B), substituted "six years" for "five years".

1996. Act Feb. 10, 1996 (applicable to persons first admitted to the United States Air Force Academy after December 31, 1991, as provided by § 531(e) of such Act, which appears as 10 USCS § 4348 note), in subsec. (a)(2)(B), substituted "five years" for "six years".

Other provisions:

Regulations implementing 1985 amendment. Secretary of the Air Force to prescribe regulations required by 10 USCS § 9348(c), as added by Act Nov. 8, 1985, P. L. 99-145, not later than the end of the 90-day period beginning on Nov. 8, 1985, see § 512(d) of such Act, which appears as 10 USCS § 4348 note.

CROSS REFERENCES

Effect upon enlisted status of acceptance of appointment as midshipman, 10 USCS § 516.

§ 9349. Cadets: organization; service; instruction

(a) A cadet shall perform duties at such places and of such type as the President may direct.

(b) The course of instruction at the Academy is four years.

(c) The Secretary of the Air Force shall so arrange the course of studies at the Academy that cadets are not required to pursue their studies on Sunday.

(d) Cadets shall be trained in the duties of members of the Air Force.

(Aug. 10, 1956, ch 1041, § 1, 70A Stat. 566.)

HISTORY; ANCILLARY LAWS AND DIRECTIVES

Prior law and revision:

Revised Section	Source (USCS)	Source (Statutes at Large)
9349(a)	10:1102.	R.S. 1322.
9349(b)	10:1043.	R.S. 1323.
9349(c)	10:1044.	Mar. 30, 1920, ch. 112 (1st par., less provisos, under ''Miscellaneous''), 41 Stat. 548.
9349(d)	10:1105.	R.S. 1324.

In subsection (a), the word ''commissioned'' is inserted for clarity. 10:1105 (2d sentence) is omitted as obsolete.

In subsection (b), the word ''perform'' is substituted for the words ''be subject at all times to do''. The words ''of such type'' are substituted for the words ''on such service''.

In subsection (e), the words ''members of the Air Force'' are substituted for the words ''private soldier, noncommissioned officer, and officer''. The words ''taught and'' are omitted as surplusage. 10:1105 (less 1st 18 words of last sentence) is omitted as inapplicable to the Air Force.

§ 9350. Cadets: clothing and equipment

(a) The Secretary of the Air Force may prescribe the amount to be credited to a cadet, upon original admission to the Academy, for the cost of his initial issue of clothing and equipment. That amount shall be deducted from his pay. If a cadet is discharged before graduation while owing the United States for pay advanced for the purchase of required clothing and equipment, he shall turn in so much of his clothing and equipment of a distinctive military nature as is necessary to repay the amount advanced. If the value of the clothing and equipment turned in does not cover the amount owed, the indebtedness shall be cancelled.

(b) Under such regulations as the Secretary may prescribe, uniforms and equipment shall be furnished to a cadet at the Academy upon his request.

(Aug. 10, 1956, ch 1041, § 1, 70A Stat. 566.)

HISTORY; ANCILLARY LAWS AND DIRECTIVES

Prior law and revision:

Revised Section	Source (USCS)	Source (Statutes at Large)
9350(a)	10:1149a.	Aug. 31, 1918, ch. 166, § 9, (17th through 22d words), 40 Stat. 957.
9350(b)	10:1106.	Aug. 22, 1951, ch. 340, § 1, 65 Stat. 196.

In subsection (a), the words "while owing the United States for pay advanced for the purpose of" are substituted for the words "who is indebted to the United States on account of advances in pay to purchase". The words "as is necessary to repay the amount advanced" are substituted for the words "to the extent required to discharge such indebtedness".

In subsection (b), the word "accouterments" is omitted as surplusage. The words "by the Government" and "such restrictions and" are omitted as surplusage. The words "at cost" are omitted to reflect Title IV of the National Security Act of 1947, as amended (63 Stat. 585), which authorized the Secretary of Defense to prescribe regulations governing the use and sale of certain inventories at cost, including applicable administrative expenses. (See opinion of the Assistant General Counsel (Fiscal Matters) of the Office of the Secretary of Defense, January 4, 1955.)

§ 9351. Cadets: deficiencies in conduct or studies; effect of failure on successor

(a) A cadet who is reported as deficient in conduct or studies and recommended to be discharged from the Academy may not, unless recommended by the Academy Board, be returned or reappointed to the Academy.

(b) Any cadet who fails to pass a required examination because he is deficient in any one subject of instruction is entitled to a reexamination of equal scope and difficulty in that subject, if he applies in writing to the Superintendent within 10 days after he is officially notified of his failure. The reexamination shall be held within 60 days after the date of his application. If the cadet passes the reexamination and is otherwise qualified, he shall be readmitted to the Academy. If he fails, he may not have another examination.

(c) The failure of a member of a graduating class to complete the course with his class does not delay the admission of his successor.

(Aug. 10, 1956, ch 1041, § 1, 70A Stat. 566.)

HISTORY; ANCILLARY LAWS AND DIRECTIVES

Prior law and revision:

Revised Section	Source (USCS)	Source (Statutes at Large)
9351(a)	10:1104.	Aug. 11, 1916, ch. 314 (3d, 4th, and 5th provisos under "Permanent Establishment"), 39 Stat. 493.
9351(b)	10:1103.	R.S. 1325.
9351(c)	10:1092b (1st proviso).	June 30, 1950, ch 421, § 2 (1st proviso), 64 Stat. 304.

In subsection (a), 10:1104 (last 20 words) is omitted as superseded by section 8287(d) of this title.

In subsection (b), the words "is entitled to" are substituted for the words "shall have the right to apply". The words "of equal scope and difficulty in that subject'' are substituted for the words ''by compliance with the requirements existing at the time of the first examination.

In subsection (c), the words ''by reason of sickness, or deficiency in his studies, or other cause'' are omitted as surplusage.

§ 9352. Cadets: hazing

(a) Subject to the approval of the Secretary of the Air Force, the superintendent of the Academy shall issue regulations—

(1) defining hazing;

(2) designed to prevent that practice; and

(3) prescribing dismissal, suspension, or other adequate punishment for violations.

(b) If a cadet who is charged with violating a regulation issued under subsection (a), the penalty for which is or may be dismissal from the Academy, requests in writing a trial by a general court-martial, he may not be dismissed for that offense except under sentence of such a court.

(c) A cadet dismissed from the Academy for hazing may not be reappointed as an Air Force cadet, and is ineligible for appointment as a commissioned officer in a regular component of the Army, Navy, Air Force, or Marine Corps, until two years after the graduation of his class.

(Aug. 10, 1956, ch 1041, § 1, 70A Stat. 566.)

HISTORY; ANCILLARY LAWS AND DIRECTIVES

Prior law and revision:

Revised Section	Source (USCS)	Source (Statutes at Large)
9352(a)	10:1163 (1st par.).	Mar. 2, 1901, ch. 804 (2d proviso under ''Permanent Establishment''); restated Apr. 19, 1910, ch. 174 (38th par. under ''Buildings and Grounds''), 36 Stat. 323.
9352(b)	10:1163 (1st 32 words of last para.).	
9352(c)	10:1163 (last para. less 1st 32 words).	

In subsection (a), the word ''violations'' is substituted for the words ''infractions of the same''. The words ''to embody a clear'' are omitted as surplusage.

In subsection (b), the words ''the penalty for which is or may be'' are substituted for the words ''which would involve''. The words ''may not be dismissed for that offense except under sentence of such a court'' are substituted for the words ''shall be granted''.

In subsection (c), the words ''a regular component'' are inserted, since the source statute historically applied only to the regular components.

§ 9353. Cadets: degree and commission on graduation

(a) The Superintendent of the Academy may, under such conditions as the Secretary of the Air Force may prescribe, confer the degree of bachelor of science upon graduates of the Academy.

(b) Notwithstanding any other provision of law, a cadet who completes the prescribed course of instruction may, upon graduation, be appointed a second lieutenant in the Regular Air Force under section 531 of this title [10 USCS § 531].

(Aug. 10, 1956, ch 1041, § 1, 70A Stat. 567; Sept. 2, 1958, P. L. 85-861, §§ 1(201), 33(a)(43), 72 Stat. 1541, 1567; Dec. 12, 1980, P.L. 96-513, Title V, Part A, § 504(25), 94 Stat. 2917; Nov. 18, 1997, P. L. 105-85, Div A, Title V, Subtitle E, Part I, § 542(d), 111 Stat. 1743.)

HISTORY; ANCILLARY LAWS AND DIRECTIVES

Prior law and revision:

1956 ACT

Revised Section	Source (USCS)	Source (Statutes at Large)
9353(a)	10:486a (less last sentence).	May 25, 1933, ch. 37 (less last sentence); restated Aug. 9, 1946, ch. 932, (less last sentence); restated Aug. 4, 1949, ch. 393, § 13; restated Aug. 18, 1949, ch. 476 (less last sentence), 63 Stat. 615.
9353(b)	10:506c(f) (1st sentence, less last 43 words).	Aug. 7, 1947, ch. 512, § 506(f) (1st sentence, less last 43 words), 61 Stat. 892.

In subsection (a), the last 27 words are substituted for 10:486a (last sentence). The words "rules and" and "from and after the date of the accrediting of said Academy" are omitted as surplusage. The word "conditions" is substituted for the word "regulations".

In subsection (b), the words "except section 541 of this title" are inserted to reflect the authority to appoint graduates of one service academy as officers of another service.

1958 ACT

Revised Section	Source (USCS)	Source (Statutes at Large)
9353(b)	10 App.:1850c(e) (1st sentence)	July 20, 1956, ch. 646, §203(e) (1st sentence), 70 Stat. 585.

It is unnecessary to include a reference to section 541 of this title, since that section does not derogate from the authority granted in this section.

The change reflects the opinion of the Judge Advocate General of the Air

Force (July 19, 1957) that the words "from and after the date of the accrediting of said academies" in the source law for section 9353(a) (Act of May 25, 1933, ch 37 (48 Stat. 73), as amended) were a condition precedent to the authority to grant degrees and should not have been omitted.

Amendments:

1958. Act Sept. 2, 1958 (effective as provided by § 33(g) of such Act, which appears as 10 USCS § 101 note), substituted the text of this section for text which read:

"(a) Under such conditions as the Secretary of the Air Force may prescribe, the Superintendent of the Academy may confer the degree of bachelor of science upon graduates of the Academy.

"(b) Notwithstanding any other provision of law except section 541 of this title, a cadet who completes the prescribed course of instruction may, upon graduation, be appointed a second lieutenant in the Regular Air Force."

1980. Act Dec. 12, 1980 (effective 9/15/81, as provided by § 701(a) of such Act, which appears as 10 USCS § 101 note), in subsec. (b), inserted "under section 531 of this title".

1997. Act Nov. 18, 1997, in subsec. (a), substituted "The" for "After the date of the accrediting of the Academy, the".

§ 9354. Buildings and grounds: buildings for religious worship

The Secretary of the Air Force may authorize any denomination, sect, or religious body to erect a building for religious worship at the Air Force Academy, if its erection will not interfere with the use of the reservation for military purposes and will be without expense to the United States. Such a building shall be removed, or its location changed, without compensation for it and without expense to the United States, by the denomination, sect, or religious body that erected it, whenever in the opinion of the Secretary public or military necessity so requires.

(Aug. 10, 1956, ch 1041, § 1, 70A Stat. 567.)

HISTORY; ANCILLARY LAWS AND DIRECTIVES

Prior law and revision:

Revised Section	Source (USCS)	Source (Statutes at Large)
9354	10:1126.	July 8, 1898, ch. 636, 30 Stat. 722.

The words "in his discretion" and "Government of" are omitted as surplusage. The words "United States" are substituted for the word "Government".

§ 9355. Board of Visitors

(a) A Board of Visitors to the Academy is constituted annually of—

(1) the chairman of the Committee on Armed Services of the Senate, or his designee;

(2) three other members of the Senate designated by the Vice President or the President pro tempore of the Senate, two of whom are members of the Committee on Appropriations of the Senate;

(3) the Chairman of the Committee on National Security of the House of Representatives, or his designee;

(4) four other members of the House of Representatives designated by the Speaker of the House of Representatives, two of whom are members of the Committee on Appropriations of the House of Representatives; and

(5) six persons designated by the President.

(b) The persons designated by the President serve for three years each except that any member whose term of office has expired shall continue to serve until his successor is appointed. The President shall designate two persons each year to succeed the members whose terms expire that year.

(c) If a member of the Board dies or resigns, a successor shall be designated for the unexpired portion of the term by the official who designated the member.

(d) The Board shall visit the Academy annually. With the approval of the Secretary of the Air Force, the Board or its members may make other visits to the Academy in connection with the duties of the Board or to consult with the Superintendent of the Academy.

(e) The Board shall inquire into the morale and discipline, the curriculum, instruction, physical equipment, fiscal affairs, academic methods, and other matters relating to the Academy which the Board decides to consider.

(f) Within 60 days after its annual visit, the Board shall submit a written report to the President of its action, and of its views and recommendations pertaining to the Academy. Any report of a visit, other than the annual visit, shall, if approved by a majority of the members of the Board, be submitted to the President within 60 days after the approval.

(g) Upon approval by the Secretary, the Board may call in advisers for consultation.

(h) While performing his duties, each member of the Board and each adviser shall be reimbursed under Government travel regulations for his travel expenses.

(Aug. 10, 1956, ch 1041, § 1, 70A Stat. 567; Dec. 23, 1980, P. L. 96-579, § 13(c), 94 Stat. 3369; Feb. 10, 1996, P. L. 104-106, Div A, Title X, Subtitle F, § 1061(e)(2), Title XV, § 1502(a)(12), 110 Stat. 443, 503.)

HISTORY; ANCILLARY LAWS AND DIRECTIVES

Prior law and revision:

Revised Section	Source (USCS)	Source (Statutes at Large)
9355(a)	10:1055. 10:1056 (1st sentence).	June 29, 1948, ch. 714, §§ 1-6, 62 Stat. 1094;

Revised Section	Source (USCS)	Source (Statutes at Large)
9355(b)	10:1056 (less 1st sentence).	June 30, 1954, ch. 432, § 732, 68 Stat. 356.
9355(c)	10:1057.	
9355(d)	10:1058.	
9355(e)	10:1059(a).	
9355(f)	10:1059(b).	
9355(g)	10:1059(c).	
9355(h)	10:1060.	

In subsections (a) and (b), the word ''designated'' is substituted for the word ''appointed'' to make it clear that the positions described are not constitutional offices.

Subsection (b) is substituted for 10:1056(e) (less 1st sentence).

In subsection (c), the words ''during the term for which such member was appointed'' and ''Such successor shall be appointed . . . who died or resigned'' are omitted as surplusage.

In subsection (g), the words ''as it may deem necessary or advisable to effectuate the duties imposed upon it by the provisions of sections 1055–1060 of this title'' are omitted as surplusage.

In subsection (h), the words ''called for consultation by the Board in connection with the business of the Board'' are omitted as surplusage.

Amendments:

1980. Act Dec. 23, 1980, substituted subsec. (b) for one which read: ''(b) Of the first six persons designated by the President, two shall be designated to serve for one year, two shall be designated to serve for two years, and two shall be designated to serve for three years. Persons designated thereafter serve for three years. Two persons shall be designated by him each year to succeed the members whose terms expire that year.''.

1996. Act Feb. 10, 1996, in subsec. (a)(3), substituted ''National Security'' for ''Armed Services''; and, in subsec. (h), deleted ''is entitled to not more than $5 a day and'' following ''adviser''.

CODE OF FEDERAL REGULATIONS

Department of the Air Force—Appointment to the United States Air Force Academy, 32 CFR Part 901.

[§ 9356. Repealed]

HISTORY; ANCILLARY LAWS AND DIRECTIVES

This section (Act Oct. 5, 1994, P. L. 103-337, Div A, Title V, Subtitle E, § 556(c)(1), 108 Stat. 2775) was repealed by Act Feb. 10, 1996, P. L. 104-106, Div A, Title V, Subtitle D, Part I, § 533(c)(1), 110 Stat. 315. It provided for an athletics program, an athletic director, and a nonappropriated fund account for the program.

CHAPTER 905. AVIATION LEADERSHIP PROGRAM

HISTORY; ANCILLARY LAWS AND DIRECTIVES

Explanatory notes:
A prior chapter 905 was repealed by Act Oct. 13, 1964, P. L. 88-647, Title III, § 301(26), 78 Stat. 107. Such chapter related to the Air Force Reserve Officers' Training Corps.

Amendments:
1993. Act Nov. 30, 1993, P. L. 103-160, Div A, Title XI, Subtitle H, § 1178(b), 107 Stat. 1769, added the chapter heading and chapter analysis.

§ 9381. Establishment of program

Under regulations prescribed by the Secretary of Defense, the Secretary of the Air Force may establish and maintain an Aviation Leadership Program to provide undergraduate pilot training and necessary related training to personnel of the air forces of friendly, less-developed foreign nations. Training under this chapter [10 USCS §§ 9381 et seq.] shall include language training and programs to promote better awareness and understanding of the democratic institutions and social framework of the United States.
(Added Nov. 30, 1993, P. L. 103-160, Div A, Title XI, Subtitle H, § 1178(b), 107 Stat. 1769.)

HISTORY; ANCILLARY LAWS AND DIRECTIVES

Explanatory notes:
A prior § 9381 (Act Aug. 10, 1956, ch 1041, § 1, 70A Stat. 568) was repealed by Act Oct. 13, 1964, P. L. 88-647, Title III, § 301(26), 78 Stat. 1073. Such section related to Air Force Reserve Officers' Training Corps. For similar provisions, see 10 USCS § 2101.

Other provisions:
Aviation leadership program; findings. Act Nov. 30, 1993, P. L. 103-160, Div A, Title XI, Subtitle H, § 1178(a), 107 Stat. 1768, provides: ''The Congress finds the following:

''(1) The training in the United States of pilots from the air forces of friendly foreign nations furthers the interests of the United States, promotes closer relations with such nations, and advances the national security.

''(2) Many friendly foreign nations cannot afford to reimburse the United States for the cost of such training.

''(3) It is in the interest of the United States that the Secretary of the Air Force establish a program to train in the United States pilots from the air forces of friendly, less developed foreign nations.''.

§ 9382. Supplies and clothing

(a) The Secretary of the Air Force may, under such conditions as the Secretary may prescribe, provide to a person receiving training under this chapter [10 USCS §§ 9381 et seq.]—

(1) transportation incident to the training;

(2) supplies and equipment to be used during the training;

(3) flight clothing and other special clothing required for the training; and

(4) billeting, food, and health services.

(b) The Secretary of the Air Force may authorize such expenditures from the appropriations of the Air Force as the Secretary considers necessary for the efficient and effective maintenance of the Program in accordance with this chapter [10 USCS §§ 9381 et seq.].

(Added Nov. 30, 1993, P. L. 103-160, Div A, Title XI, Subtitle H, § 1178(b), 107 Stat. 1769.)

HISTORY; ANCILLARY LAWS AND DIRECTIVES

Explanatory notes:

A prior § 9382 (Act Aug. 10, 1956, ch 1041, § 1, 70A Stat. 568; Sept. 2, 1958, P. L. 85-861, § 33(a)(44), 72 Stat. 1567) was repealed by Act Oct. 13, 1964, P. L. 88-647, Title III, § 301(26), 78 Stat. 1073. Such section related to Air Force Reserve Officers' Training Corps. For similar provisions, see 10 USCS § 2102.

§ 9383. Allowances

The Secretary of the Air Force may pay to a person receiving training under this chapter [10 USCS §§ 9381 et seq.] a living allowance at a rate to be prescribed by the Secretary, taking into account the amount of living allowances authorized for a member of the armed forces under similar circumstances.

(Added Nov. 30, 1993, P. L. 103-160, Div A, Title XI, Subtitle H, § 1178(b), 107 Stat. 1769.)

HISTORY; ANCILLARY LAWS AND DIRECTIVES

Explanatory notes:

A prior § 9383 (Act Aug. 10, 1956, ch 1041, § 1, 70A Stat. 569) was repealed by Act Oct. 13, 1964, P. L. 88-647, Title III, § 301(26), 78 Stat. 1073. Such section related to Air Force Reserve Officers' Training Corps. For similar provisions, see 10 USCS § 2103.

[§§ 9384–9387. Repealed]

HISTORY; ANCILLARY LAWS AND DIRECTIVES

These sections (§ 9384—Act Aug. 10, 1956, ch 1041, § 1, 70A Stat. 569; Sept. 2, 1958, P. L. 85-861, § 1(202), 72 Stat. 1541; §§ 9385, 9386, 9387—Act Aug. 10, 1956, ch 1041, § 1, 70A Stat. 569, 570) were repealed by Act Oct. 13, 1964, P. L. 88-647, Title III, § 301(26), 78 Stat. 1073. They related to the Air Force Reserve Officers' Training Corps and defined ''advanced training,'' provided for its establishment and composition, provided for admission and training of medical, dental, pharmacy and veterinary students, set out courses of training, authorized the operation and maintenance of training camps, and provided for supplies and uniforms and for advanced training and compensation therefor. For similar provisions, see 10 USCS §§ 2101 et seq.

CHAPTER 907. SCHOOLS AND CAMPS

HISTORY; ANCILLARY LAWS AND DIRECTIVES

Amendments:

1990. Act Nov. 5, 1990, P. L. 101-510, Div A, Title III, Part C, § 330(b), 104 Stat. 1535, amended the analysis of this chapter by adding item 9415.

§ 9411. Establishment: purpose

The Secretary of the Air Force may maintain schools and camps for the military instruction and training of persons selected, upon their application, from warrant officers and enlisted members of the Air Force and civilians, to qualify them for appointment as reserve officers, or enlistment as reserve noncommissioned officers, for service in the Air Force Reserve.

(Aug. 10, 1956, ch 1041, § 1, 70A Stat. 571.)

HISTORY; ANCILLARY LAWS AND DIRECTIVES

Prior law and revision:

Revised Section	Source (USCS)	Source (Statutes at Large)
9411	10:442 (words before 1st semicolon of 1st sentence).	June 3, 1916, ch. 134, § 47d (words before 1st semicolon of 1st sentence); added June 4, 1920, ch. 227, subch. I, § 34 (words before 1st semicolon of 1st sentence of last para.), 41 Stat. 779.

The words ''upon military reservations or elsewhere'' are omitted as surplusage. The words ''of the Air Force'' are inserted for clarity. The words ''or enlistment as'' are inserted for clarity.

CROSS REFERENCES

Supplies, 10 USCS § 9654.

This section is referred to in 10 USCS §§ 9412—9414.

§ 9412. Operation

In maintaining camps established under section 9411 of this title, [10 USCS § 9411], the Secretary of the Air Force may—

(1) prescribe the periods during which they will be operated;
(2) prescribe regulations for their administration;
(3) prescribe the courses to be taught;
(4) detail members of the Regular Air Force to designated duties relating to the camps;
(5) use necessary supplies and transportation;
(6) furnish uniforms, subsistence, and medical attendance and supplies to persons attending the camps; and
(7) authorize necessary expenditures from proper Air Force funds for—
(A) water;
(B) fuel;
(C) light;
(D) temporary structures, except barracks and officers' quarters;
(E) screening;
(F) damages resulting from field exercises;
(G) expenses incident to theoretical winter instruction of trainees; and
(H) other expenses incident to maintaining the camps.

(Aug. 10, 1956, ch 1041, § 1, 70A Stat. 571.)

HISTORY; ANCILLARY LAWS AND DIRECTIVES

Prior law and revision:

Revised Section	Source (USCS)	Source (Statutes at Large)
9412	10:442 (47 words after 1st semicolon, and 72 words before 3d semicolon, of 1st sentence; and last sentence).	June 3, 1916, ch. 134, § 47d (47 words after 1st semicolon, and 72 words before 3d semicolon, of 1st sentence; and last sentence); added June 4, 1920, ch. 227, subch. I, å 34 (47 words after 1st semicolon, and 72 words before 3d semicolon, of 1st sentence; and last sentence of last para.), 41 stat. 779.

The word ''supplies'' is substituted for the words ''such arms, ammunition, accoutrements, equipments, tentage, field equipage'', since, under the definition of the word ''supplies'', in section 101(26) of this title, those words are covered by the word ''supplies''. The words ''belonging to the United States'', ''and imparting military instruction and training thereat'', ''during the period of their attendance'', ''theoretical and practical instruction'', ''persons attending the camps authorized by this section'', and ''as he may deem'' are omitted as surplusage. The word ''detail'' is substituted for the word ''employ''. The word ''members'' is substituted for the words ''officers, warrant officers, and enlisted men''.

§ 9413. Transportation and subsistence during travel

(a) There may be furnished to a person attending a school or camp established under section 9411 of this title [10 USCS § 9411], for travel to and from that school or camp—

(1) transportation and subsistence;

(2) transportation in kind and a subsistence allowance of one cent a mile; or

(3) a travel allowance of five cents a mile.

(b) The travel allowance for the return trip may be paid in advance.

(c) For the purposes of this section, distance is computed by the shortest usually traveled route, within such territorial limits as the Secretary of the Air Force may prescribe, from the authorized starting point to the school or camp and return.

(Aug. 10, 1956, ch 1041, § 1, 70A Stat. 572.)

HISTORY; ANCILLARY LAWS AND DIRECTIVES

Prior law and revision:

Revised Section	Source (USCS)	Source (Statutes at Large)
9413(a), (b), (c)	10:442 (words between 1st and 3d semicolons, less 47 words after 1st semicolon, and less 72 words before 3d semicolon, of 1st sentence).	June 3, 1916, ch. 134, § 47d (words between 1st and 3d semicolons, less 47 words after 1st semicolon, and less 72 words before 3d semicolon, of 1st sentence); added June 4, 1920, ch. 227, § 34 (words between 1st and 3d semicolons, less 47 words after 1st semicolon, and less 72 words before 3d semicolon, of 1st sentence of last para.), 41 Stat. 779; Mar. 9, 1928, ch. 161, 45 Stat. 251.

In subsection (a), the introductory clause is inserted for clarity. The words "at the option of the Secretary of the Army" are omitted as surplusage.

In subsection (b), the words "of the actual performance of the same" are omitted as surplusage.

Subsection (c) is substituted for the words "the most usual and direct route within such limits as to territory as the Secretary of the Army may prescribe . . . for the distance by the shortest usually traveled route from the places from which they are authorized to proceed to the camp, and for the return travel thereto".

§ 9414. Quartermaster and ordnance property: sales

The Secretary of the Air Force may sell to a person attending a school or camp established under section 9411 of this title [10 USCS § 9411] quartermaster and ordnance property necessary for his proper equipment. Sales under this section shall be for cash.

(Aug. 10, 1956, ch 1041, § 1, 70A Stat. 572.)

HISTORY; ANCILLARY LAWS AND DIRECTIVES

Prior law and revision:

Revised Section	Source (USCS)	Source (Statutes at Large)
9414	10:442 (words after 3d semicolon of 1st sentence; and 2d sentence).	June 3, 1916, ch. 134, § 47d (words after 3d semicolon of 1st sentence; and 2d sentence); added June 4, 1920, ch. 227, § 34 (words after 3d semicolon of 1st sentence; and 2d sentence of last para.), 41 Stat. 779.

10:442 (2d sentence) is omitted as superseded by section 10 of the Act of June 26, 1934, ch 756, 48 Stat. 1229 (31 U.S.C. 725i), which limits credits to the replacing account to the actual cost of the items sold. The words ''quartermaster and ordnance property necessary for his proper equipment'' are substituted for 10:442 (last 26 words of 1st sentence). The words ''and at cost price, plus 10 per centum'' are omitted to reflect Title IV of the National Security Act of 1947, as amended (63 Stat. 585), which authorized the Secretary of Defense to prescribe regulations governing the use and sale of certain inventories at cost, including applicable administrative expenses. (See opinion of the Assistant General Counsel (Fiscal Matters) of the Office of the Secretary of Defense, January 4, 1955.)

§ 9415. Inter-American Air Forces Academy

(a) Operation. The Secretary of the Air Force may operate the Air Force education and training facility known as the Inter-American Air Forces Academy for the purpose of providing military education and training to military personnel of Central and South American countries, Caribbean countries, and other countries eligible for assistance under chapter 5 of part II of the Foreign Assistance Act of 1961 (22 U.S.C. 2347 et seq.).

(b) Costs. The fixed costs of operating and maintaining the Inter-American Air Forces Academy may be paid from funds available for operation and maintenance of the Air Force.

(Added Nov. 5, 1990, P. L. 101-510, Div A, Title III, Part C, § 330(a), 104 Stat. 1535.)

CHAPTER 909. CIVIL AIR PATROL

HISTORY; ANCILLARY LAWS AND DIRECTIVES

Amendments:

1984. Act Oct. 19, 1984, P. L. 98-525, Title XV, Part D, § 1533(b)(2), 98 Stat. 2632 (effective 10/1/84, as provided by § 1533(c) of such Act, which appears as 10 USCS § 9441 note) amended the analysis of this chapter by adding the item relating to section 9442.

§ 9441. Status: support by Air Force; employment

(a) The Civil Air Patrol is a volunteer civilian auxiliary of the Air Force.

(b) To assist the Civil Air Patrol in the fulfillment of its objectives as set forth in section 2 of the Act of July 1, 1946 (36 U.S.C. 202), the Secretary of the Air Force may, under regulations prescribed by him with the approval of the Secretary of Defense—

(1) give, lend, or sell to the Civil Air Patrol without regard to the Federal Property and Administrative Services Act of 1949, as amended (40 U.S.C. 471 et seq.)—

(A) major items of equipment, including aircraft, motor vehicles, and communication equipment; and

(B) necessary related supplies and training aids;

that are excess to the military departments;

(2) permit the use of such services and facilities of the Air Force as he considers to be needed by the Civil Air Patrol to carry out its mission;

(3) furnish such quantities of fuel and lubricants to the Civil Air Patrol as are needed by it to carry out any mission assigned to it by the Air Force, including unit capability testing missions and training missions;

(4) establish, maintain, and supply liaison offices of the Air Force at the National, State, and Territorial headquarters, and at not more than eight regional headquarters, of the Civil Air Patrol;

(5) detail or assign any member of the Air Force or any officer or employee of the Department of the Air Force to any liaison office at the National, State, or Territorial headquarters, and at not more than eight regional headquarters, of the Civil Air Patrol;

(6) detail any member of the Air Force or any officer or employee of the Department of the Air Force to any unit or installation of the Civil Air Patrol to assist in the training program of the Civil Air Patrol;

(7) in time of war, or of national emergency declared after May 27, 1954, by Congress or the President, authorize the payment of travel expenses and allowances, in accordance with subchapter I of chapter 57 of title 5 [5 USCS

§§ 5701 et seq.] to members of the Civil Air Patrol while carrying out any mission specifically assigned by the Air Force;

(8) provide funds for the national headquarters of the Civil Air Patrol, including funds for the payment of staff compensation and benefits, administrative expenses, travel, per diem and allowances, rent and utilities, and other operational expenses;

(9) authorize the payment of aircraft maintenance expenses relating to operational missions, unit capability testing missions, and training missions;

(10) authorize the payment of expenses of placing into serviceable condition major items of equipment (including aircraft, motor vehicles, and communications equipment) owned by the Civil Air Patrol;

(11) reimburse the Civil Air Patrol for costs incurred for the purchase of such major items of equipment as the Secretary considers needed by the Civil Air Patrol to carry out its missions; and

(12) furnish articles of the Air Force uniform to Civil Air Patrol cadets without cost to such cadets.

(c) The Secretary may use the services of the Civil Air Patrol in fulfilling the noncombat mission of the Department of the Air Force, and for purposes of determining the civil liability of the Civil Air Patrol (or any member thereof) with respect to any act or omission committed by the Civil Air Patrol (or any member thereof) in fulfilling such mission, the Civil Air Patrol shall be deemed to be an instrumentality of the United States.

(d)(1) The Secretary of the Air Force may authorize the Civil Air Patrol to employ, as administrators and liaison officers, persons retired from service in the Air Force whose qualifications are approved under regulations prescribed by the Secretary and who request such employment.

(2) A person employed pursuant to paragraph (1) may receive the person's retired pay and an additional amount for such employment that is not more than the difference between the person's retired pay and the pay and allowances the person would be entitled to receive if ordered to active duty in the grade in which the person retired from service in the Air Force. The additional amount shall be paid to the Civil Air Patrol by the Secretary from funds appropriated for that purpose.

(3) A person employed pursuant to paragraph (1) may not, while so employed, be considered to be on active duty or inactive-duty training for any purpose.

(Aug. 10, 1956, ch 1041, § 1, 70A Stat. 572; Sept. 8, 1980, P. L. 96-342, Title X, § 1007(a), (b)(1), 94 Stat. 1121, 1122; Dec. 12, 1980, P. L. 96-513, Title V, Part B, § 514(12), 94 Stat. 2935; Oct. 19, 1984, P. L. 98-525, Title XV, Part D, § 1533(a), 98 Stat. 2632; Nov. 8, 1985, P. L. 99-145, Title XIII, § 1303(a)(28), Title XIV, Part E, § 1458(a), 99 Stat. 740, 763; Nov. 14, 1986, P. L. 99-661, Div A, Title XIII, Part F, § 1365(a), 100 Stat. 4002; Oct. 5, 1994, P. L. 103-337, Div A, Title X, Subtitle G, § 1062, 108 Stat. 2847.)

HISTORY; ANCILLARY LAWS AND DIRECTIVES

Prior law and revision:

Revised Section	Source (USCS)	Source (Statutes at Large)
9441(a)	5:626l.	May 26, 1948, ch. 349, 62 Stat. 274, 275; Oct. 31, 1951, ch. 654, § 295, 65 Stat. 706; May 27, 1954, ch. 225, 68 Stat. 141; July 16, 1954, ch. 531, 68 Stat. 485.
9441(b)	5:626l (less 1st sentence).	
9441(c)	5:626m.	

In subsection (a), the words "established as" are omitted as executed.

In subsection (b), the words "Materials", "other equipment", and "and equip" are omitted as covered by the definition of the word "supplies" in section 101(26) of this title. The words "as he considers to be needed" are substituted for the words "as in the opinion of the Secretary of the Air Force are required". The words "any member of the Air Force or any employee of the Department of the Air Force" are substituted for the words "military and civilian personnel of the Air Force". The words "from available stock" and "the requirements of" are omitted as surplusage.

Amendments:

1980. Act Sept. 8, 1980, in subsec. (b), in para. (3), inserted "including unit capability testing missions and training missions", in para. (6), deleted "and" following the concluding semicolon, in para. (7), substituted "; and" for the concluding period, and added para. (8); in subsec. (c), inserted ", and for purposes of determining the civil liability of the Civil Air Patrol (or any member thereof) with respect to any act or omission committed by the Civil Air Patrol (or any member thereof) in fulfilling such mission, the Civil Air Patrol shall be deemed to be an instrumentality of the United States".

Act Dec. 12, 1980 (effective upon enactment on 12/12/80, as provided by § 701(b)(3) of such Act, which appears as 10 USCS § 101 note), in subsec. (b), in the introductory matter, substituted "2 of the Act of July 1, 1946 (36 U.S.C. 202)" for "202 of title 36", and, in para. (7), substituted "subchapter I of chapter 57 of title 5" for "the Travel Expense Act of 1949 (5 U.S.C. 835 et seq.)".

1984. Act Oct. 19, 1984 (effective 10/1/84, as provided by § 1533(c) of such Act, which appears as a note to this section), in subsec. (b), in para. (7), deleted "and" following "Air Force;", in para. (8), substituted "; and" for the concluding period, and added paras. (9)–(11).

1985. Act Nov. 8, 1985 (effective 10/1/85, as provided by § 1458(b) of such Act, which appears as a note to this section), in subsec. (b)(10), substituted "reimburse the Civil Air Patrol for costs incurred for the purchase" for "authorize the purchase with funds appropriated to the Air Force".

Such Act further, in subsec. (b)(8), deleted "and" following "missions;".

1986. Act Nov. 14, 1986 (applicable as provided by § 1365(b) of such Act, which appears as a note to this section), in subsec. (b)(9), substituted "major items of equipment (including aircraft, motor vehicles, and communications equipment) owned by the Civil Air Patrol'' for ''a major item of equipment furnished to the Civil Air Patrol under clause (1)''.

1994. Act Oct. 5, 1994, in subsec. (b), redesignated paras. (8)–(11) as paras. (9)–(12), respectively, and added a new para. (8); and added subsec. (d).

Other provisions:

Application of 1980 amendment of subsec. (c). Act Sept. 8, 1980, P. L. 96-342, Title X, § 1007(b)(2), 94 Stat. 1122, provides: ''The amendment made by paragraph (1) [amendment of subsec. (c) of this section; see the Amendments note] shall be effective with respect to services of the Civil Air Patrol provided to the Department of the Air Force before the date of the enactment of this Act [enacted Sept. 8, 1980] as well as to such services provided on or after such date, but such amendment shall not be construed (A) to revive any cause of action barred by an applicable statute of limitation, or (B) to serve as grounds for the reopening or appeal of any case which became final before the date of the enactment of this Act [enacted Sept. 8, 1980].''.

Effective date of amendments made by § 1533 of Act Oct. 19, 1984. Act Oct. 19, 1984, P. L. 98-525, Title XV, Part D, § 1533(c), 98 Stat. 2632, provides: ''The amendments made by this section [adding this note and 10 USCS § 9442 and amending this section and 10 USCS prec. § 9441] shall take effect on October 1, 1984.''.

Civil Air Patrol. Act Oct. 27, 1986, P. L. 99-570, Title III, Subtitle A, § 3059, 100 Stat. 3207-79; Feb. 10, 1996, P. L. 104-106, Div A, Title XV, § 1502(f)(3), 110 Stat. 509, provides:

''(a) Sense of Congress. It is the sense of Congress that—

''(1) the Civil Air Patrol, the all-volunteer civilian auxiliary of the Air force, can increase its participation in and make significant contributions to the drug interdiction efforts of the Federal Government, and

''(2) the Secretary of the Air Force should fully support that participation.

''(b) Authorization. In addition to any other amounts appropriated for the Civil Air Patrol for fiscal year 1987, there are authorized to be appropriated for the Civil Air Patrol, out of any unobligated and uncommitted balances of appropriations for the Department of Defense for fiscal year 1986 which are carried forward into fiscal year 1987, $7,000,000 for the acquisition of the major items of equipment needed by the Civil Air Patrol for drug interdiction surveillance and reporting missions.

''(c) Reports. (1) The Secretary of the Air Force shall submit to the Committee on Armed Services and the Committee on Appropriations of the Senate and the Committee on National Security and the Committee on Appropriations of the House of Representatives quarterly reports which contain the following information:

''(A) A description of the manner in which any funds are used under subsection (b).

''(B) A detailed description of the activities of the Civil Air Patrol in support of the Federal Government's drug interdiction program.

''(2) The first report under paragraph (1) shall be submitted on the last day of the first quarter ending not less than 90 days after the date of the enactment of this Act.''.

Application of 1986 amendment to subsec. (b)(9). Act Nov. 14, 1986, P. L. 99-661, Div A, Title XIII, Part F, § 1365(b), 100 Stat. 4002, provides: "The amendment made by subsection (a) [amending subsec. (b)(9) of this section] shall apply with respect to funds appropriated for fiscal years after fiscal year 1986.".

Civil Air Patrol. Act Nov. 18, 1988, P. L. 100-690, Title VII, Subtitle O, § 7606, 102 Stat. 4511; Feb. 10, 1996, P. L. 104-106, Div A, Title XV, § 1502(f)(4), 110 Stat. 509, provides:

"(a) Regulations. Within 45 days, the Secretary of the Air Force shall issue such regulations as are necessary to ensure that the Civil Air Patrol has an integral role in drug interdiction and eradication activities.

"(b) Reports. The Secretary of the Air Force shall submit to the Committee on Armed Services and the Committee on Appropriations of the Senate and the Committee on National Security and the Committee on Appropriations of the House of Representatives, quarterly reports which include a detailed description of the activities of the Civil Air Patrol in support of the Federal, State, and local government agencies' drug interdiction and eradication programs. The first report shall be submitted on the last day of the first quarter ending not less than 150 days after the date of the enactment.".

CODE OF FEDERAL REGULATIONS

Department of the Air Force—Administrative claims, 32 CFR Part 842.

CROSS REFERENCES

Military or veteran status not conferred by section, 5 USCS § 8150.

This section is referred to in 5 USCS § 8150.

INTERPRETIVE NOTES AND DECISIONS

Civil air patrol pilot, while piloting plane on loan from Air Force and carrying passenger on official indoctrination flight of Civil Air Patrol, was not employee of United States, and United States was not liable for death of passenger when plane stalled in flight and crashed. Pearl v United States (1956, CA10 Okla) 230 F2d 243.

In absence of wanton or willful misconduct of pilot, United States government was not liable for injuries received by guest in course of unauthorized flight undertaken by commissioned officer in service of the government in plane furnished by Civil Air Patrol. United States v Alexander (1956, CA4 NC) 234 F2d 861, cert den (1956) 352 US 892, 1 L Ed 2d 86, 77 S Ct 131.

Death of Civil Air Patrol member while performing under 10 USCS § 9441(c) is compensable under Federal Employees Compensation Act (5 USCS §§ 8101 et seq.). Williamson v Sartain (1982, DC Mont) 555 F Supp 487.

§ 9442. Assistance by other agencies

The Secretary of the Air Force may arrange for the use by the Civil Air Patrol of such facilities and services under the jurisdiction of the Secretary of the Army, the Secretary of the Navy, or the head of any other department or agency of the United States as the Secretary of the Air Force considers to be needed by the Civil Air Patrol to carry out its mission. Any such arrangement shall be made under regulations prescribed by the Secretary of the Air Force with the approval of the Secretary of Defense and shall be subject to the agreement of the other military department or other department or agency of the United States furnishing the facilities or services.

(Added Oct. 19, 1984, P. L. 98-525, Title XV, Part D, § 1533(b)(1), 98 Stat. 2632.)

HISTORY; ANCILLARY LAWS AND DIRECTIVES

Effective date of section:

Act Oct. 19, 1984, P. L. 98-525, Title XV, Part D, § 1533(c), 98 Stat. 2632, which appears as 10 USCS § 9441 note, provides that this section shall take effect on Oct. 1, 1984.

PART IV. SERVICE, SUPPLY, AND PROCUREMENT

HISTORY; ANCILLARY LAWS AND DIRECTIVES

Amendments:

1993. Act Nov. 30, 1993, P. L. 103-160, Div A, Title VIII, Subtitle C, § 828(c)(8)(B) 107 Stat. 1715, amended the analysis of this Part by substituting item 931 for one which read: ''931. Industrial Mobilization, Research, and Development . . . 9501''.

CHAPTER 931. CIVIL RESERVE AIR FLEET

HISTORY; ANCILLARY LAWS AND DIRECTIVES

Amendments:

1981. Act Dec. 1, 1981, P. L. 97-86, Title IX, § 915, 95 Stat. 1125, added the subchapter headings and analyses.

1989. Act Nov. 29, 1989, P. L. 101-189, Div A, Title XVI, Part D, § 1636(c)(2), 103 Stat. 1610, amended the analysis of Subchapter II by substituting items 9512 and 9513 for ones which read: ''9512. Contracts to modify aircraft: cargo-convertible features'' and ''9513. Contracts to modify aircraft: commitment of aircraft to Civil Reserve Air Fleet''.

1993. Act Nov. 30, 1993, P. L. 103-160, Div A, Title VIII, Subtitle C, § 828(c)(8), 107 Stat. 1714, deleted the analysis of Subchapter I, which read:

''9501. Industrial mobilization: orders; priorities; possession of manufacturing plants; violations

''9502. Industrial mobilization: plants; lists; Board on Mobilization of Industries Essential for Military Preparedeness

''9503. Research and development programs

"9504. Procurement for experimental purposes
"9505. Procurement of production equipment
"9506. Sale, loan, or gift of samples, drawings, and information to contractors
"9507. Sale of ordnance and ordnance stores to designers";
deleted the subchapter headings, which read: "SUBCHAPTER I. GENERAL" and "SUBCHAPTER II. CIVIL RESERVE AIR FLEET"; deleted the table of subchapters; and substituted the chapter heading for one which read: "CHAPTER 931. INDUSTRIAL MOBILIZATION, RESEARCH, AND DEVELOPMENT".

1994. Act Oct. 13, 1994, P. L. 103-355, Title III, Subtitle D, § 3033(b), 108 Stat. 3336 (effective and applicable as provided by § 10001(a) and (b) of such Act, which appear as 41 USCS § 251 note), amended the analysis of this chapter by substituting item 9513 for one which read: "9513. Commitment of aircraft to the Civil Reserve Air Fleet".

1996. Act Sept. 23, 1996, P. L. 104-201, Div A, Title X, Subtitle F, § 1079(a)(2), 110 Stat. 2669, amended the analysis of this chapter by adding item 9514.

[§§ 9501–9507. Repealed]

HISTORY; ANCILLARY LAWS AND DIRECTIVES

These sections (Act Aug. 10, 1956, ch 1041, § 1, 70A Stat. 573–575) were repealed by Act Nov. 30, 1993, P. L. 103-160, Div A, Title VIII, Subtitle C, § 822(a)(2), 107 Stat. 1705. Section 9501 provided for industrial mobilization: orders; priorities; possession of manufacturing plants; violations; § 9502 provided for industrial mobilization: plants; lists; Board on Mobilization of Industries Essential for Military Preparedness; § 9503 provided for research and development programs; § 9504 provided for procurement for experimental purposes; § 9505 provided for procurement of production equipment, § 9506 provided for sale, loan, or gift of samples, drawings, and information to contractors; and § 9507 provided for sale of ordnance and ordnance stores to designers. For provisions similar to § 9501, see 10 USCS § 2538; for provisions similar to § 9502, see 10 USCS §§ 2539, 2539a; and for provisions similar to § 9504, see 10 USCS § 2373.

§ 9511. Definitions

In this chapter [10 USCS §§ 9511 et seq.]:

(1) The terms "aircraft", "citizen of the United States", "civil aircraft", "person", and "public aircraft" have the meanings given those terms by section 40102(a) of title 49.

(2) The term "passenger-cargo combined aircraft" means a civil aircraft equipped so that its main deck can be used to carry both passengers and property (including mail) simultaneously.

(3) The term "cargo-capable aircraft" means a civil aircraft equipped so that all or substantially all of the aircraft's capacity can be used for the carriage of property or mail.

(4) The term ''passenger aircraft'' means a civil aircraft equipped so that its main deck can be used for the carriage of individuals and cannot be used principally, without major modification, for the carriage of property or mail.

(5) The term ''cargo-convertible aircraft'' means a passenger aircraft equipped or designed so that all or substantially all of the main deck of the aircraft can be readily converted for the carriage of property or mail.

(6) The term ''Civil Reserve Air Fleet'' means those aircraft allocated, or identified for allocation, to the Department of Defense under section 101 of the Defense Production Act of 1950 (50 U.S.C. App. 2071), or made available (or agreed to be made available) for use by the Department of Defense under a contract made under this title, as part of the program developed by the Department of Defense through which the Department of Defense augments its airlift capability by use of civil aircraft.

(7) The term ''contractor'' means a citizen of the United States (A) who owns or controls, or who will own or control, a new or existing aircraft and who contracts with the Secretary under section 9512 of this title to modify that aircraft by including or incorporating specified defense features in that aircraft and to commit that aircraft to the Civil Reserve Air Fleet, (B) who subsequently obtains ownership or control of a civil aircraft covered by such a contract and assumes all existing obligations under that contract, or (C) who owns or controls, or will own or control, new or existing aircraft and who, by contract, commits some or all of such aircraft to the Civil Reserve Air Fleet.

(8) The term ''existing aircraft'' means a civil aircraft other than a new aircraft.

(9) The term ''new aircraft'' means a civil aircraft that a manufacturer has not begun to assemble before the aircraft is covered by a contract under section 9512 of this title.

(10) The term ''Secretary'' means the Secretary of the Air Force.

(11) The term ''defense feature'' means equipment or design features included or incorporated in a civil aircraft which ensures the compatibility of such aircraft with the Department of Defense airlift system. Such term includes any equipment or design feature which enables such aircraft to be readily modified for use as an aeromedical aircraft or a cargo-convertible, cargo-capable, or passenger-cargo combined aircraft.

(Added Dec. 1, 1981, P.L. 97-86, Title IX, § 915(2), 95 Stat. 1125; Dec. 4, 1987, P. L. 100-180, Div A, Title XII, Part D, § 1231(17), 101 Stat. 1161; Sept. 29, 1988, P. L. 100-456, Div A, Title XII, Part D, § 1233(k)(2), 102 Stat. 2058; Nov. 29, 1989, P. L. 101-189, Div A, Title XVI, Part D, § 1636(a), 103 Stat. 1609; July 5, 1994, P. L. 103-272, § 5(b)(2), 108 Stat. 1373; Oct. 13, 1994, P. L. 103-355, Title III, Subtitle D, § 3031, 108 Stat. 3334.)

HISTORY; ANCILLARY LAWS AND DIRECTIVES

Amendments:

1987. Act Dec. 4, 1987, in paras. (1)–(11) inserted ''The term'' and, in paras. (1)–(6) and (8)–(10), revised the first quoted word in each para. so that the initial letter of such word is lower case.

1988. Act Sept. 29, 1988, in para. (1), substituted ''The terms'' for ''The term''.

1989. Act Nov. 29, 1989 substituted para. (2) for one which read: ''The term 'cargo air service' means the carriage of property or mail on the main deck of a civil aircraft.''; substituted para. (5) for one which read: ''The term 'cargo-convertible feature' means equipment or design features included or incorporated in a passenger aircraft that can readily enable all or substantially all of that aircraft's main deck to be used for the carriage of property or mail.''; in para. (8)(A), substituted ''a new or existing aircraft and who contracts with the Secretary to modify that aircraft by including or incorporating specified defense features'' for ''a civil aircraft and who contracts with the Secretary of the Air Force to modify that aircraft by including or incorporating cargo-convertible features suitable for defense purposes''; and added para. (12).

1994. Act July 5, 1994, in para. (1), substituted ''section 40102(a) of title 49'' for ''section 101 of the Federal Aviation Act of 1958 (49 U.S.C. 1301)''.

Act Oct. 13, 1994 (effective and applicable as provided by § 10001(a) and (b) of such Act, which appear as 41 USCS § 251 note), substituted the introductory matter for matter which read: ''In this subchapter:'', in para. (1), inserted '' 'civil aircraft',", and substituted ''meanings'' for ''meaning'', in para. (8), inserted ''under section 9512 of this title'', deleted ''or'' preceding ''(B) who subsequently obtains'', and inserted '', or (C) who owns or controls, or will own or control, new or existing aircraft and who, by contract, commits some or all of such aircraft to the Civil Reserve Air Fleet'', deleted para. (6), which read: ''The term 'civil aircraft' means an aircraft other than a public aircraft.'', redesignated paras. (7)–(12) as paras. (6)–(11) respectively, and in para. (11) as redesignated, substituted ''compatibility'' for ''interoperability'' and inserted ''an aeromedical aircraft or''.

Such Act further (effective and applicable as above) purported to amend para. (1) by substituting ''section 40102 of title 49'' for ''section 101 of the Federal Aviation Act of 1958 (49 U.S.C. 1301)''; however, because of a prior amendment, this amendment could not be executed.

§ 9512. Contracts for the inclusion or incorporation of defense features

(a) Authority to contract. Subject to the provisions of chapter 137 of this title [10 USCS §§ 2301 et seq.], and to the extent that funds are otherwise available for obligation, the Secretary—

(1) may contract with any citizen of the United States for the inclusion or incorporation of defense features in any new or existing aircraft to be owned or controlled by that citizen; and

(2) may contract with United States aircraft manufacturers for the inclusion or incorporation of defense features in new aircraft to be operated by a United States air carrier.

(b) Commitment to Civil Reserve Air Fleet. Each contract entered into under this section shall provide—

(1) that any aircraft covered by the contract shall be committed to the Civil Reserve Air Fleet;

(2) that, so long as the aircraft is owned or controlled by a contractor, the contractor shall operate the aircraft for the Department of Defense as needed during any activation of the Civil Reserve Air Fleet, notwithstanding any other contract or commitment of that contractor; and

(3) that the contractor operating the aircraft for the Department of Defense shall be paid for that operation at fair and reasonable rates.

(c) Terms and required repayment. Each contract entered into under subsection (a) shall include a provision that requires the contractor to repay to the United States a percentage (to be established in the contract) of any amount paid by the United States to the contractor under the contract with respect to any aircraft if—

(1) the aircraft is destroyed or becomes unusable, as defined in the contract;

(2) the defense features specified in the contract are rendered unusable or are removed from the aircraft;

(3) control over the aircraft is transferred to any person that is unable or unwilling to assume the contractor's obligations under the contract; or

(4) the registration of the aircraft under section 44103 of title 49 is terminated for any reason not beyond the control of the contractor.

(d) Authority to contract and pay directly. (1) A contract under subsection (a) for the inclusion or incorporation of defense features in an aircraft may include a provision authorizing the Secretary—

(A) to contract, with the concurrence of the contractor, directly with another person for the performance of the work necessary for the inclusion or incorporation of defense features in such aircraft; and

(B) to pay such other person directly for such work.

(2) A contract entered into pursuant to paragraph (1) may include such specifications for work and equipment as the Secretary considers necessary to meet the needs of the United States.

(e) Exclusivity of commitment to Civil Reserve Air Fleet. Notwithstanding section 101 of the Defense Production Act of 1950 (50 U.S.C. App. 2071) [50 USCS Appx § 2071], each aircraft covered by a contract entered into under this section shall be committed exclusively to the Civil Reserve Air Fleet for use by the Department of Defense as needed during any activation of the Civil Reserve Air Fleet unless the aircraft is released from that use by the Secretary of Defense.

(Added Dec. 1, 1981, P. L. 97-86, Title IX, § 915(2), 95 Stat. 1126; Oct. 19, 1984, P. L. 98-525, Title XIV, § 1405(57), 98 Stat. 2626; Nov. 29, 1989, P. L. 101-189, Div A, Title XVI, Part D, § 1636(b), 103 Stat. 1609; July 5, 1994, P. L. 103-272, § 5(b)(3), 108 Stat. 1373; Oct. 13, 1994, P. L. 103-355, Title III, Subtitle D, § 3032(1)–(8), 108 Stat. 3334; Feb. 10, 1996, P. L. 104-106, Div A, Title X, Subtitle H, § 1087, 110 Stat. 458.)

HISTORY; ANCILLARY LAWS AND DIRECTIVES

Explanatory notes:

Subecs. (b) and (e) were formerly classified to 10 USCS § 9513(a) and (b), respectively.

Amendments:

1984. Act Oct. 19, 1984, in subsec. (b)(1), inserted ''App.''

1989. Act Nov. 29, 1989 substituted this section for one which read:

''§ 9512. Contracts to modify aircraft: cargo-convertible features

''(a) Subject to chapter 137 of this title, and to the extent that funds are otherwise available for obligation, the Secretary may contract with any citizen of the United States (1) for the modification of any new aircraft to be owned or controlled by that citizen by the inclusion of cargo-convertible features suitable for defense purposes in that aircraft, or (2) for the modification of any existing passenger aircraft owned or controlled by that citizen by the incorporation of cargo-convertible features suitable for defense purposes in that aircraft.

''(b) Each contract made under subsection (a) shall include the terms required by section 9513 of this title and the following terms:

''(1) The contractor shall agree that each aircraft covered by the contract that is not already registered under section 501 of the Federal Aviation Act of 1958 (49 U.S.C. App. 1401) shall be registered under that section not later than the completion of the manufacturer of the aircraft or the completion of the modification of the aircraft under the contract.

''(2) The contractor shall agree to repay to the United States a percentage (to be established in the contract) of any amount paid by the United States to the contractor under the contract with respect to any aircraft if—

''(A) the aircraft is destroyed or becomes unusable, as defined in the contract;

''(B) the cargo-convertible features specified in the contract are rendered unusable or removed from the aircraft;

''(C) control over the aircraft is transferred to any person that is unable or unwilling to assume the contractor's obligations under the contract;

''(D) the registration of the aircraft under section 501 of the Federal Aviation Act of 1958 is terminated for any reason not beyond the control of the contractor; or

''(E) having agreed in the contract that the main deck of the aircraft will not be used for cargo air service, the contractor uses, or permits the use of, the main deck of the aircraft for cargo air service.

''(c) A contract made under subsection (a) with respect to any aircraft may include the following terms:

''(1) If the contractor agrees that the main deck of the aircraft will not be used in cargo air service, the Secretary may agree to pay the contractor—

''(A) an amount not to exceed 100 percent of the cost of modifying the aircraft to include or incorporate cargo-convertible features suitable for defense purposes in that aircraft, as described in subsection (a);

''(B) an amount to compensate the contractor for the loss of use of the aircraft during the time required to make such modification, such amount to be determined by taking into consideration the fair market rental cost of a similar aircraft (not including crews, ground facilities, or other support costs) for that time, the estimated loss of revenue by the contractor attributable to the aircraft being out of service during that time, and such other factors as the Secretary considers appropriate; and

''(C) in the case of an existing aircraft, 100 percent of the cost of positioning the aircraft for modification, recertification of that aircraft after modification, returning that aircraft to service, and other costs directly associated with the modification.

''(2) If the contractor does not agree that the main deck of the aircraft will not be used for cargo air service, the Secretary may agree to pay the contractor an amount not to exceed 50 percent of the cost of modifying the aircraft to include or incorporate cargo-convertible features suitable for defense purposes.

''(3) The Secretary may under the contract be authorized to contract directly with a person chosen by the contractor to perform the modification of the aircraft to include or incorporate cargo-convertible features suitable for defense purposes in that aircraft and to pay to that person chosen by the contractor—

''(A) if the contractor agrees that the main deck of that aircraft will not be used for cargo air service, an amount less than or equal to the amount to which the contractor would otherwise be entitled under paragraph (1)(A); or

''(B) if the contractor does not agree that the main deck of that aircraft will not be used for cargo air service, an amount less than or equal to the amount to which the contractor would otherwise be entitled to under paragraph (2).

''(d) In addition to any amount the Secretary may agree under subsection (c)(1) or (c)(3)(A) to pay under a contract made under subsection (a), the Secretary may agree under such a contract that, if the contractor agrees that the main deck of the aircraft will not be used in cargo air service, the Secretary shall make a lump sum or annual payments (or a combination thereof) to the contractor to cover any increased costs of operation or any loss of revenue attributable to the inclusion or incorporation of cargo-convertible features suitable for defense purposes in the aircraft.

''(e)(1) Subject to paragraph (2), the Secretary may agree, in any contract made under subsection (a), to pay the contractor an amount for any loss resulting from the subsequent sale of an aircraft modified under that contract if the sale of that aircraft is for a price less than the fair market value, at the time of the sale, of an aircraft substantially similar to the aircraft being sold but without the cargo-convertible features.

''(2) The Secretary may not agree to make a payment under this subsection with respect to the sale of a modified aircraft unless—

''(A) the sale is within 16 years and 6 months after the modified aircraft was initially delivered by the manufacturer to its original owner, in the case of an aircraft that was modified during manufacture, or by the modifier to the owner at the time of modification, in the case of an aircraft that was modified after manufacture;

''(B) the Secretary received written notice of the proposed sale at least 60 days before the sale;

''(C) the contractor used its best efforts to obtain bids for the purchase of the aircraft;

''(D) the sale is a bona fide, arm's length transaction made to the highest bidder for a price that is less than the fair market value of an aircraft substantially similar to the modified aircraft but without the cargo-convertible features; and

''(E) before the sale the Secretary was given an opportunity to and refused to purchase the modified aircraft for a price equal to the fair market value, at the time of the sale, of an aircraft substantially similar to the modified aircraft but without the cargo-convertible features.

''(3) Any amount that may be payable under a contract provision made under this subsection may not exceed the difference between (A) the sales price of the modified aircraft, and (B) the fair market value, at the time of the sale, of an aircraft substantially similar to the modified aircraft but without the cargo-convertible features included or incorporated into the modified aircraft under the contract.

''(4) The Secretary may use any funds appropriated for Air Force procurement for fiscal year 1982 or thereafter to pay any obligation under a contract provision made under this subsection.''.

1994. Act July 5, 1994, in subsec. (b)(4), substituted ''section 44103 of title 49'' for ''section 501 of the Federal Aviation Act of 1958 (49 U.S.C. App. 1401)''.

Act Oct. 13, 1994 (effective and applicable as provided by § 10001(a) and (b) of such Act, which appear as 41 USCS § 251 note), in subsec. (a), added the subsection heading; redesignated subsecs. (b) and (c) as subsecs. (c) and (d), respectively, and added the subsection headings; and redesignated subsecs. (a) and (b) of former 10 USCS § 9513 as subsecs. (b) and (e), respectively, transferred them to this section, and added the subsection headings.

Such Act further (effective and applicable as above), in subsec. (b) as redesignated, substituted ''entered into under this section'' for ''under section 9512 of this title''; in subsec. (c) as redesignated, deleted ''the terms required by section 9513 of this title and'' following ''(a) shall include''; and, in subsec. (e) as redesignated, substituted ''entered into under this section'' for ''under section 9512 of this title''.

1996. Act Feb. 10, 1996, in subsec. (b)(2), substituted ''Civil Reserve Air Fleet'' for ''full Civil Reserve Air Fleet''; and, in subsec. (e), substituted ''Civil Reserve Air Fleet'' for ''full Civil Reserve Air Fleet'' preceding ''unless''.

CROSS REFERENCES

This section is referred to in 10 USCS § 9511.

§ 9513. Use of military installations by Civil Reserve Air Fleet contractors

(a) Contract authority. (1) The Secretary of the Air Force—

(A) may, by contract entered into with any contractor, authorize such contractor to use one or more Air Force installations designated by the Secretary; and

(B) with the consent of the Secretary of another military department, may, by contract entered into with any contractor, authorize the contractor to use one or more installations, designated by the Secretary of the Air Force, that is under the jurisdiction of the Secretary of such other military department.

(2) The Secretary of the Air Force may include in the contract such terms and conditions as the Secretary determines appropriate to promote the national defense or to protect the interests of the United States.

(b) Purposes of use. A contract entered into under subsection (a) may authorize use of a designated installation as a weather alternate, as a technical stop not involving the enplaning or deplaning of passengers or cargo, or, in the case of an installation within the United States, for other commercial purposes. Notwithstanding any other provision of the law, the Secretary may establish different levels and types of uses for different installations for commercial operations not required by the Department of Defense and may provide in contracts under subsection (a) for different levels and types of uses by different contractors.

(c) Disposition of payments for use. Notwithstanding any other provision of law, amounts collected from the contractor for landing fees, services, supplies, or other charges authorized to be collected under the contract shall be credited to the appropriations of the armed forces having jurisdiction over the military installation to which the contract pertains. Amounts so credited to an appropriation shall be available for obligation for the same period as the appropriation to which credited.

(d) Hold harmless requirement. A contract entered into under subsection (a) shall provide that the contractor agrees to indemnify and hold harmless the United States from any action, suit, or claim of any sort resulting from, relating to, or arising out of any activities conducted, or services or supplies furnished, in connection with the contract.

(e) Reservation of right to exclude contractor. A contract entered into under subsection (a) shall provide that the Secretary concerned may, without providing prior notice, deny access to an installation designated under the contract when the Secretary determines that it is necessary to do so in order to meet military exigencies.

(Added Oct. 13, 1994, P. L. 103-355, Title III, Subtitle D, § 3033(a), 108 Stat. 3335.)

HISTORY; ANCILLARY LAWS AND DIRECTIVES

Explanatory notes:

Subsecs. (a) and (b) of a former § 9513 (Act Dec. 1, 1981, P. L. 97-86, Title IX, § 915(2), 95 Stat. 1128; Nov. 29, 1989, P. L. 101-189, Div A, Title XVI, Part D, § 1636(c)(1), 103 Stat. 1610) were redesignated subsecs. (b) and (e), respectively, and transferred to 10 USCS § 9512 by Act Oct. 13, 1994, P. L. 103-355, Title III, Subtitle D, § 3032(4), (5), 108 Stat. 3335, and the heading of the former § 9513 was deleted by § 3032(9) of such Act.

Effective date of section:
This section takes effect upon enactment, subject to certain provisions relating to promulgation of implementing regulations, as provided by § 10001(a) and (b) of Act Oct. 13, 1994, P. L. 103-355, which appear as 41 USCS § 251 note.

Other provisions:
Applicability of section. For provisions relating to applicability of this section, see § 10001(b) of Act Oct. 13, 1994, P. L. 103-355, which appears as 41 USCS § 251 note.

§ 9514. Indemnification of Department of Transportation for losses covered by defense-related aviation insurance

(a) Prompt indemnification required. (1) In the event of a loss that is covered by defense-related aviation insurance, the Secretary of Defense shall promptly indemnify the Secretary of Transportation for the amount of the loss consistent with the indemnification agreement between the two Secretaries that underlies such insurance. The Secretary of Defense shall make such indemnification—

(A) in the case of a claim for the loss of an aircraft hull, not later than 30 days after the date on which the Secretary of Transportation determines the claim to be payable or that amounts are due under the policy that provided the defense-related aviation insurance; and

(B) in the case of any other claim, not later than 180 days after the date on which the Secretary of Transportation determines the claim to be payable.

(2) When there is a loss of an aircraft hull that is (or may be) covered by defense-related aviation insurance, the Secretary of Transportation may make, during the period when a claim for such loss is pending with the Secretary of Transportation, any required periodic payments owed by the insured party to a lessor or mortgagee of such aircraft. Such payments shall commence not later than 30 days following the date of the presentment of the claim for the loss of the aircraft hull to the Secretary of Transportation. If the Secretary of Transportation determines that the claim is payable, any amount paid under this paragraph arising from such claim shall be credited against the amount payable under the aviation insurance. If the Secretary of Transportation determines that the claim is not payable, any amount paid under this paragraph arising from such claim shall constitute a debt to the United States, payable to the insurance fund. Any such amounts so returned to the United States shall be promptly credited to the fund or account from which the payments were made under this paragraph.

(b) Source of funds for payment of indemnity. The Secretary of Defense may pay an indemnity described in subsection (a) from any funds available to the Department of Defense for operation and maintenance, and such sums as may be necessary for payment of such indemnity are hereby authorized to be transferred to the Secretary of Transportation for such purpose.

(c) Notice to Congress. In the event of a loss that is covered by defense-related aviation insurance in the case of an incident in which the covered loss is (or is expected to be) in an amount in excess of $1,000,000, the Secretary of Defense shall submit to Congress—

(1) notification of the loss as soon after the occurrence of the loss as possible and in no event more than 30 days after the date of the loss; and

(2) semiannual reports thereafter updating the information submitted under paragraph (1) and showing with respect to losses arising from such incident the total amount expended to cover such losses, the source of those funds, pending litigation, and estimated total cost to the Government.

(d) Implementing matters. (1) Payment of indemnification under this section is not subject to section 2214 or 2215 of this title or any other provision of law requiring notification to Congress before funds may be transferred.

(2) Consolidation of claims arising from the same incident is not required before indemnification of the Secretary of Transportation for payment of a claim may be made under this section.

(e) Construction with other transfer authority. Authority to transfer funds under this section is in addition to any other authority provided by law to transfer funds (whether enacted before, on, or after the date of the enactment of this section [enacted Sept. 23, 1996) and is not subject to any dollar limitation or notification requirement contained in any other such authority to transfer funds.

(f) Annual report on contingent liabilities. Not later than March 1 of each year, the Secretary of Defense shall submit to Congress a report setting forth the current amount of the contingent outstanding liability of the United States under the insurance program under chapter 443 of title 49 [49 USCS §§ 44301 et seq.].

(g) Definitions. In this section:

(1) Defense-related aviation insurance. The term ''defense-related aviation insurance'' means aviation insurance and reinsurance provided through policies issued by the Secretary of Transportation under chapter 443 of title 49 [49 USCS §§ 44301 et seq.] that pursuant to section 44305(b) of that title is provided by that Secretary without premium at the request of the Secretary of Defense and is covered by an indemnity agreement between the Secretary of Transportation and the Secretary of Defense.

(2) Loss. The term ''loss'' includes damage to or destruction of property, personal injury or death, and other liabilities and expenses covered by the defense-related aviation insurance

(Added Sept. 23, 1996, P. L. 104-201, Div A, Title X, Subtitle F, § 1079(a)(1), 110 Stat. 2667.)

CHAPTER 933. PROCUREMENT

HISTORY; ANCILLARY LAWS AND DIRECTIVES

Amendments:

1982. Act Sept. 13, 1982, P. L. 97-258, § 2(b)(13)(A), 96 Stat. 1058, amended the analysis of this chapter by adding the item relating to section 9541.

1993. Act Nov. 30, 1993, P. L. 103-160, Div A, Title VIII, Subtitle C, § 828(a)(9), 107 Stat. 1713, amended the analysis of this chapter by deleting items 9531, 9534, 9535, 9537, 9538, and 9541, which read: ''9531. Authorization.'', ''9534. Subsistence supplies: contract stipulations; place of delivery on inspection.'', ''9535. Exceptional subsistence supplies: purchases without advertising.'', ''9537. Military surveys and maps: assistance of United States mapping agencies.'', ''9538. Unserviceable ammunition: exchange and reclamation.'', and ''9541. Gratuitous services of officers of the Air Force Reserve.''.

[§ 9531. Repealed]

HISTORY; ANCILLARY LAWS AND DIRECTIVES

This section (Act Aug. 10, 1956, ch 1041, § 1, 70A Stat. 575) was repealed by Act Nov. 30, 1993, P. L. 103-160, Div A, Title VIII, Subtitle C, § 823(2), 107 Stat. 1707. This section related to procurement authorization.

§ 9532. Factories, arsenals, and depots: manufacture at

The Secretary of the Air Force may have supplies needed for the Department of the Air Force made in factories, arsenals, or depots owned by the United States, so far as those factories, arsenals, or depots can make those supplies on an economical basis.

(Aug. 10, 1956, ch 1041, § 1, 70A Stat. 576.)

HISTORY; ANCILLARY LAWS AND DIRECTIVES

Prior law and revision:

Revised Section	Source (USCS)	Source (Statutes at Large)
9532	5:626-2(e).	Sept. 19, 1951, ch. 407, § 101(e), 65 Stat. 327.

The word ''made'' is substituted for the words ''manufactured or produced''. The words ''United States'' are substituted for the word ''Government''.

[§§ 9534, 9535. Repealed]

HISTORY; ANCILLARY LAWS AND DIRECTIVES

These sections (Act Aug. 10, 1956, ch 1041, § 1, 70A Stat. 576) were repealed by Act Nov. 30, 1993, P. L. 103-160, Div A, Title VIII, Subtitle C, § 823(4), 107 Stat. 1707. Section 9534 provided for subsistence supplies, contract stipulations, and place of delivery on inspection; and § 9535 provided for purchases of exceptional subsistence supplies without advertising.

§ 9536. Equipment: bakeries, schools, kitchens, and mess halls

Money necessary for the following items for the use of enlisted members of the Air Force may be spent from appropriations for regular supplies:

(1) Equipment for air base bakeries.

(2) Furniture, textbooks, paper, and equipment for air base schools.

(3) Tableware and mess furniture for kitchens and mess halls.

(Aug. 10, 1956, ch 1041, § 1, 70A Stat. 576.)

HISTORY; ANCILLARY LAWS AND DIRECTIVES

Prior law and revision:

Revised Section	Source (USCS)	Source (Statutes at Large)
9536	10:1334.	June 13, 1890, ch. 423 (1st proviso under ''Quartermaster's Department''), 26 Stat. 152.

The words ''Money necessary . . . may be spent'' are substituted for the words ''There may be expended . . . the amounts required''. The word ''bakeries'' is substituted for the words ''bake house to carry on post bakeries''. The words ''each and all'' are omitted as surplusage.

[§§ 9537, 9538. Repealed]

HISTORY; ANCILLARY LAWS AND DIRECTIVES

These sections (§ 9537–Act Aug. 10, 1956, ch 1041, § 1, 70A Stat. 576; Act Nov. 2, 1966, P. L. 89-718, § 8(a), 80 Stat. 1117; Dec. 12, 1980, P. L. 96-513, Title V, Part B, § 514(13), 94 Stat. 2936; Oct. 12, 1982, P. L. 97-295, § 6(b), 96 Stat. 1314; § 9538–Act Aug. 10, 1956, ch 1041, § 1, 70A Stat. 576; Dec. 12, 1980, P. L. 96-513, Title V, Part B, § 514(14), 94 Stat. 2936) were repealed by Act Nov. 30, 1993, P. L. 103-160, Div A, Title VIII, Subtitle C, § 823(6), 107 Stat. 1707. Section 9537 related to assistance of United States mapping agencies with military surveys and maps;

and § 9538 provided for exchange and reclamation of unserviceable ammunition.

§ 9540. Architectural and engineering services

(a) Whenever he considers that it is advantageous to the national defense and that existing facilities of the Department of the Air Force are inadequate, the Secretary of the Air Force are inadequate, the Secretary of the Air Force may, by contract or otherwise, employ the architectural or engineering services of any person outside that Department for producing and delivering designs, plans, drawings, and specifications needed for any public works or utilities project of the Department.

(b) The fee for any service under this section may not be more than 6 percent of the estimated cost, as determined by the Secretary, of the project to which it applies.

(c) Sections 305, 3324, and 7204, chapter 51, and subchapters III, IV, and VI of chapter 53 of title 5 [5 USCS §§ 305, 3324, 7204, 5101 et seq., 5331 et seq., 5341 et seq., 5361 et seq.] do not apply to employment under this section.

(Aug. 10, 1956, ch 1041, § 1, 70A Stat. 577; Nov. 2, 1966, P. L. 89-718, § 28, 80 Stat. 1119; Oct. 13, 1978, P. L. 95-454, Title VII, § 703(c)(3), Title VIII, § 801(a)(3)(I), 92 Stat. 1217, 1222; Dec. 12, 1980, P. L. 96-513, Title V, Part B, § 514(15), 94 Stat. 2936.)

HISTORY; ANCILLARY LAWS AND DIRECTIVES

Prior law and revision:

Revised Section	Source (USCS)	Source (Statutes at Large)
9540(a)	5:221 (1st sentence, less last 15 words).	Aug. 7, 1939, ch. 511, § 2, 53 Stat. 1240.
9540(b)	5:221 (less 1st sentence).	
9540(c)	5:221 (last 15 words of 1st sentence).	

In subsection (a), the words "and providing that in the opinion" are omitted as covered by the words "whenever he considers". The words "needed for" are substituted for the words "required for the accomplishment of".

In subsection (c), reference is made in substance to the Classification Act of 1949, instead of the Classification Act of 1923 referred to in the source statute, since section 1106(a) of the Classification Act of 1949, 63 Stat. 972, provides that all references in other acts to the Classification Act of 1923 should be considered to refer to the Classification Act of 1949.

Amendments:

1966. Act Nov. 2, 1966, in subsec. (c), substituted "305, 3324, 5101– 5115, 5331–5338, 5341, 5342, and 7154" for "1071–1153".

1978. Act Oct. 13, 1978, in subsec. (c), (effective 90 days after 10/13/78, as provided by § 907 of such Act, which appears as 10 USCS § 1101 note), substituted "7204" for "7154"; and, (effective on the first day of the first applicable pay period beginning on or after the 90th day after 10/13/78, as provided by § 801(a)(4)(A) of such Act, which appears as 5 USCS § 5361 note), inserted "and subchapter VI of chapter 53 of such title 5".

1980. Act Dec. 12, 1980 (effective upon enactment on 12/12/80, as provided by § 701(b)(3) of such Act, which appears as 10 USCS § 101 note), in subsec. (c), substituted "and 7204, chapter 51, and subchapters III, IV, and VI of chapter 53 of title 5" for "5101–5115, 5331–5338, 5341, 5342, and 7204 of title 5 and subchapter VI of chapter 53 of such title 5".

RESEARCH GUIDE

Am Jur:

64 Am Jur 2d, Public Works and Contracts §§ 3, 9, 11, 91.

[§ 9541. Repealed]

HISTORY; ANCILLARY LAWS AND DIRECTIVES

This section (Added Sept. 13, 1982, P. L. 97-258, § 2(b)(13)(B), 96 Stat. 1058) was repealed by Act Nov. 30, 1993, P. L. 103-160, Div A, Title VIII, Subtitle C, § 822(d)(2), 107 Stat. 1707. This section provided for gratuitous services of officers of the Air Force Reserve. For similar provisions, see 10 USCS § 10212.

CHAPTER 935. ISSUE OF SERVICEABLE MATERIAL TO ARMED FORCES

§ 9561. Rations

(a) The President may prescribe the components, and the quantities thereof, of the Air Force ration. He may direct the issue of equivalent articles in place of the prescribed components whenever, in his opinion, economy and the health and comfort of the members of the Air Force so require.

(b) An enlisted member of the Air Force on active duty is entitled to one ration daily. The emergency ration, when issued, is in addition to the regular ration.

(c) Fresh or preserved fruits, milk, butter, and eggs necessary for the proper diet of the sick in hospitals shall be provided under regulations approved by the Secretary.

(Aug. 10, 1956, ch 1041, § 1, 70A Stat. 577.)

HISTORY; ANCILLARY LAWS AND DIRECTIVES

Prior law and revision:

Revised Section	Source (USCS)	Source (Statutes at Large)
9561(a)	10:724.	Feb 2, 1901, ch. 192, § 40, 31 Stat. 758.
9561(b)	10:716b. 10:725.	
9561(c)	10:726.	R.S. 1293, July 16, 1892, ch. 195 (last 15 words before proviso under "Subsistence of the Army"), 27 Stat. 178. Mar. 2, 1907, ch. 2511 (1st proviso under "Subsistence Department"), 34 Stat. 1165. R.S. 1175.

In subsection (a), the words "the components, and the quantities thereof" are substituted for the words "the kinds and quantities of the component articles''. The words ''substitutive'' and ''a due regard'' are omitted as surplusage.

In subsection (b), the words ''on active duty'' are inserted for clarity. The words ''under such regulations as may be prescribed by the Secretary of the Army'', in 10:725, are omitted, since the Secretary has inherent authority to issue regulations appropriate to exercising his statutory functions. The words ''or reserve'', ''prescribed for use on emergent occasions'', and ''furnished'', in 10:725, are omitted as surplusage.

In subsection (c), the words ''as the Surgeon General'' are omitted, since the Air Force does not have the statutory office of Surgeon General, and functions which, for the Army, are assigned by statute to subordinate officers of the Army are, for the Air Force, assigned to the Secretary of the Air Force. The words ''Such quantities of'' and ''may be allowed'' are omitted as surplusage.

Other provisions:

Delegation of authority. Authority of President under 10 USCS § 9561(a) to prescribe uniform military ration applicable to Air Force delegated to Secretary of defense, see Ex. Or. No. 12781, Nov. 20, 1991, § 3(a), 56 Fed. Reg. 59203, which appears as 3 USCS § 301 note.

§ 9562. Clothing

The President may prescribe the quantity and kind of clothing to be issued annually to members of the Air Force.

(Aug. 10, 1956, ch 1041, § 1, 70A Stat. 577.)

HISTORY; ANCILLARY LAWS AND DIRECTIVES

Prior law and revision:

Revised Section	Source (USCS)	Source (Statutes at Large)
9562	10:831.	R.S. 1296 (less 1st 9 words).

The words ''members of the Air Force'' are substituted for the words ''troops of the United States''.

CROSS REFERENCES

Uniforms, general military law provisions, 10 USCS §§ 771 et seq.

§ 9563. Clothing: replacement when destroyed to prevent contagion

The Secretary of the Air Force may order a gratuitous issue of clothing to any enlisted member of the Air Force who has had a contagious disease, and to any hospital attendant who attended him while he had that disease, to replace clothing destroyed by order of a medical officer to prevent contagion.

(Aug. 10, 1956, ch 1041, § 1, 70A Stat. 577.)

HISTORY; ANCILLARY LAWS AND DIRECTIVES

Prior law and revision:

Revised Section	Source (USCS)	Source (Statutes at Large)
9563	10:834.	R.S. 1298.

The words "enlisted member" are substituted for the word "soldiers". The words "any articles of their" are omitted as surplusage. The words "while he had that disease" are inserted for clarity. The words "a medical officer" are substituted for the words "proper medical officers". The words "on the recommendation of the Surgeon General" are omitted, since the Air Force does not have the statutory office of Surgeon General, and functions which, for the Army, are assigned by statute to subordinate officers of the Army are, for the Air Force, assigned to the Secretary of the Air Force.

§ 9564. Navy and Marine Corps: camp equipment and transportation; when on shore duty with Air Force

While any detachment of the Navy or Marine Corps is on shore duty in cooperation with troops of the Air Force, the Secretary of the Air Force shall, upon the requisition of the officer of the Navy or Marine Corps in command of the detachment, issue rations and camp equipment, and furnish transportation, to that detachment.

(Aug. 10, 1956, ch 1041, § 1, 70A Stat. 578.)

HISTORY; ANCILLARY LAWS AND DIRECTIVES

Prior law and revision:

Revised Section	Source (USCS)	Source (Statutes at Large)
9564	10:1295d. 10:1259e.	R.S. 1143; June 28, 1950, ch. 383, § 402(a), 64 Stat. 272. R.S. 1135; June 28, 1950, ch. 383, s 402(a), 64 Stat. 272.

The words "While . . . on shore duty" are substituted for the words "under orders to act on shore", in 10:1259d and 1259e, and 34:541. The words "the Secretary of the Air Force" are substituted for the words "the branch, office, or officers of the Army, the Secretary of the Army may from time to time designate", in 10:1259d and 1259e, and 34:541, since the functions which, for the Army, are assigned by statute to subordinate officers of the Army, are, for the Air Force, assigned to the Secretary of the Air Force. The words "during the time such detachment is so acting or proceeding to act", in 10:1259d and 1259e, and 34:541, are omitted as surplusage. The words "their baggage, provisions, and cannon", in 10:1259e and 34:541, are omitted as surplusage. The words "and shall furnish the naval officer commanding any such detachment, and his necessary aides, with horses, accouterments, and forage'', in 10:1259e and 35:541, are omitted as obsolete.

§ 9565. Colors, standards, and guidons of demobilized organizations: disposition

(a) The Secretary of the Air Force may dispose of colors, standards, and guidons of demobilized organizations of the Air Force, as follows:

(1) Those brought into Federal service by the Air National Guard of a State may be returned to that State upon the request of its governor.

(2) Those that cannot be returned under clause (1) may, upon the request of its governor, be sent to the State that, as determined by the Secretary, furnished the majority of members of the organization when it was formed.

Those that cannot be returned or sent under clause (1) or (2) of this subsection shall be delivered to the Secretary, for such national use as he may direct.

(b) Title to colors, standards, and guidons of demobilized organizations of the Air Force remains in the United States.

(c) No color, standard, or guidon may be disposed of under this section unless provision satisfactory to the Secretary has been made for its preservation and care.

(Aug. 10, 1956, ch 1041, § 1, 70A Stat. 578.)

HISTORY; ANCILLARY LAWS AND DIRECTIVES

Prior law and revision:

Revised Section	Source (USCS)	Source (Statutes at Large)
9565(a)	5:202 (less 3d and last sentences).	Mar. 4, 1921, ch. 166, § 2, 41 Stat. 1438.
9565(a)	5:202 (3d sentence).	
9565(c)	5:202 (last sentence).	

In subsection (a), the words ''Any which were used during their service by such organizations and'' are omitted as surplusage. The first 15 words of the last sentence are substituted for 5:202 (1st 45 words of 2d sentence). The words ''the Quartermaster General'' are omitted, since the functions which, for the Army, are assigned by statute to subordinate officers of the Army, are, for the Air Force, assigned to the Secretary of the Air Force.

CHAPTER 937. UTILITIES AND SERVICES

Section
9591. Utilities: proceeds from overseas operations
9592. Radiograms and telegrams: forwarding charges due connecting commercial facilities
9593. Quarters: heat and light

§ 9591. Utilities: proceeds from overseas operations

During actual or threatened hostilities, proceeds from operating a public utility in connection with operations of the Air Force in the field overseas are available for that utility until the close of the fiscal year following that in which they are received.

(Aug. 10, 1956, ch 1041, § 1, 70A Stat. 578.)

HISTORY; ANCILLARY LAWS AND DIRECTIVES

Prior law and revision:

Revised Section	Source (USCS)	Source (Statutes at Large)
9591	10:1287.	July 9, 1918, ch. 143, subch. XX (1st para.), 40 Stat. 893; May 29, 1928, ch. 901 (para. 37), 45 Stat. 989; Aug. 1, 1953, ch. 305, § 645 (7th cl.), 67 Stat. 357.

The words ''Air Force'' are substituted for the word ''Engineer'', since the Air Force does not have organic corps created by statute.

§ 9592. Radiograms and telegrams: forwarding charges due connecting commercial facilities

In the operation of telegraph lines, cables, or radio stations, members of the Air Force may, in the discretion of the Secretary of the Air Force, collect forwarding charges due connecting commercial telegraph or radio companies for sending radiograms or telegrams over their lines. Under such regulations as the Secretary may prescribe, they may present a voucher to a disbursing official for payment of the forwarding charge.

(Aug. 10, 1956, ch 1041, § 1, 70A Stat. 578; Sept. 13, 1982, P. L. 97-258, § 2(b)(1)(A) in part, 96 Stat. 1052; Oct. 19, 1996, P. L. 104-316, Title I, § 105(e), 110 Stat. 3830.)

HISTORY; ANCILLARY LAWS AND DIRECTIVES

Prior law and revision:

Revised Section	Source (USCS)	Source (Statutes at Large)
9592	10:1319.	May 12, 1917, ch. 12 (proviso under ''Washington-Alaska military Cable and Telegraph System''), 40 Stat. 43.

The words ''members of the Air Force'' are substituted for the words ''Signal Corps'', since the Air Force does not have organic corps created by statute. The words ''Government'', ''and to this end'', ''as may be'', and ''amount of such'' are omitted as surplusage.

Amendments:

1982. Act Sept. 13, 1982 substituted ''official'' for ''officer''.

1996. Act Oct. 19, 1996 (effective on enactment, as provided by § 101(e) of such Act, which appears as 2 USCS § 130c note) substituted ''of'' for '', or may file a claim with the General Accounting Office for'' following ''payment''.

CROSS REFERENCES

Conclusiveness of balances certified by Comptroller, 10 USCS § 9842; 31 USCS § 3526.

§ 9593. Quarters: heat and light

The heat and light necessary for the authorized quarters of members of the Air Force shall be furnished at the expense of the United States.

(Aug. 10, 1956, ch 1041, § 1, 70A Stat. 578.)

HISTORY; ANCILLARY LAWS AND DIRECTIVES

Prior law and revision:

Revised Section	Source (USCS)	Source (Statutes at Large)
9593	10:723.	Mar. 2, 1907, ch. 2511 (1st proviso under ''Quartermaster's Department''), 34 Stat. 1167.

The word ''members'' is substituted for the words ''officers and enlisted men''. The words ''under such regulations as the Secretary of the Army may prescribe'' are omitted, since the Secretary has inherent authority to issue regulations appropriate to exercising his statutory functions.

Other provisions:

Excess energy consumption charges. For regulations, proceeds, deposit in account, applicability, and test program regarding excess consumption of energy, see Act Aug. 1, 1977, P. L. 95-82, Title V, § 507, 91 Stat. 372, set out at 10 USCS § 4593 note.

CHAPTER 939. SALE OF SERVICEABLE MATERIAL

Section
9621. Subsistence and other supplies: members of armed forces; veterans; executive or military departments and employees; prices
9622. Rations: commissioned officers in field
9623. Tobacco: enlisted members of Air Force
9624. Medical supplies: civilian employees of the Air Force; American National Red Cross; Armed Forces Retirement Home
9625. Ordnance property: officers of armed forces; civilian employees of Air Force; American National Red Cross; educational institutions; homes for veterans' orphans
9626. Aircraft supplies and services: foreign military or air attaché
9627. Supplies: educational institutions
9628. Airplane parts and accessories: civilian flying schools
9629. Proceeds: disposition

HISTORY; ANCILLARY LAWS AND DIRECTIVES

Amendments:

1980. Act Dec. 12, 1980, P.L. 96-513, Title V, Part B, § 514(17)(c), 94 Stat. 2936 (effective upon enactment on 12/12/80, as provided by § 701(b)(3) of such Act, which appears as 10 USCS § 101 note), amended the analysis of this chapter in item 9624 by inserting "the" and "and Airmen's".

1990. Act Nov. 5, 1990, P. L. 101-510, Div A, Title XV, Part B, § 1533(a)(8)(C), 104 Stat. 1735, effective 1 year after enactment as provided by § 1541(a), which appears as 24 USCS 401 note, amended the analysis of this chapter by substituting item 9624 for one which read: "9624. Medical supplies: civilian employees of the Air Force; American National Red Cross; Soldiers' and Airmen's Home.".

§ 9621. Subsistence and other supplies: members of armed forces; veterans; executive or military departments and employees; prices

(a) The Secretary of the Air Force shall procure and sell, for cash or credit—

(1) articles designated by him, to members of the Air Force; and

(2) items of individual clothing and equipment, to officers of the Air Force, under such restrictions as the Secretary may prescribe.

An account of sales on credit shall be kept and the amount due reported to the Secretary. Except for articles and items acquired through the use of working capital funds under section 2208 of this title, sales of articles shall be at cost, and sales of individual clothing and equipment shall be at average current prices, including overhead, as determined by the Secretary.

(b) The Secretary shall sell subsistence supplies to members of other armed forces at the prices at which like property is sold to members of the Air Force.

(c) The Secretary may sell serviceable quartermaster property, other than subsistence supplies, to an officer of another armed force for his use in the service, in the same manner as these articles are sold to an officer of the Air Force.

(d) A person who has been discharged honorably or under honorable conditions from the Army, Navy, Air Force, or Marine Corps and who is receiving care and medical treatment from the Public Health Service or the Veterans' Administration may buy subsistence supplies and other supplies, except articles of uniform, at the prices at which like property is sold to a member of the Air Force.

(e) Under such conditions as the Secretary may prescribe, exterior articles of uniform may be sold to a person who has been discharged from the Air Force honorably or under honorable conditions, at the prices at which like articles are sold to members of the Air Force. This subsection does not modify section 772 or 773 of this title.

(f) Whenever, under regulations to be prescribed by the Secretary, subsistence supplies are furnished to any organization of the Air Force or sold to employees of any executive department other than the Department of Defense, payment shall be made in cash or by commercial credit.

(g) The Secretary may, by regulation, provide for the procurement and sale of stores designated by him to such civilian officers and employees of the United States, and such other persons, as he considers proper—

(1) at military installations outside the United States; and

(2) at military installations inside the United States where he determines that it is impracticable for those civilian officers, employees, and persons to obtain those stores from private agencies without impairing the efficient operation of military activities.

However, sales to those officers and employees inside the United States may be made only to those residing within military installations.

(h) Appropriations for subsistence of the Air Force may be applied to the purchase of subsistence supplies for sale to members of the Air Force on active duty for the use of themselves and their families.

(Aug. 10, 1956, ch 1041, § 1, 70A Stat. 579; Sept. 7, 1962, P. L. 87-651, Title I, § 118, 76 Stat. 513; Dec. 12, 1980, P. L. 96-513, Title V, Part B, § 514(16), 94 Stat. 2936; July 10, 1981, P. L. 97-22, § 11(a)(11), 95 Stat. 138; Dec. 4, 1987, P. L. 100-180, Div A, Title III, Part B, § 313(c), 101 Stat. 1074; Nov. 29, 1989, P. L. 101-189, Div A, Title XVI, Part C, § 1621(a)(1), 103 Stat. 1602; Feb. 10, 1996, P. L. 104-106, Div A, Title III, Subtitle G, § 375(b)(2), 110 Stat. 283.)

HISTORY; ANCILLARY LAWS AND DIRECTIVES

Prior law and revision:

1956 ACT

Revised Section	Source (USCS)	Source (Statutes at Large)
9621(a)	10:904.	Aug. 31, 1918, ch. 166, § 9
	10:1231.	(less 17th through 22d
	10:1237.	words), 40 Stat. 957.
	32:156.	R.S. 1144; June 28, 1950,
9621(b)	10:1238.	ch. 333, § 402(a), 64
		Stat.
9621(c)	10:1233.	272.
9621(d)	10:1234.	June 3, 1916, ch. 134,
	34:539.	§ 109; restated June 4,
9621(e)	10:1235.	1920, ch. 227, subch. I,
9621(f)	10:1395 (less last	§ 47; restated June 3,
	sentence).	1924, ch. 244, § 3; re
9621(g)	10:1253.	stated Oct. 14, 1940, ch.
9621(h)	10:1241.	875, § 3, 54 Stat. 1136;
9621(i)	10:1196.	Mar. 25, 1948, ch. 157,
		§ 5(b), 62 Stat. 91; Oct.
		12, 1949, ch. 681,
		§ 501(f)(2) and (3) (as
		applicable to § 109 of the
		Act of June 3, 1916, ch.
		134), 63 Stat. 827; July
		9, 1952, ch. 608, § 803
		(12th para.), 66 Stat. 505.
		June 30, 1942, ch. 253,
		title I (last proviso under
		''Clothing and
		Equipage''), 42 Stat. 729.
		July 5, 1884, ch. 217 (pro-
		viso under ''Subsistence
		of the Army''), 23 Stat.
		108.
		Aug. 29, 1916, ch. 418
		(words before semicolon
		of 3d proviso under
		''Subsistence of the
		Army''), 39 Stat. 630.
		Mar. 4, 1915, ch. 143 (last
		proviso under Clothing,
		and Camp and Garrison
		Equipage''), 38 Stat.
		1079; June 28, 1950, ch.
		383, § 402(k), 64 Stat.
		273.

Revised Section	Source (USCS)	Source (Statutes at Large)
		June 5, 1920, ch. 240 (para. under ''Purchase of Army Stores by Discharged Receiving Treatment from the Public Health Service''), 41 Stat. 976.
		Feb. 14, 1927, ch. 134 (less last sentence), 44 Stat. 1096.
		Mar. 3, 1911, ch. 209 (last para. under ''Subsistence Department''), 36 Stat. 1047.
		Aug. 8, 1953, ch. 390, § 1, 67 Stat. 499.
		Mar. 1875, ch. 131 (proviso of 1st sentence of 1st para. under ''War Department''), 18 Stat. 410.

In subsection (a), the word ''members'' is substituted for the words ''officers and enlisted men'', in 10:1237. Cl. 92) is substituted for 10:904. Reference to the Secretary of the Air Force is substituted for reference to branch, office, or officers of the Army, in 10:1237, since the functions which, for the Army are assigned to subordinate officers, are, for the Air Force assigned to the Secretary of the Air Force. 32:156 is omitted as covered by 10:904, since the words ''officers of the Air Force'' necessarily cover all persons named in 32:156. The words ''Except for articles and items acquired through the use of working capital funds under sections 172–172j of title 5'' are inserted to reflect Title IV of the National Security Act of 1947, as amended (63 Stat. 585), which authorized the Secretary of Defense to prescribe regulations governing the use and sale of certain inventories at cost, including applicable administrative expenses. (See opinion of the Assistant General Counsel (Fiscal Matters) of the Office of the Secretary of Defense, January 4, 1955.)

In subsection (b), the first sentence states expressly the rule which is implicit in 10:1238. The word ''members'' is substituted for the words ''officers and enlisted men''. The words ''shall be understood, in all cases of such sales'' are omitted as surplusage. The last sentence is inserted to reflect Title IV of the National Security Act of 1947, as amended (63 Stat. 585), which authorized the Secretary of Defense to prescribe regulations governing the use and sale of certain inventories at cost, including applicable administrative expenses. (See opinion of the Deputy General Counsel of the Office of the Secretary of Defense, March 28, 1956.)

In subsection (c), the word ''members'' is substituted for the words ''officers and enlisted men''. The words ''prices at which like property is sold to'' are substituted for the words ''same price as is charged the''.

In subsections (c) and (d), the words ''other armed forces'' are substituted for the words "Navy and Marine Corps", since such sales are authorized to members of the Coast Guard by section 144(b) of title 14.

In subsection (d), the words "other than subsistence supplies" are inserted, since the sale of subsistence supplies is covered by subsection (c).

In subsection (e), the words "a person who has been discharged" are substituted for the words "discharged officers and enlisted men". The words "Navy . . . or Marine Corps", omitted from the 1952 edition of the United States Code, are inserted to conform to the source statute. The words "may buy" are substituted for the words "shall . . . be permitted to purchase". The words "at the prices at which like property is sold" are substituted for the words "at the same price as charged". The word "member" is substituted for the words "officers and enlisted men". The words "while undergoing such care and treatment" are omitted as surplusage.

In subsection (f), the words "person who has been discharged" are substituted for the words "former members . . . who have been separated therefrom". The words "at the prices at which like articles are sold to members" are inserted to conform to the last sentence of subsection (a) and subsection (e).

In subsection (g), the words "regulations to be prescribed by the Secretary" are substituted for the words "Army Regulations". The words "of the Government" are omitted as surplusage. 10:1253 (last 22 words of 1st sentence) is omitted as surplusage. The words "or to another executive department of the Government" are omitted as superseded by section 7 of the Act of May 21, 1920, ch 194, as amended (31 U.S.C. 686). The provisions of 10:1253 relating to the computation of cost are omitted to reflect Title IV of the National Security Act of 1947, as amended (63 Stat. 585), which authorized the Secretary of Defense to prescribe regulations governing the use and sale of certain inventories at cost, including applicable administrative expenses. (See opinion of the Assistant General Counsel (Fiscal Matters) of the Office of the Secretary of Defense, January 4, 1955.)

In subsection (h), the word "outside" is substituted for the words "beyond the continental limitations". The words "or in Alaska" are omitted, since, under 10 USCS § 101(1), the words "United States" are defined to include only the States and the District of Columbia. The word "continental", after the words "within the", is omitted for the same reason. The last sentence is substituted for 10:1241 (proviso).

In subsection (i), 10:1196 (last 30 words) is omitted as superseded by the Act of April 27, 1914, ch 72 (last proviso under "Subsistence of the Army"), 38 Stat. 361. The words "So much of the" and "as may be necessary" are omitted as surplusage. The words "members . . . on active duty, for the use of themselves and their families" are substituted for the words "officers for the use of themselves and their families, and to commanders of companies or other organizations, for the use of the enlisted men of their companies or organizations", to conform to 10:1237 and 1238. Those sections provide the basic authority for procurement and sale of subsistence supplies to all members. This interpretation conforms to established administrative practice under those sections. The word "supplies" is substituted for the word "stores".

1962 ACT

The change corrects an internal reference.

Amendments:

1962. Act Sept. 7, 1962, in subsecs. (a) and (b) substituted "section 2208 of this title" for "sections 172–172j of title 5".

1980. Act Dec. 12, 1980 (effective upon enactment on 12/12/80, as provided by § 701(b)(3) of such Act, which appears as 10 USCS § 101 note), in subsec. (f), substituted "or 773" for "773, or 8612".

1981. Act July 10, 1981, in subsec. (f), deleted the comma following "section 772".

1987. Act Dec. 4, 1987 deleted subsec. (b) which read: "Subsistence supplies may be sold to members of the Air Force. The selling price of each article sold under this subsection is the invoice price of the last lot of that article that the officer making the sale received before the first day of the month in which the sale is made. Activities conducted under this subsection shall be consistent with section 2208 of this title."; and redesignated subsecs. (c)–(i) as subsecs. (b)–(h), respectively.

1989. Act Nov. 29, 1989, in subsec. (d), substituted "Department of Veterans Affairs" for "Veterans' Administration".

1996. Act Feb. 10, 1996, in subsec. (b), substituted "The Secretary shall" for "The Air Force shall"; and, in subsec. (f), inserted "or by commercial credit".

CROSS REFERENCES

Settlement of accounts, deductions from pay, 10 USCS § 9837.

This section is referred to in 10 USCS § 9629; 37 USCS § 1007.

§ 9622. Rations: commissioned officers in field

Commissioned officers of the Air Force serving in the field may buy rations for their own use, on credit. Amounts due for these purchases shall be reported monthly to the Secretary of the Air Force.

(Aug. 10, 1956, ch 1041, § 1, 70A Stat. 580.)

HISTORY; ANCILLARY LAWS AND DIRECTIVES

Prior law and revision:

Revised Section	Source (USCS)	Source (Statutes at Large)
9622	10:1232.	R.S. 1145.

The words "at cost prices" are omitted to reflect Title IV of the National Security Act of 1947, as amended (63 Stat. 585), which authorized the Secretary of Defense to prescribe regulations governing the use and sale of certain inventories at cost, including applicable administrative expenses. (See opinion of the Assistant General Counsel (Fiscal Matters) of the Office of the Secretary of Defense, January 4, 1955.)

CROSS REFERENCES

Settlement of accounts, deductions from pay, 10 USCS § 9837.

INTERPRETIVE NOTES AND DECISIONS

Under predecessor of 10 USCS § 9622, only advantage which commissioned officers had in respect to rations was right to purchase rations for his own use at cost when serving in field. Reid v United States (1883) 18 Ct Cl 625.

§ 9623. Tobacco: enlisted members of Air Force

The Air Force shall sell not more than 16 ounces of tobacco a month to an enlisted member of the Air Force on active duty who requests it.

(Aug. 10, 1956, ch 1041, § 1, 70A Stat. 580.)

HISTORY; ANCILLARY LAWS AND DIRECTIVES

Prior law and revision:

Revised Section	Source (USCS)	Source (Statutes at Large)
9623	10:1239.	R.S. 1149.

The words "Air Force" are substituted for the words "Quartermaster Corps", since the Air Force does not have organic corps created by statute. The words "on active duty" are inserted for clarity. The words "shall sell" are substituted for the words "shall be furnished by". The words "in such quantities as they may require" are omitted as surplusage. The words "at cost prices, excluding the cost of transportation" are omitted to reflect Title IV of the National Security Act of 1947, as amended (63 Stat. 585), which authorized the Secretary of Defense to prescribe regulations governing the use and sale of certain inventories at cost, including applicable administrative expenses. (See opinion of the Assistant General Counsel (Fiscal Matters) of the Office of the Secretary of Defense, January 4, 1955.)

CROSS REFERENCES

Settlement of accounts, deductions from pay, 10 USCS § 9837; 37 USCS § 1007.

§ 9624. Medical supplies: civilian employees of the Air Force; American National Red Cross; Soldiers' and Airmen's Home

(a) Under regulations to be prescribed by the Secretary of the Air Force, a civilian employee of the Department of the Air Force who is stationed at an air base may buy necessary medical supplies from the Air Force when they are prescribed by a medical officer on active duty.

(b) The Secretary may sell medical supplies to the American National Red Cross for cash.

(c) The Secretary may sell medical and hospital supplies to the Armed Forces Retirement Home.

(Aug. 10, 1956, ch 1041, § 1, 70A Stat. 580; Dec. 12, 1980, P. L. 96-513, Title V, Part B, § 514(17)(A), (B), 94 Stat. 2936; Nov. 5, 1990, P. L. 101-510, Div A, Title XV, Part B, § 1533(a)(8)(A), (B), 104 Stat. 1735.)

HISTORY; ANCILLARY LAWS AND DIRECTIVES

Prior law and revision:

Revised Section	Source (USCS)	Source (Statutes at Large)
9624(a)	10:1236.	Apr. 23, 1904, ch. 1485 (last proviso under "Medical Department"), 33 Stat. 273; Mar. 2, 1905, ch. 1307 (last proviso under "Medical Department"), 33 Stat. 1080.
9624(b)	10:1254.	Mar. 4, 1915, ch. 143 (2d proviso under "Medical Department"), 38 Stat. 1080.
9624(c)	24:58.	June 4, 1897, ch 2 (para. under "Soldiers' Home, District of Columbia"), 30 Stat. 54; June 28, 1950, ch. 383, § 402(d), 64 Stat. 272.

In subsection (a), the words "on active duty" are inserted for clarity.

In subsection (b), the words "rates of charge", "to cover the cost of purchase, inspection, and so forth", and "as can be spared without detriment to the military service" are omitted as surplusage. The words "the contract prices paid therefor" are omitted to reflect title IV of the National Security Act of 1947, as amended (63 Stat. 585), which authorized the Secretary of Defense to prescribe regulations governing the use and sale of certain inventories, at cost, including applicable administrative expenses. (See opinion of the Assistant General Counsel (Fiscal Matters) of the Office of the Secretary of Defense, January 4, 1955.) The word "equipments" is omitted as covered by the word "supplies".

In subsections (b) and (c), the words "The Secretary" are substituted for the words "Medical Department of the Army", since the functions which, for the Army, are assigned by statute to subordinate organizational units of the Army, are, for the Air Force, assigned to the Secretary of the Air Force.

In subsection (c), the words "in the District of Columbia" are omitted as surplusage, since there is only one Soldiers' Home. The words "Upon proper application therefor" are omitted as surplusage. The words "its contract prices" are omitted to reflect Title IV of the National Security Act of 1947, as amended (63 Stat. 585), which authorized the Secretary of Defense to prescribe regulations governing the use and sale of certain inventories at cost, including applicable administrative expenses. (See opinion of the Assistant General Counsel (Fiscal Matters) of the Office of the Secretary of Defense, January 4, 1955.)

Amendments:

1980. Act Dec. 12, 1980 (effective upon enactment on 12/12/80, as provided by § 701(b)(3) of such Act, which appears as 10 USCS § 101 note), in the catchline, inserted "the" and "and Airmen's"; and, in subsec. (c), substituted "United States Soldiers' and Airmen's Home" for "Soldiers' Home".

1990. Act Nov. 5, 1990 (effective 1 year after enactment as provided by § 1541(a), which appears as 24 USCS § 401 note) substituted the section heading for one which read: "§ 9624. Medical supplies: civilian employees of the Air Force; American National Red Cross; Soldiers' and Airmen's Home"; and, in subsec. (c), substituted "Armed Forces Retirement Home" for "United States Soldier's and Airmen's Home".

CROSS REFERENCES

American National Red Cross–Equipment for instruction and practice, 10 USCS § 2542.

American National Red Cross–Generally, 36 USCS §§ 1 et seq.

§ 9625. Ordnance property: officers of armed forces; civilian employees of Air Force; American National Red Cross; educational institutions; homes for veterans' orphans

(a) The Secretary of the Air Force may sell articles of ordnance property to officers of other armed forces for their use in the service, in the same manner as these articles are sold to officers of the Air Force.

(b) Under such regulations as the Secretary may prescribe, ordnance stores may be sold to civilian employees of the Air Force and to the American National Red Cross.

(c) Articles of ordnance property may be sold to educational institutions and to State soldiers' and sailors' orphans' homes for maintaining the ordnance and ordnance stores issued to those institutions and homes.

(Aug. 10, 1956, ch 1041, § 1, 70A Stat. 580.)

HISTORY; ANCILLARY LAWS AND DIRECTIVES

Prior law and revision:

Revised Section	Source (USCS)	Source (Statutes at Large)
9625(a)	34:540. 50:70.	Mar. 3, 1909, ch. 252 (5th para. under "National Trophy and Medals for Rifle Contests"), 35 Stat 750.
9625(b)	50:71.	Mar. 3, 1909, ch. 252 (8th para. under "Nation Trophy and Medals for Rifle Contests"), 35 Stat. 751; June 28, 1950, ch. 383, § 402(h), 64 Stat. 273.
9625(c)	50:63.	

Revised Section	Source (USCS)	Source (Statutes at Large)
		May 11, 1908, ch. 163 (4th para. under "National Trophy and Medals for Rifle Contests), 35 Stat. 125.

In subsection (a), the words "Secretary of the Air Force" are substituted for the words "Chief of Ordnance", since the functions which, for the Army, are assigned to subordinate officers of the Army, are, for the Air Force, assigned to the Secretary of the Air Force. The words "other armed forces" are substituted for the words "the Navy and Marine Corps", in 34:540 and 50:70, since those sales may be made to officers of the Coast Guard under section 114(c) of Title 14.

CROSS REFERENCES

American National Red Cross, equipment for instruction and practice, 10 USCS § 2542.

§ 9626. Aircraft supplies and services: foreign military or air attaché

Under such conditions as he may prescribe, the Secretary of the Air Force may provide for the sale of fuel, oil, and other supplies for use in aircraft operated by a foreign military or air attaché accredited to the United States, and for the furnishing of mechanical service and other assistance to such aircraft. Shelter may be furnished to such aircraft, but only without charge.

(Aug. 10, 1956, ch 1041, § 1, 70A Stat. 581.)

HISTORY; ANCILLARY LAWS AND DIRECTIVES

Prior law and revision:

Revised Section	Source (USCS)	Source (Statutes at Large)
9626	22:259 (less last sentence).	May 31, 1939, ch. 161 (less last sentence), 53 Stat. 795.

The last sentence is substituted for the words "except for shelter for which no charge shall be made". The words "and equipment" are omitted as covered by the word "supplies". 22:259 (last 22 words of 2d sentence) is omitted to reflect Title IV of the National Security Act of 1947, as amended (63 Stat. 585), which authorized the Secretary of Defense to prescribe regulations governing the use and sale of certain inventories at cost, including applicable administrative expenses. (See opinion of the Assistant General Counsel (Fiscal Matters) of the Office of the Secretary of Defense, January 4, 1955.)

CROSS REFERENCES

This section is referred to in 10 USCS § 9629.

§ 9627. Supplies: educational institutions

Under such regulations as the Secretary of the Air Force may prescribe, supplies and military publications procured for the Air Force may be sold to any educational institution to which an officer of the Air Force is detailed as professor of air science and tactics, for the use of its military students. Sales under this section shall be for cash.

(Aug. 10, 1956, ch 1041, § 1, 70A Stat. 581.)

HISTORY; ANCILLARY LAWS AND DIRECTIVES

Prior law and revision:

Revised Section	Source (USCS)	Source (Statutes at Large)
9627	10:1179 (less proviso).	July 17, 1914, ch. 149 (less proviso), 38 Stat. 512.

The words "procured for" are substituted for the words "as are furnished to". The words "stores . . . materiel of war" are omitted as covered by the word "supplies". The words "the price listed to the Army" are omitted to reflect Title IV of the National Security Act of 1947, as amended (63 Stat. 585), which authorized the Secretary of Defense to prescribe regulations governing the use and sale of certain inventories at cost, including applicable administrative expenses. (See opinion of the Assistant General Counsel (Fiscal Matters) of the Office of the Secretary of Defense, January 4, 1955.)

CROSS REFERENCES

This section is referred to in 10 USCS § 9629.

§ 9628. Airplane parts and accessories: civilian flying schools

The Secretary of the Air Force may sell, to civilian flying schools at which personnel of the Department of the Air Force or the Department of the Army are receiving flight training under contracts requiring these schools to maintain and repair airplanes of the Air Force furnished to them for flight training, the spare parts and accessories needed for those repairs.

(Aug. 10, 1956, ch 1041, § 1, 70A Stat. 581.)

HISTORY; ANCILLARY LAWS AND DIRECTIVES

Prior law and revision:

Revised Section	Source (USCS)	Source (Statutes at Large)
9628	10:298c.	Feb. 12, 1940, ch. 27, title I (proviso under "Air Corps"), 54 Stat. 25.

The words "under the provisions of the Act of April 3, 1939, ch 35, 53 Stat. 555", are omitted as obsolete, since training formerly performed under that Act is now performed under section 9301of this title. The words "personnel of the Departments" are substituted for the words "flying cadets", since the authority is reciprocal, and to conform to section 9656 of this title. The words "flying cadet" are omitted as obsolete. 10:298c (last 28 words) is omitted to reflect Title IV of the National Security Act of 1947, as amended (63 Stat. 585), which authorized the Secretary of Defense to prescribe regulations governing the use and sale of certain inventories at cost, including applicable administrative expenses. (See opinion of the Assistant General Counsel (Fiscal Matters) of the Office of the Secretary of Defense, January 4, 1955.

CROSS REFERENCES

Issuance of aircraft and equipment to civilian aviation schools, 10 USCS § 9656.

§ 9629. Proceeds: disposition

The proceeds of sales of the following shall be paid into the Treasury to the credit of the appropriation out of which they were purchased, and are available for the purposes of that appropriation:

(1) Exterior articles of uniform sold under section 9621 of this title [10 USCS § 9621].

(2) Supplies, war material, and military publications sold to educational institutions under section 9627 of this title [10 USCS § 9627].

(3) Fuel, oil, other supplies, and services for aircraft of a foreign military or air attache sold under section 9626 of this title [10 USCS § 9626].

(Aug. 10, 1956, ch 1041, § 1, 70A Stat. 581.)

HISTORY; ANCILLARY LAWS AND DIRECTIVES

Prior law and revision:

Revised Section	Source (USCS)	Source (Statutes at Large)
9629	10:1179 (proviso). 10:1395 (last sentence). 22:259 (last sentence).	Feb. 14, 1927, ch. 134 (last sentence), 44 Stat. 1096. July 17, 1914, ch. 149 (proviso), 38 Stat. 512. May 31, 1939, ch. 161 (last sentence), 53 Stat. 796.

CHAPTER 941. ISSUE OF SERVICEABLE MATERIAL OTHER THAN TO ARMED FORCES

Section
9651. Arms, tentage, and equipment: educational institutions not maintaining units of A. F. R. O. T. C.
9652. Rifles and ammunition for target practice: educational institutions having corps of cadets
9653. Ordnance and ordnance stores: District of Columbia high schools
9654. Supplies: military instruction camps
9655. Arms and ammunition: agencies and departments of United States
9656. Aircraft and equipment: civilian aviation schools

§ 9651. Arms, tentage, and equipment: educational institutions not maintaining units of A. F. R. O. T. C.

Under such conditions as he may prescribe, the Secretary of the Air Force may issue arms, tentage, and equipment that he considers necessary for proper military training, to any educational institution at which no unit of the Air Force Reserve Officers' Training Corps is maintained, but which has a course in military training prescribed by the Secretary and which has at least 100 physically fit students over 14 years of age.

(Aug. 10, 1956, ch 1041, § 1, 70A Stat. 581; Nov. 8, 1985, P. L. 99-145, Title XIII, § 1301(d)(3), 99 Stat. 736.)

HISTORY; ANCILLARY LAWS AND DIRECTIVES

Prior law and revision:

Revised Section	Source (USCS)	Source (Statutes at Large)
9651	10:1180.	June 3, 1916, ch. 134, § 55c (words before semicolon); added June 4, 1920, ch. 227, subch. I, § 35 (words of last para. before semicolon), 41 Stat. 780.

The reference to schools ''other than those provided for in section 381 of this title'' is omitted as covered by the descriptions of the educational institutions.

Amendments:

1985. Act Nov. 8, 1985 deleted ''male'' following ''physically fit''.

§ 9652. Rifles and ammunition for target practice: Educational institutions having corps of cadets

(a) The Secretary of the Air Force may lend, without expense to the United States, magazine rifles and appendages that are not of the existing service models in use at the time, and that are not necessary for a proper reserve supply, to any educational institution having a uniformed corps of cadets of sufficient number for target practice. He may also issue 40 rounds of ball cartridges for each cadet for each range at which target practice is held, but not more than 120 rounds each year for each cadet participating in target practice.

(b) The institutions to which property is lent under subsection (a) shall use it for target practice, take proper care of it, and return it when required.

(c) The Secretary shall prescribe regulations to carry out this section, containing such other requirements as he considers necessary to safeguard the interests of the United States.

(Aug. 10, 1956, ch 1041, § 1, 70A Stat. 582.)

HISTORY; ANCILLARY LAWS AND DIRECTIVES

Prior law and revision:

Revised Section	Source (USCS)	Source (Statutes at Large)
9652(a)	10:1185 (1st para.).	Apr. 27, 1914, ch. 72 (last proviso and last para. under "Manufacture of Arms"), 38 Stat. 370.
9652(b)	10:1185 (last para., less 1st 22, and last 19, words).	
9652(c)	10:1185 (1st 22, and last 19, words of last para.).	

In subsection (a), the words, "and carrying on military training" and "the maintenance of" are omitted as surplusage. In clause (2), the words "suitable to said arm" are omitted as surplusage.

In subsection (b), the words "shall use it for target practice" are substituted for the words "insuring the designed use of the property issued". The words "take proper care of it" are substituted for the words "providing against loss to the United States through lack of proper care".

§ 9653. Ordnance and ordnance stores: District of Columbia high schools

The Secretary of the Air Force, under regulations to be prescribed by him, may issue to the high schools of the District of Columbia ordnance and ordnance stores required for military instruction and practice. The Secretary shall require a bond in double the value of the property issued under this section, for the care and safekeeping of that property and, except for property properly expended, for its return when required.

(Aug. 10, 1956, ch 1041, § 1, 70A Stat. 582.)

HISTORY; ANCILLARY LAWS AND DIRECTIVES

Prior law and revision:

Revised Section	Source (USCS)	Source (Statutes at Large)
9653	10:1183.	Feb. 5, 1891, J. Res. 9, 26 Stat. 1113.

The words ''at his discretion and'', ''belonging to the Government, and which can be spared for that purpose'', and ''in each case'' are omitted as surplusage. The words ''high schools of the'' are substituted for the words ''High School of Washington'', since the various high schools of the District of Columbia have succeeded the Washington High School that existed at the time the statute was enacted. The words ''except for property properly expended'' are inserted for clarity.

§ 9654. Supplies: military instruction camps

Under such conditions as he may prescribe, the Secretary of the Air Force may issue, to any educational institution at which an Air Force officer is detailed as professor of air science and tactics, such supplies as are necessary to establish and maintain a camp for the military instruction of its students. The Secretary shall require a bond in the value of the property issued under this section, for the care and safekeeping of that property and, except for property properly expended, for its return when required.

(Aug. 10, 1956, ch 1041, § 1, 70A Stat. 582.)

HISTORY; ANCILLARY LAWS AND DIRECTIVES

Prior law and revision:

Revised Section	Source (USCS)	Source (Statutes at Large)
9654	10:1182.	May 18, 1910, ch. 124, 39 Stat. 123.

The words ''at his discretion and'' and ''belonging to the Government, and which can be spared for that purpose, as may appear to be'' are omitted as surplusage. The words ''except for property properly expended'' are inserted for clarity. The word ''stores'' is omitted as covered by the word ''supplies''.

§ 9655. Arms and ammunition: agencies and departments of United States

(a) Whenever required for the protection of public money and property, the Secretary of the Air Force may lend arms and their accouterments, and issue ammunition, to a department or independent agency of the United States, upon request of its head. Property lent or issued under this subsection may be delivered to an officer of the department or agency designated by the head thereof, and that officer shall account for the property to the Secretary of the

Air Force. Property lent or issued under this subsection and not properly expended shall be returned when it is no longer needed.

(b) The department or agency to which property is lent or issued under subsection (a) shall transfer funds to the credit of the Department of the Air Force to cover the costs of—

(1) ammunition issued;

(2) replacing arms and accouterments that have been lost or destroyed or cannot be repaired;

(3) repairing arms and accouterments returned to the Department of the Air Force; and

(4) making and receiving shipments by the Department of the Air Force.

(Aug. 10, 1956, ch 1041, § 1, 70A Stat. 582.)

HISTORY; ANCILLARY LAWS AND DIRECTIVES

Prior law and revision:

Revised Section	Source (USCS)	Source (Statutes at Large)
9655(a)	50:61 (less proviso).	Mar. 3, 1879, ch. 183 (2d para. under ''Miscellaneous''); restated Apr. 14, 1937, ch. 79, 50 Stat. 63.
9655(b)	50:61 (proviso).	

In subsection (a), the word ''lend'' is substituted for the word ''issue'', with respect to arms and accouterments, since the property must be returned when the necessity for its use has expired. The words ''and not properly expended'' are inserted for clarity. The words ''United States'' are substituted for the word ''Government''. The word ''their'' is substituted for the words ''suitable . . . for use therewith''. The words ''it is no longer needed'' are substituted for the words ''the necessity for their use has expired''.

In subsection (b), the words ''hereafter'', ''borrowed'', and ''under the authority of this section'' are omitted as surplusage.

§ 9656. Aircraft and equipment: civilian aviation schools

The Secretary of the Air Force, under regulations to be prescribed by him, may lend aircraft, aircraft parts, and aeronautical equipment and accessories that are required for instruction, training, and maintenance, to accredited civilian aviation schools at which personnel of the Department of the Air Force or the Department of the Army are pursuing a course of instruction and training under detail by competent orders.

(Aug. 10, 1956, ch 1041, § 1, 70A Stat. 583; Oct. 12, 1982, P. L. 97-295, § 1(53), 96 Stat. 1301.)

HISTORY; ANCILLARY LAWS AND DIRECTIVES

Prior law and revision:

1956 ACT

Revised Section	Source (USCS)	Source (Statutes at Large)
9656	10:298b.	Apr. 3, 1939, ch. 35, § 4, 53 Stat. 556.

The words ''in his discretion and'', ''rules'', ''limitations'', and ''on hand and belonging to the Government such articles as may appear to be'' are omitted as surplusage. The words ''Department of the Air Force or the Department of the Army'' are substituted for the words ''Military Establishment'', since the authority is reciprocal.

1982 ACT

In 10:9656, the words '', and at least one of which is designated by the Civil Aeronautics Authority for the training of Negro air pilots'' are stricken as obsolete.

Amendments:

1982. Act Oct. 12, 1982, deleted '', and at least one of which is designated by the Civil Aeronautics Authority for the training of Negro air pilots'' following ''competent orders''.

CHAPTER 943. DISPOSAL OF OBSOLETE OR SURPLUS MATERIAL

Section
9681. Surplus war material: sale to States and foreign governments
9682. Obsolete or excess material: sale to National Council of Boy Scouts of America
9684. Surplus obsolete ordnance: sale to patriotic organizations
9685. Obsolete ordnance: loan to educational institutions and State soldiers' and sailors' orphans' homes
9686. Obsolete ordnance: gift to State homes for soldiers and sailors

§ 9681. Surplus war material: sale to States and foreign governments

Subject to regulations under section 205 of the Federal Property and Administrative Services Act of 1949 (40 U.S.C. 486), the Secretary of the Air Force may sell surplus war material and supplies, except food, of the Department of the Air Force, for which there is no adequate domestic market, to any State or to any foreign government with which the United States was at peace on June 5, 1920. Sales under this section shall be made upon terms that the Secretary considers expedient.

(Aug. 10, 1956, ch 1041, § 1, 70A Stat. 583; Dec. 12, 1980, P.L. 96-513, Title V, Part B, § 514(18), 94 Stat. 2936.)

HISTORY; ANCILLARY LAWS AND DIRECTIVES

Prior law and revision:

Revised Section	Source (USCS)	Source (Statutes at Large)
9681	10:1262.	June 5, 1920, ch. 240 (2d proviso under ''Contingencies of the Army''), 41 Stat. 949; Oct. 31, 1951, ch. 654, § 2(8), 65 Stat. 707.

The word ''may'' is substituted for the words ''is authorized in his discretion, to''. The words ''war material'' are substituted for the word ''materiel''. The words ''or equipment'' are omitted as covered by the word ''supplies''. The words ''of the Department of the Air Force'' are substituted for the words ''pertaining to the Military Establishment''. The words ''which are not needed for military purposes'' are omitted as covered by the word ''surplus''. The words ''as or may be found to be'' are omitted as surplusage.

Amendments:

1980. Act Dec. 12, 1980 (effective upon enactment on 12/12/80, as provided by § 701(b)(3) of such Act, which appears as 10 USCS § 101 note), substituted "205 of the Federal Property and Administrative Services Act of 1949 (40 U.S.C. 486)" for "486 of title 40".

INTERPRETIVE NOTES AND DECISIONS

Under predecessor of 10 USCS § 9681, where government sold its property under its own initiative, by its own officers, in accord with its own terms and conditions exclusively, and services of agent were not proximate cause of sale, agent was not entitled to commission or brokerage. Murphy v United States (1929) 68 Ct Cl 149.

§ 9682. Obsolete or excess material: sale to National Council of Boy Scouts of America

Subject to regulations under section 205 of the Federal Property and Administrative Services Act of 1949 (40 U.S.C. 486), the Secretary of the Air Force, under such conditions as he may prescribe, may sell obsolete or excess material to the National Council of the Boy Scouts of America. Sales under this section shall be at fair value to the Department of the Air Force, including packing, handling, and transportation.

(Aug. 10, 1956, ch 1041, § 1, 70A Stat. 583; Dec. 12, 1980, P.L. 96-513, Title V, Part B, § 514(18), 94 Stat. 2936.)

HISTORY; ANCILLARY LAWS AND DIRECTIVES

Prior law and revision:

Revised Section	Source (USCS)	Source (Statutes at Large)
9682	10:1259.	May 15, 1937, ch. 193, 50 Stat. 167; Oct. 31, 1951, ch. 654, § 2(7), 65 Stat. 707.

The words "obsolete or excess material" are substituted for the words "such obsolete material as may not be needed by the Department of the Army, and such other material as may be spared" to conform to the Federal Property and Administrative Services Act of 1949, as amended (40 U.S.C. 471 et seq.). The words "in his discretion" are omitted as surplusage.

Amendments:

1980. Act Dec. 12, 1980 (effective upon enactment on 12/12/80, as provided by § 701(b)(3) of such Act, which appears as 10 USCS § 101 note), substituted "205 of the Federal Property and Administrative Services Act of 1949 (40 U.S.C. 486)" for "486 of title 40".

§ 9684. Surplus obsolete ordinance: sale to patriotic organizations

Subject to regulations under section 205 of the Federal Property and Administrative Services Act of 1949 (40 U.S.C. 486), the Secretary of the Air Force may sell, without advertisement and at prices that he considers reasonable—

(1) surplus obsolete small arms and ammunition and equipment for them, to any patriotic organization for military purposes; and

(2) surplus obsolete brass or bronze cannons, carriages, and cannon balls, for public parks, public buildings, and soldiers' monuments.

(Aug. 10, 1956, ch 1041, § 1, 70A Stat. 583; Dec. 12, 1980, P.L. 96-513, Title V, Part B, § 514(18), 94 Stat. 2936.)

HISTORY; ANCILLARY LAWS AND DIRECTIVES

Prior law and revision:

Revised Section	Source (USCS)	Source (Statutes at Large)
9684	50:64. 50:68.	May 28, 1908, ch. 215, § 14, 35 Stat. 443; June 28, 1950, ch. 383, § 402(g), 64 Stat. 273; Oct. 31, 1951, ch. 654, § 2(26), 65 Stat. 707. Mar. 4, 1909, ch. 319, § 47, 35 Stat. 1075; June 28, 1950, ch. 383, § 402(i), 64 Stat. 273; Oct. 31, 1951, ch. 654, § 2(28), 65 Stat. 707.

50:64 (proviso) and 50:68 (proviso) are omitted as surplusage.

The words ''the Chief of Ordnance'' are omitted, since the functions which, for the Army, are assigned by statute to subordinate officers of the Army, are, for the Air Force, assigned to the Secretary of the Air Force.

Amendments:

1980. Act Dec. 12, 1980 (effective upon enactment on 12/12/80, as provided by § 701(b)(3) of such Act, which appears as 10 USCS § 101 note), in the introductory matter, substituted ''205 of the Federal Property and Administrative Services Act of 1949 (40 U.S.C. 486)'' for ''486 of title 40''.

§ 9685. Obsolete ordnance: loan to educational institutions and State soldiers' and sailors' orphans' homes

(a) Upon the recommendation of the Governor of the State or Territory concerned, the Secretary of the Air Force, under regulations to be prescribed by him and without cost to the United States for transportation, may lend obsolete ordnance and ordnance stores to State and Territorial educational institutions and to State soldiers' and sailors' orphans' homes, for drill and instruction. However, no loan may be made under this subsection to an institution to which ordnance or ordnance stores may be issued under any law that was in effect on June 30, 1906, and is still in effect.

(b) The Secretary shall require a bond from each institution or home to which property is lent under subsection (a), in double the value of the property lent, for the care and safekeeping of that property and, except for property properly expended, for its return when required.

(Aug. 10, 1956, ch 1041, § 1, 70A Stat. 584.)

HISTORY; ANCILLARY LAWS AND DIRECTIVES

Prior law and revision:

Revised Section	Source (USCS)	Source (Statutes at Large)
9685(a)	50:62a (1st para. and proviso of last para.).	June 30, 1906, ch. 3938, 34 Stat. 817.
9685(b)	50:62a (last para., less proviso).	

In subsection (a), the words "at his discretion" and "as may be available" are omitted as surplusage. The word "lend" is substituted for the word "issue" to reflect the intent of the section 50:62a (1st 13 words of proviso) is omitted as surplusage. The words "and which is still in effect" are inserted for clarity.

In subsection (b), the words "to the United States" are omitted as surplusage. The words "except property property expended" are inserted for clarity.

§ 9686. Obsolete ordinance: gift to State homes for soldiers and sailors

Subject to regulations under section 205 of the Federal Property and Administrative Services Act of 1949 (40 U.S.C. 486) [40 USCS § 486], the Secretary of the Air Force may give not more than two obsolete bronze and iron cannons suitable for firing salutes to any home for soldiers or sailors established and maintained under State authority.

(Aug. 10, 1956, ch 1041, § 1, 70A Stat. 584; Dec. 12, 1980, P.L. 96-513, Title V, Part B, § 514(18), 94 Stat. 2936.)

HISTORY; ANCILLARY LAWS AND DIRECTIVES

Prior law and revision:

Revised Section	Source (USCS)	Source (Statutes at Large)
9686	50:66.	Feb. 8, 1889, ch. 116, 25 Stat. 657; Oct. 31, 1951, ch. 654, § 2(27), 65 Stat. 707. Mar. 3, 1899, ch. 423 (1st proviso under Ordnance Department"), 30 Stat. 1073; May 26, 1900, ch. 586 (1st proviso under "Ordnance Department"), 31 Stat. 216; June 28, 1950, ch. 383, § 402(e), 64 Stat. 273.

The words "subject to such regulations as he may prescribe" are omitted, since the Secretary has inherent authority to issue regulations appropriate to exercising his statutory functions. The words ''to any of the 'National Homes for Disabled Volunteer Soldiers' already established or hereafter established and'', in the Act of February 8, 1889, ch 116, 25 Stat. 657, are not contained in 50:66 (2d sentence). They are also omitted from the revised section, since the National Homes for Disabled Volunteer Soldiers were dissolved by the Act of July 3, 1930, ch. 863, 46 Stat. 1016. The acts of March 3, 1899, ch. 643 (1st proviso under ''Ordnance Department''), 30 Stat. 1073; and May 26, 1900, ch 586 (1st proviso under ''Ordnance Department''), 31 Stat. 216, as amended, relating to disposal of ordnance to ''Homes for Disabled Volunteer Soldiers'' by the Chief of Ordnance of the Army, became inoperative when the Homes were dissolved. Although section 402(e) of the Army Organization Act of 1950, ch 383, 64 Stat. 273, amended the Act of May 26, 1900, it did not have the effect of reviving that Act. The word ''give'' is substituted for the word ''deliver'' to express more clearly the intent of the section. The words ''serviceable'' and ''as may be on hand undisposed of'' are omitted as surplusage. The word ''may'' is substituted for the words ''is authorized and directed'', since 10 USCS 9684 provides an alternative method for the disposal of obsolete cannon.

Amendments:

1980. Act Dec. 12, 1980 (effective upon enactment on 12/12/80, as provided by § 701(b)(3) of such Act, which appears as 10 USCS § 101 note), substituted ''205 of the Federal Property and Administrative Services Act of 1949 (40 U.S.C. 486)'' for ''486 of title 40''.

CHAPTER 945. INQUESTS; DISPOSITION OF EFFECTS OF DECEASED PERSONS

HISTORY; ANCILLARY LAWS AND DIRECTIVES

Amendments:

1980. Act Dec. 12, 1980, P.L. 96-513, Title V, Part B, § 514(20)(C), 94 Stat. 2936 (effective upon enactment on 12/12/80, as provided by § 701(b)(3) of such Act, which appears as 10 USCS § 101 note), amended the analysis of this chapter in item 9713 by inserting ''and Airmen's''.

1990. Act Nov. 5, 1990 (effective 1 year after enactment as provided by § 1541(a), which appears as 24 USCS 401 note) substituted this heading for one which read: ''§ 9624. Medical supplies: civilian employees of the Air Force; American National Red Cross; Soldiers' and Airmen's Home''; and, in subsec. (c), substituted ''Armed Forces Retirement Home'' for ''United States Soldier's and Airmen's Home''.

§ 9711. Inquests

(a) When a person is found dead under circumstances that require investigation, at a place garrisoned by the Air Force and under the exclusive jurisdiction of the United States, the commanding officer shall direct a summary court-martial to investigate the circumstances of the death.

(b) In conducting an investigation under subsection (a), the summary court-martial may summon witnesses and examine them upon oath.

(c) The summary court-martial shall promptly submit to the commanding officer a report of the investigation and findings as to the cause of death.

(Aug. 10, 1956, ch 1041, § 1, 70A Stat. 584.)

HISTORY; ANCILLARY LAWS AND DIRECTIVES

Prior law and revision:

Revised Section	Source (USCS)	Source (Statutes at Large)
9711(a)	10:15a (words before semicolon of 1st sentence).	June 4, 1920, ch. 227, subch. II, § 1 (Art. 113), 41 Stat. 810; May 5, 1950, ch. 169, § 6(d), 64 Stat. 145.
9711(b)	10:15a (1st sentence, less words before semicotlon).	
9711(c)	10:15a (less 1st sentence).	

In subsection (a), the words ''post, fort, camp, or other'' are omitted as surplusage.

In subsection (b), the words ''In conducting an investigation under subsection (a)'' are substituted for the words ''for this purpose''. The word ''may'' is substituted for the words ''shall have power to''. The words ''or affirmation'' are omitted, since the word ''oath'', as defined in section 1 of title 1, includes ''affirmation''.

In subsection (c), the words ''commanding officer'' are substituted for the words ''post or other commander'' to conform to subsec. (a).

CROSS REFERENCES

Summary courts-martial–Jurisdiction, 10 USCS § 820.

Summary courts-martial–Persons authorized to convene, 10 USCS § 824.

§ 9712. Disposition of effects of deceased persons by summary court-martial

(a) Upon the death of—

(1) a person subject to military law at a place or command under the jurisdiction of the Air Force; or

(2) a resident of the Armed Forces Retirement Home who dies in an Air Force hospital outside the District of Columbia when sent from the Home to that hospital for treatment;

the commanding officer of the place or command shall permit the legal representative or the surviving spouse of the deceased, if present, to take possession of the effects of the deceased that are then at the air base or in quarters.

(b) If there is no legal representative or surviving spouse present, the commanding officer shall direct a summary court-martial to collect the effects of the deceased that are then at the air base or in quarters.

(c) The summary court-martial may collect debts due the decedent's estate by local debtors, pay undisputed local creditors of the deceased to the extent permitted by money of the deceased in the court's possession, and shall take receipts for those payments, to be filed with the court's final report to the Department of the Air Force.

(d) As soon as practicable after the collection of the effects and money of the deceased, the summary court-martial shall send them at the expense of the United States to the living person highest on the following list who can be found by the court:

(1) The surviving spouse or legal representative.

(2) A child of the deceased.

(3) A parent of the deceased.

(4) A brother or sister of the deceased.

(5) The next-of-kin of the deceased.

(6) A beneficiary named in the will of the deceased.

(e) If the summary court-martial cannot dispose of the effects under subsection

(d) because there are no persons in those categories or because the court finds that the addresses of the persons are not known or readily ascertainable, the court may convert the effects of the deceased, except sabers, insignia, decorations, medals, watches, trinkets, manuscripts, and other articles valuable chiefly as keepsakes, into cash, by public or private sale, but not until 30 days after the date of death of the deceased.

(f) As soon as practicable after the effects have been converted into cash under subsection (e), the summary court-martial shall deposit all cash in the court's possession and belonging to the estate with the officer designated in regulations, and shall send a receipt therefor, together with any will or other papers of value, an inventory of the effects, and articles not permitted to be sold, to the executive part of the Department of the Air Force. The Secretary of the Air Force shall deliver to the Armed Forces Retirement Home all items received by the executive part of the Department of the Air Force under this subsection.

(Aug. 10, 1956, ch 1041, § 1, 70A Stat. 585; Act Nov. 2, 1966, P. L. 89-718, § 48, 80 Stat. 1121; Dec. 12, 1980, P. L. 96-513, Title V, Part B, § 514(19), 94 Stat. 2936; Nov. 8, 1985, P. L. 99-145, Title XIII, § 1301(d)(4)(A), 99 Stat. 736; Nov. 5, 1990, P. L. 101-510, Div A, Title XV, Part B, § 1533(a)(9), 104 Stat. 1735; Oct. 19, 1996, P. L. 104-316, Title II, § 202(g), 110 Stat. 3842.)

HISTORY; ANCILLARY LAWS AND DIRECTIVES

Prior law and revision:

Revised Section	Source (USCS)	Source (Statutes at Large)
9712(a)	5:150j (words before 1st semicolon of 1st para.; and last para.).	June 4, 1920, ch. 227, subch. II, § 1 (Art. 112), 41 Stat. 809; May 5, 1950, ch. 169, § 6(c), 64 Stat. 145.
9712(b)	5:150j (22 words after 1s semicolon of 1st tpara.).	
9712(c)	5:150j (words between 1st and second semicolons of 1st para., less 1st 22 words).	
9712(d)	5:150j (words between 2d and semicolons of 1st para.).	
9712(e)	5:150j (words between 3d and 4th semicolons of 1st para.).	
9712(f)	5:150j (1st para., less words before 4th semicolon, and less last 40 words).	
9712(g)	5:150j (last 40 words of 1st para.).	

In subsection (a), the words "the court-martial jurisdiction of the Air Force

or the Army at a place or command under the jurisdiction of the Air Force'' are substituted for the words ''military law'', to reflect the creation of a separate Air Force. Cl. (2) is substituted for 5:150j (last para.).
In subsections (a), (b), and (c), the words ''surviving spouse'' are substituted for the word ''widow''.
In subsection (c), the word ''may'' is substituted for the words ''shall have authority to''. The words ''to the extent permitted'' are substituted for the words ''in so far as . . . will permit''. The words ''under this article'' and ''upon its transactions'' are omitted as surplusage.
In subsection (d), the words ''through the Quartermaster Corps'' are omitted, since the Air Force does not have organic corps created by statute. The words ''if such be found by said court'' are omitted as surplusage. The words ''United States'' are substituted for the word ''Government''. 5:150j (19 words before 3d semicolon of 1st par.) is omitted as covered by subsection (g).
In subsection (e), the first 37 words are substituted for 5:150j (33 words after 3d semicolon of 1st par.). The word ''may'' is substituted for the word ''shall have the authority''.
In subsection (f), the words ''Soldiers' Home'' are inserted, since, as provided in section 9713 of this title, the Home is now the place where the mentioned articles are sent.

Amendments:

1966. Act Nov. 2, 1966, in subsec. (a)(1) substituted ''military law'' for ''the court-martial jurisdiction of the Air Force or the Army''.

1980. Act Dec. 12, 1980 (effective upon enactment on 12/12/80, as provided by § 701(b)(3) of such Act, which appears as 10 USCS § 101 note), in subsecs. (a)(2) and (f), substituted ''United States Soldiers' and Airmen's Home'' for ''Soldiers' Home''.

1985. Act Nov. 8, 1985, in subsec. (d), substituted paras. (1)–(6) for former paras. (1)–(9) which read:

''(1) Surviving spouse or legal representative.

''(2) Son.

''(3) Daughter.

''(4) Father, if he has not abandoned the support of his family.

''(5) Mother.

''(6) Brother.

''(7) Sister.

''(8) Next of kin.

''(9) Beneficiary named in the will of the deceased.''.

1990. Act Nov. 5, 1990 (effective 1 year after enactment as provided by § 1541(a), which appears as 24 USCS § 401 note), in subsec. (a)(2), substituted ''a resident of the Armed Forces Retirement Home'' for ''an inmate of the United States Soldiers' and Airmen's Home''; and, in subsec. (f), deleted ''for transmission to the United States Soldiers' and Airmen's Home'' after ''Air Force'' and inserted the sentence beginning ''The Secretary of the Air Force . . .''.

1996. Act Oct. 19, 1996 deleted subsec. (g), which read: ''(g) The summary court-martial shall make a full report of the transactions under this section, with respect to the deceased, to the Department of the Air Force for transmission to the General Accounting Office for action authorized in the settlement of accounts of deceased members of the Air Force.''.

Transfer of functions:

For transfer of functions contained in this section from the Comptroller General to the Director of the Office of Management and Budget, effective June 30, 1996, see Act Nov. 19, 1995, P. L. 104-53, Title II, § 211, 109 Stat. 535, which appears as 31 USCS § 501 note.

CROSS REFERENCES

Summary courts-martial—Jurisdiction, 10 USCS § 820.

Summary courts-martial—Persons authorized to convene, 10 USCS § 824.

General military law provisions respecting—Disposition of unclaimed property, 10 USCS § 2575.

General military law provisions respecting—Final settlement of accounts of deceased members, 10 USCS § 2771.

General military law provisions respecting—Armed Forces Retirement Home, 24 USCS §§ 401 et seq.

This section is referred to in 5 USCS § 5564; 10 USCS § 2575; 24 USCS § 420; 37 USCS § 554.

[§ 9713. Repealed]

HISTORY; ANCILLARY LAWS AND DIRECTIVES

This section (Acts Aug. 10, 1956, ch 1041, § 1, 70A Stat. 586; Dec. 12, 1980, P. L. 96-513, Title V, Part B, § 514(20)(A), (B), 94 Stat. 2936; Nov. 8, 1985, P. L. 99-145, Title XIII, § 1301(d)(4)(B), 99 Stat. 737; Nov. 29, 1989, P. L. 101-189, Div A, Title XVI, Part C, § 1621(a)(1), 103 Stat. 1602) was repealed by Act Nov. 5, 1990, P. L. 101-510, Div A, Title XV, Part B, § 1533(a)(10)(A), 104 Stat. 1735, effective 1 year after enactment as provided by § 1541(a), which appears as 24 USCS § 401 note. This section provided for disposition of effects of deceased persons by Soldiers' and Airmen's Home.

CHAPTER 947. TRANSPORTATION

HISTORY; ANCILLARY LAWS AND DIRECTIVES

Amendments:

1962. Act Sept. 7, 1962, P. L. 87-651, Title I, § 129 (2), 76 Stat. 514, amended the analysis of this chapter by deleting item ''9748, which read: ''9748. Motor vehicles: for members on permanent change of station''.

1996. Act Sept. 23, 1996, P. L. 104-201, Div A, Title IX, Subtitle A, § 906(d)(3), 110 Stat. 2620, amended the analysis of this chapter by deleting item 9742, which read: ''9742. Control of transportation systems in time of war''.

§ 9741. Control and supervision

The transportation of members, munitions of war, equipment, military property, and stores of the Air Force throughout the United States shall be under the immediate control and supervision of the Secretary of the Air Force and agents appointed or designated by him.

(Aug. 10, 1956, ch 1041, § 1, 70A Stat. 587.)

HISTORY; ANCILLARY LAWS AND DIRECTIVES

Prior law and revision:

Revised Section	Source (USCS)	Source (Statutes at Large)
9741	10:1363.	R.S. 220.

INTERPRETIVE NOTES AND DECISIONS

Widow of National Guard officer killed in crash of military aircraft while returning from fishing trip as non-paying passenger was not entitled to recover against United States under Federal Tort Claims Act (28 USCS § 2674) as officer, while aboard aircraft, was subject to immediate control and supervision of Secretary of Army by virtue of 10 USCS § 4741 and Secretary of Air Force by virtue of 10 USCS § 9741 and thus officer's activity at time of death was incident to service. Herreman v United States (1973, CA7 Wis) 476 F2d 234.

[§ 9742. Repealed]

HISTORY; ANCILLARY LAWS AND DIRECTIVES

This section (Act Aug. 10, 1956, ch 1041, § 1, 70A Stat. 587) was repealed by Act Sept. 23, 1996, P. L. 104-201, Div A, Title IX, Subtitle A, § 906(c), 110 Stat. 2620. It provided for control of transportation systems in time of war. For similar provisions, see 10 USCS § 2644.

§ 9743. Officers: Use of transportation

Under such conditions as the Secretary of the Air Force may prescribe, officers of the Air Force may, in the performance of their duties, use means of transportation provided for the Air Force and its supplies.

(Aug. 10, 1956, ch 1041, § 1, 70A Stat. 587.)

HISTORY; ANCILLARY LAWS AND DIRECTIVES

Prior law and revision:

Revised Section	Source (USCS)	Source (Statutes at Large)
9743	10:749.	Mar. 3, 1911, ch. 209 (5th proviso under ''Transportation of The Army and Its Supplies''), 36 Stat. 1051.

Since its legislative history shows that it was enacted because the Comptroller of the Treasury had disallowed certain accounts for travel expenses (46 Congressional Record, pp. 905–913, 4643–4645), the source statute is restated to preclude future disallowances. The words ''official and military'' are omitted as surplusage.

§ 9746. Civilian personnel in Alaska

Persons residing in Alaska who are and have been employed there by the United States for at least two years, and their families, may be transported on airplanes operated by Air Force transport agencies or, within bulk space allocations made to the Department of the Air Force, on vessels or airplanes operated by any military transport agency of the Department of Defense, if—

(1) the Secretary of the Air Force considers that accommodations are available;

(2) the transportation is without expense to the United States;

(3) the transportation is limited to one round trip between Alaska and the United States during any two-year period, except in an emergency such as sickness or death; and

(4) in case of travel by air—

(A) the Secretary of Transportation has not certified that commercial air carriers of the United States that can handle the transportation are operating between Alaska and the United States; and

(B) the transportation cannot be reasonably handled by a United States commercial air carrier.

(Aug. 10, 1956, ch 1041, § 1, 70A Stat. 587; Oct. 4, 1984, P. L. 98-443, § 9(k) in part, 98 Stat. 1708.)

HISTORY; ANCILLARY LAWS AND DIRECTIVES

Prior law and revision:

Revised Section	Source (USCS)	Source (Statutes at Large)
9746	10:1371a.	Nov. 21, 1941, ch. 483; restated July 25, 1947, ch. 321, 61 Stat. 423.

Before the enactment of the National Security Act of 1947, the transport functions covered by this section were performed only by the Army. Under Transfer Order 26, 15 Oct. 1948, JAAF Bull. 42, 1948; JAAFAR 4-55-1, par. 2a(1)(f), 29 Oct. 1948; AR 96-15, AFR 76-7, 5 June 1951; AR 96-20, AFR 76-6, 11 June 1953, these transport functions also became the responsibility of the Secretary of the Air Force.

Under section 2(a)(3) of the National Security Act (as it existed before August 10, 1949), the sea transportation functions of the Army and Navy, and the air transportation functions of the Army, Navy, and Air Force were respectively consolidated into the ''Military Sea Transportation Service'', under the Department of the Navy, and the ''Military Air Transport Service'', under the Department of the Air Force. Instead of having space on transport vessels and airplanes operated by it for its sole use, the Air Force is allotted bulk space on vessels and airplanes operated by military transport agencies operating for the benefit of the Department of Defense as a whole. The words ''or, within bulk space allocations made to the Department of the Air Force, on vessels or airplanes operated by any military transport agency of the Department of Defense'' are inserted, in accordance with an opinion of the Judge Advocate General of the Army (JAGA 1953/5885, 22 July 1953), concurred in by the Judge Advocate General of the Air Force, to make clear that the rule applicable to vessels and airplanes applies to the bulk space allocated to the Air Force. Since the authority to perform transportation functions could again be transferred as between the military departments, the references to airplanes of Air Force transport agencies (as distinct from bulk space allocations thereon) is retained.

The word ''considers'' is substituted for the words ''in the opinion of''.

The words ''Persons residing in Alaska who are and have been employed there by the United States'', are substituted for the words ''employees of the United States, residing in Alaska, who have been in such employment''.

The word ''commercial'' is substituted for the word ''civil'' for clarity.

The words ''from and after November 21, 1941'', ''and the carriage of all such air traffic shall be terminated'', ''dire'', ''the privilege herein granted'', and ''as to each eligible individual'' are omitted as surplusage.

The words ''the continental'' are omitted, since 10 USCS § 101(1) defines the United States as ''the States and the District of Columbia''.

Amendments:

1984. Act Oct. 4, 1984 (effective 1/1/85, as provided by § 9(v) of such Act, which appears as 5 USCS § 5314 note), in para. (4)(A), substituted ''Secretary of Transportation'' for ''Civil Aeronautics Board''.

[§ 9748. Repealed]

HISTORY; ANCILLARY LAWS AND DIRECTIVES

This section (Act Aug. 10, 1956, ch 1041, § 1, 70A Stat. 588) was repealed

by Act Sept. 7, 1962, P. L. 87-651, Title I, § 129(1), 76 Stat. 514. It related to transportation of motor vehicles for members on permanent change of station. For similar provisions, see 10 USCS § 2634.

CHAPTER 949. REAL PROPERTY

HISTORY; ANCILLARY LAWS AND DIRECTIVES

Amendments:

1958. Act Sept. 2, 1958, P. L. 85-861, § 1(203)(B), 72 Stat. 1542, amended the analysis of this chapter by adding item 9780.

1971. Act Oct. 27, 1971, P. L. 92-145, Title V, § 509(b), 85 Stat. 408, amended the analysis of this chapter by deleting item 9775, which read: ''9775. Quarters: officers.''.

1973. Act Nov. 29, 1973, P. L. 93-166, Title V, § 509(e), 87 Stat. 678, amended the analysis of this chapter by substituting item 9774 for one which read ''Construction of quarters: limitations on space and cost.''.

1980. Act Dec. 12, 1980, P.L. 96-513, Title V, Part B, § 514(21), 94 Stat. 2936 (effective upon enactment on 12/12/80, as provided by § 701(b)(3) of such Act, which appears as 10 USCS § 101 note), amended the analysis of this chapter by deleting item 9772, which read: ''9772. Reservation and use for air base and testing field.''.

1982. Act July 12, 1982, P. L. 97-214, § 10(a)(9)(B), 96 Stat. 175 (effective 10/1/82, as provided by § 12(a) of such Act, which appears as 10 USCS § 2801 note), amended the analysis of this chapter by deleting item 9774, which read: ''9774. Construction: limitations''.

1987. Act Dec. 4, 1987, P. L. 100-180, Div B, Subdiv 3, Title II, § 2325(b), 101 Stat. 1221, amended the analysis of this chapter by adding item 9781.

1997. Act Nov. 18, 1997, P. L. 105-85, Div A, Title II, Subtitle D, § 242(b), 111 Stat. 1667, amended the analysis of this chapter by adding item 9782.

§ 9771. Acceptance of donations: land for mobilization, training, supply base, or aviation field

The Secretary of the Air Force may accept for the United States a gift of—

(1) land that he considers suitable and desirable for a permanent mobilization, training, or supply base; and

(2) land that he considers suitable and desirable for an aviation field, if the gift is from a citizen of the United States and its terms authorize the use of the property by the United States for any purpose.

(Aug. 10, 1956, ch 1041, § 1, 70A Stat. 588.)

HISTORY; ANCILLARY LAWS AND DIRECTIVES

Prior law and revision:

Revised Section	Source (USCS)	Source (Statutes at Large)
9771	10:1342. 10:1344.	Aug. 29, 1916, ch. 418 (6th and 8th para. under ''Office of the Chief Signal Officer''), 39 Stat. 622, 623.

10:1344 (last 40 words) is omitted as executed. The words ''tract or tracts'', in 10:1342 and 1344, are omitted as surplusage. The words ''and remount station'', in 10:1342, are omitted, since the property and civilian personnel of the Remount Service of the Quartermaster Corps were transferred to the Department of Agriculture by the act of April 21, 1948, ch. 224, 62 Stat. 197 (7 U.S.C. 436-438). The words ''by the United States for any purpose'' are substituted for the words ''for any other service of the United States which may hereafter appear desirable'', in 10:1342. The words ''from any person'', in 10:1344, are omitted as surplusage.

[§ 9772. Repealed]

HISTORY; ANCILLARY LAWS AND DIRECTIVES

This section (Act Aug. 10, 1956, ch 1041, § 1, 70A Stat. 588) was repealed by Act Oct. 21, 1976, P. L. 94-579, § 704(a), 90 Stat. 2792 (effective on or after Oct. 21, 1978, as provided by such section). It authorized unappropriated public land or other property of the United States to be reserved or used for air bases or testing fields.

Other provisions:

Rights existing on Oct. 21, 1976. Repeal by Act Oct. 21, 1976, not to be construed as terminating any valid lease, permit, patent, etc., existing on Oct. 21, 1976, see 43 USCS § 1701 note.

§ 9773. Acquisition and construction: air bases and depots

(a) The Secretary of the Air Force shall determine the sites of such additional permanent air bases and depots in all strategic areas of the United States and the Territories, Commonwealths, possessions, and holdings as he considers necessary. He shall determine when the enlargement of existing air bases and depots is necessary for the effective peacetime training of the Air Force.

(b) In determining the sites of new air bases and depots, the Secretary shall consider the following regions for the purposes indicated—

(1) the Atlantic northeast, for training in cold weather and in fog;

(2) the Atlantic southeast and Caribbean areas, for training in long-range operations, especially those incident to reinforcing the defenses of the Panama Canal;

(3) the southeastern United States, to provide a depot necessary to maintain the Air Force;

(4) the Pacific northwest, to establish and maintain air communication with Alaska;

(5) Alaska, for training under conditions of extreme cold;

(6) the Rocky Mountain area, to provide a depot necessary to maintain the Air Force, and for training in operations from fields in high altitudes; and

(7) other regions, for the establishment of intermediate air bases to provide for transcontinental movements of the Air Force for maneuvers.

(c) In selecting sites for air bases and depots covered by this section and in determining the alteration or enlargement of existing air bases or depots, the Secretary shall consider the need—

(1) to form the nucleus for concentration of Air Force units in time of war;

(2) to permit, in time of peace, training and effective planning in each strategic area for the use and expansion of commercial, municipal, and private flying installations in time of war;

(3) to locate, in each strategic area in which it is considered necessary, adequate storage facilities for munitions and other articles necessary to facilitate the movement, concentration, maintenance, and operation of the Air Force; and

(4) to afford the maximum warning against surprise attack by enemy aircraft upon aviation of the United States and its necessary installations consistent with maintaining, in connection with existing or contemplated landing fields, the full power of the Air Force for operations necessary in the defense of the United States, and in the defense and reinforcement of the Territories, Commonwealths, possessions, and holdings.

(d) In carrying out this section, the Secretary, on behalf of the United States, may acquire title, in fee simple and free of encumbrance, to any land that he considers necessary—

(1) by accepting title without cost to the United States;

(2) by exchanging military reservations or parts thereof for that land, upon the written approval of the President; or

(3) by purchase or condemnation, if acquisition by gift or exchange is impracticable.

(e) The Secretary may, by purchase, gift, lease, or otherwise, acquire at desired locations bombing and machine gun ranges necessary for practice by, and the training of, tactical units.

(f) At each air base or depot established under this section, the Secretary shall remove or remodel existing structures as necessary; do necessary grading; and provide buildings, utilities, communication systems, landing fields and mats, roads, walks, aprons, docks, runways, facilities for the storage and distribution of ammunition, fuel, oil, necessary protection against bombs, and and all appurtenances to the foregoing.

(g) The Secretary may direct the transportation of personnel, and the purchase, renovation, and transportation of material, that he considers necessary to carry out this section.

(Aug. 10, 1956, ch 1041, § 1, 70A Stat. 588.)

HISTORY; ANCILLARY LAWS AND DIRECTIVES

Prior law and revision:

Revised Section	Source (USCS)	Source (Statutes at Large)
9773(a)	10:1343a (1st sentence).	Aug. 12, 1935, ch. 511,
9773(b)	10:1343a (2d sentence).	§§ 1-3, 49 Stat. 610.
9773(c)	10:1343a (less 1st and 2d sentences).	
9773(d)	10:1343b.	
9773(e)	10:1343c (last sentence).	
9773(f)	10:1343c (1st sentence).	
9773(g)	10:1343c (2d sentence).	

In subsection (a), the word ''shall'' is substituted for the words ''is authorized and directed to''. The words ''Territories, Commonwealths,'' are substituted for the word ''Alaska'' to make it clear that the section covers all territory of the United States. The words ''Air Force'' are substituted for the words ''General Headquarters Air Force and the Air Corps components of our overseas garrisons''.

In subsection (b), the words ''to provide'', ''to permit'', ''in addition'', and ''incident to the concentration of'' are omitted as surplusage.

In subsection (c), the introductory cl. is substituted for 10:1343a (1st 41 words of 3d sentence). The words ''to locate'' are substituted for the words ''there shall be provided''. The words ''aviation of the United States'' are substituted for the words ''our own aviation''. The words, ''Territories, Commonwealths,'' are inserted to conform to subsec. (a). The words ''The stations shall be suitably located'', ''of the set-up'', ''by responsible personnel'', ''there shall be provided'', ''General Headquarters'', ''in peace and war'', ''such close and distant . . . over land and sea'', and ''The stations and depots shall be located with a view'', and 10:1343a (4th clause of 3d sentence) are omitted as surplusage.

In subsection (d), cl. (3) is substituted for 10:1343b (last 26 words), 10:1043b (24 words before 1st proviso) is omitted as surplusage.

In subsection (f), the word ''shall'' is substituted for the words ''is further authorized and directed to''. The word ''provide'' is substituted for the words ''construct, install, and equip, or complete the construction, installation, and equipment''. The words ''technical buildings and utilities'' are omitted as covered by the words ''buildings'' and ''utilities''. The words ''sewer, water, power station and aerodrome lighting'' are omitted as covered by the word ''utilities''. The words ''communication systems'' are substituted for the words ''telephone and signal communications''. The words ''appurtenances to the foregoing'' are substituted for the words ''other essentials''.

RESEARCH GUIDE

Federal Procedure:

7 Fed Proc L Ed, Condemnation of Property § 14:247.

INTERPRETIVE NOTES AND DECISIONS

1. Condemnation of land
2. Miscellaneous

1. Condemnation of land

In proceeding to condemn land for use in connection with air force base, determination of Secretary as to what was necessary to be taken was not reviewable by courts; hence, court erred in holding that state's mineral interest in land, fee title to which was sought, was not necessary and in dismissing that interest from taking. United States v South Dakota (1954, CA8 SD) 212 F2d 14, 3 OGR 1435.

Where declaration of taking in condemnation described estate taken as right to clear and keep clear trees, perennial growth and construction above prescribed height, only clearance or obstruction easement, and not aviation or flight easement, was taken, and trial court erred in construing it as latter. United States v Brondum (1959, CA5 Ala) 272 F2d 642.

In condemnation proceeding by United States, declaration of taking by Secretary of War reciting that land sought was taken under predecessor of 10 USCS § 9773 and that use for which the same was acquired was for purpose described in said acts was not insufficient as not containing sufficient statement of public use for which lands were taken; original declaration of taking by Secretary which took entire fee was not shown to be void, because Secretary later attempted to amend it by eliminating from proceedings oil, gas, and other minerals in said lands. United States v 16572 Acres of Land (1942, DC Tex) 45 F Supp 23.

2. Miscellaneous

State Public Service Commission cannot designate utility company from whom federal government must purchase electricity, nor can commission dictate area of government owned property in which government must use electricity it has purchased for Air Force base acquired and constructed pursuant to 10 USCS § 9773. Arkansas Power & Light Co. v Arkansas Public Service Com. (1959) 231 Ark 142, 330 SW2d 51, cert den (1960) 362 US 975, 4 L Ed 2d 1011, 80 S Ct 1060.

[§ 9774. Repealed]

HISTORY; ANCILLARY LAWS AND DIRECTIVES

This section (Act Aug. 10, 1956, ch 1041, § 1, 70A Stat. 590; Aug. 30, 1957, P. L. 85-241, Title IV, § 404(c), 71 Stat. 556; Aug. 10, 1959, P. L. 86-149, Title IV, § 410(c), 73 Stat. 322; July 27, 1962, P. L. 87-554, Title V, § 504(a), (c), 76 Stat. 239; Nov. 7, 1963, P. L. 88-174, Title V, § 503, 77 Stat. 325; Dec. 5, 1969, P. L. 91-142, Title V, § 510(b), 83 Stat. 312; Oct. 27, 1971, P. L. 92-145, Title V, § 508(a), (c), 85 Stat. 408; Nov. 29, 1973, P. L. 93-166, Title V, § 509(e), 87 Stat. 678) was repealed by Act July 12, 1982, P. L. 97-214, § 7(1) in part, 96 Stat. 173, effective Oct. 1, 1982, as provided by § 12(a) of such Act, which appears as 10 USCS § 2801 note. This section provided for construction and limitations thereon. For similar provisions, see 10 USCS §§ 2801 et seq.

[§ 9775. Repealed]

HISTORY; ANCILLARY LAWS AND DIRECTIVES

This section (Act Aug. 10, 1956, ch 1041, § 1, 70A Stat. 590), was repealed by Act Oct. 27, 1971, P. L. 92-145, § 509(b), 85 Stat. 408. It authorized assignment of quarters belonging to the United States at an air base or other Air Force installation to officers, grade lieutenant general down to second lieutenant, 10 to 2 rooms, respectively, and prohibited other assignment where quarters existed.

§ 9776. Emergency construction: fortifications

If in an emergency the President considers it urgent, a temporary air base or fortification may be built on private land if the owner consents in writing.
(Aug. 10, 1956, ch 1041, § 1, 70A Stat. 591; Act Sept. 1, 1970, P. L. 91-393, § 5, 84 Stat. 835.)

HISTORY; ANCILLARY LAWS AND DIRECTIVES

Prior law and revision:

Revised Section	Source (USCS)	Source (Statutes at Large)
9776	50:178.	Apr. 11, 1898, J. Res. 21, 30 Stat. 737.

The word "important" is omitted as covered by the word "urgent". The words "upon which such work is to be placed" are omitted as surplusage.

Amendments:

1970. Act Sept. 1, 1970, after the sentence beginning "If in an emergency. . . .", deleted one which read "In such a case, section 175 of title 50 does not apply.".

§ 9777. Permits: military reservations; landing ferries, erecting bridges, driving livestock

Whenever the Secretary of the Air Force considers that it can be done without injury to the reservation or inconvenience to the military forces stationed there, he may permit—

(1) the landing of ferries at a military reservation;

(2) the erection of bridges on a military reservation; and

(3) the driving of livestock across a military reservation.

(Aug. 10, 1956, ch 1041, § 1, 70A Stat. 591.)

HISTORY; ANCILLARY LAWS AND DIRECTIVES

Prior law and revision:

Revised Section	Source (USCS)	Source (Statutes at Large)
9777	10:1348.	July 5, 1884, ch. 214, § 6, 23 Stat. 104.

The words "may permit" are substituted for the words "shall have authority, in his discretion, to permit". The words "to permit the extension of State, county, and Territorial roads across military reservations" are omitted as superseded by section 2668 of this title. In clause (3), the word "livestock" is substituted for the words "cattle, sheep or other stock animals".

INTERPRETIVE NOTES AND DECISIONS

Exercise of Secretary's discretion pursuant to predecessor of 10 USCS § 9777 was not making of law and Congress could properly delegate such power. United States v Golden Gate Bridge & Highway Dist. (1941, DC Cal) 37 F Supp 505, affd (1942, CA9 Cal) 125 F2d 872, cert den (1942) 316 US 700, 86 L Ed 1769, 62 S Ct 1298.

§ 9778. Licenses: military reservations; erection and use of buildings; Young Men's Christian Association

Under such conditions as he may prescribe, the Secretary of the Air Force may issue a revocable license to the International Committee of Young Men's Christian Associations of North America to erect and maintain, on military reservations within the United States and the Territories, Commonwealths, and possessions, buildings needed by that organization for the promotion of the social, physical, intellectual, and moral welfare of the members of the Air Force on those reservations.

(Aug. 10, 1956, ch 1041, § 1, 70A Stat. 591.)

HISTORY; ANCILLARY LAWS AND DIRECTIVES

Prior law and revision:

Revised Section	Source (USCS)	Source (Statutes at Large)
9778	10:1346.	May 31, 1902, ch. 943, 32 Stat. 282.

The words "may issue" are substituted for the words "Authority is given to . . . in his discretion, to grant permission". The words "Under such conditions as he may prescribe" are substituted for the words "under such regulations as the Secretary of the Army may impose". The words "members of the Air Force" are substituted for the word "garrisons". The words "the Territories, Commonwealths, and possessions" are substituted for the words "or its island possessions", for clarity.

INTERPRETIVE NOTES AND DECISIONS

As evidenced by predecessor of 10 USCS § 9778, it was Congress' intent that even temporary or transient occupation of land reserved for military purposes would require express permission of appropriate authorities. (1897) 21 Op Atty Gen. 537.

§ 9779. Use of public property

(a) When the economy of the Air Force so requires, the Secretary of the Air Force shall establish military headquarters in places where suitable buildings are owned by the United States.

(b) No money appropriated for the support of the Air Force may be spent for base gardens or Air Force exchanges. However, this does not prevent Air Force exchanges from using public buildings or public transportation that, in the opinion of the Secretary, are not needed for other purposes.

(Aug. 10, 1956, ch 1041, § 1, 70A Stat. 591; Nov. 14, 1986, P. L. 99-661, Div B, Title VII, Part C, § 2721 in part, 100 Stat. 4042.)

HISTORY; ANCILLARY LAWS AND DIRECTIVES

Prior law and revision:

Revised Section	Source (USCS)	Source (Statutes at Large)
9779(a)	10:1332.	June 23, 1879, ch. 35, § 8, 21 Stat. 35.
9779(b)	10:1345.	Aug. 1, 1914, ch. 223 (2d para. under "Quartermaster Corps"), 38 Stat. 629.
9779(c)	10:1335.	July 16, 1892, ch. 195 (last proviso under "Quartermaster's Department"), 27 Stat. 178; June 28, 1950, ch. 383, § 402(c), 64 Stat. 272.

In subsection (a), the words "United States" are substituted for the word "Government".

In subsection (b), the words "suitable space" are substituted for the words "proper and suitable room or rooms". The words "there is a" are substituted for the words "have been established".

In subsection (c), the words "the Secretary" are substituted for the words "the Quartermaster General", since the functions which, for the Army, are assigned by statute to subordinate officers of the Army, are, for the Air Force, assigned to the Secretary.

Amendments:

1986. Act Nov. 14, 1986 deleted subsec. (b), which read: "The Secretary shall assign suitable space for postal purposes at each air base where there is a post office."; and redesignated subsec. (c) as subsec. (b).

§ 9780. Acquisition of buildings in District of Columbia

(a) In time of war or when war is imminent, the Secretary of the Air Force may acquire by lease any building, or part of a building, in the District of Columbia that may be needed for military purposes.

(b) At any time, the Secretary may, for the purposes of the Department of the Air Force, requisition the use and take possession of any building or space in any building, and its appurtenances, in the District of Columbia, other than—

(1) a dwelling house occupied as such;

(2) a building occupied by any other agency of the United States; or

(3) space in such a dwelling house or building.

The Secretary shall determine, and pay out of funds appropriated for the payment of rent by the Department of the Air Force, just compensation for that use. If the amount of the compensation is not satisfactory to the person entitled to it, the Secretary shall pay 75 percent of it to that person, and the claimant is entitled to recover by action against the United States an additional amount that, when added to the amount paid by the Secretary, is determined by the court to be just compensation for that use.

(Added Sept 2, 1958, P. L. 85-861, § 1(203)(A), 72 Stat. 1542.)

HISTORY; ANCILLARY LAWS AND DIRECTIVES

Prior law and revision:

Revised Section	Source (USCS)	Source (Statutes at Large)
9780(a)	40:37.	July 9, 1918, ch. 143 (3d proviso under ''Barracks and Quarters''), 40 Stat. 861.
9780(b)	40:41.	July 8, 1918, ch. 139, (2d para. under ''War Department''), 40 Stat. 826.

In subsection (a), the words ''may acquire by lease'' are substituted for the words ''is authorized, in his discretion, to rent or lease''. The word ''needed'' is substituted for the word ''required''.

In subsection (b), the words ''At any time'' are inserted for clarity. The word ''may'' is substituted for the words ''is authorized''. The word ''agency'' is substituted for the word ''branch''. Clause (3) is inserted for clarity. The word ''determine'' is substituted for the word ''ascertain''. The words ''out of funds appropriated for the payment of rent by'' are substituted for the words ''within the limits of the appropriations for rent made by any act making appropriations for''. The word ''is'' is substituted for the word ''be''. The words ''so ascertained'' and ''in the manner provided by sections 41(20) and 250 of Title 28'' are omitted as surplusage, since those sections were repealed in 1948 and replaced by sections 1346, 1491, 1496, 1501, 1503, 2401, 2402, and 2501 of that title.

§ 9781. Disposition of real property at missile sites

(a)(1) The Administrator of General Services shall dispose of the interest of the United States in any tract of real property described in paragraph (2) or in any easement held in connection with any such tract of real property only as provided in this section.

(2) The real property referred to in paragraph (1) is any tract of land (including improvements thereon) owned by the Air Force that—

(A) is not required for the needs of the Air Force and the discharge of the responsibilities of the Air Force, as determined by the Secretary of the Air Force;

(B) does not exceed 25 acres;

(C) was used by the Air Force as a site for one or more missile launch facilities, missile launch control buildings, or other facilities to support missile launch operations; and

(D) is surrounded by lands that are adjacent to such tract and that—

(i) are owned in fee simple by one owner, either individually or by more than one person jointly, in common, or by the entirety; or

(ii) are owned separately by two or more owners.

(b)(1)(A) Whenever the interest of the United States in a tract of real property or easement referred to in subsection (a) is available for disposition under this section, the Administrator shall transmit a notice of the availability of the real property or easement to each person described in subsection (a)(2)(D)(i) who owns lands adjacent to that real property or easement.

(B) The Administrator shall convey, for fair market value, the interest of the United States in a tract of land referred to in subsection (a), or in any easement in connection with such a tract of land, to any person or persons described in subsection (a)(2)(D)(i) who, with respect to such land, are ready, willing, and able to purchase such interest for the fair market value of such interest.

(2)(A) In the case of a tract of real property referred to in subsection (a) that is surrounded by adjacent lands that are owned separately by two or more owners, the Administrator shall dispose of that tract of real property in accordance with this paragraph. In disposing of the real property, the Administrator shall satisfy the requirements specified in paragraph (1) regarding notice to owners, sale at fair market value, and the determination of the qualifications of the purchaser.

(B) The Administrator shall dispose of such a tract of real property through a sealed bid competitive sale. The Administrator shall afford an opportunity to compete to acquire the interest of the United States in the real property to all of the persons described in subsection (a)(2)(D)(ii) who own lands adjacent to that real property. The Administrator shall restrict to these persons the opportunity to compete in the sealed bid competitive sale.

(C) Subject to subparagraph (D), the Administrator shall convey the interest of the United States in the tract of real property to the highest bidder.

(D) If all of the bids received by the Administrator in the sealed bid competitive sale of the tract of real property are less than the fair market value of the real property, the Administrator shall dispose of the real property in accordance with the provisions of title II of the Federal Property and Administrative Services Act of 1949 (40 U.S.C. 481 et seq.).

(c) The Administrator shall determine the fair market value of the interest of the United States to be conveyed under this section.

(d) The requirement to determine whether any tract of land described in subsection (a)(2) is excess property or surplus property under title II of the Federal Property and Administrative Services Act of 1949 (40 U.S.C. 481 et seq.) before disposing of such tract shall not be applicable to the disposition of such tract under this section.

(e) The disposition of a tract of land under this section to any person shall be subject to (1) any easement retained by the Secretary of the Air Force with respect to such tract, and (2) such additional terms and conditions as the Administrator considers necessary or appropriate to protect the interests of the United States.

(f) The exact acreage and legal description of any tract of land to be conveyed under this section shall be determined in any manner that is satisfactory to the Administrator. The cost of any survey conducted for the purpose of this subsection in the case of any tract of land shall be borne by the person or persons to whom the conveyance of such tract of land is made.

(g) If any real property interest of the United States described in subsection (a) is not purchased under the procedures provided in subsections (a) through (f), such tract may be disposed of only in accordance with the Federal Property and Administrative Services Act of 1949.

(Added Dec. 4, 1987, P. L. 100-180, Div B, Subdiv 3, Title II, § 2325(a), 101 Stat. 1220; Nov. 30, 1993, P. L. 103-160, Div B, Title XXVIII, Subtitle E, § 2851, 107 Stat. 1906.)

HISTORY; ANCILLARY LAWS AND DIRECTIVES

References in text:

The ''Federal Property and Administrative Services Act of 1949'', referred to in this section, is Act June 30, 1949, ch 288, 63 Stat. 377, which appears generally as 40 USCS §§ 471 et seq. For full classification of such Act, consult USCS Tables volumes.

Amendments:

1993. Act Nov. 30, 1993, in subsec. (a), in para. (1), substituted ''Administrator of General Services'' for ''Secretary of the Air Force'' and, in para. (2), substituted subpara. (D) for one which read: ''(D) is surrounded by lands that are adjacent to such tract and that are owned in fee simple by one owner or by more than one owner jointly, in common, or by the entirety.''; substituted subsec. (b) for one which read: ''(b) The Secretary shall convey, for fair market value, the interest of the United States in any tract of land referred to in subsection (a) or in any easement in connection with any such tract of land to any person or persons who, with respect to such tract of land, own lands referred to in paragraph (2)(D) of such subsection and are ready, willing, and able to purchase such interest for the fair market value of such interest. Whenever such interest of the United States is available for purchase under this section, the Secretary shall transmit a notice of the availability of such interest to each such person.''; in subsec. (c), substituted ''Administrator'' for ''Secretary''; in subsec. (e), substituted ''Secretary of the Air Force'' for ''Secretary'' and substituted ''Administrator'' for ''Secretary''; and, in subsec. (f), substituted ''"Administrator'' for ''Secretary''.

§ 9782. Maintenance and repair of real property

(a) Allocation of funds. The Secretary of the Air Force shall allocate funds authorized to be appropriated by a provision described in subsection (c) and a provision described in subsection (d) for maintenance and repair of real property at military installations of the Department of the Air Force without regard to whether the installation is supported with funds authorized by a provision described in subsection (c) or (d).

(b) Mixing of funds prohibited on individual projects. The Secretary of the Air Force may not combine funds authorized to be appropriated by a provision described in subsection (c) and funds authorized to be appropriated by a provision described in subsection (d) for an individual project for maintenance and repair of real property at a military installation of the Department of the Air Force.

(c) Research, development, test, and evaluation funds. The provision described in this subsection is a provision of a national defense authorization Act that authorizes funds to be appropriated for a fiscal year to the Air Force for research, development, test, and evaluation.

(d) Operation and maintenance funds. The provision described in this subsection is a provision of a national defense authorization Act that authorizes funds to be appropriated for a fiscal year to the Air Force for operation and maintenance.

(Added Nov. 18, 1997, P. L. 105-85, Div A, Title II, Subtitle D, § 242(a), 111 Stat. 1666.)

CHAPTER 951. MILITARY CLAIMS

HISTORY; ANCILLARY LAWS AND DIRECTIVES

Amendments:

1960. Act June 29, 1960, P. L. 86-533, § 1(7)(B), 74 Stat. 247, amended the analysis of this chapter by deleting item 9805, which read: ''9805. Reports to Congress.''.

1972. Act August 29, 1972, P. L. 92-417, § 1(7), 86 Stat. 655, amended the analysis of this chapter by substituting item 9802 for one which read: ''Damage by United States vessels; towage and salvage of United States vessels.''.

§ 9801. Definition

In this chapter [10 USCS §§ 9801 et seq.], the term ''settle'' means consider, ascertain, adjust, determine, and dispose of a claim, whether by full or partial allowance or by disallowance.

(Aug. 10, 1956, ch 1041, § 1, 70A Stat. 591; Dec. 4, 1987, P. L. 100-180, Div A, Title XII, Part D, § 1231(19)(B), 101 Stat. 1161.)

HISTORY; ANCILLARY LAWS AND DIRECTIVES

Prior law and revision:

Revised Section	Source (USCS)	Source (Statutes at Large)
9801	[No source].	[No source].

The revised section is inserted for clarity, and is based on usage in the source laws for this revised chapter.

Amendments:

1987. Act Dec. 4, 1987 inserted ''the term''.

CODE OF FEDERAL REGULATIONS

Department of the Air Force—Administrative claims, 32 CFR Part 842.

§ 9802. Admiralty claims against the United States

(a) The Secretary of the Air Force may settle or compromise an admiralty claim against the United States for—

(1) damage caused by a vessel of, or in the service of, the Department of the

Air Force or by other property under the jurisdiction of the Department of the Air Force;

(2) compensation for towage and salvage service, including contract salvage, rendered to a vessel of, or in the service of, the Department of the Air Force or to other property under the jurisdiction of the Department of the Air Force; or

(3) damage caused by a maritime tort committed by any agent or employee of the Department of the Air Force or by property under the jurisdiction of the Department of the Air Force.

(b) If a claim under subsection (a) is settled or compromised for $500,000 or less, the Secretary of the Air Force may pay it. If it is settled or compromised for more than $500,000, he shall certify it to Congress.

(c) In any case where the amount to be paid is not more than $100,000, the Secretary of the Air Force may delegate his authority under subsection (a) to any person in the Department of the Air Force designated by him.

(Aug. 10, 1956, ch 1041, § 1, 70A Stat. 592; July 7, 1965, P. L. 89-67, 79 Stat. 212; Aug. 29, 1972, P. L. 92-417, § 1(6), 86 Stat. 655; Nov. 29, 1989, P. L. 101-189, Div A, Title XVI, Part D, § 1633, 103 Stat. 1608.)

HISTORY; ANCILLARY LAWS AND DIRECTIVES

Prior law and revision:

Revised Section	Source (USCS)	Source (Statutes at Large)
9802(a)	10:1861 (less 35 words before proviso, and less last proviso).	Oct. 20, 1951, ch. 524, §§ 1 (less 35 words before 1st proviso), 6 (as applicable to § 1), 65 Stat. 572, 573.
9802(b)	10:1861 (last proviso).	
9802(c)	10:1866 (as applicable to 10:1861).	

In subsection (a), the words "consider, ascertain, adjust, determine, compromise" are omitted as covered by the word "settle", as defined in section 9801 of this title. 10:1861 (1st proviso) is omitted as unnecessary, since other applicable claims laws are restated in this title. 10:1861 (2d proviso) is omitted as surplusage.

Amendments:

1965. Act July 7, 1965, in subsec. (c), substituted "$10,000" for "$1,000".

1972. Act Aug. 29, 1972, substituted the catchline for one which read: "Damage by United States vessels; towage and salvage of United States vessels"; and substituted subsec. (a) for one which read:

"(a) Under the direction of the Secretary of Defense, the Secretary of the Air Force may settle or compromise a claim against the United States for—

"(1) damage caused by a vessel of, or in the service of, the Department of the Air Force; or

"(2) compensation for towage and salvage service, including contract salvage, rendered to a vessel of, or in the service of, the Department of the Air Force.".

1989. Act Nov. 29, 1989, in subsec. (c), substituted "$100,000" for "$10,000".

CODE OF FEDERAL REGULATIONS

Department of the Air Force—Administrative claims, 32 CFR Part 842.

CROSS REFERENCES

This section is referred to in 10 USCS § 9806.

RESEARCH GUIDE

Federal Procedure:

23 Fed Proc L Ed, Maritime Law and Procedure §§ 53:162, 163.

Am Jur:

68 Am Jur 2d, Salvage § 60.

§ 9803. Admiralty claims by United States

(a) Under the direction of the Secretary of Defense, the Secretary of the Air Force may settle, or compromise, and receive payment of a claim by the United States for damage to property under the jurisdiction of the Department of the Air Force or property for which the Department has assumed an obligation to respond for damage, if—

(1) the claim is—

(A) of a kind that is within the admiralty jurisdiction of a district court of the United States; or

(B) for damage caused by a vessel or floating object; and

(2) the amount to be received by the United States is not more than $500,000.

(b) In exchange for payment of an amount found to be due the United States under subsection (a), the Secretary of the Air Force may execute a release of the claim on behalf of the United States. Amounts received under this section shall be covered into the Treasury.

(c) In any case where the amount to be received by the United States is not more than $100,000, the Secretary of the Air Force may delegate his authority under subsections (a) and (b) to any person in the Department of the Air Force designated by him.

(Aug. 10, 1956, ch 1041, § 1, 70A Stat. 592; July 7, 1965, P. L. 89-67, 79 Stat. 212; Nov. 29, 1989, P. L. 101-189, Div A, Title XVI, Part D, § 1633, 103 Stat. 1608.)

HISTORY; ANCILLARY LAWS AND DIRECTIVES

Prior law and revision:

Revised Section	Source (USCS)	Source (Statutes at Large)
9803(a)	10:1862 (1st sentence; 2d sentence, less last 32 words; and provisos of last sentence).	Oct. 20, 1951, ch. 524, §§ 2 (less last 32 words of 2d sentence), 6 (less applicability to § 1), 65 Stat. 572, 573.
9803(b)	10:1862 (3d sentence; and last sentence, less provisos).	
9803(c)	10:1866 (less applicability to 10:1861).	

In subsection (a), the words ''consider, ascertain, adjust, determine'' are omitted as covered by the word ''settle'', as defined in section 9801 this title. The words ''receive payment'' are substituted for 10:1862 (2d sentence, less last 32 words). The words ''of a kind that is within the admiralty jurisdiction'' are substituted for the words ''cognizable in admiralty''. Clause (2) is substituted for 10:1862 (last proviso of last sentence). 10:1862 (1st proviso of last sentence) is omitted as unnecessary, since other applicable claims laws are restated in this title. The words ''by contract or otherwise'' are omitted as surplusage.

In subsection (b), the words ''of the United States as miscellaneous receipts'' and ''to deliver'' are omitted as surplusage.

Amendments:

1965. Act July 7, 1965, in subsec. (c), substituted ''$10,000'' for ''$1,000''.

1989. Act Nov. 29, 1989, in subsec. (c), substituted ''$100,000'' for ''$10,000''.

CODE OF FEDERAL REGULATIONS

Department of the Air Force—Administrative claims, 32 CFR Part 842.

CROSS REFERENCES

Admiralty and maritime jurisdiction, Const. Art. 3, § 2 cl. 1; 28 USCS § 1333; 46 USCS § 740.

This section is referred to in 10 USCS § 9806.

RESEARCH GUIDE

Federal Procedure:

23 Fed Proc L Ed, Maritime Law and Procedure § 53:160.

§ 9804. Salvage claims by United States

(a) The Secretary of the Air Force may settle, or compromise, and receive payment of a claim by the United States for salvage services performed by the Department of the Air Force. Amounts received under this section shall be covered into the Treasury.

(b) In any case where the amount to be received by the United States is not more than $10,000, the Secretary of the Air Force may delegate his authority under subsection (a) to any person designated by him.

(Aug. 10, 1956, ch 1041, § 1, 70A Stat. 592; Aug. 29, 1972, P. L. 92-417, § 1(8), 86 Stat. 655.)

HISTORY; ANCILLARY LAWS AND DIRECTIVES

Prior law and revision:

Revised Section	Source (USCS)	Source (Statutes at Large)
9804	10:1863.	Oct. 20, 1951, ch. 524, § 3, 65 Stat. 573.

The words ''under this section'' are substituted for the words ''for salvage services rendered''. The words ''consider, ascertain, adjust, determine'' are omitted as covered by the word ''settle'', as defined in section 9801 of this title. The words ''and receive payment of'' are inserted for clarity and to conform to 9803 of this title. The words ''as miscellaneous receipts'' are omitted as surplusage.

Amendments:

1972. Act Aug. 29, 1972, subject to subsequent amendment, substituted this section for one which read: ''Under the direction of the Secretary of Defense, the Secretary of the Air Force may settle, or compromise, and receive payment of a claim by the United States for salvage services performed by the Department of the Air Force for any vessel. Amounts received under this section shall be covered into the Treasury.''.

CODE OF FEDERAL REGULATIONS

Department of the Air Force—Administrative claims, 32 CFR Part 842.

RESEARCH GUIDE

Federal Procedure:

23 Fed Proc L Ed, Maritime Law and Procedure § 53:161.

Am Jur:

68 Am Jur 2d, Salvage § 59.

[§ 9805. Repealed]

HISTORY; ANCILLARY LAWS AND DIRECTIVES

This section (Act Aug. 10, 1956, ch 1041, § 1, 70A Stat. 592) was repealed by Act June 29, 1960, P. L. 86-533, § 1(7)(A), 74 Stat. 246. It related to reports to the Congress with respect to claims under 10 USCS §§ 9802–9804.

§ 9806. Settlement of compromise: final and conclusive

Notwithstanding any other provision of law, upon acceptance of payment the settlement or compromise of a claim under section 9802 or 9803 of this title [10 USCS § 9802 or 9803] is final and conclusive.

(Aug. 10, 1956, ch 1041, § 1, 70A Stat. 593.)

HISTORY; ANCILLARY LAWS AND DIRECTIVES

Prior law and revision:

Revised Section	Source (USCS)	Source (Statutes at Large)
9806	10:861 (35 words before 1st proviso). 10:862 (last 32 words of 2d sentence).	Oct. 20, 1951, ch. 524, §§ 1 (35 words before 1st proviso), 2 (last 32 words of 2d sentence), 65 Stat. 572, 573.

The words ''for all purposes'' and ''to the contrary'', in 10:1861 and 1862; ''by the claimant and not until then'', in 10:1861; and ''but not until then'', in 10:1862; are omitted as surplusage.

CODE OF FEDERAL REGULATIONS

Department of the Air Force—Administrative claims, 32 CFR Part 842.

RESEARCH GUIDE

Federal Procedure:

23 Fed Proc L Ed, Maritime Law and Procedure §§ 53:160, 162.

CHAPTER 953. ACCOUNTABILITY AND RESPONSIBILITY

HISTORY; ANCILLARY LAWS AND DIRECTIVES

Amendments:

1962. Act June 8, 1962, P. L. 87-480, § 1(5), 76 Stat. 94, amended the analysis of this chapter by deleting item 9833, which read: ''9833. Accountability for public money: disbursing officers; agent officers.''.

1980. Act Dec. 12, 1980, P.L. 96-513, Title V, Part B, § 514(22)(C), 94 Stat. 2937 (effective upon enactment on 12/12/80, as provided by § 701(b)(3) of such Act, which appears as 10 USCS § 101 note), amended the analysis of this chapter in item 9837 by substituting ''remission or cancellation of indebtedness of enlisted members'' for ''deductions from pay''.

1982. Act Sept. 13, 1982, P.L. 97-258, § 2(b)(14)(A), 96 Stat. 1058, amended the analysis of this chapter by adding the items relating to sections 9841 and 9842.

§ 9831. Custody of departmental records and property

The Secretary of the Air Force has custody and charge of all books, records, papers, furniture, fixtures, and other property under the lawful control of the executive part of the Department of the Air Force.

(Aug. 10, 1956, ch 1041, § 1, 70A Stat. 593.)

HISTORY; ANCILLARY LAWS AND DIRECTIVES

Prior law and revision:

Revised Section	Source (USCS)	Source (Statutes at Large)
9831	5:191.	R.S. 217.

The words ''under the lawful control of the executive part of the Department of the Air Force'' are substituted for the words ''appertaining to the Department''.

CROSS REFERENCES

Federal records, maintenance of, 44 USCS §§ 2101 et seq.

RESEARCH GUIDE

Am Jur:

53 Am Jur 2d, Military, and Civil Defense § 24.

§ 9832. Property accountability: regulations

The Secretary of the Air Force may prescribe regulations for the accounting for Air Force property and the fixing of responsibility for that property.
(Aug. 10, 1956, ch 1041, § 1, 70A Stat. 593.)

HISTORY; ANCILLARY LAWS AND DIRECTIVES

Prior law and revision:

Revised Section	Source (USCS)	Source (Statutes at Large)
9832	10:1301.	Aug. 29, 1916, ch. 418 (3d proviso under "Clothing and Camp and Garrison Equipment"), 39 Stat. 635.

The word "supplies" is omitted as covered by the word "property".

[§ 9833. Repealed]

HISTORY; ANCILLARY LAWS AND DIRECTIVES

This section (Act Aug. 10, 1956, ch 1041, § 1, 70A Stat. 593) was repealed by Act June 8, 1962, P. L. 87-480, § 1(4), 76 Stat. 94. It related to the accountability of Air Force officers for public money. For similar provisions, see 10 USCS § 2773.

§ 9835. Reports of survey

(a) Under such regulations as the Secretary of the Air Force may prescribe, any officer of the Air Force designated by him may act upon reports of surveys and vouchers pertaining to the loss, spoilage, unserviceability, unsuitability, or destruction of or damage to property of the United States under the control of the Department of the Air Force.

(b) Action taken under subsection (a) is final, except that action holding a person pecuniarily liable for loss, spoilage, destruction, or damage is not final until approved by the Secretary or an officer of the Air Force designated by him.

(Aug. 10, 1956, ch 1041, § 1, 70A Stat. 593.)

HISTORY; ANCILLARY LAWS AND DIRECTIVES

Prior law and revision:

Revised Section	Source (USCS)	Source (Statutes at Large)
9835(a)	10:1305 (less 16 words before proviso, and less proviso).	Oct. 11, 1951, ch. 484, 65 Stat. 387.
9835(b)	10:1305 (16 words before proviso and proviso).	

In subsection (b), the words ''or concern'' are omitted as covered by the definition of ''person'', in section 1 of title 1.

INTERPRETIVE NOTES AND DECISIONS

The word ''final'' in 10 USCS § 9835 seems to refer to finality within the Air Force hierarchy rather than to a determination binding on the courts; in any event, it requires much stronger language, or a powerful showing from legislative history, to find that Congress intended, in a statute relating to pecuniary liability of an individual to the Government, to bar judicial review even where the crucial administrative findings are supported by no evidence or no substantial evidence. Abel v United States (1970) 191 Ct Cl 89, 423 F2d 339.

§ 9836. Individual equipment: unauthorized disposition

(a) No enlisted member of the Air Force may sell, lend, pledge, barter, or give any clothing, arms, or equipment furnished him by the United States to any person other than a member of the Air Force, or an officer of the United States, authorized to receive it.

(b) If a member of the Air Force has disposed of property in violation of subsection (a) and it is in the possession of a person who is neither a member of the Air Force, nor an officer of the United States, authorized to receive it, that person has no right to or interest in the property, and any civil or military officer of the United States may seize it, wherever found. Possession of such property furnished by the United States to a member of the Air Force, by a person who is neither a member of the Air Force nor an officer of the United States, is prima facie evidence that it has been disposed of in violation of subsection (a).

(c) If an officer who seizes property under subsection (b) is not authorized to retain it for the United States, he shall deliver it to a person who is authorized to retain it.

(Aug. 10, 1956, ch 1041, § 1, 70A Stat. 594.)

HISTORY; ANCILLARY LAWS AND DIRECTIVES

Prior law and revision:

Revised Section	Source (USCS)	Source (Statutes at Large)
9836(a)	10:1316 (words before semicolon of 1st sentence).	R.S. 1242.
	10:1317 (words before semicolon of 1st sentence).	R.S. 3748.
9836(b)	10:1316 (less words before semicolon, and less last 16 words of 1st sentence).	
	10:1317 (less words before semicolon of 1st sentence and less last 16 words of last sentence).	
9836(c)	10:1316 (last 16 words of 1st sentence).	
	10:1317 (last 16 words of last sentence).	

In subsection (a), the word ''equipment'' is substituted for the words ''military outfits, and accouterments'', in 10:1316 and 1317. The word ''exchanged'' is omitted as surplusage. The last 22 words are inserted to reflect various provisions authorizing transfer of the enumerated items of property.

In subsections (a) and (b), the words ''enlisted member'' and ''member'' are substituted for the word ''soldier'', in 10:1316 and 1317.

In subsections (b), the first 16 words of the first sentence are inserted for clarity. The words ''authorized to receive it'' are substituted for the words ''duly authorized'', in 10:1316. The words ''such property furnished by the United States'' are substituted for the words ''any such clothes, arms, military outfits, or accouterments'', in 10:1316.

In subsections (c), the first 19 words are inserted for clarity. The words ''person who is authorized to retain it'' are substituted for the words ''quartermaster [,] or other officer authorized to receive the same'', in 10:1316 and 1317.

CROSS REFERENCES

Federal offenses—Embezzlement and theft of public property, 18 USCS § 641.

Federal offenses—Purchase or receipt of military property, 18 USCS § 1024.

Federal offenses—Malicious mischief, government property, 18 USCS § 1361.

RESEARCH GUIDE

Am Jur:

53 Am Jur 2d, Military, and Civil Defense § 26.

53 Am Jur 2d, Military and Civil Defense § 9.

INTERPRETIVE NOTES AND DECISIONS

Predecessors of 10 USCS § 9836 were not criminal statutes, but simply prohibited disposition of military stores of United States, except as they are issued to soldiers in service of United States. United States v Smith (1907, CCD Wash) 156 F 859.

§ 9837. Settlement of accounts: remission or cancellation of indebtedness of enlisted members

If he considers it in the best interest of the United States, the Secretary may have remitted or cancelled any part of an enlisted member's indebtedness to the United States or any of its instrumentalities remaining unpaid before, or at the time of, that member's honorable discharge.

(Aug. 10, 1956, ch 1041, § 1, 70A Stat. 594; Sept. 2, 1958, P. L. 85-861, § 33(a)(45), 72 Stat. 1567; Sept. 7, 1962, P. L. 87-649, § 14(c)(58), 76 Stat. 502; Dec. 12, 1980, P. L. 96-513, Title V, Part B, § 514(22)(A), (B), 94 Stat. 2936.)

HISTORY; ANCILLARY LAWS AND DIRECTIVES

Prior law and revision:

1956 ACT

Revised Section	Source (USCS)	Source (Statutes at Large)
9837(a)	10:875. 10:875b.	R.S. 1300. R.S. 1301.
9837(b)	10:875a (less 3d and last provisos).	May 22, 1928, ch. 676, 45 Stat. 698; June 26, 1934, ch. 751, 48 Stat. 1222.
9837(c)	10:875a (last proviso).	
9837(d)	10:875 (3d proviso).	R.S. 1303.
9837(e)	10:871.	R.S. 1304.
9837(f)	10:872.	R.S. 1299.
9837(g)	10:875c.	

In subsection (a), the words ''sold to the member on credit under section 9621(a)(1) of this title'' are substituted for the words ''articles designated by the inspectors general of the Army, and sold to him on credit by officers of the Quartermaster Corps'', in 10:875. The words ''at cost prices'' are omitted to reflect section 9623 of this title.

In subsection (b), the last sentence is substituted for 10:875a (1st and 2d provisos). The words ''on current payrolls'' are omitted as surplusage.

In subsection (c), the words ''Subject to subsection (b)'' are substituted for the words ''in the proportions herein before indicated''.

In subsection (d), the words ''If he considers it in the best interests of the United States'' are substituted for the words ''when in his opinion the interests of the Government are best served by such action''. The words ''before, or at the time of'' are substituted for the words ''either on . . . or prior thereto''.

In subsection (e), the words ''member'' and ''his'' are substituted for the words ''officer or soldier''. The words ''or implement'' are omitted as surplusage.

In subsection (f), the words ''or if an article of military supply with whose issue a commissioned officer is charged is damaged'' are substituted for 10:872 (last sentence). The words ''that he was not at fault'' are substituted for the words ''that said deficiency [such damage] was not occasioned by any fault on his part''.
In subsection (g), the words ''bought on credit under section 9621(a)(1) of this title'' are substituted for the words ''designated by the officers of the Inspector-General's Department of the Army and purchased on credit from commissaries of subsistence''.

1958 ACT

The change [in subsec. (b)] reflects the opinion of the Judge Advocate General of the Air Force (June 10, 1957) that the term ''rate of pay'', as used in the source law for section 9837(b) (Act of May 22, 1928, ch 676 (45 Stat. 698), as amended), included special pay and incentive pay.
The change [in subsec. (f)] reflects the opinion of the Assistant General Counsel (Fiscal Matters), Department of Defense (July 19, 1957), that section 1304, Revised Statutes (formerly 10 U.S.C. 872), the source law for this section, applied to warrant officers as well as to commissioned officers.

Amendments:

1958. Act Sept. 2, 1958 (effective 8/10/56, as provided by § 33(g) of such Act, which appears as 10 USCS § 101 note), in subsec. (b), in the sentence beginning ''However . . .'', deleted ''basic'' following ''his''; in subsec. (f) substituted ''an'' for ''a commissioned'' in two places.
1962. Act Sept. 7, 1962 (effective 11/1/62, as provided by § 15 of such Act, which appears as 10 USCS § 101 note), deleted subsecs. (a)–(c) and (e)–(g) which read:
''(a) An amount due the United States from an enlisted member of the Air Force for articles sold to the member on credit under section 9621 (a) (1) of this title shall be deducted from the next pay due that member after the sale is reported. An amount due the United States from an enlisted member of the Air Force for tobacco sold to him by the United States under section 9623 of this title shall be deducted from his pay in the manner provided for the settlement of clothing accounts.
''(b) Under regulations to be prescribed by the Secretary of the Air Force, any amount that an enlisted member is administratively determined to owe the United States or any of its instrumentalities may be deducted from his pay in monthly installments. However, after the deduction of pay forfeited by the sentence of a court-martial, if any, or otherwise authorized by law to be withheld, the deductions authorized by this section may not reduce the pay actually received for any month to less than one-third of his basic pay for that month.
''(c) Subject to subsection (b), an amount due the United States from an enlisted member may be deducted from his pay on final statement, or from his savings on his clothing allowance.
''(e) The amount of any damage, or cost of repairs, to arms or equipment caused by the abuse or negligence of a member of the Air Force who had the care of, or was using, the property when it was damaged shall be deducted from his pay.

"(f) If, upon final settlement of the accounts of a commissioned officer of the Air Force charged with the issue of an article of military supply, there is a deficiency of that article, or if an article of military supply with whose issue a commissioned officer is charged is damaged, the value of the lost article or the amount of the damage shall be charged against the officer and deducted from his monthly pay, unless he shows to the satisfaction of the Secretary, by one or more affidavits setting forth the circumstances, that he was not at fault.

"(g) An amount due the United States from an officer of the Air Force for rations bought on credit, and for articles bought on credit under section 9621 (a) (1) of this title, shall be deducted from the next pay due that officer after the sale is reported.".

For similar provisions, see 37 USCS § 1007(b)–(g).

1980. Act Dec. 12, 1980 (effective upon enactment on 12/12/80, as provided by § 701(b)(3) of such Act, which appears as 10 USCS § 101 note), in the catchline, substituted "remission or cancellation of indebtedness of enlisted members" for "deductions from pay"; and deleted "(d)" before "If he considers".

CROSS REFERENCES

Military property of United States; loss, damage, destruction, or wrongful disposition, punishment, 10 USCS § 908.

Public Accounts to be submitted to Comptroller General; rendition of current accounts, 31 USCS § 3522.

Property returns by officers, 31 USCS § 3531.

This section is referred to in 5 USCS § 5514.

§ 9838. Settlement of accounts: affidavit of squadron commander

In the settlement of the accounts of the commanding officer of a squadron for clothing and other military supplies, his affidavit may be received to show—

(1) that vouchers or squadron books were lost;

(2) anything tending to prove that any apparent deficiency of those articles was caused by unavoidable accident, or by loss in actual service without his fault; or

(3) that all or part of the clothing and supplies was properly used.

The affidavit may be used as evidence of the facts set forth, with or without other evidence, as determined by the Secretary of the Air Force to be just and proper under the circumstances.

(Aug. 10, 1956, ch 1041, § 1, 70A Stat. 595.)

HISTORY; ANCILLARY LAWS AND DIRECTIVES

Prior law and revision:

Revised Section	Source (USCS)	Source (Statutes at Large)
9838	10:1302.	R.S. 225 (less 1st sentence); added Feb. 27, 1877, ch. 69 (3d para.), 19 Stat. 241.

The word ''anything'' is substituted for the words ''any matter or circumstance''. The words ''properly used'' are substituted for the words ''legally used and appropriated''. The words ''of the case'' are omitted as surplusage.

§ 9839. Settlement of accounts: oaths

The Secretary of the Air Force may detail any employee of the Department of the Air Force to administer oaths required by law in the settlement of an officer's accounts for clothing and other military supplies. An oath administered under this section shall be without expense to the person to whom it is administered.

(Aug. 10, 1956, ch 1041, § 1, 70A Stat. 595.)

HISTORY; ANCILLARY LAWS AND DIRECTIVES

Prior law and revision:

Revised Section	Source (USCS)	Source (Statutes at Large)
9839	10:1303.	R.S. 225 (1st sentence).

The words ''and other military supplies'' are substituted for the words ''camp and garrison equipage, quartermaster's stores, and ordnance'' to conform to section 9838 of this title. The words ''person to whom administered'' are substituted for the words ''parties taking them.'' The words ''for the purpose of'' are omitted as surplusage.

CROSS REFERENCES

Administration of oaths by employee of Executive department, 5 USCS § 303.

Authority to administer oaths, 10 USCS § 936.

§ 9840. Final settlement of officer's accounts

Before final payment upon discharge may be made to an officer of the Air Force who has been accountable or responsible for public property, he must obtain a certificate of nonindebtedness to the United States from each officer to whom he was accountable or responsible for property. He must also make an affidavit, certified by his commanding officer to be correct, that he is not accountable or responsible for property to any other officer. An officer who has not been responsible for public property must make an affidavit of that fact,

certified by his commanding officer. Compliance with this section warrants the final payment of the officer concerned.
(Aug. 10, 1956, ch 1041, § 1, 70A Stat. 595.)

HISTORY; ANCILLARY LAWS AND DIRECTIVES
Prior law and revision:

Revised Section	Source (USCS)	Source (Statutes at Large)
9840	10:878.	Jan. 12, 1899, ch. 46, § 2, 30 Stat. 784.

The words ''Before final payment upon discharge may be made'' are substituted for the words ''shall warrant their final payment''. The words ''at any time'' are omitted as surplusage. The word ''must'' is substituted for the words ''shall be required . . . to''. The words ''He must also make'' are substituted for the words ''accompanied by''. The words ''from each officer to whom he was accountable or responsible for property'' are substituted for the words ''from only such of the bureaus of the Department of the Army to which the property for which they were accountable or responsible pertains'', since the Air Force does not have organic bureaus created by statute. The words ''that he is not accountable or responsible for property to any other officer'' are substituted for the words ''accompanied by the affidavits of officers, of nonaccountability, or nonresponsibility to other bureaus of the Department of the Army'' for the same reason. The reference to certificates from the General Accounting Office is omitted as obsolete. The last sentence is substituted for 10:878 (last 18 words). The last proviso of section 2 of the Act of January 12, 1899, ch 46, 30 Stat. 784, is not contained in 10:878. It is also omitted from the revised section, since it related to authority of mustering officers to administer oaths, and the general authority to administer oaths is now contained in section 936 of this title (Article 136 of the Uniform Code of Military Justice).

§ 9841. Payment of small amounts to public creditors

When authorized by the Secretary of the Air Force, a disbursing official of Air Force subsistence funds may keep a limited amount of those funds in the personal possession and at the risk of the disbursing official to pay small amounts to public creditors.
(Added Sept. 13, 1982, P. L. 97-258, § 2(b)(14)(B) in part, 96 Stat. 1058.)

HISTORY; ANCILLARY LAWS AND DIRECTIVES
Prior law and revision:

Revised Section	Source (USCS)	Source (Statutes at Large)
9841	31:493.	Mar. 2, 1907, ch. 2511 (proviso on p. 1166), 34 Stat. 1166.

The words Secretary of the Air Force'' are substituted for ''Secretary of War'' because of section 205(a) and 207(a) and (f) of the Act of July 26, 1947 (ch. 343, 61 Stat. 501, 502), and sections 1 and 53 of the Act of August 10, 1956 (ch. 1041, 70A Stat. 157, 488, 676). For comparable provisions that apply to the Army, see the revision note for 10:4841.

§ 9842. Settlement of accounts of line officers

The Comptroller General shall settle the account of a line officer of the Air Force for pay due the officer even if the officer cannot account for property entrusted to the officer or cannot make a monthly report or return, when the Comptroller General is satisfied that the inability to account for property or make a report or return was the result of the officer having been a prisoner, or of an accident or casualty of war

(Added Sept. 13, 1982, P. L. 97-258, § 2(b)(14)(B) in part, 97 Stat. 1058.)

HISTORY; ANCILLARY LAWS AND DIRECTIVES

Prior law and revision:

Revised Section	Source (USCS)	Source (Statutes at Large)
9842	31:44 (1st sentence). 31:95.	June 10, 1921, ch. 18, § 304 (1st par. 1st sentence), 42 Stat. 24. R.S. § 278.

The section is made applicable to the Air Force by section 207(a) and (f) of the Act of July 26, 1947 (ch. 343, 61 Stat. 502). For comparable provisions that apply to the Army, see the revision note for 10:4842.

SUBTITLE E. RESERVE COMPONENTS

PART I. ORGANIZATION AND ADMINISTRATION

PART II. PERSONNEL GENERALLY

PART III. PROMOTION AND RETENTION OF OFFICERS ON THE RESERVE ACTIVE-STATUS LIST

PART IV. TRAINING FOR RESERVE COMPONENTS AND EDUCATIONAL ASSISTANCE PROGRAMS

PART V. SERVICE, SUPPLY, AND PROCUREMENT

HISTORY; ANCILLARY LAWS AND DIRECTIVES

Amendments:

1994. Act Oct. 5, 1994, P. L. 103-337, Div A, Title XVI, Subtitle A, Part I, § 1611, 108 Stat. 2921, added the subtitle heading and analysis.

1996. Act Feb. 10, 1996, P. L. 104-106, Div A, Title V, Subtitle B, § 512(a)(2), 110 Stat. 305, amended the analysis of this subtitle by adding item 1214.

Act Feb. 10, 1996, P. L. 104-106, Div A, Title XV, § 1501(b)(1), 110 Stat. 495, amended the analysis of this subtitle by substituting ''Repayment Programs'' for ''Repayments'' in item 1609.

Act Sept. 23, 1996, P. L. 104-201, Div A, Title XII, Subtitle A, § 1211(a)(2), 110 Stat. 2691, amended the analysis of this subtitle by adding item 1006.

1997. Act Nov. 18, 1997, P. L. 105-85, Div A, Title V, Subtitle B, § 515(b), 111 Stat. 1733, amended the analysis of this subtitle by substituting item 1215 for one which read: ''1215. Miscellaneous Prohibitions and Penalties . . . [No present sections]''.

PART I. ORGANIZATION AND ADMINISTRATION

HISTORY; ANCILLARY LAWS AND DIRECTIVES

Amendments:

1994. Act Oct. 5, 1994, P. L. 103-337, Div A, Title XVI, Subtitle C, § 1661, 108 Stat. 2969 (effective 12/1/94 as provided by § 1691(a) of such Act, which appears as 10 USCS § 10001 note), added the part heading and analysis.

1996. Act Sept. 23, 1996, P. L. 104-201, Div A, Title XII, Subtitle A, § 1211(a)(2), 110 Stat. 2691, amended the analysis of this part by adding item 1006.

CHAPTER 1001. DEFINITIONS

HISTORY; ANCILLARY LAWS AND DIRECTIVES

Amendments:

1994. Oct. 5, 1994, P. L. 103-337, Div A, Title XVI, Subtitle C, § 1661(a)(1), 108 Stat. 2969 (effective 12/1/94 as provided by § 1691 of such Act, which appears as 10 USCS § 10001 note) added the chapter heading and analysis.

§ 10001. Definition of State

In this subtitle [10 USCS §§ 10001 et seq.], the term ''State'' includes the District of Columbia, the Commonwealth of Puerto Rico, the Virgin Islands, and Guam.

(Added Oct. 5, 1994, P. L. 103-337, Div A, Title XVI, Subtitle C, § 1661(a)(1), 108 Stat. 2969.)

HISTORY; ANCILLARY LAWS AND DIRECTIVES

Effective date of section:

This section took effect on Dec. 1, 1994, pursuant to Act Oct. 5, 1994, P. L. 103-337, Div A, Title XVI, Subtitle F, § 1691, 108 Stat. 3026, which appears as a note to this section.

Short title:

Act Oct. 5, 1994, P. L. 103-337, Div A, Title XVI, § 1601, 108 Stat. 2921, provides: ''This title may be cited as the 'Reserve Officer Personnel Management Act'.''. Such Title added Subtitle E of Title 10, USCS (10 USCS §§ 10001 et seq.), among other things; for full classification, consult USCS Tables volumes.

Act Sept. 23, 1996, P. L. 104-201, Div A, Title XII, § 1201, 110 Stat. 2689, provides: ''This title may be cited as the 'Reserve Forces Revitalization Act of 1996'.''. For full classification of such Title, consult USCS Tables volumes.

Other provisions:

Reserve Officer Personnel Management Act; effective dates. Act Oct. 5, 1994, P. L. 103-337, Div A, Title XVI, Subtitle F, § 1691, 108 Stat. 3026, provides:

''(a) Effective date for amendments. Except as provided in subsection (b), the amendment made by section 1611 [adding Subtitle E of Title 10 [10 USCS §§ 10001 et seq.] and the amendments made by subtitles C and D [for full classification, consult USCS Tables volumes] shall take effect on December 1, 1994.

''(b) Effective date for new Reserve officer personnel policies. (1) The provisions of part III of subtitle E of title 10, United States Code [10 USCS §§ 14001 et seq.], as added by section 1611, shall become effective on October 1, 1996. The amendments made by part II of subtitle A, by subtitle B, and by section 1671(c)(2) and paragraphs (2), (3)(B), (3)(C), and (4) of section 1675(d) [for full classification, consult USCS Tables volumes] shall take effect on October 1, 1996.

''(2) Any reference in subtitle E of this title [for full classification, consult USCS Tables volumes] to the effective date of this title is a reference to the effective date prescribed in paragraph (1).

''(3) The personnel policies applicable to Reserve officers under the provisions of law in effect on the day before the date prescribed in subsection (a) and replaced by the Reserve officer personnel policies prescribed in part III of subtitle E of title 10, United States Code [10 USCS §§ 14001 et seq.], as added by section 1611, shall, notwithstanding the provisions of subsection (a), continue in effect until the effective date prescribed in paragraph (1).

''(4) The authority to prescribe regulations under the provisions of part III of subtitle E of title 10, United States Code [10 USCS §§ 14001 et seq.], as added by section 1611, shall take effect on the date of the enactment of this Act.''.

Preservation of suspended status of laws suspended as of effective date. Act Oct. 5, 1994, P. L. 103-337, Div A, Title XVI, Subtitle F, § 1692, 108 Stat. 3027, provides: ''If a provision of law that is in a suspended status on the day before the effective date of this title under section 1691(b)(1) [note to this section] is transferred or amended by this title, the suspended status of that provision is not affected by that transfer or amendment.''.

Preservation of pre-existing rights, duties, penalties, and proceedings. Act Oct. 5, 1994, P. L. 103-337, Div A, Title XVI, Subtitle F, § 1693, 108 Stat. 3027, provides: ''Except as otherwise provided in this title, the provisions of this title and the amendments made by this title [for full classification, consult USCS Tables volumes] do not affect rights and duties that matured, penalties that were incurred, or proceedings that were begun before the effective date of this title under section 1691(b)(1) [note to this section].''.

Effective date of certain Oct. 5, 1994 amendments to subtitle and chapter analyses. Act Feb. 10, 1996, P. L. 104-106, Div A, Title XV, § 1501(f)(2), 110 Stat. 501; Nov. 18, 1997, P. L. 105-85, Div A, Title X, Subtitle G, § 1073(d)(1)(E)(ii), 111 Stat. 1905 (effective and applicable as provided by § 1073(d)(1) and (i) of such Act, which appear as notes to 10 USCS §§ 1076 and 101, respectively), provides: ''The amendments made by sections 1672(a), 1673(a) (with respect to chapters 541 and 549), 1673(b)(2), 1673(b)(4), 1674(a), and 1674(b)(7) of the Reserve Officer Personnel Management Act [Act Oct. 5, 1994, P. L. 103-337, 108 Stat. 3015–3117; for full classification, consult USCS Tables volumes] shall take effect on the effective date specified in section 1691(b)(1) of the Reserve Officer Personnel Management Act [i.e., Oct. 1, 1996] (notwithstanding section 1691(a) of such Act).''.

Reserve Forces Revitalization Act of 1996; purpose. Act Sept. 23, 1996, P. L. 104-201, Div A, Title XII, § 1202, 110 Stat. 2689, provides: ''The purpose of this title [for full classification, consult USCS Tables volumes] is to revise the basic statutory authorities governing the organization and administration of the reserve components of the Armed Forces in order to recognize the realities of reserve component partnership in the Total Force and to better prepare the American citizen-soldier, sailor, airman, and Marine in time of peace for duties in war.''.

CHAPTER 1003. RESERVE COMPONENTS GENERALLY

HISTORY; ANCILLARY LAWS AND DIRECTIVES

Amendments:

1994. Act Oct. 5, 1994, P. L. 103-337, Div A, Title XVI, Subtitle C, § 1661(a)(1), 108 Stat. 2969 (effective 12/1/94 as provided by § 1691 of such Act, which appears as 10 USCS § 10001 note), added the chapter heading and analysis.

1996. Act Feb. 10, 1996, P. L. 104-106, Div A, Title XV, § 1501(b)(2)(B), 110 Stat. 495 (effective as if included in Act Oct. 5, 1994, P. L. 103-337, as enacted on Oct. 5, 1994, as provided by § 1501(f)(3) of Act Feb. 10, 1996, which appears as 10 USCS § 113 note), amended the analysis of this chapter by substituting item 10103 for one which read: ''10103. Basic policy for order of National Guard into Federal service''.

§ 10101. Reserve components named

The reserve components of the armed forces are:

(1) The Army National Guard of the United States.

(2) The Army Reserve.

(3) The Naval Reserve.

(4) The Marine Corps Reserve.

(5) The Air National Guard of the United States.

(6) The Air Force Reserve.

(7) The Coast Guard Reserve.

(Added Oct. 5, 1994, P. L. 103-337, Div A, Title XVI, Subtitle C, § 1661(a)(1), 108 Stat. 2970.)

HISTORY; ANCILLARY LAWS AND DIRECTIVES

Effective date of section:

This section took effect on Dec. 1, 1994, pursuant to Act Oct. 5, 1994, P. L. 103-337, Div A, Title XVI, Subtitle F, § 1691, 108 Stat. 3026, which appears as 10 USCS 10001 note.

Other provisions:

Repeal of prohibition against use of funds for pay of technicians who are not military members of Army Reserve troop program units they are employed to support. Act Dec. 1, 1995, P. L. 104-61, Title VIII, § 8016, 109 Stat. 654, which formerly appeared as a note to this section, was repealed by Act Nov. 18, 1997, P. L. 105-85, Div A, Title V, Subtitle C, § 522(e), 111 Stat. 1735. Such note prohibited use of funds for pay of technicians who are not military members of the Army Reserve troop program units they are employed to support.

Similar provisions were contained in Acts Dec. 8, 1983, P. L. 98-212, Title VII, § 783, 97 Stat. 1453; Oct. 12, 1984, P. L. 98-473, Title I, § 101(h) [Title VIII, § 8076],98 Stat. 1904, 1938; Dec. 19, 1985, P. L. 99-190, § 101(b) [Title VIII, § 8059], 99 Stat. 1185, 1212; Oct. 18, 1986, P. L. 99-500, § 101(c) [Title IX, § 9054], 100 Stat. 1783-82, 1783-111; Oct. 30, 1986, P. L. 99-591, § 101(c) [Title IX, § 9054], 100 Stat. 3341-82, 3341-111; Dec. 22, 1987, P. L. 100-202, § 101(b) [Title VII, § 8055], 101 Stat. 1329-43, 1329-72; Oct. 1, 1988, P. L. 100-463, Title VIII, § 8045, 102 Stat. 2270-25; Nov. 21, 1989, P. L. 101-165, Title IX, § 9027, 103 Stat. 1135; Nov. 5, 1990, P. L. 101-511, Title VIII, § 8018, 104 Stat. 1178; Nov. 26, 1991, P. L. 102-172, Title VIII, § 8018, 105 Stat. 1175; Oct. 6, 1992, P. L. 102-396, Title IX, § 9019, 106 Stat. 1904; Nov. 11, 1993, P. L. 103-139, Title VIII, § 8016, 107 Stat. 1440; Sept. 30, 1994, P. L. 103-335, Title VIII, § 8015, 108 Stat. 2620.

Retention in active status until age 60 of National Guard or Reserve technician. Act Dec. 1, 1995, P. L. 104-61, Title VIII, § 8017, 109 Stat. 654, provides: ''Notwithstanding any other provision of law, during the current fiscal year and hereafter, the Secretaries of the Army and Air Force may authorize the retention in an active status until age sixty of any person who would otherwise be removed from an active status and who is employed as a National Guard or Reserve technician in a position in which active status in a reserve component of the Army or Air Force is required as a condition of that employment.''.

Similar provisions were contained in Acts Oct. 12, 1984, P. L. 98-473, Title I, § 101(h) [Title VIII, § 8106], 98 Stat. 1904, 1943; Dec. 19, 1985, P. L. 99-190, § 101(b) [Title VIII, § 8073], 99 Stat. 1185, 1214; Oct. 18, 1986, P. L. 99-500, § 101(c) [Title IX, § 9063], 100 Stat. 1783-82, 1783-112; Oct. 30, 1986, P. L. 99-591, § 101(c) [Title IX, § 9063], 100 Stat. 3341-82, 3341-112; Dec. 22, 1987, P. L. 100-202, § 101(b) [Title VII, § 8064], 101 Stat. 1329-43, 1329-73; Oct. 1, 1988, P. L. 100-463, Title VIII, § 8052, 102 Stat. 2270-26; Nov. 21, 1989, P. L. 101-165, Title IX, § 9032, 103 Stat. 1136; Nov. 5, 1990, P. L. 101-511, Title VIII, § 8022, 104 Stat. 1879; Nov. 26, 1991, P. l. 102-172, Title VIII, § 8022, 105 Stat. 1176; Oct. 6, 1992, P. L. 102-396, Title IX, § 9022, 106 Stat. 1905; Nov. 11, 1993, P. L. 103-139, Title VIII, § 8018, 107 Stat. 1441; Sept. 30, 1994, P. L. 103-335, Title VIII, § 8016, 108 Stat. 2620.

CROSS REFERENCES

This section is referred to in 5 USCS §§ 6323, 8401, 8456; 26 USCS § 219.

§ 10102. Purpose of reserve components

The purpose of each reserve component is to provide trained units and qualified persons available for active duty in the armed forces, in time of war or national emergency, and at such other times as the national security may require, to fill the needs of the armed forces whenever, during and after the period needed to procure and train additional units and qualified persons to achieve the planned mobilization, more units and persons are needed than are in the regular components.

(Added Oct. 5, 1994, P. L. 103-337, Div A, Title XVI, Subtitle C, § 1661(a)(1), 108 Stat. 2970.)

HISTORY; ANCILLARY LAWS AND DIRECTIVES

Effective date of section:

This section took effect on Dec. 1, 1994, pursuant to Act Oct. 5, 1994, P. L. 103-337, Div A, Title XVI, Subtitle F, § 1691, 108 Stat. 3026, which appears as 10 USCS 10001 note.

INTERPRETIVE NOTES AND DECISIONS

Congress clearly intended United States Army Reserve, Ready Reserve, to constitute integral part of Army, and since reserve forces are geared toward possibility of active military duty, required qualifications of any soldier are same whether he be on active duty or in reserves; even though reservist on inactive duty is in status of relatively reduced military responsibility, he has obligation to maintain himself in state of readiness for full-time military service. Olenick v Brucker (1959, DC Dist Col) 173 F Supp 493, set aside (1959) 107 US App DC 5, 273 F2d 819.

Accurate inference regarding meaning of ''mobilization'' could be drawn from former 10 USCS § 262 which set out purpose of Reserve components, so that meaning of ''mobilization'' was not limited to ''total mobilization in time of war'' and could imply activation by President. Goldstein v Clifford (1968, DC NJ) 290 F Supp 275.

§ 10103. Basic policy for order into Federal service

Whenever Congress determines that more units and organizations are needed for the national security than are in the regular components of the ground and air forces, the Army National Guard of the United States and the Air National Guard of the United States, or such parts of them as are needed, together with units of other reserve components necessary for a balanced force, shall be ordered to active duty and retained as long as so needed.

(Added Oct. 5, 1994, P. L. 103-337, Div A, Title XVI, Subtitle C, § 1661(a)(1), 108 Stat. 2970; Feb. 10, 1996, P. L. 104-106, Div A, Title XV, § 1501(b)(2)(A), 110 Stat. 495.)

HISTORY; ANCILLARY LAWS AND DIRECTIVES

Effective date of section:

This section took effect on Dec. 1, 1994, pursuant to Act Oct. 5, 1994, P. L. 103-337, Div A, Title XVI, Subtitle F, § 1691, 108 Stat. 3026, which appears as 10 USCS 10001 note.

Amendments:

1996. Act Feb. 10, 1996 (effective as if included in Act Oct. 5, 1994, P. L. 103-337, as enacted on Oct. 5, 1994, as provided by § 1501(f)(3) of Act Feb. 10, 1996, which appears as 10 USCS § 113 note) substituted the section heading for one which read: "§ 10103. Basic policy for order of the National Guard and reserve components to active duty".

CROSS REFERENCES

Similar provision, 32 USCS § 102.

INTERPRETIVE NOTES AND DECISIONS

Former 10 USCS § 263 did not violate equal protection concepts merely because it applied only to units, not to individuals; words "national security" as used in such § 263 did not relate only to defense of borders of United States. Morse v Boswell (1968, DC Md) 289 F Supp 812, affd (1968, CA4 Md) 401 F2d 544, cert den (1969) 393 US 1052, 21 L Ed 2d 694, 89 S Ct 687.

§ 10104. Army Reserve: composition

The Army Reserve includes all Reserves of the Army who are not members of the Army National Guard of the United States.

(Added Oct. 5, 1994, P. L. 103-337, Div A, Title XVI, Subtitle C, § 1661(a)(1), 108 Stat. 2970.)

HISTORY; ANCILLARY LAWS AND DIRECTIVES

Effective date of section:

This section took effect on Dec. 1, 1994, pursuant to Act Oct. 5, 1994, P. L. 103-337, Div A, Title XVI, Subtitle F, § 1691, 108 Stat. 3026, which appears as 10 USCS 10001 note.

§ 10105. Army National Guard of the United States: composition

The Army National Guard of the United States is the reserve component of the Army that consists of—

(1) federally recognized units and organizations of the Army National Guard; and

(2) members of the Army National Guard who are also Reserves of the Army.

(Added Oct. 5, 1994, P. L. 103-337, Div A, Title XVI, Subtitle C, § 1661(a)(1), 108 Stat. 2970.)

HISTORY; ANCILLARY LAWS AND DIRECTIVES

Effective date of section:

This section took effect on Dec. 1, 1994, pursuant to Act Oct. 5, 1994, P. L. 103-337, Div A, Title XVI, Subtitle F, § 1691, 108 Stat. 3026, which appears as 10 USCS 10001 note.

Other provisions:

Army Guard combat reform initiative. Act Oct. 23, 1992, P. L. 102-484, Div A, Title XI, 106 Stat. 2536; May 31, 1993, P. L. 103-35, Title II, § 202(a)(11), 107 Stat. 101 (applicable as if included in the enactment of Act Oct. 23, 1992, P. L. 102-484, as provided by § 202(b) of Act May 31, 1993); Nov. 30, 1993, P. L. 103-160, Div A, Title V, Subtitle B, § 520, 107 Stat. 1651; Oct. 5, 1994, P. L. 103-337, Div A, Title V, Subtitle B, § 516, 108 Stat. 2754; Feb. 10, 1996, P. L. 104-106, Div A, Title V, Subtitle B, §§ 514, 515, Title VII, Subtitle A, § 704(b), 110 Stat. 307, 372, provided:

''Sec. 1101. Short title.

''This title may be cited as the 'Army National Guard Combat Readiness Reform Act of 1992'.

''Deployability Enhancements

''Sec. 1111. Prior active-duty personnel.

''(a) Additional prior active duty officers. The Secretary of the Army shall increase the number of qualified prior active-duty officers in the Army National Guard by providing a program that permits the separation of officers on active duty with at least two, but less than three, years of active service upon condition that the officer is accepted for appointment in the Army National Guard. The Secretary shall have a goal of having not fewer than 150 officers become members of the Army National Guard each year under this section.

''(b) Additional prior active duty enlisted members. The Secretary of the Army shall increase the number of qualified prior active-duty enlisted members in the Army National Guard through the use of enlistments as described in section 8020 of the Department of Defense Appropriations Act, 1994 (Public Law 103-139) [unclassified]. The Secretary shall enlist not fewer than 1,000 new enlisted members each year under enlistments described in that section.

''(c) Qualified prior active-duty personnel. For purposes of this section, qualified prior active-duty personnel are members of the Army National Guard with not less than two years of active duty.

''Sec. 1112. Service in Selected Reserve in lieu of active-duty service.

''(a) Academy graduates and distinguished ROTC graduates to serve in selected reserve for period of active-duty service obligation not served on active duty. ''(1) An officer who is a graduate of one of the service academies or who was commissioned as a distinguished Reserve Officers' Training Corps graduate and who is permitted to be released from active duty before the completion of the active-duty service obligation applicable to that officer shall serve the remaining period of such active-duty service obligation as a member of the Selected Reserve.

''(2) The Secretary concerned may waive paragraph (1) in a case in which the Secretary determines that there is no unit position available for the officer.

''(b) ROTC graduates. The Secretary of the Army shall provide a program under which graduates of the Reserve Officers' Training Corps program may perform their minimum period of obligated service by a combination of (A) two years of active duty, and (B) such additional period of service as is necessary to complete the remainder of such obligation, to be served in the Selected Reserve.

''Sec. 1113. Review of officer promotions by commander of associated active duty unit.

''(a) Review. Whenever an officer in an Army Selected Reserve unit as defined in subsection (b) is recommended for a unit vacancy promotion to a grade above first lieutenant, the recommended promotion shall be reviewed by the commander of the active duty unit associated with the Selected Reserve unit of that officer or another active-duty officer designated by the Secretary of the Army. The commander or other active-duty officer designated by the Secretary of the Army shall provide to the promoting authority, through the promotion board convened by the promotion authority to consider unit vacancy promotion candidates, before the promotion is made, a recommendation of concurrence or nonconcurrence in the promotion. The recommendation shall be provided to the promoting authority within 60 days after receipt of notice of the recommended promotion.

"(b) Coverage of Selected Reserve combat and early deploying units. (1) Subsection (a) applies to officers in all units of the Selected Reserve that are designated as combat units or that are designated for deployment within 75 days of mobilization.

"(2) Subsection (a) shall take effect with respect to officers of the Army Reserve, and with respect to officers of the Army National Guard in units not subject to subsection (a) as of the date of the enactment of the National Defense Authorization Act for Fiscal Year 1996 [enacted Feb. 10, 1996], at the end of the 90-day period beginning on such date of enactment.

"(c) Report on feasibility. The Secretary of the Army shall submit to the Committees on Armed Services of the Senate and House of Representatives a report, not later than March 1, 1993, containing a plan for implementation of subsection (a). The Secretary may include with the report such proposals for legislation to clarify, improve, or modify the provisions of subsection (a) in order to better carry out the purposes of those provisions as the Secretary considers appropriate.

"Sec. 1114. Noncommissioned officer education requirements.

"(a) Nonwaivability. Any standard prescribed by the Secretary of the Army establishing a military education requirement for noncommissioned officers that must be met as a requirement for promotion to a higher noncommissioned officer grade may be waived only if the Secretary determines that the waiver is necessary in order to preserve unit leadership continuity under combat conditions.

"(b) Availability of training positions. The Secretary of the Army shall ensure that there are sufficient training positions available to enable compliance with subsection (a).

"Sec. 1115. Initial entry training and nondeployable personnel account.

"(a) Establishment of personnel account. The Secretary of the Army shall establish a personnel accounting category for members of the Army Selected Reserve to be used for categorizing members of the Selected Reserve who have not completed the minimum training required for deployment or who are otherwise not available for deployment. The account shall be designed so that it is compatible with the decentralized personnel systems of the Army Guard and Reserve. The account shall be used for the reporting of personnel readiness and may not be used as a factor in establishing the level of Army Guard and Reserve force structure.

"(b) Use of account. Until a member of the Army Selected Reserve has completed the minimum training necessary for deployment, the member may not be assigned to fill a position in a Selected Reserve unit but shall be carried in the account established under subsection (a).

"(c) Time for qualification for deployment. (1) If at the end of 24 months after a member of the Army Selected Reserve enters the Army Selected Reserve, the member has not completed the minimum training required for deployment, the member shall be discharged.

"(2) The Secretary of the Army may waive the requirement in paragraph

(1) in the case of health care providers and in other cases determined necessary. The authority to make such a waiver may not be delegated.

''Sec. 1116. Minimum physical deployability standards.

''The Secretary of the Army shall transfer the personnel classification of a member of the Army Selected Reserve from the Selected Reserve unit of the member to the personnel account established pursuant to section 1115 if the member does not meet minimum physical profile standards required for deployment. Any such transfer shall be made not later than 90 days after the date on which the determination that the member does not meet such standards is made.

''Secs. 1117, 1118. [Repealed]

''Sec. 1119. Combat unit training.

''The Secretary of the Army shall establish a program to minimize the post-mobilization training time required for combat units of the Army National Guard. The program shall require—

''(1) that unit premobilization training emphasize—

''(A) individual soldier qualification and training;

''(B) collective training and qualification at the crew, section, team, and squad level; and

''(C) maneuver training at the platoon level as required of all Army units; and

''(2) that combat training for command and staff leadership include annual multi-echelon training to develop battalion, brigade, and division level skills, as appropriate.

''Sec. 1120. Use of combat simulators.

''The Secretary of the Army shall expand the use of simulations, simulators, and advanced training devices and technologies in order to increase training opportunities for members and units of the Army National Guard and the Army Reserve.

''Assessment of National Guard Capability

''Sec. 1121. Deployability rating system.

'' The Secretary of the Army shall modify the readiness rating system for units of the Army Reserve and Army National Guard to ensure that the rating system provides an accurate assessment of the deployability of a unit and those shortfalls of a unit that require the provision of additional resources. In making such modifications, the Secretary shall ensure that the unit readiness rating system is designed so—

''(1) that the personnel readiness rating of a unit reflects—

''(A) both the percentage of the overall personnel requirement of the unit that is manned and deployable and the fill and deployability rate for critical occupational specialties necessary for the unit to carry out its basic mission requirements; and

''(B) the number of personnel in the unit who are qualified in their primary military occupational specialty; and

''(2) that the equipment readiness assessment of a unit—

''(A) documents all equipment required for deployment;

''(B) reflects only that equipment that is directly possessed by the unit;

''(C) specifies the effect of substitute items; and

''(D) assesses the effect of missing components and sets on the readiness of major equipments items.

''Sec. 1122. Inspections.

''Section 105 of title 32, United States Code, is amended—

''(1) in subsection (a)—

''(A) by striking out 'may' in the matter preceding paragraph (1) and inserting in lieu thereof 'shall';

''(B) by striking out 'and' at the end of paragraph (5);

''(C) by striking out the period at the end of paragraph (6) and inserting in lieu thereof '; and'; and

''(D) by inserting after paragraph (6) the following:

'' '(7) the units of the Army National Guard meet requirements for deployment.'; and

''(2) in subsection (b), by inserting '; and for determining which units of the National Guard meet deployability standards' before the period.

''Compatibility of Guard Units With Active Component Units

''Sec. 1131. Active duty associate unit responsibility.

''(a) Associate units. The Secretary of the Army shall require—

''(1) that each ground combat maneuver brigade of the Army National Guard that (as determined by the Secretary) is essential for the execution of the National Military Strategy be associated with an active-duty combat unit; and

''(2) that combat support and combat service support units of the Army Selected Reserve that (as determined by the Secretary) are essential for the execution of the National Military Strategy be associated with active-duty units.

''(b) Responsibilities. The commander (at a brigade or higher level) of the associated active duty unit for any National Guard unit or Army Selected Reserve unit that (as determined by the Secretary under subsection (a)) is essential for the execution of the National Military Strategy shall be responsible for—

''(1) approving the training program of that unit;

''(2) reviewing the readiness report of that unit;

''(3) assessing the manpower, equipment, and training resources requirements of that unit; and

''(4) validating, not less often than annually, the compatibility of that unit with the active duty forces.

''(c) Implementation. The Secretary of the Army shall begin to implement subsection (a) during fiscal year 1993 and shall achieve full implementation of the plan not later than October 1, 1995.

''Sec. 1132. Training compatibility.

''Section 414(c) of the National Defense Authorization Act for Fiscal Years 1992 and 1993 (105 Stat. 1353) is amended by adding at the end the following new paragraph:

'' '(4) After September 30, 1994, not less than 3,000 warrant officers and enlisted members in addition to those assigned under paragraph (2) shall be assigned to serve as advisers under the program.'.

''Sec. 1133. Systems compatibility.

''(a) Compatibility program. The Secretary of the Army shall develop and implement a program to ensure that Army personnel systems, Army supply systems, Army maintenance management systems, and Army finance systems are compatible across all Army components.

''(b) Report. Not later than September 30, 1993, the Secretary shall submit to the Committees on Armed Services of the Senate and House of Representatives a report describing the program under subsection (a) and setting forth a plan for implementation of the program by the end of fiscal year 1997.

''Sec. 1134. Equipment compatibility.

''Section 115b(b) of title 10, United States Code, is amended by adding at the end the following new paragraph:

'' '(8) A statement of the current status of the compatibility of equipment between the Army reserve components and active forces of the Army, the effect of that level of incompatibility on combat effectiveness, and a plan to achieve full equipment compatibility.'.

''Sec. 1135. Deployment planning reform.

''(a) Requirement for priority system. The Secretary of the Army shall develop a system for identifying the priority for mobilization of Army reserve component units. The priority system shall be based on regional contingency planning requirements and doctrine to be integrated into the Army war planning process.

''(b) Unit deployment designators. The system shall include the use of Unit Deployment Designators to specify the post-mobilization training days allocated to a unit before deployment. The Secretary shall specify standard designator categories in order to group units according to the timing of deployment after mobilization.

''(c) Use of designators. (1) The Secretary shall establish procedures to link the Unit Deployment Designator system to the process by which resources are provided for National Guard units.

''(2) The Secretary shall develop a plan that allocates greater funding for training, full-time support, equipment, and manpower in excess of 100 percent of authorized strength to units assigned Unit Deployment Designators that allow fewer post-mobilization training days.

''(3) The Secretary shall establish procedures to identify the command level at which combat units would, upon deployment, be integrated with active component forces consistent with the Unit Deployment Designator system.

''Sec. 1136. Qualification for prior-service enlistment bonus.

''Section 308i(c) of title 37, United States Code, is amended by striking out the period at the end and inserting in lieu thereof 'and may not be paid a bonus under this section unless the specialty associated with the position the member is projected to occupy is a specialty in which the member successfully served while on active duty and attained a level of qualification commensurate with the member's grade and years of service.'.

''Sec. 1137. Study of implementation for all reserve components.

''The Secretary of Defense shall conduct an assessment of the feasibility of implementing the provisions of this title for all reserve components. Not later than December 31, 1993, the Secretary shall submit to the Committees on Armed Services of the Senate and House of Representatives a report containing a plan for such implementation.''.

Active component support for reserve training. Act Nov. 30, 1993, P. L. 103-160, Div A, Title V, Subtitle B, § 515, 107 Stat. 1650, provided:

''(a) Requirement to establish. The Secretary of the Army shall, not later than September 30, 1995, establish one or more active-component units of the Army with the primary mission of providing training support to reserve units. Each such unit shall be part of the active Army force structure and shall have a commander who is on the active-duty list of the Army.

''(b) Implementation plan. The Secretary of the Army shall during fiscal year 1994 submit to the Committees on Armed Services of the Senate and House of Representatives a plan to meet the requirement in subsection (a). The plan shall include a proposal for any statutory changes that the Secretary considers to be necessary for the implementation of the plan.''.

Test program for reserve combat maneuver unit integration. Act Nov. 30, 1993, P. L. 103-160, Div A, Title V, Subtitle B, § 516, 107 Stat. 1650, directed the Secretary of the Army to prepare a plan for carrying out a test program to determine the feasibility and advisability of applying the roundout and roundup models for integration of active and reserve component Army units at the battalion and company levels and submit to Congress not later than March 31, 1994, a report that includes the plan for the test program.

§ 10106. Army National Guard: when a component of the Army

The Army National Guard while in the service of the United States is a component of the Army.

(Added Oct. 5, 1994, P. L. 103-337, Div A, Title XVI, Subtitle C, § 1661(a)(1), 108 Stat. 2970.)

HISTORY; ANCILLARY LAWS AND DIRECTIVES

Effective date of section:

This section took effect on Dec. 1, 1994, pursuant to Act Oct. 5, 1994, P. L. 103-337, Div A, Title XVI, Subtitle F, § 1691, 108 Stat. 3026, which appears as 10 USCS 10001 note.

INTERPRETIVE NOTES AND DECISIONS

National Guard did not become part of army until Congress declared emergency to exist, and until then governor was commander-in-chief. Bianco v Austin (1922) 204 App Div 34, 197 NYS 328.

§ 10107. Army National Guard of the United States: status when not in Federal service

When not on active duty, members of the Army National Guard of the United States shall be administered, armed, equipped, and trained in their status as members of the Army National Guard.

(Added Oct. 5, 1994, P. L. 103-337, Div A, Title XVI, Subtitle C, § 1661(a)(1), 108 Stat. 2971.)

HISTORY; ANCILLARY LAWS AND DIRECTIVES

Effective date of section:

This section took effect on Dec. 1, 1994, pursuant to Act Oct. 5, 1994, P. L. 103-337, Div A, Title XVI, Subtitle F, § 1691, 108 Stat. 3026, which appears as 10 USCS 10001 note.

CROSS REFERENCES

Active duty, 10 USCS § 12401.

INTERPRETIVE NOTES AND DECISIONS

Member of state national guard awaiting extended active duty in United States Army was neither employee of United States nor member of United States Army, and therefore cause of action arising from his negligent driving of automobile while awaiting reporting date did not come within purview of Tort Claims Act. Smither v United States (1972, ED Ky) 342 F Supp 1384.

Critical element in determining whether National Guardsman is employee of United States is whether or not he is in active, federal service. Ursulich v Puerto Rico Nat'l Guard (1974, DC Puerto Rico) 384 F Supp 736.

§ 10108. Naval Reserve: administration

(a) The Naval Reserve is the reserve component of the Navy. It shall be organized, administered, trained, and supplied under the direction of the Chief of Naval Operations.

(b) The bureaus and offices of the executive part of the Department of the Navy have the same relation and responsibility to the Naval Reserve as they do to the Regular Navy.

(Added Oct. 5, 1994, P. L. 103-337, Div A, Title XVI, Subtitle C, § 1661(a)(1), 108 Stat. 2971.)

HISTORY; ANCILLARY LAWS AND DIRECTIVES

Effective date of section:

This section took effect on Dec. 1, 1994, pursuant to Act Oct. 5, 1994, P. L. 103-337, Div A, Title XVI, Subtitle F, § 1691, 108 Stat. 3026, which appears as 10 USCS 10001 note.

§ 10109. Marine Corps Reserve: administration

(a) The Marine Corps Reserve is the reserve component of the Marine Corps. It shall be organized, administered, trained, and supplied under the direction of the Commandant of the Marine Corps.

(b) The departments and offices of Headquarters, Marine Corps have the same relation and responsibilities to the Marine Corps Reserve as they do to the Regular Marine Corps.

(Added Oct. 5, 1994, P. L. 103-337, Div A, Title XVI, Subtitle C, § 1661(a)(1), 108 Stat. 2971.)

HISTORY; ANCILLARY LAWS AND DIRECTIVES

Effective date of section:

This section took effect on Dec. 1, 1994, pursuant to Act Oct. 5, 1994, P. L. 103-337, Div A, Title XVI, Subtitle F, § 1691, 108 Stat. 3026, which appears as 10 USCS 10001 note.

§ 10110. Air Force Reserve: composition

The Air Force Reserve is a reserve component of the Air Force to provide a reserve for active duty. It consists of the members of the officers' section of the Air Force Reserve and of the enlisted section of the Air Force Reserve. It includes all Reserves of the Air Force who are not members of the Air National Guard of the United States.

(Added Oct. 5, 1994, P. L. 103-337, Div A, Title XVI, Subtitle C, § 1661(a)(1), 108 Stat. 2971.)

HISTORY; ANCILLARY LAWS AND DIRECTIVES

Effective date of section:

This section took effect on Dec. 1, 1994, pursuant to Act Oct. 5, 1994, P. L. 103-337, Div A, Title XVI, Subtitle F, § 1691, 108 Stat. 3026, which appears as 10 USCS 10001 note.

§ 10111. Air National Guard of the United States: composition

The Air National Guard of the United States is the reserve component of the Air Force that consists of—

(1) federally recognized units and organizations of the Air National Guard; and

(2) members of the Air National Guard who are also Reserves of the Air Force.

(Added Oct. 5, 1994, P. L. 103-337, Div A, Title XVI, Subtitle C, § 1661(a)(1), 108 Stat. 2971.)

HISTORY; ANCILLARY LAWS AND DIRECTIVES

Effective date of section:

This section took effect on Dec. 1, 1994, pursuant to Act Oct. 5, 1994, P. L. 103-337, Div A, Title XVI, Subtitle F, § 1691, 108 Stat. 3026, which appears as 10 USCS 10001 note.

CROSS REFERENCES

Air National Guard generally, 32 USCS §§ 101 et seq.

§ 10112. Air National Guard: when a component of the Air Force

The Air National Guard while in the service of the United States is a component of the Air Force.

(Added Oct. 5, 1994, P. L. 103-337, Div A, Title XVI, Subtitle C, § 1661(a)(1), 108 Stat. 2971.)

HISTORY; ANCILLARY LAWS AND DIRECTIVES

Effective date of section:

This section took effect on Dec. 1, 1994, pursuant to Act Oct. 5, 1994, P. L. 103-337, Div A, Title XVI, Subtitle F, § 1691, 108 Stat. 3026, which appears as 10 USCS 10001 note.

§ 10113. Air National Guard of the United States: status when not in Federal service

When not on active duty, members of the Air National Guard of the United States shall be administered, armed, equipped, and trained in their status as members of the Air National Guard.

(Added Oct. 5, 1994, P. L. 103-337, Div A, Title XVI, Subtitle C, § 1661(a)(1), 108 Stat. 2971.)

HISTORY; ANCILLARY LAWS AND DIRECTIVES

Effective date of section:

This section took effect on Dec. 1, 1994, pursuant to Act Oct. 5, 1994, P. L. 103-337, Div A, Title XVI, Subtitle F, § 1691, 108 Stat. 3026, which appears as 10 USCS 10001 note.

CROSS REFERENCES

Air National Guard generally, 32 USCS §§ 101 et seq.

§ 10114. Coast Guard Reserve

As provided in section 701 of title 14, the Coast Guard Reserve is a component of the Coast Guard and is organized, administered, trained, and supplied under the direction of the Commandant of the Coast Guard. Laws applicable to the Coast Guard Reserve are set forth in chapter 21 of title 14 (14 U.S.C. 701 et seq.).

(Added Oct. 5, 1994, P. L. 103-337, Div A, Title XVI, Subtitle C, § 1661(a)(1), 108 Stat. 2971.)

HISTORY; ANCILLARY LAWS AND DIRECTIVES

Effective date of section:

This section took effect on Dec. 1, 1994, pursuant to Act Oct. 5, 1994, P. L. 103-337, Div A, Title XVI, Subtitle F, § 1691, 108 Stat. 3026, which appears as 10 USCS 10001 note.

CHAPTER 1005. ELEMENTS OF RESERVE COMPONENTS

HISTORY; ANCILLARY LAWS AND DIRECTIVES

Amendments:

1994. Act Oct. 5, 1994, P. L. 103-337, Div A, Title XVI, Subtitle C, § 1661(a)(1), 108 Stat. 2972 (effective 12/1/94 as provided by § 1691 of such Act, which appears as 10 USCS § 10001 note), added the chapter heading and analysis.

1996. Act Feb. 10, 1996, P. L. 104-106, Div A, Title XV, § 1501(b)(3), 110 Stat. 496 (effective as if included in Act Oct. 5, 1995, P. L. 103-337, as enacted on Oct. 5, 1994, as provided by § 1501(f)(3) of Act Feb. 10, 1996, which appears as 10 USCS § 113 note), amended the analysis of this chapter by deleting ''generally'' following ''Reserve'' in item 10142.

§ 10141. Ready Reserve; Standby Reserve; Retired Reserve: placement and status of members; training categories

(a) There are in each armed force a Ready Reserve, a Standby Reserve, and a Retired Reserve. Each Reserve shall be placed in one of those categories.

(b) Reserves who are on the inactive status list of a reserve component, or who are assigned to the inactive Army National Guard or the inactive Air National Guard, are in an inactive status. Members in the Retired Reserve are in a retired status. All other Reserves are in an active status.

(c) As prescribed by the Secretary concerned, each reserve component except the Army National Guard of the United States and the Air National Guard of the United States shall be divided into training categories according to the degrees of training, including the number and duration of drills or equivalent duties to be completed in stated periods. The designation of training categories shall be the same for all armed forces and the same within the Ready Reserve and the Standby Reserve.

(Added Oct. 5, 1994, P. L. 103-337, Div A, Title XVI, Subtitle C, § 1661(a)(1), 108 Stat. 2972.)

HISTORY; ANCILLARY LAWS AND DIRECTIVES

Effective date of section:

This section took effect on Dec. 1, 1994, pursuant to Act Oct. 5, 1994, P. L. 103-337, Div A, Title XVI, Subtitle F, § 1691, 108 Stat. 3026, which appears as 10 USCS 10001 note.

CROSS REFERENCES

This section is referred to in 10 USCS § 261.

§ 10142. Ready Reserve

(a) The Ready Reserve consists of units or Reserves, or both, liable for active duty as provided in sections 12301 and 12302 of this title.

(b) The authorized strength of the Ready Reserve is 2,900,000.

(Added Oct. 5, 1994, P. L. 103-337, Div A, Title XVI, Subtitle C, § 1661(a)(1), 108 Stat. 2972.)

HISTORY; ANCILLARY LAWS AND DIRECTIVES

Effective date of section:

This section took effect on Dec. 1, 1994, pursuant to Act Oct. 5, 1994, P. L. 103-337, Div A, Title XVI, Subtitle F, § 1691, 108 Stat. 3026, which appears as 10 USCS 10001 note.

§ 10143. Ready Reserve: Selected Reserve

(a) Within the Ready Reserve of each of the reserve components there is a Selected Reserve. The Selected Reserve consists of units, and, as designated by the Secretary concerned, of Reserves, trained as prescribed in section 10147(a)(1) of this title or section 502(a) of title 32, as appropriate.

(b) The organization and unit structure of the Selected Reserve shall be approved—

(1) in the case of all reserve components other than the Coast Guard Reserve, by the Secretary of Defense based upon recommendations from the military departments as approved by the Chairman of the Joint Chiefs of Staff in accordance with contingency and war plans; and

(2) in the case of the Coast Guard Reserve, by the Secretary of Transportation upon the recommendation of the Commandant of the Coast Guard.

(Added Oct. 5, 1994, P. L. 103-337, Div A, Title XVI, Subtitle C, § 1661(a)(1), 108 Stat. 2972.)

HISTORY; ANCILLARY LAWS AND DIRECTIVES

Effective date of section:

This section took effect on Dec. 1, 1994, pursuant to Act Oct. 5, 1994, P. L. 103-337, Div A, Title XVI, Subtitle F, § 1691, 108 Stat. 3026, which appears as 10 USCS 10001 note.

CROSS REFERENCES

This section is referred to in 10 USCS §§ 12304, 16133; 38 USCS §§ 3002, 3012, 3701.

§ 10144. Ready Reserve: Individual Ready Reserve

(a) Within the Ready Reserve of each of the reserve components there is an Individual Ready Reserve. The Individual Ready Reserve consists of those members of the Ready Reserve who are not in the Selected Reserve or the inactive National Guard.

(b)(1) Within the Individual Ready Reserve of each reserve component there is a category of members, as designated by the Secretary concerned, who are subject to being ordered to active duty involuntarily in accordance with section 12304 of this title. A member may not be placed in that mobilization category unless—

(A) the member volunteers for that category; and

(B) the member is selected for that category by the Secretary concerned, based upon the needs of the service and the grade and military skills of that member.

(2) A member of the Individual Ready Reserve may not be carried in such mobilization category of members after the end of the 24-month period beginning on the date of the separation of the member from active service.

(3) The Secretary shall designate the grades and military skills or specialities of members to be eligible for placement in such mobilization category.

(4) A member in such mobilization category shall be eligible for benefits (other than pay and training) as are normally available to members of the Selected Reserve, as determined by the Secretary of Defense.

(Added Oct. 5, 1994, P. L. 103-337, Div A, Title XVI, Subtitle C, § 1661(a)(1), 108 Stat. 2973; Nov. 18, 1997, P. L. 105-85, Div A, Title V, Subtitle B, § 511(a), 111 Stat. 1728.)

HISTORY; ANCILLARY LAWS AND DIRECTIVES

Effective date of section:

This section took effect on Dec. 1, 1994, pursuant to § 1691 of Act Oct. 5, 1994, P. L. 103-337, which appears as 10 USCS 10001 note.

Amendments:

1997. Act Nov. 18, 1997 designated the existing provisions as subsec. (a); and added subsec. (b).

§ 10145. Ready Reserve: placement in

(a) Each person required under law to serve in a reserve component shall, upon becoming a member, be placed in the Ready Reserve of his armed force for his prescribed term of service, unless he is transferred to the Standby Reserve under section 10146(a) of this title.

(b) The units and members of the Army National Guard of the United States and of the Air National Guard of the United States are in the Ready Reserve of the Army and the Ready Reserve of the Air Force, respectively.

(c) All Reserves assigned to units organized to serve as units and designated as units in the Ready Reserve are in the Ready Reserve.

(d) Under such regulations as the Secretary concerned may prescribe, any qualified member of a reserve component or any qualified retired enlisted member of a regular component may, upon his request, be placed in the Ready Reserve. However, a member of the Retired Reserve entitled to retired pay or a retired enlisted member of a regular component may not be placed in the Ready Reserve unless the Secretary concerned makes a special finding that the member's services in the Ready Reserve are indispensable. The Secretary concerned may not delegate his authority under the preceding sentence.

(Added Oct. 5, 1994, P. L. 103-337, Div A, Title XVI, Subtitle C, § 1661(a)(1), 108 Stat. 2973.)

HISTORY; ANCILLARY LAWS AND DIRECTIVES

Effective date of section:

This section took effect on Dec. 1, 1994, pursuant to Act Oct. 5, 1994, P. L. 103-337, Div A, Title XVI, Subtitle F, § 1691, 108 Stat. 3026, which appears as 10 USCS 10001 note.

CROSS REFERENCES

This section is referred to in 10 USCS § 10147.

INTERPRETIVE NOTES AND DECISIONS

1. Generally
2. Consent of governor
3. Review

1. Generally

Making Army National Guard part of reserve force and members of National Guard members of Ready Reserve of Army insure that training of National Guard will be consistent throughout all states and will produce fighting force readily assimilated into Army in case of activation. Hoersch v Froehlke (1974, ED Pa) 382 F Supp 1235.

Membership in National Guard can automatically make one member of Ready Reserve of Army without violating Constitution, Article I, § 8 clauses 15, 16. Hoersch v Froehlke (1974, ED Pa) 382 F Supp 1235.

Navy's age-in-grade regulations under which Navy Reserve officers are involuntarily transferred from Ready Reserve to Standby Reserve are valid. Corwin v Lehman (1984, CA) 724 F2d 1577, cert den (1984) 467 US 1227, 81 L Ed 2d 876, 104 S Ct 2680.

2. Consent of governor

Change of manner in which governor exercised discretion vested in him by former 10 USCS § 269(g), in forbidding transfer to Standby Reserve of reservists who were away from their units serving on active duty in training while in meantime their units were called up in connection with postal strike, based on distinction in hardship and disruption of civilian life of those reservists already away from their units serving in active duty on one hand and of those actually called up in connection with postal strike, on other hand, was clearly within power given to governor under former 10 USCS § 269(g); where governor's consent to transfer to Standby Reserve given to National Guardsmen who were away from their units serving on active duty in training while their units were called up in connection with postal strike was changed by new governor so that these men could not longer transfer to Standby Reserve, only those National Guardsmen who had already applied for such transfer before governor's consent was changed were to have their applications for transfer granted, as new consent did not operate retroactively. Kurlan v Callaway (1974, CA2 NY) 510 F2d 274.

State interests of having National Guard serve state in time of civil emergencies within state were protected by requirement in former 10 USCS § 269(g) that members of National Guard not be transferred by Army to Standby Reserve without governor's consent. Mela v Callaway (1974, SD NY) 378 F Supp 25.

3. Review

Contention that plaintiff was wrongfully induced to re-enlist in Ready Reserve by misrepresentation that he was not then eligible to apply for Standby Reserve will not be entertained by court after plaintiff has served portion of his re-enlistment and has done so unsatisfactorily. Metz v United States (1969, WD Pa) 304 F Supp 207.

Burden of establishing unconstitutionality of former 10 USCS § 269(b) was upon party attacking it. Hoersch v Froehlke (1974, ED Pa) 382 F Supp 1235.

§ 10146. Ready Reserve: transfer from

(a) Subject to subsection (c) and under regulations prescribed by the Secretary of Defense, or by the Secretary of Transportation with respect to the Coast Guard when it is not operating as a service in the Navy, a member in the Ready Reserve may be transferred to the Standby Reserve.

(b) A Reserve who is qualified and so requests may be transferred to the Retired Reserve under regulations prescribed by the Secretary concerned and, in the case of the Secretary of a military department, approved by the Secretary of Defense.

(c) A member of the Army National Guard of the United States or the Air National Guard of the United States may be transferred to the Standby Reserve only with the consent of the governor or other appropriate authority of the State.

(Added Oct. 5, 1994, P. L. 103-337, Div A, Title XVI, Subtitle C, § 1661(a)(1), 108 Stat. 2973.)

HISTORY; ANCILLARY LAWS AND DIRECTIVES

Effective date of section:

This section took effect on Dec. 1, 1994, pursuant to Act Oct. 5, 1994, P. L. 103-337, Div A, Title XVI, Subtitle F, § 1691, 108 Stat. 3026, which appears as 10 USCS 10001 note.

CROSS REFERENCES

This section is referred to in 10 USCS § 10147.

§ 10147. Ready Reserve: training requirements

(a) Except as specifically provided in regulations to be prescribed by the Secretary of Defense, or by the Secretary of Transportation with respect to the Coast Guard when it is not operating as a service in the Navy, each person who is enlisted, inducted, or appointed in an armed force, and who becomes a member of the Ready Reserve under any provision of law except section 513 or 10145(b) of this title, shall be required, while in the Ready Reserve, to—

(1) participate in at least 48 scheduled drills or training periods during each year and serve on active duty for training of not less than 14 days (exclusive of traveltime) during each year; or

(2) serve on active duty for training not more than 30 days during each year.

(b) A member who has served on active duty for one year or longer may not be required to perform a period of active duty for training if the first day of that period falls during the last 120 days of the member's required membership in the Ready Reserve.

(Added Oct. 5, 1994, P. L. 103-337, Div A, Title XVI, Subtitle C, § 1661(a)(1), 108 Stat. 2973.)

HISTORY; ANCILLARY LAWS AND DIRECTIVES

Effective date of section:

This section took effect on Dec. 1, 1994, pursuant to Act Oct. 5, 1994, P. L. 103-337, Div A, Title XVI, Subtitle F, § 1691, 108 Stat. 3026, which appears as 10 USCS 10001 note.

Other provisions:

Application of subsec. (a). Act Oct. 5, 1994, P. L. 103-337, Div A, Title XVI, Subtitle C, § 1661(a)(5)(A), 108 Stat. 2980, provides: "Section 10147(a), as added by paragraph (1), applies only to persons who were inducted, enlisted, or appointed in an armed force after August 9, 1955.".

CROSS REFERENCES

This section is referred to in 5 USCS § 5517; 10 USCS §§ 10143, 10148; 14 USCS § 712; 50 USCS App. § 456.

INTERPRETIVE NOTES AND DECISIONS

Even though 32 CFR § 100.3, embracing approach of ordering ready reservist to active duty for up to 24 months for unsatisfactory performance, largely superseded provisions of former 10 USCS § 270(b) in practice, regulations of Secretary of Defense under former § 270(b) continued in effect. Winters v United States (1968, ED NY) 281 F Supp 289, affd (1968, CA2 NY) 390 F2d 879, cert den (1968) 393 US 896, 21 L Ed 2d 177, 89 S Ct 188.

Petitioner who failed to participate satisfactorily in reserve unit was not entitled to read into his contract of enlistment, entered into in 1962, former 10 USCS § 270(b), which was statute in force at time of his enlistment, providing that member of Ready Reserve who failed to satisfactorily perform his training duties could be ordered without his consent to perform additional active duty for training for not more than 45 days, to exclusion of applicability of later statute providing that reservist ordered to active duty for failure to participate satisfactorily in reserve unit could be required to serve on active duty for training for 24 months; petitioner did not acquire vested right in provisions of relevant statute as they existed in 1962. Fox v Brown (1968, SD NY) 286 F Supp 855, affd (1968, CA2 NY) 402 F2d 837, cert den (1969) 394 US 938, 22 L Ed 2d 471, 89 S Ct 1219.

10 USCS § 673a did not eliminate former 10 USCS § 270(b); application of requirement of former § 270(b) which authorized 45 days involuntary active duty for unsatisfactory drill participation to prior service obligors was discretionary. Even v Clifford (1968, SD Cal) 287 F Supp 334.

§ 10148. Ready Reserve: failure to satisfactorily perform prescribed training

(a) A member of the Ready Reserve covered by section 10147 of this title who fails in any year to perform satisfactorily the training duty prescribed in that section, as determined by the Secretary concerned under regulations prescribed by the Secretary of Defense, may be ordered without his consent to perform additional active duty for training for not more than 45 days. If the failure occurs during the last year of his required membership in the Ready Reserve, his membership is extended until he performs that additional active duty for training, but not for more than six months.

(b) A member of the Army National Guard of the United States or the Air National Guard of the United States who fails in any year to perform satisfactorily the training duty prescribed by or under law for members of the Army National Guard or the Air National Guard, as the case may be, as determined by the Secretary concerned, may, upon the request of the Governor of the State (or, in the case of the District of Columbia, the commanding general of the District of Columbia National Guard) be ordered, without his consent, to perform additional active duty for training for not more than 45 days. A member ordered to active duty under this subsection shall be ordered to duty as a Reserve of the Army or as a Reserve of the Air Force, as the case may be.

(Added Oct. 5, 1994, P. L. 103-337, Div A, Title XVI, Subtitle C, § 1661(a)(1), 108 Stat. 2974.)

HISTORY; ANCILLARY LAWS AND DIRECTIVES

Effective date of section:

This section took effect on Dec. 1, 1994, pursuant to Act Oct. 5, 1994, P. L. 103-337, Div A, Title XVI, Subtitle F, § 1691, 108 Stat. 3026, which appears as 10 USCS 10001 note.

Other provisions:

Application of subsec. (b). Act Oct. 5, 1994, P. L. 103-337, Div A, Title XVI, Subtitle C, § 1661(a)(5)(B), 108 Stat. 2980, provides: ''Section 10148(b), as added by paragraph (1), applies only to persons who became members of the Army National Guard of the United States or the Air National Guard of the United States after October 4, 1961.''.

CROSS REFERENCES

This section is referred to in 10 USCS § 1201.

§ 10149. Ready Reserve: continuous screening

(a) Under regulations to be prescribed by the President, the Secretary concerned shall provide a system of continuous screening of units and members of the Ready Reserve to ensure the following:

(1) That there will be no significant attrition of those members or units during a mobilization.

(2) That there is a proper balance of military skills.

(3) That except for those with military skills for which there is an overriding requirement, members having critical civilian skills are not retained in numbers beyond the need for those skills.

(4) That with due regard to national security and military requirements, recognition will be given to participation in combat.

(5) That members whose mobilization in an emergency would result in an extreme personal or community hardship are not retained in the Ready Reserve.

(b) Under regulations to be prescribed by the Secretary of Defense, and by the Secretary of Transportation with respect to the Coast Guard when it is not operating as a service in the Navy, a member of the Ready Reserve who is designated as a member not to be retained in the Ready Reserve as a result of screening under subsection (a) shall, as appropriate, be—

(1) transferred to the Standby Reserve;

(2) discharged; or

(3) if the member is eligible and applies therefor, transferred to the Retired Reserve.

(Added Oct. 5, 1994, P. L. 103-337, Div A, Title XVI, Subtitle C, § 1661(a)(1), 108 Stat. 2974.)

HISTORY; ANCILLARY LAWS AND DIRECTIVES

Effective date of section:

This section took effect on Dec. 1, 1994, pursuant to Act Oct. 5, 1994, P. L. 103-337, Div A, Title XVI, Subtitle F, § 1691, 108 Stat. 3026, which appears as 10 USCS 10001 note.

Other provisions:

Screening of ready reserve. Ex. Or. No. 11190 of Dec. 29, 1964, 29 Fed. Reg. 19183; Ex. Or. No. 11382 of Nov. 28, 1967, 32 Fed.Reg. 16247, provided:

"By virtue of the authority vested in me by section 301 of title 3 of the United States Code, and as President of the United States and Commander in Chief of the Armed Forces of the United States, it is ordered as follows:

"Section 1. There is delegated to the Secretary of Defense (and to the Secretary of Transportation with regard to the United States Coast Guard) the authority vested in the President by section 271 of title 10 of the United States Code [10 USCS § 10149] to prescribe regulations for the screening of units and members of the Ready Reserve of the Armed Forces.

"Sec. 2. Executive Order No. 10651 of January 6, 1956, is revoked."

INTERPRETIVE NOTES AND DECISIONS

Former 10 USCS § 271 did not repeal former 10 USCS § 270, and former § 271(a)(5) merely permitted service to release member of Ready Reserve prior to completion of his enlistment period upon finding of extreme personal or community hardship but did not otherwise affect obligations assumed by enlistee. Petition of La Plata on behalf of Fisher (1959, DC Mich) 174 F Supp 884.

Transfer to Stand-by Reserve from Ready Reserve of reservist holding key civilian position (federal district judge) is valid, since Ready Reserve Service Agreement is not contract, and exemption of reservists from Dual Compensation Act (5 USCS §§ 5531-5533) does not exempt reservists from military readiness criteria. Sharp v Weinberger (1984, DC Dist Col) 593 F Supp 886, affd in part and vacated in part on other grounds (1986, App DC) 255 US App DC 90, 798 F2d 1521.

Army Reserve psychiatrist was not entitled to temporary restraining order blocking his impending mobilization into active duty on ground that loss of his services to substance abuse treatment program would work extreme hardship on community under former 10 USCS § 271, where country's involvement in Persian Gulf war took priority over war on drugs at time, because hardship imposed on large city by psychiatrist's mobilization was not "extreme" but rather much like hardship on thousands of families and on every community and occupational calling throughout U.S. Blocher v Fonville (1991, SD Tex) 756 F Supp 306.

§ 10150. Ready Reserve: transfer back from Standby Reserve

Under regulations to be prescribed by the Secretary of Defense, and by the Secretary of Transportation with respect to the Coast Guard when it is not operating as a service in the Navy, a member of the Standby Reserve who has not completed his required period of service in the Ready Reserve may be transferred to the Ready Reserve when the reason for his transfer to the Standby Reserve no longer exists.

(Added Oct. 5, 1994, P. L. 103-337, Div A, Title XVI, Subtitle C, § 1661(a)(1), 108 Stat. 2975.)

HISTORY; ANCILLARY LAWS AND DIRECTIVES

Effective date of section:

This section took effect on Dec. 1, 1994, pursuant to Act Oct. 5, 1994, P. L. 103-337, Div A, Title XVI, Subtitle F, § 1691, 108 Stat. 3026, which appears as 10 USCS 10001 note.

§ 10151. Standby Reserve: composition

The Standby Reserve consists of those units or members, or both, of the reserve components, other than those in the Ready Reserve or Retired Reserve, who are liable for active duty only as provided in sections 12301 and 12306 of this title.
(Added Oct. 5, 1994, P. L. 103-337, Div A, Title XVI, Subtitle C, § 1661(a)(1), 108 Stat. 2975.)

HISTORY; ANCILLARY LAWS AND DIRECTIVES

Effective date of section:

This section took effect on Dec. 1, 1994, pursuant to Act Oct. 5, 1994, P. L. 103-337, Div A, Title XVI, Subtitle F, § 1691, 108 Stat. 3026, which appears as 10 USCS 10001 note.

§ 10152. Standby Reserve: inactive status list

An inactive status list shall be maintained in the Standby Reserve. Whenever an authority designated by the Secretary concerned considers that it is in the best interest of the armed force concerned, a member in the Standby Reserve who is not required to remain a Reserve, and who cannot participate in prescribed training, may, if qualified, be transferred to the inactive status list under regulations to be prescribed by the Secretary concerned. These regulations shall fix the conditions under which such a member is entitled to be returned to an active status.
(Added Oct. 5, 1994, P. L. 103-337, Div A, Title XVI, Subtitle C, § 1661(a)(1), 108 Stat. 2975.)

HISTORY; ANCILLARY LAWS AND DIRECTIVES

Effective date of section:

This section took effect on Dec. 1, 1994, pursuant to Act Oct. 5, 1994, P. L. 103-337, Div A, Title XVI, Subtitle F, § 1691, 108 Stat. 3026, which appears as 10 USCS 10001 note.

INTERPRETIVE NOTES AND DECISIONS

Navy's age-in-grade regulations under which Navy Reserve officers are involuntarily transferred from Ready Reserve to Standby Reserve are valid. Corwin v Lehman (1984, CA) 724 F2d 1577, cert den (1984) 467 US 1227, 81 L Ed 2d 876, 104 S Ct 2680.

§ 10153. Standby Reserve: status of members

While in an inactive status, a Reserve is not eligible for pay or promotion and (as provided in section 12734(a) of this title) does not accrue credit for years of service under chapter 1223 of this title [10 USCS §§ 12731 et seq.].

(Added Oct. 5, 1994, P. L. 103-337, Div A, Title XVI, Subtitle C, § 1661(a)(1), 108 Stat. 2975.)

HISTORY; ANCILLARY LAWS AND DIRECTIVES

Effective date of section:

This section took effect on Dec. 1, 1994, pursuant to Act Oct. 5, 1994, P. L. 103-337, Div A, Title XVI, Subtitle F, § 1691, 108 Stat. 3026, which appears as 10 USCS 10001 note.

§ 10154. Retired Reserve

The Retired Reserve consists of the following Reserves:

(1) Reserves who are or have been retired under section 3911, 6323, or 8911 of this title or under section 291 of title 14.

(2) Reserves who have been transferred to the Retired Reserve upon their request, retain their status as Reserves, and are otherwise qualified.

(Added Oct. 5, 1994, P. L. 103-337, Div A, Title XVI, Subtitle C, § 1661(a)(1), 108 Stat. 2975.)

HISTORY; ANCILLARY LAWS AND DIRECTIVES

Effective date of section:

This section took effect on Dec. 1, 1994, pursuant to Act Oct. 5, 1994, P. L. 103-337, Div A, Title XVI, Subtitle F, § 1691, 108 Stat. 3026, which appears as 10 USCS 10001 note.

Other provisions:

Authority to issue military identification cards to so-called honorary retirees of the Naval and Marine Corps Reserves. Act Oct. 5, 1994, P. L. 103-337, Div A, Title III, Subtitle H, § 377, 108 Stat. 2737; Feb. 10, 1996, P. L. 104-106, Div A, Title XV, § 1501, 110 Stat. 500; Nov. 18, 1997, P. L. 105-85, Div A, Title X, Subtitle G, § 1073(d)(1)(E)(i), 111 Stat. 1905 (effective and applicable as provided by § 1073(d)(1) and (i) of such Act, which appear as notes to 10 USCS §§ 1076 and 101, respectively), provided:

''(a) Authority. The Secretary of the Navy may issue a military identification card to a member of the Retired Reserve described in subsection (b).

''(b) Covered members. A member of the Retired Reserve referred to in subsection (a) is a member of the Naval Reserve or Marine Corps Reserve who transferred to the Retired Reserve under section 274(2) of title 10, United States Code, without having completed the years of service required under section 1331(a)(2) of such title for eligibility for retired pay under chapter 67 of such title [10 USCS §§ 1331 et seq.] or who after November 30, 1994, transferred to the Retired Reserve under section 10154(2) of title 10, United States Code, without having completed the years of service required under section 12731(a)(2) of such title for eligibility for retired pay under chapter 1223 of such title [10 USCS §§ 12731 et seq.].

''(c) Effect on commissary and exchange benefits. The issuance of a military identification card under subsection (a) to a member of the Retired

Reserve does not confer eligibility for commissary and exchange benefits on that member.

''(d) Limitation on color and format. The Secretary shall ensure that the color and format in which a military identification card is issued under subsection (a) is not similar to the color and format in which a military identification card is issued by the Department of Defense to individuals other than members described in subsection (b).''.

CHAPTER 1006. RESERVE COMPONENT COMMANDS

HISTORY; ANCILLARY LAWS AND DIRECTIVES

Amendments:

1996. Act Sept. 23, 1996, P. L. 104-201, Div A, Title XII, Subtitle A, § 1211(a)(1), 110 Stat. 2689, added the chapter heading and chapter analysis.

§ 10171. United States Army Reserve Command

(a) Command. The United States Army Reserve Command is a separate command of the Army commanded by the Chief of Army Reserve.

(b) Chain of command. Except as otherwise prescribed by the Secretary of Defense, the Secretary of the Army shall prescribe the chain of command for the United States Army Reserve Command.

(c) Assignment of forces. The Secretary of the Army—

(1) shall assign to the United States Army Reserve Command all forces of the Army Reserve in the continental United States other than forces assigned to the unified combatant command for special operations forces established pursuant to section 167 of this title; and

(2) except as otherwise directed by the Secretary of Defense in the case of forces assigned to carry out functions of the Secretary of the Army specified in section 3013 of this title, shall assign all such forces of the Army Reserve to the commander of the United States Atlantic Command.

(Added Sept. 23, 1996, P. L. 104-201, Div A, Title XII, Subtitle A, § 1211(a)(1), 110 Stat. 2689.)

HISTORY; ANCILLARY LAWS AND DIRECTIVES

Other provisions:

Implementation schedule. Act Sept. 23, 1996, P. L. 104-201, Div A, Title XII, Subtitle A, § 1211(c), 110 Stat. 2691, provided: ''Implementation of chapter 1006 of title 10, United States Code [10 USCS §§ 10171 et seq.], as added by subsection (a), shall begin not later than 90 days after the date of the enactment of this Act and shall be completed not later than one year after such date.''.

§ 10172. Naval Reserve Force

(a) Establishment of command. The Secretary of the Navy, with the advice and assistance of the Chief of Naval Operations, shall establish a Naval Reserve

Force. The Naval Reserve Force shall be operated as a separate command of the Navy.

(b) Commander. The Chief of Naval Reserve shall be the commander of the Naval Reserve Force. The commander of the Naval Reserve Force reports directly to the Chief of Naval Operations.

(c) Assignment of forces. The Secretary of the Navy—

(1) shall assign to the Naval Reserve Force specified portions of the Naval Reserve other than forces assigned to the unified combatant command for special operations forces established pursuant to section 167 of this title; and

(2) except as otherwise directed by the Secretary of Defense in the case of forces assigned to carry out functions of the Secretary of the Navy specified in section 5013 of this title, shall assign to the combatant commands all such forces assigned to the Naval Reserve Force under paragraph (1) in the manner specified by the Secretary of Defense.

(Added Sept. 23, 1996, P. L. 104-201, Div A, Title XII, Subtitle A, § 1211(a)(1), 110 Stat. 2689.)

§ 10173. Marine Forces Reserve

(a) Establishment. The Secretary of the Navy, with the advice and assistance of the Commandant of the Marine Corps, shall establish in the Marine Corps a command known as the Marine Forces Reserve.

(b) Commander. The Marine Forces Reserve is commanded by the Commander, Marine Forces Reserve. The Commander, Marine Forces Reserve, reports directly to the Commandant of the Marine Corps.

(c) Assignment of forces. The Commandant of the Marine Corps—

(1) shall assign to the Marine Forces Reserve the forces of the Marine Corps Reserve stationed in the continental United States other than forces assigned to the unified combatant command for special operations forces established pursuant to section 167 of this title; and

(2) except as otherwise directed by the Secretary of Defense in the case of forces assigned to carry out functions of the Secretary of the Navy specified in section 5013 of this title, shall assign to the combatant commands (through the Marine Corps component commander for each such command) all such forces assigned to the Marine Forces Reserve under paragraph (1) in the manner specified by the Secretary of Defense.

(Added Sept. 23, 1996, P. L. 104-201, Div A, Title XII, Subtitle A, § 1211(a)(1), 110 Stat. 2690.)

§ 10174. Air Force Reserve Command

(a) Establishment of Command. The Secretary of the Air Force, with the advice and assistance of the Chief of Staff of the Air Force, shall establish an Air Force Reserve Command. The Air Force Reserve Command shall be operated as a separate command of the Air Force.

(b) Commander. The Chief of Air Force Reserve is the Commander of the Air Force Reserve Command. The commander of the Air Force Reserve Command reports directly to the Chief of Staff of the Air Force.

(c) Assignment of forces. The Secretary of the Air Force—

(1) shall assign to the Air Force Reserve Command all forces of the Air Force Reserve stationed in the continental United States other than forces assigned to the unified combatant command for special operations forces established pursuant to section 167 of this title; and

(2) except as otherwise directed by the Secretary of Defense in the case of forces assigned to carry out functions of the Secretary of the Air Force specified in section 8013 of this title, shall assign to the combatant commands all such forces assigned to the Air Force Reserve Command under paragraph (1) in the manner specified by the Secretary of Defense.

(Added Sept. 23, 1996, P. L. 104-201, Div A, Title XII, Subtitle A, § 1211(a)(1), 110 Stat. 2690.)

CHAPTER 1007. ADMINISTRATION OF RESERVE COMPONENTS

HISTORY; ANCILLARY LAWS AND DIRECTIVES

Amendments:

1994. Act Oct. 5, 1994, P. L. 103-337, Div A, Title XVI, Subtitle C, § 1661(a)(1), 108 Stat. 2976, added the chapter heading and analysis.

1996. Act Feb. 10, 1996, P. L. 104-106, Div A, Title V, Subtitle B, § 513(c)(2), 110 Stat. 306, amended the analysis of this chapter by adding item 10216.

Act Feb. 10, 1996, P. L. 104-106, Div A, Title XV, § 1501(b), 110 Stat. 496, amended the analysis of this chapter by deleting ''Individual'' preceding ''Ready'' in item 10205, and by capitalizing ''Reserve'' in item 10211.

1997. Act Nov. 18, 1997, P. L. 105-85, Div A, Title V, Subtitle C, §§ 522(h)(2), 523(a)(2), 111 Stat. 1736, 1737, amended the analysis of this chapter by substituting item 10216 for one which read: ''10216. Military technicians'', and by adding item 10217.

§ 10201. Assistant Secretary of Defense for Reserve Affairs

As provided in section 138(b)(2) of this title, the official in the Department of Defense with responsibility for overall supervision of reserve component affairs of the Department of Defense is the Assistant Secretary of Defense for Reserve Affairs.

(Added Oct. 5, 1994, P. L. 103-337, Div A, Title XVI, Subtitle C, § 1661(a)(1), 108 Stat. 2976; Feb. 10, 1996, P. L. 104-106, Div A, Title IX, Subtitle A, § 903(f)(4), 110 Stat. 402; Sept. 23, 1996, P. L. 104-201, Div A, Title IX, Subtitle A, § 901, 110 Stat. 2617.)

HISTORY; ANCILLARY LAWS AND DIRECTIVES

Effective date of section:

This section took effect on Dec. 1, 1994, pursuant to Act Oct. 5, 1994, P. L. 103-337, Div A, Title XVI, Subtitle F, § 1691, 108 Stat. 3026, which appears as 10 USCS 10001 note.

Amendments:

1996. Act Sept. 23, 1996, § 901, repealed § 903(f)(4) of Act Feb. 10, 1996, which provided for amendment of this section effective January 31, 1997.

CROSS REFERENCES

This section is referred to in 10 USCS § 261.

§ 10202. Regulations

(a) Subject to standards, policies, and procedures prescribed by the Secretary of Defense, the Secretary of each military department shall prescribe such regulations as the Secretary considers necessary to carry out provisions of law relating to the reserve components under the Secretary's jurisdiction.

(b) The Secretary of Transportation, with the concurrence of the Secretary of the Navy, shall prescribe such regulations as the Secretary considers necessary to carry out all provisions of law relating to the reserve components insofar as they relate to the Coast Guard, except when the Coast Guard is operating as a service in the Navy.

(c) So far as practicable, regulations for all reserve components shall be uniform.

(Added Oct. 5, 1994, P. L. 103-337, Div A, Title XVI, Subtitle C, § 1661(a)(1), 108 Stat. 2976.)

HISTORY; ANCILLARY LAWS AND DIRECTIVES

Effective date of section:

This section took effect on Dec. 1, 1994, pursuant to Act Oct. 5, 1994, P. L. 103-337, Div A, Title XVI, Subtitle F, § 1691, 108 Stat. 3026, which appears as 10 USCS 10001 note.

INTERPRETIVE NOTES AND DECISIONS

Navy's age-in-grade regulations under which Navy Reserve officers are involuntarily transferred from Ready Reserve to Standby Reserve are valid. Corwin v Lehman (1984, CA) 724 F2d 1577, cert den (1984) 467 US 1227, 81 L Ed 2d 876, 104 S Ct 2680.

§ 10203. Reserve affairs: designation of general or flag officer of each armed force

(a) The Secretary of the Army may designate a general officer of the Army to be directly responsible for reserve affairs to the Chief of Staff of the Army.

(b) The Secretary of the Navy may designate a flag officer of the Navy to be directly responsible for reserve affairs to the Chief of Naval Operations and a general officer of the Marine Corps to be directly responsible for reserve affairs to the Commandant of the Marine Corps.

(c) The Secretary of the Air Force may designate a general officer of the Air Force to be directly responsible for reserve affairs to the Chief of Staff of the Air Force.

(d) The Secretary of Transportation may designate a flag officer of the Coast Guard to be directly responsible for reserve affairs to the Commandant of the Coast Guard.

(e) This section does not affect the functions of the Chief of the National Guard Bureau, the Chief of Army Reserve, or the Chief of Air Force Reserve.

(Added Oct. 5, 1994, P. L. 103-337, Div A, Title XVI, Subtitle C, § 1661(a)(1), 108 Stat. 2976.)

HISTORY; ANCILLARY LAWS AND DIRECTIVES

Effective date of section:

This section took effect on Dec. 1, 1994, pursuant to Act Oct. 5, 1994, P. L. 103-337, Div A, Title XVI, Subtitle F, § 1691, 108 Stat. 3026, which appears as 10 USCS 10001 note.

§ 10204. Personnel records

(a) The Secretary concerned shall maintain adequate and current personnel records of each member of the reserve components under the Secretary's jurisdiction showing the following with respect to the member:

(1) Physical condition.
(2) Dependency status.
(3) Military qualifications.
(4) Civilian occupational skills.
(5) Availability for service.
(6) Such other information as the Secretary concerned may prescribe.

(b) Under regulations to be prescribed by the Secretary of Defense, the Secretary of each military department shall maintain a record of the number of members of each class of each reserve component who, during each fiscal year, have participated satisfactorily in active duty for training and inactive duty training with pay.

(Added Oct. 5, 1994, P. L. 103-337, Div A, Title XVI, Subtitle C, § 1661(a)(1), 108 Stat. 2977.)

HISTORY; ANCILLARY LAWS AND DIRECTIVES

Effective date of section:

This section took effect on Dec. 1, 1994, pursuant to Act Oct. 5, 1994, P. L. 103-337, Div A, Title XVI, Subtitle F, § 1691, 108 Stat. 3026, which appears as 10 USCS 10001 note.

RESEARCH GUIDE

Law Review Articles:

Bryant. The Posse Comitatus Act, the military, and drug interdiction: just how far can we go? 1990 Army Law 3, December 1990.

§ 10205. Members of Ready Reserve: requirement of notification of change of status

(a) Each member of the Ready Reserve shall notify the Secretary concerned of any change in the member's address, marital status, number of dependents, or civilian employment and of any change in the member's physical condition that would prevent the member from meeting the physical or mental standards prescribed for the member's armed force.

(b) This section shall be administered under regulations prescribed by the Secretary of Defense and by the Secretary of Transportation with respect to the Coast Guard when it is not operating as a service in the Navy.

(Added Oct. 5, 1994, P. L. 103-337, Div A, Title XVI, Subtitle C, § 1661(a)(1), 108 Stat. 2977.)

HISTORY; ANCILLARY LAWS AND DIRECTIVES

Effective date of section:

This section took effect on Dec. 1, 1994, pursuant to Act Oct. 5, 1994, P. L. 103-337, Div A, Title XVI, Subtitle F, § 1691, 108 Stat. 3026, which appears as 10 USCS 10001 note.

§ 10206. Members: periodic physical examinations

(a) Each member of the Ready Reserve who is not on active duty shall—

(1) be examined as to his physical fitness every five years, or more often as the Secretary concerned considers necessary; and

(2) execute and submit annually to the Secretary concerned a certificate of physical condition.

Each Reserve in an active status, or on an inactive status list, who is not on active duty shall execute and submit annually to the Secretary concerned a certificate of physical condition.

(b) The kind of duty to which a Reserve ordered to active duty may be assigned shall be considered in determining physical qualifications for active duty.

(Added Oct. 5, 1994, P. L. 103-337, Div A, Title XVI, Subtitle C, § 1661(a)(1), 108 Stat. 2977.)

HISTORY; ANCILLARY LAWS AND DIRECTIVES

Effective date of section:

This section took effect on Dec. 1, 1994, pursuant to Act Oct. 5, 1994, P. L. 103-337, Div A, Title XVI, Subtitle F, § 1691, 108 Stat. 3026, which appears as 10 USCS 10001 note.

§ 10207. Mobilization forces: maintenance

(a) Whenever units or members of the reserve components are ordered to active duty (other than for training) during a period of partial mobilization, the Secretary concerned shall continue to maintain mobilization forces by planning and budgeting for the continued organization and training of the reserve components not mobilized, and make the fullest practicable use of the Federal facilities vacated by mobilized units, consistent with approved joint mobilization plans.

(b) In this section, the term 'partial mobilization' means the mobilization resulting from action by Congress or the President, under any law, to bring units of any reserve component, and members not assigned to units organized to serve as units, to active duty for a limited expansion of the active armed forces.

(Added Oct. 5, 1994, P. L. 103-337, Div A, Title XVI, Subtitle C, § 1661(a)(1), 108 Stat. 2977.)

HISTORY; ANCILLARY LAWS AND DIRECTIVES

Effective date of section:

This section took effect on Dec. 1, 1994, pursuant to Act Oct. 5, 1994, P. L. 103-337, Div A, Title XVI, Subtitle F, § 1691, 108 Stat. 3026, which appears as 10 USCS 10001 note.

§ 10208. Annual mobilization exercise

(a) The Secretary of Defense shall conduct at least one major mobilization exercise each year. The exercise should be as comprehensive and as realistic as possible and should include the participation of associated active component and reserve component units.

(b) The Secretary shall maintain a plan to test periodically each active component and reserve component unit based in the United States and all interactions of such units, as well as the sustainment of the forces mobilized as part of the exercise, with the objective of permitting an evaluation of the adequacy of resource allocation and planning.

(Added Oct. 5, 1994, P. L. 103-337, Div A, Title XVI, Subtitle C, § 1661(a)(1), 108 Stat. 2978.)

HISTORY; ANCILLARY LAWS AND DIRECTIVES

Effective date of section:

This section took effect on Dec. 1, 1994, pursuant to Act Oct. 5, 1994, P. L. 103-337, Div A, Title XVI, Subtitle F, § 1691, 108 Stat. 3026, which appears as 10 USCS 10001 note.

§ 10209. Regular and reserve components: discrimination prohibited

Laws applying to both Regulars and Reserves shall be administered without discrimination—

(1) among Regulars;
(2) among Reserves; and
(3) between Regulars and Reserves.

(Added Oct. 5, 1994, P. L. 103-337, Div A, Title XVI, Subtitle C, § 1661(a)(1), 108 Stat. 2978.)

HISTORY; ANCILLARY LAWS AND DIRECTIVES

Effective date of section:

This section took effect on Dec. 1, 1994, pursuant to Act Oct. 5, 1994, P. L. 103-337, Div A, Title XVI, Subtitle F, § 1691, 108 Stat. 3026, which appears as 10 USCS 10001 note.

INTERPRETIVE NOTES AND DECISIONS

1. "Laws applying to both Regulars and Reserves"
2. Promotions
3. Miscellaneous

1. "Laws applying to both Regulars and Reserves"

Former 10 USCS § 277 did not apply to Marine Corps bulletin which required Marine reservists to attend 100 percent of reserve drills while reservists in other branches of armed forces had to attend only 90 percent of their reserve drills, as such § 277 applied only to "laws applying to both Regulars and Reserves." Winters v United States (1969, CA9 Cal) 412 F2d 140, cert den (1969) 396 US 920, 24 L Ed 2d 200, 90 S Ct 248.

Former 10 USCS § 277 was not applicable to review order of governor which withdrew consent to transfer to Standby Reserve National Guardsmen who did not perform full-time duty with their units at time of postal workers' strike even though they were absent from their unit for active duty for training, as such § 277 by its terms covered only "laws applying to both Regulars and Reserves." Kurlan v Callaway (1974, SD NY) 381 F Supp 594, affd in part and revd in part on other grounds (1974, CA2 NY) 510 F2d 274.

2. Promotions

State national guard was not prohibited by Total Force concept nor by former 10 USCS § 277 from employing policy of internal promotions. MacFarlane v Grasso (1982, CA2 Conn) 696 F2d 217.

Officer was illegally discharged where Standby Advisory Board which considered him for promotion consisted of officers who had been members of regular selection board which had previously rejected plaintiff, as overlapping membership on regular and standby boards discriminated against officer by denying him fair and equitable evaluation. Evensen v United States (1981) 228 Ct Cl 207, 654 F2d 68.

3. Miscellaneous

Statute did not require that regulations established by respective secretaries of boards for correction of military records be identical. Edison v United States (1989) 18 Cl Ct 362, affd without op (1990, CA) 909 F2d 1496, reported in full (1990, CA FC) 1990 US App LEXIS 12426.

§ 10210. Dissemination of information

The Secretary of Defense shall require the complete and current dissemination, to all Reserves and to the public, of information of interest to the reserve components.

(Added Oct. 5, 1994, P. L. 103-337, Div A, Title XVI, Subtitle C, § 1661(a)(1), 108 Stat. 2978.)

HISTORY; ANCILLARY LAWS AND DIRECTIVES

Effective date of section:

This section took effect on Dec. 1, 1994, pursuant to Act Oct. 5, 1994, P. L. 103-337, Div A, Title XVI, Subtitle F, § 1691, 108 Stat. 3026, which appears as 10 USCS 10001 note.

RESEARCH GUIDE

Law Review Articles:

Bryant. The Posse Comitatus Act, the military, and drug interdiction: just how far can we go? 1990 Army Law 3, December 1990.

INTERPRETIVE NOTES AND DECISIONS

Former 10 USCS § 278 did not impose affirmative obligation on Air Force to advise reserve officers of membership of promotion boards. Foster v United States (1984, CA) 733 F2d 88.

§ 10211. Policies and regulations: participation of Reserve officers in preparation and administration

Within such numbers and in such grades and assignments as the Secretary concerned may prescribe, each armed force shall have officers of its reserve components on active duty (other than for training) at the seat of government, and at headquarters responsible for reserve affairs, to participate in preparing and administering the policies and regulations affecting those reserve components. While so serving, such an officer is an additional number of any staff with which he is serving.

(Added Oct. 5, 1994, P. L. 103-337, Div A, Title XVI, Subtitle C, § 1661(a)(1), 108 Stat. 2978.)

HISTORY; ANCILLARY LAWS AND DIRECTIVES

Effective date of section:

This section took effect on Dec. 1, 1994, pursuant to Act Oct. 5, 1994, P. L. 103-337, Div A, Title XVI, Subtitle F, § 1691, 108 Stat. 3026, which appears as 10 USCS 10001 note.

CROSS REFERENCES

This section is referred to in 10 USCS §§ 523, 641, 3038, 8038.

§ 10212. Gratuitous services of officers: authority to accept

(a) Notwithstanding section 1342 of title 31, the Secretary of Defense may accept the gratuitous services of an officer of a reserve component (other than an officer of the Army National Guard of the United States or the Air National Guard of the United States) in consultation upon matters relating to the armed forces.

(b) Notwithstanding section 1342 of title 31, the Secretary of a military department may accept the gratuitous services of an officer of a reserve component under the Secretary's jurisdiction (other than an officer of the Army National Guard of the United States or the Air National Guard of the United States)—

(1) in the furtherance of the enrollment, organization, and training of that officer's reserve component or the Reserve Officers' Training Corps; or

(2) in consultation upon matters relating to the armed forces.

(Added Oct. 5, 1994, P. L. 103-337, Div A, Title XVI, Subtitle C, § 1661(a)(1), 108 Stat. 2978; Oct. 13, 1994, P. L. 103-355, Title III, Subtitle C, § 3021(a), 108 Stat. 3333.)

HISTORY; ANCILLARY LAWS AND DIRECTIVES

Effective date of section:

This section took effect on Dec. 1, 1994, pursuant to Act Oct. 5, 1994, P. L. 103-337, Div A, Title XVI, Subtitle F, § 1691, 108 Stat. 3026, which appears as 10 USCS 10001 note.

Amendments:

1994. Act Oct. 13, 1994 (effective as provided by § 3021(b) of such Act, which appears as a note to this section), designated the existing provisions as subsec. (b), and added subsec. (a).

Other provisions:

Effective date of Oct. 13, 1994 amendments. Act Oct. 13, 1994, P. L. 103-355, Title III, Subtitle C, § 3021(b), 108 Stat. 3333, provides: "Notwithstanding section 10001 [41 USCS § 251 note], the amendments made by subsection (a) [amending this section] shall take effect on December 1, 1994, immediately after the amendments made by the Reserve Officer Personnel Management Act [adding this section, among other things; for full classification, consult USCS Tables volumes].".

§ 10213. Reserve components: dual membership prohibited

Except as otherwise provided in this title, no person may be a member of more than one reserve component at the same time.

(Added Oct. 5, 1994, P. L. 103-337, Div A, Title XVI, Subtitle C, § 1661(a)(1), 108 Stat. 2979.)

HISTORY; ANCILLARY LAWS AND DIRECTIVES

Effective date of section:

This section took effect on Dec. 1, 1994, pursuant to Act Oct. 5, 1994, P. L. 103-337, Div A, Title XVI, Subtitle F, § 1691, 108 Stat. 3026, which appears as 10 USCS 10001 note.

CROSS REFERENCES

This section is referred to in 10 USCS § 14317.

§ 10214. Adjutants general and assistant adjutants general: reference to other officers of National Guard

In any case in which, under the laws of a State, an officer of the National Guard of that jurisdiction, other than the adjutant general or an assistant adjutant general, normally performs the duties of that office, the references in sections 12004(b)(1), 12215, 12642(c), 14507(b), 14508(e), and 14512 of this title to the adjutant general or the assistant adjutant general shall be applied to that officer instead of to the adjutant general or assistant adjutant general.

(Added Oct. 5, 1994, P. L. 103-337, Div A, Title XVI, Subtitle C, § 1661(a)(1), 108 Stat. 2979.)

HISTORY; ANCILLARY LAWS AND DIRECTIVES

Effective date of section:

This section took effect on Dec. 1, 1994, pursuant to Act Oct. 5, 1994, P. L. 103-337, Div A, Title XVI, Subtitle F, § 1691, 108 Stat. 3026, which appears as 10 USCS 10001 note.

§ 10215. Officers of Army National Guard of the United States and Air National Guard of the United States: authority with respect to Federal status

(a)(1) Officers of the Army National Guard of the United States who are not on active duty—

(A) may order members of the Army National Guard of the United States to active duty for training under section 12301(d) of this title; and

(B) with the approval of the Secretary of the Air Force, may order members of the Air National Guard of the United States to active duty for training under that section.

(2) Officers of the Air National Guard of the United States who are not on active duty—

(A) may order members of the Air National Guard of the United States to active duty for training under section 12301(d) of this title; and

(B) with the approval of the Secretary of the Army, may order members of the Army National Guard of the United States to active duty for training under that section.

(b) Officers of the Army National Guard of the United States or the Air National Guard of the United States who are not on active duty—

(1) may enlist, reenlist, or extend the enlistments of persons as Reserves of the Army or Reserves of the Air Force for service in the Army National Guard of the United States or the Air National Guard of the United States, as the case may be; and

(2) with respect to their Federal status, may promote or discharge persons enlisted or reenlisted as Reserves of the Army or Reserves of the Air Force for that service.

(c) This section shall be carried out under regulations prescribed by the Secretary of the Army, with respect to matters concerning the Army, and by the Secretary of the Air Force, with respect to matters concerning the Air Force.

(Added Oct. 5, 1994, P. L. 103-337, Div A, Title XVI, Subtitle C, § 1661(a)(1), 108 Stat. 2979.)

HISTORY; ANCILLARY LAWS AND DIRECTIVES

Effective date of section:

This section took effect on Dec. 1, 1994, pursuant to Act Oct. 5, 1994, P. L. 103-337, Div A, Title XVI, Subtitle F, § 1691, 108 Stat. 3026, which appears as 10 USCS 10001 note.

§ 10216. Military technicians (dual status)

(a) In general. (1) For purposes of this section and any other provision of law, a military technician (dual status) is a Federal civilian employee who—

(A) is employed under section 3101 of title 5 or section 709 of title 32;

(B) is required as a condition of that employment to maintain membership in the Selected Reserve; and

(C) is assigned to a position as a technician in the administration and training of the Selected Reserve or in the maintenance and repair of supplies or equipment issued to the Selected Reserve or the armed forces.

(2) Military technicians (dual status) shall be authorized and accounted for as a separate category of civilian employees.

(b) Priority for management of military technicians (dual status). (1) As a basis for making the annual request to Congress pursuant to section 115(g) of this title for authorization of end strengths for military technicians (dual status) of the Army and Air Force reserve components, the Secretary of Defense shall give priority to supporting authorizations for military technicians (dual status) in the following high-priority units and organizations:

(A) Units of the Selected Reserve that are scheduled to deploy no later than 90 days after mobilization.

(B) Units of the Selected Reserve that are or will deploy to relieve active duty peacetime operations tempo.

(C) Those organizations with the primary mission of providing direct support surface and aviation maintenance for the reserve components of the Army and Air Force, to the extent that the military technicians (dual status) in such units would mobilize and deploy in a skill that is compatible with their civilian position skill.

(2) For each fiscal year, the Secretary of Defense shall, for the high-priority units and organizations referred to in paragraph (1), seek to achieve a programmed manning level for military technicians (dual status) that is not less than 90 percent of the programmed manpower structure for those units and organizations for military technicians (dual status) for that fiscal year.

(3) Military technician (dual status) authorizations and personnel shall be exempt from any requirement (imposed by law or otherwise) for reductions in Department of Defense civilian personnel and shall only be reduced as part of military force structure reductions.

(c) Information required to be submitted with annual end strength authorization request. (1) The Secretary of Defense shall include as part of the budget justification documents submitted to Congress with the budget of the Department of Defense for any fiscal year the following information with respect to the end strengths for military technicians (dual status) requested in that budget pursuant to section 115(g) of this title, shown separately for each of the Army and Air Force reserve components:

(A) The number of military technicians (dual status) in the high priority units and organizations specified in subsection (b)(1).

(B) The number of technicians other than military technicians (dual status) in the high priority units and organizations specified in subsection (b)(1).

(C) The number of military technicians (dual status) in other than high priority units and organizations specified in subsection (b)(1).

(D) The number of technicians other than military technicians (dual status) in other than high priority units and organizations specified in subsection (b)(1).

(2)(A) If the budget submitted to Congress for any fiscal year requests authorization for that fiscal year under section 115(g) of this title of a military technician (dual status) end strength for a reserve component of the Army or Air Force in a number that constitutes a reduction from the end strength minimum established by law for that reserve component for the fiscal year during which the budget is submitted, the Secretary of Defense shall submit to the congressional defense committees with that budget a justification providing the basis for that requested reduction in technician end strength.

(B) Any justification submitted under subparagraph (A) shall clearly delineate the specific force structure reductions forming the basis for such requested technician reduction (and the numbers related to those reductions).

(d) Unit membership requirement. (1) Unless specifically exempted by law, each individual who is hired as a military technician (dual status) after December 1, 1995, shall be required as a condition of that employment to maintain membership in—

(A) the unit of the Selected Reserve by which the individual is employed as a military technician; or

(B) a unit of the Selected Reserve that the individual is employed as a military technician to support.

(2) Paragraph (1) does not apply to a military technician (dual status) who is employed by the Army Reserve in an area other than Army Reserve troop program units.

(e) Dual status requirement. (1) Funds appropriated for the Department of Defense may not (except as provided in paragraph (2)) be used for compensation as a military technician of any individual hired as a military technician after February 10, 1996, who is no longer a member of the Selected Reserve.

(2) The Secretary concerned may pay compensation described in paragraph (1) to an individual described in that paragraph who is no longer a member of the Selected Reserve for a period not to exceed six months following the individual's loss of membership in the Selected Reserve if the Secretary determines that such loss of membership was not due to the failure of that individual to meet military standards.

(Added Feb. 10, 1996, P. L. 104-106, Div A, Title V, Subtitle B, § 513(c)(1), 110 Stat. 306; Sept. 23, 1996, P. L. 104-201, Div A, Title IV, Subtitle A, § 413(b), (c), Title XII, Subtitle A, § 1214, 110 Stat. 2507, 2695; Nov. 18, 1997, P. L. 105-85, Div A, Title V, Subtitle C, § 522(a), (b), (f)–(h)(1), 111 Stat. 1734, 1735.)

HISTORY; ANCILLARY LAWS AND DIRECTIVES

Amendments:

1996. Act Sept. 23, 1996, in subsec. (a)(1), in the introductory matter, substituted "section 115(g)" for "section 115"; redesignated subsec. (b) as subsec. (c); added new subsec. (b); and, in subsec. (c) as redesignated, substituted ''after February 10, 1996,'' for ''after the date of the enactment of this section'' in two places.

Such Act further redesignated subsecs. (a), (b), and (c), as subsecs. (b), (c), and (d), respectively; added a new subsec. (a); and, in subsec. (b) as redesignated, in para. (3), deleted ''in high-priority units and organizations specified in paragraph (1)'' following ''authorizations and personnel''.

1997. Act Nov. 18, 1997 substituted the section heading for one which read: ''§ 10216. Military technicians''; substituted subsec. (a) for one which read: ''(a) In general. Military technicians are Federal civilian employees hired under title 5 and title 32 who are required to maintain dual-status as drilling reserve component members as a condition of their Federal civilian employment. Such employees shall be authorized and accounted for as a separate category of dual-status civilian employees, exempt as specified in subsection (b)(3) from any general or regulatory requirement for adjustments in Department of Defense civilian personnel.''; in subsec. (b), in the heading, inserted ''(dual status)'', in para. (1), in the introductory matter, inserted ''(dual status)'' and substituted ''military technicians (dual status)'' for ''dual status military technicians'' and, in subpara. (C), inserted ''(dual status)'', and, in paras. (2) and (3), inserted ''(dual status)'' wherever appearing; in subsec. (c), in the introductory matter, inserted ''(dual status)'' and, in para. (1), in subparas. (A)–(D), substituted ''military technicians (dual status)'' for ''dual-status technicians'' and substituted ''subsection (b)(1)'' for ''subsection (a)(1)'', in para. (2), in subpara. (A), inserted ''(dual status)'' and, in subpara. (B), substituted ''delineate the specific force structure reductions'' for ''delineate—

''(i) in the case of a reduction that includes a reduction in technicians described in subparagraph (A) or (C) of paragraph (1), the specific force structure reductions forming the basis for such requested technician reduction (and the numbers related to those force structure reductions); and

''(ii) in the case of a reduction that includes reductions in technicians described in subparagraphs (B) or (D) of paragraph (1), the specific force structure reductions, Department of Defense civilian personnel reductions, or other reasons'';

and substituted subsecs. (d) and (e) for former subsec. (d), which read: ''(d) Dual-status requirement. The Secretary of Defense shall require the Secretary of the Army and the Secretary of the Air Force to establish as a condition of employment for each individual who is hired after February 10, 1996, as a military technician that the individual maintain membership in the Selected Reserve (so as to be a so-called 'dual-status' technician) and shall require that the civilian and military position skill requirements of dual-status military technicians be compatible. No Department of Defense funds may be spent for compensation for any military technician hired after February 10, 1996, who is not a member of the Selected Reserve, except that compensation may be paid for up to six months following loss of membership in the Selected Reserve if such loss of membership was not due to the failure to meet military standards.''.

CROSS REFERENCES

This section is referred to in 10 USCS § 115a.

§ 10217. Non-dual status military technicians

(a) Definition. For the purposes of this section and any other provision of law, a non-dual status military technician is a civilian employee of the Department of Defense serving in a military technician position who—

(1) was hired as a military technician before the date of the enactment of the National Defense Authorization Act for Fiscal Year 1998 [enacted Nov. 18, 1996] under any of the authorities specified in subsection (c)[(b)]; and

(2) as of the date of the enactment of that Act [enacted Nov. 18, 1996] is not a member of the Selected Reserve or after such date ceased to be a member of the Selected Reserve.

(b) Employment authorities. The authorities referred to in subsection (a) are the following:

(1) Section 10216 of this title.

(2) Section 709 of title 32.

(3) The requirements referred to in section 8401 of title 5.

(4) Section 8016 of the Department of Defense Appropriations Act, 1996 (Public Law 104-61; 109 Stat. 654) [former 10 USCS § 10101 note], and any comparable provision of law enacted on an annual basis in the Department of Defense Appropriations Acts for fiscal years 1984 through 1995.

(5) Any memorandum of agreement between the Department of Defense and the Office of Personnel Management providing for the hiring of military technicians.

(Added Nov. 18, 1997, P. L. 105-85, Div A, Title V, Subtitle C, § 523(a)(1), 111 Stat. 1736.)

HISTORY; ANCILLARY LAWS AND DIRECTIVES

Explanatory notes:

The bracketed subsection designator "(b)" has been inserted in subsec. (a)(1) as the reference probably intended by Congress.

Other provisions:

Plan for full utilization of military technicians (dual status). Act Nov. 18, 1997, P. L. 105-85, Div A, Title V, Subtitle C, § 523(d), (e), 111 Stat. 1737, provides:

"(d) Plan for full utilization of military technicians (dual status). (1) Not later than 180 days after the date of the enactment of this Act, the Secretary of Defense shall submit to Congress a plan for ensuring that, on and after September 30, 2007, all military technician positions are held only by military technicians (dual status).

"(2) The plan shall provide for achieving, by September 30, 2002, a 50 percent reduction, by conversion of positions or otherwise, in the number of non-dual status military technicians that are holding military technicians positions, as compared with the number of non-dual status technicians that held military technician positions as of September 30, 1997, as specified in the report under subsection (c).

"(3) Among the alternative actions to be considered in developing the plan, the Secretary shall consider the feasibility and cost of each of the following:

''(A) Eliminating or consolidating technician functions and positions.

''(B) Contracting with private sector sources for the performance of functions performed by military technicians.

''(C) Converting non-dual status military technician positions to military technician (dual status) positions or to positions in the competitive service or, in the case of positions of the Army National Guard of the United States or the Air National Guard of the United States, to positions of State employment.

''(D) Use of incentives to facilitate attainment of the objectives specified for the plan in paragraphs (1) and (2).

''(4) The Secretary shall submit with the plan any recommendations for legislation that the Secretary considers necessary to carry out the plan.

''(e) Definitions for categories of military technicians. In this section:

''(1) The term 'non-dual status military technician' has the meaning given that term in section 10217 of title 10, United States Code, as added by subsection (a).

''(2) The term 'military technician (dual status)' has the meaning given the term in section 10216(a) of such title.''.

CHAPTER 1009. RESERVE FORCES POLICY BOARDS AND COMMITTEES

HISTORY; ANCILLARY LAWS AND DIRECTIVES

Amendments:

1994. Act Oct. 5, 1994, P. L. 103-337, Div A, Title XVI, Subtitle C, § 1661(b)(1), 108 Stat. 2980 (effective Dec. 1, 1994, as provided by § 1691 of such Act, which appears as 10 USCS § 10001 note), added the chapter heading and analysis.

§ 10301. Reserve Forces Policy Board

(a) There is in the Office of the Secretary of Defense a Reserve Forces Policy Board. The Board consists of the following:

(1) A civilian chairman appointed by the Secretary of Defense.

(2) The Assistant Secretary of the Army for Manpower and Reserve Affairs, the Assistant Secretary of the Navy for Manpower and Reserve Affairs, and the Assistant Secretary of the Air Force for Manpower and Reserve Affairs.

(3) An officer of the Regular Army designated by the Secretary of the Army.

(4) An officer of the Regular Navy and an officer of the Regular Marine Corps, each designated by the Secretary of the Navy.

(5) An officer of the Regular Air Force designated by the Secretary of the Air Force.

(6) Four reserve officers designated by the Secretary of Defense upon the recommendation of the Secretary of the Army, two of whom must be members of the Army National Guard of the United States, and two of whom must be members of the Army Reserve.

(7) Four reserve officers designated by the Secretary of Defense upon the recommendation of the Secretary of the Navy, two of whom must be members of the Naval Reserve, and two of whom must be members of the Marine Corps Reserve.

(8) Four reserve officers designated by the Secretary of Defense upon the recommendation of the Secretary of the Air Force, two of whom must be members of the Air National Guard of the United States, and two of whom must be members of the Air Force Reserve.

(9) A reserve officer of the Army, Navy, Air Force, or Marine Corps who is a general officer or flag officer designated by the Chairman of the Board with the approval of the Secretary of Defense, and who serves without vote as military adviser to the Chairman and as executive officer of the Board.

(10) An officer of the Regular Army, Regular Navy, Regular Air Force, or Regular Marine Corps serving in a position on the Joint Staff who is designated by the Chairman of the Joint Chiefs of Staff.

(b) Whenever the Coast Guard is not operating as a service in the Navy, the Secretary of Transportation may designate two officers of the Coast Guard, Regular or Reserve, to serve as voting members of the Board.

(c) The Board, acting through the Assistant Secretary of Defense for Reserve Affairs, is the principal policy adviser to the Secretary of Defense on matters relating to the reserve components.

(d) This section does not affect the committees on reserve policies prescribed within the military departments by sections 10302 through 10305 of this title.

(e) A member of a committee or board prescribed under a section listed in subsection (d) may, if otherwise eligible, be a member of the Reserve Forces Policy Board.

(f) The Board shall act on those matters referred to it by the Chairman and, in addition, on any matter raised by a member of the Board.

(Added Oct. 5, 1994, P. L. 103-337, Div A, Title XVI, Subtitle C, § 1661(b)(1), 108 Stat. 2980.)

HISTORY; ANCILLARY LAWS AND DIRECTIVES

Effective date of section:

This section took effect on Dec. 1, 1994, pursuant to Act Oct. 5, 1994, P. L. 103-337, Div A, Title XVI, Subtitle F, § 1691, 108 Stat. 3026, which appears as 10 USCS 10001 note.

CROSS REFERENCES

This section is referred to in 10 USCS §§ 175, 641.

§ 10302. Army Reserve Forces Policy Committee

(a) There is in the Office of the Secretary of the Army an Army Reserve Forces Policy Committee. The Committee shall review and comment upon major policy matters directly affecting the reserve components and the mobilization preparedness of the Army. The Committee's comments on such policy matters shall accompany the final report regarding any such matters submitted to the Secretary of the Army and the Chief of Staff.

(b) The Committee consists of officers in the grade of colonel or above, as follows:

(1) five members of the Regular Army on duty with the Army General Staff;

(2) five members of the Army National Guard of the United States not on active duty; and

(3) five members of the Army Reserve not on active duty.

(c) The members of the Committee shall select the Chairman from among the members on the Committee not on active duty.

(d) A majority of the members of the Committee shall act whenever matters affecting both the Army National Guard of the United States and Army Reserve are being considered. However, when any matter solely affecting one of the reserve components of the Army is being considered, it shall be acted upon only by the Subcommittee on Army National Guard Policy or the Subcommittee on Army Reserve Policy, as appropriate.

(e) The Subcommittee on Army National Guard Policy consists of the members of the Committee other than the Army Reserve members.

(f) The Subcommittee on Army Reserve Policy consists of the members of the Committee other than the Army National Guard members.

(g) Membership on the Committee is determined by the Secretary of the Army and is for a minimum period of three years. Except in the case of members of the Committee from the Regular Army, the Secretary of the Army, when appointing new members, shall insure that among the officers of each component on the Committee there will at all times be two or more members with more than one year of continuous service on the Committee.

(h) There shall be not less than 10 officers of the Army National Guard of the United States and the Army Reserve on duty with the Army Staff, one-half of whom shall be from each of those components. These officers shall be considered as additional members of the Army Staff while on that duty.

(Aug. 10, 1956, ch 1041, § 1, 70A Stat. 161; Sept. 2, 1958, P. L. 85-861, § 33(a)(17), 72 Stat. 1565; Dec. 1, 1967, P. L. 90-168, § 2(18), 81 Stat. 524; Oct. 1, 1986, P. L. 99-433, Title V, Part A, § 501(a)(8), 100 Stat. 1039; Oct. 5, 1994, P. L. 103-337, Div A, Title XVI, Subtitle C, § 1661(b)(2)(A), 108 Stat. 2981.)

HISTORY; ANCILLARY LAWS AND DIRECTIVES

Prior law and revision:

1956 ACT

Revised Section	Source (USCS)	Source (Statutes at Large)
3033(a)	10:38 (1st para. less last 37 words).	June 3, 1916, ch. 134, § 5 (less last para.); June 4,
3033(b)	10:38 (last 37 words of 1st para).	1920, ch. 227, subch. I, § 5 (1st 7 paras.); Sept.
3033(c)	10:38 (1st sentence, less proviso of 2d para).	22, 1922, ch. 423, § 1; July 2, 1926, ch. 721, § 5;
3033(d)	10:38 (proviso of 1st sentence on 2d para).	May 21, 1928, ch, 647; added June 15, 1933, ch.
3033(e)	10:38 (2d sentence, and 3d sentence less proviso, of 2d para).	87, § 2 (less last para.), 48 Stat. 153; June 3, 1938, ch. 319; July 14, 1939, ch.
3033(f).............	10:38 (proviso of 3d sentence, and last sentence, of 2d para).	269; June 28, 1950, ch. 383, § 401(b), 64 Stat. 271.

In subsection (a), the words ''the following subjects'' are inserted for clarity.

In subsections, (a) and (c), the words ''of officers'', after the word ''committee'', are inserted for clarity. The words ''and of'' are substituted for the words ''to which shall be added''.

In subsection (e), the words ''For the purpose specified herein'' are omitted as surplusage. The words ''on that duty'' are substituted for the words ''so serving''.

1958 ACT

The change is necessary to make subsection (d) coextensive with subsection (c), to which it was a proviso in the source law, the Act of June 3, 1916, ch 134, § 5 (1st sentence of 2d par.) (formerly 10 U.S.C. 38 (1st sentence of 2d para.)).

Amendments:

1958. Act Sept. 2, 1958 (effective 8/10/56, as provided by section 33(g) of such Act; see 10 USCS § 101 note), in subsec. (d), inserted ''the organization, distribution, training, appointment, assignment, promotion, or discharge of members of'' and ''those of''.

1967. Act Dec. 1, 1967 (effective on the first day of the first calendar month following enactment on 12/1/67, as provided by § 7 of such Act, which appears as 10 USCS § 138 note), substituted this section for one which read:

''(a) Each policy or regulation affecting the following subjects shall be prepared by a committee of officers of the appropriate division or divisions of the Army General Staff and of an equal number of officers of the Army National Guard of the United States:

''(1) The organization or distribution of the Army National Guard of the United States.

''(2) The organization, distribution, or training of the Army National Guard.

''(b) The members of each committee under subsection (a) who are officers of the Army National Guard of the United States must be selected from lists of officers of that component who are suitable for that duty, submitted by the governors of the States and Territories of whose Army National Guard they are members, respectively, and by the commanding general of the District of Columbia National Guard for the District of Columbia.

''(c) Each policy or regulation affecting the organization, distribution, training, appointment, assignment, promotion, or discharge of members of the Army Reserve shall be prepared by a committee of officers of the appropriate divisions of the Army General Staff and of an equal number of officers of the Army Reserve.

''(d) Each policy or regulation affecting the organization, distribution, training, appointment, assignment, promotion, or discharge of members of the Army Reserve and those of either the Army National Guard of the United States or the Army National Guard shall be prepared by a committee composed of equal numbers of officers of the Regular Army, of the Army National Guard of the United States, and of the Army Reserve.

''(e) There shall be not less than 10 officers of the Army National Guard of the United States and the Army Reserve on duty with the Army General Staff, one-half of whom shall be from each of those components. These officers shall be considered as additional members of the Army General Staff while on that duty.

"(f) The Chief of Staff shall—

"(1) send the statements of policies and regulations prepared under this section to the Secretary of the Army;

"(2) advise him with regard thereto; and

"(3) after action on those policies and regulations by the Secretary, act as the agent of the Secretary in carrying them into effect.".

1986. Act Oct. 1, 1986 redesignated this section, formerly 10 USCS § 3033, as 10 USCS § 3021, and in such section as redesignated, substituted the catchline for one which read: "§ 3033. Reserve components of Army; policies and regulations for government of" in subsec. (a), substituted "Office" for "office" and "Committee. The Committee" for "Committee which", inserted "and the mobilization preparedness", substituted "Army. The" for "Army, and the", and substituted "Secretary of the Army and the Chief of Staff" for "Chief of Staff and the Assistant Secretary responsible for reserve affairs"; and, in subsec. (h), deleted "General" preceding "Staff" in two places.

1994. Act Oct. 5, 1994 (effective 12/1/94 as provided by § 1691 of such Act, which appears as 10 USCS § 10001 note) transferred this section, enacted as 10 USCS § 3021, to Chapter 1009 and redesignated it as 10 USCS § 10302.

CROSS REFERENCES

This section is referred to in 10 USCS §§ 523, 641, 3021, 10301; 37 USCS § 204.

§ 10303. Naval Reserve Policy Board

A Naval Reserve Policy Board shall be convened at least once annually at the seat of government to consider, recommend, and report to the Secretary of the Navy on reserve policy matters. At least half of the members of the Board must be officers of the Naval Reserve.

(Added Oct. 5, 1994, P. L. 103-337, Div A, Title XVI, Subtitle C, § 1661(b)(1), 108 Stat. 2981.)

HISTORY; ANCILLARY LAWS AND DIRECTIVES

Effective date of section:

This section took effect on Dec. 1, 1994, pursuant to Act Oct. 5, 1994, P. L. 103-337, Div A, Title XVI, Subtitle F, § 1691, 108 Stat. 3026, which appears as 10 USCS 10001 note.

CROSS REFERENCES

This section is referred to in 10 USCS §§ 523, 641, 10301.

§ 10304. Marine Corps Reserve Policy Board

A Marine Corps Reserve Policy Board shall be convened at least once annually at the seat of government to consider, recommend, and report to the Secretary of the Navy on reserve policy matters. At least half of the members of the Board must be officers of the Marine Corps Reserve.

(Added Oct. 5, 1994, P. L. 103-337, Div A, Title XVI, Subtitle C, § 1661(b)(1), 108 Stat. 2981.)

HISTORY; ANCILLARY LAWS AND DIRECTIVES

Effective date of section:

This section took effect on Dec. 1, 1994, pursuant to Act Oct. 5, 1994, P. L. 103-337, Div A, Title XVI, Subtitle F, § 1691, 108 Stat. 3026, which appears as 10 USCS 10001 note.

CROSS REFERENCES

This section is referred to in 10 USCS §§ 523, 641, 10301.

§ 10305. Air Force Reserve Forces Policy Committee

(a) There is in the Office of the Secretary of the Air Force an Air Reserve Forces Policy Committee on Air National Guard and Air Force Reserve Policy. The Committee shall review and comment upon major policy matters directly affecting the reserve components and the mobilization preparedness of the Air Force. The Committee's comments on such policy matters shall accompany the final report regarding any such matters submitted to the Secretary of the Air Force and the Chief of Staff.

(b) The Committee consists of officers in the grade of colonel or above, as follows:

(1) five members of the Regular Air Force on duty with the Air Staff;

(2) five members of the Air National Guard of the United States not on active duty; and

(3) five members of the Air Force Reserve not on active duty.

(c) The members of the Committee shall select the Chairman from among the members on the Committee not on active duty.

(d) A majority of the members of the Committee shall act whenever matters affecting both the Air National Guard of the United States and Air Force Reserve are being considered. However, when any matter solely affecting one of the Air Force Reserve components is being considered, it shall be acted upon only by the Subcommittee on Air National Guard Policy or the Subcommittee on Air Force Reserve Policy, as appropriate.

(e) The Subcommittee on Air National Guard Policy consists of the members of the Committee other than the Air Force Reserve members.

(f) The Subcommittee on Air Force Reserve Policy consists of the members or the Committee other than the Air National Guard members.

(g) Membership on the Air Staff Committee is determined by the Secretary of the Air Force and is for a minimum period of three years. Except in the case of members of the Committee from the Regular Air Force, the Secretary of the Air Force, when appointing new members, shall insure that among the officers of each component on the Committee there will at all times be two or more members with more than one year of continuous service on the Committee.

(h) There shall be not less than 10 officers of the Air National Guard of the United States and the Air Force Reserve on duty with the Air Staff, one-half of whom shall be from each of those components. These officers shall be considered as additional members of the Air Staff while on that duty.

(Aug. 10, 1956, ch 1041, § 1, 70A Stat. 491; Sept. 2, 1958, P. L. 85-861, § 33(a)(17), 72 Stat. 1565; Dec. 1, 1967, P. L. 90-168, § 2(21), 81 Stat. 525; Oct. 1, 1986, P. L. 99-433, Title V, Part C, § 521(a)(6), 100 Stat. 1059; Oct. 5, 1994, P. L. 103-337, Div A, Title XVI, Subtitle C, § 1661(b)(2)(B), 108 Stat. 2981.)

HISTORY; ANCILLARY LAWS AND DIRECTIVES

Prior law and revision:

1956 ACT

Revised Section	Source (USCS)	Source (Statutes at Large)
8033(a)	10:38 (1st para., less last 37 words).	June 3, 1916, ch. 134, § 5 (less last para.); June 4, 1920, ch. 227, subch. I, § 5 (1st 7 paras.); Sept. 22, 1922, ch. 423, § 1; July 2, 1926, ch. 721, § 5; May 21, 1928, ch. 647; added June 15, 1933, ch. 87, § 2 (less last para.), 48 Stat. 153; June 3, ch. 319; July 14, 1939, ch. 269; June 28, 1950, ch. 383, § 401(b), 64 Stat. 271.
8033(b)	10:38 (last 37 words of 1st para.).	
8033(c)	10:38 (1st sentence, less proviso, of 2d para.).	
8033(d)	10:38 (proviso of 1st sentence of 2d para.).	
8033(e)	10:38 (2d sentence, and 3d sentence less proviso, of 2d para.).	
8033(f)	10:38 (proviso of 3d sentence, and last sentence, of 2d para.).	
8033(g)	5:626(f).	July 26, 1947, ch. 343, § 207(f), 61 Stat. 503.

In subsection (a), the words "the following subjects" are inserted for clarity.

In subsections (a) and (c), the words "of officers", after the word "committee", are inserted for clarity. The words "and of" are substituted for the words "to which shall be added".

In subsection (e), the words "For the purpose specified herein" are omitted as surplusage. The words "on that duty" are substituted for the words "so serving".

In subsection (g), the word "perform" is substituted for the words "be charged with". All of 5:626(f) except the first proviso of the first sentence is omitted as executed. The words "Territories, Puerto Rico, the Canal Zone, and the District of Columbia" are inserted to conform to other sections of this title which, in describing the National Guard, also include these jurisdictions.

1958 ACT

The change is necessary to make subsec. (d) co-extensive with subsec. (c), to which it was a proviso in the source law, the Act of June 3, 1916, ch 134, § 5 (1st sentence of 2d para.) (formerly 10 U.S.C. 38 (1st sentence of 2d para.)).

Amendments:

1958. Act Sept. 2, 1958 (effective 8/10/56, as provided by § 33(g) of such

Act, which appears as 10 USCS § 101 note), in subsec. (d), inserted "the organization, distribution, training, appointment, assignment, promotion, or discharge of members of" and "those of".

1967. Act Dec. 1, 1967 (effective on the first day of the first calendar month following 12/1/67, as provided by § 7 of such Act, which appears as 10 USCS § 138 note), substituted this section for one which read:

"(a) Each policy or regulation affecting the following subjects shall be prepared by a committee of officers of the appropriate division or divisions of the Air Staff and of an equal number of officers of the Air National Guard of the United States:

"(1) The organization or distribution of the Air National Guard of the United States.

"(2) The organization, distribution, or training of the Air National Guard.

"(b) The members of each committee under subsection (a) who are officers of the Air National Guard of the United States must be selected from lists of officers of that component who are suitable for that duty, submitted by the governors of the States and Territories of whose Air National Guard they are members, respectively, and by the commanding general of the District of Columbia National Guard for the District of Columbia.

"(c) Each policy or regulation affecting the organization, distribution, training, assignment, promotion, or discharge of members of the Air Force Reserve shall be prepared by a committee of officers of the appropriate divisions of the Air Staff and of an equal number of officers of the Air Force Reserve.

"(d) Each policy or regulation affecting the organization, distribution, training, appointment, assignment, promotion, or discharge of members of the Air Force Reserve and those of either the Air National Guard of the United States or the Air National Guard shall be prepared by a committee composed of equal numbers of officers of the Regular Air Force, of the Air National Guard of the United States, and of the Air Force Reserve.

"(e) There shall be not less than 10 officers of the Air National Guard of the United States and the Air Force Reserve on duty with the Air Staff, one-half of whom shall be from each of those components. These officers shall be considered as additional members of the Air Staff while on that duty.

"(f) The Chief of Staff shall—

"(1) send the statements of policies and regulations prepared under this section to the Secretary of the Air Force;

"(2) advise him with regard thereto; and

"(3) after action on those policies and regulations by the Secretary, act as the agent of the Secretary in carrying them into effect.

"(g) In addition to the function and duties performed by it for the Department of the Army, the National Guard Bureau shall perform similar functions and duties for the Department of the Air Force, and shall be the channel of communication between the Department of the Air Force and the States and Territories, Puerto Rico, the Canal Zone, and the District of Columbia on all matters affecting the Air National Guard.".

1986. Act Oct. 1, 1986 redesignated this section, formerly 10 USCS § 8033, as 10 USCS § 8021, and in such section as redesignated, substituted this catchline for one which read:
''§ 8021. Reserve components of Air Force; policies and regulations for government of: functions of National Guard Bureau with respect to Air National Guard''; in subsec. (a), substituted ''Policy. The Committee'' for ''Policy which'', inserted ''and the mobilization preparedness'', and substituted ''Air Force. The'' for ''Air Force and the'' and substituted ''Secretary of the Air Force and the Chief of Staff'' for ''Chief of Staff, and the Assistant Secretary responsible for reserve affairs''; and, in subsec. (b), in para. (2) inserted ''and'' following the semicolon.
1994. Act Oct. 5, 1994 (effective 12/1/94 as provided by § 1691 of such Act, which appears as 10 USCS § 10001 note) transferred this section, enacted as 10 USCS § 8021, to Chapter 1009 and redesignated it as 10 USCS § 10305.

CROSS REFERENCES

Air National Guard, 32 USCS §§ 101 et seq.

This section is referred to in 10 USCS §§ 523, 641, 8021, 10301; 37 USCS § 204.

CHAPTER 1011. NATIONAL GUARD BUREAU

HISTORY; ANCILLARY LAWS AND DIRECTIVES

Amendments:

1994. Act Oct. 5, 1994, P. L. 103-337, Div A, Title IX, Subtitle A, § 904(a), 108 Stat. 2824 added the chapter heading and chapter analysis.

Act Oct. 5, 1994, P. L. 103-337, Div A, Title XVI, Subtitle C, § 1661(c)(1)(B), 108 Stat. 2982 (effective 12/1/94 as provided by § 1691 of such Act, which appears as 10 USCS § 10001 note), added item 10507.

1996. Act Feb. 10, 1996, P. L. 104-106, Div A, Title XV, § 1501(b)(5), (7)(B), 110 Stat. 496 (effective as if included in Act Oct. 5, 1994, P. L. 103-337, as enacted on Oct. 5, 1994, as provided by § 1501(f)(3) of Act Feb. 10, 1996, which appears as 10 USCS § 113 note), amended the analysis of this chapter by inserting a heading at the top of the column of section numbers and by deleting item 10508, which read: ''10508. Definition''.

§ 10501. National Guard Bureau

(a) National Guard Bureau. There is in the Department of Defense the National Guard Bureau, which is a joint bureau of the Department of the Army and the Department of the Air Force.

(b) Purposes. The National Guard Bureau is the channel of communications on all matters pertaining to the National Guard, the Army National Guard of the United States, and the Air National Guard of the United States between (1) the Department of the Army and Department of the Air Force, and (2) the several States.

(Added Oct. 5, 1994, P. L. 103-337, Div A, Title IX, Subtitle A, § 904(a), 108 Stat. 2824.)

HISTORY; ANCILLARY LAWS AND DIRECTIVES

Effective date of section:

This section became effective at the end of the 90-day period beginning on enactment, as provided by Act Oct. 5, 1994, P. L. 103-337, Div A, Title IX, Subtitle A, § 904(d), 108 Stat. 2827, which appears as a note to this section.

Other provisions:

Effective date of Oct. 5, 1994 amendments. Act Oct. 5, 1994, P. L. 103-337, Div A, Title IX, Subtitle A, § 904(d), 108 Stat. 2827; Feb. 10, 1996, P. L. 104-106, Div A, Title XV, § 1504(a)(6), 110 Stat. 513 (effective 10/5/94, and as if included in Act Oct. 5, 1994, as enacted, as provided by § 1504(a)(1) of Act Feb. 10, 1996, which appears as 10 USCS § 2701 note), provides: "The provisions of chapter 1011 of title 10, United States Code [10 USCS §§ 10501 et seq.], as added by subsection (a), shall become effective, and the repeal made by subsection (b) [repealing 10 USCS § 3040] and the amendment made by subsection (c) [amending 32 USCS § 108] shall take effect, at the end of the 90-day period beginning on the date of the enactment of this Act.".

CROSS REFERENCES

This section is referred to in 10 USCS § 641.

§ 10502. Chief of the National Guard Bureau: appointment; adviser on National Guard matters; grade

(a) Appointment. There is a Chief of the National Guard Bureau, who is responsible for the organization and operations of the National Guard Bureau. The Chief of the National Guard Bureau is appointed by the President, by and with the advice and consent of the Senate. Such appointment shall be made from officers of the Army National Guard of the United States or the Air National Guard of the United States who—

(1) are recommended for such appointment by their respective Governors or, in the case of the District of Columbia, the commanding general of the District of Columbia National Guard;

(2) have had at least 10 years of federally recognized commissioned service in an active status in the National Guard; and

(3) are in a grade above the grade of brigadier general.

(b) Term of office. An officer appointed as Chief of the National Guard Bureau serves at the pleasure of the President for a term of four years. An officer may not hold that office after becoming 64 years of age. An officer may be reappointed as Chief of the National Guard Bureau. While holding that office, the Chief of the National Guard Bureau may not be removed from the reserve active-status list, or from an active status, under any provision of law that otherwise would require such removal due to completion of a specified number of years of service or a specified number of years of service in grade.

(c) Adviser on National Guard matters. The Chief of the National Guard Bureau is the principal adviser to the Secretary of the Army and the Chief of Staff of the Army, and to the Secretary of the Air Force and the Chief of Staff of the Air Force, on matters relating to the National Guard, the Army National Guard of the United States, and the Air National Guard of the United States.

(d) Grade. The Chief of the National Guard Bureau shall be appointed to serve in the grade of lieutenant general.

(Added Oct. 5, 1994, P. L. 103-337, Div A, Title IX, Subtitle A, § 904(a), 108 Stat. 2824.)

HISTORY; ANCILLARY LAWS AND DIRECTIVES

Effective date of section:

This section became effective at the end of the 90-day period beginning on enactment, as provided by Act Oct. 5, 1994, P. L. 103-337, Div A, Title IX, Subtitle A, § 904(d), 108 Stat. 2827, which appears as 10 USCS § 10501 note.

CROSS REFERENCES

Provisions respecting responsibility for reserve affairs as not affecting functions of Chief of National Guard Bureau, 10 USCS § 10203.

National Guard Bureau—Appropriations, 32 USCS § 107.

Chief's issuance of certificate of eligibility for Federal recognition of officers, 32 USCS § 307.

This section is referred to in 10 USCS § 641; 37 USCS § 204.

President's appointing power, Const. Art. II, § 2, cl. 2.

§ 10503. Functions of National Guard Bureau: charter from Secretaries of the Army and Air Force

The Secretary of the Army and the Secretary of the Air Force shall jointly develop and prescribe a charter for the National Guard Bureau. The charter shall cover the following matters:

(1) Allocating unit structure, strength authorizations, and other resources to the Army National Guard of the United States and the Air National Guard of the United States.

(2) Prescribing the training discipline and training requirements for the Army National Guard and the Air National Guard and the allocation of Federal funds for the training of the Army National Guard and the Air National Guard.

(3) Ensuring that units and members of the Army National Guard and the Air National Guard are trained by the States in accordance with approved programs and policies of, and guidance from, the Chief, the Secretary of the Army, and the Secretary of the Air Force.

(4) Monitoring and assisting the States in the organization, maintenance, and operation of National Guard units so as to provide well-trained and well-equipped units capable of augmenting the active forces in time of war or national emergency.

(5) Planning and administering the budget for the Army National Guard of the United States and the Air National Guard of the United States.

(6) Supervising the acquisition and supply of, and accountability of the States for, Federal property issued to the National Guard through the property and fiscal officers designated, detailed, or appointed under section 708 of title 32.

(7) Granting and withdrawing, in accordance with applicable laws and regulations, Federal recognition of (A) National Guard units, and (B) officers of the National Guard.

(8) Establishing policies and programs for the employment and use of National Guard technicians under section 709 of title 32.

(9) Supervising and administering the Active Guard and Reserve program as it pertains to the National Guard.

(10) Issuing directives, regulations, and publications consistent with approved policies of the Army and Air Force, as appropriate.

(11) Facilitating and supporting the training of members and units of the National Guard to meet State requirements.

(12) Such other functions as the Secretaries may prescribe.

(Added Oct. 5, 1994, P. L. 103-337, Div A, Title IX, Subtitle A, § 904(a), 108 Stat. 2825.)

HISTORY; ANCILLARY LAWS AND DIRECTIVES

Effective date of section:

This section became effective at the end of the 90-day period beginning on enactment, as provided by Act Oct. 5, 1994, P. L. 103-337, Div A, Title IX, Subtitle A, § 904(d), 108 Stat. 2827, which appears as 10 USCS § 10501 note.

Other provisions:

Annual preparation of future years defense plan. Act Sept. 16, 1996, P. L. 104-196, § 123, 110 Stat. 2392, provides: "The National Guard Bureau shall annually prepare a future years defense plan based on the requirement and priorities of the National Guard: *Provided,* That this plan shall be presented to the committees of Congress concurrent with the President's budget submission for each fiscal year.".

§ 10504. Chief of National Guard Bureau: annual report

(a) Annual report. The Chief of the National Guard Bureau shall submit to the Secretary of Defense, through the Secretaries of the Army and the Air Force, an annual report on the state of the National Guard and the ability of the National Guard to meet its missions. The report shall be prepared in conjunction with the Secretary of the Army and the Secretary of the Air Force and may be submitted in classified and unclassified versions.

(b) Submission of report to Congress. The Secretary of Defense shall transmit the annual report of the Chief of the National Guard Bureau to Congress, together with such comments on the report as the Secretary considers appropriate. The report shall be transmitted at the same time each year that the annual report of the Secretary under section 113(c) of this title is submitted to Congress.

(Added Oct. 5, 1994, P. L. 103-337, Div A, Title IX, Subtitle A, § 904(a), 108 Stat. 2825.)

HISTORY; ANCILLARY LAWS AND DIRECTIVES

Effective date of section:

This section became effective at the end of the 90-day period beginning on enactment, as provided by Act Oct. 5, 1994, P. L. 103-337, Div A, Title IX, Subtitle A, § 904(d), 108 Stat. 2827, which appears as 10 USCS § 10501 note.

§ 10505. Vice Chief of the National Guard Bureau

(a) Appointment. (1) There is a Vice Chief of the National Guard Bureau, selected by the Secretary of Defense from officers of the Army National Guard of the United States or the Air National Guard of the United States who—

(A) are recommended for such appointment by their respective Governors or, in the case of the District of Columbia, the commanding general of the District of Columbia National Guard;

(B) have had at least 10 years of federally recognized commissioned service in an active status in the National Guard; and

(C) are in a grade above the grade of colonel.

(2) The Chief and Vice Chief of the National Guard Bureau may not both be members of the Army or of the Air Force.

(3)(A) Except as provided in subparagraph (B), an officer appointed as Vice Chief of the National Guard Bureau serves for a term of four years, but may be removed from office at any time for cause.

(B) The term of the Vice Chief of the National Guard Bureau shall end upon the appointment of a Chief of the National Guard Bureau who is a member of the same armed force as the Vice Chief.

(4) The Secretary of Defense may waive the restrictions in paragraph (2) and the provisions of paragraph (3)(B) for a limited period of time to provide for the orderly transition of officers appointed to serve in the positions of Chief and Vice Chief of the National Guard Bureau.

(b) Duties. The Vice Chief of the National Guard Bureau performs such duties as may be prescribed by the Chief of the National Guard Bureau.

(c) Grade. The Vice Chief of the National Guard Bureau shall be appointed to serve in the grade of major general.

(d) Functions as acting Chief. When there is a vacancy in the office of the Chief of the National Guard Bureau or in the absence or disability of the Chief, the Vice Chief of the National Guard Bureau acts as Chief and performs the duties of the Chief until a successor is appointed or the absence or disability ceases.

(e) Succession after Chief and Vice Chief. When there is a vacancy in the offices of both Chief and Vice Chief of the National Guard Bureau or in the absence or disability of both the Chief and Vice Chief of the National Guard Bureau, or when there is a vacancy in one such office and in the absence or disability of the officer holding the other, the senior officer of the Army National Guard of the United States or the Air National Guard of the United States on duty with the National Guard Bureau shall perform the duties of the Chief until a successor to the Chief or Vice Chief is appointed or the absence or disability of the Chief or Vice Chief ceases, as the case may be.

(Added Oct. 5, 1994, P. L. 103-337, Div A, Title IX, Subtitle A, § 904(a), 108 Stat. 2826.)

HISTORY; ANCILLARY LAWS AND DIRECTIVES

Effective date of section:

This section became effective at the end of the 90-day period beginning on enactment, as provided by Act Oct. 5, 1994, P. L. 103-337, Div A, Title IX, Subtitle A, § 904(d), 108 Stat. 2827, which appears as 10 USCS § 10501 note.

CROSS REFERENCES

This section is referred to in 10 USCS § 641.

§ 10506. Other senior National Guard Bureau officers

(a) Additional general officers. (1) In addition to the Chief and Vice Chief of the National Guard Bureau, there shall be assigned to the National Guard Bureau—

(A) two general officers selected by the Secretary of the Army from officers of the Army National Guard of the United States who have been nominated by their respective Governors or, in the case of the District of Columbia, the commanding general of the District of Columbia National Guard, the senior of whom while so serving shall hold the grade of major general and serve as Director, Army National Guard, with the other serving as Deputy Director, Army National Guard; and

(B) two general officers selected by the Secretary of the Air Force from officers of the Air National Guard of the United States who have been nominated by their respective Governors or, in the case of the District of Columbia, the commanding general of the District of Columbia National Guard, the senior of whom while so serving shall hold the grade of major general and serve as Director, Air National Guard, with the other serving as Deputy Director, Air National Guard.

(2) The officers so selected shall assist the Chief of the National Guard Bureau in carrying out the functions of the National Guard Bureau as they relate to their respective branches.

(b) Other officers. There are in the National Guard Bureau a legal counsel, a comptroller, and an inspector general, each of whom shall be appointed by the Chief of the National Guard Bureau. They shall perform such duties as the Chief may prescribe.

(Added Oct. 5, 1994, P. L. 103-337, Div A, Title IX, Subtitle A, § 904(a), 108 Stat. 2827.)

HISTORY; ANCILLARY LAWS AND DIRECTIVES

Effective date of section:

This section became effective at the end of the 90-day period beginning on enactment, as provided by Act Oct. 5, 1994, P. L. 103-337, Div A, Title IX, Subtitle A, § 904(d), 108 Stat. 2827, which appears as 10 USCS § 10501 note.

CROSS REFERENCES

This section is referred to in 10 USCS § 641.

§ 10507. National Guard Bureau: assignment of officers of regular or reserve components

Except as provided in section 12402(b) of this title, the President may assign to duty in the National Guard Bureau as many regular or reserve officers of the Army or Air Force as he considers necessary.

(Added Oct. 5, 1994, P. L. 103-337, Div A, Title XVI, Subtitle C, § 1661(c)(1)(A), 108 Stat. 2982; Feb. 10, 1996, P. L. 104-106, Div A, Title XV, § 1501(b)(6), 110 Stat. 496.)

HISTORY; ANCILLARY LAWS AND DIRECTIVES

Effective date of section:

This section took effect on December 1, 1994, as provided by Act Oct. 5, 1994, P. L. 103-337, Div A, Title XVI, Subtitle F, § 1691, 108 Stat. 3026, which appears as 10 USCS § 10001 note.

Amendments:

1996. Act Feb. 10, 1996, P. L. 104-106, Div A, Title XV, § 1501, 110 Stat. 496 (effective as if included in Act Oct. 5, 1994, P. L. 103-337, as enacted on Oct. 5, 1994, as provided by § 1501(f)(3) of Act Feb. 10, 1996, which appears as 10 USCS § 113 note), substituted ''section 12402(b)'' for ''section 124402(b)'' and substituted ''Air Force'' for ''Air Forces''.

CROSS REFERENCES

This section is referred to in 10 USCS § 641.

[§ 10508. Repealed]

HISTORY; ANCILLARY LAWS AND DIRECTIVES

This section (Act Oct. 5, 1994, P. L. 103-337, Div A, Title IX, Subtitle A, § 904(a), 108 Stat. 2827) was repealed by Act Feb. 10, 1996, P. L. 104-106, Div A, Title XV, § 1501(b)(7)(A), 110 Stat. 496 (effective as if included in Act Oct. 5, 1994, P. L. 103-337, as enacted on Oct. 5, 1994, as provided by § 1501(f)(3) of Act Feb. 10, 1996, which appears as 10 USCS § 113 note). It provided a definition for the term ''State''.

CHAPTER 1013. BUDGET INFORMATION AND ANNUAL REPORTS TO CONGRESS

HISTORY; ANCILLARY LAWS AND DIRECTIVES

Amendments:

1994. Act Oct. 5, 1994, P. L. 103-337, Div A, Title XVI, Subtitle C, § 1661(d)(1), 108 Stat. 2982 (effective 12/1/94 as provided by § 1691 of such Act, which appears as 10 USCS § 10001 note), added the chapter heading and analysis.

1996. Act Sept. 23, 1996, P. L. 104-201, Div A, Title XII, Subtitle C, § 1257(a)(2), 110 Stat. 2699, amended the analysis of this chapter by adding item 10543.

§ 10541. National Guard and reserve component equipment: annual report to Congress

(a) The Secretary of Defense shall submit to the Congress each year, not later than February 15, a written report concerning the equipment of the National Guard and the reserve components of the armed forces for each of the three succeeding fiscal years.

(b) Each report under this section shall include the following:

(1) Recommendations as to the type and quantity of each major item of equipment which should be in the inventory of the Selected Reserve of the Ready Reserve of each reserve component of the armed forces.

(2) A statement of the quantity and average age of each type of major item of equipment which is expected to be physically available in the inventory of the Selected Reserve of the Ready Reserve of each reserve component as of the beginning of each fiscal year covered by the report.

(3) A statement of the quantity and cost of each type of major item of equipment which is expected to be procured for the Selective Reserve of the Ready Reserve of each reserve component from commercial sources or to be transferred to each such Selected Reserve from the active-duty components of the armed forces.

(4) A statement of the quantity of each type of major item of equipment which is expected to be retired, decommissioned, transferred, or otherwise removed from the physical inventory of the Selected Reserve of the Ready Reserve of each reserve component and the plans for replacement of that equipment.

(5) A listing of each major item of equipment required by the Selected Reserve of the Ready Reserve of each reserve component indicating—

(A) the full war-time requirement of that component for that item, shown in accordance with deployment schedules and requirements over successive 30-day periods following mobilization;

(B) the number of each such item in the inventory of the component;

(C) a separate listing of each such item in the inventory that is a deployable item and is not the most desired item;

(D) the number of each such item projected to be in the inventory at the end of the third succeeding fiscal year; and

(E) the number of nondeployable items in the inventory as a substitute for a required major item of equipment.

(6) A narrative explanation of the plan of the Secretary concerned to provide equipment needed to fill the war-time requirement for each major item of equipment to all units of the Selected Reserve, including an explanation of the plan to equip units of the Selected Reserve that are short of major items of equipment at the outset of war.

(7) For each item of major equipment reported under paragraph (3) in a report for one of the three previous years under this section as an item expected to be procured for the Selected Reserve or to be transferred to the Selected Reserve, the quantity of such equipment actually procured for or transferred to the Selected Reserve.

(8) A statement of the current status of the compatibility of equipment between the Army reserve components and active forces of the Army, the effect of that level of incompatibility on combat effectiveness, and a plan to achieve full equipment compatibility.

(c) Each report under this section shall be expressed in the same format and with the same level of detail as the information presented in the annual Five Year Defense Program Procurement Annex prepared by the Department of Defense.

(Added Nov. 5, 1990, P. L. 101-510, Div A, Title XIV, Part H, § 1483(a), 104 Stat. 1714; Oct. 23, 1992, P. L. 102-484, Div A, Title XI, Subtitle C, § 1134, 106 Stat. 2541; Oct. 5, 1994, P. L. 103-337, Div A, Title XVI, Subtitle C, § 1661(d)(2), 108 Stat. 2982.)

HISTORY; ANCILLARY LAWS AND DIRECTIVES

Amendments:

1992. Act Oct. 23, 1992, in subsec. (b), added para. (8).

1994. Oct. 5, 1994 (effective 12/1/94 as provided by § 1691 of such Act, which appears as 10 USCS § 10001 note) transferred this section, enacted as 10 USCS § 115b, to Chapter 1013, inserted it after the chapter analysis, redesignated it as 10 USCS § 10541, and substituted the heading for one which read: ''Annual report on National Guard and reserve component equipment''.

§ 10542. Army National Guard combat readiness: annual report

(a) In general. The Secretary of the Army shall include in the annual report of the Secretary to Congress known as the Army Posture Statement a detailed presentation concerning the Army National Guard, including particularly information relating to the implementation of the Army National Guard Combat Readiness Reform Act of 1992 (title XI of Public Law 102-484; 106 Stat. 2536) (hereinafter in this section referred to as ''ANGCRRA'').

(b) Matters to be included in report. Each presentation under subsection (a) shall include, with respect to the period covered by the report, the following information concerning the Army National Guard:

(1) The number and percentage of officers with at least two years of active-duty before becoming a member of the Army National Guard.

(2) The number and percentage of enlisted personnel with at least two years of active-duty before becoming a member of the Army National Guard.

(3) The number of officers who are graduates of one of the service academies and were released from active duty before the completion of their active-duty service obligation and, of those officers—

(A) the number who are serving the remaining period of their active-duty service obligation as a member of the Selected Reserve pursuant to section 1112(a)(1) of ANGCRRA [10 USCS § 3077 note]; and

(B) the number for whom waivers were granted by the Secretary under section 1112(a)(2) of ANGCRRA [10 USCS § 3077 note], together with the reason for each waiver.

(4) The number of officers who were commissioned as distinguished Reserve Officers' Training Corps graduates and were released from active duty before the completion of their active-duty service obligation and, of those officers—

(A) the number who are serving the remaining period of their active-duty service obligation as a member of the Selected Reserve pursuant to section 1112(a)(1) of ANGCRRA [10 USCS § 3077 note]; and

(B) the number for whom waivers were granted by the Secretary under section 1112(a)(2) of ANGCRRA [10 USCS § 3077 note], together with the reason for each waiver.

(5) The number of officers who are graduates of the Reserve Officers' Training Corps program and who are performing their minimum period of obligated service in accordance with section 1112(b) of ANGCRRA [10 USCS § 3077 note] by a combination of (A) two years of active duty, and (B) such additional period of service as is necessary to complete the remainder of such obligation served in the National Guard and, of those officers, the number for whom permission to perform their minimum period of obligated service in accordance with that section was granted during the preceding fiscal year.

(6) The number of officers for whom recommendations were made during the preceding fiscal year for a unit vacancy promotion to a grade above first lieutenant and, of those recommendations, the number and percentage that were concurred in by an active-duty officer under section 1113(a) of ANGCRRA [10 USCS § 3077 note], shown separately for each of the three categories of officers set forth in section 1113(b) of ANGCRRA [10 USCS § 3077 note].

(7) The number of waivers during the preceding fiscal year under section 1114(a) of ANGCRRA [10 USCS § 3077 note] of any standard prescribed by the Secretary establishing a military education requirement for noncommissioned officers and the reason for each such waiver.

(8) The number and distribution by grade, shown for each State, of personnel in the initial entry training and nondeployability personnel accounting category established under section 1115 of ANGCRRA [10 USCS § 3077 note] for members of the Army National Guard who have not completed the minimum training required for deployment or who are otherwise not available for deployment.

(9) The number of members of the Army National Guard, shown for each State, that were discharged during the previous fiscal year pursuant to section 1115(c)(1) of ANGCRRA [10 USCS § 3077 note] for not completing the minimum training required for deployment within 24 months after entering the National Guard.

(10) The number of waivers, shown for each State, that were granted by the Secretary during the previous fiscal year under section 1115(c)(2) of ANGCRRA [10 USCS § 3077 note] of the requirement in section 1115(c)(1) of ANGCRRA [10 USCS § 3077 note] described in paragraph (9), together with the reason for each waiver.

(11) The number of members, shown for each State, who were screened during the preceding fiscal year to determine whether they meet minimum physical profile standards required for deployment and, of those members—

(A) the number and percentage who did not meet minimum physical profile standards required for deployment; and

(B) the number and percentage who were transferred pursuant to section 1116 of ANGCRRA [10 USCS § 3077 note] to the personnel accounting category described in paragraph (8).

(12) The number of members, and the percentage of the total membership, of the Army National Guard, shown for each State, who underwent a medical screening during the previous fiscal year as provided in section 1117 of ANGCRRA [10 USCS § 3077 note].

(13) The number of members, and the percentage of the total membership, of the Army National Guard, shown for each State, who underwent a dental screening during the previous fiscal year as provided in section 1117 of ANGCRRA [10 USCS § 3077 note].

(14) The number of members, and the percentage of the total membership, of the Army National Guard, shown for each State, over the age of 40 who underwent a full physical examination during the previous fiscal year for purposes of section 1117 of ANGCRRA [10 USCS § 3077 note].

(15) The number of units of the Army National Guard that are scheduled for early deployment in the event of a mobilization and, of those units, the number that are dentally ready for deployment in accordance with section 1118 of ANGCRRA [10 USCS § 3077 note].

(16) The estimated post-mobilization training time for each Army National Guard combat unit, and a description, displayed in broad categories and by

State, of what training would need to be accomplished for Army National Guard combat units in a post-mobilization period for purposes of section 1119 of ANGCRRA [10 USCS § 3077 note].

(17) A description of the measures taken during the preceding fiscal year to comply with the requirement in section 1120 of ANGCRRA [10 USCS § 3077 note] to expand the use of simulations, simulators, and advanced training devices and technologies for members and units of the Army National Guard.

(18) Summary tables of unit readiness, shown for each State, and drawn from the unit readiness rating system as required by section 1121 of ANGCRRA [10 USCS § 3077 note], including the personnel readiness rating information and the equipment readiness assessment information required by that section, together with—

(A) explanations of the information shown in the table; and

(B) based on the information shown in the tables, the Secretary's overall assessment of the deployability of units of the Army National Guard, including a discussion of personnel deficiencies and equipment shortfalls in accordance with such section 1121.

(19) Summary tables, shown for each State, of the results of inspections of units of the Army National Guard by inspectors general or other commissioned officers of the Regular Army under the provisions of section 105 of title 32, together with explanations of the information shown in the tables, and including display of—

(A) the number of such inspections;

(B) identification of the entity conducting each inspection;

(C) the number of units inspected; and

(D) the overall results of such inspections, including the inspector's determination for each inspected unit of whether the unit met deployability standards and, for those units not meeting deployability standards, the reasons for such failure and the status of corrective actions.

(20) A listing, for each Army National Guard combat unit, of the active-duty combat unit associated with that Army National Guard unit in accordance with section 1131(a) of ANGCRRA [10 USCS § 3077 note], shown by State and to be accompanied, for each such National Guard unit, by—

(A) the assessment of the commander of that associated active-duty unit of the manpower, equipment, and training resource requirements of that National Guard unit in accordance with section 1131(b)(3) of ANGCRRA [10 USCS § 3077 note]; and

(B) the results of the validation by the commander of that associated active- duty unit of the compatibility of that National Guard unit with active duty forces in accordance with section 1131(b)(4) of ANGCRRA [10 USCS § 3077 note].

(21) A specification of the active-duty personnel assigned to units of the Selected Reserve pursuant to section 414(c) of the National Defense Authorization Act for Fiscal Years 1992 and 1993 (10 U.S.C. 12001 note), shown (A) by State, (B) by rank of officers, warrant officers, and enlisted members assigned, and (C) by unit or other organizational entity of assignment.

(Added Nov. 30, 1993, P. L. 103-160, Div A, Title V, Subtitle B, § 521(a), 107 Stat. 1652; Oct. 5, 1994, P. L. 103-337, Div A, Title XVI, Subtitle C, § 1661(d)(3), 108 Stat. 2982; Feb. 10, 1996, P. L. 104-106, Div A, Title XV, § 1501(b)(8), 110 Stat. 496; Sept. 23, 1996, P. L. 104-201, Div A, Title X, Subtitle F, § 1074(a)(21), 110 Stat. 2660.)

HISTORY; ANCILLARY LAWS AND DIRECTIVES

References in text:

The ''Army National Guard Combat Readiness Reform Act of 1992'' and ''ANGCRRA'', referred to in this section, are references to Title XI of Act Oct. 23, 1992, P. L. 102-484, 106 Stat. 2536, which appears generally as 10 USCS § 3077 note. For full classification of such Act, consult USCS Tables volumes.

Amendments:

1994. Act Oct. 5, 1994 (effective 12/1/94 as provided by § 1691 of such Act, which appears as 10 USCS § 10001 note) transferred this section, enacted as 10 USCS § 3082, to Chapter 1013, inserted it after 10 USCS § 10541, and redesignated it as 10 USCS § 10542.

Such Act further (effective as above), in the heading, deleted ''reform'' preceding the colon and deleted subsec. (c), which read: ''(c) Implementation. The requirement to include in a presentation required by subsection (a) information under any paragraph of subsection (b) shall take effect with respect to the year following the year in which the provision of ANGCRRA to which that paragraph pertains has taken effect. Before then, in the case of any such paragraph, the Secretary shall include any information that may be available concerning the topic covered by that paragraph.''.

1996. Act Feb. 10, 1996 (effective as if included in Act Oct. 5, 1994, P. L. 103-337, as enacted on Oct. 5, 1994, as provided by § 1501(f)(3) of Act Feb. 10, 1996, which appears as 10 USCS § 113 note) deleted subsec. (d), which read: ''(d) Definition. In this section, the term 'State' includes the District of Columbia, Puerto Rico, Guam, and the Virgin Islands.''.

Act Sept. 23, 1996, in subsec. (b)(21), substituted ''12001'' for ''261''.

§ 10543. National Guard and reserve component equipment procurement and military construction funding: inclusion in future-years defense program

(a) In general. The Secretary of Defense shall specify in each future-years defense program submitted to Congress under section 221 of this title the estimated expenditures and the proposed appropriations, for each fiscal year of the period covered by that program, for the procurement of equipment and for military construction for each of the reserve components of the armed forces.

(b) Associated annexes. The associated annexes of the future-years defense program shall specify, at the same level of detail as is set forth in the annexes for the active components, the amount requested for—

(1) procurement of each item of equipment to be procured for each reserve component; and

(2) each military construction project to be carried out for each reserve component, together with the location of the project.

(c) Report. (1) If the aggregate of the amounts specified in paragraphs (1) and (2) of subsection (b) for a fiscal year is less than the amount equal to 90 percent of the average authorized amount applicable for that fiscal year under paragraph (2), the Secretary of Defense shall submit to Congress a report specifying for each reserve component the additional items of equipment that would be procured, and the additional military construction projects that would be carried out, if that aggregate amount were an amount equal to such average authorized amount. The report shall be at the same level of detail as is required by subsection (b).

(2) In this subsection, the term ''average authorized amount'', with respect to a fiscal year, means the average of—

(A) the aggregate of the amounts authorized to be appropriated for the preceding fiscal year for the procurement of items of equipment, and for military construction, for the reserve components; and

(B) the aggregate of the amounts authorized to be appropriated for the fiscal year preceding the fiscal year referred to in subparagraph (A) for the procurement of items of equipment, and for military construction, for the reserve components.

(Added Sept. 23, 1996, P. L. 104-201, Div A, Title XII, Subtitle C, § 1257(a)(1), 110 Stat. 2699; Nov. 18, 1997, P. L. 105-85, Div A, Title X, Subtitle A, § 1009(a), 111 Stat. 1872.)

HISTORY; ANCILLARY LAWS AND DIRECTIVES

Amendments:

1997. Act Nov. 18, 1997, designated the existing provisions as subsec. (a) and, in such subsection, added the heading; and added subsecs. (b) and (c).

Other provisions:

Applicability of section. Act Sept. 23, 1996, P. L. 104-201, Div A, Title XII, Subtitle C, § 1257(b), 110 Stat. 2699, provides: ''Section 10543 of title 10, United States Code, as added by subsection (a), shall apply with respect to each future-years defense program submitted to Congress after the date of the enactment of this Act.''.

Level of detail for procurement and military construction. Act Nov. 18, 1997, P. L. 105-85, Div A, Title X, Subtitle A, § 1009(b), 111 Stat. 1872, provides: ''The level of detail provided for procurement and military construction in the future-years defense programs for fiscal years after fiscal year 1998 may not be less than the level of detail provided for procurement and military construction in the future-years defense program for fiscal year 1998.''.

PART II. PERSONNEL GENERALLY

HISTORY; ANCILLARY LAWS AND DIRECTIVES

Amendments:

1994. Act Oct. 5, 1994, P. L. 103-337, Div A, Title XVI, Subtitle C, § 1662(a)(1), 108 Stat. 2983, added the part heading and analysis.

1996. Act Feb. 10, 1996, P. L. 104-106, Div A, Title V, Subtitle B, § 512(a)(2), 110 Stat. 305, amended the analysis of this part by adding item 1214.

1997. Act Nov. 18, 1997, P. L. 105-85, Div A, Title V, Subtitle B, § 515(b), 111 Stat. 1733, amended the analysis of this part by substituting item 1215 for one which read: "1215. Miscellaneous Prohibitions and Penalties . . . [No present sections]".

CHAPTER 1201. AUTHORIZED STRENGTHS AND DISTRIBUTION IN GRADE

time National Guard duty for administration of the reserves or the National Guard

12012. Authorized strengths: senior enlisted members on active duty or on full-time National Guard duty for administration of the reserves or the National Guard

HISTORY; ANCILLARY LAWS AND DIRECTIVES

Explanatory notes:

Item 12003 does not conform to section catchline.

Amendments:

1994. Act Oct. 5, 1994, P. L. 103-337, Div A, Title XVI, Subtitle C, § 1662(a)(1), 108 Stat. 2983 (effective 12/1/94 as provided by § 1691 of such Act, which appears as 10 USCS § 10001 note), added the chapter heading and analysis.

§ 12001. Authorized strengths: reserve components

(a) Whenever the authorized strength of a reserve component (other than the Coast Guard Reserve) is not prescribed by law, it shall be prescribed by the President.

(b) Subject to the authorized strength of the reserve component concerned, the authorized strength of each reserve component (other than the Coast Guard Reserve) in members in each grade is that which the Secretary concerned determines to be necessary to provide for mobilization requirements. The Secretary shall review these determinations at least once each year and revise them if he considers it necessary. However, a member of the reserve component concerned may not, as a result of such a determination, be reduced in the member's reserve grade without the member's consent.

(Added Oct. 5, 1994, P. L. 103-337, Div A, Title XVI, Subtitle C, § 1662(a)(1), 108 Stat. 2983.)

HISTORY; ANCILLARY LAWS AND DIRECTIVES

Effective date of section:

This section took effect on Dec. 1, 1994, pursuant to Act Oct. 5, 1994, P. L. 103-337, Div A, Title XVI, Subtitle F, § 1691, 108 Stat. 3026, which appears as 10 USCS 10001 note.

Other provisions:

Reserve forces readiness; report, study. Act Oct. 19, 1984, P. L. 98-525, Title V, Part E, § 552(a)–(e), (g), 98 Stat. 2530; Oct. 5, 1994, P. L. 103-337, Div A, Title XVI, Subtitle C, § 1661(a)(2)(A), 108 Stat. 2980 (effective Dec. 1, 1994, as provided by § 1691 of such Act, which appears as 10 USCS § 10001 note), provides:

"(a)(1) The Secretary of Defense shall conduct a review of the various systems used to measure the readiness of reserve units of the Armed Forces and shall implement a measurement system for the active and reserve components of the Armed Forces to provide an objective and uniform evaluation of the readiness of all units of the Armed Forces. The measurement system should be designed to produce information adequate to provide comparisons concerning the readiness of all units. The system for evaluation of the readiness of a unit of an active component should incorporate the performance of any unit of a reserve component affiliated with the active component unit, including the effect of the reserve component unit on the mobilization capability of the active component unit.

''(2) Not later than March 31, 1985, the Secretary shall submit a report to the Committees on Armed Services of the Senate and House of Representatives describing the results of the review under paragraph (1) and the measurement system implemented in accordance with that paragraph.

''(b)(1) The Secretary of Defense, acting through the Assistant Secretary of Defense for Reserve Affairs, shall conduct a study to evaluate the feasibility of allocating equipment to units of reserve components based on a measure of effectiveness of such units. The study should consider the effects of allocating equipment by comparing units with similar deployment times and similar capabilities in terms of training and equipment rather than by comparing all reserve component units with each other. The study should be integrated with an evaluation of the system for measuring unit effectiveness to be implemented in accordance with subsection (a).

''(2) As part of the report under subsection (a)(2), the Secretary of Defense shall submit to the Committees on Armed Services of the Senate and House of Representatives a report on the study carried out under paragraph (1).

''(c) It is the sense of Congress that the number of members of the Army Reserve and of the Army National Guard assigned to full-time manning duty should be increased to 14 percent of the total membership of the Army Reserve and of the Army National Guard, respectively, by fiscal year 1989.

''(d)(1)(A) The Secretary of Defense, acting through the Assistant Secretary of Defense for Reserve Affairs, shall conduct a study of the benefits of a longer training program for certain units of the reserve components and shall conduct a test of such a program. The test program should begin at the earliest realistic date.

''(B) In developing training programs for the reserve components, the Secretary shall give increased attention to innovative training technologies, techniques, and schedules that recognize the limitations on time and the geographic dispersion of the reserve components.

''(2) Not later than March 31, 1985, the Secretary shall submit a report to the Committees on Armed Services of the Senate and House of Representatives describing the study under paragraph (1).

''(e) [Repealed]

''(f) [Omitted]

''(g) This section does not apply to the Coast Guard.''.

Authority to waive end strength laws; fiscal year 1991 end strength. Act April 6, 1991, P. L. 102-25, Title II, § 201(a), 105 Stat. 79, provides: ''The Secretary of a military department may waive any end strength prescribed in section 401(a), 411, or 412(a) of the National Defense Authorization Act for Fiscal Year 1991 (Public Law 101-510; 104 Stat. 1485) [notes to this section and 10 USCS § 115] that applies to any of the armed forces under the jurisdiction of that Secretary.''.

Certification. Act April 6, 1991, P. L. 102-25, Title II, § 202, 105 Stat. 79, provides: "The Secretary of a military department may exercise the authority provided in subsection (a) or (b) of section 201 [note to this section or 10 USCS § 527 note] only after the Secretary submits to the congressional defense committees a certification in writing that the exercise of that authority is necessary because of personnel actions associated with Operation Desert Storm.".

Relationship to other waiver authorities. Act April 6, 1991, P. L. 102-25, Title II, § 205(a), 105 Stat. 80, provides: "The authority provided in section 201(a) [note to this section] is in addition to the waiver authority provided in sections 401(c) and 411(b) of the National Defense Authorization Act for Fiscal Year 1991 (Public Law 101-510) [notes to this section and 10 USCS § 115] and the waiver authority provided in section 115(c)(1) of title 10, United States Code.".

Pilot program for active component support of the reserves. Act Dec. 5, 1991, P. L. 102-190, Div A, Title IV, Part B, § 414(a)–(d), 105 Stat. 1352; Oct. 23, 1992, P. L. 102-484, Div A, Title V, Subtitle B, § 511(b), Title XI, Subtitle C, § 1132, 106 Stat. 2405, 2541; Nov. 30, 1993, P. L. 103-160, Div A, Title V, Subtitle B, § 517(a), 107 Stat. 1650; Oct. 5, 1994, P. L. 103-337, Div A, Title IV, Subtitle B, § 413, 108 Stat. 2747; Feb. 10, 1996, P. L. 104-106, Div A, Title IV, Subtitle B, § 413, 110 Stat. 288; Sept. 23, 1996, P. L. 104-201, Div A, Title V, Subtitle E, § 545(b), 110 Stat. 2524, provides:

"(a) Pilot program required. The Secretary of the Army shall carry out a pilot program to provide active component advisers to combat units, combat support units, and combat service support units in the Selected Reserve of the Ready Reserve that have a high priority for deployment on a time-phased troop deployment list or have another contingent high priority for deployment. The advisers shall be assigned to full-time duty in connection with organizing, administering, recruiting, instructing, or training such units.

"(b) Objectives of program. The objectives of the program are as follows:

"(1) To improve the readiness of units in the reserve components of the Army.

"(2) To increase substantially the number of active component personnel directly advising reserve component unit personnel.

"(3) To provide a basis for determining the most effective mix of reserve component personnel and active component personnel in organizing, administering, recruiting, instructing, or training reserve component units.

"(4) To provide a basis for determining the most effective mix of active component officer and enlisted personnel in advising reserve component units regarding organizing, administering, recruiting, instructing, or training reserve component units.

"(c) Personnel to be assigned. (1) The Secretary shall assign not less than 2,000 active component personnel to serve as advisers under the program. After September 30, 1996, the number under the preceding sentence shall be increased to not less than 5,000.

"(2) The Secretary of Defense may count toward the number of active component personnel required under paragraph (1) to be assigned to serve as advisers under the program under this section any active component personnel who are assigned to an active component unit (A) that was established principally for the purpose of providing dedicated training support to reserve component units, and (B) the primary mission of which is to provide such dedicated training support.

''(d) Action on the basis of program results. Based on the experience under the pilot program, the Secretary of the Army shall by April 1, 1993, submit to the Committees on Armed Services of the Senate and House of Representatives a report containing the Secretary's evaluation of the program to that date. As part of the budget submission for fiscal year 1995, the Secretary shall submit any recommendations for expansion or modification of the program, together with a proposal for any statutory changes that the Secretary considers necessary to implement the program on a permanent basis. In no case may the number of active duty personnel assigned to the program decrease below the number specified for the pilot program.''.

Reserve component force structure. Act Oct. 23, 1992, P. L. 102-484, Div A, Title IV, Subtitle B, § 413, 106 Stat. 2399, provides:

''(a) Requirement to prescribe reserve component force structure. The Secretary of each military department shall prescribe a force structure allowance for each reserve component under the jurisdiction of the Secretary. Each such force structure allowance for a reserve component—

''(1) shall be consistent with, but in no case include a number of personnel spaces that is less than, the authorized end strength for that component; and

''(2) shall be prescribed in accordance with historic service policies.

''(b) Definition. For purposes of this section, the term 'force structure allowance' means the number and types of units and organizations, and the number of authorized personnel spaces allocated to those units and organizations, in a military force.''.

Repeal of provision limiting reduction in number of reserve component medical personnel. Act Oct. 23, 1992, P. L. 102-484, Div A, Title V, Subtitle B, § 518, 106 Stat. 2407; Oct. 5, 1994, P. L. 103-337, Div A, Title VII, Subtitle B, § 716, 108 Stat. 2803, which formerly appeared as a note to this section, was repealed by Act Feb. 10, 1996, P. L. 104-106, Div A, Title V, Subtitle F, § 564(d)(3), 110 Stat. 327. Such note provided for limitation on reduction in number of reserve component medical personnel.

Annual report on implementation of the Pilot Program for Active Component Support of the Reserves. Act Nov. 30, 1993, P. L. 103-160, Div A, Title V, Subtitle B, § 517(b), 107 Stat. 1651, provides:

''(1) The Secretary of the Army shall include in the annual report of the Secretary to Congress known as the Army Posture Statement a presentation relating to the implementation of the Pilot Program for Active Component Support of the Reserves under section 414 of the National Defense Authorization Act for Fiscal Years 1992 and 1993 (Public Law 102-190; 10 U.S.C. 261 note), as amended by subsection (a).

''(2) Each such presentation shall include, with respect to the period covered by the report, the following information:

''(A) The promotion rate for officers considered for promotion from within the promotion zone who are serving as active component advisers to units of the Selected Reserve of the Ready Reserve (in accordance with that program) compared with the promotion rate for other officers considered for promotion from within the promotion zone in the same pay grade and the same competitive category, shown for all officers of the Army.

''(B) The promotion rate for officers considered for promotion from below the promotion zone who are serving as active component advisers to units of the Selected Reserve of the Ready Reserve (in accordance with that program) compared in the same manner as specified in subparagraph (A).''.

End strengths for Selected Reserve as of 9/30/97. Act Sept. 23, 1996, P. L. 104-201, Div A, Title IV, Subtitle B, §§ 411, 110 Stat. 2506, provides:

''(a) In general. The Armed Forces are authorized strengths for Selected Reserve personnel of the reserve components as of September 30, 1997, as follows:

''(1) The Army National Guard of the United States, 366,758.

''(2) The Army Reserve, 215,179.

''(3) The Naval Reserve, 96,304.

''(4) The Marine Corps Reserve, 42,000.

''(5) The Air National Guard of the United States, 109,178.

''(6) The Air Force Reserve, 73,311.

''(7) The Coast Guard Reserve, 8,000.

''(b) Waiver authority. The Secretary of Defense may vary the end strength authorized by subsection (a) by not more than 2 percent.

''(c) Adjustments. The end strengths prescribed by subsection (a) for the Selected Reserve of any reserve component for a fiscal year shall be proportionately reduced by—

''(1) the total authorized strength of units organized to serve as units of the Selected Reserve of such component which are on active duty (other than for training) at the end of the fiscal year, and

''(2) the total number of individual members not in units organized to serve as units of the Selected Reserve of such component who are on active duty (other than for training or for unsatisfactory participation in training) without their consent at the end of the fiscal year.

Whenever such units or such individual members are released from active duty during any fiscal year, the end strength prescribed for such fiscal year for the Selected Reserve of such reserve component shall be proportionately increased by the total authorized strengths of such units and by the total number of such individual members.''.

End strengths for Reserve on active duty in support of the Reserves as of 9/30/97. Act Sept. 23, 1996, P. L. 104-201, Div A, Title IV, Subtitle B, §§ 412, 110 Stat. 2506, provides:

''Within the end strengths prescribed in section 411(a) [note to this section], the reserve components of the Armed Forces are authorized, as of September 30, 1997, the following number of Reserves to be serving on full-time active duty or full-time duty, in the case of members of the National Guard, for the purpose of organizing, administering, recruiting, instructing, or training the reserve components:

''(1) The Army National Guard of the United States, 22,798.

''(2) The Army Reserve, 11,729.

''(3) The Naval Reserve, 16,603.

"(4) The Marine Corps Reserve, 2,559.

"(5) The Air National Guard of the United States, 10,403.

"(6) The Air Force Reserve, 655.".

Provisions prescribing specific strengths for Selected Reserve personnel of the reserve components of the armed forces for specific fiscal years, providing waiver authority, and providing criteria for proportionate reductions or increases in the prescribed strengths were contained in the following authorization acts: Sept. 20, 1968, P. L. 90-500, Title III, §§ 301, 302, 82 Stat. 850; Nov. 19, 1969, P. L. 91-121, Title III, §§ 301, 302, 83 Stat. 206; Oct. 7, 1970, P. L. 91-441, Title III, §§ 301, 302, 84 Stat. 908; Nov. 17, 1971, P. L. 92-156, Title III, §§ 301, 302, 85 Stat. 425; Sept. 26, 1972, P. L. 92-436, Title IV, §§ 401, 402, 86 Stat. 736; Nov. 16, 1973, P. L. 93-155, Title IV, §§ 401, 402, 87 Stat. 608; Aug. 5, 1974, P. L. 93-365, Title IV, §§ 401, 402, 88 Stat. 402, 403; Oct 7, 1975, P. L. 94-106, Title IV, § 401, 89 Stat. 352; July 14, 1976, P. L. 94-361, Title IV, § 401, 90 Stat. 926; July 30, 1977, P. L. 95-79, Title IV, § 401, 91 Stat. 327; Oct. 20, 1978, P. L. 95-485, Title IV, § 401, 92 Stat. 1613; Nov. 9, 1979, P. L. 96-107, Title IV, § 401, 93 Stat. 807; Sept. 8, 1980, P. L. 96-342, Title IV, § 401, 94 Stat; 1084; Dec. 1, 1981, P. L. 97-86, Title V, § 501, 95 Stat. 1107; Sept. 8, 1982, P. L. 97-252, Title V, § 501, 96 Stat. 726; Act Sept. 24, 1983, P. L. 98-94, Title V, § 501, 97 Stat. 630; Oct. 19, 1984, P. L. 98-525, Title IV, Part B, § 411, 98 Stat. 2516; Nov. 8, 1985, P. L. 99-145, Title IV, Part B, § 411, 99 Stat. 618; Nov. 14, 1986, P. L. 99-661, Div A, Title IV, Part B, § 411(a)–(c), 100 Stat. 3860; Dec. 4, 1987, P. L. 100-180, Div A, Title IV, Part B, § 411, 101 Stat. 1082; Sept. 29, 1988, P. L. 100-456, Div A, Title IV, Part B, § 411(b), 102 Stat. 1964; Nov. 29, 1989, P. L. 101-189, Div A, Title IV, Part B, § 411, 103 Stat. 1432; Nov. 5, 1990, P. L. 101-510, Div A, Title IV, Part B, §§ 411(a)–(c), 412, 104 Stat. 1546, 1547; Dec. 5, 1991, P. L. 102-190, Div A, Title IV, Part B, §§ 411, 412, 414(e), 105 Stat. 1351, 1353; Nov. 30, 1993, P. L. 103-160, Div A, Title V, Subtitle B, § 513, 107 Stat. 1649; Oct. 23, 1992, P. L. 102-484, Div A, Title IV, Subtitle B, §§ 411, 412, 106 Stat. 2399; Oct. 5, 1994, P. L. 103-337, Div A, Title IV, Subtitle B, §§ 411, 412, 108 Stat. 2746; Feb. 10, 1996, P. L. 104-106, Div A, Title IV, Subtitle B, §§ 411, 412, 110 Stat. 287.

End strengths for Selected Reserve as of 9/30/98. Act Nov. 18, 1997, P. L. 105-85, Div A, Title IV, Subtitle B, § 411, 111 Stat. 1719, provides:

"(a) In general. The Armed Forces are authorized strengths for Selected Reserve personnel of the reserve components as of September 30, 1998, as follows:

"(1) The Army National Guard of the United States, 361,516.

"(2) The Army Reserve, 208,000.

"(3) The Naval Reserve, 94,294.

"(4) The Marine Corps Reserve, 42,000.

"(5) The Air National Guard of the United States, 108,002.

"(6) The Air Force Reserve, 73,447.

"(7) The Coast Guard Reserve, 8,000.

"(b) Adjustments. The end strengths prescribed by subsection (a) for the Selected Reserve of any reserve component shall be proportionately reduced by—

"(1) the total authorized strength of units organized to serve as units of the Selected Reserve of such component which are on active duty (other than for training) at the end of the fiscal year, and

''(2) the total number of individual members not in units organized to serve as units of the Selected Reserve of such component who are on active duty (other than for training or for unsatisfactory participation in training) without their consent at the end of the fiscal year.

Whenever such units or such individual members are released from active duty during any fiscal year, the end strength prescribed for such fiscal year for the Selected Reserve of such reserve component shall be proportionately increased by the total authorized strengths of such units and by the total number of such individual members.''.

End strengths for reserves on active duty in support of the Reserves as of 9/30/98. Act Nov. 18, 1997, P. L. 105-85, Div A, Title IV, Subtitle B, § 412, 111 Stat. 1720, provides:

''Within the end strengths prescribed in section 411(a) [note to this section], the reserve components of the Armed Forces are authorized, as of September 30, 1998, the following number of Reserves to be serving on full-time active duty or full-time duty, in the case of members of the National Guard, for the purpose of organizing, administering, recruiting, instructing, or training the reserve components:

''(1) The Army National Guard of the United States, 22,310.

''(2) The Army Reserve, 11,500.

''(3) The Naval Reserve, 16,136.

''(4) The Marine Corps Reserve, 2,559.

''(5) The Air National Guard of the United States, 10,671.

''(6) The Air Force Reserve, 867.''.

CROSS REFERENCES

Authorization of end strength of Selected Reserve of each reserve component of the armed forces, prerequisite to appropriation of funds to or for use of Selected Reserve, 10 USCS § 115.

§ 12002. Authorized strengths: Army and Air Force reserve components, exclusive of members on active duty

(a) The authorized strengths of the National Guard and the reserve components of the Army and the Air Force, exclusive of members who are included in the strengths authorized for members of the Army and Air Force, respectively, on active duty, are as follows:

Army National Guard and the Army National Guard of the United States	600,000
Army Reserve	980,000
Air National Guard and the Air National Guard of the United States	150,000
Air Force Reserve	500,000.

(b) The strength authorized by this section for the Army National Guard and the Army National Guard of the United States, and the strength authorized by this section for the Air National Guard and the Air National Guard of the United States, shall be allocated among the States.

(Added Oct. 5, 1994, P. L. 103-337, Div A, Title XVI, Subtitle C, § 1662(a)(1), 108 Stat. 2983.)

HISTORY; ANCILLARY LAWS AND DIRECTIVES

Effective date of section:

This section took effect on Dec. 1, 1994, pursuant to Act Oct. 5, 1994, P. L. 103-337, Div A, Title XVI, Subtitle F, § 1691, 108 Stat. 3026, which appears as 10 USCS 10001 note.

§ 12003. Authorized strengths: commissioned officers in an active status

(a) The authorized strengths of the Army, Navy, Air Force, and Marine Corps in reserve commissioned officers, other than commissioned warrant officers and officers on an active-duty list, in an active status are as follows:

Army	275,000
Air Force	200,000
Navy	150,000
Marine Corps	24,500.

(b) The authorized strengths prescribed by subsection (a) may not be exceeded unless—

(1) the Secretary concerned determines that a greater number is necessary for planned mobilization requirements; or

(2) the excess results directly from the operation of a nondiscretionary provision of law.

(Added Oct. 5, 1994, P. L. 103-337, Div A, Title XVI, Subtitle C, § 1662(a)(1), 108 Stat. 2984.)

HISTORY; ANCILLARY LAWS AND DIRECTIVES

Effective date of section:

This section took effect on Dec. 1, 1994, pursuant to Act Oct. 5, 1994, P. L. 103-337, Div A, Title XVI, Subtitle F, § 1691, 108 Stat. 3026, which appears as 10 USCS 10001 note.

CROSS REFERENCES

This section is referred to in 10 USCS §§ 123, 12005, 12006.

§ 12004. Strength in grade: reserve general and flag officers in an active status

(a) The authorized strengths of the Army, Air Force, and Marine Corps in reserve general officers in an active status, and the authorized strength of the Navy in reserve officers in the grades of rear admiral (lower half) and rear admiral in an active status, are as follows:

Army	207
Air Force	157
Navy	48
Marine Corps	10.

(b) The following Army and Air Force reserve officers shall not be counted for purposes of this section:

(1) Those serving as adjutants general or assistant adjutants general of a State.

(2) Those serving in the National Guard Bureau.

(3) Those counted under section 526 of this title.

(c)(1) The authorized strength of the Navy under subsection (a) is exclusive of officers counted under section 526 of this title. Of the number authorized under subsection (a), 39 are distributed among the line and the staff corps as follows:

Line	28
Medical Corps	5
Chaplain Corps	1
Judge Advocate General's Corps	1
Dental Corps	2
Nurses Corps	1
Medical Service Corps	1

(2) The remaining authorizations for the Navy under subsection (a) shall be distributed among such other staff corps as are established by the Secretary of the Navy under the authority provided by section 5150(b) of this title, except that—

(A) if the Secretary has established a Supply Corps, the authorized strength for the Supply Corps shall be seven; and

(B) if the Secretary has established a Civil Engineering Corps, the authorized strength for the Civil Engineering Corps shall be two.

(3) Not more than 50 percent of the officers in an active status authorized under this section for the Navy may serve in the grade of rear admiral.

(d) The authorized strength of the Marine Corps under subsection (a) is exclusive of those counted under section 526 of this title.

(e)(1) A reserve general officer of the Army or Air Force may not be reduced in grade because of a reduction in the number of general officers authorized under subsection (a).

(2) An officer of the Naval Reserve or the Marine Corps Reserve may not be reduced in permanent grade because of a reduction in the number authorized by this section for his grade.

(Added Oct. 5, 1994, P. L. 103-337, Div A, Title XVI, Subtitle C, § 1662(a)(1), 108 Stat. 2984; Feb. 10, 1996, P. L. 104-106, Div A, Title XV, § 1501(b)(9), 110 Stat. 496.)

HISTORY; ANCILLARY LAWS AND DIRECTIVES

Effective date of section:

This section took effect on Dec. 1, 1994, pursuant to Act Oct. 5, 1994, P. L. 103-337, Div A, Title XVI, Subtitle F, § 1691, 108 Stat. 3026, which appears as 10 USCS 10001 note.

Amendments:

1996. Act Feb. 10, 1996 (effective as if included in Act Oct. 5, 1994, P. L. 103-337, as enacted on Oct. 5, 1994, as provided by § 1501(f)(3) of Act Feb. 10, 1996, which appears as 10 USCS § 113 note), in subsec. (a), in the introductory matter, substituted ''active status'' for ''active-status'' following ''rear admiral in an''.

CROSS REFERENCES

Adjutants general and assistant adjutants general, reference as applicable to other officers of National Guard, 10 USCS § 10214.

This section is referred to in 10 USCS §§ 10214, 12005, 12006.

§ 12005. Strength in grade: commissioned officers in grades below brigadier general or rear admiral (lower half) in an active status

(a)(1) Subject to paragraph (2), the authorized strength of the Army and the Air Force in reserve commissioned officers in an active status in each grade named in paragraph (2) is as prescribed by the Secretary of the Army or the Secretary of the Air Force, respectively. A vacancy in any grade may be filled by an authorized appointment in any lower grade.

(2) A strength prescribed by the Secretary concerned under paragraph (1) for a grade may not be higher than the percentage of the strength authorized for the Army or the Air Force, as the case may be, under section 12003 of this title that is specified for that grade as follows:

Grade	Army percentage	Air Force percentage
Colonel	2	1.8
Lieutenant colonel	6	4.6
Major	13	14.0
Captain	35	32.0
First lieutenant and second lieutenant (when combined with the number authorized for general officer grades under section 12004 of this title)	44	47.6

(b)(1) The authorized strengths of the Naval Reserve in line officers in an active status in the grades of captain, commander, lieutenant commander, and lieutenant, and in the grades of lieutenant (junior grade) and ensign combined, are the following percentages of the total authorized number of those officers:

Captain	1.5 percent
Commander	7 percent
Lieutenant commander	22 percent
Lieutenant	37 percent
Lieutenant (junior grade) and ensign (when combined with the number authorized for flag officer grades under section 12004 of this title)	32.5 percent.

(2) When the actual number of line officers in an active status in any grade is less than the number authorized by paragraph (1) for that grade, the difference may be applied to increase the number authorized by that paragraph for any lower grade or grades.

(c)(1) The authorized strengths of the Marine Corps Reserve in officers in an active status in the grades of colonel, lieutenant colonel, major, and captain, and in the grades of first lieutenant and second lieutenant combined, are the following percentages of the total authorized number of those officers:

Colonel	2 percent
Lieutenant colonel	6 percent
Major	12 percent
Captain	35 percent
First lieutenant and second lieutenant (when combined with the number authorized for general officer grades under section 12004 of this title)	32.5 percent.

(2) When the actual number of officers in an active status in any grade is less than the number authorized by paragraph (1) for that grade, the difference may be applied to increase the number authorized by that paragraph for any lower grade or grades.

(d)(1) An officer of the Army or Air Force may not be reduced in grade because of a reduction in the number of commissioned officers authorized for the officer's grade under this section.

(2) An officer of the Naval Reserve or the Marine Corps Reserve may not be reduced in permanent grade because of a reduction in the number authorized by this section for his grade.

(Added Oct. 5, 1994, P. L. 103-337, Div A, Title XVI, Subtitle C, § 1662(a)(1), 108 Stat. 2985.)

HISTORY; ANCILLARY LAWS AND DIRECTIVES

Effective date of section:

This section took effect on Dec. 1, 1994, pursuant to Act Oct. 5, 1994, P. L. 103-337, Div A, Title XVI, Subtitle F, § 1691, 108 Stat. 3026, which appears as 10 USCS 10001 note.

CROSS REFERENCES

This section is referred to in 10 USCS § 12006.

§ 12006. Strength limitations: authority to waive in time of war or national emergency

(a) In time of war, or of national emergency declared by Congress or the President, the President may suspend the operation of any provision of section 12003, 12004, or 12005 of this title. So long as any such war or national emergency continues, any such suspension may be extended by the President.

(b) Any suspension under subsection (a) shall, if not sooner ended, end on the last day of the two-year period beginning on the date on which the suspension (or the last extension thereof) takes effect or on the last day of the one-year period beginning on the date of the termination of the war or national emergency, whichever occurs first. With respect to the end of any such suspension, the preceding sentence supersedes the provisions of title II of the National Emergencies Act (50 U.S.C. 1621, 1622) which provide that powers or authori-

ties exercised by reason of a national emergency shall cease to be exercised after the date of termination of the emergency.
(Added Oct. 5, 1994, P. L. 103-337, Div A, Title XVI, Subtitle C, § 1662(a)(1), 108 Stat. 2986.)

HISTORY; ANCILLARY LAWS AND DIRECTIVES

Effective date of section:

This section took effect on Dec. 1, 1994, pursuant to Act Oct. 5, 1994, P. L. 103-337, Div A, Title XVI, Subtitle F, § 1691, 108 Stat. 3026, which appears as 10 USCS 10001 note.

§ 12007. Reserve officers of the Army: distribution

The Secretary of the Army shall distribute the number of reserve commissioned officers, other than commissioned warrant officers, authorized in each commissioned grade between those assigned to reserve units organized to serve as units and those not assigned to such units. The Secretary shall distribute the number who are assigned to reserve units organized to serve as units among the units of each reserve component by prescribing appropriate tables of organization and tables of distribution. The Secretary shall distribute the number who are not assigned to such units between—
(1) each special branch; and
(2) all other branches taken together.
(Added Oct. 5, 1994, P. L. 103-337, Div A, Title XVI, Subtitle C, § 1662(a)(1), 108 Stat. 2986.)

HISTORY; ANCILLARY LAWS AND DIRECTIVES

Effective date of section:

This section took effect on Dec. 1, 1994, pursuant to Act Oct. 5, 1994, P. L. 103-337, Div A, Title XVI, Subtitle F, § 1691, 108 Stat. 3026, which appears as 10 USCS 10001 note.

§ 12008. Army Reserve and Air Force Reserve: warrant officers

The Secretary of the Army may prescribe the authorized strength of the Army Reserve in warrant officers. The Secretary of the Air Force may prescribe the authorized strength of the Air Force Reserve in warrant officers.
(Added Oct. 5, 1994, P. L. 103-337, Div A, Title XVI, Subtitle C, § 1662(a)(1), 108 Stat. 2987.)

HISTORY; ANCILLARY LAWS AND DIRECTIVES

Effective date of section:

This section took effect on Dec. 1, 1994, pursuant to Act Oct. 5, 1994, P. L. 103-337, Div A, Title XVI, Subtitle F, § 1691, 108 Stat. 3026, which appears as 10 USCS 10001 note.

§ 12009. Army and Air Force reserve components: temporary increases

(a) The authorized strength in any reserve grade, as prescribed under this chapter [10 USCS §§ 12001 et seq.], for any reserve component under the jurisdiction of the Secretary of the Army or the Secretary of the Air Force is automatically increased to the minimum extent necessary to give effect to each appointment made in that grade under section 1211(a), 3036, 14304(b), 14314, or 14317 of this title.

(b) An authorized strength so increased is increased for no other purpose. While an officer holds that grade, the officer whose appointment caused the increase is counted for the purpose of determining when other appointments, not under those sections, may be made in that grade.

(Added Oct. 5, 1994, P. L. 103-337, Div A, Title XVI, Subtitle C, § 1662(a)(1), 108 Stat. 2987.)

HISTORY; ANCILLARY LAWS AND DIRECTIVES

Effective date of section:

This section took effect on Dec. 1, 1994, pursuant to Act Oct. 5, 1994, P. L. 103-337, Div A, Title XVI, Subtitle F, § 1691, 108 Stat. 3026, which appears as 10 USCS 10001 note.

§ 12010. Computations for Naval Reserve and Marine Corps Reserve: rule when fraction occurs in final result

When there is a fraction in the final result of any computation under this chapter [10 USCS §§ 12001 et seq.] for the Naval Reserve or the Marine Corps Reserve, a fraction of one-half or more is counted as one, and a fraction of less than one-half is disregarded.

(Added Oct. 5, 1994, P. L. 103-337, Div A, Title XVI, Subtitle C, § 1662(a)(1), 108 Stat. 2987.)

HISTORY; ANCILLARY LAWS AND DIRECTIVES

Effective date of section:

This section took effect on Dec. 1, 1994, pursuant to Act Oct. 5, 1994, P. L. 103-337, Div A, Title XVI, Subtitle F, § 1691, 108 Stat. 3026, which appears as 10 USCS 10001 note.

§ 12011. Authorized strengths: reserve officers on active duty or on full-time National Guard duty for administration of the reserves or the National Guard

(a) The number of reserve officers of the Army, Air Force, and Marine Corps who may be on active duty or full-time National Guard duty in each of the grades of major, lieutenant colonel, and colonel, and of the Navy who may be on active duty in each of the grades of lieutenant commander, commander, and captain, as of the end of any fiscal year for duty described in subclauses (B) and (C) of section 523(b)(1) of this title or full-time National Guard duty (other than for training) under section 502(f) of title 32 may not exceed the number for that grade and armed force in the following table:

"Grade	Army	Navy	Air Force	Marine Corps
Major or Lieutenant Commander . .	3,219	1,071	643	140
Lieutenant Colonel or Commander .	1,524	520	672	90
Colonel or Navy Captain	412	188	264	30''

(b) Whenever the number of officers serving in any grade is less than the number authorized for that grade under this section, the difference between the two numbers may be applied to increase the number authorized under this section for any lower grade.

(Added Dec. 12, 1980, P. L. 96-513, Title I, § 103, 94 Stat. 2844; Dec. 1, 1981, P. L. 97-86, Title V, § 503(b), 95 Stat. 1108; Sept. 8, 1982, P. L. 97-252, Title V, § 503(b), 96 Stat. 727; Sept. 24, 1983, P. L. 98-94, Title V, § 503(b), 97 Stat. 631; Oct. 19, 1984, P. L. 98-525, Title IV, Part B, §§ 413(b), 414(a)(4)(A), (B)(i), 98 Stat. 2518; Nov. 8, 1985, P. L. 99-145, Title IV, Part B, § 413(b), 99 Stat. 619; Dec. 4, 1987, P. L. 100-180, Div A Title IV, Part B, § 413(b)(1), (2), 101 Stat. 1083; Nov. 29, 1989, P. L. 101-189, Div A, Title IV, Part B, § 413(b)(1), (2), 103 Stat. 1433; Dec. 5, 1991, P. L. 102-190, Div A, Title IV, Part B, § 413(b), 105 Stat. 1352; Nov. 30, 1993, P. L. 103-160, Div A, Title IV, Subtitle B, § 413(b), 107 Stat. 1642; Oct. 5, 1994, P. L. 103-337, Div A, Title XVI, Subtitle C, § 1662(a)(2), 108 Stat. 2988; Feb. 10, 1996, P. L. 104-106, Div A, Title IV, Subtitle B, § 414(a), 110 Stat. 288.)

HISTORY; ANCILLARY LAWS AND DIRECTIVES

Effective date of section:

Act Dec. 12, 1980, P. L. 96-513, Title VII, § 701(a), 94 Stat. 2955, provided that this section shall take effect on September 15, 1981, except as provided in § 701(b)(1) of such Act, which appears as 10 USCS § 101 note.

Amendments:

1981. Act Dec. 1, 1981, in subsec. (a), substituted the tabular matter for matter which read:

"Grade	Army	Navy	Air Force	Marine Corps
"Major or lieutenant commander . .	821	823	170	51
"Lieutenant colonel or commander .	503	425	183	35
"Colonel or Navy captain	163	177	146	19''

1982. Act Sept. 8, 1982, in subsec. (a), in the tabular matter, for the Army, substituted "1,351", "671" and "234" for "1,105", "551" and "171", respectively, for the Air Force, substituted "281", "267" and "170" for "189", "194" and "147", respectively, and, for the Marine Corps, substituted "95", "40" and "21" for "51", "35" and "19", respectively.

1983. Act Sept. 24, 1983 (effective 10/1/83, as provided by § 503(c) of such Act, which appears as 10 USCS § 517 note), in subsec. (a), substituted the tabular matter for matter which read:

"Grade	Army	Navy	Air Force	Marine Corps
"Major or lieutenant commander ..	1,351	823	281	95
"Lieutenant colonel or commander .	671	425	267	40
"Colonel or Navy captain	234	177	170	21"

1984. Act Oct. 19, 1984 (effective 10/1/84, as provided by § 413(c) of such Act, which appears as 10 USCS § 517 note), in subsec. (a), substituted the tabular matter for matter which read:

Grade	Army	Navy	Air Force	Marine Corps
"Major or Lieutenant Commander .	1,948	823	408	95
"Lieutenant Colonel or Commander	967	520	303	48
"Colonel or Navy Captain	338	177	171	23

Section 414(a)(4)(A), (B)(i) of such Act substituted the catchline for one which read: "524. Authorized strengths: reserve officers on active duty for administration of the reserves in grades of major, lieutenant colonel, and colonel and Navy grades of lieutenant commander, commander, and captain"; and in subsec. (a), inserted "or full-time National Guard duty" and "or full-time National Guard duty (other than for training) under section 502(f) of title 32".

1985. Act Nov. 8, 1985 (effective 10/1/85, as provided by § 413(c) of such Act, which appears as 10 USCS § 517 note), in subsec. (a), substituted the table for one which read:

"Grade	Army	Navy	Air Force	Marine Corps
"Major or lieutenant commander ..	2,261	823	471	100
"Lieutenant colonel or commander .	1,121	520	293	50
"Colonel or Navy captain	345	177	172	25"

1987. Act Dec. 4, 1987, in subsec. (a), substituted the table for one which read:

Grade	Army	Navy	Air Force	Marine Corps
"Major or Lieutenant Commander .	2,317	850	476	100
"Lieutenant Colonel or Commander	1,152	520	318	60
"Colonel or Navy Captain	348	177	189	25"

Such Act further (effective 10/1/88 as provided by § 413(b)(2) of such Act), in subsec. (a), substituted the table for one which read:

"Grade	Army	Navy	Air Force	Marine Corps
"Major or Lieutenant Commander .	2,550	850	575	105
"Lieutenant Colonel or Commander	1,152	520	322	70
"Colonel or Navy Captain	348	185	184	25"

1989. Act Nov. 29, 1989, in subsec. (a), substituted the table for one which read:

"Grade	Army	Navy	Air Force	Marine Corps
"Major or Lieutenant Commander .	2,600	875	575	110
"Lieutenant Colonel or Commander	1,250	520	476	75
"Colonel or Navy Captain	348	185	190	15"

Such Act further (effective 10/1/90), in subsec. (a), substituted the table for one which read:

"Grade	Army	Navy	Air Force	Marine Corps
"Major or Lieutenant Commander .	3,030	1,065	575	110
"Lieutenant Colonel or Commander	1,448	520	476	75
"Colonel or Navy Captain	351	188	190	25"

1991. Act Dec. 5, 1991, in subsec. (a), substituted the table for one which read:

"Grade	Army	Navy	Air Force	Marine Corps
"Major or Lieutenant Commander .	3,219	1,071	575	110
"Lieutenant Colonel or Commander	1,524	520	532	75
"Colonel or Navy Captain	364	188	194	25"

1993. Act Nov. 30, 1993, in subsec. (a), substituted the table for one which read:

"Grade	Army	Navy	Air Force	Marine Corps
"Major or Lieutenant Commander .	3,219	1,071	575	110
"Lieutenant Colonel or Commander	1,524	520	595	75
"Colonel or Navy Captain	372	188	227	25"

1994. Act Oct. 5, 1994 (effective 12/1/94 as provided by § 1691 of such Act, which appears as 10 USCS § 10001 note) transferred this section, enacted as 10 USCS § 524, to Chapter 1201, inserted it after 10 USCS § 12010, redesignated it as 10 USCS § 12011, and substituted the heading for one which read: "Authorized strengths: reserve officers on active duty or on full-time National Guard duty for administration of the reserves or the National Guard in grades of major, lieutenant colonel, and colonel and Navy grades of lieutenant commander, commander, and captain".

1996. Act Feb. 10, 1996, in subsec. (a), substituted the table for one which read:

"Grade	Army	Navy	Air Force	Marine Corps
"Major or Lieutenant Commander .	3,219	1,071	575	110
"Lieutenant Colonel or Commander	1,524	520	636	75
"Colonel or Navy Captain	372	188	274	25"

CROSS REFERENCES

This section is referred to in 10 USCS §§ 3380, 8380, 14304, 14311; 32 USCS § 112.

INTERPRETIVE NOTES AND DECISIONS

Total number of commissioned line officers on active list should be calculated upon basis of total authorized number of enlisted personnel in Navy. 33 Op Atty Gen 311.

When computing total strength of active list line officers in Navy, Secretary should not apply percentage established by statute as basis for this computation to enlisted personnel receiving training in trade schools under temporary authorization, as well as to permanent strength of enlisted personnel. 36 Op Atty Gen 423.

§ 12012. Authorized strengths: senior enlisted members on active duty or on full-time National Guard duty for administration of the reserves or the National Guard

(a) The number of enlisted members in pay grades E-8 and E-9 who may be on active duty (other than for training) or on full-time National Guard duty under the authority of section 502(f) of title 32 (other than for training) as of the end of any fiscal year in connection with organizing, administering, recruiting, instructing, or training the reserve components or the National Guard may not exceed the number for that grade and armed force in the following table:

Grade	Army	Navy	Air Force	Marine Corps
E-9	603	202	366	20
E-8	2,585	429	890	94

(b) Whenever the number of members serving in pay grade E-9 for duty described in subsection (a) is less than the number authorized for that grade under subsection (a), the difference between the two numbers may be applied to increase the number authorized under such subsection for pay grade E-8.

(Added Oct. 5, 1994, P. L. 103-337, Div A, Title XVI, Subtitle C, § 1662(a)(1), 108 Stat. 2987; Feb. 10, 1996, P. L. 104-106, Div A, Title IV, Subtitle B, § 414(b), Title XV, § 1501(b)(10), 110 Stat. 288, 496.)

HISTORY; ANCILLARY LAWS AND DIRECTIVES

Effective date of section:

This section took effect on Dec. 1, 1994, pursuant to Act Oct. 5, 1994, P. L. 103-337, Div A, Title XVI, Subtitle F, § 1691, 108 Stat. 3026, which appears as 10 USCS 10001 note.

Amendments:

1996. Act Feb. 10, 1996, in subsec. (b), substituted the table for one which read:

"Grade	Army	Navy	Air Force	Marine Corps
E-9	569	202	328	14
E-8	2,585	429	840	74".

Such Act further (effective as if included in Act Oct. 5, 1994, P. L. 103-337, as enacted on Oct. 5, 1994, as provided by § 1501(f)(3) of Act Feb. 10, 1996, which appears as 10 USCS § 113 note), in the section heading, inserted ''the'' preceding ''National Guard''.

CHAPTER 1203. ENLISTED MEMBERS

HISTORY; ANCILLARY LAWS AND DIRECTIVES

Amendments:

1994. Act Oct. 5, 1994, P. L. 103-337, Div A, Title XVI, Subtitle C, § 1662(b)(1), 108 Stat. 2988 (effective 12/1/94 as provided by § 1691 of such Act, which appears as 10 USCS § 10001 note), added the chapter heading and analysis.

§ 12101. Definition

In this chapter [10 USCS §§ 12101 et seq.], the term ''enlistment'' means original enlistment or reenlistment.

(Added Oct. 5, 1994, P. L. 103-337, Div A, Title XVI, Subtitle C, § 1662(b)(1), 108 Stat. 2988.)

HISTORY; ANCILLARY LAWS AND DIRECTIVES

Effective date of section:

This section took effect on Dec. 1, 1994, pursuant to Act Oct. 5, 1994, P. L. 103-337, Div A, Title XVI, Subtitle F, § 1691, 108 Stat. 3026, which appears as 10 USCS 10001 note.

§ 12102. Reserve components: qualifications

(a) To become an enlisted member of a reserve component a person must be enlisted as a Reserve of an armed force and subscribe to the oath prescribed by section 502 of this title, or be transferred to that component according to law. In addition, to become an enlisted member of the Army National Guard of the United States or the Air National Guard of the United States, he must meet the requirements of section 12107 of this title.

(b) Except as otherwise provided by law, the Secretary concerned shall prescribe physical, mental, moral, professional, and age qualifications for the enlistment of persons as Reserves of the armed forces under his jurisdiction. However, no person may be enlisted as a Reserve unless—

(1) he is a citizen of the United States or has been lawfully admitted to the

United States for permanent residence under the Immigration and Nationality Act (8 U.S.C. 1101 et seq.); or

(2) he has previously served in the armed forces or in the National Security Training Corps.

(c) A person who is otherwise qualified, but who has a physical defect that the Secretary concerned determines will not interfere with the performance of the duties to which that person may be assigned, may be enlisted as a Reserve of any armed force under the jurisdiction of that Secretary.

(Aug. 10, 1956, ch 1041, § 1, 70A Stat. 17; Dec. 23, 1963, P. L. 88-236, 77 Stat. 474; Nov. 8, 1967, P. L. 90-193, § 1(2), 81 Stat. 374; Oct. 22, 1968, P. L. 90-623, § 2(3), 82 Stat. 1314; Dec. 12, 1980, P. L. 96-513, Title V, Part B, § 511(13), 94 Stat. 2921; Oct. 5, 1994, P. L. 103-337, Div A, Title XVI, Subtitle B, Part I, § 1631(a), Subtitle C, § 1662(b)(2), Subtitle D, § 1675(a), 108 Stat. 2964, 2989, 3017; Feb. 10, 1996, P. L. 104-106, Div A, Title XV, § 1501(a)(5)(A), 110 Stat. 495.)

HISTORY; ANCILLARY LAWS AND DIRECTIVES

Prior law and revision:

Revised Section	Source (USCS)	Source (Statutes at Large)
510(a)	50:952 (less proviso).	July 9, 1952, ch. 608,
510(b)	50:941(a) (as applicable to enlistments).	§§ 217 (less (c), as applicable to enlistments), 228
510(c)	50:941(b) (as applicable to enlistments).	(less proviso), 232 (as applicable to enlistments),
510(d)	50:956 (as applicable to enlistments).	66 Stat. 486, 488, 489.

In subsection (a), the last sentence is inserted to reflect sections 3261 and 8261 of this title.

In subsection (b), the word "However" is substituted for the words "Subject to the limitation that". The words "as Reserves in the armed forces under his jurisdiction" are substituted for the words "of Reserve members of the Armed Forces of the United States". The words "its Territories" are omitted as surplusage, since citizens of the Territories are citizens of the United States.

In subsection (c), the words "armed force concerned" are substituted for the words "of the appropriate Armed Force of the United States". The words "in which she previously served satisfactorily" are substituted for the words "satisfactorily held by her".

In subsection (d), the words "under the jurisdiction of that Secretary" are inserted for clarity. The words "general or special" are omitted as surplusage.

References in text:

The "Immigration and Nationality Act (8 U.S.C. 1101 et seq.)", referred to in this section, is Act June 27, 1952, ch 477, 66 Stat. 166, which appears generally as 8 USCS §§ 1101 et seq. For full classification of such Act, consult USCS Tables volumes.

Amendments:

1963. Act Dec. 23, 1963, in subsec. (b)(1), substituted "he is a citizen of the United States or has been lawfully admitted to the United States for permanent residence under chapter 12 of title 8" for "he is, or has made a declaration of intention to become, a citizen of the United States or of a possession thereof".

1967. Act Nov. 8, 1967, P. L. 90-130, § 1(2), 81 Stat. 374, in subsec. (c), deleted "for service in the Army Reserve, Naval Reserve, Air Force Reserve, Marine Corps Reserve, and Coast Guard Reserve" after "Women may be enlisted as Reserves of the armed forces".

1968. Act Oct. 22, 1968, in subsec. (a), substituted "section 502" for "section 501".

1980. Act Dec. 12, 1980 (effective upon enactment 12/12/80, as provided by § 701(b)(3) of such Act, which appears as 10 USCS § 101 note), in subsec. (b)(1), substituted "the Immigration and Nationality Act (8 U.S.C. 1101 et seq.)" for "chapter 12 of title 8".

1994. Act Oct. 5, 1994 (effective 12/1/94 as provided by § 1691 of such Act, which appears as 10 USCS § 10001 note), transferred this section, enacted as 10 USCS § 510, to Chapter 1203, inserted it after 10 USCS § 12101, redesignated it as 10 USCS § 12102; and, in subsec. (a), substituted "section 12107" for "section 3261 or 8261".

Such Act further (effective 10/1/96, as provided by § 1691(b)(1) of such Act, which appears as 10 USCS § 10001 note), as amended Feb. 10, 1996 (effective as if included in Act Oct. 5, 1994, P. L. 103-337, as enacted on Oct. 5, 1994, as provided by § 1501(f)(3) of Act Feb. 10, 1996, which appears as 10 USCS § 113 note) deleted subsec. (c), which read: "(c) Women may be enlisted as Reserves of the armed forces. Women are enlisted in the grades and ratings authorized for enlisted women of the regular component of the armed force concerned. Any female former enlisted member of an armed force may, if otherwise qualified, be enlisted as a Reserve of that armed force in the highest grade or rating in which she previously served satisfactorily on active duty (other than for training)."; and redesignated subsec. (d) as subsec. (c).

1996. Act Feb. 10, 1996 (effective as if included in Act Oct. 5, 1994, P. L. 103-337, as enacted on Oct. 5, 1994, as provided by § 1501(f)(3) of Act Feb. 10, 1996, which appears as 10 USCS § 113 note) amended the directory language of § 1631(a) of Act Oct. 5, 1994.

Other provisions:

Purpose of 1968 amendment; restatement of existing laws. Act Oct. 22, 1968, P. L. 90-623, § 6, 82 Stat. 1315, which appears as 5 USCS § 5334 note, provided that the amendments made by that Act were intended to restate without substantive change the law in effect on Oct. 22, 1968.

Termination of provisions for treatment of single parents enlisting in reserve components of the Armed Forces. Act Nov. 14, 1986, P. L. 99-661, Div A, Title V, Part B, § 523, 100 Stat. 3871; Dec. 4, 1987, P. L. 100-180, Div A, Title V, § 503, 101 Stat. 1085; Nov. 29, 1989, P. L. 101-189, Div A, Title V, Part A, § 504, 103 Stat. 1437, terminated Sept. 30, 1991, as provided by former subsec. (d) of such section.

CROSS REFERENCES

National Security Training Corps, 50 USCS App. § 454.

This section is referred to in 10 USCS § 641.

§ 12103. Reserve components: terms

(a) Except as otherwise prescribed by law, enlistments as Reserves are for terms prescribed by the Secretary concerned. However, an enlistment that is in effect at the beginning of a war or of a national emergency declared by Congress, or entered into during such a war or emergency, and that would otherwise expire, continues in effect until the expiration of six months after the end of that war or emergency, whichever is later, unless sooner terminated by the Secretary concerned.

(b) Under regulations to be prescribed by the Secretary of Defense, and by the Secretary of Transportation with respect to the Coast Guard when it is not operating as a service in the Navy, a person who is qualified for enlistment for active duty in an armed force, and who is not under orders to report for induction into an armed force under the Military Selective Service Act (50 U.S.C. App. 451 et seq.) may be enlisted as a Reserve for service in the Army Reserve, Naval Reserve, Air Force Reserve, Marine Corps Reserve, or Coast Guard Reserve, for a term of not less than six years nor more than eight years. Each person enlisted under this subsection shall serve—

(1) on active duty for a period of not less than two years; and

(2) the rest of his period of enlistment as a member of the Ready Reserve.

(c) In time of war or of national emergency declared by Congress the term of service of an enlisted member transferred to a reserve component according to law, that would otherwise expire, continues until the expiration of six months after the end of that war or emergency, whichever is later, unless sooner terminated by the Secretary concerned.

(d) Under regulations to be prescribed by the Secretary of Defense, or the Secretary of Transportation with respect to the Coast Guard when it is not operating as a service in the Navy, a non-prior-service person who is qualified for induction for active duty in an armed force and who is not under orders to report for induction into an armed force under the Military Selective Service Act (50 U.S.C. App. 451 et seq.), except as provided in section 6(c)(2)(A)(ii) and (iii) of such Act [50 USCS Appx. § 456(c)(2)(A)(ii), (iii)], may be enlisted in the Army National Guard or the Air National Guard, or as a Reserve for service in the Army Reserve, Naval Reserve, Air Force Reserve, Marine Corps Reserve, or Coast Guard Reserve, for a term of not less than six years nor more than eight years. Each person enlisted under this subsection shall perform an initial period of active duty for training of not less than twelve weeks to commence insofar as practicable within 270 days after the date of that enlistment.

(Aug. 10, 1956, ch 1041, § 1, 70A Stat. 18; Sept. 2, 1958, P. L. 85-861, § 1(8), 72 Stat. 1439; Sept. 3, 1963, P. L. 88-110, § 3, 77 Stat. 135; Dec. 1, 1967, P. L. 90-168, § 2(11), 81 Stat. 523; Oct. 7, 1975, P. L. 94-106, Title VIII, § 802(a), 89 Stat. 537; Oct. 20, 1978, P. L. 95-485, Title IV, § 405(c)(1), 92 Stat. 1615; Nov. 9, 1979, P. L. 96-107, Title VIII, § 805(a), 93 Stat. 812; Dec. 12, 1980, P. L. 96-513, Title V, Part B, § 511(14), 94 Stat. 2921; Sept. 8, 1982, P. L.

97-252, Title XI, § 1115(a), 96 Stat. 750; Oct. 12, 1982, P. L. 97-295, § 1(6), 96 Stat. 1289; Sept. 24, 1983, P. L. 98-94, Title X, Part C, § 1022(a)(1), 97 Stat. 670; Oct. 5, 1994, P. L. 103-337, Div A, Title XVI, Subtitle C, § 1662(b)(2), 108 Stat. 2989.)

HISTORY; ANCILLARY LAWS AND DIRECTIVES

Prior law and revision:

1956 ACT

Revised Section	Source (USCS)	Source (Statutes at Large)
511(a)	50:951 (less (c)).	July 9, ch. 608, § 227, 66 Stat. 488.
511(b)	50:951(c).	

In subsection (a), the first sentence is substituted for 50:951(a). The words "as Reserves in the Armed Forces of the United States" and "the existence of" are omitted as surplusage.

In subsections (a) and (b), the word "hereafter" is omitted as surplusage. The words "the expiration of" are inserted for clarity.

In subsection (b), the word "continues" is substituted for the words "shall . . . be extended".

1958 ACT

Revised Section	Source (USCS)	Source (Statutes at Large)
511(b)	50:1012.	Aug. 9, 1955, ch. 665, § 2(i) (1st 2 paras.), 69 Stat. 600.

In subsection (b), the words "respectively, pursuant to the provisions of this section" are omitted as surplusage. The words "as a Reserve for service" are inserted to reflect section 510 of this title. The last six words of the first sentence are substituted for 50:1012(b) (1st sentence).

Amendments:

1958. Act Sept. 2, 1958, redesignated (b) as subsec. (c); and added new subsec. (b).

1963. Act Sept. 3, 1963, added subsec. (d).

1967. Act Dec. 1, 1967 (effective on the first day of the first calendar month following enactment on Dec. 1, 1967, as provided by § 7 of such Act, which appears as 10 USCS § 138 note), substituted subsec. (d) for one which read; "(d) Under regulations to be prescribed by the Secretary of Defense, or the Secretary of the Treasury with respect to the Coast Guard when it is not operating as a service in the Navy, a non-prior-service person who is under twenty-six years of age, who is qualified for induction for active duty in an armed force, and who is not under orders to report for induction into an armed force under section 451–473 of title 50, appendix, may be enlisted in the Army National Guard or the Air National Guard, or as a Reserve for service in the Army Reserve, Naval Reserve, Air Force Reserve, Marine Corps Reserve, or Coast Guard Reserve, for a term of six years. Each person enlisted under this subsection shall perform an initial period of active duty for training of not less than four months and shall subject to section 269(e)(4) of this title, serve the rest of his period of enlistment as a member of the Ready Reserve.''.

1975. Act Oct. 7, 1975, in subsec. (d), substituted ''twelve weeks'' for ''four months''.

1978. Act Oct. 20, 1978 (effective as provided by § 405(c)(2) of such Act, which appears as a note to this section), in subsec. (b), in the introductory matter, substituted ''the Secretary of Defense, and by the Secretary of Transportation with respect to the Coast Guard when it is not operating as a service in the Navy'' for ''the Secretary concerned'', and substituted ''the Military Selective Service Act (50 U. S. C. App.451–473)'' for ''sections 451–473 of title 50, appendix'', in cl. (1), inserted ''not less than'' and inserted ''and'', deleted cl. (2), which read: ''satisfactorily as a member of the Ready Reserve for a period that, when added to his active duty under clause (1), totals five years; and'', and redesignated former cl. (3) as cl. (2), and, as so redesignated, substituted ''Ready Reserve'' for ''Standby Reserve''.

1979. Act Nov. 9, 1979 (effective as provided by § 805(c) of such Act, which appears as a note to this section), in subsec. (d), deleted ''who is under 26 years of age'' following ''non-prior-service person'' and deleted the comma following ''in an armed force''.

1980. Act Dec. 12, 1980 (effective upon enactment on 12/12/80, as provided by § 701(b)(3) of such Act, which appears as a note to 10 USCS § 101), in subsec. (d), substituted ''Military Selective Service Act (50 U.S.C. App. 451 et seq.)'' for ''Military Selective Service Act of 1967 (50 App. U.S.C. 451–473)''.

1982. Act Sept. 8, 1982 (effective as provided by § 1115(b) of such Act, which appears as a note to this section), in subsec. (d), substituted ''270 days'' for ''180 days''.

Act Oct. 12, 1982, in subsec. (b), substituted ''451 et seq.'' for ''451–473''.

1983. Act Sept. 24, 1983, in subsecs. (b) and (d), substituted ''not less than six years nor more than eight years'' for ''six years''.

1994. Act Oct. 5, 1994 (effective 12/1/94 as provided by § 1691 of such Act, which appears as 10 USCS § 10001 note) transferred this section, enacted as 10 USCS § 511, to Chapter 1203 and redesignated it as 10 USCS § 12103.

Other provisions:

Applicability of 1978 amendment. Act Oct. 20, 1978, P. L. 95-485, Title IV, § 405(c)(2), 92 Stat. 1616, provided that: ''The amendments made by paragraph (1) [amending this section] shall not apply with respect to a person who enlisted as a Reserve for service in the Armed Forces under section 511(b) of title 10, United States Code [subsec. (b) of this section], before the date of the enactment of this Act.''

Application of 1979 amendments. Act Nov. 9, 1979, P. L. 96-107, Title VIII, § 805(c), 93 Stat. 813, provided that: ''The amendments made by this section shall apply only to individuals who become members of an Armed Force after the date of the enactment of this Act [enacted Nov. 9, 1979].''.

Application of Sept. 8, 1982 amendment. Act Sept. 8, 1983, P. L. 97-252,

Title XI, § 1115(b), 96 Stat. 750, provides: "The amendment made by this section [amending this section] shall be effective with respect to persons enlisting in a reserve component of the Armed Forces after the end of the ninety-day period beginning on the date of the enactment of this Act.".

Application of Sept. 24, 1983 amendments. Act Sept. 24, 1983, P. L. 98-94, Title X, Part C, § 1022(a)(2), 97 Stat. 670, provides: "The amendments made by paragraph (1) [amending subsecs. (b) and (d) of this section] shall apply only with respect to persons who enlist under the authority of subsection (b) or (d) of section 511 of title 10, United States Code [subsecs. (b), (d) of this section], 60 or more days after the date of the enactment of this Act.".

CROSS REFERENCES

Extension of enlistment term of officer candidates, 10 USCS § 12209.

This section is referred to in 5 USCS § 2108; 14 USCS § 713; 37 USCS § 205, 38 USCS §§ 3002, 3202, 3452, 3501; 50 USCS App. § 456.

§ 12104. Reserve components: transfers

(a) A person who would otherwise be required to be transferred to a reserve component under section 651 of this title or under the Military Selective Service Act (50 U.S.C. App. 451 et seq.), is entitled, if he is qualified and accepted, to be enlisted in any armed force that he chooses and to participate in the programs authorized for that armed force. However, unless the two Secretaries concerned consent, he may not be enlisted as a Reserve of an armed force other than that from which he is transferred. All periods of his participation shall be credited against the total period of service required of him under section 651 of this title or under the Military Selective Service Act (50 U.S.C. App. 451 et seq.). However, no period may be credited more than once.

(b) A person covered by subsection (a) shall perform the rest of his required term of service in the armed force in which he is so enlisted or in any other armed force in which he is later enlisted or appointed.

(c) This section does not change any term of service under an appointment, enlistment, or agreement, including an agreement made before or at the time when the member entered upon a program authorized by an armed force.

(Aug. 10, 1956, ch 1041, § 1, 70A Stat. 18; Dec. 12, 1980, P. L. 96-513, Title V, Part B, § 511(15), 94 Stat. 2921; Oct. 5, 1994, P. L. 103-337, Div A, Title XVI, Subtitle C, § 1662(b)(2), 108 Stat. 2989.)

HISTORY; ANCILLARY LAWS AND DIRECTIVES

Prior law and revision:

Revised Section	Source (USCS)	Source (Statutes at Large)
512(a)	50:929(a) (less 2d sentence, as applicable to enlistments).	July 9, 1952, ch. 608, § 209 (as applicable to enlistments), 66 Stat. 484.

Revised Section	Source (USCS)	Source (Statutes at Large)
512(b)	50:929(a) (2d sentence, as applicable to enlistments).	
512(c)	50:929(b) (as applicable to enlistments).	

In subsection (a), the words "is entitled . . . to be enlisted in any armed force that he chooses" are substituted for the words "shall . . . be permitted to enlist . . . in such Armed Force of the United States as he may elect". The second sentence is substituted for 50:929(a) (words within parentheses). The words "of an Armed Force of the United States" are omitted as surplusage.

In subsection (b), the word "rest" is substituted for the words "remaining period". The words "be required to" are omitted as surplusage.

In subsection (c), the words "This section does not" are substituted for the words "Nothing in this section shall be construed". The word "change" is substituted for the words "reduce, limit, or modify". The words "which any person may undertake to perform" are omitted as surplusage.

Amendments:

1980. Act Dec. 12, 1980 (effective upon enactment on 12/12/80, as provided by § 701(b)(3) of such Act, which appears as 10 USCS § 101 note), in subsec. (a), substituted "the Military Selective Service Act (50 U.S.C. App. 451 et seq.)" for "sections 451–473 of title 50, appendix".

1994. Act Oct. 5, 1994 (effective 12/1/94 as provided by § 1691 of such Act, which appears as 10 USCS § 10001 note) transferred this section, enacted as 10 USCS § 512, to Chapter 1203 and redesignated it as 10 USCS § 12104.

CROSS REFERENCES

Active Duty agreements, 10 USCS §§ 12311, 12312.

§ 12105. Army Reserve and Air Force Reserve: transfer from Guard components

(a) Under such regulations as the Secretary concerned may prescribe—

(1) an enlisted member of the Army National Guard of the United States may be transferred in grade to the Army Reserve; and

(2) an enlisted member of the Air National Guard of the United States may be transferred in grade to the Air Force Reserve.

(b) Upon such a transfer, the member transferred is eligible for promotion to the highest regular or reserve grade ever held by him in the Army, if transferred under subsection (a)(1), or the Air Force, if transferred under subsection (a)(2), if his service has been honorable.

(c) A transfer under this section may only be made with the consent of the governor or other appropriate authority of the State concerned.

(Added Oct. 5, 1994, P. L. 103-337, Div A, Title XVI, Subtitle C, § 1662(b)(1), 108 Stat. 2988.)

HISTORY; ANCILLARY LAWS AND DIRECTIVES

Effective date of section:

This section took effect on Dec. 1, 1994, pursuant to Act Oct. 5, 1994, P. L. 103-337, Div A, Title XVI, Subtitle F, § 1691, 108 Stat. 3026, which appears as 10 USCS 10001 note.

CROSS REFERENCES

This section is referred to in 32 USCS § 323.

§ 12106. Army and Air Force Reserve: transfer to upon withdrawal as member of National Guard

(a) An enlisted member of the Army National Guard of the United States who ceases to be a member of the Army National Guard becomes a member of the Army Reserve unless he is also discharged from his enlistment as a Reserve.

(b) An enlisted member of the Air National Guard of the United States who ceases to be a member of the Air National Guard becomes a member of the Air Force Reserve unless he is also discharged from his enlistment as a Reserve.

(c) An enlisted member who becomes a member of the Army Reserve or the Air Force Reserve under this section ceases to be a member of the Army National Guard of the United States or the Air National Guard of the United States, as the case may be.

(Added Oct. 5, 1994, P. L. 103-337, Div A, Title XVI, Subtitle C, § 1662(b)(1), 108 Stat. 2989.)

HISTORY; ANCILLARY LAWS AND DIRECTIVES

Effective date of section:

This section took effect on Dec. 1, 1994, pursuant to Act Oct. 5, 1994, P. L. 103-337, Div A, Title XVI, Subtitle F, § 1691, 108 Stat. 3026, which appears as 10 USCS 10001 note.

§ 12107. Army National Guard of United States; Air National Guard of the United States: enlistment in

(a) Except as provided in subsection (c), to become an enlisted member of the Army National Guard of the United States or the Air National Guard of the United States, a person must—

(1) be enlisted in the Army National Guard or the Air National Guard, as the case may be;

(2) subscribe to the oath set forth in section 304 of title 32; and

(3) be a member of a federally recognized unit or organization of the Army National Guard or the Air National Guard, as the case may be, in the grade in which he is to be enlisted as a Reserve.

(b)(1) Under regulations to be prescribed by the Secretary of the Army, a person who enlists in the Army National Guard, or whose term of enlistment in the Army National Guard is extended, shall be concurrently enlisted, or his term of enlistment shall be concurrently extended, as the case may be, as a

Reserve of the Army for service in the Army National Guard of the United States.

(2) Under regulations to be prescribed by the Secretary of the Air Force, a person who enlists in the Air National Guard, or whose term of enlistment in the Air National Guard is extended, shall be concurrently enlisted, or his term of enlistment shall be concurrently extended, as the case may be, as a Reserve of the Air Force for service in the Air National Guard of the United States.

(c)(1) A member of the Army Reserve who enlists in the Army National Guard in his reserve grade, and is a member of a federally recognized unit or organization of the Army National Guard, becomes a member of the Army National Guard of the United States and ceases to be a member of the Army Reserve.

(2) A member of the Air Force Reserve who enlists in the Air National Guard in his reserve grade, and is a member of a federally recognized unit or organization of the Air National Guard, becomes a member of the Air National Guard of the United States and ceases to be a member of the Air Force Reserve.

(Added Oct. 5, 1994, P. L. 103-337, Div A, Title XVI, Subtitle C, § 1662(b)(1), 108 Stat. 2989.)

HISTORY; ANCILLARY LAWS AND DIRECTIVES

Effective date of section:

This section took effect on Dec. 1, 1994, pursuant to Act Oct. 5, 1994, P. L. 103-337, Div A, Title XVI, Subtitle F, § 1691, 108 Stat. 3026, which appears as 10 USCS 10001 note.

CROSS REFERENCES

This section is referred to in 10 USCS § 12102.

RESEARCH GUIDE

Annotations:

Enlistment or re-enlistment in branches of United States Armed Forces as protected by Federal Constitution or by federal statutes. 64 ALR Fed 489.

CHAPTER 1205. APPOINTMENT OF RESERVE OFFICERS

HISTORY; ANCILLARY LAWS AND DIRECTIVES

Amendments:

1994. Act Oct. 5, 1994, P. L. 103-337, Div A, Title XVI, Subtitle C, § 1662(c)(3), 108 Stat. 2990 (effective 12/1/94 as provided by § 1691 of such Act, which appears as 10 USCS § 10001 note) added the chapter heading and analysis.

1996. Act Feb. 10, 1996, P. L. 104-106, Div A, Title XV, § 1501(b)(11)(B), (13)(B), 110 Stat. 496 (effective as if included in Act Oct. 5, 1994, P. L. 103-337, as enacted on Oct. 5, 1994, as provided by § 1501(f)(3) of Act Feb. 10, 1996, which appears as 10 USCS § 113 note), amended the analysis of this chapter by substituting item 12201 for one which read: ''12201. Qualifications for appointment'' and by inserting ''the'' in items 12211, 12212, 12213, and 12214.

§ 12201. Reserve officers: qualifications for appointment

(a) To become an officer of a reserve component a person must be appointed as a Reserve of an armed force in a grade corresponding to a grade authorized for the regular component of the armed force concerned and subscribe to the oath prescribed by section 3331 of title 5. In addition, to become an officer of the Army National Guard of the United States or the Air National Guard of the United States, he must first be appointed to, and be federally recognized in, the same grade in the Army National Guard or the Air National Guard, as the case may be.

(b) Except as otherwise provided by law, the Secretary concerned shall prescribe physical, mental, moral, professional, and age qualifications for the appointment of persons as Reserves of the armed forces under his jurisdiction. However, no person may be appointed as a Reserve unless he is at least 18 years of age and—

(1) he is a citizen of the United States or has been lawfully admitted to the United States for permanent residence under the Immigration and Nationality Act (8 U.S.C. 1101 et seq.); or

(2) he has previously served in the armed forces or in the National Security Training Corps.

(c) A person who is otherwise qualified, but who has a physical defect that the Secretary concerned determines will not interfere with the performance of the duties to which that person may be assigned, may be appointed as a Reserve of any armed force under the jurisdiction of that Secretary.

(d) In prescribing age qualifications under subsection (b) for the appointment of persons as Reserves of the armed forces under his jurisdiction, the Secretary concerned may not prescribe a maximum age qualification of less than 47 years of age for the initial appointment of a person as a Reserve to serve in a health profession specialty which has been designated by the Secretary concerned as a specialty critically needed in wartime.

(Aug. 10, 1956, ch 1041, § 1, 70A Stat. 24; Sept. 2, 1958, P. L. 85-861, § 1(10)(A), 72 Stat. 1440; Dec. 23, 1963, P. L. 88-236, 77 Stat. 474; Nov. 2, 1966, P. L. 89-718, § 4, 80 Stat. 1115; Nov. 8, 1967, P. L. 90-130, § 1(3), 81 Stat. 374; Dec. 12, 1980, P. L. 96-513, Title V, Part B, § 511(16), 94 Stat. 2921; Dec. 4, 1987, P. L. 100-180, Div A, Title VII, Part A, § 718(a), 101 Stat. 1115; Oct. 5, 1994, P. L. 103-337, Div A, Title XVI, Subtitle B, Part I, § 1631(b), Subtitle C, § 1662(c)(2), 108 Stat. 2964, 2990; Feb. 10, 1996, P. L. 104-106, Div A, Title XV, § 1501(a)(5)(B), (b)(11)(A), 110 Stat. 495, 496.)

HISTORY; ANCILLARY LAWS AND DIRECTIVES

Prior law and revision:

1956 ACT

Revised Section	Source (USCS)	Source (Statutes at Large)
591(a)	50:946.	July 9, 1952, ch. 608, §§ 217 (less (c), and less applicability to enlist ments), 222, 232 (less applicability to enlistments), 66 Stat. 486, 487, 489.
591(b)	50:941(a) (less applicability to enlistments).	
591(c)	50:941(b) (less applicability to enlistments).	
591(d)	50:956 (less applicability to enlistments).	

In subsection (a), 50:946(a) (last 12 words of proviso) is omitted as covered by section 312 of title 32, 50:946(b) is omitted as covered by the revised subsection.

In subsection (b), the word "However" is substituted for the words "Subject to the limitation that". The exception as to section 4(i)(7) of the

Universal Military Training and Service Act is inserted for clarity. The words ''as Reserves of the armed forces under his jurisdiction'' are substituted for the words ''of Reserve members of the Armed Forces of the United States''. The words ''unless he is at least 18 years of age'' are substituted for 50:941(a) (last sentence). The words ''its Territories'' are omitted as surplusage, since citizens of the Territories are citizens of the United States.

In subsection (c), the words ''armed force concerned'' are substituted for the words ''of the appropriate Armed Force of the United States''. The words ''in the grades corresponding to the grades authorized for female officers of the'' are substituted for the words ''in the same grades . . . as are authorized for women in the'', to conform to subsection (a). The words ''in which she previously served satisfactorily'' are substituted for the words ''satisfactorily held by her''.

In subsection (d), the words ''under the jurisdiction of that Secretary'' are inserted for clarity. The words ''general or special'' are omitted as surplusage.

1958 ACT

Revised Section	Source (USCS)	Source (Statutes at Large)
591(c)	50:941(b).	July 30, 1956, ch. 789, § 4(a), 70 Stat. 729.

The words ''Subject to section 946(a) of this title'' are omitted, since that section is restated in subsection (a) of the revised section and is applicable to all reserve appointments. 50:941(b) (last 2 sentences) is omitted as covered by sections 510 and 591 of this title.

Amendments:

1958. Act Sept. 2, 1958, in subsec. (c), added ''Women who are otherwise qualified may be appointed as Reserves of the armed forces with a view to serving as nurses or medical specialists in the Army National Guard of the United States or the Air National Guard of the United States.''.

1963. Act Dec. 23, 1963, in subsec. (b)(1), substituted ''he is a citizen of the United States or has been lawfully admitted to the United States for permanent residence under chapter 12 of title 8'' for ''he is, or has made a declaration of intention to become, a citizen of the United States or of a possession thereof''.

1966. Act Nov. 2, 1966, in subsec. (a), substituted ''3331'' for ''16''.

1967. Act Nov. 8, 1967, in subsec. (c), deleted ''as nurses or medical specialists'', following ''Women who are otherwise qualified may be appointed as Reserves of the armed forces with a view to serving''.

1980. Act Dec. 12, 1980 (effective upon enactment, as provided by § 701(b)(3) of such Act, which appears as 10 USCS § 101 note), in subsec. (b), in the introductory matter, deleted ''except as provided in section 454(i)(7) of title 50, appendix,'' after ''However,'' and, in para, (1), substituted ''the Immigration and Nationality Act (8 U.S.C. 1101 et seq.)'' for ''chapter 12 of title 8''.

1987. Act Dec. 4, 1987 added subsec. (e).

1994. Act Oct. 5, 1994 (effective 12/1/94 as provided by § 1691 of such

Act, which appears as 10 USCS § 10001 note) transferred this section, enacted as 10 USCS § 591, to Chapter 1205 and redesignated it as 10 USCS § 12201.

Such Act further (effective 10/1/96, as provided by § 1691(b)(1) of such Act, which appears as 10 USCS § 10001 note), as amended Feb. 10, 1996 (effective as if included in Act Oct. 5, 1994, P. L. 103-337, as enacted on Oct. 5, 1994, as provided by § 1501(f)(3) of Act Feb. 10, 1996, which appears as 10 USCS § 113 note) deleted subsec. (c), which read: ''(c) Women may be appointed as Reserves of the armed forces for service in the Army Reserve, Naval Reserve, Air Force Reserve, Marine Corps Reserve, and Coast Guard Reserve. Women who are otherwise qualified may be appointed as Reserves of the armed forces with a view to serving in the Army National Guard of the United States or the Air National Guard of the United States. Women are appointed in grades corresponding to the grades authorized for female officers of the regular component of the armed force concerned. Any female former officer of an armed force may, if otherwise qualified, be appointed as a Reserve of that armed force in the highest grade in which she previously served satisfactorily on active duty (other than for training).''; and redesignated subsecs. (d) and (e) as subsecs. (c) and (d), respectively.

1996. Act Feb. 10, 1996 (effective as if included in Act Oct. 5, 1994, P. L. 103-337, as enacted on Oct. 5, 1994, as provided by § 1501(f)(3) of Act Feb. 10, 1996, which appears as 10 USCS § 113 note) substituted the section heading for one which read: ''§ 12201. Reserve components: qualifications''.

Such Act further (effective as if included in Act Oct. 5, 1994, P. L. 103-337, as enacted on Oct. 5, 1994, as provided by § 1501(f)(3) of Act Feb. 10, 1996, which appears as 10 USCS § 113 note) amended the directory language of § 1631(b) of Act Oct. 5, 1994.

Other provisions:

Deadline for regulations. Act Dec. 4, 1987, P. L. 100-180, Div A, Title VII, Part A, § 718(b), 101 Stat. 1115, provides: ''The Secretary concerned shall prescribe regulations implementing subsection (e) of section 591 of title 10, United States Code, as added by subsection (a), not later than 90 days after the date of the enactment of this Act.''.

Report on initial appointment of all officers as Reserve officers and on the appropriate active duty obligation of graduates of the service academies. Act Nov. 5, 1990, P. L. 101-510, Div A, Title V, Part B, § 524, 104 Stat. 1562, provides:

''(a) Report required. The Secretary of Defense shall submit to the Committees on Armed Services of the Senate and House of Representatives a report on—

''(1) the advantages, disadvantages, and desirability of initially appointing all persons commissioned as officers in the Army, Navy, Air Force, or Marine Corps as Reserve officers, and

''(2) what the appropriate active duty service obligation should be for graduates of the service academies.

''(b) Deadline for report. (1) The Secretary shall submit the report required by subsection (a), together with such comments and recommendations as the Secretary considers appropriate, not later than 60 days after the date of the enactment of this Act.

"(2) If the report is not submitted within 60 days after the date of the enactment of this Act, then—

"(A) all persons initially appointed as commissioned officers in the Army, Navy, Air Force, and Marine Corps after the 60th day following the date of the enactment of this Act shall be appointed as commissioned officers in a Reserve component of the Armed Forces; and

"(B) all persons entering the service academies after the 60th day following the date of the enactment of this Act shall incur an obligation to serve on active duty for a period of five years.

"(c) Service academy defined. For purposes of this section, the term 'service academies' means the United States Military Academy, the United States Naval Academy, and the United States Air Force Academy.".

Repeal of provision requiring baccalaureate degree for certain appointments or promotions of reserve officers. Act Dec. 5, 1991, P. L. 102-190, Div A, Title V, Part C, § 523, 105 Stat. 1363, which formerly appeared as a note to this section, was repealed by Act May 31, 1993, P. L. 103-35, Title II, § 203(a), 107 Stat. 102. Such section required a baccalaureate degree for appointment or promotion of reserve officers to grades above first lieutenant or lieutenant (junior grade).

Priority in making original appointments in guard and reserve components for ROTC scholarship program graduates. Act Dec. 5, 1991, P. L. 102-190, Title V, Part C, § 524, 105 Stat. 1363, provides: "In making appointments of persons as second lieutenants in the Army Reserve, Air Force Reserve, or Marine Corps Reserve or to the grade of ensign in the Naval Reserve, or in granting federal recognition in the grade of second lieutenant to members of the Army National Guard or Air National Guard, the Secretary of the military department concerned shall give preference to persons who have completed a post-secondary program of education pursued under a ROTC scholarship program at a college or university accredited to award baccalaureate degrees or pursued under a ROTC scholarship program at an accredited two-year or four-year military college.".

CROSS REFERENCES

National Guard, Federal recognition of commissioned officers, 32 USCS §§ 305 et seq.

This section is referred to in 10 USCS §§ 591, 2130a.

INTERPRETIVE NOTES AND DECISIONS

As to question of physical qualification for commissioned officers of Naval Reserve, specific authority in 10 USCS §§ 591 [12201] and 5579 must take precedence over general guidelines of 29 USCS § 794 prohibiting discrimination against otherwise qualified handicapped individual under any federally assisted program or any activity conducted by Executive agency solely by reason of handicap. Smith v Christian (1985, CA11 Fla) 763 F2d 1322, 1 AD Cas 756, 38 BNA FEP Cas 545, 38 CCH EPD ¶ 35669.

Rehabilitation Act (29 USCS § 794) does not apply to uniformed military personnel; it would be incongruous to allow uniformed military personnel to bring discrimination claims against military based on handicapped, when statutory claims based on sex, race, religion, or national origin are barred. Doe v Garrett (1990, CA11 Fla) 903 F2d 1455, 1 AD Cas 1606, 53 BNA FEP Cas 335, 54 CCH EPD ¶ 40053, cert den (1991) 499 US 904, 113 L Ed 2d 213, 111 S Ct 1102, 2 AD Cas 214, 55 BNA FEP Cas 144, 55 CCH EPD ¶ 40570.

Rehabilitation Act (29 USCS § 794) does not apply to military commissioning programs. Smith v United States Navy (1983, SD Fla) 573 F Supp 1361, 38 BNA FEP Cas 540, 39 CCH EPD ¶ 36056, affd (1985, CA11 Fla) 763 F2d 1322, 1 AD Cas 756, 38 BNA FEP Cas 545, 38 CCH EPD P 35669.

§ 12202. Commissioned officer grades

Except for commissioned warrant officers, the reserve commissioned officer grades in each armed force are those authorized for regular commissioned officers of that armed force.

(Added Sept. 2, 1958, P. L. 85-861, § 1(10)(B), 72 Stat. 1440; Oct. 5, 1994, P. L. 103-337, Div A, Title XVI, Subtitle C, § 1662(c)(2), 108 Stat. 2990.)

HISTORY; ANCILLARY LAWS AND DIRECTIVES

Prior law and revision:

Revised Section	Source (USCS)	Source (Statutes at Large)
592	50:1181(1) (as applicable to 50:1201). 50:1201.	Sept. 3, 1954, ch. 1257, §§ 102(1) (as applicable to § 211), 68 Stat. 1149, 1153.

The words ''including those heretofore or hereafter transferred to the Retired Reserve'', ''permanent'', and ''pursuant to the Officer Personnel Act of 1947, as amended'' are omitted as surplusage. The rule as to the Coast Guard is consolidated with the rule applicable to the other armed forces, since 14:754 prescribes the same substantive result as that prescribed by 50:1201 for the other armed forces.

Amendments:

1994. Act Oct. 5, 1994 (effective 12/1/94 as provided by § 1691 of such Act, which appears as 10 USCS § 10001 note) transferred this section, enacted as 10 USCS § 592, to Chapter 1205 and redesignated it as 10 USCS § 12202.

§ 12203. Commissioned officers: appointment, how made; term

(a) Appointments of reserve officers in commissioned grades of lieutenant colonel and commander or below, except commissioned warrant officer, shall be made by the President alone. Appointments of reserve officers in commissioned grades above lieutenant colonel and commander shall be made by the President, by and with the advice and consent of the Senate, except as provided in section 624, 12213, or 12214 of this title.

(b) Appointments of Reserves in commissioned grades are for an indefinite term and are held during the pleasure of the President.

(Aug. 10, 1956, ch 1041, § 1, 70A Stat. 25; Sept. 2, 1958, P. L. 85-861, § 1(10)(C), 72 Stat. 1440; Sept. 28, 1971, P. L. 92-129, Title VI, § 601, 85 Stat. 361; Dec. 12, 1980, P. L. 96-513, Title V, Part A, § 501(7), 94 Stat. 2907; Oct. 5, 1994, P. L. 103-337, Div A, Title XVI, Subtitle B, Part I, § 1632, Subtitle C, § 1662(c)(2), Subtitle D, § 1675(b)(1), 108 Stat. 2965, 2990, 3017; Feb. 10, 1996, P. L. 104-106, Div A, Title XV, § 1501(a)(6), 110 Stat. 495.)

HISTORY; ANCILLARY LAWS AND DIRECTIVES

Prior law and revision:

1956 ACT

Revised Section	Source (USCS)	Source (Statutes at Large)
593(a)	50:942. 50:943.	July 1952, ch. 608, §§ 218, 219, 221, 224 (less 3d and 4th sentences, as appli cable to commissioned officers), 66 Stat. 487.
593(b)	50:945. 50:948 (less 3d and 4th sentences, as applicable to commissioned officers).	

In subsection (a), the word "alone" is inserted for clarity. The exception as to commissioned warrant officers is inserted to reflect section 597 of this title, since reserve chief warrant officers of the Navy, Marine Corps, and Coast Guard are appointed by commission by the Secretary concerned.
In subsection (b), 50:948 (2d and last sentences) is omitted as executed.

1958 ACT

Revised Section	Source (USCS)	Source (Statutes at Large)
593(a)	[No source].	[No source].

The exception is inserted to reflect section 3352(b) of title 10, United States Code.

Amendments:

1958. Act Sept. 2, 1958, in subsec. (a), inserted ", except as provided in section 3352 of this title".

1971. Act Sept. 28, 1971, substituted subsec. (a) for one which read: "(a) Appointments of Reserves in commissioned grades below general officer and flag officer, except commissioned warrant officer, shall be made by the President alone. Appointments of Reserves as general and flag officers shall be made by the President, by and with the advice and consent of the Senate, except as provided in section 3352 of this title.".

1980. Act Dec. 12, 1980 (effective 9/15/81, as provided by § 701(a) of such Act, which appears as 10 USCS § 101 note), in subsec. (a), substituted "624, 3352, or 8352" for " 3352 or 8352".

1994. Act Oct. 5, 1994 (effective 12/1/94 as provided by § 1691 of such Act, which appears as 10 USCS § 10001 note) transferred this section, enacted as 10 USCS § 593, to Chapter 1205 and redesignated it as 10 USCS § 12203; and, in subsec. (a), substituted "12213, or 12214" for "3352, or 8352".

Such Act further (effective 10/1/96, as provided by § 1691(b)(1) of such Act, which appears as 10 USCS § 10001 note), as amended Feb. 10, 1996 (effective as if included in Act Oct. 5, 1994, P. L. 103-337, as enacted on Oct. 5, 1994, as provided by § 1501(f)(3) of Act Feb. 10, 1996, which appears as 10 USCS § 113 note), in subsec. (a), substituted "reserve officers in commissioned grades of lieutenant colonel and commander or below" for "Reserves in commissioned grades below lieutenant colonel and commander" and substituted "reserve officers in commissioned grades above lieutenant colonel and commander'' for ''Reserves in commissioned grades above major and lieutenant commander''.

1996. Act Feb. 10, 1996 (effective as if included in Act Oct. 5, 1994, P. L. 103-337, as enacted on Oct. 5, 1994, as provided by § 1501(f)(3) of Act Feb. 10, 1996, which appears as 10 USCS § 113 note) amended the directory language of § 1632 of Act Oct. 5, 1994.

Other provisions:

Indefinite appointments for certain reserve officers. Act Aug. 10, 1956, ch 1041, § 41, 70A Stat. 636, provided: ''Each person who was a reserve officer on July 9, 1952, and who did not hold an appointment for an indefinite term on that date, shall be given an appointment for an indefinite term in place of the appointment he then held, if after written notification by competent authority before July 2, 1953, the officer agrees in writing to have that appointment continued for an indefinite term. In the event such officer does not agree in writing, the term of his current appointment shall not be changed by this section.''.

CROSS REFERENCES

Reserve warrant officer, appointment, 10 USCS § 12241.

Coast Guard Reserve officers, appointment as prescribed in this section, 14 USCS § 271.

This section is referred to in 10 USCS §§ 12213, 14308; 14 USCS § 271.

INTERPRETIVE NOTES AND DECISIONS

10 USCS § 593 (now § 12203) should be read together with eligibility requirements for promotion of Title 10 and such requirements must be met before promotion is considered valid; word ''alone'' used in 10 USCS § 593 (now § 12203) does not mean that President can establish his own criteria for appointments and appoint anyone regardless of qualifications. Jamerson v United States (1968) 185 Ct Cl 471, 401 F2d 808.

Action of Air Force in imposing three-year service commitment upon career reserve officer as result of his involuntary attendance at pilot instruction training course was not arbitrary, capricious, or unreasonable. De Long v Davis (1966, WD Tex) 261 F Supp 860.

Rehabilitation Act (29 USCS § 794) does not apply to military commissioning programs. Smith v United States Navy (1983, SD Fla) 573 F Supp 1361, 38 BNA FEP Cas 540, 39 CCH EPD ¶ 36056, affd (1985, CA11 Fla) 763 F2d 1322, 1 AD Cas 756, 38 BNA FEP Cas 545, 38 CCH EPD P 35669.

§ 12204. Commissioned officers: original appointment; limitation

(a) No person may be appointed as a Reserve in a commissioned grade above major or lieutenant commander, unless—

(1) he was formerly a commissioned officer of an armed force; or

(2) such an appointment is recommended by a board of officers convened by the Secretary concerned.

(b) This section does not apply to adjutants general and assistant adjutants general of the several States and Territories, Puerto Rico, and the District of Columbia.

(Aug. 10, 1956, ch 1041, § 1, 70A Stat. 25; Sept. 29, 1988, P. L. 100-456, Div A, Title XII, Part D, § 1234(a)(1), 102 Stat. 2059; Oct. 5, 1994, P. L. 103-337, Div A, Title XVI, Subtitle C, § 1662(c)(2), 108 Stat. 2990.)

HISTORY; ANCILLARY LAWS AND DIRECTIVES

Prior law and revision:

Revised Section	Source (USCS)	Source (Statutes at Large)
594(a)	50:941(c) (less 1st 21 words).	July 9, 1952, ch. 608, § 217(c), 66 Stat. 487.
594(b)	50:941(c) (1st 21 words).	

In subsection (a), the words "unless . . . he was formerly" are substituted for the words "has not held an appointment as". The words "or any component thereof" are omitted as surplusage.

Amendments:

1988. Act Sept. 29, 1988, in subsec. (b), deleted "the Canal Zone," following "Puerto Rico,".

1994. Act Oct. 5, 1994 (effective 12/1/94 as provided by § 1691 of such Act, which appears as 10 USCS § 10001 note) transferred this section, enacted as 10 USCS § 594, to Chapter 1205 and redesignated it as 10 USCS § 12204.

CROSS REFERENCES

Adjutants general, 32 USCS § 314.

§ 12205. Commissioned officers: appointment; educational requirement

(a) In general. No person may be appointed to a grade above the grade of first lieutenant in the Army Reserve, Air Force Reserve, or Marine Corps Reserve or to a grade above the grade of lieutenant (junior grade) in the Naval Reserve, or be federally recognized in a grade above the grade of first lieutenant as a member of the Army National Guard or Air National Guard, unless that person has been awarded a baccalaureate degree by a qualifying educational institution.

(b) Exceptions. Subsection (a) does not apply to the following:

(1) The appointment to or recognition in a higher grade of a person who is appointed in or assigned for service in a health profession for which a baccalaureate degree is not a condition of original appointment or assignment.

(2) The appointment in the Naval Reserve or Marine Corps Reserve of a person appointed for service as an officer designated as a limited duty officer.

(3) The appointment in the Naval Reserve of a person appointed for service under the Naval Aviation Cadet (NAVCAD) program or the Seaman to Admiral program.

(4) The appointment to or recognition in a higher grade of any person who was appointed to, or federally recognized in, the grade of captain or, in the case of the Navy, lieutenant before October 1, 1995.

(5) Recognition in the grade of captain or major in the Alaska Army National Guard of a person who resides permanently at a location in Alaska that is

more than 50 miles from each of the cities of Anchorage, Fairbanks, and Juneau, Alaska, by paved road and who is serving in a Scout unit or a Scout supporting unit.

(c) Qualifying educational institutions. (1) A qualifying educational institution for purposes of this section is an educational institution that is accredited or that meets the requirements of paragraph (2).

(2)(A) An unaccredited educational institution shall be considered to be a qualifying educational institution for purposes of the appointment or recognition of a person who is a graduate of that institution if the Secretary concerned determines that (as of the year of the graduation of that person from that institution) at least three educational institutions that are accredited and that maintain Reserve Officers' Training Corps programs each generally grant baccalaureate degree credit for completion of courses of the unaccredited institution equivalent to the baccalaureate degree credit granted by the unaccredited institution for the completion of those courses.

(B) In order to assist the Secretary concerned in making determinations under subparagraph (A), any unaccredited institution that seeks to be considered to be a qualifying educational institution for purposes of this paragraph shall submit to the Secretary of Defense each year such information as the Secretary may require concerning the program of instruction at that institution.

(C) In the case of a person with a degree from an unaccredited institution that is a qualifying educational institution under this paragraph, the degree may not have been awarded more than eight years before the date on which the person is to be appointed to, or recognized in, the grade of captain or, in the case of the Naval Reserve, lieutenant, in order for that person to be considered for purposes of subsection (a) to have been awarded a baccalaureate degree by a qualifying educational institution.

(Added Oct. 23, 1992, P. L. 102-484, Div A, Title V, Subtitle B, § 515(a), 106 Stat. 2406; Oct. 5, 1994, P. L. 103-337, Div A, Title V, Subtitle B, §§ 519, 520, Title XVI, Subtitle C, § 1662(c)(2), 108 Stat. 2755, 2990; Sept. 23, 1996, P. L. 104-201, Div A, Title V, Subtitle A, §§ 504, 505, Title X, Subtile F, § 1074(a)(22), 110 Stat. 2512, 2660.)

HISTORY; ANCILLARY LAWS AND DIRECTIVES

Amendments:

1994. Act Oct. 5, 1994, in subsec. (a), substituted ''a qualifying educational institution'' for ''an accredited educational institution''; in subsec. (b), in paras. (2) and (3), substituted ''a person'' for ''an individual'', and added para. (5); and added subsec. (c).

Such Act further (effective 12/1/94 as provided by § 1691 of such Act, which appears as 10 USCS § 10001 note) transferred this section, enacted as 10 USCS § 596, to Chapter 1205 and redesignated it as 10 USCS § 12205.

1996. Act Sept. 23, 1996, in subsec. (a), substituted ''No person'' for ''After September 30, 1995, no person''; in subsec. (b)(3), inserted ''or the Seaman to Admiral program''; and, in subsec. (c)(2)(C), substituted ''eight years'' for ''three years''.

CODE OF FEDERAL REGULATIONS

Office of the Secretary of Defense—Educational requirements for appointment of reserve component officers to a grade above First Lieutenant or Lieutenant (Junior Grade), 32 CFR Part 67.

§ 12206. Commissioned officers: appointment of former commissioned officers

Under regulations prescribed by the Secretary of Defense, a person who is a former commissioned officer may, if otherwise qualified, be appointed as a reserve officer of the Army, Navy, Air Force, or Marine Corps. A person so appointed—

(1) may be placed on the reserve active-status list of that armed force in the grade equivalent to the permanent regular or reserve grade, and in the same competitive category, in which the person previously served satisfactorily on active duty or in an active status; and

(2) may be credited for the purpose of determining date of rank under section 741(d) of this title with service in grade equal to that held by that person when discharged or separated.

(Added and amended Oct. 5, 1994, P. L. 103-337, Div A, Title XVI, Subtitle B, Part I, § 1633, Subtitle C, § 1662(c)(2), 108 Stat. 2965, 2990.)

HISTORY; ANCILLARY LAWS AND DIRECTIVES

Effective date of section:

This section became effective on Oct. 1, 1996, as provided by Act Oct. 5, 1994, P. L. 103-337, Div A, Title XVI, Subtitle F, § 1691(b)(1), 108 Stat. 3026, which appears as 10 USCS 10001 note.

Amendments:

1994. Act Oct. 5, 1994 (effective 12/1/94 as provided by § 1691 of such Act, which appears as 10 USCS § 10001 note) transferred this section, enacted as 10 USCS § 596a, to Chapter 1205 and redesignated it as 10 USCS § 12206.

§ 12207. Commissioned officers: service credit upon original appointment

(a)(1) For the purpose of determining the grade and the rank within grade of a person receiving an original appointment as a reserve commissioned officer (other than a commissioned warrant officer) in the Army, Navy, Air Force, or Marine Corps, the person shall be credited at the time of the appointment with any commissioned service (other than service as a commissioned warrant officer) performed before such appointment as a regular officer, or as a reserve officer in an active status, in any armed force, the National Oceanic and Atmospheric Administration, or the Public Health Service.

(2) The Secretary of Defense shall prescribe regulations, which shall apply uniformly among the Army, Navy, Air Force, and Marine Corps, to authorize the Secretary of the military department concerned to limit the amount of prior commissioned service with which a person receiving an original ap-

pointment may be credited under paragraph (1), or to deny any such credit, in the case of a person who at the time of such appointment is credited with constructive service under subsection (b).

(b)(1) Under regulations prescribed by the Secretary of Defense, a person who is receiving an original appointment as a reserve commissioned officer (other than a commissioned warrant officer) of the Army, Navy, Air Force, or Marine Corps, or a designation in, or an assignment to, an officer category in which advanced education or training is required and who has advanced education or training, shall be credited with constructive service for such education, training, or experience, as follows:

(A) One year for each year of advanced education beyond the baccalaureate degree level, for persons appointed or designated in, or assigned to, officer categories requiring such advanced education or an advanced degree as a prerequisite for such appointment, designation, or assignment. In determining the number of years of constructive service to be credited under this subparagraph to officers in any professional field, the Secretary concerned shall credit an officer with, but with not more than, the number of years of advanced education required by a majority of institutions that award degrees in that professional field for completion of the advanced education or award of the advanced degree.

(B)(i) Credit for any period of advanced education in a health profession (other than medicine and dentistry) beyond the baccalaureate degree level which exceeds the basic education criteria for such appointment, designation, or assignment, if such advanced education will be directly used by the armed force concerned.

(ii) Credit for experience in a health profession (other than medicine or dentistry), if such experience will be directly used by the armed force concerned.

(C) Additional credit of (i) not more than one year for internship or equivalent graduate medical, dental, or other formal health professional training required by the armed forces, and (ii) not more than one year for each additional year of such graduate-level training or experience creditable toward certification in a speciality required by the armed force concerned.

(D) Additional credit, in unusual cases, based on special experience in a particular field.

(E) Additional credit for experience as a physician or dentist, if appointed, assigned, or designated as a medical or dental officer.

(2) If the Secretary of Defense determines that the number of medical or dental officers serving in an active status in a reserve component of the Army, Navy, or Air Force in grades below major or lieutenant commander is critically below the number needed by such reserve component in such grades, the Secretary of Defense may authorize the Secretary of the military department concerned to credit any person who is receiving an original appointment for service as a medical or dental officer with a period of constructive credit in such amount (in addition to any amount credited such person under subsection (b)) as will result in the grade of such person being that of captain or, in the case of the Naval Reserve, lieutenant.

(3) Except as authorized by the Secretary concerned in individual cases and under regulations prescribed by the Secretary of Defense in the case of a medical or dental officer, the amount of constructive service credited an officer under this subsection may not exceed the amount required in order for the officer to be eligible for an original appointment as a reserve officer of the Army, Air Force, or Marine Corps in the grade of major or as a reserve officer of the Navy in the grade of lieutenant commander.

(4) Constructive service credited an officer under this subsection is in addition to any service credited that officer under subsection (a) and shall be credited at the time of the original appointment of the officer or assignment to or designation in an officer category in which advanced education or training or special experience is required.

(c) Constructive service may not be credited under subsection (b) for education, training, or experience obtained while serving as a commissioned officer (other than a warrant officer) on active duty or in an active status. However, in the case of an officer who completes advanced education or receives an advanced degree while on active duty or in an active status and in less than the number of years normally required to complete such advanced education or receive such advanced degree, constructive service may, subject to regulations prescribed under subsection (a)(2), be credited to the officer under subsection (b)(1)(A) to the extent that the number of years normally required to complete such advanced education or receive such advanced degree exceeds the actual number of years in which such advanced education or degree is obtained by the officer.

(d) If the Secretary of Defense determines that the number of qualified judge advocates serving on the active-duty list of the Army, Navy, Air Force, or Marine Corps in grades below lieutenant commander or major is critically below the number needed by that armed force in those grades, the Secretary of Defense may authorize the Secretary of the military department concerned to credit any person who is receiving an original appointment with a view to assignment to the Judge Advocate General's Corps of the Army or appointment to the Judge Advocate General's Corps of the Navy, or who is receiving an original appointment in the Air Force or Marine Corps with a view to designation as a judge advocate, with a period of constructive service in such an amount (in addition to any amount credited such person under subsection (b)) as will result in the grade of such person being that of captain or, in the case of the Navy, lieutenant, and the date of rank of such person being junior to that of all other officers of the same grade serving on the active-duty list.

(e) Constructive service credited an officer under subsection (b) or (d) shall be used only for determining the officer's—

(1) initial grade as a reserve officer;

(2) rank in grade; and

(3) service in grade for promotion eligibility.

(f) The grade and position on the reserve active-status list of a person receiving an appointment as a reserve officer who at the time of appointment is credited with service under this section shall be determined under regulations prescribed by the Secretary of Defense based upon the amount of service credited.

(Added and amended Oct. 5, 1994, P. L. 103-337, Div A, Title XVI, Subtitle B, Part I, § 1634, Subtitle C, § 1662(c)(2), 108 Stat. 2965, 2990.)

HISTORY; ANCILLARY LAWS AND DIRECTIVES

Effective date of section:

This section became effective on Oct. 1, 1996, as provided by Act Oct. 5, 1994, P. L. 103-337, Div A, Title XVI, Subtitle F, § 1691(b)(1), 108 Stat. 3026, which appears as 10 USCS 10001 note.

Amendments:

1994. Act Oct. 5, 1994 (effective 12/1/94 as provided by § 1691 of such Act, which appears as 10 USCS § 10001 note) transferred this section, enacted as 10 USCS § 596b, to Chapter 1205 and redesignated it as 10 USCS § 12207.

CROSS REFERENCES

Commissioned officers in Navy and Marine Corps, 10 USCS § 5600.

This section is referred to in 10 USCS §§ 2121, 12102, 12320.

§ 12208. Officers: appointment upon transfer

(a) A person who would otherwise be required to be transferred to a reserve component under section 651 of this title or under the Military Selective Service Act (50 U.S.C. App. 451 et seq.), is entitled, if he is qualified and accepted, to be appointed as an officer of any armed force that he chooses and to participate in the programs authorized for that armed force. However, unless the two Secretaries concerned consent, he may not be appointed as a Reserve of an armed force other than that from which he is transferred. All periods of his participation shall be credited against the total period of service required of him under section 651 of this title or under the Military Selective Service Act (50 U.S.C. App. 451 et seq.). However, no period may be credited more than once.

(b) A person covered by subsection (a) shall perform the rest of his required term of service in the armed force in which he is so appointed or in any other armed force in which he is later appointed or enlisted.

(c) This section does not change any term of service under an appointment, enlistment, or agreement, including an agreement made before or at the time when the member entered upon a program authorized by an armed force.

(Aug. 10, 1956, ch 1041, § 1, 70A Stat. 25; Dec 12, 1980, P. L. 96-513, Title V, Part B, § 511(17), 94 Stat. 2921; Oct. 5, 1994, P. L. 103-337, Div A, Title XVI, Subtitle C, § 1662(c)(2), 108 Stat. 2990.)

HISTORY; ANCILLARY LAWS AND DIRECTIVES

Prior law and revision:

Revised Section	Source (USCS)	Source (Statutes at Large)
595(a)	50:929(a) (less 2d sentence, less applicability to enlistments).	July 9, 1952, ch. 608, § 209 (less applicability to enlistments), 66 Stat. 484.
595(b)	50:929(a) (2d sentence, and less applicability to enlistments).	
595(c)	50:929(b) (less applicability to enlistments).	

In subsection (a), the words ''is entitled . . . to be appointed as an officer of any armed force that he chooses'' are substituted for the words ''shall be permitted to . . . accept an appointment in such armed force of the United States as he may elect''. The last sentence is substituted for 50:929(a) (words within parentheses). The words ''of an armed force of the United States'' are omitted as surplusage.

In subsection (b), the word ''rest'' is substituted for the words ''remaining period''. The words ''be required to'' are omitted as surplusage.

In subsection (c), the words ''This section does not'' are substituted for the words ''Nothing in this section shall be construed''. The word ''change'' is substituted for the words ''reduce, limit, or modify''. The words ''which any person may undertake to perform'' are omitted as surplusage.

Amendments:

1980. Act Dec. 12, 1980 (effective upon enactment as provided by § 701(b)(3) of such Act, which appears as 10 USCS § 101 note), in subsec. (a), substituted ''the Military Selective Service Act (50 U.S.C. App. 451 et seq.)'' for ''sections 451–473 of title 50, appendix'' in two places.

1994. Act Oct. 5, 1994 (effective 12/1/94 as provided by § 1691 of such Act, which appears as 10 USCS § 10001 note) transferred this section, enacted as 10 USCS § 595, to Chapter 1205 and redesignated it as 10 USCS § 12208.

CROSS REFERENCES

Active duty agreements, 10 USCS §§ 12311, 12312.

§ 12209. Officer candidates: enlisted Reserves

(a) Within such numbers as the Secretary concerned may prescribe, enlisted Reserves may, with their consent, be selected for training as officer candidates. Enlisted Reserves so selected shall be designated as officer candidates during that training. However, no member of the Army National Guard of the United States or the Air National Guard of the United States may be so selected or designated unless—

(1) he is on active duty; or

(2) the governor or other appropriate authority of the jurisdiction concerned consents.

(b) The enlistment or term of service of a Reserve who is designated as an officer candidate under this section is extended to include any period, beyond its normal expiration date, during which he is an officer candidate.

(c) While he is on active duty, other than active duty for training without pay, or performing authorized travel to and from that duty, an officer candidate designated under this section is entitled to the pay and allowances of his enlisted grade, but not less than those prescribed for pay grade E-2.

(d) An officer candidate designated under this section may not participate in the program of a reserve officer training corps of any armed force.

(Aug. 10, 1956, ch 1041, § 1, 70A Stat. 26; Oct. 5, 1994, P. L. 103-337, Div A, Title XVI, Subtitle C, § 1662(c)(3), 108 Stat. 2990; Feb. 10, 1996, P. L. 104-106, Div A, Title XV, § 1501(b)(12)(A), 110 Stat. 496.)

HISTORY; ANCILLARY LAWS AND DIRECTIVES

Prior law and revision:

Revised Section	Source (USCS)	Source (Statutes at Large)
600(a)	50:935(a).	July 9, 1952, ch. 608,
600(b)	50:954(a).	§§ 215(a), 230, 242, 66
600(c)	50:973.	Stat. 486, 489, 491.
600(d)	50:954(b).	

In subsection (a), the words "who is not in active Federal service" are substituted for the words "when not in the active military service of the United States". The word "during" is substituted for the words "for the period of".

In subsection (c), the words "active duty other than active duty for training without pay" are substituted for the words "active duty or active duty for training with pay". The words "enlisted members of the reserve components designated as", "enlisted", and "under the Career Compensation Act of 1949, as amended" are omitted as surplusage.

Amendments:

1994. Act Oct. 5, 1994 (effective 12/1/94 as provided by § 1691 of such Act, which appears as 10 USCS § 10001 note) transferred this section, enacted as 10 USCS § 600, to Chapter 1205 and redesignated it as 10 USCS § 12209.

1996. Act Feb. 10, 1996 (effective as if included in Act Oct. 5, 1994, P. L. 103-337, as enacted on Oct. 5, 1994, as provided by § 1501(f)(3) of Act Feb. 10, 1996, which appears as 10 USCS § 113 note) substituted the section heading for one which read: "§ 12209. Officer candidates".

CROSS REFERENCES

Basic pay and allowances, 37 USCS §§ 203, 402.

This section is referred to in 14 USCS § 705.

§ 12210. Attending Physician to the Congress: reserve grade while so serving

While serving as Attending Physician to the Congress, a Reserve who holds a reserve grade lower than major general or rear admiral shall hold the reserve grade of major general or rear admiral, as appropriate, if appointed to that grade by the President, by and with the advice and consent of the Senate.

(Added Nov. 14, 1986, P. L. 99-661, Div A, Title V, Part A, § 508(d)(1)(A), 100 Stat. 3867; Oct. 5, 1994, P. L. 103-337, Div A, Title XVI, Subtitle C, § 1662(c)(3), 108 Stat. 2990; Feb. 10, 1996, P. L. 104-106, Div A, Title XV, § 1501(b)(12)(B), 110 Stat. 496.)

HISTORY; ANCILLARY LAWS AND DIRECTIVES

Amendments:

1994. Act Oct. 5, 1994 (effective 12/1/94 as provided by § 1691 of such Act, which appears as 10 USCS § 10001 note) transferred this section, enacted as 10 USCS § 600a, to Chapter 1205 and redesignated it as 10 USCS § 12210.

1996. Act Feb. 10, 1996 (effective as if included in Act Oct. 5, 1994, P. L. 103-337, as enacted on Oct. 5, 1994, as provided by § 1501(f)(3) of Act Feb. 10, 1996, which appears as 10 USCS § 113 note) substituted the section heading for one which read: "§ 12210. Attending Physician to the Congress".

Other provisions:

Application of Nov. 14, 1986 amendments. Act Nov. 14, 1986, P. L. 99-661, Div A, Title V, Part A, § 508(f), 100 Stat. 3868, provides: "The amendments made by this section [adding this section, among other things; for full classification, consult USCS Tables volumes] shall apply only with respect to appointments or details made on or after the date of the enactment of this Act."

§ 12211. Officers: Army National Guard of the United States

(a) Upon being federally recognized, an officer of the Army National Guard shall be appointed as a Reserve for service as a member of the Army National Guard of the United States in the grade that he holds in the Army National Guard. However, an officer of the Army Reserve who is federally recognized as an officer of the Army National Guard becomes an officer of the Army National Guard of the United States and ceases to be an officer of the Army Reserve. The acceptance of an appointment as a Reserve for service as a member of the Army National Guard of the United States by an officer of the Army National Guard does not vacate his office in the Army National Guard.

(b) When an officer of the Army National Guard to whom temporary Federal recognition has been extended is appointed as a Reserve for service as a member of the Army National Guard of the United States, his appointment shall bear the date of the temporary recognition and shall be considered to have been accepted and effective on that date.

(c) When the Army National Guard of the United States is ordered to active duty, any officer of the Army National Guard who is not a Reserve of the Army may be appointed by the President as a Reserve for service as a member of the Army National Guard of the United States in the grade that he holds in the Army National Guard.

(Aug. 10, 1956, ch 1041, § 1, 70A Stat. 193; Oct. 5, 1994, P. L. 103-337, Div A, Title XVI, Subtitle C, § 1662(c)(3), 108 Stat. 2990; Feb. 10, 1996, P. L. 104-106, Div A, Title XV, § 1501(b)(13)(A), 110 Stat. 496.)

HISTORY; ANCILLARY LAWS AND DIRECTIVES

Prior law and revision:

Revised Section	Source (USCS)	Source (Statutes at Large)
3351(a)	50:1113 (less (a)). 50:1115(a) (last 39 words).	July 9, 1952, ch. 608, §§ 703 (less (a)), 704 (2d sentence), 705(a) (last 39 words), 713 (less (a)), 66 Stat. 502, 504.
3351(b)	50:1114 (2d sentence).	
3351(c)	50:1123 (less (a)).	

In subsection (a), the words "as a Reserve" are substituted for the words "as Reserve officers of the appropriate Armed Force of the United States" and "as a Reserve officer of the Armed Force of the United States concerned", in 50:1113(b). The words "federally recognized appointments" and "in the same grade and branch", in 50:1113(b), are omitted as surplusage. The words "those officers who do not hold appointments as Reserve officers of the appropriate Armed Force of the United States", in 50:1113(b), are omitted as covered by the second sentence of the revised subsection.

In subsection (c), the words "active duty" are substituted for the words "active military service of the United States". The words "and branch" are omitted as surplusage. The words "of the Army National Guard of the United States" are inserted for clarity.

Amendments:

1994. Act Oct. 5, 1994 (effective 12/1/94 as provided by § 1691 of such Act, which appears as 10 USCS § 10001 note) transferred this section, enacted as 10 USCS § 3351, to Chapter 1205 and redesignated it as 10 USCS § 12211.

1996. Act Feb. 10, 1996 (effective as if included in Act Oct. 5, 1994, P. L. 103-337, as enacted on Oct. 5, 1994, as provided by § 1501(f)(3) of Act Feb. 10, 1996, which appears as 10 USCS § 113 note), in the section heading, inserted "the".

§ 12212. Officers: Air National Guard of the United States

(a) Upon being federally recognized, an officer of the Air National Guard shall be appointed as a Reserve for service as a member of the Air National Guard of the United States in the grade that he holds in the Air National Guard. However, an officer of the Air Force Reserve who is federally recognized as an officer of the Air National Guard becomes an officer of the Air National Guard of the United States and ceases to be an officer of the Air Force Reserve. The acceptance of an appointment as a Reserve for service as a member of the Air National Guard of the United States by an officer of the Air National Guard does not vacate his office in the Air National Guard.

(b) When an officer of the Air National Guard to whom temporary Federal recognition has been extended is appointed as a Reserve for service as a member of the Air National Guard of the United States, his appointment shall bear the date of the temporary recognition and shall be considered to have been accepted and effective on that date.

(c) When the Air National Guard of the United States is ordered to active duty, any officer of the Air National Guard who is not a Reserve of the Air Force may be appointed by the President as a Reserve for service as a member of the Air National Guard of the United States in the grade that he holds in the Air National Guard.

(Aug. 10, 1956, ch 1041, § 1, 70A Stat. 519; Oct. 5, 1994, P. L. 103-337, Div A, Title XVI, Subtitle C, § 1662(c)(3), 108 Stat. 2990; Feb. 10, 1996, P. L. 104-106, Div A, Title XV, § 1501(b)(13)(A), 110 Stat. 496.)

HISTORY; ANCILLARY LAWS AND DIRECTIVES

Prior law and revision:

Revised Section	Source (USCS)	Source (Statutes at Large)
8351(a)	50:1113 (less (a)). 50:1115(a) (last 39 words).	July 9, 1952, ch. 608, §§ 703 (less (a)), 704 (2d sentence), 705(a) (last 39 words), 713 (less (a)), 66 Stat. 502-504.
8351(b)	50:1114 (2d sentence).	
8351(c)	50:1123 (less (a)).	

In subsection (a), the words "as a Reserve" are substituted for the words "as Reserve officers of the appropriate Armed Force of the United States" and "as a Reserve officer of the Armed Force of the United States concerned" in 50:1113(b). The words "federally recognized appointments" and "in the same grade and branch", in 50:1113(b), are omitted as surplusage. The words "those officers who do not hold appointments as reserve officers of the appropriate Armed Force of the United States", in 50:1113(b), are omitted as covered by the second sentence of the revised subsec.

In subsection (c), the words "active duty" are substituted for the words "active military service of the United States". The words "and branch" are omitted as surplusage. The words "of the Air National Guard of the United States" are inserted for clarity.

Amendments:

1994. Act Oct. 5, 1994 (effective 12/1/94 as provided by § 1691 of such Act, which appears as 10 USCS § 10001 note) transferred this section, enacted as 10 USCS § 8351, to Chapter 1205 and redesignated it as 10 USCS § 12212.

1996. Act Feb. 10, 1996 (effective as if included in Act Oct. 5, 1994, P. L. 103-337, as enacted on Oct. 5, 1994, as provided by § 1501(f)(3) of Act Feb. 10, 1996, which appears as 10 USCS § 113 note), in the section heading, inserted "the".

§ 12213. Officers; Army Reserve: transfer from Army National Guard of the United States

(a) Under such regulations as the Secretary of the Army may prescribe and with the consent of the governor or other appropriate authority of the State concerned, an officer of the Army National Guard of the United States may be transferred in grade to the Army Reserve.

(b) Unless discharged from his appointment as a Reserve, an officer of the Army National Guard of the United States whose Federal recognition as a member of the Army National Guard is withdrawn becomes a member of the Army Reserve. An officer who so becomes a member of the Army Reserve ceases to be a member of the Army National Guard of the United States.

(Aug. 10, 1956, ch 1041, § 1, 70A Stat. 194; Sept. 2, 1958, P. L. 85-861, § 1(80)(A), 72 Stat. 1468; June 30, 1960, P. L. 86-559, § 1(7), 74 Stat. 265; Sept. 29, 1988, P. L. 100-456, Div A, Title XII, Part D, § 1234(a)(1), 102 Stat. 2059; Oct. 5, 1994, P. L. 103-337, Div A, Title XVI, Subtitle B, Part I, § 1636(a), Subtitle C, § 1662(c)(3), Subtitle D, § 1675(b)(2), 108 Stat. 2968, 2990, 3017; Feb. 10, 1996, P. L. 104-106, Div A, Title XV, § 1501(b)(13)(A), (14), 110 Stat. 496.)

HISTORY; ANCILLARY LAWS AND DIRECTIVES

Prior law and revision:

1956 ACT

Revised Section	Source (USCS)	Source (Statutes at Large)
3352(a)	50:1116 (less last 15 words of 1st sentence, and less applicability to enlistments).	July 9, 1952, ch. 608, §§ 706 (less last 15 words of 1st sentence, and less applicability to enlist ments), 707 (less applicability to enlistments), 66 Stat. 503.
3352(b)	50:1117 (less applicability to enlistments).	

In subsection (a), the words "at any time", "of any person", and "from the National Guard of the United States or from the Air National Guard of the United States" are omitted as surplusage. The words "highest regular or reserve grade ever held by him in the Army" are substituted for the words "highest permanent grade previously held in the Army or any component thereof", since "permanent" grades are held only in a component and there are no "non-permanent" grades held in a component.

In subsection (b), the words "appointment as a Reserve" are substituted for the words "appointment or . . . as a Reserve officer or". The words "whose Federal recognition as a member . . . is withdrawn" are substituted for the words "ceases to hold a status as a federally recognized member".

1958 ACT

Revised Section	Source (USCS)	Source (Statutes at Large)
3352(a)	50:1254.	Sept. 3, 1954, ch. 1257, § 322, 68 Stat. 1161.

Amendments:

1958. Act Sept. 2, 1958, in subsec. (a), substituted "Notwithstanding any other provision of this chapter or section 593 of this title, an officer who is transferred under this section shall be advanced to the highest regular or reserve grade ever held by him in the Army, unless the Secretary determines that it is not in the best interests of the service" for "Upon transfer, he is eligible for promotion to the highest regular or reserve grade ever held by him in the Army, if his service has been honorable".

1960. Act June 30, 1960, in subsec. (a), substituted "temporary, regular," for "regular".

1988. Act Sept. 29, 1988, in subsec. (a), deleted "the Canal Zone," following "Puerto Rico,".

1994. Act Oct. 5, 1994 (effective 12/1/94 as provided by § 1691 of such Act, which appears as 10 USCS § 10001 note) transferred this section, enacted as 10 USCS § 3352, to Chapter 1205 and redesignated it as 10 USCS § 12213; and, in subsec. (a), deleted "or Territory, Puerto Rico, or the District of Columbia, whichever is" following "State".

Such Act Oct. 5, 1994 further (effective 2/10/96 as provided by § 1501(f)(1) of Act Feb. 10, 1996, which appears as a note to this section), in subsec. (a), deleted "Notwithstanding any other provision of this chapter or section 12203 of this title, an officer who is transferred under this section shall be advanced to the highest temporary, regular, or reserve grade ever held by him in the Army, unless the Secretary determines that it is not in the best interests of the service." following "Reserve.".

1996. Act Feb. 10, 1996 (effective as if included in Act Oct. 5, 1994, P. L. 103-337, as enacted on Oct. 5, 1994, as provided by § 1501(f)(3) of Act Feb. 10, 1996, which appears as 10 USCS § 113 note), in the section heading, inserted "the"; and, in subsec. (a), substituted "section 12203" for "section 593".

Other provisions:

Effective date of Oct. 5, 1994 amendment of subsec. (a). Act Feb. 10, 1996, P. L. 104-106, Div A, Title XV, § 1501(f)(1), 110 Stat. 501, provides: "Section 1636 of the Reserve Officer Personnel Management Act [§ 1636 of Act Oct. 5, 1994, P. L. 103-337; deleting the second sentence of subsec. (a) of this section and repealing 10 USCS §§ 8356 and 8379] shall take effect on the date of the enactment of this Act.".

CROSS REFERENCES

This section is referred to in 10 USCS §§ 123, 12203, 12683; 32 USCS § 323.

§ 12214. Officers; Air Force Reserve: transfer from Air National Guard of the United States

(a) Under such regulations as the Secretary of the Air Force may prescribe, and with the consent of the governor or other appropriate authority of the State concerned, an officer of the Air National Guard of the United States may be transferred in grade to the Air Force Reserve.

(b) Unless discharged from his appointment as a Reserve, an officer of the Air National Guard of the United States whose Federal recognition as a member of the Air National Guard is withdrawn becomes a member of the Air Force Reserve. An officer who so becomes a member of the Air Force Reserve ceases to be a member of the Air National Guard of the United States.

(Aug. 10, 1956, ch 1041, § 1, 70A Stat. 520; Sept. 7, 1962, P. L. 87-651, Title I, § 126, 76 Stat. 514; Sept. 29, 1988, P. L. 100-456, Div A, Title XII, Part D, § 1234(a)(1), 102 Stat. 2059; Oct. 5, 1994, P. L. 103-337, Div A, Title XVI, Subtitle C, § 1662(c)(3), Subtitle D, § 1675(b)(2), 108 Stat. 2990, 3017; Feb. 10, 1996, P. L. 104-106, Div A, Title XV, § 1501(b)(13)(A), 110 Stat. 496.)

HISTORY; ANCILLARY LAWS AND DIRECTIVES

Prior law and revision:

Revised Section	Source (USCS)	Source (Statutes at Large)
8352(a)	50:1116 (less last 15 words of 1st sentence, and less applicability to enlistments).	July 9, 1952, ch. 608, §§ 706 (less last 15 words of 1st sentence, and less applicability to enlistments), 707 (less applicability to enlistments), 66 Stat. 503.
8352(b)	50:1117 (less applicability to enlistments).	

In subsection (a), the words "at any time", "of any person", and "from the National Guard of the United States or from the Air National Guard of the United States" are omitted as surplusage. The words "highest regular or reserve grade ever held by him in the Air Force" are substituted for the words "highest permanent grade previously held in . . . the Air Force or any component thereof", since "permanent" grades are held only in a component and there are no "nonpermanent" grades held in a component.

In subsection (b), the words "appointment as a Reserve" are substituted for the words "appointment or . . . as a Reserve officer or". The words "whose Federal recognition as a member . . . is withdrawn" are substituted for the words "ceases to hold a status as a federally recognized member".

1962 ACT

The change reflects the implied repeal of the second sentence of 10 USCS § 8352(a) by section 502(a) of the Reserve Officer Personnel Act of 1954 (68 Stat. 1172).

Amendments:

1962. Act Sept. 7, 1962, in subsec (a), after the sentence beginning "Under such regulations . . .", deleted one which read: "Upon transfer, he is eligible for promotion to the highest regular or reserve grade ever held by him in the Air Force, if his service has been honorable.".

1988. Act Sept. 29, 1988, in subsec. (a), deleted ''the Canal Zone,'' following ''Puerto Rico,''.

1994. Act Oct. 5, 1994 (effective 12/1/94 as provided by § 1691 of such Act, which appears as 10 USCS § 10001 note) transferred this section, enacted as 10 USCS § 8352, to Chapter 1205 and redesignated it as 10 USCS § 12214; and, in subsec. (a), deleted ''or Territory, Puerto Rico, or the District of Columbia, whichever is'' following ''State''.

1996. Act Feb. 10, 1996 (effective as if included in Act Oct. 5, 1994, P. L. 103-337, as enacted on Oct. 5, 1994, as provided by § 1501(f)(3) of Act Feb. 10, 1996, which appears as 10 USCS § 113 note), in the section heading, inserted ''the''.

CROSS REFERENCES

This section is referred to in 10 USCS §§ 12203, 12683; 32 USCS § 323.

§ 12215. Commissioned officers: reserve grade of adjutants general and assistant adjutants general

(a) The adjutant general or an assistant adjutant general of the Army National Guard of a State may, upon being extended Federal recognition, be appointed as a reserve officer of the Army as of the date on which he is so recognized.

(b) The adjutant general or an assistant adjutant general of the Air National Guard of a State may be appointed in the reserve commissioned grade in which Federal recognition in the Air National Guard is extended to him.

(Added Oct. 5, 1994, P. L. 103-337, Div A, Title XVI, Subtitle C, § 1662(c)(1), 108 Stat. 2990.)

HISTORY; ANCILLARY LAWS AND DIRECTIVES

Effective date of section:

This section took effect on Dec. 1, 1994, pursuant to Act Oct. 5, 1994, P. L. 103-337, Div A, Title XVI, Subtitle F, § 1691, 108 Stat. 3026, which appears as 10 USCS 10001 note.

CROSS REFERENCES

Adjutants general and assistant adjutants general, reference as applicable to other officers of National Guard, 10 USCS § 10214.

This section is referred to in 10 USCS § 10214.

CHAPTER 1207. WARRANT OFFICERS

HISTORY; ANCILLARY LAWS AND DIRECTIVES

Amendments:

1994. Act Oct. 5, 1994, P. L. 103-337, Div A, Title XVI, Subtitle C, § 1662(d)(1), 108 Stat. 2991 (effective 12/1/94 as provided by § 1691 of such Act, which appears as 10 USCS § 10001 note), added the chapter heading and analysis.

1996. Act Feb. 10, 1996, P. L. 104-106, Div A, Title XV, § 1501(b)(15), 110 Stat. 496 (effective as if included in Act Oct. 5, 1994, P. L. 103-337, as enacted on Oct. 5, 1994, as provided by § 1501(f)(3) of Act Feb. 10, 1996, which appears as 10 USCS § 113 note), amended the analysis of this chapter by substituting ''promotion'' for ''promotions'' in item 12243.

§ 12241. Warrant officers: grades; appointment, how made; term

(a) The permanent reserve warrant officer grades in each armed force are those prescribed for regular warrant officers by section 571(a) of this title.

(b) Appointments made in the permanent reserve grade of warrant officer, W-1, shall be made by warrant by the Secretary concerned. Appointments made in a permanent reserve grade of chief warrant officer shall be made by commission by the Secretary concerned.

(c) Appointments as Reserves in permanent warrant officer grades are for an indefinite term and are held during the pleasure of the Secretary concerned.

(Aug. 10, 1956, ch 1041, § 1, 70A Stat. 26; Nov. 8, 1985, P. L. 99-145, Title V, Part D, § 531(b), 99 Stat. 633; Dec. 5, 1991, P. L. 102-190, Div A, Title XI, Part C, § 1131(2), 105 Stat. 1505; Oct. 5, 1994, P. L. 103-337, Div A, Title XVI, Subtitle C, § 1662(d)(2), 108 Stat. 2991.)

HISTORY; ANCILLARY LAWS AND DIRECTIVES

Prior law and revision:

Revised Section	Source (USCS)	Source (Statutes at Large)
597(a)	10:600a(a) (less 3d and last sentences, as applicable to permanent reserve appointments).	May 29, 1954, ch. 249, §§ 3(a) (less last sentence, as applicable to permanent reserve appoint-

Revised Section	Source (USCS)	Source (Statutes at Large)
	34:135a(a) (less last sentence, as applicable to permanent reserve appointments).	ments), 5(a) (last sentence, as applicable to permanent reserve appointments), 68 Stat. 157, 159.
597(b)	10:600a(a) (3d sentence, as applicable to permanent reserve appointments). 10:600c(a) (last sentence, as applicable to permanent reserve appointments). 34:135a(a) (last sentence, as applicable to permanent reserve appointments). 34:135c(a) (last sentence, as applicable to permanent reserve appointments). 50:944.	July 9, 1952, ch. 608, §§ 220, 223, 224, (less 3d and 4th sentences, and less applicability to commissioned officers), 66 Stat. 487
597(c)	50:947. 50:948 (less 3d and 4th sentences, and less applicability to commissioned officers).	

In subsection (b), the words ''W-4, W-3, and W-2'' and ''persons'' are omitted as surplusage.

In subsection (c), the words ''After July 9, 1952'' are omitted as executed. 50:948 (2d and last sentence) is omitted as executed.

Amendments:

1985. Act Nov. 8, 1985 (effective 6 months after enactment on 11/8/85, as provided by § 531(d) of such Act, which appears as a note to this section) substituted subsec. (b) for one which read:

''Reserve chief warrant officers of the Army and the Air Force shall be appointed in those grades, by warrant, by the Secretary concerned. Permanent reserve chief warrant officers of the Navy, Marine Corps, and Coast Guard shall be appointed in those grades, by commission, by the Secretary concerned. Permanent reserve warrant officers, W-1, shall be appointed in those grades, by warrant, by the Secretary concerned.''

1991. Act Dec. 5, 1991 (effective 2/1/92 as provided by § 1132 of such Act, which appears as 10 USCS § 521 note), in subsec. (a), substituted ''section 571(a)'' for ''section 555(a)''.

1994. Oct. 5, 1994 (generally effective Dec. 1, 1994, except as otherwise provided in § 1691 of such Act, as provided by § 1691 of such Act, which appears as 10 USCS § 10001 note) transferred this section, enacted as 10 USCS § 597, to Chapter 1205 and redesignated it as 10 USCS § 12241.

Other provisions:

Transition provisions for 1985 amendment. Act Nov. 8, 1985, P. L. 99-145, Title V, Part D, § 531(c), 99 Stat. 633, provided:

"(1) The amendments made by subsections (a) and (b) apply to any appointment of a warrant officer or chief warrant officer on or after the effective date of this section.

"(2) An officer who on the effective date of this section is serving in a chief warrant officer grade under an appointment by warrant may be appointed in that grade by commission under section 555(b) or 597(b) of title 10 [10 USCS § 12241(b)], United States Code, as appropriate. The date of rank of an officer who receives an appointment under this paragraph is the date of rank for the officer's appointment by warrant to that grade."

Effective date of 1985 amendment. Act Nov. 8, 1985, P. L. 99-145, Title V, Part D, § 531(d), 99 Stat. 633, provided: "This section takes effect six months after the date of the enactment of this Act."

CROSS REFERENCES

Regular warrant officers, appointments, 10 USCS § 571.

This section is referred to in 10 USCS § 591.

INTERPRETIVE NOTES AND DECISIONS

Punitive separation from services of commissioned warrant officers is by way of dismissal, while such separation of other warrant officers is by way of dishonorable discharge. United States v Briscoe (1963) 13 USCMA 510, 33 CMR 42.

§ 12242. Warrant officers: promotion

The promotion of permanent reserve warrant officers not on the warrant officer active-duty list to permanent reserve warrant officer grades shall be governed by such regulations as the Secretary concerned may prescribe.

(Aug. 10, 1956, ch 1041, § 1, 70A Stat. 26; Dec. 5, 1991, P. L. 102-190, Div A, Title XI, Part C, § 1131(3), 105 Stat. 1505; Oct. 5, 1994, P. L. 103-337, Div A, Title XVI, Subtitle C, § 1662(d)(2), 108 Stat. 2991.)

HISTORY; ANCILLARY LAWS AND DIRECTIVES

Prior law and revision:

Revised Section	Source (USCS)	Source (Statutes at Large)
598	10:600e (last sentence, less applicabilty to temporary promotions). 34:330 (last sentence, less applicability to temporary promotions).	May 29, 1954, ch. 249, § 7 (last sentence, less applicability to temporary promotions), 68 Stat. 159.

1991. Act Dec. 5, 1991 (effective 2/1/92 as provided by § 1132 of such Act, which appears as 10 USCS § 521 note) inserted "not on the warrant officer active-duty list".

1994. Oct. 5, 1994 (generally effective Dec. 1, 1994, except as otherwise provided in § 1691 of such Act, as provided by § 1691 of such Act, which appears as 10 USCS § 10001 note) transferred this section, enacted as 10 USCS § 598, to Chapter 1205 and redesignated it as 10 USCS § 12242.

§ 12243. Warrant officers: suspension of laws for promotion or mandatory retirement or separation during war or emergency

In time of war, or of emergency declared after May 29, 1954, by Congress or the President, the President may suspend the operation of any provision of law relating to promotion, or mandatory retirement or separation, of permanent reserve warrant officers of any armed force.

(Aug. 10, 1956, ch 1041, § 1, 70A Stat. 26; Oct. 5, 1994, P. L. 103-337, Div A, Title XVI, Subtitle C, § 1662(d)(2), 108 Stat. 2991.)

HISTORY; ANCILLARY LAWS AND DIRECTIVES

Prior law and revision:

Revised Section	Source (USCS)	Source (Statutes at Large)
599	10:600p (as applicable to reserve warrant officers). 34:330g (as applicable to reserve warrant officers. 34:430d (as applicable to reserve warrant officers).	May 29, 1954, ch. 249, § 18 (as applicable to reserve warrant officers), 68 Stat. 165.

The word ''may'' is substituted for the words ''is authorized, in his discretion''. The words ''any provision of law'' are substituted for the words ''all or any part or parts of the several provisions of law''.

Amendments:

1994. Oct. 5, 1994 (generally effective Dec. 1, 1994, except as otherwise provided in § 1691 of such Act, as provided by § 1691 of such Act, which appears as 10 USCS § 10001 note) transferred this section, enacted as 10 USCS § 599, to Chapter 1205 and redesignated it as 10 USCS § 12243.

Other provisions:

Delegation of functions to the Secretary of Defense. Section 1(4) of Ex. Or. No. 11390 of January 22, 1968, 33 Fed. Reg. 841, provided: ''The Secretary of Defense, and, as designated by the said Secretary for this purpose, any of the Secretaries, Under Secretaries, and Assistant Secretaries of the military departments, are hereby designated and empowered to perform the following-described functions of the President without the approval, ratification, or other action of the President:

''(4) The authority vested in the President by sections 565, 599, 3450, and 8450 of title 10, United States Code [this section and 10 USCS §§ 565, 3450, 8450], to suspend, in time of war or emergency, any provision of law relative to promotion and mandatory retirement or separation of warrant officers of the armed forces.''.

CHAPTER 1209. ACTIVE DUTY

HISTORY; ANCILLARY LAWS AND DIRECTIVES

Amendments:

1994. Act Oct. 5, 1994, P. L. 103-337, Div A, Title XVI, Subtitle C, § 1662(e)(1), 108 Stat. 2991, added the chapter heading and analysis.

1996. Act Feb. 10, 1996, P. L. 104-106, Div A, Title XV, § 1501(b)(16), 110 Stat. 496, amended the analysis of this chapter by substituting a semicolon for a colon in item 12304 and by deleting ''on active duty'' following ''Retention'' in item 12308.

1997. Act Nov. 18, 1997, P. L. 105-85, Div A, Title V, Subtitle B, § 511(e)(2), 111 Stat. 1729, amended the analysis of this chapter by substituting item 12304 for one which read: ''12304. Selected Reserve; order to active duty other than during war or national emergency''.

§ 12301. Reserve components generally

(a) In time of war or of national emergency declared by Congress, or when otherwise authorized by law, an authority designated by the Secretary concerned may, without the consent of the persons affected, order any unit, and any member not assigned to a unit organized to serve as a unit, of a reserve component under the jurisdiction of that Secretary to active duty (other than for training) for the duration of the war or emergency and for six months thereafter. However a member on an inactive status list or in a retired status may not be ordered to active duty under this subsection unless the Secretary concerned, with the approval of the Secretary of Defense in the case of the Secretary of a military department, determines that there are not enough qualified Reserves in an active status or in the inactive National Guard in the required category who are readily available.

(b) At any time, an authority designated by the Secretary concerned may, without the consent of the persons affected, order any unit, and any member not assigned to a unit organized to serve as a unit, in an active status in a reserve component under the jurisdiction of that Secretary to active duty for not more than 15 days a year. However, units and members of the Army National Guard of the United States or the Air National Guard of the United States may not be ordered to active duty under this subsection without the consent of the governor of the State (or, in the case of the District of Columbia National Guard, the commanding general of the District of Columbia National Guard).

(c) So far as practicable, during any expansion of the active armed forces that requires that units and members of the reserve components be ordered to active duty (other than for training), members of units organized and trained to serve as units who are ordered to that duty without their consent shall be so ordered with their units. However, members of those units may be reassigned after being ordered to active duty (other than for training).

(d) At any time, an authority designated by the Secretary concerned may order a member of a reserve component under his jurisdiction to active duty, or retain him on active duty, with the consent of that member. However, a member of the Army National Guard of the United States or the Air National Guard of the United States may not be ordered to active duty under this subsection without the consent of the governor or other appropriate authority of the State concerned.

(e) The period of time allowed between the date when a Reserve ordered to active duty (other than for training) is alerted for that duty and the date when the Reserve is required to enter upon that duty shall be determined by the Secretary concerned based upon military requirements at that time.

(f) The consent of a Governor described in subsections (b) and (d) may not be withheld (in whole or in part) with regard to active duty outside the United States, its territories, and its possessions, because of any objection to the location, purpose, type, or schedule of such active duty.

(g)(1) A member of a reserve component may be ordered to active duty without his consent if the Secretary concerned determines that the member is in a captive status. A member ordered to active duty under this section may not be retained on active duty, without his consent, for more than 30 days after his captive status is terminated.

(2) The Secretary of Defense shall prescribe regulations to carry out this section. Such regulations shall apply uniformly among the armed forces

under the jurisdiction of the Secretary. A determination for the purposes of this subsection that a member is in a captive status shall be made pursuant to such regulations.

(3) In this section, the term ''captive status'' means the status of a member of the armed forces who is in a missing status (as defined in section 551(2) of title 37) which occurs as the result of a hostile action and is related to the member's military status.

(Aug. 10, 1956, ch 1041, § 1, 70A Stat. 27; Sept. 2, 1958, P. L. 85-861, §§ 1(13), 33(a)(5), 72 Stat. 1440, 1564; Sept. 24, 1980, P. L. 96-357, § 6, 94 Stat. 1182; Dec. 23, 1980, P. L. 96-584, § 1, 94 Stat. 3377; Oct. 18, 1986, P. L. 99-500; Oct. 30, 1986, P. L. 99-591, Title I, § 101(c) in part, 100 Stat. 3341-127; Nov. 14, 1986, P. L. 99-661, Div A, Title V, Part B, §§ 522, 524(a), 100 Stat. 3871; Sept. 29, 1988, P. L. 100-456, Div A, Title XII, Part D, § 1234(a)(1), (2), 102 Stat. 2059; Oct. 5, 1994, P. L. 103-337, Div A, Title XVI, Subtitle C, § 1662(e)(2), Subtitle D, § 1675(c)(1), 108 Stat. 2992, 3017.)

HISTORY; ANCILLARY LAWS AND DIRECTIVES

Prior law and revision:

1956 ACT

Revised Section	Source (USCS)	Source (Statutes at Large)
672(a)	50:961(a).	July 9, 1952, ch. 608, §§ 233 (loss (b) and (f)), 234 (1st sentence), 66 Stat. 489, 490.
672(b)	50:961(c).	
672(c)	50:961(g).	
672(d)	50:961(d). 50:962 (1st sentence).	
672(e)	50:961(e).	

In subsection (a), the word ''hereafter'' is omitted as surplusage. The words ''there are not enough . . . who are'' are substituted for the words ''adequate numbers of . . . are not''. The words ''without the consent of the persons affected'' and ''under the jurisdiction of that Secretary'' are inserted for clarity. The words ''and the members thereof'' are omitted as surplusage.

In subsection (b), the words ''without the consent of the persons affected'' are substituted for the words ''without his consent'', since units as well as individuals are covered by the revised subsection. The words ''and the members thereof'', ''and required to perform'', ''or required to serve on'', and ''in the service of the United States'' are omitted as surplusage.

In subsections (b) and (d), the words ''active duty for training'' are omitted as covered by the words ''active duty''.

In subsection (c), the words ''to active duty'' are substituted for the words ''into the active military service of the United States'', in 50:961(g) (1st and last sentences). The words ''to serve'' are substituted for the words ''for the purpose of serving''. The words ''without their consent'' are substituted for the word ''involuntarily''. The words ''to that duty'' are substituted for the words ''into active duty''. The last sentence of the revised subsection is substituted for 50:961(g) (last sentence).

In subsection (d), the words "the consent of that member" are substituted for the words "his consent". The words "under his jurisdiction" are inserted for clarity. 50:962 (last 15 words of 1st sentence) is omitted as covered by 50:961(d).

In subsection (e), the words "to active duty (other than for training)" are substituted for the words "into the active military service of the United States". The words "period of" are omitted as surplusage. The word "requirements" is substituted for the word "condition" for clarity.

1958 ACT

Revised Section	Source (USCS)	Source (Statutes at Large)
672(a)	50:961(a).	Aug. 9, 1955, ch. 665, § 2(e), 69 Stat. 599.

The word "hereafter" is omitted as surplusage. The words "there are not enough . . . who are" are substituted for the words "adequate numbers of . . . are not". The words "without the consent of the persons affected" and "under the jurisdiction of that Secretary" are inserted for clarity.

The changes are necessary to reflect section 101(b) of the Armed Forces Reserve Act of 1952 (50 U.S.C. 901(b)), which defines the term "active duty" to exclude active duty for training. This definition applied to the source law for these sections, section 233(a), (b)(1), and (c) of the Armed Forces Reserve Act of 1952 (50 U.S.C. 961(a), (b)(1), (c)).

Explanatory notes:

Act Oct. 30, 1986, P. L. 99-591, is a corrected version of Act Oct. 18, 1986, P. L. 99-500.

Amendments:

1958. Act Sept. 2, 1958, § 1(13) (effective as provided by § 33(g) of such Act, which appears as 10 USCS § 101 note), substituted subsec. (a) for one which read "(a) In time of war or of national emergency declared by Congress, or when otherwise authorized by law, an authority designated by the Secretary concerned may, without the consent of the persons affected, order any unit, and any member not assigned to a unit organized to serve as a unit, of a reserve component under the jurisdiction of that Secretary to active duty for the duration of the war or emergency and for six months thereafter. However, a member on an inactive status list or in a retired status may not be ordered to active duty under this subsection unless the Secretary concerned, with the approval of the Secretary of Defense in the case of a Secretary of a military department, determines that there are not enough qualified Reserves in an active status or in the inactive Army National Guard or in the inactive Air National Guard in the required category who are readily available."

Section 33(a)(5) of such Act (effective as of Aug. 10, 1956, as provided by § 33(g) of that Act), in subsec. (a), as amended, and in subsec. (c), added "(other than for training)" after "active duty".

1980. Act Sept. 24, 1980, in subsec. (a), substituted the sentence beginning "However . . ." for "However—" and paras. (1) and (2).

Act Dec. 23, 1980, substituted subsec. (e) for one which read: "A reasonable time shall be allowed between the date when a Reserve ordered to active duty (other than for training) is alerted for that duty and the date when he is required to enter upon that duty. Unless the Secretary concerned determines that the military requirements do not allow it, this period shall be at least 30 days.''.

1986. Acts Oct. 18, 1986 and Oct. 30, 1986 added subsec. (f).

Act Nov. 14, 1986 (effective as provided by § 524(b) of such Act, which appears as a note to this section), made the same amendment as Acts Oct. 18, 1986 and Oct. 30, 1986.

1988. Act Sept. 29, 1988, in subsec. (b), substituted ''or Puerto Rico'' for '', Puerto Rico, or the Canal Zone,''; and, in subsec. (d), deleted ''the Canal Zone,'' following ''Puerto Rico,''.

1994. Act Oct. 5, 1994 (effective 12/1/94 as provided by § 1691 of such Act, which appears as 10 USCS § 10001 note) transferred this section, enacted as 10 USCS § 672, to Chapter 1209 and redesignated it as 10 USCS § 12301; in subsec. (b), substituted ''(or, in the case of the District of Columbia National Guard, the commanding general of the District of Columbia National Guard).'' for ''or Territory or Puerto Rico or the commanding general of the District of Columbia National Guard, as the case may be.''; and, in subsec. (d), deleted ''or Territory, Puerto Rico, or the District of Columbia, whichever is'' following ''State''.

Other provisions:

Application of subsec. (g). Act Nov. 14, 1986, P. L. 99-661, Div A, Title V, Part B, § 524(b), 100 Stat. 3872, provides: ''Section 672(g) of title 10, United States Code, as added by subsection (a), does not authorize a member of a reserve component to be ordered to active duty for a period before the date of the enactment of this Act.''.

Construction of duplicate authorization and appropriation provisions. For construction of the duplicate provisions of Act Oct. 18, 1986, P. L. 99-500, Act Oct. 30, 1986, P. L. 99-591, and Act Nov. 14, 1986, P. L. 99-661 and for the rule for the date of enactment of such Acts, see Act April 21, 1987, P. L. 100-26, § 6, 101 Stat. 274, which appears as 10 USCS § 2301 note.

CROSS REFERENCES

Ready Reserve, composition and authorized strength of, 10 USCS § 10142.

Standby Reserve, composition of, 10 USCS § 10151.

This section is referred to in 10 USCS §§ 101, 523, 582, 641, 672, 10142, 10151, 10215, 12305–12307 12310, 16131, 16133; 38 USCS §§ 3011, 3013, 3231, 3511, 4211; 50 USCS App. § 592.

INTERPRETIVE NOTES AND DECISIONS

1. Generally
2. Constitutionality
3. Discretion of service
4. Circumstances warranting call to active duty
5. Notice
6. Retention after active duty

1. Generally

If Congress intended to limit its own or President's power over each enlistee to that which laws authorized at time of enactments of 10 USCS §§ 672, 673 (now §§ 12301, 12302), it would have specified ''or otherwise authorized by law'' in §§ 672, 673 (now §§ 12301, 12302), phrase more clearly contemplating laws already in existence at that time, rather than employing ''when'' terminology which clearly looks to future. Linsalata v Clifford (1968, SD NY) 290 F Supp 338.

2. Constitutionality

Federal Constitution's militia clauses are not violated by 10 USCS § 672(f) (now § 12301(f)) limits on governors' authority to withhold consent to National Guard training outside United States. Perpich v Department of Defense (1990) 496 US 334, 110 L Ed 2d 312, 110 S Ct 2418.

State governor's challenge to constitutionality of 10 USCS § 672(f) (now § 12301(f)) must fail, where 10 USCS § 672(b) and (d) (now § 12301(b) and (d)) granted Defense Secretary authority to order National Guard units to active duty with consent of governor of state or territory, Minnesota governor threatened to withhold consent to ordering of Minnesota unit to active duty training missions in Central America, then Congress passed § 672(f) (now § 12301(f)) which prohibited withholding of consent by governor based on objection to location, purpose, type or schedule of active duty ordered, because Congress retains full authority to train National Guard units while in active federal service under Article I, § 8, cl. 16, unlimited by reservation to states of authority of training militia according to discipline prescribed by Congress. Perpich v United States Dep't of Defense (1987, DC Minn) 666 F Supp 1319, revd (1988, CA8) 1988 US App LEXIS 16494, vacated, en banc (1989, CA8) 1989 US App LEXIS 2104 and affd, on reh, en banc (1989, CA8 Minn) 880 F2d 11, affd (1990) 496 US 334, 110 L Ed 2d 312, 110 S Ct 2418.

3. Discretion of service

It is within Air Force's discretion whether or not to call reserve officer to active duty. De Bow v United States (1970) 193 Ct Cl 499, 434 F2d 1333, cert den (1971) 404 US 846, 30 L Ed 2d 84, 92 S Ct 150.

It rests within discretion of particular armed service whether to place reserve officer on active duty. Abruzzo v United States (1975) 206 Ct Cl 731, 513 F2d 608.

4. Circumstances warranting call to active duty

Congress did not intend all of 10 USCS § 672 (now § 12301) to operate solely under one set of circumstances, as § 672(a) (now § 12301(a)) operates in time of war or of national emergency or when otherwise authorized by law, § 672(b) (now § 12301(b)) operates at any time and § 672(c) (now § 12301(c)) operates during any expansion of active Armed Forces which requires that units and members of reserve components be ordered for active duty. Linsalata v Clifford (1968, SD NY) 290 F Supp 338.

Even though there was no war or national emergency, army reservists could be called to active duty "when otherwise authorized by law" without breaching enlistment contract as rules of ordinary contract law did not apply automatically to those in military service. Adams v Clifford (1969, DC Hawaii) 294 F Supp 1318.

5. Notice

Despite failure of petitioners to receive 60 days' notice, in conformity with Air Force Manual provision, in advance of date on which they were to be permanently reassigned, order of permanent reassignment is not invalid as Air Force regulation allows waiver of 60-day rule for operational reasons. Linsalata v Clifford (1968, SD NY) 290 F Supp 338.

6. Retention after active duty

Under 10 USCS § 672 (now § 12301), retention of national guardsmen after term of active duty specified in orders by state officials without further authorization by them is not allowable. United States v Peel (1977, CMA) 4 MJ 28.

§ 12302. Ready Reserve

(a) In time of national emergency declared by the President after January 1, 1953, or when otherwise authorized by law, an authority designated by the Secretary concerned may, without the consent of the persons concerned, order any unit, and any member not assigned to a unit organized to serve as a unit, in the Ready Reserve under the jurisdiction of that Secretary to active duty (other than for training) for not more than 24 consecutive months.

(b) To achieve fair treatment as between members in the Ready Reserve who are being considered for recall to duty without their consent, consideration shall be given to—

(1) the length and nature of previous service, to assure such sharing of exposure to hazards as the national security and military requirements will reasonably allow;

(2) family responsibilities; and

(3) employment necessary to maintain the national health, safety, or interest.

The Secretary of Defense shall prescribe such policies and procedures as he considers necessary to carry out this subsection. He shall report on those policies and procedures at least once a year to the Committee on Armed Services of the Senate and the Committee on National Security of the House of Representatives.

(c) Not more than 1,000,000 members of the Ready Reserve may be on active duty (other than for training), without their consent, under this section at any one time.

(d) Whenever one or more units of the Ready Reserve are ordered to active duty, the President shall, on the first day of the second fiscal year quarter immediately following the quarter in which the first unit or units are ordered to active duty and on the first day of each succeeding six-month period thereafter, so long as such unit is retained on active duty, submit a report to the Congress regarding the necessity for such unit or units being ordered to and retained on active duty. The President shall include in each such report a statement of the mission of each such unit ordered to active duty, an evaluation of such unit's performance of that mission, where each such unit is being deployed at the time of the report, and such other information regarding each unit as the President deems appropriate.

(Aug. 10, 1956, ch 1041, § 1, 70A Stat. 28; Sept. 2, 1958, P. L. 85-861, §§ 1(14), 33(a)(5), 72 Stat. 1441, 1564; Nov. 16, 1973, P. L. 93-155, Title III, § 303(a), 87 Stat. 607; Oct. 5, 1994, P. L. 103-337, Div A, Title XVI, Subtitle C, § 1662(e)(2), 108 Stat. 2992; Feb. 10, 1996, P. L. 104-106, Div A, Title XV, § 1502(a)(2), 110 Stat. 502.)

HISTORY; ANCILLARY LAWS AND DIRECTIVES

Prior law and revision:

1956 ACT

Revised Section	Source (USCS)	Source (Statutes at Large)
673(a)	50:961(b)(1).	July 9, 1952, ch. 608,
673(b)	50:961(b)(2).	§ 233(b), 66 Stat. 489.

In subsection (a), the words "after January 1, 1953" are substituted for the word "hereafter", to reflect the effective date of the source statute. The words "without the consent of the persons concerned" are substituted for the word "involuntarily".

The words "under the jurisdiction of that Secretary" are inserted for clarity. The last sentence of the revised subsection is substituted for 50:961(b)(1) (proviso). The words "and the members thereof" and "and required to perform" are omitted as surplusage.

In subsection (b), the words "to achieve" are substituted for the words "in the interest of". The words "without their consent" are substituted for the word "involuntarily". The words "who are being considered for" are inserted for clarity. The words ''prescribe such policies and procedures'' are substituted for the words ''promulgate such policies and establish such procedures''. The words ''as he considers necessary'' are substituted for the words ''as may be required in his opinion''. The words ''this subsection'' are substituted for the words ''our intent here declared''. The words ''at least once a year'' are substituted for the words ''from time to time, and at least annually''. The words ''Senate and the House of Representatives'' are substituted for the word ''Congress''. 50:961(b)(2) (1st 18 words) is omitted as surplusage. The words ''with the objective'' and ''found to be'' are omitted as surplusage.

1958 ACT

Revised Section	Source (USCS)	Source (Statutes at Large)
673(a)	50:961(b)(1) (less proviso).	Aug. 9, 1955, ch. 665, § 2(f), 69 Stat. 599.
673(c)	50:961(b)(1) (proviso).	

In subsection (c), the words ''on active duty (other than for training)'' are substituted for the words ''may be required to perform active duty'' for clarity. The words ''without their consent'' are substituted for the word ''involuntarily''. The words ''of all reserve components'' and ''unless the Congress shall have authorized the exercise of the authority contained in this subsection'' are omitted as surplusage.

The changes are necessary to reflect section 101(b) of the Armed Forces Reserve Act of 1952 (50 U.S.C. 901(b)), which defines the term ''active duty'' to exclude active duty for training. This definition applied to the source law for these sections, section 233(a), (b)(1), and (c) of the Armed Forces Reserve Act of 1952 (50 U.S.C. 961(a), (b)(1), (c)).

Amendments:

1958. Act Sept. 2, 1958 (effective as provided by § 33(g) of such Act, which appears as 10 USCS § 101 note), in subsec. (a), inserted ''(other than for training)'' in the first sentence and deleted a second sentence which read: ''This subsection does not apply unless Congress determines how many members of the reserve components are necessary, in the interest of national security, to be ordered to active duty hereunder.''; and added subsec. (c).

1973. Act Nov. 16, 1973, added subsec. (d).

1994. Act Oct. 5, 1994 (effective 12/1/94 as provided by § 1691 of such Act, which appears as 10 USCS § 10001 note) transferred this section, enacted as 10 USCS § 673, to Chapter 1209 and redesignated it as 10 USCS § 12302.

1996. Act Feb. 10, 1996, in subsec. (b), in the concluding matter, substituted ''Committee on Armed Services of the Senate and the Committee on National Security of the House of Representatives'' for ''Committees on Armed Services of the Senate and the House of Representatives''.

Other provisions:

Ordering the Ready Reserve of the Armed Forces to active duty. Ex. Or. No. 12743 of Jan. 18, 1991, 56 Fed. Reg. 2661, provides:

''By the authority vested in me as President by the Constitution and the laws of the United States of America, including the National Emergencies Act (50 U.S.C. 1601 et seq.), and section 301 of title 3 of the United States Code; in furtherance of Executive Order No. 12722, dated August 2, 1990 [former 50 USCS § 1701 note], which declared a national emergency to address the threat to the national security and foreign policy of the United States posed by the invasion of Kuwait by Iraq; and, in accordance with the requirements contained in section 301 of the National Emergencies Act, 50 U.S.C. 1631, I hereby order as follows:

''Section 1. To provide additional authority to the Department of Defense and the Department of Transportation to respond to the continuing threat posed by Iraq's invasion of Kuwait, the authority under section 673 [now § 12302] of title 10, United States Code, to order any unit, and any member not assigned to a unit organized to serve as a unit, in the Ready Reserve to active duty (other than for training) for not more than 24 consecutive months, is invoked and made available, according to its terms, to the Secretary concerned, subject, in the case of the Secretaries of the Army, Navy, and Air Force, to the direction of the Secretary of Defense. The term 'Secretary concerned' is defined in section 101(8) of title 10, United States Code, to mean the Secretary of the Army with respect to the Army; the Secretary of the Navy with respect to the Navy, the Marine Corps, and the Coast Guard when it is operating as a service in the Navy; the Secretary of the Air Force with respect to the Air Force; and, the Secretary of Transportation with respect to the Coast Guard when it is not operating as a service in the Navy.

''Sec. 2. To allow for the orderly administration of personnel within the armed forces, the authority vested in the President by section 527 of title 10, United States Code, to suspend the operation of sections 523-526 of title 10, United States Code, regarding officer strength and officer distribution in grade, is invoked to the full extent provided by the terms thereof.

''Sec. 3. To allow for the orderly administration of personnel within the armed forces, the authority vested in the President by section 644 of title 10, United States Code, to suspend the operation of any provision of law relating to the promotion, involuntary retirement, or separation of commissioned officers of the Army, Navy, Air Force, or Marine Corps, is invoked to the full extent provided by the terms thereof.

''Sec. 4. The Secretary of Defense is hereby designated and empowered, without the approval, ratification, or other action by the President, to exercise the authority vested in the President by sections 527 and 644 of title 10, United States Code, as invoked by sections 2 and 3 of this order, to suspend the operation of certain provisions of law.

''Sec. 5. The authorities delegated by sections 1 and 4 of this order may be redelegated and further subdelegated to civilian subordinates who are appointed to their offices by the President, by and with the advice and consent of the Senate.

''Sec. 6. This order is intended to improve the internal management of the executive branch, and is not intended to create any right or benefit, substantive or procedural, enforceable at law by a party against the United States, its agencies, its officers, or any person.

''Sec. 7. This order is effective immediately, and shall be transmitted to the Congress and published in the Federal Register.''.

CROSS REFERENCES

Ready Reserve—Ordering to active duty during national emergency, 10 USCS § 10103.

Ready Reserve—Composition and authorized strength, 10 USCS § 10142.

This section is referred to in 10 USCS §§ 101, 115, 10142, 12304, 12305, 12318, 16131, 16133; 50 USCS App. § 592.

INTERPRETIVE NOTES AND DECISIONS

1. ''When otherwise authorized by law''
2. Right to hearing
3. Failure of service to comply with its regulations

1. ''When otherwise authorized by law''

10 USCS § 673(a) (now § 12302(a)), regarding ''when otherwise authorized by law'' language, should be given prospective meaning so as to include laws enacted after § 673 (now § 12302) was enacted. Johnson v Powell (1969, CA5 Tex) 414 F2d 1060.

Words ''when otherwise authorized by law'' have prospective meaning and clearly look to future. Morse v Boswell (1968, DC Md) 289 F Supp 812, affd (1968, CA4 Md) 401 F2d 544, cert den (1969) 393 US 1052, 21 L Ed 2d 694, 89 S Ct 687; Goldstein v Clifford (1968, DC NJ) 290 F Supp 275.

If Congress intended to limit its own or President's power over each enlistee to that which laws authorized at time of enactments of 10 USCS §§ 672, 673 (now §§ 12301, 12302), it would have specified ''or otherwise authorized by law'' in §§ 672, 673 (now §§ 12301, 12302), phrase more clearly contemplating laws already in existence at that time, rather than employing ''when'' terminology which clearly looks to future. Linsalata v Clifford (1968, SD NY) 290 F Supp 338.

2. Right to hearing

10 USCS § 673(a) (now § 12302(a)) does not give involuntary activated reservist right to personal hearing in appeal of his orders to involuntary active duty. Ansted v Resor (1971, CA7 Ind) 437 F2d 1020, cert den (1971) 404 US 827, 30 L Ed 2d 56, 92 S Ct 61, reh den (1971) 404 US 960, 30 L Ed 2d 278, 92 S Ct 306.

3. Failure of service to comply with its regulations

Failure of service to comply with its own regulation does not preclude application of Feres doctrine under Federal Torts Claim Act (28 USCS § 2674). Anderson v United States (1983, CA8 Minn) 724 F2d 608.

Army will be enjoined from ordering reservist into involuntary active reserve where order for active duty is predicated on reservist's failure to attend unit meetings as required, but unit commander fails to follow Army regulations requiring commander to make investigation as to whether absences were due to cogent or emergency reasons and where prescribed procedures for involuntary active service were not followed in notifying reservist of such orders; that reservist pursued appeal is not substitute for Army's failure to follow regulations. Febus Nevarez v Schlesinger (1977, DC Puerto Rico) 440 F Supp 741.

§ 12303. Ready Reserve: members not assigned to, or participating satisfactorily in, units

(a) Notwithstanding any other provision of law, the President may order to active duty any member of the Ready Reserve of an armed force who—

(1) is not assigned to, or participating satisfactorily in, a unit of the Ready Reserve;

(2) has not fulfilled his statutory reserve obligation; and

(3) has not served on active duty for a total of 24 months.

(b) A member who is ordered to active duty under this section may be required to serve on active duty until his total service on active duty equals 24 months. If his enlistment or other period of military service would expire before he has served the required period under this section, it may be extended until he has served the required period.

(c) To achieve fair treatment among members of the Ready Reserve who are being considered for active duty under this section, appropriate consideration shall be given to—

(1) family responsibilities; and

(2) employment necessary to maintain the national health, safety, or interest.

(Added June 30, 1967, P. L. 90-40, § 6(1), 81 Stat. 105; Oct. 5, 1994, P. L. 103-337, Div A, Title XVI, Subtitle C, § 1662(e)(2), 108 Stat. 2992.)

HISTORY; ANCILLARY LAWS AND DIRECTIVES

Amendments:

1994. Act Oct. 5, 1994 (effective 12/1/94 as provided by § 1691 of such Act, which appears as 10 USCS § 10001 note) transferred this section, enacted as 10 USCS § 673a, to Chapter 1209 and redesignated it as 10 USCS § 12303.

Other provisions:

Assigning authority to order certain persons in the Ready Reserve to active duty. Ex. Or. No. 11366 of Aug. 8, 1967, 32 Fed. Reg. 11411, provided: "Section 1. (a) The Secretary of Defense is hereby authorized and empowered to exercise the authority vested in the President by section 673a [now § 12303] of title 10 of the United States Code, to order to active duty any member of the Ready Reserve of an armed force (except the Coast Guard when not operating as a service in the Navy) who—

"(1) is not assigned to, or participating satisfactorily in, a unit of the Ready Reserve;

"(2) has not fulfilled his statutory reserve obligation; and

"(3) has not served on active duty for a total of 24 months.

"(b) In pursuance of the provisions of section 673a [now § 12303] of title 10 of the United States Code, the Secretary of Defense is hereby authorized to require a member ordered to active duty under the authority of this Order to serve on active duty until his total service on active duty equals 24 months. If the enlistment or period of military service of a member of the Ready Reserve ordered to active duty under this authority would expire before he has served the required period of active duty prescribed herein, his enlistment or period of military service may be extended until he has served the required period.

"(c) In pursuance of the provisions of section 673a [now § 12303] of title 10 of the United States Code, and in order to achieve fair treatment among members of the Ready Reserve who are being considered for active duty under this authority, appropriate consideration shall be given to—

"(1) family responsibilities; and

"(2) employment necessary to maintain the national health, safety, or interest.

"Sec. 2. The Secretary of Transportation is hereby authorized and empowered to exercise the authority vested in the President by section 673a [now § 12303] of title 10 of the United States Code, with respect to any member of the Ready Reserve of the Coast Guard when it is not operating as a service in the Navy, under the same conditions as such authority may be exercised by the Secretary of Defense under this Order with respect to any member of the Ready Reserve of any other armed force.

"Sec. 3. (a) The Secretary of Defense may designate any of the Secretaries of the military departments of the Department of Defense to exercise the authority vested in him by section 1 of this Order.

"(b) The Secretary of Transportation may designate the Commandant of the United States Coast Guard to exercise the authority vested in him by section 2 of this Order.

"Sec. 4. Executive Order No. 11327 of February 15, 1967, is superseded except with respect to members of the Ready Reserve ordered to active duty under the authority of that Order.".

Assigning authority to order Ready Reserve to active duty. Ex. Or. No. 11406, April 10, 1968, 33 Fed. Reg. 5735, authorized the Secretary of Defense and, when designated by him, any of the Secretaries of the military departments of the Department of Defense to exercise the authority vested in the President until June 30, 1968 by paragraph (e) of Title I of the Department of Defense Appropriation Act, 1967 (Act Oct 15, 1966, P. L. 89-687, 80 Stat. 981 [unclassified]) to order any unit in the Ready Reserve to active duty for a period not to exceed 24 months.

Auto-Cite®: Cases and annotations referred to herein can be further researched through the Auto-Cite® computer-assisted research service. Use Auto-Cite to check citations for form, parallel references, prior and later history, and annotation references.

INTERPRETIVE NOTES AND DECISIONS

I. IN GENERAL

1. Generally
2. Purpose
3. Constitutionality
4. Applicability
5. Relation to other laws
6. Relation to Selective Service System
7. Nature of activation
8. Activation as alteration of enlistment contract

II. FACTORS AFFECTING ACTIVATION

9. Unsatisfactory performance
10. Unexcused absences
11. —Determining valid reasons for nonattendance
12. Proper attire and appearance at assembly
13. —Hair, beards and wigs
14. Deactivation of reservist's unit
15. Failure to join new unit
16. Discharge of reservist
17. Consideration of family responsibilities, employment, and hardship claims

III. PRACTICE AND PROCEDURE

18. Notice to reservist
19. Administrative appeal procedures
20. —Hearings
21. Waiver of right to challenge activation
22. Immunity from suit of officer issuing activation order
23. Judicial review
24. —Burden of proof
25. —Exhaustion of administrative remedies
26. Relief

I. IN GENERAL

1. Generally

In computing permissible extended active duty under 10 USCS § 673a(b) (now § 12303(b)), which allows such extension until reservist's total service on active duty equals 24 months, reservist's summer camp training is not "active duty" within § 673a(a) (now § 12303(a)). Fox v Brown (1968, CA2 NY) 402 F2d 837, cert den (1969) 394 US 938, 22 L Ed 2d 471, 89 S Ct 1219.

10 USCS § 673a (now § 12303) vests broad powers in President to call all members of Ready Reserve to active duty, and it does not require promulgation of regulations to implement it. Dix v Rollins (1969, CA8 Mo) 413 F2d 711.

2. Purpose

Primary purpose of involuntary activation appears to be to maintain military proficiency that is otherwise maintained by attendance at unit training assemblies. O'Mara v Zebrowski (1971, CA3 Pa) 447 F2d 1085; Wolf v Secretary of Defense (1975, MD Pa) 399 F Supp 446.

10 USCS § 673a (now § 12303) was intended by

Congress to assure Reservist of more equitable treatment than formerly in fulfillment of his military obligation. Even v Clifford (1968, SD Cal) 287 F Supp 334.

One purpose of 10 USCS § 673a (now § 12303) was to provide large pool of men who could be called into active duty without necessity of activating whole units and without presidential declaration of national emergency. Pfile v Corcoran (1968, DC Colo) 287 F Supp 554.

Congressional intent behind 10 USCS § 673a (now § 12303) is clearly to equalize obligation of reservists who have not previously served on active duty with that of draftees who spend 24 months on active duty. Heuchan v Laird (1969, DC Mo) 314 F Supp 796, affd (1970, CA8 Mo) 427 F2d 980.

3. Constitutionality

10 USCS § 673a (now § 12303) is clearly within power of Congress to enact and does not infringe on constitutional rights. Karpinski v Resor (1969, CA3 Pa) 419 F2d 531.

10 USCS § 673a (now § 12303) appears within war powers afforded Congress because it clearly provides more efficient procedure for processing delinquent reservists. Even v Clifford (1968, SD Cal) 287 F Supp 334.

Plaintiff's allegation that 10 USCS § 673a (now § 12303) is unconstitutional on its face in that it is void for vagueness since it lacks standards by which ''unsatisfactory participation'' can be ascertained, and it authorizes administrative punishment without procedural due process is plainly insubstantial and does not warrant convening of three-judge court under 28 USCS § 2282. Mickey v Barclay (1971, ED Pa) 328 F Supp 1108.

10 USCS § 673a (now § 12303) is not constitutionally infirm on grounds that (1) term ''unsatisfactory participation'' lacks sufficient standards to withstand void for vagueness test, (2) it authorizes administrative punishment without procedural due process and (3) it subjects reservist to cruel and unusual punishment. Mellinger v Laird (1972, ED Pa) 339 F Supp 434.

Reservist's involuntary activation as result of excessive unexcused absences does not constitute cruel and unusual punishment in violation of Eighth Amendment, since involuntary activation is not punishment primary purpose of involuntary order to active duty being to maintain military proficiency that is otherwise maintained by attendance at unit drills. Wolf v Secretary of Defense (1975, MD Pa) 399 F Supp 446.

Involuntary order to active duty of reservist found to be performing unsatisfactorily does not constitute cruel and unusual punishment. Caruso v Toothaker (1971, MD Pa) 331 F Supp 294.

4. Applicability

Fact that there has been hiatus in training, due to unsatisfactory performance on part of trainee, training being resumed within one month, did not prevent trainee from being lawfully member of the Air National Guard and subject, under 10 USCS § 673a (now § 12303), to be called up for active duty for not participating satisfactorily in his unit. Rasmussen v Seamans (1970, CA10 Colo) 432 F2d 346.

10 USCS § 673a (now § 12303) applies to member of Coast Guard. Bates v Commander, First Coast Guard Dist. (1969, DC Mass) 297 F Supp 193, vacated on other grounds (1969, CA1 Mass) 413 F2d 475.

5. Relation to other laws

Since 10 USCS § 673a (now § 12303), authority for activation order, is applicable by its terms notwithstanding any other provision of law, activation order is not invalid where consent of governor under 10 USCS § 672 (now § 12301)or request of governor under 10 USCS § 270(c) (now repealed) was not shown; even though 32 USCS § 303(c) (now repealed) provides that in time of peace, no enlisted member may be required to serve for period longer than that for which he enlisted in active or inactive National Guard, 10 USCS § 673a(a) (now § 12303(a)), which provided for involuntary activation of reservist for his unsatisfactory participation in reserves, applies notwithstanding any other provision of law. Fox v Brown (1968, CA2 NY) 402 F2d 837, cert den (1969) 394 US 938, 22 L Ed 2d 471, 89 S Ct 1219.

10 USCS § 673a (now § 12303) as statutory basis for military reservist's involuntary activation, was not qualified or modified by 10 USCS § 886(1) (which concerns absence without leave) nor 10 USCS § 815 (which concerns a commanding officer's non-judicial punishment) since these statutes were enacted prior to § 673a (now § 12303) which begins with unequivocal language ''Notwithstanding any other provision of law''. O'Mara v Zebrowski (1971, CA3 Pa) 447 F2d 1085.

10 USCS § 673a (now § 12303) did not eliminate 10 USCS § 270(b) (now repealed). Even v Clifford (1968, SD Cal) 287 F Supp 334.

6. Relation to Selective Service System

Retroactive application of 10 USCS § 673a (now § 12303) to order appellant, who enlisted in National Guard prior to enactment of § 673a (now § 12303) did not harm appellant in any tangible way, where, although appellant's enlistment contract provided that any induction was to be through Selective Service System, applicable regulations at time of appellant's enlistment made clear that local board's responsibility was solely ministerial, to bring into active service soldier who had already enlisted and whose reserve status had been terminated; appellant would have had no right to reclassification if he were processed through Selective Service, so he lost no right by being activated through procedure which bypassed local draft board. Gianatasio v Whyte (1970, CA2 Conn) 426 F2d 908, cert den (1970) 400 US 941, 27 L Ed 2d 244, 91 S Ct 234.

By virtue of 10 USCS § 673a (now § 12303), delinquent reservist is ordered to involuntary active duty without induction by Selective Service System. Even v Clifford (1968, SD Cal) 287 F Supp 334.

Effect of 10 USCS § 673a (now § 12303) was to give reserve organization power to call up reservist without processing him through Selective Service System, but reservist could only be called up for period such that his total active duty time, including prior active duty, did not exceed 24 months, so that reservist with prior active duty time receives credit for that time, which he would not have received if inducted through Selective Service System and thus, § 673a (now § 12303) is in this limited sense, ameliorating measure. Pfile v Corcoran (1968, DC Colo) 287 F Supp 554.

7. Nature of activation

Activation of unsatisfactory participating reservist is not punitive, but administrative. Keister v Resor (1972, CA3 Pa) 462 F2d 471, cert den (1972) 409 US 894, 34 L Ed 2d 151, 93 S Ct 116.

Activation order issued pursuant to 10 USCS § 673a (now § 12303) is not punitive administrative action but rather is simply administrative or contractual sanction imposed for failure to perform duties voluntarily accepted in return for exemption from service in the regular army. Mickey v Barclay (1971, ED Pa) 328 F Supp 1108.

8. Activation as alteration of enlistment contract

Activation under 10 USCS § 673a (now § 12303) of member of reserves was not unconstitutional as violation of his prior enlistment contract with reserves which provided for order to active duty for training for 45 days or report to selective service for immediate induction. Schwartz v Franklin (1969, CA9 Cal) 412 F2d 736; Dellaverson v Laird (1972, SD Cal) 351 F Supp 134.

Where period for which reservist was called to active duty for failure to comply with his reserve obligation, under 10 USCS § 673a (now § 12303), would extend beyond expiration date of his enlistment, there has been no violation of reservist's constitutional rights. Karpinski v Resor (1969, CA3 Pa) 419 F2d 531.

Retroactive application of 10 USCS § 673a (now § 12303) to order appellant, who enlisted in National Guard prior to enactment of § 673a (now § 12303), did not harm appellant in any tangible way, where, although appellant's enlistment contract provided that any induction was to be through Selective Service System, applicable regulations at time of appellant's enlistment made clear that local board's responsibility was solely ministerial, to bring into active service soldier who had already enlisted and whose reserve status had been terminated; appellant would have had no right to reclassification if he were processed through Selective Service, so he lost no right by being activated through a procedure which bypassed the local draft board. Gianatasio v Whyte (1970, CA2 Conn) 426 F2d 908, cert den (1970) 400 US 941, 27 L Ed 2d 244, 91 S Ct 234.

Statutory enactment of 10 USCS § 673a (now § 12303) and its implementation by executive order and military directives may validly modify contractual provision which limits duration of time for which reservist may be activated for unsatisfactory participation. Heuchan v Laird (1970, CA8 Mo) 427 F2d 980.

Petitioner was not deprived of any substantial contract rights which may have arisen under provisions of his enlistment contract by 10 USCS § 673a (now § 12303), which eliminated role of local draft board in ordering delinquent reservist to involuntary active duty. Even v Clifford (1968, SD Cal) 287 F Supp 334.

10 USCS § 673a (now § 12303) may be applied retroactively to petitioner who entered enlistment contract prior to enactment of § 673a (now § 12303), even though contract provided for different circumstances under which petitioner could be assigned to active duty. Pfile v Corcoran (1968, DC Colo) 287 F Supp 554.

Since 10 USCS § 262 (now repealed) provides that purpose of reserves is to provide trained units and qualified persons available for active duty in armed forces at such times as national security requires, amendment of petitioners' enlistment contract by enactment of 10 USCS § 673a (now § 12303) authorizing activation without declaration of national emergency, was not violation of due process or denial of equal protection. Sullivan v Cushman (1968, DC Mass) 290 F Supp 659.

Where petitioner was subject to priority induction for 24 months under his enlistment agreement and for active duty for extended period under other statutes, application of 10 USCS § 673a (now § 12303), in light of petitioner's unsatisfactory participation in Ready Reserve, does not deprive petitioner of any substantial contract rights without due process of law. Schultz v Clifford (1968, DC Minn) 303 F Supp 965, affd (1969, CA8 Minn) 417 F2d 775, cert den (1970) 397 US 1007, 25 L Ed 2d 420, 90 S Ct 1234.

Call to active duty pursuant to 10 USCS § 673a (now § 12303) for unsatisfactory participation in Ready Reserve does not effectively abrogate contractual rights of one who has enlisted in Ready Reserve under laws existing prior thereto. Metz v United States (1969, WD Pa) 304 F Supp 207.

Where at time reservist signed enlistment contract, Army had additional consequence available for all delinquent reservists, regardless of exact language of their contracts, in addition to activation for 45 days, whereby reservist who fails to serve satisfactorily during his obligated period of service could be inducted and required to serve at least 2 years in armed force of which such reserve component was part, under 50 USCS Appendix § 456, there is no change in substance of reservist's contractual burdens by retroactive application of 10 USCS § 673a (now § 12303), so no constitutional violation has occurred; even though reservist's enlistment contract expressly provided that upon unsatisfactory participation in Ready Reserves he could be activated only for period of 45 days, application of 10 USCS § 673a (now § 12303), which was enacted after his enlistment, and allowed activation for up to 2 years, does not violate Fifth Amendment's prohibition against retroactive impairment of contracts. Mellinger v Laird (1972, ED Pa) 339 F Supp 434.

Involuntary activation of plaintiff pursuant to 10 USCS § 673a (now § 12303) would not be effective where active duty orders did not become effective until day after plaintiff's enlistment term had expired, as plaintiff was not activated nor his enlistment properly extended during his 6-year period of enlistment, so to subject him to activation would violate terms of his enlistment contract and possibly contravene Navy regulations. Musikov v United States Secretary of Defense (1973, DC Minn) 357 F Supp 526.

II. FACTORS AFFECTING ACTIVATION

9. Unsatisfactory performance

Regulations promulgated pursuant to 10 USCS § 673a (now § 12303) which provided that unsatisfactory performance leading to activation would include failure to progress satisfactorily in training, which are of prospective force, may constitutionally provide for determinations based upon past events and apply to persons possessing continuing status. Heuchan v Laird (1970, CA8 Mo) 427 F2d 980.

When one opts for 6-year reserve status in lieu of 2 years' active duty, such reservist in signing his enlistment contract agrees to be subject to applicable federal statutes and military regulations and consents to induction into active service should he fail to participate satisfactorily as reservist. Schulz v Resor (1971, ED Wis) 332 F Supp 708.

Under 10 USCS § 673a (now § 12303), member of National Guard who is not satisfactorily participating in drills may be extended as to time he must serve. Baugh v Bennett (1972, DC Idaho) 350 F Supp 1248.

10. Unexcused absences

Unexcused absences from scheduled drills comes within meaning of "unsatisfactory participation" especially in view of specific advice petitioner was given concerning what would constitute unsatisfactory participation. Mickey v Barclay (1971, ED Pa) 328 F Supp 1108.

Regulation providing that 5 unexcused absences within 1 year would result in reservist's activation contemplates merely that 5 absences must accrue within 1 year period, not that order to active duty itself must be issued within that period. Mellinger v Laird (1972, ED Pa) 339 F Supp 434.

11. —Determining valid reasons for nonattendance

Given Army regulation providing that Army commander had to determine that reservist's absence was for reasons within reservist's control before commander could conclude that reservist's absence from annual training was unexcused and that involuntary activation was indicated, where before making decision as to activation, commander was aware that reservist had been attempting to obtain medical discharge from service, that reservist had taken physical exam only 11 days before summer camp which showed him to be medically qualified for military service, that reservist had signed statement acknowledging his obligation to attend annual training less than 2 weeks before summer camp session began, that reservist had failed to appear for summer camp as required, that reservist knew he was subject to involuntary activation if he did not satisfactorily perform his reserve obligation, that reservist had been contacted by member of commander's staff about his absence, that reservist had stated he was not going to summer camp because he had discharge due him and that reservist had not contacted his commander to give any emergency or cogent reasons for his absence, commander has sufficiently complied with regulation and he was not required to secure additional information, speak with reservist personally or undertake some kind of formalized investigation. White v Callaway (1974, CA5 Tex) 501 F2d 672, reh den (1974, CA5 Tex) 503 F2d 1403.

Where Army commander fails to follow Army regulations providing that before commander shall initiate request that reservist who has five or more unexcused absences be ordered to active duty, such commander must first make determination as to whether there was good reason for absences, prejudice will result to reservist in question even if he was later permitted to offer his excuse in various military appellate reviews of commander's request that reservist be placed on active duty. Hall v Fry (1975, CA10 Kan) 509 F2d 1105.

Where plaintiff has been ordered to active duty under Army regulation providing that any reservist who is absent from 5 or more unit training assemblies during 1-year period will be ordered to active duty for certain period, other regulation requiring plaintiff's commanding officer to determine if any cogent or emergency reasons exist which prevent member from attending, did not require commanding officer to do more than determine what nature of member's excuse for nonattendance is, and if that excuse is related to employment conflicts, to forward case to area commander: reservist was not entitled to full-blown, judicial style hearing. Homfeld v United States (1972, ED Mich) 353 F Supp 862.

Investigation called for by Army regulation into reason for unexcused absence from scheduled unit training assembly need be made only for fifth absence, which results in involuntary activation under regulation in question; where reservist is absent for fifth time, resulting in involuntary activation, even though excuse for such absence is not offered within 14 day period as prescribed by Army regulations, commander nonetheless has obligation of making investigation which will enable him to certify whether or not any cogent or emergency reasons exist which prevented reservist from attending drill, and simply stating excuse was not received in time is not discharge of obligations which investigating officer has under regulation in question. Feeny v Smith (1973, DC Utah) 371 F Supp 319.

Where Army regulation mandates that before unit commander may recommend involuntary activation of member for reason of absence from drills, he must determine if any cogent or emergency reason existed which prevented member from attending, failure of unit commander to consider medical report detailing reservist's disability which led to such absences will prevent activation of reservist. Tobiczyk v United States (1974, ED Mich) 381 F Supp 345.

Determination by officer that reserve member has failed to participate satisfactorily is immune from complaint that officer failed to determine whether any cogent or emergency reasons existed which prevented member from attending his drill periods where facts show that officer questioned member as to whether there were any facts he should be aware of before deciding whether to deny credit for periods and received no reply. Caruso v Toothaker (1971, MD Pa) 331 F Supp 294.

12. Proper attire and appearance at assembly

Determination of "neat and soldierly appearance" is determination within discretion of military and failure to give reservist credit for drills was proper exercise of discretion when it was shown that he did not comply with appearance standard of army regulation. Raderman v Kaine (1969, CA2 NY) 411 F2d 1102, cert dismd (1969) 396 US 976, 24 L Ed 2d 447, 90 S Ct 467.

Determination that reserve member was absent without excuse will be upheld where, although physically present at assembly, reservist did not fulfill regulation requirements that he appear in prescribed uniform, that his appearance be neat and soldierly, and that he perform his assigned duties in satisfactory manner. Caruso v Toothaker (1971, MD Pa) 331 F Supp 294.

13. —Hair, beards and wigs

Where Army failed to follow its own regulation requiring that proof submitted by reservist as to necessity of his long hair for his civilian livelihood be made part of reservist's official record, reservist may not be involuntarily activated on basis of excessive unexcused absences arising from his long hair. Smith v Resor (1969, CA2 NY) 406 F2d 141.

It is proper to deny credit for attendance to member whose hair style did not conform to commander's standard. Anderson v Laird (1971, CA7 Ill) 437 F2d 912, cert den (1971) 404 US 865, 30 L Ed 2d 109, 92 S Ct 68.

Regulations governing length of hair and beards of men in army reserve were not unconstitutional on ground that enforcement of such regulations would subject reservists to additional unexcused absences, and that accumulation of five such absences during 12-month period would make them liable for involuntary active duty. Krill v Bauer (1970, ED Wis) 314 F Supp 965.

As applied to Army Reservists, regulation which prohibits wearing of wig or hairpiece while in uniform or on duty, except for cosmetic reasons to cover natural baldness and when appropriate to cover physical disfiguration caused by accident or medical procedure, exceeds statutory authorization; prohibiting plaintiff from wearing short-haired wig over his long hair at reserve meetings impinges upon his freedom to govern his appearance which is protected by due process clauses of the Fifth and the Fourteenth Amendments. Harris v Kaine (1972, SD NY) 352 F Supp 769.

Reservist may not be activated under 10 USCS § 673a (now § 12303) on basis that his wearing short-hair wig to cover long hair, in contravention of Navy regulation permitting wearing of wigs only for bald men, led to unexcused absences in excess of number allowed, since Navy regulation in question unconstitutionally distinguishes between plaintiff's wearing wig and bald men wearing wigs. Etheridge v Schlesinger (1973, ED Va) 362 F Supp 198.

14. Deactivation of reservist's unit

Even though petitioner's unit had been deactivated and was eligible for retention in Ready Reserve Pool, petitioner was not permanently exempted from call to active duty under 10 USCS § 673a (now § 12303), as he was not called to active duty for failure to observe drill requirements or reserve duties but was only called after proper determination was made that substantial need existed for calling reservists to active duty. Dix v Rollins (1969, CA8 Mo) 413 F2d 711.

15. Failure to join new unit

Petitioner was not wrongfully activated under 10 USCS § 673a (now § 12303) on basis that he failed to join new unit within 60 days as prescribed by Army regulations and short grace period granted thereafter, after change of residence, where petitioner was ill on day he was to take oath of enlistment in new unit, which marked end of grace period, since petitioner was aware of his duty to locate and join new unit within time specified. Shadle v United States (1970, MD Pa) 315 F Supp 102.

16. Discharge of reservist

Marine Corps reservist who was called to active duty for not participating 100 percent in reserve drills and who was discharged and subsequently reactivated was not subjected to double jeopardy due to administrative error in discharge action. Winters v United States (1969, CA9 Cal) 412 F2d 140, cert den (1969) 396 US 920, 24 L Ed 2d 200, 90 S Ct 248.

National Guard has no responsibility to process application for discharge of delinquent reservist who first files his application after he has already been issued orders to report for active duty. Johnson v Laird (1970, CA9 Wash) 435 F2d 493.

Department of Defense directive which provides that reservist who does not satisfactorily participate in reserves for any of several enumerated reasons will be processed, upon application, for discharge and provides that only those eligible for discharge for any of enumerated reasons will be discharged, does not mandate determination of reservist's eligibility for discharge before his activation for unexcused absences pursuant to 10 USCS § 673a (now § 12303). Keister v Resor (1972, CA3 Pa) 462 F2d 471, cert den (1972) 409 US 894, 34 L Ed 2d 151, 93 S Ct 116.

17. Consideration of family responsibilities, employment, and hardship claims

Appropriate consideration was not given to hardship claim of Marine Corps reservist, ordered to involuntary active duty under authority of 10 USCS § 673a (now § 12303) as implemented by Marine Corps order requiring commanding officers to investigate personal hardship claims, where record showed that reservist was not specifically questioned concerning hardship claim, or advised of right to make hardship claim, by interviewing officers, but that commandant could have assumed that he had been so questioned, and Marine Corps would be directed to give appropriate consideration to whatever hardship claim reservist could make. United States ex rel. United States ex rel. Sledjeski v Commanding Officer, Armed Forces (1973, CA2 Conn) 478 F2d 1147.

Failure, in involuntary assignment of Ready Reservist to active duty, to render effective consideration of Reservist's family responsibilities and employment in its relation to national health, safety or interest as required by 10 USCS § 673a(c) (now § 12303(c)) would not operate to invalidate order sending plaintiff to active duty, where record showed that reservist had no dependents and disclosed that he was single and childless, and no claim based on employment was advanced. Winters v United States (1968, ED NY) 281 F Supp 289, affd (1968, CA2 NY) 390 F2d 879, cert den (1968) 393 US 896, 21 L Ed 2d 177, 89 S Ct 188.

Where no consideration was given by Marine Corps to pregnancy of petitioner's wife and his family responsibilities, as required by 10 USCS § 673a(c) (now § 12303(c)), in issuing orders for petitioner's involuntary active duty in connection with petitioner's alleged unexcused absence from reserve meetings, petitioner may not be activated. McSweeney v United States (1971, ND Ohio) 338 F Supp 350.

Provision in 10 USCS § 673a(c) (now § 12303(c)) requiring that "appropriate consideration" be given to "family responsibilities," when ordering reservist to involuntary active duty under § 673a (now § 12303) does not require investigation into reservist's family situation by officer issuing order; it is sufficient that reservist's superior officers know of his family responsibilities and consider them before recommending his activation. Santos v Franklin (1980, ED Pa) 493 F Supp 847.

III. PRACTICE AND PROCEDURE

18. Notice to reservist

Lack of notice of scheduling of drills and meetings is factor to be considered in determination of whether reservist's absences from such drills and meetings should be recorded as unexcused for purposes of determining if reservist should be involuntarily activated. Schatten v United States (1969, CA6 Mich) 419 F2d 187.

Order which involuntarily activates reservist for too many unexcused absences must be revoked where Army failed to follow its own regulation in that upon being notified that he was involuntarily activated, reservist was not notified that he was not required or authorized to attend unit assemblies while awaiting his entry on active duty and that he would be granted excused absence during period involved. Konn v Laird (1972, CA7 Wis) 460 F2d 1318.

Failure of Army to follow its own regulations requiring that letters advising reservist that his performance at particular drill was unsatisfactory must be submitted to reservist prior to next scheduled drill so as to keep reservist advised as to his absences or unsatisfactory performances so that he can be fully apprised of his record before approaching fifth absence which will result in involuntary activation, does work to prejudice of reservist in question. Hall v Fry (1975, CA10 Kan) 509 F2d 1105.

Where Army fails to follow its own regulation in involuntarily activating petitioner for petitioner's alleged unexcused absences from training, in that petitioner was not notified of order transferring him to active duty and was not notified of his right to appeal activation order, petitioner was improperly ordered to active duty. Horn v Musick (1971, SD Ohio) 347 F Supp 1307, 31 Ohio Misc 115, 60 Ohio Ops 2d 250.

Where Army fails to follow its own regulation providing that reservist must be notified promptly when his participation in any training assembly is unsatisfactory or where he was inexcusably absent, reservist in question may not be involuntarily activated on basis of such unsatisfactory performances or unexcused absences. United States ex rel. United States ex rel. Moravetz v Resor (1972, DC Minn) 349 F Supp 1182.

Where petitioner has received several notices prior to dates on which he was inexcusably absent from drills and which gave rise to his order to involuntary active duty, Army's failure to give notice prior to these particular occasions giving rise to order in question was not prejudicial to petitioner. Feeny v Smith (1973, DC Utah) 371 F Supp 319.

Army Reservist ordered to active duty under 10 USCS § 673a (now § 12303) due to his failure to satisfactorily participate in scheduled Army Reserve drills could not complain of absence of notice where evidence showed he systematically and intentionally failed to claim correspondence directed to him by his Reserve unit. United States ex rel. Niemann v Greer (1975, DC NJ) 394 F Supp 249.

When Army fails to follow its own regulations in connection with reservist's alleged excessive absences leading to activation, in not furnishing reservist with letter of instruction after unexcused absence and before next scheduled training assembly advising him of consequences of absence and in not advising reservist of his right to appeal his order to active duty, involuntary activation of reservist will not be allowed. United States v Kilbreth (1973) 22 USCMA 390, 47 CMR 327.

19. Administrative appeal procedures

Reservist's administrative activation under 10 USCS § 673a (now § 12303) must be affirmed where Army followed its appropriate regulations in processing his appeal, even though that regulation only indicates what authority would consider his appeal and does not detail what must and may be submitted with appeal or enumerate reasons for which appeal may be taken. Antonuk v United States (1971, CA6 Mich) 445 F2d 592.

Selective service regulations devised to implement 10 USCS § 673a (now § 12303) which governs involuntary activation of military reservist who has more than five unexcused absences from "unit training assemblies" are not invalid on due process grounds where procedure permits reservist to take matter up with his unit commander and also permits appeal in which reservist has opportunity to explain facts pertinent to his case which he feels have not been fully considered and to include any additional appropriate evidence. O'Mara v Zebrowski (1971, CA3 Pa) 447 F2d 1085.

Army regulation providing that reservist shall be informed of his right to appeal order to active duty and that any such appeal must be submitted no later than 15 days from receipt of right to appeal letter is in accord with 10 USCS § 673a (now § 12303). Cruz-Matos v Laird (1971, DC Puerto Rico) 324 F Supp 1325.

When Army regulations provide for appeal by reservist from orders to involuntary active duty, these regulations must be held to require that meaningful appeal be afforded and anything less deprives individual of due process of law. Baugh v Bennett (1971, DC Idaho) 329 F Supp 20.

Admitted failure of State Adjutant General to personally inquire into substance of each unexcused absence rather than just administrative details in connection with reservist's activation does not violate Army regulation requiring State Adjutant General to personally verify circumstances in each case and determine that administrative requirements have been complied with. Mellinger v Laird (1972, ED Pa) 339 F Supp 434.

Army reservist has been denied meaningful appeal of order calling him to active service upon alleged unexcused absences from drills, where he did not have his military personnel records available to him to persuade those having authority to act that decision appealed from was incorrect. Feeny v Smith (1973, DC Utah) 371 F Supp 319.

It is not constitutionally required that reservist called to active duty be supplied copy of his Appeal Board record. Caruso v Toothaker (1971, MD Pa) 331 F Supp 294.

20. —Hearings

Full personal hearing is not required as matter of contractual law or as matter of constitutional law when appealing involuntary activation order. Ansted v Resor (1971, CA7 Ind) 437 F2d 1020, cert den (1971) 404 US 827, 30 L Ed 2d 56, 92 S Ct 61, reh den (1971) 404 US 960, 30 L Ed 2d 278, 92 S Ct 306.

Due process does not require full formal hearing before administrative activation of Army reservist, and reservists may be activated pursuant to 10 USCS § 673a (now § 12303) notwithstanding clauses in their enlistment contracts to contrary. Antonuk v United States (1971, CA6 Mich) 445 F2d 592.

No constitutional infirmity arises from absence of hearing before involuntary activation of reservist. Keister v Resor (1972, CA3 Pa) 462 F2d 471, cert den (1972) 409 US 894, 34 L Ed 2d 151, 93 S Ct 116.

There is no violation of Army regulations where reservist was not provided with personal hearing, including representation and right of cross-examination, before Delay Appeal Board, body charged with acting on appeals from active duty orders, since reservist received personal hearing under Uniform Code of Military Justice (10 USCS § 938) at which he was afforded opportunity to have counsel present, testify and cross-examine witnesses against him. Mellinger v Laird (1972, ED Pa) 339 F Supp 434.

Where plaintiff has been ordered to active duty under Army regulation providing that any reservist who is absent from 5 or more unit training assemblies during 1-year period will be ordered to active duty for certain period, other regulation requiring plaintiff's commanding officer to determine if any cogent or emergency reasons exist which prevent member from attending, did not require commanding officer to do more than determine what nature of member's excuse for nonattendance is, and if that excuse is related to employment conflicts, to forward case to area commander: reservist was not entitled to full-blown, judicial style hearing. Homfeld v United States (1972, ED Mich) 353 F Supp 862.

Reservist has no right to formal hearing when faced with involuntary call to active duty due to unsatisfactory participation in Ready Reserve under provisions of 10 USCS § 673a (now § 12303). Herrick v Cushman (1974, ED NC) 379 F Supp 1143.

Even though there are punitive aspects to involuntary activation, full due process hearing is not required. Tobiczyk v United States (1974, ED Mich) 381 F Supp 345.

21. Waiver of right to challenge activation

Reservist involuntarily activated under 10 USCS § 673a (now § 12303) is subject to court-martial jurisdiction even though he challenges propriety of call-up where failure to challenge activation within reasonable time and through provided procedures constitutes knowing and voluntary waiver of right to challenge, on constitutional due process grounds, his involuntary activation orders. United States v Barraza (1978, CMA) 5 MJ 230.

22. Immunity from suit of officer issuing activation order

Officer who ordered reservist to active duty under authority of 10 USCS § 673a (now § 12303) for failure to attend required number of training drills is immune from suit for damages by reservist where officer complied with all applicable regulations and acted within scope of his official function and discretion. Santos v Franklin (1980, ED Pa) 493 F Supp 847.

23. Judicial review

Activation order under 10 USCS § 673a (now § 12303) for unsatisfactory performance in reserves may only be reviewed to extent of determining whether military had acted within its jurisdiction under valid law. Fox v Brown (1968, CA2 NY) 402 F2d 837, cert den (1969) 394 US 938, 22 L Ed 2d 471, 89 S Ct 1219; Metz v United States (1969, WD Pa) 304 F Supp 207.

Federal court may properly examine decision to call reservist for active duty in order to determine if reservist's procedural rights under applicable statutes and military procedures and regulations were violated in manner which caused substantial prejudice to reservist, and this examination does not involve any undue interference with proper and efficient operation of military forces, because it is required only that Army carry out procedures and regulations it created itself. Smith v Resor (1969, CA2 NY) 406 F2d 141.

Definition of ''satisfactory participation'' is matter properly within area of military discretion, which prevents civil courts to judge whether military has properly determined balance between military needs and personal rights. Anderson v Laird (1971, CA7 Ill) 437 F2d 912, cert den (1971) 404 US 865, 30 L Ed 2d 109, 92 S Ct 68.

Courts may examine order that reservist be activated in order to ascertain whether military's rules and regulations were violated in manner resulting in substantial prejudice; whether reservist's hair was too long for one drill and whether his conduct at another drill was unsatisfactory, which resulted in unexcused absences and involuntary activation, were matters peculiarly within discretion of reservist's commanding officer and over which court could not exercise jurisdiction. Hall v Fry (1975, CA10 Kan) 509 F2d 1105.

Exercise of discretion by plaintiff's commanding officer in finding that plaintiff performed unsatisfactorily in year in which he had 2 unexcused absences from required drill, is not reviewable by court. Winters v United States (1968, ED NY) 281 F Supp 289, affd (1968, CA2 NY) 390 F2d 879, cert den (1968) 393 US 896, 21 L Ed 2d 177, 89 S Ct 188.

Allowable scope of review in case whereby reservist would be involuntarily activated under 10 USCS § 673a (now § 12303) is confined to determination of (1) whether military orders were promulgated in violation of military's own regulation, (2) whether procedures employed by military comport with requirements of due process in light of context in which procedures operate and (3) whether military has acted within jurisdiction conferred on it by valid law. Feeny v Smith (1973, DC Utah) 371 F Supp 319.

In reviewing Army order sending reservist to active duty for his alleged unsatisfactory participation in scheduled training drills, court is limited to determining whether or not military has complied with its regulations in ordering reservist to active duty, as discretionary administrative decisions of military authorities consistent with procedures mandated by military regulations are not subject to review; determinations of validity or invalidity of excuses for absences from scheduled drills which may lead to involuntary activation are vested within sound discretion of military authorities and allegation that reservist's unit erroneously refused to accept valid excuses is not properly before court. Russo v Luba (1975, WD Pa) 400 F Supp 370.

Discretionary decision of military officials, ordering reservist to active duty due to his excessive unexcused absences, made within their valid jurisdiction is beyond permissible scope of review of federal courts. Wolf v Secretary of Defense (1975, MD Pa) 399 F Supp 446.

Determination by officer that reserve member is not performing satisfactorily will not be disturbed for failure by officer to make findings if those findings are not required by Army regulations. Caruso v Toothaker (1971, MD Pa) 331 F Supp 294.

24. —Burden of proof

Reservist questioning military's right to order him to active duty in proceeding before courts bears heavy burden to show that President and his authorized representatives abused discretion vested in them in calling him to active service. Dix v Rollins (1969, CA8 Mo) 413 F2d 711.

Summary judgment was precluded where marine corps failed to meet burden of proof of showing that involuntary activation was precipitated by fact that reservist, on numerous occasions, was allegedly voluntarily, and without cause, absent from mandatory drills rather than precipitated as punishment for wearing wig during drills which met marine corps standards but not those of his commanding officer. Narez v Wilson (1979, CA8 Mo) 591 F2d 459.

25. —Exhaustion of administrative remedies

Before court may determine whether plaintiff received meaningful appeal from order of involuntary activation arising from absences which reservist maintains resulted from legitimate medical condition, reservist must comply with pertinent Army regulation which states that each member ordered to active duty must undergo medical examination, and until reservist complies with such regulation, he has not exhausted administrative remedies. Lizzio v Richardson (1974, ED Pa) 378 F Supp 986.

Administrative remedies under 10 USCS § 938 must be exhausted before habeas corpus action in federal court may be brought challenging involuntary activation. Herrick v Cushman (1974, ED NC) 379 F Supp 1143.

In proceeding challenging call-up under 10 USCS § 673a (now § 12303), doctrine of exhaustion of administrative remedies will be applied to involuntary activation cases on ground that they involve challenges to factual determinations which formed basis for call-up rather than attacks on compliance with essential procedural requirements in administrative procedure; one challenging involuntary call-up waives constitutional rights to challenge on due process ground where there is no evidence that he protested his activation prior to, during, or immediately after his entrance into active duty nor is there evidence that within reasonable time after reporting for active duty he attempted to secure his release on constitutional grounds in federal civil court by writ of habeas corpus and did not raise constitutional challenge to activation orders until 6 months after call-up at court-martial for drug offenses which were unrelated to initial order to report for active duty. United States v Barraza (1978, CMA) 5 MJ 230.

26. Relief

Reservist contesting legality of his call-up to active duty is entitled to stay preventing his transfer to combat area, pending appeal from Federal District Court to Court of Appeals, where important federal questions are presented on which no appellate court has passed and on which there is conflict among District Courts within same circuit and where denial of stay might result in irreparable damage to reservist. Winters v United States (1968, US) 21 L Ed 2d 80, 89 S Ct 57.

Mandamus is proper action to test validity of activation order based upon unexcused absences from training assemblies claimed to be illegal in that unit commander did not follow army regulations prior to activation for unsatisfactory participation. Papaioannou v Commanding Officer, 1st U.S. Army (1975, CA1 RI) 509 F2d 692.

Failure of reservist's drill commander to accept wig worn by reservist, which wig met Marine Corps standards, refusal to grant request of reservist for MAST, and apparent intent of commander to make example of reservist, raises such questions of harassment and violation of Marine Corps regulations, that summary judgment will not be granted in favor of government on reservist's suit to preclude involuntary transfer to active duty pursuant to 10 USCS § 673a (now § 12303). Narez v Wilson (1979, CA8 Mo) 591 F2d 459.

Petitioner, who was member of national guard unit, was not entitled to relief via habeas corpus petition on grounds that he was civilian and should be released from military, when military had jurisdiction over him because he had missed more than required number of drills and was subsequently called to active duty. Colon-Rios v Perrin (1969, DC Puerto Rico) 306 F Supp 1314.

§ 12304. Selected Reserve and certain Individual Ready Reserve members; order to active duty other than during war or national emergency

(a) Notwithstanding the provisions of section 12302(a) or any other provision of law, when the President determines that it is necessary to augment the active forces for any operational mission, he may authorize the Secretary of Defense and the Secretary of Transportation with respect to the Coast Guard when it is not operating as a service in the Navy, without the consent of the members concerned, to order any unit, and any member not assigned to a unit organized to serve as a unit, of the Selected Reserve (as defined in section 10143(a) of this title), or any member in the Individual Ready Reserve mobilization category and designated as essential under regulations prescribed by the Secretary concerned, under their respective jurisdictions, to active duty (other than for training) for not more than 270 days.

(b) No unit or member of a reserve component may be ordered to active duty under this section to perform any of the functions authorized by chapter 15 [10 USCS §§ 331 et seq.] or section 12406 of this title, or to provide assistance to either the Federal Government or a State in time of a serious natural or manmade disaster, accident, or catastrophe.

(c) Not more than 200,000 members of the Selected Reserve and the Individual Ready Reserve may be on active duty under this section at any one time, of whom not more than 30,000 may be members of the Individual Ready Reserve.

(d) Members ordered to active duty under this section shall not be counted in computing authorized strength in members on active duty or members in grade under this title or any other law.

(e) The Secretary of Defense and the Secretary of Transportation shall prescribe such policies and procedures for the armed forces under their respective jurisdictions as they consider necessary to carry out this section.

(f) Whenever the President authorizes the Secretary of Defense or the Secretary of Transportation to order any unit or member of the Selected Reserve or Individual Ready Reserve to active duty, under the authority of subsection (a), he shall, within 24 hours after exercising such authority, submit to Congress a report, in writing, setting forth the circumstances necessitating the action taken under this section and describing the anticipated use of these units or members.

(g) Whenever any unit of the Selected Reserve or any member of the Selected Reserve not assigned to a unit organized to serve as a unit, or any member of the Individual Ready Reserve, is ordered to active duty under authority of subsection (a), the service of all units or members so ordered to active duty may be terminated by—

(1) order of the President, or

(2) law.

(h) Nothing contained in this section shall be construed as amending or limiting the application of the provisions of the War Powers Resolution (50 U.S.C. 1541 et seq.).

(i) For purposes of this section, the term ''Individual Ready Reserve mobilization category'' means, in the case of any reserve component, the category of the Individual Ready Reserve described in section 10144(b) of this title.

(Added May 14, 1976, P. L. 94-286, § 1 in part, 90 Stat. 517; Dec. 23, 1980, P. L. 96-584, § 2, 94 Stat. 3377; Oct. 12, 1982, P. L. 97-295, § 1(9), 96 Stat. 1289; Nov. 14, 1986, P. L. 99-661, Div A, Title V, Part B, § 521, 100 Stat. 3870; Oct. 5, 1994, P. L. 103-337, Div A, Title V, Subtitle B, § 511(a), Title XVI, Subtitle C, § 1662(e)(2), Subtitle D, § 1675(c)(2), 108 Stat. 2752, 2992, 3017; Nov. 18, 1997, P. L. 105-85, Div A, Title V, Subtitle B, § 511(b)–(d), (e)(1), 111 Stat. 1728.)

HISTORY; ANCILLARY LAWS AND DIRECTIVES

Amendments:

1980. Act Dec. 23, 1980, in subsec. (c), substituted "100,000" for "50,000".

1982. Act Oct. 12, 1982 (effective as provided by § 5 of such Act, which appears as 10 USCS § 101 note), in subsec. (h), inserted "(50 U.S.C. 1541 et seq.)".

1986. Act Nov. 14, 1986, in subsec. (b), substituted "reserve component" for "Reserve component"; in subsec. (c), substituted "200,000" for "100,000"; in subsec. (e), substituted "armed forces" for "Armed Forces"; in subsec. (f), substituted "Congress" for "the Speaker of the House of Representatives and to the President pro tempore of the Senate"; in subsec. (g)(2), substituted "law" for "a concurrent resolution of the Congress"; and added subsec. (i).

1994. Act Oct. 5, 1994, in subsec. (a), substituted "270 days" for "90 days"; and deleted subsec. (i), which read: "(i) When a unit of the Selected Reserve, or a member of the Selected Reserve not assigned to a unit organized to serve as a unit of the Selected Reserve, is ordered to active duty under this section and the President determines that an extension of the service of such unit or member on active duty is necessary in the interests of national security, he may authorize the Secretary of Defense and the Secretary of Transportation with respect to the Coast Guard when it is not operating as a service in the Navy to extend the period of such order to active duty for a period of not more than 90 additional days. Whenever the President exercises his authority under this subsection, he shall immediately notify Congress of such action and shall include in the notification a statement of reasons for the action. Nothing in this subsection shall be construed as limiting the authorities to terminate the service of units or members ordered to active duty under this section under subsection (g).".

Such Act further (effective 12/1/94 as provided by § 1691 of such Act, which appears as 10 USCS § 10001 note) transferred this section, enacted as 10 USCS § 673b, to Chapter 1209 and redesignated it as 10 USCS § 12304; in subsec. (a), substituted "section 12302(a)" for "673(a)" and substituted "section 10143(a)" for "section 268(b)"; and, in subsec. (b), substituted "section 12406" for "section 3500 or 8500".

1997. Act Nov. 18, 1997 substituted the section heading for one which read: "§ 12304. Selected Reserve; order to active duty other than during war or national emergency"; in subsec. (a), inserted "or any member in the Individual Ready Reserve mobilization category and designated as essential under regulations prescribed by the Secretary concerned,"; in subsec. (c), inserted "and the Individual Ready Reserve" and ", of whom not more than 30,000 may be members of the Individual Ready Reserve''; in subsec. (f), inserted ''or Individual Ready Reserve''; in subsec. (g), inserted '', or any member of the Individual Ready Reserve,''; and added subsec. (i).

Other provisions:

Ordering the Selected Reserve of the armed forces to active duty. Ex. Or. No. 12727 of Aug. 22, 1990, 55 Fed. Reg. 35027, provides:

''By the authority vested in me as President by the Constitution and the laws of the United States of America, including sections 121 and 673b [now § 12304] of title 10 of the United States Code, I hereby determine that it is necessary to augment the active armed forces of the United States for the effective conduct of operational missions in and around the Arabian Peninsula. Further, under the stated authority, I hereby authorize the Secretary of Defense, and the Secretary of Transportation with respect to the Coast Guard when the latter is not operating as a service in the Department of the Navy, to order to active duty units and individual members not assigned to units, of the Selected Reserve.

''This order is intended only to improve the internal management of the executive branch, and is not intended to create any right or benefit, substantive or procedural, enforceable at law by a party against the United States, its agencies, its officers, or any person.

''This order shall be published in the Federal Register and transmitted promptly to the Congress.''.

Duration of active duty for Selected Reserve extended to 180 days. Act Nov. 5, 1990, P. L. 101-511, Title VIII, § 8132, 104 Stat. 1908, provides:

''During fiscal year 1991, in exercising the authority provided the President under section 673b [now § 12304] of title 10, United States Code, to authorize the order to active duty of units and members of the Selected Reserve, the President may use that authority in the case of orders to active duty in support of operations in and around the Arabian Peninsula and Operation Desert Shield as if '180 days' were substituted for '90 days' in subsection (a) of that section and '180 additional days' were substituted for '90 additional days' in subsection (i) of that section: Provided, That this section applies only to Selected Reserve combat units.''.

Authorizing the extension of the period of active duty of personnel of the Selected Reserve of the Armed Forces. Ex. Or. No. 12733 of Nov. 13, 1990, 55 Fed. Reg. 47837, provides:

''By the authority vested in me as President by the Constitution and the laws of the United States of America, including sections 121 and 673b(i) [now § 12304(i)] of title 10 of the United States Code, I hereby determine that, in the interests of national security, extending the period of active duty is necessary for the following: units of the Selected Reserve, and members of the Selected Reserve not assigned to a unit organized to serve as a unit of the Selected Reserve, now serving on or hereafter ordered to active duty pursuant to section 673b(a) [now § 12304(a)] of title 10 of the United States Code and Executive Order No. 12727 of August 22, 1990 [note to this section]. Further, under the stated authority, I hereby authorize the Secretary of Defense, and the Secretary of Transportation with respect to the Coast Guard when the latter is not operating as a service in the Department of the Navy, to extend the period of active duty of such units and members of the Selected Reserve.

"This order is intended only to improve the internal management of the executive branch, and is not intended to create any right or benefit, substantive or procedural, enforceable at law by a party against the United States, its agencies, its officers, or any person.".

Ordering the Selected Reserve of the Armed Forces to active duty. Ex. Or. No. 12927 of Sept. 15, 1994, 59 Fed. Reg. 47781, provides:

"By the authority vested in me as President by the Constitution and the laws of the United States of America, including sections 121 and 673b of title 10 of the United States Code, I hereby determine that it is necessary to augment the active armed forces of the United States for the effective conduct of operational missions to restore the civilian government in Haiti. Further, under the stated authority, I hereby authorize the Secretary of Defense, and the Secretary of Transportation with respect to the Coast Guard when it is not operating as a service in the Department of the Navy, to order to active duty any units, and any individual members not assigned to a unit organized to serve as a unit, of the Selected Reserve.

"This order is intended only to improve the internal management of the executive branch, and is not intended to create any right or benefit, substantive or procedural, enforceable at law by a party against the United States, its agencies, its officers, or any person.

"This order is effective immediately and shall be published in the Federal Register and transmitted to the Congress.".

Ordering the Selected Reserve of the Armed Forces to active duty. Ex. Or. No. 12982 of Dec. 8, 1995, 60 Fed. Reg. 68395, provides:

"By the authority vested in me as President by the Constitution and the laws of the United States of America, including sections 121 and 12304 of title 10, United States Code, I hereby determine that it is necessary to augment the active armed forces of the United States for the effective conduct of operations in and around former Yugoslavia. Further, under the stated authority, I hereby authorize the Secretary of Defense, and the Secretary of Transportation with respect to the Coast Guard when it is not operating as a service in the Department of the Navy, to order to active duty any units, and any individual members not assigned to a unit organized to serve as a unit, of the Selected Reserve.

"This order is intended only to improve the internal management of the executive branch and is not intended to create any right or benefit, substantive or procedural, enforceable at law by a party against the United States, its agencies, its officers, or any person.

"This order shall be published in the Federal Register and transmitted to the Congress.".

Ordering the Selected Reserve of the Armed Forces to active duty. Ex. Or. 13076 of February 24, 1998, 63 Fed. Reg. 9719 (Feb. 26, 1998), provides:

"By the authority vested in me as President by the Constitution and the laws of the United States of America, including sections 121 and 12304 of title 10, United States Code, I hereby determine that it is necessary to augment the active armed forces of the United States for the effective conduct of operations in and around Southwest Asia. Further, under the stated authority, I hereby authorize the Secretary of Defense, and the Secretary of Transportation with respect to the Coast Guard when it is not operating as a service in the Department of the Navy, to order to active duty any units, and any individual members not assigned to a unit organized to serve as a unit, of the Selected Reserve.

"This order is intended only to improve the internal management of the executive branch and is not intended to create any right or benefit, substantive or procedural, enforceable at law by a party against the United States, its agencies, its officers, or any person.".

CROSS REFERENCES

This section is referred to in 10 USCS §§ 101, 115, 523, 582, 641, 12305, 12318, 16131, 16133; 38 USCS §§ 3011, 3013, 3231, 3511, 4211, 4304; 50 USCS App. § 592.

§ 12305. Authority of President to suspend certain laws relating to promotion, retirement, and separation

(a) Notwithstanding any other provision of law, during any period members of a reserve component are serving on active duty pursuant to an order to active duty under authority of section 12301, 12302, or 12304 of this title, the President may suspend any provision of law relating to promotion, retirement, or separation applicable to any member of the armed forces who the President determines is essential to the national security of the United States.

(b) A suspension made under the authority of subsection (a) shall terminate (1) upon release from active duty of members of the reserve component ordered to active duty under the authority of section 12301, 12302, or 12304 of this title, as the case may be, or (2) at such time as the President determines the circumstances which required the action of ordering members of the reserve component to active duty no longer exist, whichever is earlier.

(Added Sept. 24, 1983, P. L. 98-94, Title X, Part C, § 1021(a), 97 Stat. 670; Oct. 19, 1984, P. L. 98-525, Title XIV, § 1405(16), 98 Stat. 2622; Oct. 5, 1994, P. L. 103-337, Div A, Title XVI, Subtitle C, § 1662(e)(2), Subtitle D, § 1675(c)(3), 108 Stat. 2992, 3017.)

HISTORY; ANCILLARY LAWS AND DIRECTIVES

Amendments:

1984. Act Oct. 19, 1984, in subsec. (b)(1), inserted "of this title".

1994. Act Oct. 5, 1994 (effective 12/1/94 as provided by § 1691 of such Act, which appears as 10 USCS § 10001 note) transferred this section, enacted as 10 USCS § 673c, to Chapter 1209 and redesignated it as 10 USCS § 12305; and, in subsecs. (a) and (b), substituted "section 12301, 12302, or 12304" for "section 672, 673, or 673b".

Other provisions:

Delegating the President's authority to suspend any provision of law relating to the promotion, retirement, or separation of members of the armed forces. Ex. Or. No. 12728 of Aug. 22, 1990, 55 Fed. Reg. 35029, provides:

"By the authority vested in me as President by the Constitution and the laws of the United States of America, including section 673c [now § 12305] of title 10 of the United States Code and section 301 of title 3 of the United States Code, I hereby order:

"Section 1. The Secretary of Defense, and the Secretary of Transportation with respect to the Coast Guard when it is not operating as a service in the Department of the Navy, are hereby designated and empowered to exercise, without the approval, ratification, or other action of the President, the authority vested in the President by section 673c [now § 12305] of title 10 of the United States Code (1) to suspend any provision of law relating to promotion, retirement, or separation applicable to any member of the armed forces determined to be essential to the national security of the United States, and (2) to determine, for the purposes of said section, that members of the armed forces are essential to the national security of the United States.

"Sec. 2. The authority delegated to the Secretary of Defense and the Secretary of Transportation by this order may be redelegated and further subdelegated to subordinates who are appointed to their offices by the President, by and with the advice and consent of the Senate.

"Sec. 3. This order is intended only to improve the internal management of the executive branch and is not intended to create any right or benefit, substantive or procedural, enforceable at law by a party against the United States, its agencies, its officers, or any person.".

CROSS REFERENCES

This section is referred to in 10 USCS §§ 101, 1047b, 37 USCS § 302f.

INTERPRETIVE NOTES AND DECISIONS

Air Force sergeant is denied habeas corpus relief from "Stop Loss" program extension of his term of service, even though statute at issue begins by referring to "members of reserve component," because it would make little sense that President is allowed to extend enlistments of reservists in case of war but not of active duty personnel, and fair interpretation is that 10 USCS § 673c (now § 12305) acts as specific exception to prohibition on involuntary extensions found in 50 USCS Appx § 454(c)(1), permitting extensions to enlistments of both active and reserve personnel. Sherman v United States (1991, MD Ga) 755 F Supp 385.

§ 12306. Standby Reserve

(a) Units and members in the Standby Reserve may be ordered to active duty (other than for training) only as provided in section 12301 of this title.

(b) In time of emergency—

(1) no unit in the Standby Reserve organized to serve as a unit or any member thereof may be ordered to active duty (other than for training), unless the Secretary concerned, with the approval of the Secretary of Defense in the case of a Secretary of a military department, determines that there are not enough of the required kinds of units in the Ready Reserve that are readily available; and

(2) no other member in the Standby Reserve may be ordered to active duty (other than for training) as an individual without his consent, unless the Secretary concerned, with the approval of the Secretary of Defense in the case of a Secretary of a military department, determines that there are not enough qualified members in the Ready Reserve in the required category who are readily available.

(Aug. 10, 1956, ch 1041, § 1, 70A Stat. 29; Sept. 7, 1962, P. L. 87-651, Title

I, § 130, 76 Stat. 514; Oct. 5, 1994, P. L. 103-337, Div A, Title XVI, Subtitle C, § 1662(e)(2), Subtitle D, § 1675(c)(4), 108 Stat. 2992, 3017.)

HISTORY; ANCILLARY LAWS AND DIRECTIVES

Prior law and revision:

1956 ACT

Revised Section	Source (USCS)	Source (Statutes at Large)
674(a)	50:926(a) (less 1st 28 words).	July 9, 1952, ch. 606, § 206 (less 1st 28 words of (a)), 66 Stat. 483.
674(b)	50:926(b).	

In subsection (b), the words "to serve" are substituted for the words "for the purpose of serving". The words "there are not enough . . . that are" are substituted for the words "adequate numbers of . . . are not". The words "(other than for training)" are inserted, since the words "active duty" were defined in the source statute cited above to exclude "active duty for training".

1962 ACT

The change is made to conform section 674(a) more closely to the source law for that section, section 206(a) of the Armed Forces Reserve Act of 1952 (66 Stat. 483). Section 206(a) of that Act defined the Standby Reserve in terms of units and members of the reserve components according to their liability to be ordered to active duty. It did not provide authority to order units and members of the Standby Reserve to active duty. This authority was provided by section 233(a) of the Armed Forces Reserve Act of 1952 (66 Stat. 489), which is restated in section 672(a) of title 10. Since the present language of section 674(a) may be interpreted to provide independent authority to order units and members of the Standby Reserve to active duty, it is revised to make clear that this is not the case and that section 672 is the authority for that action.

Amendments:

1962. Act Sept. 7, 1962, in subsec. (a), substituted "as provided in section 672 of this title" for "in time of war, of national emergency declared by Congress, or when otherwise authorized by law".

1994. Act Oct. 5, 1994 (effective 12/1/94 as provided by § 1691 of such Act, which appears as 10 USCS § 10001 note) transferred this section, enacted as 10 USCS § 674, to Chapter 1209 and redesignated it as 10 USCS § 12306; and, in subsec. (a), substituted "section 12301" for "section 672"..

CROSS REFERENCES

Standby Reserve, composition of, 10 USCS § 10151.

This section is referred to in 10 USCS §§ 10151; 38 USCS § 3011; 50 App. § 592.

§ 12307. Retired Reserve

A member in the Retired Reserve may, if qualified, be ordered to active duty without his consent, but only as provided in section 688 or 12301(a) of this title. A member of the Retired Reserve (other than a member transferred to the Retired Reserve under section 12641(b) of this title) who is ordered to active duty or other appropriate duty in a retired status may be credited under chapter 1223 of this title [10 USCS §§ 12731 et seq.] with service performed pursuant to such order. A member in a retired status is not eligible for promotion (or for consideration for promotion) as a Reserve.

(Aug. 10, 1956, ch 1041, § 1, 70A Stat. 29; Sept. 24, 1983, P. L. 98-94, Title X, Part B, § 1017(a), 97 Stat. 669; Nov. 29, 1989, P. L. 101-189, Div A, Title VI, Part F, § 651(d), 103 Stat. 1461; Oct. 5, 1994, P. L. 103-337, Div A, Title XVI, Subtitle C, § 1662(e)(2), Subtitle D, § 1675(c)(5), 108 Stat. 2992, 3017; Feb. 10, 1996, P. L. 104-106, Div A, Title XV, § 1501(b)(17), 110 Stat. 497.)

HISTORY; ANCILLARY LAWS AND DIRECTIVES

Prior law and revision:

Revised Section	Source (USCS)	Source (Statutes at Large)
675	50:927(c).	July 9, 1952, ch. 608, § 207(c), 66 Stat. 483.

Amendments:

1983. Act Sept. 24, 1983, inserted "or 688".

1989. Act Nov. 29, 1989 added the sentence beginning "A member of the Ready Reserve . . .".

1994. Act Oct. 5, 1994 (effective 12/1/94 as provided by § 1691 of such Act, which appears as 10 USCS § 10001 note) transferred this section, enacted as 10 USCS § 675, to Chapter 1209 and redesignated it as 10 USCS § 12307; and substituted "section 688 or 12301(a)" for "section 672(a) or 688", substituted "section 12641(b)" for "section 1001(b)", and substituted "chapter 1223" for "chapter 67".

1996. Act Feb. 10, 1996 (effective as if included in Act Oct. 5, 1994, P. L. 103-337, as enacted on Oct. 5, 1994, as provided by § 1501(f)(3) of Act Feb. 10, 1996, which appears as 10 USCS § 113 note) substituted "Retired Reserve" for "Ready Reserve" preceding "(other".

CROSS REFERENCES

Retired Reserve, composition of, 10 USCS § 10154.

Retired lists, 10 USCS § 12774.

This section is referred to in 38 USCS § 3011; 50 App. USCS § 592.

INTERPRETIVE NOTES AND DECISIONS

Person in Retired Reserve may serve on active duty although by definition, member of Retired Reserve cannot be in "active status" Jamerson v United States (1968) 185 Ct Cl 471, 401 F2d 808.

§ 12308. Retention after becoming qualified for retired pay

Any person who has qualified for retired pay under chapter 1223 of this title [10 USCS §§ 12731 et seq.] may, with his consent and by order of the Secretary concerned, be retained on active duty, or in service in a reserve component other than that listed in section 12732(b) of this title. A member so retained shall be credited with that service for all purposes.

(Aug. 10, 1956, ch 1041, § 1, 70A Stat. 29; Oct. 5, 1994, P. L. 103-337, Div A, Title XVI, Subtitle C, § 1662(e)(2), Subtitle D, § 1675(c)(6), 108 Stat. 2992, 3017.)

HISTORY; ANCILLARY LAWS AND DIRECTIVES

Prior law and revision:

Revised Section	Source (USCS)	Source (Statutes at Large)
676	10:1036a(e). 34:440i(e).	June 29, 1948, ch. 708, § 302(e), 62 Stat. 1088.

The words "active duty, or in service, in a reserve component other than that listed in section 1332(b) of this title" are inserted to reflect the words "Federal service", as used in Title III of the source statute. The words "that service for all purposes" are substituted for 10:1036a(e) (last 11 words) and 34:4401(e) (last 11 words). The words "upon attaining the age of sixty years" are omitted as surplusage.

Amendments:

1994. Act Oct. 5, 1994 (effective 12/1/94 as provided by § 1691 of such Act, which appears as 10 USCS § 10001 note) transferred this section, enacted as 10 USCS § 676, to Chapter 1209 and redesignated it as 10 USCS § 12308; and substituted "chapter 1223" for "chapter 67" and substituted "section 12732(b)" for "section 1332(b)".

INTERPRETIVE NOTES AND DECISIONS

10 USCS § 676 (now § 12308) makes no requirement that retention on active duty must be continuation of service as reserve officer; § 676 (now § 12308) contemplates retention on active duty of officer serving in active status at time Secretarial discretion is exercised, as distinguished from recall to duty of officer in retired status. Grahl v United States (1964) 167 Ct Cl 80, 336 F2d 199.

Plaintiff was validly retained on active duty pursuant to 10 USCS § 676 (now § 12308) when he was appointed reserve colonel, although he was over age of 60 and consequently, he was "reserved commissioned officer of the Army" within meaning of 10 USCS § 3911 when he was retired from Army, and since he had more than 20 years of service as computed under 10 USCS § 3926(a), he was properly accorded retirement under Chapter 67 (10 USCS §§ 1331 et seq.); § 676 (now § 12308), by its terms, applies to officer who has qualified for retired pay under "point system" by which officer may not receive retired pay unless and until he has reached 60 years of age, so § 676 (now § 12308) must permit retention on active duty of overage officer whose release from duty would otherwise be required by 10 USCS § 3843(b) (now repealed) which requires retirement or discharge of reserve officers below general officer grades who have reached age 60; Army regulation forbidding officers to be appointed to reserve grade of colonel if they would reach mandatory retirement age within 2 years of appointment is applicable only to initial commissioning of officer and not to commission conferred in order to retain him on active duty under authority of § 676 (now § 12308). Grahl v United States (1964) 167 Ct Cl 80, 336 F2d 199.

Nothing in Title 10 prevents officer's retention on active duty while being listed as Retired Reserve officer; person in Retired Reserve may serve on active duty although by definition, member of Retired Reserve cannot be in "active status"; § 676 (now § 12308) does not indicate that person qualifying for retirement must be retained in active status and cannot be transferred to Retired Reserve. Jamerson v United States (1968) 185 Ct Cl 471, 401 F2d 808.

Navy Reserve officer who was recalled to duty and who then performed 19 years' active service could not be "re-retired" anew on basis of that additional service as statute authorizing military and naval reservists who are qualified for retirement to be retained in active status to receive credit for all purposes for subsequent service does not apply to reservists who have in effect been retired, since retirement orders are not subject to cancellation, and while retirees may be recalled to active service from retirement they cannot be retired and retained on active duty simultaneously. (1986) 65 Op Comp Gen 774.

§ 12309. Reserve officers: use of in expansion of armed forces

When an expansion of the active armed forces requires that officers of the reserve components who are not members of units organized to serve as such be ordered as individuals to active duty (other than for training) without their consent, the services of qualified and available reserve officers in all grades shall be used, so far as practicable, according to the needs of the branches, grades, or specialties concerned.

(Aug. 10, 1956, ch 1041, § 1, 70A Stat. 29; Oct. 5, 1994, P. L. 103-337, Div A, Title XVI, Subtitle C, § 1662(e)(2), 108 Stat. 2992.)

HISTORY; ANCILLARY LAWS AND DIRECTIVES

Prior law and revision:

Revised Section	Source (USCS)	Source (Statutes at Large)
677	50:961(f).	July 9, 1952, ch. 608, § 233(f), 66 Stat. 490.

The words ''without their consent'' are substituted for the word ''involuntarily''. The words ''it shall be the policy'' are omitted as surplusage. The words ''to active duty (other than for training)'' are substituted for the words ''into the active military service''.

Amendments:

1994. Act Oct. 5, 1994 (effective 12/1/94 as provided by § 1691 of such Act, which appears as 10 USCS § 10001 note) transferred this section, enacted as 10 USCS § 677, to Chapter 1209 and redesignated it as 10 USCS § 12309.

§ 12310. Reserves: for organizing, administering, etc., reserve components

(a) A Reserve ordered to active duty under section 12301(d) of this title in connection with organizing, administering, recruiting, instructing, or training the reserve components shall be ordered in his reserve grade. While so serving, he continues to be eligible for promotion as a Reserve, if he is otherwise qualified.

(b) A Reserve on active duty as described in subsection (a) may be provided training consistent with training provided to other members on active duty, as the Secretary concerned sees fit.

(Aug. 10, 1956, ch 1041, § 1, 70A Stat. 30; Oct. 5, 1994, P. L. 103-337, Div A, Title XVI, Subtitle C, § 1662(e)(2), Subtitle D, § 1675(c)(7), 108 Stat. 2992, 3017; Sept. 23, 1996, P. L. 104-201, Div A, Title V, Subtitle E, § 541, 110 Stat. 2521.)

HISTORY; ANCILLARY LAWS AND DIRECTIVES

Prior law and revision:

Revised Section	Source (USCS)	Source (Statutes at Large)
678(a)	50:962 (2d sentence).	July 2, 1952, ch. 608, § 234, (less 1st sentence), 66 Stat. 490.
678(b)	50:962 (less 1st and 2d sentences).	

In subsection (a), the words ''to active duty under section 672(d) of this title in connection with organizing, administering, recruiting, instructing, or training the reserve components'' are substituted for the words ''into the active military service of the United States under the provisions of this section''. The words ''his reserve grade'' are substituted for the words ''held by them in the Reserve of their Armed Force''. The words ''as a Reserve'', in the last sentence of the revised subsection, are substituted for the words ''in the Reserve of their Armed Force''. The word ''Hereafter'' is omitted as surplusage.

Subsection (b) is substituted for 50:962 (less 1st and 2d sentences).

Amendments:

1994. Act Oct. 5, 1994 (effective 12/1/94 as provided by § 1691 of such Act, which appears as 10 USCS § 10001 note) transferred this section, enacted as 10 USCS § 678, to Chapter 1209 and redesignated it as 10 USCS § 12310; and, in subsec. (a), substituted ''section 12301(d)'' for ''section 672(d)''.

1996. Act Sept. 23, 1996 substituted subsec. (b) for one which read: ''(b) To assure that a Reserve on duty under subsection (a) receives periodic refresher training in the categories for which he is qualified, the Secretary concerned may detail him to duty with any armed force, or otherwise as the Secretary sees fit.''.

CROSS REFERENCES

This section is referred to in 10 USCS § 12318.

§ 12311. Active duty agreements

(a) To provide definite terms of active duty (other than for training) for Reserves with their consent, the Secretary concerned may make a standard written agreement with any member of a reserve component under his jurisdiction requiring the member to serve for a period of active duty (other than for training) of not more than five years. When such an agreement expires, a new one may be made. This subsection does not apply in time of war declared by Congress.

(b) An agreement may not be made under subsection (a) unless the specified period of duty is at least 12 months longer than any period of active duty that the member is otherwise required to perform.

(c) Agreements made under subsection (a) shall be uniform so far as practicable, and are subject to such standards and policies as may be prescribed by the Secretary of Defense for the armed forces under his jurisdiction or by the

Secretary of Transportation for the Coast Guard when the Coast Guard is not operating as a service in the Navy.

(d) If an agreement made under subsection (a) expires during a war or during a national emergency declared by Congress or the President after January 1, 1953, the Reserve concerned may be kept on active duty, without his consent, as otherwise prescribed by law.

(Aug. 10, 1956, ch 1041, § 1, 70A Stat. 30; Dec. 12, 1980, P. L. 96-513, Title V, Part B, § 511(19), 94 Stat. 2921; Oct. 5, 1994, P. L. 103-337, Div A, Title XVI, Subtitle C, § 1662(e)(2), 108 Stat. 2992.)

HISTORY; ANCILLARY LAWS AND DIRECTIVES

Prior law and revision:

Revised Section	Source (USCS)	Source (Statutes at Large)
679(a)	50:963(a) (less last sentence).	July 9, 1952, ch. 608, §§ 235 (less last sentence of (a), and less (b)), 236, 66 Stat. 491.
	50:963(c).	
	50:963(f).	
679(b)	50:963(d).	
679(c)	50:963(e).	
679(d)	50:964.	

In subsection (a), the words "To provide definite terms of active duty for" are substituted for the words "In order that . . . may remain on or be ordered to active duty . . . for terms of service of definite duration". The words "with their consent" are substituted for the word "voluntarily". The words "requiring the member to serve" are substituted for 50:963(c). The words "more than" are substituted for the words "to exceed". The second sentence is substituted for 50:963(a) (2d sentence). The word "hereafter" is omitted as surplusage. 50:963(f) is omitted as executed. The words "under his jurisdiction" are inserted for clarity.

In subsection (b), the words "is at least . . . longer" are substituted for the words "exceeds by at least". The words "active duty that the member is otherwise required to perform" are substituted for the words "obligated or involuntary active duty to which he is otherwise liable".

In subsection (c) the words "for the armed forces under his jurisdiction" are inserted for clarity.

Amendments:

1980. Act Dec. 12, 1980 (effective upon enactment as provided by § 701(b)(3) of such Act, which appears as 10 USCS § 101 note), in subsec. (c), substituted "Secretary of Transportation" for "Secretary of the Treasury".

1994. Act Oct. 5, 1994 (effective 12/1/94 as provided by § 1691 of such Act, which appears as 10 USCS § 10001 note) transferred this section, enacted as 10 USCS § 679, to Chapter 1209 and redesignated it as 10 USCS § 12311.

CROSS REFERENCES

This section is referred to in 10 USCS § 12312; 14 USCS § 41a.

INTERPRETIVE NOTES AND DECISIONS

1. Construction of agreements
2. Regulations

1. Construction of agreements

Active duty agreement executed between reservist and Navy was not contract of type authorized by 10 USCS § 679 (now § 12311), and therefore procedural requirements of § 680 (now § 12312) were not applicable, where terms of agreement did not explicitly incorporate provisions of § 680 (now § 12312). Alley v United States (1984) 5 Cl Ct 280, reh den (1984) 6 Cl Ct 99.

Where contract between Air Force officer and Secretary of Air Force, alleged to be contract authorized by 10 USCS § 679(a) (now § 12311(a)), provided that officer would be continued on active duty until Secretary determines that Southeast Asia Mission is such that officer's services are no longer required, Secretary's decree that officers of certain status be separated for budgetary reasons did not constitute breach of such contract since contract's language was broad enough for Secretary's determination respecting "mission" to be that he would spend less money on it. Sidoran v United States (1977) 213 Ct Cl 110, 550 F2d 636 (ovrld in part on other grounds by Deering v United States (1980) 223 Ct Cl 342, 620 F2d 242).

Transfer to Stand-by Reserve from Ready Reserve of reservist holding key civilian position (federal district judge) is valid, since Ready Reserve Service Agreement is not contract, and exemption of reservists from Dual Compensation Act (5 USCS §§ 5531-5533) does not exempt reservists from military readiness criteria. Sharp v Weinberger (1984, DC Dist Col) 593 F Supp 886, affd in part and vacated in part on other grounds (1986, App DC) 255 US App DC 90, 798 F2d 1521.

2. Regulations

Regulations issued pursuant to 10 USCS § 679 (now § 12311), providing that when member volunteers for period of active duty contingent upon assignments to particular type of duty or geographical location or contingent upon being tendered specific type of contract (active duty agreement), he has, by his own action, placed restrictions on his request which are incompatible with requirement that he volunteer for additional regular tour of duty and consequently should such conditional request be denied he may not be regarded as having been involuntarily released from active duty, were reasonably designed to carry into effect acts enacted by Congress and have force and effect of law. Henneberger v United States (1968) 185 Ct Cl 614, 403 F2d 237, reh den (1969) 187 Ct Cl 265, 407 F2d 1340.

§ 12312. Active duty agreements: release from duty

(a) Each agreement made under section 12311(a) of this title shall provide that the member may not be released from active duty without his consent during the period of the agreement—

(1) because of a reduction in the actual personnel strength of the armed force concerned, unless the release is in accordance with the recommendation of a board of officers appointed by an authority designated by the Secretary concerned to determine the members to be released from active duty under regulations prescribed by the Secretary; or

(2) for any other reason, without an opportunity to be heard by a board of officers before the release, unless he is (A) dismissed or discharged under the sentence of a court-martial, (B) released because of an unexplained absence without leave for at least three months, (C) released because he is convicted and sentenced to confinement in a Federal or State penitentiary or correctional institution and the sentence has become final, or (D) released because he has been considered at least twice and has not been recommended for promotion to the next higher grade or because he is considered as having failed of selection for promotion to the next higher grade and has not been recommended for promotion to that grade, under conditions that would require the release or separation of a reserve officer who is not serving under such agreement.

(b) A member who is released from active duty without his consent before the end of his agreement made under section 12311(a) of this title is entitled to an amount computed by multiplying the number of years and fractions of a year of his unexpired period of service under the agreement by the sum of one month's basic pay, special pay, and allowances to which he is entitled on the day of his release. The amount to which a member is entitled under this subsection is in addition to any pay and allowances to which he is otherwise entitled. For the purposes of this subsection, a fraction of a month of 15 days or more is counted as a whole month, and a fraction of a month of less than 15 days is disregarded. This subsection does not apply to a member if he is—

(1) released for a reason described in subsection (a)(2)(A)–(C);

(2) released because of a physical disability resulting from his intentional misconduct or wilful neglect;

(3) eligible for retired pay, separation pay, or severance pay under another provision of law;

(4) placed on a temporary disability retired list; or

(5) released to accept an appointment, or to be enlisted, in a regular component of an armed force.

(Aug. 10, 1956, ch 1041, § 1, 70A Stat. 30; June 28, 1962, P. L. 87-509, § 2, 76 Stat. 121; Oct. 19, 1984, P. L. 98-525, Title V, Part C, § 533(b), Title XIV, § 1405(17), 98 Stat. 2528, 2622; Oct. 5, 1994, P. L. 103-337, Div A, Title XVI, Subtitle C, § 1662(e)(2), Subtitle D, § 1675(c)(8), 108 Stat. 2992, 3017.)

HISTORY; ANCILLARY LAWS AND DIRECTIVES

Prior law and revision:

Revised Section	Source (USCS)	Source (Statutes at Large)
680(a)	50:963(a) (last sentence).	July 9, 1952, ch. 608, § 235(a) (last sentence), (b), 66 Stat. 491.
680(b)	50:963(b).	

In subsections (a) and (b), the words "without his consent" are substituted for the word "involuntary".

In subsection (a)(1), the word "because" is substituted for the words "by reason". The words "actual personnel strength" are substituted for the words "numerical strength of the military personnel".

In subsection (a)(2), the words "for any other reason" are substituted for the words "for reasons other than that prescribed in paragraph (1)". The words "dismissed or discharged" are inserted for clarity. The words "at least" are substituted for the word "duration". The words "is convicted and sentenced . . . and the sentence has become final" are substituted for the words "final conviction and sentence". The words "from active duty" are omitted as surplusage.

In subsection (b), the words "before the end of" are substituted for the words "prior to the expiration of the period of service under". The words "computed by multiplying . . . and fractions of a year of his unexpired period of service under the agreement by the sum of one month's . . . pay, and allowances" are substituted for the words "equal to one month's pay and allowances multiplied by . . . (including any pro rata part thereof) remaining as the unexpired period of his agreement for active duty''. The words ''basic . . . special pay . . . to which he is entitled on the day of his release'' are substituted for 50:963(b) (2d sentence). The third sentence is substituted for 50:963(b) (last sentence). The last sentence is substituted for 50:963(b) (words within 1st parentheses).

In subsection (b)(2), the words ''because of'' are substituted for the words ''when such release is due to''.

In subsection (b)(5), the words ''to accept'' are substituted for the words ''for the purpose of accepting''. The words ''of an armed force'' are inserted for clarity.

Amendments:

1962. Act June 28, 1962, in subsec. (a)(2), deleted ''or'' before ''(C)'' and added clause (D).

1984. Act Oct. 19, 1984, in subsec. (a)(2)(D), substituted ''reserve officer'' for ''Reserve Officer''; and, in subsec. (b)(3), inserted '', separation pay,''.

1994. Act Oct. 5, 1994 (effective 12/1/94 as provided by § 1691 of such Act, which appears as 10 USCS § 10001 note) transferred this section, enacted as 10 USCS § 680, to Chapter 1209 and redesignated it as 10 USCS § 12312; and, in subsecs. (a) and (b), substituted ''section 12311(a)'' for ''section 679(a)''.

CROSS REFERENCES

Temporary disability retired lists, 10 USCS §§ 1202, 1205.

Disability from intentional misconduct or wilful neglect, separation, 10 USCS § 1207.

Basic pay, special pay, and allowances, 37 USCS §§ 203 et seq.

INTERPRETIVE NOTES AND DECISIONS

1. Construction of agreements
2. Validity of release

1. Construction of agreements

Active duty agreement executed between reservist and Navy was not contract of type authorized by 10 USCS § 679 (now § 12311)), and therefore procedural requirements of § 680 (now § 12312) were not applicable, where terms of agreement did not explicitly incorporate provisions of § 680 (now § 12312). Alley v United States (1984) 5 Cl Ct 280, reh den (1984) 6 Cl Ct 99.

Service under active duty agreement is quite different from service on active duty without such agreement, as officer serving without active duty agreement can be dismissed at any time without notice and is not entitled to pay received by officer who is dismissed while serving under active duty agreement. Henneberger v United States (1968) 185 Ct Cl 614, 403 F2d 237, reh den (1969) 187 Ct Cl 265, 407 F2d 1340.

Transfer to Stand-by Reserve from Ready Reserve of reservist holding key civilian position (federal district judge) is valid, since Ready Reserve Service Agreement is not contract, and exemption of reservists from Dual Compensation Act (5 USCS §§ 5531-5533) does not exempt reservists from military readiness criteria. Sharp v Weinberger (1984, DC Dist Col) 593 F Supp 886, affd in part and vacated in part (1986, App DC) 255 US App DC 90, 798 F2d 1521.

2. Validity of release

Where plaintiff was compensated for period of time up until his release from active duty, thereafter had no entitlement to active duty pay, and pointed to no statute or regulation to show that his release from active duty was invalid, Claims Court lacked jurisdiction since plaintiff had been fully compensated for period over which court could act. Jagnandan v United States (1989) 17 Cl Ct 107, affd without op (1990, CA) 897 F2d 538.

§ 12313. Reserves; release from active duty

(a) Except as otherwise provided in this title, the Secretary concerned may at any time release a Reserve under his jurisdiction from active duty.

(b) In time of war or of national emergency declared by Congress or the President after January 1, 1953, a member of a reserve component may be released from active duty (other than for training) only if—

(1) a board of officers convened at his request by an authority designated by the Secretary concerned recommends the release and the recommendation is approved;

(2) the member does not request that a board be convened; or

(3) his release is otherwise authorized by law.

This subsection does not apply to an armed force during a period of demobilization or reduction in strength of that armed force.

(Aug. 10, 1956, ch 1041, § 1, 70A Stat. 31; Oct. 5, 1994, P. L. 103-337, Div A, Title XVI, Subtitle C, § 1662(e)(2), 108 Stat. 2992.)

HISTORY; ANCILLARY LAWS AND DIRECTIVES

Prior law and revision:

Revised Section	Source (USCS)	Source (Statutes at Large)
681(a)	50:967(a).	July 9, 1952, ch. 608, § 239,
681(b)	50:967 (less (a)).	66 Stat. 492.

In subsection (a), the word "title" is substituted for the word "chapter". The provisions of this title relating to active duty of Reserves are based on the Armed Forces Reserve Act of 1952. The words "under his jurisdiction" are inserted for clarity. The words "or active duty for training" are omitted as covered by the words "active duty".

Subsection (b) is substituted for 50:967(b). Clause (3) is inserted, since other provisions of law are necessarily exceptions to the general rule here stated.

Amendments:

1994. Act Oct. 5, 1994 (effective 12/1/94 as provided by § 1691 of such Act, which appears as 10 USCS § 10001 note) transferred this section, enacted as 10 USCS § 681, to Chapter 1209 and redesignated it as 10 USCS § 12313.

INTERPRETIVE NOTES AND DECISIONS

1. Generally
2. Procedures for release
3. Particular requests for release

1. Generally

Secretary's discretionary power of release from active duty is subject to compliance with departmental regulations which, once prescribed by Secretary, serve to limit permissible exercise of that discretion. Murphy v United States (1989) 16 Cl Ct 385, revd on other grounds (1993, CA) 993 F2d 871, reh, en banc, den (1993, CA FC) 1993 US App LEXIS 18599 and cert den (1994) 511 US 1019, 128 L Ed 2d 75, 114 S Ct 1402, reh den (1994) 511 US 1118, 128 L Ed 2d 681, 114 S Ct 2123.

Secretary's refusal to correct record of officer whom he had previously discharged to show that officer had remained on active duty from date of such discharge to date of his later retirement, was neither illegal or arbitrary since Secretary has authority under 10 USCS § 681 (now § 12313) to release reserve officer under his jurisdiction from active duty. Mercereau v United States (1961) 155 Ct Cl 157.

Under 10 USCS § 681(a) (now § 12313(a)), reserve officers can be released from active duty at any time and conditions and circumstances governing that release rest within sound discretion of service. Abruzzo v United States (1975) 206 Ct Cl 731, 513 F2d 608.

2. Procedures for release

Secretary of Army must abide by his own regulations in exercising his authority under 10 USCS § 681 (now § 12313), so reservist may not be involuntarily released from duty by order of Secretary alone; regulations must be followed despite 10 USCS § 1163(d) (now repealed) which provides that Secretary must personally authorize release of reservists who are within 2 years of qualifying for retirement, since § 1163(d) (now repealed) is additional requirement. Roberts v Vance (1964) 119 US App DC 367, 343 F2d 236.

Although plaintiff's interservice transfer request was mishandled by Marine Corps, plaintiff's release was not thereby rendered illegal, since service was not obligated to retain plaintiff on active duty until request was finally approved or disapproved. Abruzzo v United States (1975) 206 Ct Cl 731, 513 F2d 608.

Private involuntarily discharged from Army was entitled to challenge results of urinalysis under 10 USCS § 681(a) (now § 12313(a)), where urinalysis formed basis for his discharge, because statute does not defeat property interest in continued service that is within protection of due process clause. May v Gray (1988, ED NC) 708 F Supp 716.

3. Particular requests for release

Navy was not required to delineate guidelines as to basis upon which it would grant delays or exemptions from obligation under "Berry" plan for naval reserve officers to report for active duty; Navy's action in refusing reserve officer's request for exemption was not arbitrary or irrational where based on fact that Navy expected shortfall in ensuing year of 43 specialists in officer's category of family practice. West v Chafee (1977, CA8 Minn) 560 F2d 942.

Work stoppage by United States Postal Service employees does not require that board of officers be convened under 10 USCS § 681(b) (now § 12313(b)) where strike was short-lived and its effects were long over by time of reservist's reassignment and release from active status. Woodward v Moore (1978, DC Dist Col) 451 F Supp 346, 25 BNA FEP Cas 693, vacated on other grounds (1981, DC Dist Col) 25 BNA FEP Cas 695, remanded without op (1982, App DC) 684 F2d 1033.

§ 12314. Reserves: kinds of duty

Notwithstanding any other provision of law, a member of a reserve component who is on active duty other than for training may, under regulations prescribed by the Secretary concerned, be detailed or assigned to any duty authorized by law for members of the regular component of the armed force concerned.

(Aug. 10, 1956, ch 1041, § 1, 70A Stat. 31; Oct. 5, 1994, P. L. 103-337, Div A, Title XVI, Subtitle C, § 1662(e)(2), 108 Stat. 2992.)

HISTORY; ANCILLARY LAWS AND DIRECTIVES

Prior law and revision:

Revised Section	Source (USCS)	Source (Statutes at Large)
682	50:965.	July 9, 1952, ch. 608, § 237, 66 Stat. 492.

The words "armed force concerned" are substituted for the words "Armed Forces of the United States". The words "now or hereafter" and "officers and enlisted" are omitted as surplusage. The words "other than for training" are inserted, since the words "active duty" were defined in the source statute cited above to exclude active duty for training.

Amendments:

1994. Act Oct. 5, 1994 (effective 12/1/94 as provided by § 1691 of such

Act, which appears as 10 USCS § 10001 note) transferred this section, enacted as 10 USCS § 682, to Chapter 1209 and redesignated it as 10 USCS § 12314.

§ 12315. Reserves: duty with or without pay

(a) Subject to other provisions of this title, any Reserve may be ordered to active duty or other duty—

(1) with the pay and allowances provided by law; or

(2) with his consent, without pay.

Duty without pay shall be considered for all purposes as if it were duty with pay.

(b) A Reserve who is kept on active duty after his term of service expires is entitled to pay and allowances while on that duty, except as they may be forfeited under the approved sentence of a court-martial or by non-judicial punishment by a commanding officer or when he is otherwise in a non-pay status.

(Aug 10, 1956, ch 1041, § 1, 70A Stat. 31; Oct. 5, 1994, P. L. 103-337, Div A, Title XVI, Subtitle C, § 1662(e)(2), 108 Stat. 2992.)

HISTORY; ANCILLARY LAWS AND DIRECTIVES

Prior law and revision:

Revised Section	Source (USCS)	Source (Statutes at Large)
683(a)	50:971.	July 9, 1952, ch. 608,
683(b)	50:972.	§§ 240, 241, 66 Stat. 492.

In subsection (a), the word "title" is substituted for the word "chapter". The provisions of this title relating to active duty of reservists are based on the Armed Forces Reserve Act of 1952. The words "shall be considered . . . as if it were" are substituted for the words "shall be counted . . . the same as like".

In subsections (a) and (b), the words "active duty for training" are omitted as covered by the words "active duty".

In subsection (b), the word "kept" is substituted for the words "retained or continued". The words "pursuant to law" are omitted as surplusage.

Amendments:

1994. Act Oct. 5, 1994 (effective 12/1/94 as provided by § 1691 of such Act, which appears as 10 USCS § 10001 note) transferred this section, enacted as 10 USCS § 683, to Chapter 1209 and redesignated it as 10 USCS § 12315.

CROSS REFERENCES

Pay and allowances, 37 USCS §§ 101 et seq.

INTERPRETIVE NOTES AND DECISIONS

Nothing in 10 USCS § 683 (now § 12315) could be construed to authorize payment to reservist if ordered to additional training without pay and without his consent, as statute merely authorized one method of additional duty, i. e., without pay if one consents, and in no way speaks or authorizes payment of money if reservist is ordered to additional nonpaid duty without consent. O'Hanlon v United States (1986) 11 Cl Ct 192.

Where plaintiff, in response to orders dated July 12, 1940, reported for active duty training on July 31, 1940 and performed active duty until August 9, 1940, and where on August 17, 1940, order was issued revoking orders of July 12, 1940, orders were in full force and effect during period of active service, and plaintiff was entitled to recover pay and allowances for such period. Jones v United States (1944) 102 Ct Cl 188.

§ 12316. Payment of certain Reserves while on duty

(a) Except as provided by subsection (b), a Reserve of the Army, Navy, Air Force, Marine Corps, or Coast Guard who because of his earlier military service is entitled to a pension, retired or retainer pay, or disability compensation, and who performs duty for which he is entitled to compensation, may elect to receive for that duty either—

(1) the payments to which he is entitled because of his earlier military service; or

(2) if he specifically waives those payments, the pay and allowances authorized by law for the duty that he is performing.

(b) Unless the payments because of his earlier military service are greater than the compensation prescribed by subsection (a)(2), a Reserve of the Army, Navy, Air Force, Marine Corps, or Coast Guard who because of his earlier military service is entitled to a pension, retired or retainer pay, or disability compensation, and who upon being ordered to active duty for a period of more than 30 days in time of war or national emergency is found physically qualified to perform that duty, ceases to be entitled to the payments because of his earlier military service until the period of active duty ends. While on that active duty, he is entitled to the compensation prescribed by subsection (a)(2). Other rights and benefits of the member or his dependents are unaffected by this subsection.

(Added Sept. 2, 1958, P. L. 85-861, § 1(15), 72 Stat. 1441; Jan. 2, 1975, P. L. 93-586, § 1, 88 Stat. 1920; Oct. 5, 1994, P. L. 103-337, Div A, Title XVI, Subtitle C, § 1662(e)(2), 108 Stat. 2992.)

HISTORY; ANCILLARY LAWS AND DIRECTIVES

Prior law and revision:

Revised Section	Source (USCS)	Source (Statutes at Large)
684(a)	10 App.:369b (less proviso and last 3 sentences). 34 App.:853e-1 (less provisos and last 3 sentences).	Aug. 2, 1946, ch. 756, § 10; restated Sept. 27, 1950, ch. 1053, § 1, 64 Stat. 1067; July 12, 1955, ch. 337, §§ 1, 4, 69 Stat. 300, 301.
684(b)	10 App.:369b (proviso and last 3 sentences).	Sept. 27, 1950, ch. 1053, § 2, 64 Stat. 1067; July

Revised Section	Source (USCS)	Source (Statutes at Large)
	34 App.:853e-1 (provisos and last 3 sentences).	12, 1955, ch. 337, §§ 2, 4, 69 Stat. 301.

In subsections (a) and (b), the words ''retirement pay'' are omitted as covered by the words ''retired pay''.

In subsection (a), the words ''Except as provided by subsection (b)'' are inserted for clarity. The words ''who performs duty for which he is entitled to compensation, may elect to receive for that duty'' are substituted for the words ''may elect, with reference to periods of active duty, active duty for training, drill, training, instruction, or other duty for which they may be entitled to receive compensation pursuant to any provisions of law''. The words ''Notwithstanding the provisions of any other law'', in 10 App.:369b, and ''or relinquish'' are omitted as surplusage.

Subsection (a)(1) is substituted for clause (2) of 10 App.:369b, and clause (2) of 34 App.:853e-1.

In subsection (a)(2), the words ''pay and allowances authorized by law for the duty that he is performing'' are substituted for clause (1) of 10 App.:369b and 34 App.:853e-1.

In subsection (b), the word ''extended'', the next to the last sentence of 10 App.:369b and of 34 App.:853e-1, and the first proviso of 34 App.:853e-1, are omitted as surplusage.

Amendments:

1975. Act Jan. 2, 1975, in subsecs. (a) and (b), substituted a comma for ''or'' before ''Marine Corps'', and added '', or Coast Guard''.

1994. Act Oct. 5, 1994 (effective 12/1/94 as provided by § 1691 of such Act, which appears as 10 USCS § 10001 note) transferred this section, enacted as 10 USCS § 684, to Chapter 1209 and redesignated it as 10 USCS § 12316.

INTERPRETIVE NOTES AND DECISIONS

Retired members of armed services who perform reserve duty, active or inactive, on 31st day of calendar month must waive one day retired pay in order to be entitled to active duty pay or inactive duty pay which would otherwise accrue for that day. (1983) 62 Op Comp Gen 266.

§ 12317. Reserves: theological students; limitations

A Reserve may not be required to serve on active duty, or to participate in inactive duty training, while preparing for the ministry in a recognized theological or divinity school.

(Added Sept. 2, 1958, P. L. 85-861, § 1(15), 72 Stat. 1441; Oct. 5, 1994, P. L. 103-337, Div A, Title XVI, Subtitle C, § 1662(e)(2), 108 Stat. 2992.)

HISTORY; ANCILLARY LAWS AND DIRECTIVES

Prior law and revision:

Revised Section	Source (USCS)	Source (Statutes at Large)
686	50:961(h) (last sentence).	Aug. 9, ch. 665, § 2(g) (last sentence), 69 Stat. 599.

The words ''active training and service, active duty for training'' are omitted as covered by the words ''active duty'' as defined in section 101(22) of this title.

Amendments:

1994. Act Oct. 5, 1994 (effective 12/1/94 as provided by § 1691 of such Act, which appears as 10 USCS § 10001 note) transferred this section, enacted as 10 USCS § 685, to Chapter 1209 and redesignated it as 10 USCS § 12317.

INTERPRETIVE NOTES AND DECISIONS

Soldier seeking discharge on grounds of being theological student or duly ordained minister of recognized religion must demonstrate that his religious activity constitutes vocation. Wright v Hendershot (1976, ED Pa) 420 F Supp 904.

§ 12318. Reserves on active duty; duties; funding

(a) During a period that members of a reserve component are serving on active duty pursuant to an order under section 12302 or 12304 of this title, members of reserve components serving on active duty may perform duties in connection with either such section.

(b) Funds available for the pay and allowances of Reserves referred to section 12310 of this title shall be available for the pay and allowances of such Reserves who perform duties in connection with section 12302 or 12304 of this title under the authority of subsection (a).

(Added Nov. 14, 1986, P. L. 99-661, Div A, Title IV, Part B, § 412(b)(1), 100 Stat. 3862; Oct. 5, 1994, P. L. 103-337, Div A, Title XVI, Subtitle C, § 1662(e)(2), Subtitle D, § 1675(c)(9), 108 Stat. 2992, 3017.)

HISTORY; ANCILLARY LAWS AND DIRECTIVES

Amendments:

1994. Act Oct. 5, 1994 (effective 12/1/94 as provided by § 1691 of such Act, which appears as 10 USCS § 10001 note) transferred this section, enacted as 10 USCS § 686, to Chapter 1209 and redesignated it as 10 USCS § 12318; in subsec. (a), substituted ''section 12301 or 12304'' for ''section 673 or 673b''; and, in subsec. (b), substituted ''section 12310'' for ''section 678'' and substituted ''section 12301 or 12304'' for ''section 673 or 673b''.

§ 12319. Ready Reserve: muster duty

(a) Under regulations prescribed by the Secretary of Defense, a member of the

Ready Reserve may be ordered without his consent to muster duty one time each year. A member ordered to muster duty under this section shall be required to perform a minimum of two hours of muster duty on the day of muster.

(b) The period which a member may be required to devote to muster duty under this section, including round-trip travel to and from the location of that duty, may not total more than one day each calendar year.

(c) Except as specified in subsection (d), muster duty (and travel directly to and from that duty) under this section shall be treated as the equivalent of inactive-duty training (and travel directly to and from that training) for the purposes of this title and the provisions of title 37 (other than section 206(a)) and title 38, including provisions relating to the determination of eligibility for and the receipt of benefits and entitlements provided under those titles for Reserves performing inactive-duty training and for their dependents and survivors.

(d) Muster duty under this section shall not be credited in determining entitlement to, or in computing, retired pay under chapter 1223 of this title [10 USCS §§ 12731 et seq.].

(Added Nov. 29, 1989, P. L. 101-189, Div A, Title V, Part A, § 502(a)(1), 103 Stat. 1436; Oct. 5, 1994, P. L. 103-337, Div A, Title XVI, Subtitle C, § 1662(e)(2), Subtitle D, § 1675(c)(10), 108 Stat. 2992, 3018.)

HISTORY; ANCILLARY LAWS AND DIRECTIVES

Amendments:

1994. Act Oct. 5, 1994 (effective 12/1/94 as provided by § 1691 of such Act, which appears as 10 USCS § 10001 note) transferred this section, enacted as 10 USCS § 687, to Chapter 1209 and redesignated it as 10 USCS § 12319; and, in subsec. (d), substituted "chapter 1223" for "chapter 67".

CROSS REFERENCES

This section is referred to in 37 USCS § 433.

§ 12320. Reserve officers: grade in which ordered to active duty

A reserve officer who is ordered to active duty or full-time National Guard duty shall be ordered to active duty or full-time National Guard duty in his reserve grade, except that a reserve officer who is credited with service under section 12207 of this title and is ordered to active duty and placed on the active-duty list may be ordered to active duty in a reserve grade and with a date of rank and position on the active-duty list determined under regulations prescribed by the Secretary of Defense based upon the amount of service credited.

(Added Dec. 12, 1980, P. L. 96-513, Title I, § 106, 94 Stat. 2868; July 10, 1981, P. L. 97-22, § 4(g), 95 Stat. 127; Oct. 5, 1994, P. L. 103-337, Div A, Title XVI, Subtitle A, Part II, § 1625, Subtitle C, § 1662(e)(2), Subtitle D, § 1675(c)(11), 108 Stat. 2962, 2992, 3018; Feb. 10, 1996, P. L. 104-106, Div A, Title XV, § 1501(a)(2), 110 Stat. 495.)

HISTORY; ANCILLARY LAWS AND DIRECTIVES

Effective date of section:

Act Dec. 12, 1980, P. L. 96-513, Title VII, § 701(a), 94 Stat. 2955, provided that this section shall take effect on September 15, 1981, except as provided in § 701(b)(1) of such Act, which appears as 10 USCS § 101 note.

Amendments:

1981. Act July 10, 1981, inserted ", except that a reserve officer who is credited with service under section 3353, 5600, or 8353 of this title and is ordered to active duty may be ordered to active duty in a reserve grade and with a date of rank and position on the active-duty list determined under regulations prescribed by the Secretary of Defense based upon the amount of service credited".

1994. Act Oct. 5, 1994 (effective 12/1/94 as provided by § 1691 of such Act, which appears as 10 USCS § 10001 note) transferred this section, enacted as 10 USCS § 689, to Chapter 1209 and redesignated it as 10 USCS § 12320, and substituted "section 12207" for "section 3353, 5600, or 8353".

Such Act further (effective 10/1/96, as provided by § 1691(b)(1) of such Act, which appears as 10 USCS § 10001 note), as amended Feb. 10, 1996 (effective as if included in Act Oct. 5, 1994, P. L. 103-337, as enacted on Oct. 5, 1994, as provided by § 1501(f)(3) of Act Feb. 10, 1996, which appears as 10 USCS § 113 note) inserted "or full-time National Guard duty" in two places, and inserted "and placed on the active-duty list".

1996. Act Feb. 10, 1996 (effective as if included in Act Oct. 5, 1994, P. L. 103-337, as enacted on Oct. 5, 1994, as provided by § 1501(f)(3) of Act Feb. 10, 1996, which appears as 10 USCS § 113 note) amended the directory language of § 1625 of Act Oct. 5, 1994.

§ 12321. Reserve Officer Training Corps units: limitation on number of Reserves assigned

The number of members of the reserve components serving on active duty or full-time National Guard duty for the purpose of organizing, administering, recruiting, instructing, or training the reserve components who are assigned to duty with a unit of the Reserve Officer Training Corps program may not exceed 275.

(Added Nov. 5, 1990, P. L. 101-510, P. L. 101-510, Div A, Title V, Part E, § 559(a)(1), 105 Stat. 1571; April 6, 1991, P. L. 102-25, Title VII, § 704(a)(3)(A), (B), 105 Stat. 118; Dec. 5, 1991, P. L. 102-190, Div A, Title X, Part E, § 1061(a)(4)(A), 105 Stat. 1472; Oct. 23, 1992, P. L. 102-484, Div A, Title V, Subtitle B, § 512, 106 Stat. 2405; Nov. 30, 1993, P. L. 103-160, Div A, Title V, Subtitle B § 512, 107 Stat. 1649; Oct. 5, 1994, P. L. 103-337, Div A, Title XVI, Subtitle C, § 1662(e)(2), (3), 108 Stat. 2992.)

HISTORY; ANCILLARY LAWS AND DIRECTIVES

Effective date of section:

Act Nov. 5, 1990, P. L. 101-510, Div A, Title V, Part E, § 559(b), 104 Stat. 1571; April 6, 1991, P. L. 102-25, Title VII, § 704(a)(3)(C), 105 Stat. 118 (effective as if included in P. L. 101-510, as provided by § 704(e) of Act April 6, 1991, which appears as 10 USCS § 690 note), provides: "Section 690 of title 10, United States Code, as added by subsection (a), shall take effect on September 30, 1991.".

Amendments:

1991. Act April 6, 1991 (effective as if included in Act Nov. 5, 1990, as provided by § 704(e) of Act April 6, 1991, which appears as 10 USCS § 690 note) amended Act Nov. 5, 1990 so as to redesignate this section, enacted as 10 USCS § 687, as 10 USCS § 690, and to position this section at the end of this chapter.

Act Dec. 5, 1991 substituted ''Corps'' for ''Corp'' in the section heading.

1992. Act Oct. 23, 1992 substituted ''The number of members of the reserve components'' for ''A member of a reserve component'', substituted ''who are assigned'' for ''may not be assigned'', and inserted ''may not exceed 200''.

1993. Act Nov. 30, 1993 substituted ''may not exceed 275'' for ''may not exceed 200''.

1994. Act Oct. 5, 1994 (effective 12/1/94 as provided by § 1691 of such Act, which appears as 10 USCS § 10001 note) transferred this section, enacted as 10 USCS § 690, to Chapter 1209 and redesignated it as 10 USCS § 12321; and substituted the heading for one which read: ''Limitation on duty with Reserve Officer Training Corps units''.

Other provisions:

Application of amendments made by § 704 of Act April 6, 1991. Act April 6, 1991, P. L. 102-25, Title VII, § 704(e), 105 Stat. 120, provides: ''The amendments made by this section [for full classification, consult USCS Tables volumes] shall apply as if included in the enactment of the National Defense Authorization Act for Fiscal Year 1991 (Public Law 101-510) [enacted Nov. 5, 1990].''.

Waiver of prohibition on certain reserve service with the ROTC program. Act Dec. 5, 1991, P. L. 102-190, Div A, Title V, Part C, § 525, 105 Stat. 1363; Feb. 10, 1996, P. L. 104-106, Div A, Title XV, § 1501(d)(2), 110 Stat. 500 (effective as if included in Act Oct. 5, 1994, P. L. 103-337, as enacted on Oct. 5, 1994, as provided by § 1501(f)(3) of Act Feb. 10, 1996, which appears as 10 USCS § 113 note), provides: ''The Secretary of the military department concerned may waive the prohibition in section 12321 of title 10, United States Code, in the case of a member of a reserve component of the Armed Forces referred to in that section who is serving in an assignment to duty with a unit of the Reserve Officer Training Corps program on September 30, 1991, it the Secretary determines that the removal of the member from that assignment will cause a financial hardship for that member.''.

CHAPTER 1211. NATIONAL GUARD MEMBERS IN FEDERAL SERVICE

HISTORY; ANCILLARY LAWS AND DIRECTIVES

Amendments:

1994. Act Oct. 5, 1994, P. L. 103-337, Div A, Title XVI, Subtitle C, § 1662(f)(1), 108 Stat. 2992 (effective 12/1/94 as provided by § 1691 of such Act, which appears as 10 USCS § 10001 note), added the chapter heading and analysis.

1996. Act Feb. 10, 1996, P. L. 104-106, Div A, Title XV, § 1501(b)(18)(A), 110 Stat. 497 (effective as if included in Act Oct. 5, 1994, P. L. 103-337, as enacted on Oct. 5, 1994, as provided by § 1501(f)(3) of Act Feb. 10, 1996, which appears as 10 USCS § 113 note), amended the analysis of this chapter by inserting ''the'' in items 12401, 12402, 12403, and 12404.

§ 12401. Army and Air National Guard of the United States: status

Members of the Army National Guard of the United States and the Air National Guard of the United States are not in active Federal service except when ordered thereto under law.

(Added Oct. 5, 1994, P. L. 103-337, Div A, Title XVI, Subtitle C, § 1662(f)(1), 108 Stat. 2993.)

HISTORY; ANCILLARY LAWS AND DIRECTIVES

Effective date of section:

This section took effect on Dec. 1, 1994, pursuant to Act Oct. 5, 1994, P. L. 103-337, Div A, Title XVI, Subtitle F, § 1691, 108 Stat. 3026, which appears as 10 USCS 10001 note.

CROSS REFERENCES

Status when not in Federal service, 10 USCS § 10107.

Call into Federal service, 10 USCS § 12406.

INTERPRETIVE NOTES AND DECISIONS

Critical element in determining whether National Guardsman is employee of United States is whether or not he is in active, federal service. Ursulich v Puerto Rico Nat'l Guard (1974, DC Puerto Rico) 384 F Supp 736.

Member of New York Army National Guard who sustained injuries in state armory while attending regularly scheduled drill of his unit, since he had not been called into active service by order of President, was not employee of United States Government, but of state. Sadowski v State (1966) 51 Misc 2d 832, 274 NYS2d 368.

§ 12402. Army and Air National Guard of the United States: commissioned officers; duty in National Guard Bureau

(a) The President may, with their consent, order commissioned officers of the Army National Guard of the United States and the Air National Guard of the United States to active duty in the National Guard Bureau.

(b)(1) The number of officers of the Army National Guard of the United States in grades below brigadier general who are ordered to active duty in the National Guard Bureau may not be more than 40 percent of the number of officers of the Army authorized for duty in that Bureau and, to the extent practicable, shall not exceed 40 percent of the number of officers of the Army serving in that Bureau in any grade below brigadier general.

(2) The number of officers of the Air National Guard of the United States in grades below brigadier general who are ordered to active duty in the National Guard Bureau may not be more than 40 percent of the number of officers of the Air Force authorized for duty in that Bureau and, to the extent practicable, shall not exceed 40 percent of the number of officers of the Air Force serving in that Bureau in any grade below brigadier general.

(Added Oct. 5, 1994, P. L. 103-337, Div A, Title XVI, Subtitle C, § 1662(f)(1), 108 Stat. 2993; Feb. 10, 1996, P. L. 104-106, Div A, Title XV, § 1501(b)(18)(B), 110 Stat. 497.)

HISTORY; ANCILLARY LAWS AND DIRECTIVES

Effective date of section:

This section took effect on Dec. 1, 1994, pursuant to Act Oct. 5, 1994, P. L. 103-337, Div A, Title XVI, Subtitle F, § 1691, 108 Stat. 3026, which appears as 10 USCS 10001 note.

Amendments:

1996. Act Feb. 10, 1996 (effective as if included in Act Oct. 5, 1994, P. L. 103-337, as enacted on Oct. 5, 1994, as provided by § 1501(f)(3) of Act Feb. 10, 1996, which appears as 10 USCS § 113 note), in the section heading, inserted "the".

CROSS REFERENCES

National Guard Bureau, assignment of officers of regular or reserve components, 10 USCS § 10507.

Payment of pay and allowances for the Chief of the National Guard Bureau and officers ordered to active duty under this section, 32 USCS § 107; 37 USCS § 204.

This section is referred to in 10 USCS §§ 523, 641, 10507; 32 USCS § 107; 37 USCS § 204.

§ 12403. Army and Air National Guard of the United States: members; status in which ordered into Federal service

Members of the Army National Guard of the United States ordered to active duty shall be ordered to duty as Reserves of the Army. Members of the Air National Guard of the United States ordered to active duty shall be ordered to duty as Reserves of the Air Force.
(Added Oct. 5, 1994, P. L. 103-337, Div A, Title XVI, Subtitle C, § 1662(f)(1), 108 Stat. 2993; Feb. 10, 1996, P. L. 104-106, Div A, Title XV, § 1501(b)(18)(B), 110 Stat. 497.)

HISTORY; ANCILLARY LAWS AND DIRECTIVES

Effective date of section:
This section took effect on Dec. 1, 1994, pursuant to Act Oct. 5, 1994, P. L. 103-337, Div A, Title XVI, Subtitle F, § 1691, 108 Stat. 3026, which appears as 10 USCS 10001 note.

Amendments:
1996. Act Feb. 10, 1996 (effective as if included in Act Oct. 5, 1994, P. L. 103-337, as enacted on Oct. 5, 1994, as provided by § 1501(f)(3) of Act Feb. 10, 1996, which appears as 10 USCS § 113 note), in the section heading, inserted "the".

§ 12404. Army and Air National Guard of the United States: mobilization; maintenance of organization

During an initial mobilization, the organization of a unit of the Army National Guard of the United States or of the Air National Guard of the United States ordered into active Federal service shall, so far as practicable, be maintained as it existed on the date of the order to duty.
(Added Oct. 5, 1994, P. L. 103-337, Div A, Title XVI, Subtitle C, § 1662(f)(1), 108 Stat. 2993; Feb. 10, 1996, P. L. 104-106, Div A, Title XV, § 1501(b)(18)(B), 110 Stat. 497.)

HISTORY; ANCILLARY LAWS AND DIRECTIVES

Effective date of section:
This section took effect on Dec. 1, 1994, pursuant to Act Oct. 5, 1994, P. L. 103-337, Div A, Title XVI, Subtitle F, § 1691, 108 Stat. 3026, which appears as 10 USCS 10001 note.

Amendments:
1996. Act Feb. 10, 1996 (effective as if included in Act Oct. 5, 1994, P. L. 103-337, as enacted on Oct. 5, 1994, as provided by § 1501(f)(3) of Act Feb. 10, 1996, which appears as 10 USCS § 113 note), in the section heading, inserted "the".

§ 12405. National Guard in Federal service: status

Members of the National Guard called into Federal service are, from the time when they are required to respond to the call, subject to the laws and regulations governing the Army or the Air Force, as the case may be, except those applicable only to members of the Regular Army or Regular Air Force, as the case may be.

(Added Oct. 5, 1994, P. L. 103-337, Div A, Title XVI, Subtitle C, § 1662(f)(1), 108 Stat. 2993.)

HISTORY; ANCILLARY LAWS AND DIRECTIVES

Effective date of section:

This section took effect on Dec. 1, 1994, pursuant to Act Oct. 5, 1994, P. L. 103-337, Div A, Title XVI, Subtitle F, § 1691, 108 Stat. 3026, which appears as 10 USCS 10001 note.

§ 12406. National Guard in Federal service: call

Whenever—

(1) the United States, or any of the Territories, Commonwealths, or possessions, is invaded or is in danger of invasion by a foreign nation;

(2) there is a rebellion or danger of a rebellion against the authority of the Government of the United States; or

(3) the President is unable with the regular forces to execute the laws of the United States;

the President may call into Federal service members and units of the National Guard of any State in such numbers as he considers necessary to repel the invasion, suppress the rebellion, or execute those laws. Orders for these purposes shall be issued through the governors of the States or, in the case of the District of Columbia, through the commanding general of the National Guard of the District of Columbia.

(Added Oct. 5, 1994, P. L. 103-337, Div A, Title XVI, Subtitle C, § 1662(f)(1), 108 Stat. 2994.)

HISTORY; ANCILLARY LAWS AND DIRECTIVES

Effective date of section:

This section took effect on Dec. 1, 1994, pursuant to Act Oct. 5, 1994, P. L. 103-337, Div A, Title XVI, Subtitle F, § 1691, 108 Stat. 3026, which appears as 10 USCS 10001 note.

CROSS REFERENCES

This section is referred to in 5 USCS § 6323; 10 USCS §§ 101, 115, 523, 641, 10507, 12304; 32 USCS § 107; 37 USCS § 204.

INTERPRETIVE NOTES AND DECISIONS

1. Power of President
2. Power of Congress
3. Power of states
4. Refusal to serve

1. Power of President

Under former 10 USCS § 3500, National Guard units of states were subject to be mustered into Regular Army of United States under directive of President when Congress had declared national emergency; until such assigning of unit was ordered, unit remained component of state militia, not of federal Armed Forces. Satcher v United States (1952, DC SC) 101 F Supp 919.

Under USCS Constitution Art. 1, § 8, Congress could provide for calling forth militia to execute laws of Union, suppress insurrections, and repel invasions; authority to call forth militia had been vested in President, who was sole judge of exigency justifying call. Alabama Great Southern R. Co. v. U. S., 49 Ct Cl 522.

President had no authority to call forth organized militia of states and send it into foreign country with regular army as part of army of occupation. 29 Op Atty Gen 322.

Under USCS Constitution, Art. 2, §§ 2 and 3 President had authority to call militia of District of Columbia to aid civil authorities. U. S. v. Stewart, (DC Cir), F Cas 16,401a, 2 Hayw & H 280.

President had authority to call into service militia in any part of Union, and persons subject to militia duty in such district were subject to military law. Johnson v. Duncan, 3 Mart (La) 530, 6 Am Dec 675.

President was sole judge as to necessity of calling forth militia. Vanderheyden v. Young, 11 Johns (NY) 150.

President, who had power to call forth militia, had power to prescribe manner in which members should have been drafted and detached, where states did not make sufficient provisions for that purpose. In re Griner (1863) 16 Wis 423.

2. Power of Congress

Congress had no power to place militia under command of officer, not member of militia, when militia was performing services for United States. Opinion of Justices (1812) 8 Mass 548.

3. Power of states

Court-martial organized under authority of state had no power to assess fines on delinquent members of state militia for failure to enter service when called by Secretary of War. Meade v Deputy Marshal, (CC-Va), F Cas 9,372, 1 Brock 324.

Power to determine whether necessary exigencies existed for calling forth militia by President rested with states. Opinion of Justices (1812) 8 Mass 548.

4. Refusal to serve

Although militiaman, who refused to obey orders of President calling him to public service, was not in service of United States, yet he was liable to be tried by court-martial under authority of United States. Houston v Moore (1820) 18 US 1, 5 Wheat 1, 5 L Ed 19; Martin v Mott (1827) 25 US 19, 6 L Ed 537.

§ 12407. National Guard in Federal service: period of service; apportionment

(a) Whenever the President calls the National Guard of a State into Federal service, he may specify in the call the period of the service. Members and units called shall serve inside or outside the territory of the United States during the term specified, unless sooner relieved by the President. However, no member of the National Guard may be kept in Federal service beyond the term of his commission or enlistment.

(b) When the National Guard of a State is called into Federal service with the National Guard of another State, the President may apportion the total number called from the Army National Guard or from the Air National Guard, as the case may be, on the basis of the populations of the States affected by the call.

(Added Oct. 5, 1994, P. L. 103-337, Div A, Title XVI, Subtitle C, § 1662(f)(1), 108 Stat. 2994; Feb. 10, 1996, P. L. 104-106, Div A, Title XV, § 1501(b)(19), 110 Stat. 497.)

HISTORY; ANCILLARY LAWS AND DIRECTIVES

Effective date of section:

This section took effect on Dec. 1, 1994, pursuant to Act Oct. 5, 1994, P. L. 103-337, Div A, Title XVI, Subtitle F, § 1691, 108 Stat. 3026, which appears as 10 USCS 10001 note.

Amendments:

1996. Act Feb. 10, 1996 (effective as if included in Act Oct. 5, 1994, P. L. 103-337, as enacted on Oct. 5, 1994, as provided by § 1501(f)(3) of Act Feb. 10, 1996, which appears as 10 USCS § 113 note), in subsec. (b), substituted ''State'' for ''of those jurisdictions'' and substituted ''States'' for ''jurisdictions''.

§ 12408. National Guard in Federal service: physical examination

(a) Under regulations prescribed by the President, each member of the National Guard called into Federal service under section 12301(a), 12302, or 12304 of this title shall be examined as to physical fitness, without further commission or enlistment.

(b) Immediately before such a member is mustered out of Federal service, he shall be examined as to physical fitness. The record of this examination shall be retained by the United States.

(Added Oct. 5, 1994, P. L. 103-337, Div A, Title XVI, Subtitle C, § 1662(f)(1), 108 Stat. 2994; Sept. 23, 1996, P. L. 104-201, Div A, Title V, Subtitle C, § 523, 110 Stat. 2517.)

HISTORY; ANCILLARY LAWS AND DIRECTIVES

Effective date of section:

This section took effect on Dec. 1, 1994, pursuant to Act Oct. 5, 1994, P. L. 103-337, Div A, Title XVI, Subtitle F, § 1691, 108 Stat. 3026, which appears as 10 USCS 10001 note.

Amendments:

1996. Act Sept. 23, 1996, in subsec. (a), inserted ''under section 12301(a), 12302, or 12304 of this title''.

INTERPRETIVE NOTES AND DECISIONS

Where person was drafted into United States army according to National Conscription Act of May 18, 1917, and at such time was regularly examined by federal medical officers, it made no difference if at time of enlistment into national guard there were irregularities in medical examination. Blackington v United States (1918, CA1 Mass) 248 F 124.

Physical examination was not prerequisite to entry into active federal service by national guardsman responding to call of President. United States v Carlson (1930, CA9 Wash) 44 F2d 5.

CHAPTER 1213. SPECIAL APPOINTMENTS, ASSIGNMENTS, DETAILS, AND DUTIES

HISTORY; ANCILLARY LAWS AND DIRECTIVES

Amendments:

1994. Act Oct. 5, 1994, P. L. 103-337, Div A, Title XVI, Subtitle C, § 1662(g)(1), 108 Stat. 2994 (effective 12/1/94 as provided by § 1691 of such Act, which appears as 10 USCS § 10001 note), added the chapter heading and analysis.

§ 12501. Reserve components: detail of members of regular and reserve components to assist

The Secretary concerned shall detail such members of the regular and reserve components under his jurisdiction as are necessary to effectively develop, train, instruct, and administer those reserve components.

(Added Oct. 5, 1994, P. L. 103-337, Div A, Title XVI, Subtitle C, § 1662(g)(1), 108 Stat. 2995.)

HISTORY; ANCILLARY LAWS AND DIRECTIVES

Effective date of section:

This section took effect on Dec. 1, 1994, pursuant to Act Oct. 5, 1994, P. L. 103-337, Div A, Title XVI, Subtitle F, § 1691, 108 Stat. 3026, which appears as 10 USCS 10001 note.

CROSS REFERENCES

Detail of regular members of Army and Air Force, 32 USCS § 315.

§ 12502. Chief and assistant chief of staff of National Guard divisions and wings in Federal service: detail

(a) The President may detail a regular or reserve officer of the Army as chief of staff, and a regular or reserve officer or an officer of the Army National Guard as assistant to the chief of staff, of any division of the Army National Guard that is in Federal service as an Army National Guard organization.

(b) The President may detail a regular or reserve officer of the Air Force as chief of staff, and a regular or reserve officer or an officer of the Air National Guard as assistant to the chief of staff, of any wing of the Air National Guard that is in Federal service as an Air National Guard organization.

(Added Oct. 5, 1994, P. L. 103-337, Div A, Title XVI, Subtitle C, § 1662(g)(1), 108 Stat. 2995.)

HISTORY; ANCILLARY LAWS AND DIRECTIVES

Effective date of section:

This section took effect on Dec. 1, 1994, pursuant to Act Oct. 5, 1994, P. L. 103-337, Div A, Title XVI, Subtitle F, § 1691, 108 Stat. 3026, which appears as 10 USCS 10001 note.

CROSS REFERENCES

Army Staff, 10 USCS §§ 3031 et seq.

Air Staff, 10 USCS §§ 8031 et seq.

Organization of National Guard, 32 USCS § 104.

CHAPTER 1214. READY RESERVE MOBILIZATION INCOME INSURANCE

HISTORY; ANCILLARY LAWS AND DIRECTIVES

Amendments:

1996. Act Feb. 10, 1996, P. L. 104-106, Div A, Title V, Subtitle B, § 512(a)(1), 110 Stat. 299, added the chapter heading and chapter analysis.
1997. Act Nov. 18, 1997, P. L. 105-85, Div A, Title V, Subtitle B, § 512(b), 111 Stat. 1729, amended the analysis of this chapter by adding item 12533.

§ 12521. Definitions

In this chapter [10 USCS §§ 12521 et seq.]:

(1) The term ''insurance program'' means the Ready Reserve Mobilization Income Insurance Program established under section 12522 of this title.

(2) The term ''covered service'' means active duty performed by a member of a reserve component under an order to active duty for a period of more than 30 days which specifies that the member's service—

(A) is in support of an operational mission for which members of the reserve components have been ordered to active duty without their consent; or

(B) is in support of forces activated during a period of war declared by Congress or a period of national emergency declared by the President or Congress.

(3) The term ''insured member'' means a member of the Ready Reserve who is enrolled for coverage under the insurance program in accordance with section 12524 of this title.

(4) The term ''Secretary'' means the Secretary of Defense.

(5) The term ''Department'' means the Department of Defense.

(6) The term ''Board of Actuaries'' means the Department of Defense Education Benefits Board of Actuaries referred to in section 2006(e)(1) of this title.

(7) The term ''Fund'' means the Reserve Mobilization Income Insurance Fund established by section 12528(a) of this title.

(Added Feb. 10, 1996, P. L. 104-106, Div A, Title V, Subtitle B, § 512(a)(1), 110 Stat. 299.)

HISTORY; ANCILLARY LAWS AND DIRECTIVES

Other provisions:

Effective date of insurance program. Act Feb. 10, 1996, P. L. 104-106, Div A, Title V, Subtitle B, § 512(b), 110 Stat. 305, provides: ''The insurance program provided for in chapter 1214 of title 10, United States Code [10 USCS §§ 12521 et seq.], as added by subsection (a), and the requirement for deductions and contributions for that program shall take effect on September 30, 1996, or on any earlier date declared by the Secretary and published in the Federal Register.''.

CROSS REFERENCES

This section is referred to in 10 USCS § 12529.

§ 12522. Establishment of insurance program

(a) Establishment. The Secretary shall establish for members of the Ready Reserve (including the Coast Guard Reserve) an insurance program to be known as the ''Ready Reserve Mobilization Income Insurance Program''.

(b) Administration. The insurance program shall be administered by the Secretary. The Secretary may prescribe in regulations such rules, procedures, and policies as the Secretary considers necessary or appropriate to carry out the insurance program.

(c) Agreement with Secretary of Transportation. The Secretary and the Secretary of Transportation shall enter into an agreement with respect to the administration of the insurance program for the Coast Guard Reserve.

(Added Feb. 10, 1996, P. L. 104-106, Div A, Title V, Subtitle B, § 512(a)(1), 110 Stat. 299.)

CROSS REFERENCES

This section is referred to in 10 USCS § 12521.

§ 12523. Risk insured

(a) In general. The insurance program shall insure members of the Ready Reserve against the risk of being ordered into covered service.

(b) Entitlement to benefits. (1) An insured member ordered into covered service shall be entitled to payment of a benefit for each month (and fraction thereof) of covered service that exceeds 30 days of covered service, except that no member may be paid under the insurance program for more than 12 months of covered service served during any period of 18 consecutive months.

(2) Payment shall be based solely on the insured status of a member and on

the period of covered service served by the member. Proof of loss of income or of expenses incurred as a result of covered service may not be required.

(Added Feb. 10, 1996, P. L. 104-106, Div A, Title V, Subtitle B, § 512(a)(1), 110 Stat. 300.)

§ 12524. Enrollment and election of benefits

(a) Enrollment. (1) Except as provided in subsection (f), upon first becoming a member of the Ready Reserve, a member shall be automatically enrolled for coverage under the insurance program. An automatic enrollment of a member shall be void if within 60 days after first becoming a member of the Ready Reserve the member declines insurance under the program in accordance with the regulations prescribed by the Secretary.

(2) Promptly after the insurance program is established, the Secretary shall offer to members of the reserve components who are then members of the Ready Reserve (other than members ineligible under subsection (f)) an opportunity to enroll for coverage under the insurance program. A member who fails to enroll within 60 days after being offered the opportunity shall be considered as having declined to be insured under the program.

(3) A member of the Ready Reserve ineligible to enroll under subsection (f) shall be afforded an opportunity to enroll upon being released from active duty in accordance with regulations prescribed by the Secretary if the member has not previously had the opportunity to be enrolled under paragraph (1) or (2). A member who fails to enroll within 60 days after being afforded that opportunity shall be considered as having declined to be insured under the program.

(b) Election of benefit amount. The amount of a member's monthly benefit under an enrollment shall be the basic benefit under subsection (a) of section 12525 of this title unless the member elects a different benefit under subsection (b) of such section within 60 days after first becoming a member of the Ready Reserve or within 60 days after being offered the opportunity to enroll, as the case may be.

(c) Elections irrevocable. (1) An election to decline insurance pursuant to paragraph (1) or (2) of subsection (a) is irrevocable.

(2) The amount of coverage may not be increased after enrollment.

(d) Election to terminate. A member may terminate an enrollment at any time.

(e) Information to be furnished. The Secretary shall ensure that members referred to in subsection (a) are given a written explanation of the insurance program and are advised that they have the right to decline to be insured and, if not declined, to elect coverage for a reduced benefit or an enhanced benefit under subsection (b).

(f) Members ineligible to enroll. Members of the Ready Reserve serving on active duty (or full-time National Guard duty) are not eligible to enroll for coverage under the insurance program. The Secretary may define any additional category of members of the Ready Reserve to be excluded from eligibility to purchase insurance under this chapter [10 USCS §§ 12521 et seq.].

(g) Members of Individual Ready Reserve. Notwithstanding any other provision of this section, and pursuant to regulations issued by the Secretary, a member of the Individual Ready Reserve who becomes a member of the Selected Reserve shall not be denied eligibility to purchase insurance under this chapter upon becoming a member of the Selected Reserve unless the member previously declined to enroll in the program of insurance under this chapter while a member of the Selected Reserve.

(Added Feb. 10, 1996, P. L. 104-106, Div A, Title V, Subtitle B, § 512(a)(1), 110 Stat. 300; Sept. 23, 1996, P. L. 104-201, Div A, Title V, Subtitle E, § 542, 110 Stat. 2521.)

HISTORY; ANCILLARY LAWS AND DIRECTIVES

Amendments:

1996. Act Sept. 23, 1996 added subsec. (g).

CROSS REFERENCES

This section is referred to in 10 USCS § 12521.

§ 12525. Benefit amounts

(a) Basic benefit. The basic benefit for an insured member under the insurance program is $1,000 per month (as adjusted under subsection (d)).

(b) Reduced and enhanced benefits. Under the regulations prescribed by the Secretary, a person enrolled for coverage under the insurance program may elect—

(1) a reduced coverage benefit equal to one-half the amount of the basic benefit; or

(2) an enhanced benefit in the amount of $1,500, $2,000, $2,500, $3,000, $3,500, $4,000, $4,500, or $5,000 per month (as adjusted under subsection (d)).

(c) Amount for partial month. The amount of insurance payable to an insured member for any period of covered service that is less than one month shall be determined by multiplying 1/30 of the monthly benefit rate for the member by the number of days of the covered service served by the member during such period.

(d) Adjustment of amounts. (1) The Secretary shall determine annually the effect of inflation on benefits and shall adjust the amounts set forth in subsections (a) and (b)(2) to maintain the constant dollar value of the benefit.

(2) If the amount of a benefit as adjusted under paragraph (1) is not evenly divisible by $10, the amount shall be rounded to the nearest multiple of $10, except that an amount evenly divisible by $5 but not by $10 shall be rounded to the next lower amount that is evenly divisible by $10.

(Added Feb. 10, 1996, P. L. 104-106, Div A, Title V, Subtitle B, § 512(a)(1), 110 Stat. 301.)

CROSS REFERENCES

This section is referred to in 10 USCS § 12524 .

§ 12526. Premiums

(a) Establishment of rates. (1) The Secretary, in consultation with the Board of Actuaries, shall prescribe the premium rates for insurance under the insurance program.

(2) The Secretary shall prescribe a fixed premium rate for each $1,000 of monthly insurance benefit. The premium amount shall be equal to the share of the cost attributable to insuring the member and shall be the same for all members of the Ready Reserve who are insured under the insurance program for the same benefit amount. The Secretary shall prescribe the rate on the basis of the best available estimate of risk and financial exposure, levels of subscription by members, and other relevant factors.

(b) Level premiums. The premium rate prescribed for the first year of insurance coverage of an insured member shall be continued without change for subsequent years of insurance coverage, except that the Secretary, after consultation with the Board of Actuaries, may adjust the premium rate in order to fund inflation-adjusted benefit increases on an actuarially sound basis.

(Added Feb. 10, 1996, P. L. 104-106, Div A, Title V, Subtitle B, § 512(a)(1), 110 Stat. 301.)

§ 12527. Payment of premiums

(a) Methods of payment. (1) The monthly premium for coverage of a member of the Selected Reserve under the insurance program shall be deducted and withheld from the insured member's pay for each month.

(2) The Secretary of Defense, in consultation with the Secretary of Transportation, shall prescribe regulations which specify the procedures for payment of premiums by members of the Individual Ready Reserve and other members who do not receive pay on a monthly basis.

(b) Advance pay for premium. The Secretary concerned may advance to an insured member the amount equal to the first insurance premium payment due under this chapter [10 USCS §§ 12521 et seq.]. The advance may be paid out of appropriations for military pay. An advance to a member shall be collected from the member either by deducting and withholding the amount from basic pay payable for the member or by collecting it from the member directly. No disbursing or certifying officer shall be responsible for any loss resulting from an advance under this subsection.

(c) Premiums to be deposited in Fund. Premium amounts deducted and withheld from the pay of insured members and premium amounts paid directly to the Secretary shall be credited monthly to the Fund.

(Added Feb. 10, 1996, P. L. 104-106, Div A, Title V, Subtitle B, § 512(a)(1), 110 Stat. 302; Sept. 23, 1996, P. L. 104-201, Div A, Title V, Subtitle E, § 547, 110 Stat. 2524.)

HISTORY; ANCILLARY LAWS AND DIRECTIVES

Amendments:

1996. Act Sept. 23, 1996, in subsec. (a), in para. (1), inserted "of the Selected Reserve", and substituted para. (2) for one which read: "(2) An insured member who does not receive pay on a monthly basis shall pay the Secretary directly the premium amount applicable for the level of benefits for which the member is insured.".

CROSS REFERENCES

This section is referred to in 10 USCS § 12528.

§ 12528. Reserve Mobilization Income Insurance Fund

(a) Establishment. There is established on the books of the Treasury a fund to be known as the "Reserve Mobilization Income Insurance Fund", which shall be administered by the Secretary of the Treasury. The Fund shall be used for the accumulation of funds in order to finance the liabilities of the insurance program on an actuarially sound basis.

(b) Assets of Fund. There shall be deposited into the Fund the following:

(1) Premiums paid under section 12527 of this title.

(2) Any amount appropriated to the Fund.

(3) Any return on investment of the assets of the Fund.

(c) Availability. Amounts in the Fund shall be available for paying insurance benefits under the insurance program.

(d) Investment of assets of Fund. The Secretary of the Treasury shall invest such portion of the Fund as is not in the judgment of the Secretary of Defense required to meet current liabilities. Such investments shall be in public debt securities with maturities suitable to the needs of the Fund, as determined by the Secretary of Defense, and bearing interest at rates determined by the Secretary of the Treasury, taking into consideration current market yields on outstanding marketable obligations of the United States of comparable maturities. The income on such investments shall be credited to the Fund.

(e) Annual accounting. At the beginning of each fiscal year, the Secretary, in consultation with the Board of Actuaries and the Secretary of the Treasury, shall determine the following:

(1) The projected amount of the premiums to be collected, investment earnings to be received, and any transfers or appropriations to be made for the Fund for that fiscal year.

(2) The amount for that fiscal year of any cumulative unfunded liability (including any negative amount or any gain to the Fund) resulting from payments of benefits.

(3) The amount for that fiscal year (including any negative amount) of any cumulative actuarial gain or loss to the Fund.

(Added Feb. 10, 1996, P. L. 104-106, Div A, Title V, Subtitle B, § 512(a)(1), 110 Stat. 302.)

CROSS REFERENCES

This section is referred to in 10 USCS § 12521.

§ 12529. Board of Actuaries

(a) Actuarial responsibility. The Board of Actuaries shall have the actuarial responsibility for the insurance program.

(b) Valuations and premium recommendations. The Board of Actuaries shall carry out periodic actuarial valuations of the benefits under the insurance program and determine a premium rate methodology for the Secretary to use in setting premium rates for the insurance program. The Board shall conduct the first valuation and determine a premium rate methodology not later than six months after the insurance program is established.

(c) Effects of changed benefits. If at the time of any actuarial valuation under subsection (b) there has been a change in benefits under the insurance program that has been made since the last such valuation and such change in benefits increases or decreases the present value of amounts payable from the Fund, the Board of Actuaries shall determine a premium rate methodology, and recommend to the Secretary a premium schedule, for the liquidation of any liability (or actuarial gain to the Fund) resulting from such change and any previous such changes so that the present value of the sum of the scheduled premium payments (or reduction in payments that would otherwise be made) equals the cumulative increase (or decrease) in the present value of such benefits.

(d) Actuarial gains or losses. If at the time of any such valuation the Board of Actuaries determines that there has been an actuarial gain or loss to the Fund as a result of changes in actuarial assumptions since the last valuation or as a result of any differences, between actual and expected experience since the last valuation, the Board shall recommend to the Secretary a premium rate schedule for the amortization of the cumulative gain or loss to the Fund resulting from such changes in assumptions and any previous such changes in assumptions or from the differences in actual and expected experience, respectively, through an increase or decrease in the payments that would otherwise be made to the Fund.

(e) Insufficient assets. If at any time liabilities of the Fund exceed assets of the Fund as a result of members of the Ready Reserve being ordered to active duty as described in section 12521(2) of this title, and funds are unavailable to pay benefits completely, the Secretary shall request the President to submit to Congress a request for a special appropriation to cover the unfunded liability. If appropriations are not made to cover an unfunded liability in any fiscal year, the Secretary shall reduce the amount of the benefits paid under the insurance program to a total amount that does not exceed the assets of the Fund expected to accrue by the end of such fiscal year. Benefits that cannot be paid because of such a reduction shall be deferred and may be paid only after and to the extent that additional funds become available.

(f) Definition of present value. The Board of Actuaries shall define the term "present value" for purposes of this subsection.

(Added Feb. 10, 1996, P. L. 104-106, Div A, Title V, Subtitle B, § 512(a)(1), 110 Stat. 303.)

§ 12530. Payment of benefits

(a) Commencement of payment. An insured member who serves in excess of

30 days of covered service shall be paid the amount to which such member is entitled on a monthly basis beginning not later than one month after the 30th day of covered service.

(b) Method of payment. The Secretary shall prescribe in the regulations the manner in which payments shall be made to the member or to a person designated in accordance with subsection (c).

(c) Designated recipients. (1) A member may designate in writing another person (including a spouse, parent, or other person with an insurable interest, as determined in accordance with the regulations prescribed by the Secretary) to receive payments of insurance benefits under the insurance program.

(2) A member may direct that payments of insurance benefits for a person designated under paragraph (1) be deposited with a bank or other financial institution to the credit of the designated person.

(d) Recipients in event of death of insured member. Any insurance payable under the insurance program on account of a deceased member's period of covered service shall be paid, upon the establishment of a valid claim, to the beneficiary or beneficiaries which the deceased member designated in writing. If no such designation has been made, the amount shall be payable in accordance with the laws of the State of the member's domicile.

(Added Feb. 10, 1996, P. L. 104-106, Div A, Title V, Subtitle B, § 512(a)(1), 110 Stat. 304.)

§ 12531. Purchase of insurance

(a) Purchase authorized. The Secretary may, instead of or in addition to underwriting the insurance program through the Fund, purchase from one or more insurance companies a policy or policies of group insurance in order to provide the benefits required under this chapter [10 USCS §§ 12521 et seq.]. The Secretary may waive any requirement for full and open competition in order to purchase an insurance policy under this subsection.

(b) Eligible insurers. In order to be eligible to sell insurance to the Secretary for purposes of subsection (a), an insurance company shall—

(1) be licensed to issue insurance in each of the 50 States and in the District of Columbia; and

(2) as of the most recent December 31 for which information is available to the Secretary, have in effect at least one percent of the total amount of insurance that all such insurance companies have in effect in the United States.

(c) Administrative provisions. (1) An insurance company that issues a policy for purposes of subsection (a) shall establish an administrative office at a place and under a name designated by the Secretary.

(2) For the purposes of carrying out this chapter [10 USCS §§ 12521 et seq.], the Secretary may use the facilities and services of any insurance company issuing any policy for purposes of subsection (a), may designate one such company as the representative of the other companies for such purposes, and

may contract to pay a reasonable fee to the designated company for its services.

(d) Reinsurance. The Secretary shall arrange with each insurance company issuing any policy for purposes of subsection (a) to reinsure, under conditions approved by the Secretary, portions of the total amount of the insurance under such policy or policies with such other insurance companies (which meet qualifying criteria prescribed by the Secretary) as may elect to participate in such reinsurance.

(e) Termination. The Secretary may at any time terminate any policy purchased under this section.

(Added Feb. 10, 1996, P. L. 104-106, Div A, Title V, Subtitle B, § 512(a)(1), 110 Stat. 304.)

§ 12532. Termination for nonpayment of premiums; forfeiture

(a) Termination for nonpayment. The coverage of a member under the insurance program shall terminate without prior notice upon a failure of the member to make required monthly payments of premiums for two consecutive months. The Secretary may provide in the regulations for reinstatement of insurance coverage terminated under this subsection.

(b) Forfeiture. Any person convicted of mutiny, treason, spying, or desertion, or who refuses to perform service in the armed forces or refuses to wear the uniform of any of the armed forces shall forfeit all rights to insurance under this chapter [10 USCS §§ 12521 et seq.].

(Added Feb. 10, 1996, P. L. 104-106, Div A, Title V, Subtitle B, § 512(a)(1), 110 Stat. 305.)

§ 12533. Termination of program

(a) In general. The Secretary shall terminate the insurance program in accordance with this section.

(b) Termination of new enrollments. The Secretary may not enroll a member of the Ready Reserve for coverage under the insurance program after the date of the enactment of this section [enacted Nov. 18, 1997].

(c) Termination of coverage. (1) The enrollment under the insurance program of insured members other than insured members described in paragraph (2) is terminated as of the date of the enactment of this section [enacted Nov. 18, 1997]. The enrollment of an insured member described in paragraph (2) is terminated as of the date of the termination of the period of covered service of that member described in that paragraph.

(2) An insured member described in this paragraph is an insured member who on the date of the enactment of this section [enacted Nov. 18, 1997] is serving on covered service for a period of service, or has been issued an order directing the performance of covered service, that satisfies or would satisfy the entitlement-to-benefits provisions of this chapter [10 USCS §§ 12521 et seq.].

(d) Termination of payment of benefits. The Secretary may not make any benefit payment under the insurance program after the date of the enactment of this section [enacted Nov. 18, 1997] other than to an insured member who on that date (1) is serving on an order to covered service, (2) has been issued an order directing performance of covered service, or (3) has served on covered service before that date for which benefits under the program have not been paid to the member.

(e) Termination of Insurance Fund. The Secretary shall close the Fund not later than 60 days after the date on which the last benefit payment from the Fund is made. Any amount remaining in the Fund when closed shall be covered into the Treasury as miscellaneous receipts.

(Added Nov. 18, 1997, P. L. 105-85, Div A, Title V, Subtitle B, § 512(a), 111 Stat. 1729.)

CHAPTER 1215. MISCELLANEOUS PROHIBITIONS AND PENALTIES

HISTORY; ANCILLARY LAWS AND DIRECTIVES

Amendments:

1994. Act Oct. 5, 1994, P. L. 103-337, Div A, Title XVI, Subtitle C, § 1662(g)(1), 108 Stat. 2991 (effective 12/1/94 as provided by § 1691 of such Act, which appears as 10 USCS § 10001 note) added the chapter heading.

1997. Act Nov. 18, 1997, P. L. 105-85, Div A, Title V, Subtitle B, § 515(a), 111 Stat. 1733, substituted the chapter analysis for ''[No present sections]''.

§ 12551. Prohibition of use of Air Force Reserve AGR personnel for Air Force base security functions

(a) Limitation. The Secretary of the Air Force may not use members of the Air Force Reserve who are AGR personnel for the performance of force protection, base security, or security police functions at an Air Force facility in the United States.

(b) AGR personnel defined. In this section, the term ''AGR personnel'' means members of the Air Force Reserve who are on active duty (other than for training) in connection with organizing, administering, recruiting, instructing, or training the Air Force Reserve.

(Added Nov. 18, 1997, P. L. 105-85, Div A, Title V, Subtitle B, § 515(a), 111 Stat. 1733.)

CHAPTER 1217. MISCELLANEOUS RIGHTS AND BENEFITS

HISTORY; ANCILLARY LAWS AND DIRECTIVES

Amendments:

1994. Act Oct. 5, 1994, P. L. 103-337, Div A, Title XVI, Subtitle C, § 1662(g)(1), 108 Stat. 2995 (effective 12/1/94 as provided by § 1691 of such Act, which appears as 10 USCS § 10001 note), added the chapter heading and analysis.

§ 12601. Compensation: Reserve on active duty accepting from any person

Any Reserve who, before being ordered to active duty, was receiving compensation from any person may, while he is on that duty, receive compensation from that person.

(Added Oct. 5, 1994, P. L. 103-337, Div A, Title XVI, Subtitle C, § 1662(g)(1), 108 Stat. 2995.)

HISTORY; ANCILLARY LAWS AND DIRECTIVES

Effective date of section:

This section took effect on Dec. 1, 1994, pursuant to Act Oct. 5, 1994, P. L. 103-337, Div A, Title XVI, Subtitle F, § 1691, 108 Stat. 3026, which appears as 10 USCS 10001 note.

§ 12602. Members of Army National Guard of United States and Air National Guard of United States: credit for service as members of National Guard

(a) For the purposes of laws providing benefits for members of the Army National Guard of the United States and their dependents and beneficiaries—

(1) military training, duty, or other service performed by a member of the Army National Guard of the United States in his status as a member of the Army National Guard for which he is entitled to pay from the United States shall be considered military training, duty, or other service, as the case may be, in Federal service as a Reserve of the Army;

(2) full-time National Guard duty performed by a member of the Army National Guard of the United States shall be considered active duty in Federal service as a Reserve of the Army; and

(3) inactive-duty training performed by a member of the Army National Guard of the United States in his status as a member of the Army National

Guard, in accordance with regulations prescribed under section 502 of title 32 or other express provision of law, shall be considered inactive-duty training in Federal service as a Reserve of the Army.

(b) For the purposes of laws providing benefits for members of the Air National Guard of the United States and their dependents and beneficiaries—

(1) military training, duty, or other service performed by a member of the Air National Guard of the United States in his status as a member of the Air National Guard for which he is entitled to pay from the United States shall be considered military training, duty, or other service, as the case may be, in Federal service as a Reserve of the Air Force;

(2) full-time National Guard duty performed by a member of the Air National Guard of the United States shall be considered active duty in Federal service as a Reserve of the Air Force; and

(3) inactive-duty training performed by a member of the Air National Guard of the United States in his status as a member of the Air National Guard, in accordance with regulations prescribed under section 502 of title 32 or other express provision of law, shall be considered inactive-duty training in Federal service as a Reserve of the Air Force.

(Added Oct. 5, 1994, P. L. 103-337, Div A, Title XVI, Subtitle C, § 1662(g)(1), 108 Stat. 2995.)

HISTORY; ANCILLARY LAWS AND DIRECTIVES

Effective date of section:

This section took effect on Dec. 1, 1994, pursuant to Act Oct. 5, 1994, P. L. 103-337, Div A, Title XVI, Subtitle F, § 1691, 108 Stat. 3026, which appears as 10 USCS 10001 note.

CHAPTER 1219. STANDARDS AND PROCEDURES FOR RETENTION AND PROMOTION

HISTORY; ANCILLARY LAWS AND DIRECTIVES

Amendments:

1994. Act Oct. 5, 1994, P. L. 103-337, Div A, Title XVI, Subtitle C, § 1662(h)(1), 108 Stat. 2996 (effective 12/1/94 as provided by § 1691 of such Act, which appears as 10 USCS § 10001 note), added the chapter heading and analysis.

§ 12641. Standards and procedures: Secretary to prescribe

(a) The Secretary concerned shall, by regulation, prescribe—

(1) standards and qualifications for the retention and promotion of members of the reserve components under his jurisdiction; and

(2) equitable procedures for the periodic determination of the compliance of each such Reserve with those standards and qualifications.

(b) If a Reserve fails to comply with the standards and qualifications prescribed under subsection (a), he shall—

(1) if qualified, be transferred to an inactive reserve status;

(2) if qualified, be retired without pay; or

(3) have his appointment or enlistment terminated.

(Aug. 10, 1956, ch 1041, § 1, 70A Stat. 79; Oct. 5, 1994, P. L. 103-337, Div A, Title XVI, Subtitle C, § 1662(h)(2), (4)(A), 108 Stat. 2996.)

HISTORY; ANCILLARY LAWS AND DIRECTIVES

Prior law and revision:

Revised Section	Source (USCS)	Source (Statutes at Large)
1001(a)	10:1036c (1st sentence). 34:440k (1st sentence).	June 29, 1948, ch. 708, § 304 (less last sentence),

Revised Section	Source (USCS)	Source (Statutes at Large)
1001(b)	10:1036c (2d sentence). 34:440k (2d sentence).	62 Stat. 1088.

In subsection (a), the words ''As soon as may be practicable after the effective date of sections 1036–1036i [440h–440q] of this title'' are omitted as executed. The words ''not inconsistent with said sections or any other Act'' and ''appropriate'' are omitted as surplusage.

Amendments:

1994. Act Oct. 5, 1994 (effective 12/1/94 as provided by § 1691 of such Act, which appears as 10 USCS § 10001 note) transferred this section, enacted as 10 USCS § 1001, to Chapter 1219 and redesignated it as 10 USCS § 12641; and substituted the section heading for one which read: ''Members physically not qualified for active duty: discharge or transfer to retired status''.

CROSS REFERENCES

Qualifications—Enlisted members, 10 USCS § 12102.

Qualifications—Officers, 10 USCS § 12201.

This section is referred to in 10 USCS §§ 1001, 12307, 12734.

INTERPRETIVE NOTES AND DECISIONS

Regulation promulgated by Secretary of Defense which required minimum two years of service-in-grade at rank of colonel prior to eligibility of state adjutant general for federal recognition as brigadier general was valid where lawfully adopted pursuant to authority conferred by 10 USCS § 1001 (now § 12641), notwithstanding fact that numerous other sections of United States Code exempted adjutants general or assistant adjutants general from particular provisions, requirements or qualifications prescribed for various military officers. Jones v Hoffman (1976, MD Ala) 419 F Supp 79.

§ 12642. Standards and qualifications: result of failure to comply with

(a) To be retained in an active status, a reserve commissioned officer must, in any applicable yearly period, attain the number of points under section 12732(a)(2) of this title prescribed by the Secretary concerned, with the approval of the Secretary of Defense in the case of a Secretary of a military department, and must conform to such other standards and qualifications as the Secretary concerned may prescribe. The Secretary may not prescribe a minimum of more than 50 points under this subsection.

(b) Subject to section 12645 of this title, a reserve commissioned officer who fails to attain the number of points, or to conform to the standards and qualifications, prescribed in subsection (a) shall—

(1) be transferred to the Retired Reserve if he is qualified and applies therefor;

(2) if he is not qualified or does not apply for transfer to the Retired Reserve, be transferred to an inactive status, if he is qualified therefor; or

(3) if he is not transferred to the Retired Reserve or an inactive status, be discharged from his reserve appointment.

(c) This section does not apply to commissioned warrant officers or to adjutants general or assistant adjutants general of States and Territories, Puerto Rico, and the District of Columbia.

(Added Sept. 2, 1958, P. L. 85-861, § 1(22)(A), 72 Stat. 1443; Sept. 29, 1988, P. L. 100-456, Div A, Title XII, Part D, § 1234(a)(1), 102 Stat. 2059; Oct. 5, 1994, P. L. 103-337, Div A, Title XVI, Subtitle C, § 1662(h)(2), Subtitle D, § 1675(d)(1), 108 Stat. 2996, 3018.)

HISTORY; ANCILLARY LAWS AND DIRECTIVES

Prior law and revision:

Revised Section	Source (USCS)	Source (Statutes at Large)
1002(a)	50:1192(b) (1st sentence, less 11th through 29th words). 50:1181(4).	Sept. 3, 1954, ch. 1257, §§ 102(1) (as applicable to § 202(b))), 102(4), 202(b), 68 Stat. 1149, 1150.
1002(b)	50:1192(b) (less 1st sentence).	
1002(c)	50:1181(1) (as applicable to 50:1192(b)). 50:1192(b) (11th through 29th words of 1st sentence).	

In subsection (a), the word ''minimum'' is omitted as surplusage. The last sentence is substituted for the words ''(not to exceed fifty)''.

Amendments:

1988. Act Sept. 29, 1988, in subsec. (c), deleted ''the Canal Zone,'' following ''Puerto Rico,''.

1994. Act Oct. 5, 1994 (effective 12/1/94 as provided by § 1691 of such Act, which appears as 10 USCS § 10001 note) transferred this section, enacted as 10 USCS § 1002, to Chapter 1219 and redesignated it as 10 USCS § 12642; in subsec. (a), substituted ''section 12732(a)(2)'' for ''section 1332(a)(2)''; and, in subsec. (b), substituted ''section 12645'' for ''section 1005''.

CROSS REFERENCES

Adjutants general and assistant adjutants general, reference as applicable to other officers of National Guard, 10 USCS § 10214.

Grade of reserve commissioned officer on transfer to Retired Reserve, 10 USCS §§ 12771, 12772.

This section is referred to in 10 USCS §§ 8360, 10214.

RESEARCH GUIDE

Am Jur:

53A Am Jur 2d, Military and Civil Defense § 218.

§ 12643. Boards for appointment, promotion, and certain other purposes: composition

(a) Except as provided in section 612(a)(3) of this title and except for boards that may be convened to select Reserves for appointment in the Regular Army, Regular Navy, Regular Air Force, or Regular Marine Corps, each board convened for the appointment, promotion, demotion, involuntary release from active duty, discharge, or retirement of Reserves shall include at least one member of the Reserves, with the exact number of Reserves determined by the Secretary concerned in his discretion.

(b) Each member of a board convened for the selection for promotion, or for the demotion or discharge, of Reserves must be senior in rank to the persons under consideration by that board. However, a member serving in a legal advisory capacity may be junior in rank to any person, other than a judge advocate or law specialist, being considered by that board; and a member serving in a medical advisory capacity may be junior in rank to any person, other than a medical officer, being considered by that board.

(Aug. 10, 1956, ch 1041, § 1, 70A Stat. 11; Dec. 12, 1980, P. L. 96-513, Title V, Part A, § 501(4), 94 Stat. 2907; July 10, 1981, P. L. 97-22, § 2(c), 95 Stat. 124 ; Oct. 5, 1994, P. L. 103-337, Div A, Title XVI, Subtitle C, § 1662(h)(2), 108 Stat. 2996.)

HISTORY; ANCILLARY LAWS AND DIRECTIVES

Prior law and revision:

Revised Section	Source (USCS)	Source (Statutes at Large)
266(a)	50:1005(a).	July 9, 1952, ch. 608, § 254,
366(b)	50:1005(b).	66 Stat. 496.

In subsection (a), the words ''under . . . prescribed'' are substituted for the words ''in accordance . . . established''.

In subsection (b), the words ''in rank'' and ''by that board'' are inserted for clarity.

Amendments:

1980. Act Dec. 12, 1980 (effective 9/15/81, as provided by § 701(a) of such Act, which appears as 10 USCS § 101 note), in subsec. (a), substituted ''Except as provided in section 612(a)(3) of this title, each'' for ''Each''.

1981. Act July 10, 1981, in subsec. (a), substituted ''title and except for boards that may be convened to select Reserves for appointment in the Regular Army, Regular Navy, Regular Air Force, or Regular Marine Corps,''; for ''title,'' and substituted ''at least one member of the Reserves, with the exact number of Reserves determined by the Secretary concerned in his discretion'' for ''an appropriate number of Reserves, as prescribed by the Secretary concerned under standards and policies prescribed by the Secretary of Defense''.

1994. Act Oct. 5, 1994 (effective 12/1/94 as provided by § 1691 of such Act, which appears as 10 USCS § 10001 note) transferred this section, enacted as 10 USCS § 266, to Chapter 1219 and redesignated it as 10 USCS § 12643.

INTERPRETIVE NOTES AND DECISIONS

1. Generally
2. Improperly constituted board
3. Reconvened board
4. Review

1. Generally

Air Force Reserve captain recommended for involuntary release from active duty by Air Force Reserve Officers Screening Board is bound to know statutory requirement of representation of appropriate number of reservists, and is under duty to diligently pursue his claim by discharging affirmative duty to inquire as to whether representation was appropriate and to act on facts discovered. Jones v United States (1984) 6 Cl Ct 531.

10 USCS § 266 (now § 12643) does not require Secretary of Army to appoint to selection boards number of reservists that is proportionately equal to number of reservists board would consider for promotion; § 266(a) (now § 12643(a)) gives Secretary substantial discretion to determine what constitutes "appropriate number" of reservists. Palmer v United States (1984) 6 Cl Ct 541.

Training and Administration of Reserves officer is Reserve officer under mandatory Reserve representation requirements enumerated in 10 USCS § 266(a) (now § 12643(a)). Keltner v United States (1984) 6 Cl Ct 824.

Faculty Board proceedings are administrative and non-penal in nature, such boards being authorized only to hold hearings and make recommendations to be acted upon by convening authority after review of proceedings, findings and recommendations, and proceedings are less formal than courts-martial and are not bound by strict rules of evidence; 10 USCS § 266 (now § 12643) does not require that majority of members of Faculty Board be members of Reserve components, nor does it prohibit Career Reservists from serving on such boards, and where Board is convened to rate students, not to rate officers, medical representation on such Board is not necessary. Henderson v United States (1966) 175 Ct Cl 690, cert den (1967) 386 US 1016, 18 L Ed 2d 455, 87 S Ct 1373.

Even though 10 USCS § 266 provided that all boards convened for appointment, promotion, release from duty, etc., should include "appropriate" number [now "at least one member"] from reserve components as prescribed by appropriate Secretary in accordance with standards and policies established by Secretary of Defense, it did not require that any particular number or that majority of the voting members of such boards be Reserve officers, but rather left matter to administrative discretion. Henderson v United States (1966) 175 Ct Cl 690, cert den (1967) 386 US 1016, 18 L Ed 2d 455, 87 S Ct 1373.

2. Improperly constituted board

Action of board in passing over reservists for promotion is void since provisions of 10 USCS § 266 (now § 12643) are mandatory rather than permissive and since legislative history reveals congressional intent to establish selection boards that would protect Reserve Officers against whatever generic bias may exist against them in selection boards composed entirely of regular Army Officers. Dilley v Alexander (1979) 195 US App DC 332, 603 F2d 914.

Promotion passover by improperly constituted selection board is not void per se; Secretary is within his discretion in appointing relook board to review action of prior selection board. Jones v Alexander (1980, CA5 Ga) 609 F2d 778, reh den (1980, CA5 Ga) 613 F2d 314 and cert den (1980) 449 US 832, 66 L Ed 2d 37, 101 S Ct 100.

Secretary of Defense's decision to assign only one reserve officer, out of 27 officers who were members of election boards to consider promotion groups with reserve components of 25.4 percent and 35 percent was arbitrary and capricious, and thus abuse of discretion, as discretion in assignment of officers to selection boards, although broad, is not unfettered, and ratios clearly did not reflect appropriate number of reserves. Yerxa v United States (1986) 11 Cl Ct 110, affd without op (1987, CA) 824 F2d 978.

Plaintiffs' removal from active duty in Army was wrongful as 1974 and 1975 selection boards, before which plaintiffs were considered for promotion and then passed over, were illegally composed by not including any Reservists, resulting in prejudicial error to plaintiffs; statutory command as to board composition is clear and unequivocal expression of legislative intent; there was no way of evaluating what impact error had on original proceedings. Doyle v United States (1979) 220 Ct Cl 285, 599 F2d 984, amd on other grounds (1979) 220 Ct Cl 326, 609 F2d 990, cert den (1980) 446 US 982, 64 L Ed 2d 837, 100 S Ct 2961.

Even if board's composition did not comply with statute, reservist released from active duty could not have been prejudiced since only reserve officers were being considered by board. Sargisson v United States (1990, CA) 913 F2d 918.

3. Reconvened board

Reconvening of "relook" boards properly staffed with reservists does not cure defects in decisions of earlier improperly constituted boards since record of earlier nonselection of applicants was in front of later board and other selection factors militated against fair consideration of these applicants previously deprived of their rights under 10 USCS § 266 (now § 12643). Dilley v Alexander (1979) 195 US App DC 332, 603 F2d 914.

Reserve officer may be released from active duty because of 2 consecutive nonselections for promotion, even though promotion boards did not include reserve officers, as required by 10 USCS § 266(a) (now § 12643(a)), where promotion boards were subsequently reconvened to include reserve officers, as officer was not selected for promotion by reconstituted promotion boards. Whitehead v Alexander (1977, DC Dist Col) 439 F Supp 910.

4. Review

In action by Reserve officers challenging nonselection for promotion on grounds that promotion board did not include Rserve officers, government is precluded from arguing failure to exhaust administrative remedies upon petition for rehearing since officers alleged exhaustion at earlier stages and government failed then to challenge such allegations. Dilley v Alexander (1979) 195 US App DC 332, 603 F2d 914.

Even though 2 selection boards which refused to promote officer in 1974 and 1975 may have been improperly constituted by not including appropriate number of Reserves as required by 10 USCS § 266 (now § 12643), officer is barred under doctrine of res judicata from relitigating propriety of his involuntary discharge, where he exhausted his administrative remedies, brought suit in federal court and lost on merits of case, and failed to appeal from adverse decision, notwithstanding that Army subsequently retained him on active duty and reconsidered him for promotion several additional times before finally discharging him. Hardison v Alexander (1981, App DC) 211 US App DC 51, 655 F2d 1281.

Plaintiff cannot be excused for delay in bringing claim, laches bars claims of military personnel who challenge their nonselection for promotion by selection boards that were not constituted as required by law when personnel have re-enlisted and thereby obtain protection of 50 USCS Appx § 525 from this court's 6-year statute of limitations. Hankins v United States (1985) 7 Cl Ct 698.

Case of serviceman who is denied promotion and who, under 10 USCS § 266 (now § 12643), questions composition of selection board containing only one reservist among 25 members is remanded to Air Force Board for Correction of Military Records since exhaustion of administrative remedies is not required for relief and since serviceman has not argued this issue before Board. Stewart v United States (1979) 222 Ct Cl 42, 611 F2d 1356.

§ 12644. Members physically not qualified for active duty: discharge or transfer to retired status

Except as otherwise provided by law, the Secretary concerned may provide for the honorable discharge or the transfer to a retired status of members of the reserve components under his jurisdiction who are found to be not physically qualified for active duty. However, no member of the Army National Guard of the United States or the Air National Guard of the United States may be transferred under this subsection without the consent of the governor or other appropriate authority of the jurisdiction concerned.

(Aug. 10, 1956, ch 1041, § 1, 70A Stat. 79; July 7, 1960, P. L. 86-603, § 1(1), 74 Stat. 357; Nov. 30, 1993, P. L. 103-160, Div A, Title V, Subtitle B, § 519, 107 Stat. 1651; Oct. 5, 1994, P. L. 103-337, Div A, Title XVI, Subtitle C, §§ 1661(a)(4), 1662(h)(2), (4)(B), 108 Stat. 2980, 2996, 2997.)

HISTORY; ANCILLARY LAWS AND DIRECTIVES

Prior law and revision:

Revised Section	Source (USCS)	Source (Statutes at Large)
1004(a)	50:949.	July 9, 1952, ch. 608,
1004(b)	50:950 (last sentence).	§§ 225, 226, 66 Stat. 488.

Revised Section	Source (USCS)	Source (Statutes at Large)
1004(c)	50:950 (less last sentence).	

In subsection (a), the words "Each . . . who is not on active duty" are substituted for the words "when not on active duty all". The words "examined as to his physical fitness" are substituted for the words "given physical examinations". The words "be required to" are omitted as surplusage. The words "execute and" are inserted for clarity.

In subsection (c), the words "under his jurisdiction" are inserted for clarity.

Amendments:

1960. Act July 7, 1960 substituted subsec. (a) for one which read: "Each Reserve who is not on active duty and not in the Retired Reserve shall be examined as to his physical fitness at least once every four years, or more often as the Secretary concerned considers necessary, and shall execute and submit annually a certificate of physical condition.".

1993. Act Nov. 30, 1993, in subsec. (a)(1), substituted "five years" for "four years".

1994. Act Oct. 5, 1994 (effective 12/1/94 as provided by § 1691 of such Act, which appears as 10 USCS § 10001 note) deleted subsecs. (a) and (b), which read:

"(a) Each member of the Ready Reserve who is not on active duty shall—

"(1) be examined as to his physical fitness every five years, or more often as the Secretary concerned considers necessary; and

"(2) execute and submit annually a certificate of physical condition.

Each Reserve in an active status, or on an inactive status list, who is not on active duty shall execute and submit annually a certificate of physical condition.

"(b) The kind of duty to which a Reserve ordered to active duty may be assigned shall be considered in determining physical qualifications for active duty.";

and deleted the subsection designator "(c)" preceding "Except as otherwise provided".

Such Act further (effective as above) transferred this section, enacted as 10 USCS § 1004, to Chapter 1219, redesignated it as 10 USCS § 12644, and substituted the section heading for one which read: "Physical examination".

CROSS REFERENCES

Suspension of laws during war or emergency as to warrant officers, 10 USCS § 12243.

Discharge of reserves, 10 USCS §§ 12681, 12682.

§ 12645. Commissioned officers: retention until completion of required service

(a) Except as provided in subsection (b), a reserve commissioned officer who has not completed the period of service required of him by section 651 of this title or any other provision of law may not be discharged or transferred from an active status under chapter 573, 1407, 1409, or 1411 of this title [10 USCS §§ 6371 et seq., 14501 et seq., 14701 et seq., or 14901 et seq.] or chapter 21 of title 14 [14 USCS §§ 751a et seq.]. Unless, under regulations prescribed by the Secretary concerned, he is promoted to a higher reserve grade, he shall be retained in an active status in his reserve grade for the rest of his period of required service and shall be an additional number to the authorized strength of his grade.

(b) Subsection (a) does not prevent the discharge or transfer from an active status of—

(1) a commissioned warrant officer; or

(2) an officer on the active-duty list or a reserve active-status list who is found not qualified for promotion to the grade of first lieutenant, in the case of an officer of the Army, Air force, or Marine Corps, or lieutenant (junior grade), in the case of an officer of the Navy;

(3) an officer on the active-duty list or reserve active-status list who has failed of selection for promotion for the second time to the grade of captain, in the case of an officer of the Army, Air Force, or Marine Corps, or to the grade of lieutenant, in the case of an officer of the Navy; or

(4) an officer whose discharge or transfer from an active status is required by law.

(Added Sept. 2, 1958, P. L. 85-861, § 1(22)(B), 72 Stat. 1444; Jan. 2, 1975, P. L. 93-586, § 2, 88 Stat. 1920; Oct. 19, 1984, P. L. 98-525, Title V, Part C, § 528(a), 98 Stat. 2525; Oct. 5, 1994, P. L. 103-337, Div A, Title XVI, Subtitle A, Part II, § 1627, Subtitle C, § 1662(h)(2), Subtitle D, § 1675(d)(2), 108 Stat. 2962, 2996, 3018; Feb. 10, 1996, P. L. 104-106, Div A, Title XV, § 1501(a)(4), 110 Stat. 495; Sept. 23, 1996, P. L. 104-201, Div A, Title V, Subtitle E, § 544(b), 110 Stat. 2523.)

HISTORY; ANCILLARY LAWS AND DIRECTIVES

Prior law and revision:

Revised Section	Source (USCS)	Source (Statutes at Large)
1005	50:1181(1) (as appli cable to 50:1194). 50:1194.	Sept. 3, 1954, ch. 1257, §§ 102(1) (as applicable to § 204), 204, 68 Stat. 1149, 1151.

The word ''subsequently'' is omitted as surplusage.

Amendments:

1975. Act Jan. 2, 1975 inserted ''or chapter 21 of title 14''.

1984. Act Oct. 19, 1984, designated the existing provisions as subsec. (a), and in subsec (a), as so designated, substituted ''Except as provided in subsection (b), a reserve commissioned officer'' for ''A reserve commissioned officer, other than a commissioned warrant officer,'', and deleted the comma following ''provision of law''; and added subsec. (b).

1994. Act Oct. 5, 1994 (effective 12/1/94 as provided by § 1691 of such Act, which appears as 10 USCS § 10001 note) transferred this section, enacted as 10 USCS § 1005, to Chapter 1219 and redesignated it as 10 USCS § 12645.

Such Act further (effective 10/1/96, as provided by § 1691(b)(1), which appears as 10 USCS § 10001 note), in subsection (a), substituted "chapter 573, 1407, 1409, or 1411" for "chapter 337, 361, 363, 573, 837, 861, or 863".

Such Act further (effective as above), as amended Feb. 10, 1996 (effective as if included in Act Oct. 5, 1994, P. L. 103-337, as enacted on Oct. 5, 1994, as provided by § 1501(f)(3) of such Act, which appears as 10 USCS § 113 note), in subsec. (b), in para. (1), deleted "or" after the concluding semicolon, in para. (2), substituted a concluding semicolon for a concluding period, and added paras. (3) and (4).

1996. Act Feb. 10, 1996 (effective as if included in Act Oct. 5, 1994, P. L. 103-337, as enacted on Oct. 5, 1994, as provided by § 1501(f)(3) of such Act, which appears as 10 USCS § 113 note) amended the directory language of § 1627 of Act Oct. 5, 1994.

Act Sept. 23, 1996, in subsec. (b)(2), inserted "or a reserve active-status list".

CROSS REFERENCES

This section is referred to in 10 USCS §§ 3819, 3846, 6389, 6410, 8819, 8846, 12642, 14503, 14901; 32 USCS § 323.

§ 12646. Commissioned officers: retention of after completing 18 or more, but less than 20, years of service

(a) If on the date prescribed for the discharge or transfer from an active status of a reserve commissioned officer he is entitled to be credited with at least 18, but less than 19, years of service computed under section 12732 of this title, he may not be discharged or transferred from an active status under chapter 573, 1407, or 1409 of this title [10 USCS §§ 6371 et seq., 14501 et seq., or 14701 et seq.] or chapter 21 of title 14 [14 USCS §§ 701 et seq.], without his consent before the earlier of the following dates—

(1) the date on which he is entitled to be credited with 20 years of service computed under section 12732 of this title; or

(2) the third anniversary of the date on which he would otherwise be discharged or transferred from an active status.

(b) If on the date prescribed for the discharge or transfer from an active status of a reserve commissioned officer he is entitled to be credited with at least 19, but less than 20, years of service computed under section 12732 of this title, he may not be discharged or transferred from an active status under chapter 573, 1407, or 1409 of this title [10 USCS §§ 6371 et seq., 14501 et seq., or 14701 et seq.] or chapter 21 of title 14 [14 USCS §§ 701 et seq.], without his consent before the earlier of the following dates—

(1) the date on which he is entitled to be credited with 20 years of service computed under section 12732 of this title; or

(2) the second anniversary of the date on which he would otherwise be discharged or transferred from an active status.

(c) An officer who is retained in an active status under subsection (a) or (b) is an additional number to those otherwise authorized.

(d) Subsections (a) and (b) do not apply to—

(1) officers who are discharged or transferred from an active status for physical disability, for cause, or because they have reached the age at which transfer from an active status or discharge is required by law; or

(2) commissioned warrant officers.

(e)(1) A reserve commissioned officer on active duty (other than for training) or full-time National Guard duty (other than full-time National Guard duty for training only) who, on the date on which the officer would otherwise be removed from an active status under section 6389, 14513, or 14514 of this title or section 740 of title 14, is within two years of qualifying for retirement under section 3911, 6323, or 8911 of this title may, in the discretion of the Secretary concerned and subject to paragraph (2), be retained on that duty for a period of not more than two years.

(2) An officer may be retained on active duty or full-time National Guard duty under paragraph (1) only if—

(A) at the end of the period for which the officer is retained the officer will be qualified for retirement under section 3911, 6323, or 8911 of this title; and

(B) the officer will not, before the end of that period, reach the age at which transfer from an active status or discharge is required by this title or title 14.

(3) An officer who is retained on active duty or full-time National Guard duty under this section may not be removed from an active status while on that duty.

(Added Sept. 2, 1958, P. L. 85-861, § 1(22)(B), 72 Stat. 1444; June 30, 1960, P. L. 86-559, § 1(3)(A), 74 Stat. 264; Sept. 7, 1962, P. L. 87-651, Title I, § 105, 76 Stat. 508; Nov. 8, 1967, P. L. 90-130, § 1(4), 81 Stat. 374; Jan. 2, 1975, P. L. 93-586, § 3, 88 Stat. 1920; Aug. 4, 1980, P. L. 96-322, § 2, 94 Stat. 1015; Dec. 12, 1980, P. L. 96-513, Title V, Part B, § 511(30), 94 Stat. 2922; Oct. 5, 1994, P. L. 103-337, Div A, Title XVI, Subtitle C, § 1662(h)(2), Subtitle D, § 1675(d)(3), 108 Stat. 2996, 3018.)

HISTORY; ANCILLARY LAWS AND DIRECTIVES

Prior law and revision:

1958 ACT

Revised Section	Source (USCS)	Source (Statutes at Large)
1006(a)	50:1195(a) (less last 30 words).	Sept. 3, 1954, ch. 1257, §§ 102(1) (as applicable

Revised Section	Source (USCS)	Source (Statutes at Large)
1006(b)	50:1195(b) (less last 30 words).	to § 205), 205, 307(c), 503(c), 68 Stat. 1149, 1151, 1155, 1173; June 30, 1955, ch. 247, § 1(b), 69 Stat. 218.
1006(c)	50:1227(c). 50:1333(c).	
1006(d)	50:1181(1) (as applicable to 50:1195). 50:1195(a) (last 30 words). 50:1195(b) (last 30 words).	
1006(e)	50:1195(c).	

In subsections (a) and (b), the words ''Notwithstanding any other provisions of this chapter, except as provided in sections 1265 and 1279 of this title'' and ''has been credited with, or'' are omitted as surplusage. The words ''entitled to be'' in clause (1) are inserted for clarity.

In subsection (e), the words ''at the end of that period'' are substituted for the word ''then'' for clarity. The words ''before the end of that period'' are substituted for the word ''earlier'' for clarity.

1962 ACT

The change reflects the repeal of section 611 of the Reserve Officer Personnel Act of 1954, ch. 1257 (68 Stat. 1186), formerly section 1391 of title 50, and its restatement in section 787 of title 14 (see sections 5(2) and 36A of the Act of September 2, 1958, Pub. L. 85-861 (72 Stat. 1547 and 1569)).

Amendments:

1960. Act June 30, 1960, in subsec. (e), deleted ''3849,'' following ''3848,'' wherever appearing and deleted ''8849,'' following ''8848,''.

1962. Act Sept. 7, 1962, in subsec. (e), substituted ''787 of title 14'' for ''1391 of title 50''.

1967. Act Nov. 8, 1967, in subsec. (e), deleted ''3847,'' following ''3846,'' wherever appearing and deleted ''8847,'' following ''8846,''.

1975. Act Jan. 2, 1975, in subsecs (a) and (b), inserted ''or chapter 21 of title 14,''; in subsec. (c), deleted ''of the Army or the Air Force'' after ''An officer''; and, in subsec. (e), inserted ''or title 14''.

1980. Act Aug. 4, 1980, in subsec. (e), substituted ''740'' for ''787''.

Act Dec. 12, 1980 (effective upon enactment on 12/12/80, as provided by § 701(b)(3) of such Act, which appears as 10 USCS § 101 note), in subsec. (e), substituted ''Public Law 85-861'' for ''the Act enacting this section''.

1994. Act Oct. 5, 1994 (effective 12/1/94 as provided by § 1691 of such Act, which appears as 10 USCS § 10001 note) transferred this section, enacted as 10 USCS § 1006, to Chapter 1219 and redesignated it as 10 USCS § 12646; and, in subsecs. (a) and (b), substituted ''section 12732'' for ''section 1332'' wherever appearing.

Such Act further (effective 10/1/96, as provided by § 1691(b)(1), which appears as 10 USCS § 10001 note), in subsecs. (a) and (b), substituted ''chapter 573, 1407, or 1409'' for ''chapter 337, 361, 363, 573, 837, 861, or 863''; and substituted subsec. (e) for one which read: ''(e) A reserve commissioned officer on active duty (other than for training) who, on the date on which he would otherwise be removed from an active status under section 3846, 3848, 3851, 3852, 6389, 6397, 6403, 6410, 8846, 8848, 8851, or 8852 of this title or section 740 of title 14, and who is within two years of qualifying for retirement under section 3911, 6323, or 8911 of this title, may, in the discretion of the Secretary concerned, be retained on active duty for a period of not more than two years, if at the end of that period he will be qualified for retirement under one of those sections and will not, before the end of that period, reach the age at which transfer from an active status or discharge is required by this title or title 14. An officer who is retained on active duty under this section may not be removed from an active status while he is on that duty. For officers covered by section 3846, 3848, 3851, or 3852 of this title, the ages at which transfer from an active status or discharge is required are those set forth in section 3843, 3844, or 3845 of this title, or section 21(e) of Public Law 85-861, as the case may be.''.

CROSS REFERENCES

This section is referred to in 10 USCS §§ 3819, 3846, 8819, 8846, 14504–14907; 14 USCS §§ 740, 741; 32 USCS § 323.

§ 12647. Commissioned officers: retention in active status while assigned to Selective Service System or serving as United States property and fiscal officers

Notwithstanding chapters 573, 1407, and 1409 of this title [10 USCS §§ 6371 et seq., 14501 et seq., 14701 et seq.], a reserve commissioned officer, other than a commissioned warrant officer, who is assigned to the Selective Service System or who is a property and fiscal officer appointed, designated, or detailed under section 708 of title 32, may be retained in an active status in that assignment or position until he becomes 60 years of age.

(Added Sept. 2, 1958, P. L. 85-861, § 1(22)(B), 72 Stat. 1445; June 30, 1960, P. L. 86-559, § 1(3), (B), 74 Stat. 265; Oct. 5, 1994, P. L. 103-337, Div A, Title XVI, Subtitle C, § 1662(h)(2), Subtitle D, § 1675(d)(4), 108 Stat. 2996, 3018.)

HISTORY; ANCILLARY LAWS AND DIRECTIVES

Prior law and revision:

Revised Section	Source (USCS)	Source (Statutes at Large)
1007	50:1181(1) (as applicable to 50:1202). 50:1202.	Sept. 3, 1954, ch. 1257, §§ 102(1) (as applicable to § 212), 212, 68 Stat. 1149, 1153.

The words ''this title'' are substituted for the words ''this chapter'', since the provisions of this title requiring transfer from an active status are based on the source statute for this section (the Reserve Officer Personnel Act of 1954).

Amendments:

1960. Act June 30, 1960, in the catchline, inserted ‘‘or serving as United States property and fiscal officers’’; and, in the body, added ‘‘or who is a property and fiscal officer appointed, designated, or detailed under section 708 of title 32,’’ and ‘‘or position’’.

1994. Act Oct. 5, 1994 (effective 12/1/94 as provided by § 1691 of such Act, which appears as 10 USCS § 10001 note) transferred this section, enacted as 10 USCS § 1007, to Chapter 1219 and redesignated it as 10 USCS § 12647.

Such Act further (effective 10/1/96, as provided by § 1691(b)(1), which appears as 10 USCS § 10001 note) substituted ‘‘chapters 573, 1407, and 1409’’ for ‘‘chapters 337, 363, 573, 837, and 863’’.

CHAPTER 1221. SEPARATION

HISTORY; ANCILLARY LAWS AND DIRECTIVES

Amendments:

1994. Act Oct. 5, 1994, P. L. 103-337, Div A, Title XVI, Subtitle C, § 1662(i)(1), 108 Stat. 2997 (effective 12/1/94 as provided by § 1691 of such Act, which appears as 10 USCS § 10001 note), added the chapter heading and analysis.

1996. Act Feb. 10, 1996, P. L. 104-106, Div A, Title V, Subtitle F, § 563(a)(2)(B), 110 Stat. 325, amended the analysis of this chapter by adding item 12687.

§ 12681. Reserves: discharge authority

Subject to other provisions of this title, reserve commissioned officers may be discharged at the pleasure of the President. Other Reserves may be discharged under regulations prescribed by the Secretary concerned.

(Added Oct. 5, 1994, P. L. 103-337, Div A, Title XVI, Subtitle C, § 1662(i)(1), 108 Stat. 2997.)

HISTORY; ANCILLARY LAWS AND DIRECTIVES

Effective date of section:

This section took effect on Dec. 1, 1994, pursuant to Act Oct. 5, 1994, P. L. 103-337, Div A, Title XVI, Subtitle F, § 1691, 108 Stat. 3026, which appears as 10 USCS 10001 note.

Other provisions:

Guard and Reserve transition initiatives. Act Oct. 23, 1992, P. L. 102-484, Div D, Title XLIV, Subtitle B, 106 Stat. 2712; May 31, 1993, P. L. 103-35, Title II, § 202(a)(17), 107 Stat. 102 (applicable as if included in the enactment of Act Oct. 23, 1992, P. L. 102-484, as provided by § 202(b) of Act May 31, 1993); Nov. 30, 1993, P. L. 103-160, Div A, Title V, Subtitle F, § 561(f)(1)–(3), 107 Stat. 1667; Oct. 5, 1994, P. L. 103-337, Div A, Title V, Subtitle B, § 518(a), (b), 108 Stat. 2754 (applicable only to payments to a member of the Armed Forces under § 4416(b) of this note that are granted by the Secretary of Defense to that member after enactment, as provided by § 518(c) of Act Oct. 5, 1994); Feb. 10, 1996, P. L. 104-106, Div A, Title XV, § 1501(d)(3), 110 Stat. 500 (effective as if included in Act Oct. 5,

1994, P. L. 103-337, as enacted on Oct. 5, 1994, as provided by § 1501(f)(3) of Act Feb. 10, 1996, which appears as 10 USCS § 113 note), provides:

''Sec. 4411. Force reduction transition period defined.

''In this subtitle, the term 'force reduction transition period' means the period beginning on October 1, 1991, and ending on September 30, 1999.

''Sec. 4412. Member of Selected Reserve defined.

''In this subtitle, the term 'member of the Selected Reserve' means—

''(1) a member of a unit in the Selected Reserve of the Ready Reserve; and

''(2) a Reserve designated pursuant to section 268(b) of title 10, United States Code, who is assigned to an authorized position the performance of the duties of which qualify the member for basic pay or compensation for inactive-duty training or both.

''Sec. 4413. Restriction on reserve force reduction.

''(a) In general. During the force reduction transition period, a member of the Selected Reserve may not be involuntarily discharged from a reserve component of the Armed Forces, or involuntarily transferred from the Selected Reserve, before the Secretary of Defense has prescribed and implemented regulations that govern the treatment of members of the Selected Reserve assigned to such units and members of the Selected Reserve that are being subjected to such actions and a copy of such regulations has been transmitted to the Committees on Armed Services of the Senate and House of Representatives.

''(b) Savings provision. Subsection (a) shall not apply to actions completed before the date of the enactment of this Act.

''Sec. 4414. Transition plan requirements.

''(a) Purpose of plan. The purpose of the regulations referred to in section 4413 shall be to ensure that the members of the Selected Reserve are treated with fairness, with respect for their service to their country, and with attention to the adverse personal consequences of Selected Reserve unit inactivations, involuntary discharges of such members from the reserve components of the Armed Forces, and involuntary transfers of such members from the Selected Reserve.

''(b) Scope of plan. The regulations shall include—

''(1) such provisions as are necessary to implement the provisions of this subtitle and the amendments made by this subtitle; and

''(2) such other policies and procedures for the recruitment of personnel for service in the Selected Reserve of the Ready Reserve, and for the reassignment, retraining, separation, and retirement of members of the Selected Reserve, as are appropriate for satisfying the needs of the Selected Reserve together with the purpose set out in subsection (a).

''(c) Minimum requirements for plan. The regulations shall include the following:

''(1) The giving of a priority for enrollment in, or reassignment to, Selected Reserve units not being inactivated to—

''(A) personnel being separated from active-duty or full-time National Guard duty; and

''(B) members of the Selected Reserve whose units are inactivated.

"(2) The giving of a priority to such personnel for transfer among the reserve components of the Armed Forces in order to facilitate reassignment to such units.

"(3) A requirement that the Secretaries of the military departments take diligent actions to ensure that members of the reserve components of the Armed Forces are informed in easily understandable terms of the rights and benefits conferred upon such personnel by this subtitle, by the amendments made by this subtitle, and by such regulations.

"(4) Such other protections, preferences, and benefits as the Secretary of Defense considers appropriate.

"(d) Uniform applicability. The regulations shall apply uniformly to the Army, Navy, Air Force, and Marine Corps.

"Sec. 4415. Inapplicability to certain discharges and transfers.

"The protections, preferences, and benefits provided for in regulations prescribed in accordance with this subtitle do not apply with respect to a member of the Selected Reserve who is discharged from a reserve component of the Armed Forces or is transferred from the Selected Reserve to another category of the Ready Reserve, to the Standby Reserve, or to the Retired Reserve—

"(1) at the request of the member unless such request was made and approved under a provision of this subtitle or section 12731a of title 10, United States Code (as added by section 4417);

"(2) because the member no longer meets the qualifications for membership in the Selected Reserve set forth in any provision of law as in effect on the day before the date of the enactment of this Act;

"(3) under adverse conditions, as characterized by the Secretary of the military department concerned; or

"(4) if the member—

"(A) is immediately eligible for retired pay based on military service under any provision of law;

"(B) is serving as a military technician, as defined in section 8401(30) of title 5, United States Code, and would be immediately eligible for an unreduced annuity under the provisions of subchapter III of chapter 83 of such title [5 USCS §§ 8331 et seq.], relating to the Civil Service Retirement and Disability System, or the provisions of chapter 84 of such title [5 USCS §§ 8401 et seq.], relating to the Federal Employees' Retirement System; or

"(C) is eligible for separation pay under section 1174 of title 10, United States Code.

"Sec. 4416. Force reduction period retirements.

"(a) Temporary special authority for elimination of officers from active status. (1) During the force reduction transition period, the Secretary of the Army and the Secretary of the Air Force may, whenever the Secretary determines that such action is necessary, convene a board to recommend an appropriate number of officers in the reserve components of the Army or the Air Force, as the case may be, who (A) have met the age and service requirements specified in section 12731 of title 10, United States Code, for entitlement to retired pay for nonregular service except for not being at least 60 years of age, or (B) are immediately eligible for retired pay based on military service under any provision of law, for elimination from an active status.

''(2) An officer who is to be eliminated from an active status under this section, shall, if qualified, be given an opportunity to request transfer to the appropriate Retired Reserve and, if the officer requests it, shall be so transferred. If the officer is not transferred to the Retired Reserve, the officer shall, in the discretion of the Secretary concerned, be transferred to the appropriate inactive status list or be discharged.

''(3) A member of the Army National Guard of the United States or the Air National Guard of the United States may not be eliminated from an active status under this section without the consent of the Governor or other appropriate authority of the State or territory, Puerto Rico, or the District of Columbia, whichever is concerned.

''(b) Temporary special authority. During the force reduction transition period, the Secretary concerned may grant a member of the Selected Reserve under the age of 60 years the annual payments provided for under this section if—

''(1) as of October 1, 1991, that member has completed at least 20 years of service computed under section 1332 of title 10, United States Code, or after that date and before October 1, 1999, such member completes 20 years of service computed under that section or section 12732;

''(2) the member satisfies the requirements of paragraphs (3) and (4) of section 1331(a) or 12731a of title 10, United States Code; and

''(3) the member applies for transfer to the Retired Reserve.

''(c) [Deleted]

''(d) Annual payment period. An annual payment granted to a member under this section shall be paid for for a period of years prescribed by the Secretary concerned, except that if the member attains 60 years of age during that period the entitlement to the annual payment shall terminate on the member's 60th birthday. A period prescribed for purposes of this subsection may not be less than one year nor more than five years.

''(e) Computation of annual payment. (1) The annual payment for a member shall be equal to the amount determined by multiplying the product of 12 and the applicable percent under paragraph (2) by the monthly basic pay to which the member would be entitled if the member were serving on active duty as of the date the member is transferred to the Retired Reserve.

''(2)(A) Subject to subparagraph (B) the percent applicable to a member for purposes of paragraph (1) is 5 percent plus 0.5 percent for each full year of service, computed under section 12732 of title 10, United States Code, that a member has completed in excess of 20 years before transfer to the Retired Reserve.

''(B) The maximum percent applicable under this paragraph is 10 percent.

''(3) In the case of a member who will attain 60 years of age during the 12-month period following the date on which an annual payment is due, the payment shall be paid on a prorated basis of one-twelfth of the annual payment for each full month between the date on which the payment is due and the date on which the member attains age 60.

''(f) Applicability subject to needs of the service. (1) Subject to regulations prescribed by the Secretary of Defense, the Secretary concerned may limit the applicability of this section to any category of personnel defined by the Secretary concerned in order to meet a need of the armed force under the jurisdiction of the Secretary concerned to reduce the number of members in certain grades, the number of members who have completed a certain number of years of service, or the number of members who possess certain military skills or are serving in designated competitive categories.

"(2) A limitation under paragraph (1) shall be consistent with the purpose set forth in section 4414(a).

"(g) Nonduplication of benefits. A member transferred to the Retired Reserve under the authority of section 12731a of title 10, United States Code (as added by section 4417), may not be paid annual payments under this section.

"(h) Funding. To the extent provided in appropriations Acts, payments under this section in a fiscal year shall be made out of amounts available to the Department of Defense for that fiscal year for the pay of reserve component personnel.

"Sec. 4417. Retirement with 15 years of service.

"(a) Authority. Chapter 67 of title 10, United States Code, is amended by inserting after section 1331 the following new section:

" '§ 1331a. Temporary special retirement qualification authority

" '(a) Retirement with at least 15 years of service. For the purposes of section 1331 of this title, the Secretary of a military department may—

" '(1) during the period described in subsection (b), determine to treat a member of the Selected Reserve of a reserve component of the armed force under the jurisdiction of that Secretary as having met the service requirements of subsection (a)(2) of that section and provide the member with the notification required by subsection (d) of that section if the member—

" '(A) as of October 1, 1991, has completed at least 15, and less than 20, years of service computed under section 1332 of this title; or

" '(B) after that date and before October 1, 1995, completes 15 years of service computed under that section; and

" '(2) upon the request of the member submitted to the Secretary within one year after the date of the notification referred to in paragraph (1), transfer the member to the Retired Reserve.

" '(b) Period of authority. The period referred to in subsection (a)(1) is the period beginning on the date of the enactment of the National Defense Authorization Act for Fiscal Year 1993 [enacted Oct. 23, 1992] and ending on October 1, 1995.

" '(c) Applicability subject to needs of the service. (1) The Secretary of the military department concerned may limit the applicability of subsection (a) to any category of personnel defined by the Secretary in order to meet a need of the armed force under the jurisdiction of the Secretary to reduce the number of members in certain grades, the number of members who have completed a certain number of years of service, or the number of members who possess certain military skills or are serving in designated competitive categories.

" '(2) A limitation under paragraph (1) shall be consistent with the purpose set forth in section 4414(a) of the National Defense Authorization Act for Fiscal Year 1993 [this note].

" '(d) Exclusion. This section does not apply to persons referred to in section 1331(c) of this title.

" '(e) Regulations. The authority provided in this section shall be subject to regulations prescribed by the Secretary of Defense.'.

"(b) Clerical amendment. The table of sections at the beginning of such chapter is amended by inserting after the item relating to section 1331 the following new item:

" '1331a. Temporary special retirement qualification authority.'.

"Sec. 4418. Separation pay.

"(a) Eligibility. Subject to section 4415, a member of the Selected Reserve who, after completing at least 6 years of service computed under section 12732 of title 10, United States Code, and before completing 15 years of service computed under that section, is involuntarily discharged from a reserve component of the Armed Forces or is involuntarily transferred from the Selected Reserve during the force reduction transition period is entitled to separation pay.

"(b) Amount of separation pay. (1) The amount of separation pay which may be paid to a person under this section is 15 percent of the product of—

"(A) the years of service credited to that person under section 12733 of title 10, United States Code; and

"(B) 62 times the daily equivalent of the monthly basic pay to which the person would have been entitled had the person been serving on active duty at the time of the person's discharge or transfer.

"(2) In the case of a person who receives separation pay under this section and who later receives basic pay, compensation for inactive duty training, or retired pay under any provision of law, such basic pay, compensation, or retired pay, as the case may be, shall be reduced by 75 percent until the total amount withheld through such reduction equals the total amount of the separation pay received by that person under this section.

"(c) Relationship to other service-related pay. Subsections (g) and (h) of section 1174 of title 10, United States Code, shall apply to separation pay under this section.

"(d) Regulations. The Secretary of Defense shall prescribe regulations, which shall be uniform for the Army, Navy, Air Force, and Marine Corps, for the administration of this section.

"Sec. 4419. Waiver of continued service requirement for certain reservists for Montgomery GI Bill benefits.

"(a) Chapter 106. Section 2133(b)(1) of title 10, United States Code, is amended to read as follows:

" '(b)(1) In the case of a person—

" '(A) who is separated from the Selected Reserve because of a disability which was not the result of the individual's own willful misconduct incurred on or after the date on which such person became entitled to educational assistance under this chapter [10 USCS §§ 2131 et seq.]; or

" '(B) who, on or after the date on which such person became entitled to educational assistance under this chapter [10 USCS §§ 2131 et seq.] ceases to be a member of the Selected Reserve during the period beginning on October 1, 1991, and ending on September 30, 1995, by reason of the inactivation of the person's unit of assignment or by reason of involuntarily ceasing to be designated as a member of the Selected Reserve pursuant to section 268(b) of this title,

the period for using entitlement prescribed by subsection (a) shall be determined without regard to clause (2) of such subsection.'.

"(b) Chapter 30. Section 3012(b)(1)(B) of title 38, United States Code, is amended—

"(1) by striking out 'or' at the end of clause (i);

"(2) by striking out the period at the end of clause (ii) and inserting in lieu thereof '; or'; and

"(3) by adding after clause (ii) the following:

" '(iii) who, before completing the four years of service described in clauses (1)(A)(ii) and (1)(B)(ii) of subsection (a) of this section, ceases to be a member of the Selected Reserve during the period beginning on October 1, 1991, and ending on September 30, 1995, by reason of the inactivation of the person's unit of assignment or by reason of involuntarily ceasing to be designated as a member of the Selected Reserve pursuant to section 268(b) of title 10.'.

"Sec. 4420. Commissary and exchange privileges.

"The Secretary of Defense shall prescribe regulations to authorize a person who involuntarily ceases to be a member of the Selected Reserve during the force reduction transition period to continue to use commissary and exchange stores in the same manner as a member of the Selected Reserve for a period of two years beginning on the later of—

"(1) the date on which that person ceases to be a member of the Selected Reserve; or

"(2) the date of the enactment of this Act.

"Sec. 4421. Applicability and termination of benefits.

"(a) Applicability subject to needs of the service. (1) Subject to regulations prescribed by the Secretary of Defense, the Secretary of the military department concerned may limit the applicability of a benefit provided under sections 4418 through 4420 to any category of personnel defined by the Secretary concerned in order to meet a need of the armed force under the jurisdiction of the Secretary concerned to reduce the number of members in certain grades, the number of members who have completed a certain number of years of service, or the number of members who possess certain military skills or are serving in designated competitive categories.

"(2) A limitation under paragraph (1) shall be consistent with the purpose set forth in section 4414(a).

"(b) Inapplicability to certain separations and reassignments. Sections 4418 through 4420 do not apply with respect to personnel who cease to be members of the Selected Reserve under adverse conditions, as characterized by the Secretary of the military department concerned.

"(c) Termination of benefits. The eligibility of a member of a reserve component of the Armed Forces (after having involuntarily ceased to be a member of the Selected Reserve) to receive benefits and privileges under sections 4418 through 4420 terminates upon the involuntary separation of such member from the Armed Forces under adverse conditions, as characterized by the Secretary of the military department concerned.

"Sec. 4422. Readjustment benefits for certain voluntarily separated members of the reserve components.

"(a) Special separation benefits. Section 1174a of title 10, United States Code, is amended—

"(1) in subsection (b)(1), by inserting 'or full-time National Guard duty' after 'active duty';

"(2) in subsection (c)(2), by inserting 'or full-time National Guard duty or any combination of active duty and full-time National Guard duty' after 'active duty';

"(3) in subsection (c)(3), by inserting 'or full-time National Guard duty or any combination of active duty and full-time National Guard duty' after 'active duty';

"(4) in subsection (c)(4), by inserting 'or full-time National Guard duty or any combination of active duty and full-time National Guard duty' after the first reference to 'active duty', and by inserting 'and' after the semicolon at the end; and

"(5) in subsection (c), by striking out paragraph (5) and redesignating paragraph (6) as paragraph (5).

"(b) Voluntary separation incentive. Section 1175 of title 10, United States Code, is amended—

"(1) in subsection (b)(1), by inserting 'or full-time National Guard duty or any combination of active duty and full-time National Guard duty' after 'active duty';

"(2) in subsection (b)(2), by inserting 'or full-time National Guard duty or any combination of active duty and full-time National Guard duty' after 'active duty'; and

"(3) in subsection (b), by striking out paragraph (3) and redesignating paragraph (4) as paragraph (3).".

Implementation of agreement on the restructuring of the Army National Guard and the Army Reserve. Act Sept. 30, 1994, P. L. 103-335, Title VIII, § 8129, 108 Stat. 2652, provides:

"(a) Finding. Congress finds that the implementation of the off-site agreement may result in the loss to the Armed Forces of military personnel who have significant military experience and expertise.

"(b) Reassignment of members. (1) To the maximum extent practicable, the Secretary of the Army shall ensure that members of the Armed Forces who would otherwise be separated from service as a result of the deactivation of military units of the Army National Guard and the Army Reserve under the off-site agreement be reassigned instead to units that are not being deactivated.

"(2) The reassignment of a member under paragraph (1) shall not affect the grade or rank in grade of the member.

"(c) Reports. Not later than April 15 and October 15 of each calendar year while the off-site agreement is in effect, the Secretary of the Army shall submit to the congressional defense committees a semi-annual report on the number of members of the Armed Forces who were reassigned under subsection (b)(1) during the preceding six months.

"(d) Definitions. In this section:

"(1) The term 'congressional defense committees' means the Committees on Armed Services and the Committees on Appropriations of the Senate and the House of Representatives.

"(2) The term 'off-site agreement' means the agreement on the restructuring of the Army National Guard and the Army Reserve.".

Payments for force reduction period retirements. Act Sept. 30, 1996, P. L. 104-208, Div A, Title I, § 101(b) [Title VIII, § 8050], 110 Stat. 3009-, provides: "During the current fiscal year and hereafter, annual payments granted under the provisions of section 4416 of the National Defense Authorization Act for Fiscal Year 1993 (Public Law 102-484; 106 Stat. 2714) [note to this section] shall be made from appropriations in this Act [Department of Defense Appropriations Act] which are available for the pay of reserve component personnel.".

CROSS REFERENCES

Discharge of members not physically qualified, 10 USCS § 12644.

RESEARCH GUIDE

Annotations:

Judicial review of military action with respect to type of discharge given member of Armed Forces. 92 ALR Fed 333.

Auto-Cite®: Cases and annotations referred to herein can be further researched through the Auto-Cite® computer-assisted research service. Use Auto-Cite to check citations for form, parallel references, prior and later history, and annotation references.

INTERPRETIVE NOTES AND DECISIONS

1. Discretion of military
2. Property right in employment
3. Requirements for initiating discharge process
4. Right to trial or hearing upon discharge
5. Permissible grounds for discharge
6. Statement of reasons
7. Role and power of court

1. Discretion of military

Determination whether it is practicable and equitable under facts and circumstances of case to discharge conscientious objector, once enlisted or legally inducted into armed forces, is ultimately vested by statute, directive and regulation within discretion of military itself. United States ex rel. United States ex rel. O'Hare v Eichstaedt (1967, ND Cal) 285 F Supp 476.

2. Property right in employment

Since former 10 USCS § 1162 explicitly provided that reserve commissioned officer had no vested right to continue in employment of United States Armed Forces, officer in question had no property right in continued employment with Air Force. Sims v Fox (1974, CA5 Ga) 505 F2d 857, cert den (1975) 421 US 1011, 44 L Ed 2d 678, 95 S Ct 2415.

Since reservists may be discharged at pleasure of President, they do not have property right in their commissions. Carter v United States (1975) 206 Ct Cl 61, 509 F2d 1150, reh den (1975) 207 Ct Cl 316, 518 F2d 1199, cert den (1976) 423 US 1076, 47 L Ed 2d 86, 96 S Ct 861, reh den (1976) 424 US 950, 47 L Ed 2d 356, 96 S Ct 1423.

Reservist can show no constitutionally protected property right to continued service where regulations prescribe that Army reservist may be discharged at any time; neither can reservist claim deprivation of due process liberty interest where discharge was honorable and there was no public disclosure of reasons for discharge. Ben Shalom v Secretary of Army (1980, ED Wis) 489 F Supp 964, 22 BNA FEP Cas 1396.

Reserve commissioned officer dropped from rolls pursuant to Army rule after being convicted in federal court of criminal offense and sentenced to federal correctional institution, was not denied due process, since officer had no property interest in continued military status, neither did nondisciplinary administrative action of dropping officer from rolls, with no stigma attached, deprive him of liberty interest, neither was his life endangered by removal from rolls. Helmich v Nibert (1982, DC Md) 543 F Supp 725, affd without op (1982, CA4 Md) 696 F2d 990.

3. Requirements for initiating discharge process

Letter of army reservist sent to appropriate army

authorities adverting to crisis in conscience and requesting requisite forms to apply for discharge falls far short of formal application army regulations require in order to initiate discharge process. Earls v Resor (1971, CA2 NY) 451 F2d 1126.

4. Right to trial or hearing upon discharge

Regular air force officer was entitled to "fair and impartial" hearing on separation under 10 USCS § 8792, but there was no similar provision for reserve officers in former 10 USCS §§ 1162, 1163; however, Air Force Regulation 36-2, applying to both regular and reserve officers, guaranteed "fair and impartial" hearing, and United States Court of Appeals had jurisdiction of action seeking declaration that discharge of reserve officer was illegal because hearing guaranteed by regulations was denied. Denton v Secretary of Air Force (1973, CA9 Cal) 483 F2d 21, cert den (1974) 414 US 1146, 39 L Ed 2d 102, 94 S Ct 900.

Air force action in discharging reserve commissioned officer on ground of sexual deviancy without pre-discharge hearing does not violate officer's due process guarantees. Sims v Fox (1974, CA5 Ga) 505 F2d 857, cert den (1975) 421 US 1011, 44 L Ed 2d 678, 95 S Ct 2415.

Due process was not violated where reserve air force officer was honorably discharged from service after he expressed to his superiors apprehensions concerning flying in combat and requested assignment to ground duties notwithstanding fact that under applicable regulations such officer did not receive hearing in person, and that his burden of proof was to establish, against charges made, that he should be retained in service. Ampleman v Schlesinger (1976, CA8 Mo) 534 F2d 825.

Plaintiff, Reserve officer honorably discharged by Army for academic deficiencies, was not denied due process where Army gave plaintiff notice, adversary-type hearing, appointed counsel, and opportunity to question witnesses, respond to evidence, and to present evidence, character witnesses and extenuating circumstances. Woodard v Marsh (1981, CA5 Tex) 658 F2d 989, cert den (1982) 455 US 1022, 72 L Ed 2d 141, 102 S Ct 1721.

A probationary officer had no right to a court-martial or Board of Inquiry after being informed that he was being dismissed from the service with a discharge under other than honorable conditions because of homosexual activities. Courtney v Secretary of Air Force (1967, CD Cal) 267 F Supp 305.

5. Permissible grounds for discharge

Navy officer could not be administratively discharged without regard to his guilt or innocence of alleged crime, sodomy, under former 10 USCS § 1162(a), since it would have forced navy to improperly assume officer was guilty, and administrative discharge was not available if officer involved happened to be member of regular military force as opposed to being reservist. Silvero v Chief of Naval Air Basic Training (1970, CA5 Fla) 428 F2d 1009.

Discharge of reservist as unsuitable for service, because reservist evidences homosexual behavior or interest, but is without overt homosexual acts, is violation of First Amendment right to personal privacy and Fifth Amendment substantive due process. Ben Shalom v Secretary of Army (1980, ED Wis) 489 F Supp 964, 22 BNA FEP Cas 1396.

6. Statement of reasons

Even though initial denial by Marine Corps of reservist's application for discharge on conscientious objector grounds was defective for failure to assign reason for such action, it does not follow that reservist's application for discharge must necessarily be granted, as proper procedure would be to remand proceedings to service for reprocessing and for compliance with requirement of statement of reasons. United States ex rel. Coates v Laird (1974, CA4 NC) 494 F2d 709.

7. Role and power of court

Court of Appeals is empowered to determine whether officer in Army Reserve had his procedural rights violated by army's failure to follow pertinent regulations and statutes in regard to his application for discharge as conscientious objector. Earls v Resor (1971, CA2 NY) 451 F2d 1126.

Regular air force officer was entitled to "fair and impartial" hearing on separation under 10 USCS § 8792, but there was no similar provision for reserve officers in former 10 USCS §§ 1162, 1163; however, Air Force Regulation 36-2, applying to both regular and reserve officers, guaranteed "fair and impartial" hearing, and United States Court of Appeals had jurisdiction of action seeking declaration that discharge of reserve officer was illegal because hearing guaranteed by regulations was denied. Denton v Secretary of Air Force (1973, CA9 Cal) 483 F2d 21, cert den (1974) 414 US 1146, 39 L Ed 2d 102, 94 S Ct 900.

Although courts are extremely reluctant to interfere with military's internal affairs, particularly those involving personnel changes, courts will review without hesitation cases where it is alleged that military violated Constitution, statutes or its own regulations; mandamus for reinstatement is appropriate remedy where reservist's discharge is found to be unconstitutional. Ben Shalom v Secretary of Army (1980, ED Wis) 489 F Supp 964, 22 BNA FEP Cas 1396.

§ 12682. Reserves: discharge upon becoming ordained minister of religion

Under regulations to be prescribed by the Secretary of Defense, a Reserve who becomes a regular or ordained minister of religion is entitled upon his request to a discharge from his reserve enlistment or appointment.

(Added Oct. 5, 1994, P. L. 103-337, Div A, Title XVI, Subtitle C, § 1662(i)(1), 108 Stat. 2997.)

HISTORY; ANCILLARY LAWS AND DIRECTIVES

Effective date of section:

This section took effect on Dec. 1, 1994, pursuant to Act Oct. 5, 1994, P. L. 103-337, Div A, Title XVI, Subtitle F, § 1691, 108 Stat. 3026, which appears as 10 USCS 10001 note.

§ 12683. Reserve officers: limitation on involuntary separation

(a) An officer of a reserve component who has at least five years of service as a commissioned officer may not be separated from that component without his consent except—

(1) under an approved recommendation of a board of officers convened by an authority designated by the Secretary concerned; or

(2) by the approved sentence of a court-martial.

(b) Subsection (a) does not apply to any of the following:

(1) A separation under section 12684, 14901, or 14907 of this title.

(2) A dismissal under section 1161(a) of this title.

(3) A transfer under section 12213, 12214, 14514, or 14515 of this title.

(4) A separation of an officer who is in an inactive status in the Standby Reserve and who is not qualified for transfer to the Retired Reserve or is qualified for transfer to the Retired Reserve and does not apply for such a transfer.

(Added Oct. 5, 1994, P. L. 103-337, Div A, Title XVI, Subtitle C, § 1662(i)(1), 108 Stat. 2997; Nov. 18, 1997, P. L. 105-85, Div A, Title V, Subtitle B, § 516, 111 Stat. 1733.)

HISTORY; ANCILLARY LAWS AND DIRECTIVES

Effective date of section:

This section took effect on Dec. 1, 1994, pursuant to § 1691 of Act Oct. 5, 1994, P. L. 103-337, which appears as 10 USCS § 10001 note.

Amendments:

1997. Act Nov. 18, 1997, in subsec. (b), in the introductory matter, substituted "apply to any of the following:" for "apply—", in para. (1), substituted "A" for "to a" and substituted the concluding period for a semicolon, in para. (2), substituted "A" for "to a" and substituted the concluding period for "; and", in para. (3), substituted "A" for "to a", and added para. (4).

RESEARCH GUIDE

Annotations:

Judicial review of military action with respect to type of discharge given serviceman. 4 ALR Fed 343.

Auto-Cite®: Cases and annotations referred to herein can be further researched through the Auto-Cite® computer-assisted research service. Use Auto-Cite to check citations for form, parallel references, prior and later history, and annotation references.

INTERPRETIVE NOTES AND DECISIONS

1. Purpose
2. Release within two years of retirement
3. Basis for and type of discharge
4. Right to hearing
5. Burden of proof

1. Purpose

Purpose of enactment of former 10 USCS § 1163(d) was twofold: to provide lump-sum payments to reservists who were involuntarily released from active duty, and to provide economic security as inducement for reservists to stay in active service and thus reduce expense of personnel turnover and increase effectiveness of armed services. Fairbank v Brown (1980, DC Dist Col) 506 F Supp 336.

2. Release within two years of retirement

Eighteen year army reservist could not be involuntarily released from duty by order of Secretary of Army alone as two step procedure set out in army regulations had to be followed despite former 10 USCS § 1163(d) which provided that Secretary must personally authorize release of reservists who were within 2 years of qualifying for retirement, since this was meant as additional requirement, not alternative one. Roberts v Vance (1964) 119 US App DC 367, 343 F2d 236.

Protection from discharge afforded by former 10 USCS § 1163(d) did not apply to officer who, at time of separation, could meet two year requirement of qualifying for retirement only when such active duty time as was obtained solely through improperly issued restraining order and injunction was counted towards two year period. Pauls v Seamans (1972, CA1 Puerto Rico) 468 F2d 361.

Amended "sanctuary" provision barring applicability to individuals on training duty would not be applied retroactively to case pending at time of amendment in absence of statutory direction or legislative history indicating that it should be applied retroactively or that amendment represented what had always been the law. Ulmet v United States (1989) 17 Cl Ct 679, affd without op (1991, CA) 935 F2d 280, reported in full (1991, CA FC) 1991 US App LEXIS 10714.

It is only reasonable that Army first obtained reserve member's request for extension and resulting knowledge of member's willingness and ability to continue on active duty before it can be assessed liability for continuing backpay on basis that expiration of training tour of duty ordered resulted in "involuntary" release. Green v United States (1989) 17 Cl Ct 716.

Plaintiff, scheduled for release from active duty due to reductions in officer strength, did not challenge such release, but rather, by use of stay, sought to preserve status quo, that is, reenlistment rights which had been denied, and thus did not create any new rights and did not reach statutory period which precludes discharge of reservist with 18 years of service except with agreement of Army Secretary. Fairbank v Brown (1980, DC Dist Col) 506 F Supp 336.

Former § 1163(d) providing that member of reserve component who was on active duty and was within 2 years of becoming eligible for retired pay or retainer pay could not be involuntarily released from that duty before he became eligible for that pay unless release was approved by Secretary did not protect serviceman from being released from active duty for training tour on ground that serviceman, who had completed over 16 years of active duty Army service prior to being relieved from active duty and who later performed periods of active duty for training in Army Reserve since his release, accrued more than 18 years of active federal service. Steenson v Marsh (1985, ND Ala) 609 F Supp 800.

Service member's acceptance of readjustment payment did not affect his entitlement to retirement benefits, given legislative history which clearly showed that Congress considered situation of person who collected readjustment pay, and who later became qualified for retirement benefits, and given fact that current statute which governs separation pay upon involuntary release from active duty prevents double retirement benefit for persons who accept readjustment pay, and who later become qualified for regular retirement benefits by requiring deduction from each retirement payment until total amount deducted equals readjustment pay received. Ulmet v United States (1987, CA) 822 F2d 1079 (ovrld in part on other grounds by Wilson v United States (1990, CA FC) 1990 US App LEXIS 23208).

"Continuous active duty" language contained in

Armed Forces Reserve Act of 1952 and exclusion of reservists released from active duty for training does not apply to "sanctuary" provision, but rather refers only to readjustment payments, as later enactment of readjustment pay provision clarifies point by stating that requirement of continuous active duty is for "purposes of this subsection" only, and thus fact that reservist did not serve "continuous active duty" did not bar him from entitlement to sanctuary. Ulmet v United States (1987, CA) 822 F2d 1079 (ovrld on other grounds in part by Wilson v United States (1990, CA FC) 1990 US App LEXIS 23208).

Phrase "on active duty" in former 10 USCS § 1163(d) did not include active duty for training. Wilson v United States (1990, CA) 917 F2d 529.

3. Basis for and type of discharge

Secretary of Navy was without authority to issue punitive discharge to inactive reservist on basis of secret information relating to his associations subsequent to separation from active duty. Bland v Connally (1961) 110 US App DC 375, 293 F2d 852; Davis v Stahr (1961) 110 US App DC, 293 F2d 860.

District Court did not err in determining that record of Board of Naval Officers proceeding at which it was recommended that reserve officer be separated with honorable discharge on ground of his admitted homosexuality displayed nothing more than permissible policy bias, notwithstanding that Board members all stated that in light of Secretary of Navy instruction there were no conceivable circumstances under which they would retain homosexual in Navy, since, inter alia, each Board member had stated that he could keep open mind toward argument as to whether or not instruction was binding on Board. Urban Jacksonville, Inc. v Chalbeck (1985, CA11 Fla) 765 F2d 1085, 38 BNA FEP Cas 750, 38 CCH EPD ¶ 35531.

Department of Defense exceeded its statutory authority in characterizing administrative discharges as being issued under other than honorable conditions to members of inactive reserve having no military duties, based on civilian misconduct, where Department regulation and policy require no connection between members' civilian misconduct and their military service and there is no showing that civilian misconduct affected quality of individuals' service to military or had adverse impact on overall effectiveness of military service. Wood v Secretary of Defense (1980, DC Dist Col) 496 F Supp 192 (disapproved on other grounds Walters v Secretary of Defense (1983) 233 US App DC 148, 725 F2d 107, reh, en banc, den 237 US App DC 333, 737 F2d 1038).

4. Right to hearing

Regular air force officer was entitled to "fair and impartial" hearing on separation under 10 USCS § 8792, but there was no similar provision for reserve officers in former 10 USCS §§ 1162, 1163; however, Air Force Regulation 36-2, applying to both regular and reserve officers, guaranteed "fair and impartial" hearing, and United States Court of Appeals had jurisdiction of action seeking declaration that discharge of reserve officer was illegal because hearing guaranteed by regulations was denied. Denton v Secretary of Air Force (1973, CA9 Cal) 483 F2d 21, cert den (1974) 414 US 1146, 39 L Ed 2d 102, 94 S Ct 900.

5. Burden of proof

Nowhere in former 10 USCS § 1163 or its legislative history was there hint of authority to conduct proceeding in which defendant bore burden of proof; consequently, dishonorable discharge of air force reserve officer under regulation shifting burden of proof to accused was unlawful. Carter v United States (1975) 206 Ct Cl 61, 509 F2d 1150, reh den (1975) 207 Ct Cl 316, 518 F2d 1199, cert den (1976) 423 US 1076, 47 L Ed 2d 86, 96 S Ct 861, reh den (1976) 424 US 950, 47 L Ed 2d 356, 96 S Ct 1423.

§ 12684. Reserves: separation for absence without authority or sentence to imprisonment

The President or the Secretary concerned may drop from the rolls of the armed force concerned any Reserve—

(1) who has been absent without authority for at least three months;

(2) who may be separated under section 12687 of this title by reason of a sentence to confinement adjudged by a court-martial; or

(3) who is sentenced to confinement in a Federal or State penitentiary or correctional institution after having been found guilty of an offense by a court other than a court-martial or other military court, and whose sentence has become final.

(Added Oct. 5, 1994, P. L. 103-337, Div A, Title XVI, Subtitle C, § 1662(i)(1),

108 Stat. 2997; Feb. 10, 1996, P. L. 104-106, Div A, Title V, Subtitle F, § 563(b)(2), 110 Stat. 325.)

HISTORY; ANCILLARY LAWS AND DIRECTIVES

Effective date of section:

This section took effect on Dec. 1, 1994, pursuant to Act Oct. 5, 1994, P. L. 103-337, Div A, Title XVI, Subtitle F, § 1691, 108 Stat. 3026, which appears as 10 USCS 10001 note.

Amendments:

1996. Act Feb. 10, 1996, in para. (1), deleted ''or'' after the concluding semicolon, redesignated para. (2) as para. (3), and added new para. (2).

CROSS REFERENCES

This section is referred to in 10 USCS §§ 14504–1450.

§ 12685. Reserves separated for cause: character of discharge

A member of a reserve component who is separated for cause, except under section 12684 of this title, is entitled to a discharge under honorable conditions unless—

(1) the member is discharged under conditions other than honorable under an approved sentence of a court-martial or under the approved findings of a board of officers convened by an authority designated by the Secretary concerned; or

(2) the member consents to a discharge under conditions other than honorable with a waiver of proceedings of a court-martial or a board.

(Added Oct. 5, 1994, P. L. 103-337, Div A, Title XVI, Subtitle C, § 1662(i)(1), 108 Stat. 2998.)

HISTORY; ANCILLARY LAWS AND DIRECTIVES

Effective date of section:

This section took effect on Dec. 1, 1994, pursuant to Act Oct. 5, 1994, P. L. 103-337, Div A, Title XVI, Subtitle F, § 1691, 108 Stat. 3026, which appears as 10 USCS 10001 note.

§ 12686. Reserves on active duty within two years of retirement eligibility: limitation on release from active duty

(a) Limitation. Under regulations to be prescribed by the Secretary concerned, which shall be as uniform as practicable, a member of a reserve component who is on active duty (other than for training) and is within two years of becoming eligible for retired pay or retainer pay under a purely military retirement system, may not be involuntarily released from that duty before he becomes eligible for that pay, unless the release is approved by the Secretary.

(b) Waiver. With respect to a member of a reserve component who is to be ordered to active duty (other than for training) under section 12301 of this title pursuant to an order to active duty that specifies a period of less than 180 days and who (but for this subsection) would be covered by subsection (a), the Secretary concerned may require, as a condition of such order to active duty, that the member waive the applicability of subsection (a) to the member for the period of active duty covered by that order. In carrying out this subsection, the Secretary concerned may require that a waiver under the preceding sentence be executed before the period of active duty begins.

(Added Oct. 5, 1994, P. L. 103-337, Div A, Title XVI, Subtitle C, § 1662(i)(1), 108 Stat. 2998; Sept. 23, 1996, P. L. 104-201, Div A, Title V, Subtitle D, § 533, 110 Stat. 2520.)

HISTORY; ANCILLARY LAWS AND DIRECTIVES

Effective date of section:

This section took effect on Dec. 1, 1994, pursuant to Act Oct. 5, 1994, P. L. 103-337, Div A, Title XVI, Subtitle F, § 1691, 108 Stat. 3026, which appears as 10 USCS 10001 note.

Amendments:

1996. Act Sept. 23, 1996 designated the existing text as subsec. (a), added the subsection heading, and added subsec. (b).

§ 12687. Reserves under confinement by sentence of court-martial: separation after six months confinement

Except as otherwise provided in regulations prescribed by the Secretary of Defense, a Reserve sentenced by a court-martial to a period of confinement for more than six months may be separated from that Reserve's armed force at any time after the sentence to confinement has become final under chapter 47 of this title [10 USCS §§ 801 et seq.] and the Reserve has served in confinement for a period of six months.

(Added Feb. 10, 1996, P. L. 104-106, Div A, Title V, Subtitle F, § 563(a)(2)(A), 110 Stat. 325.)

CROSS REFERENCES

This section is referred to in 10 USCS § 12684.

CHAPTER 1223. RETIRED PAY FOR NONREGULAR SERVICE

HISTORY; ANCILLARY LAWS AND DIRECTIVES

Amendments:

1986. Act July 1, 1986, P. L. 99-348, Title III, § 304(b)(1), 100 Stat. 703, amended the analysis of this chapter by adding item 1338.

1992. Act Oct. 23, 1992, P. L. 102-484, Div D, Title XLIV, Subtitle B, § 4417(b), 106 Stat. 2717, amended the analysis of this chapter by adding item 1331a.

1994. Act Oct. 5, 1994, P. L. 103-337, Div A, Title XVI, Subtitle C, § 1662(j)(1), 108 Stat. 2998 (effective 12/1/94 as provided by § 1691 of such Act, which appears as 10 USCS § 10001 note) transferred this chapter, formerly Chapter 67, to Part II of Subtitle E, inserted it after Chapter 1221, and substituted the chapter analysis for one which read:

"1331. Age and service requirements

"1331a. Temporary special retirement qualification authority

"1332. Computation of years of service in determining entitlement to retired pay

"1333. Computation of years of service in computing retired pay

"1334. Time not creditable toward years of service

"1335. Inactive status list

"1336. Service credited for retired pay benefits not excluded for other benefits

"1337. Limitation on active duty

"1338. Limitations on revocation of retired pay".

1996. Act Feb. 10, 1996, P. L. 104-106, Div A, Title VI, Subtitle D, § 632(a)(2), 110 Stat. 365, amended the analysis of this chapter by adding item 12740.

§ 12731. Age and service requirements

(a) Except as provided in subsection (c), a person is entitled, upon application, to retired pay computed under section 12739 of this title, if the person—

(1) is at least 60 years of age;

(2) has performed at least 20 years of service computed under section 12732 of this title;

(3) performed the last eight years of qualifying service while a member of any category named in section 12732(a)(1) of this title, but not while a member of a regular component, the Fleet Reserve, or the Fleet Marine Corps Reserve; and

(4) is not entitled, under any other provision of law, to retired pay from an armed force or retainer pay as a member of the Fleet Reserve or the Fleet Marine Corps Reserve.

(b) Application for retired pay under this section must be made to the Secretary of the military department, or the Secretary of Transportation, as the case may be, having jurisdiction at the time of application over the armed force in which the applicant is serving or last served.

(c)(1) A person who, before August 16, 1945, was a Reserve of an armed force, or a member of the Army without component or other category covered by section 12732(a)(1) of this title except a regular component, is not eligible for retired pay under this chapter unless—

(A) the person performed active duty during World War I or World War II; or

(B) the person performed active duty (other than for training) during the Korean conflict, the Berlin crisis, or the Vietnam era.

(2) In this subsection:

(A) The term ''World War I'' means the period beginning on April 6, 1917, and ending on November 11, 1918.

(B) The term ''World War II'' means the period beginning on September 9, 1940, and ending on December 31, 1946.

(C) The term ''Korean conflict'' means the period beginning on June 27, 1950, and ending on July 27, 1953.

(D) The term ''Berlin crisis'' means the period beginning on August 14, 1961, and ending on May 30, 1963.

(E) The term ''Vietnam era'' means the period beginning on August 5, 1964, and ending on March 27, 1973.

(d) The Secretary concerned shall notify each person who has completed the years of service required for eligibility for retired pay under this chapter. The notice shall be sent, in writing, to the person concerned within one year after the person completes that service. The notice shall include notice of the elections available to such person under the Survivor Benefit Plan established under subchapter II of chapter 73 of this title [10 USCS §§ 1447 et seq.] and the Supplemental Survivor Benefit Plan established under subchapter III of that chapter [10 USCS §§ 1456 et seq.], and the effects of such elections.

(e) Notwithstanding section 8301 of title 5, the date of entitlement to retired pay under this section shall be the date on which the requirements of subsection (a) have been completed.

(f) In the case of a person who completes the service requirements of subsection (a)(2) during the period beginning on October 5, 1994, and ending on September 30, 1999, the provisions of subsection (a)(3) shall be applied by substituting "the last six years" for "the last eight years".

(Aug. 10, 1956, ch 1041, § 1, 70A Stat. 102; Aug. 21, 1958, P. L. 85-704, 72 Stat. 702; Sept. 2, 1958, P. L. 85-861, § 33(a)(8), 72 Stat. 1564; Oct. 14, 1966, P. L. 89-652, § 1, 80 Stat. 902; Aug. 13, 1968, P. L. 90-485, § 2, 82 Stat. 754; Sept. 30, 1978, P. L. 95-397, Title II, § 206, 92 Stat. 847; Dec. 12, 1980, P. L. 96-513, Title V, Part B, § 511(47), 94 Stat. 2924; Sept. 24, 1983, P. L. 98-94, Title IX, Part B, § 924(a), 97 Stat. 644; Nov. 29, 1989, P. L. 101-189, Div A, Title XIV, § 1404(b)(1), 103 Stat. 1586; Oct. 5, 1994, P. L. 103-337, Div A, Title VI, Subtitle D, § 636, Title XVI, Subtitle C, § 1662(j)(1), 108 Stat. 2790, 2998; Feb. 10, 1996, P. L. 104-106, Div A, Title XV, § 1501(b)(20), 110 Stat. 497.)

HISTORY; ANCILLARY LAWS AND DIRECTIVES

Prior law and revision:

1956 ACT

Revised Section	Source (USCS)	Source (Statutes at Large)
1331(a)	10:1036a(a) (less last proviso). 10:1036d (1st sentence). 34:440i(a) (less last proviso). 34:440*l* (1st sentence).	June 29, 1948, ch. 708, §§ 302(a), (d), 305 (1st sentence), 62 Stat. 1087-1089; July 12, 1952, ch. 698, 66 Stat. 590.
1331(b)	10:1036a(d). 34:440i(d).	
1331(c)	10:1036a(a) (last proviso). 34:440i(a) (last proviso).	

In subsection (a), the words "is entitled" are substituted for the words "shall . . . be granted". The words "in the status of a commissioned officer, warrant officer, flight officer, or enlisted person" and the references to reserve components are omitted as surplusage. Reference to the Army and the Air Force without component is inserted, since the words "reserve component", as used in 10:1036a(a), include all members of the Army and the Air Force except members of the regular components thereof. The words "service, computed under section 1332 of this title" are substituted for the words "satisfactory Federal service" to make it clear that some service that is not normally covered by the latter term may be counted in determining rights to retired pay under this chapter. Section 311 of the source statute, which made title III of that act applicable to the Coast Guard, was expressly repealed by the act of August 4, 1949, ch. 393, § 20, 63 Stat. 565, the act which codified Title 14 of the United States Code. 14 U.S.C. 755(e) provides for Coast Guard Reservists the same retirement benefits as those prescribed by law for the Naval Reserve, and, for this purpose, confers upon the Secretary of the Treasury the same authority as that conferred upon the Secretary of the Navy, when the Coast Guard is operating under the Treasury Department. Accordingly, the revised chapter is made expressly applicable to the Coast Guard.

In subsection (c), the words "the Army without component or other category covered by section 1332(a)(1) of this title" are inserted, since the words "reserve component", as used in 10:1036a(a), also cover members without component and members of the other special categories listed. The words "annual training duty, or attendance at a school designated as a service school by law or by the Secretary of the appropriate military department" are inserted since the words "active Federal service", as used in 10:1036a(a), also cover the additional service listed. The words "active duty" are substituted for the words "active Federal service" for uniformity.

1958 ACT

The change makes clear that in the determination of eligibility for retired pay for non-regular service, the service of a Regular serving in a temporary grade (that is, without component) may not be counted. See opinion of the Judge Advocate General of the Army, JAGA 1957/4463, May 13, 1957.

Amendments:

1958. Act Aug. 21, 1958, in subsec. (c), inserted ", or unless he performed active duty (other than for training) after June 26, 1950, and before July 28, 1953".

Act Sept. 2, 1958 (effective as of 8/10/56, for all purposes, as provided by § 33(g) of such Act, which appears as 10 USCS § 101 note), substituted subsec. (a)(3) for one which read: "he performed the last eight years of qualifying service as a member of a reserve component of any of the armed forces, of the Army or the Air Force without component, or of any other category named in section 1332(a)(1) of this title except as a member of (A) a regular component of an armed force, (B) the Fleet Reserve and the Fleet Marine Corps Reserve, or (C) a regular and a reserve component of an armed force at the same time; and".

1966. Act Oct. 14, 1966 added subsec. (d).

1968. Act Aug. 13, 1968 (effective 8/13/68, as provided by § 6 of such Act, 2hich appears as 10 USCS § 1431 note) added subsec. (e).

1978. Act Sept. 30, 1978 (effective as provided by § 210(b) of such Act, which appears as 10 USCS § 1447 note, in subsec. (d), inserted "Such notice shall include notification of the elections available to such person under the Survivor Benefit Plan established under subchapter II of chapter 73 of this title and the effects of such elections.".

1980. Act Dec. 12, 1980 (effective upon enactment on 12/12/80, as provided by § 701(b)(3) of such Act, which appears as 10 USCS § 101 note), in subsec. (b), substituted "Transportation" for "the Treasury"; and, in subsec. (e), deleted "United States Code," after "title 5".

1983. Act Sept. 24, 1983 (effective as provided by § 924(b) of such Act, which appears as a note to this section), in subsec. (c), substituted "unless—" for "unless he performed active duty after April 5, 1917, and before November 12, 1918, or after September 8, 1940, and before January 1, 1947, or unless he performed active duty (other than for training) after June 26, 1950, and before July 28, 1953.", and added paras. (1) and (2).

1989. Act Nov. 29, 1989 (effective 4/1/92, as provided by § 1404(b)(3) of such Act, which appears as a note to this section), in subsec. (d), inserted "and the Supplemental Survivor Benefit Plan established under subchapter III of that chapter,".

1994. Act Oct. 5, 1994 added subsec. (f).

Such Act further (effective 12/1/94 as provided by § 1691 of such Act, which appears as 10 USCS § 10001 note) transferred this section, enacted as part of Chapter 67, to Chapter 1223, and substituted the section heading and text for ones which read:

"§ 1331. Age and service requirements

"(a) Except as provided in subsection (c), a person is entitled, upon application, to retired pay computed under section 1401 of this title, if—

"(1) he is at least 60 years of age;

"(2) he has performed at least 20 years of service computed under section 1332 of this title;

"(3) he performed the last eight years of qualifying service while a member of any category named in section 1332(a)(1) of this title, but not while a member of a regular component, the Fleet Reserve, or the Fleet Marine Corps Reserve; and

"(4) he is not entitled, under any other provision of law, to retired pay from an armed force or retainer pay as a member of the Fleet Reserve or the Fleet Marine Corps Reserve.

"(b) Application for retired pay under this section must be made to the Secretary of the military department, or the Secretary of Transportation, as the case may be, having jurisdiction at the time of application over the armed force in which the applicant is serving or last served.

"(c) No person who, before August 16, 1945, was a Reserve of an armed force, or a member of the Army without component or other category covered by section 1332(a)(1) of this title except a regular component, is eligible for retired pay under this chapter, unless—

"(1) he performed active duty after April 5, 1917, and before November 12, 1918, or after September 8, 1940, and before January 1, 1947; or

"(2) he performed active duty (other than for training) after June 26, 1950, and before July 28, 1953, after August 13, 1961, and before May 31, 1963, or after August 4, 1964, and before March 28, 1973.

"(d) The Secretary concerned shall provide for notifying each person who has completed the years of service required for eligibility for retired pay under this chapter. The notice must be sent, in writing, to the person concerned within one year after he has completed that service. Such notice shall include notification of the elections available to such person under the Survivor Benefit Plan established under subchapter II of chapter 73 of this title and the Supplemental Survivor Benefit Plan established under subchapter III of that chapter, and the effects of such elections.

"(e) Notwithstanding section 8301 of title 5, the date of entitlement to retired pay under this section shall be the date on which the requirements of subsection (a) have been completed.

"(f) In the case of a person who completes the service requirements of subsection (a)(2) during the period beginning on the date of the enactment of this subsection and ending on September 30, 1999, the provisions of subsection (a)(3) shall be applied by substituting 'the last six years' for 'the last eight years'.".

1996. Act Feb. 10, 1996 (effective as if included in Act Oct. 5, 1994, P. L. 103-337, as enacted on Oct. 5, 1994, as provided by § 1501(f)(3) of Act Feb. 10, 1996, which appears as 10 USCS § 113 note), in subsec. (f), substituted "October 5, 1994," for "the date of the enactment of this subsection".

Other provisions:

Entitlement to retirement pay after October 14, 1966; conclusiveness. For conclusive nature of notification of completion of requisite years of service for entitlement to retirement pay if made after Oct. 14, 1966 see Act Oct. 14, 1966, P. L. 89-652, § 3, 80 Stat. 902, which appears at 10 USCS § 1406 note.

Survivor annuities; effective date. Act Oct. 1, 1976, P. L. 94-448, § 1, 90 Stat. 1499, provided: "For the purposes of survivor annuities under subchapter I of chapter 73 of title 10, United States Code [10 USCS §§ 1431 et seq.] and under prior corresponding provisions of law, the provisions of [former] section 1331(e) of such title 10 relating to the date of entitlement to retired pay under [former] chapter 67 of such title 10, shall be effective as of November 1, 1953.".

Payment of survivor annuities benefits prior to October 1, 1976. Act Oct. 1, 1976, P. L. 94-448, § 2, 90 Stat. 1499, provided: "No benefits shall be paid to any person for any period prior to the date of enactment of this Act as a result of the enactment of this Act.".

Application of Sept. 24, 1983 amendment. Act Sept. 24, 1983, P. L. 98-94, Title IX, Part B, § 924 (b), 97 Stat. 644, provided: "The amendment made by subsection (a) [amending subsec. (c) of this section] shall apply with respect to retired pay payable for months beginning after September 30, 1983, or the date of the enactment of this Act, whichever is later.".

Report on reserve retirement system. Act July 1, 1986, P. L. 99-348, Title III, § 302, 100 Stat. 702, provides:

"(a) Report requirement. The Secretary of Defense shall submit to Congress a report on the retirement system provided under [former] chapter 67 of title 10, United States Code, for members of the Armed Forces performing non-regular-service. The Secretary shall include in the report any proposals of the Secretary for modifications to such system.

"(b) Deadline for report. The report under subsection (a) shall be submitted not later than February 1, 1988.".

Effective date of Nov. 29, 1989 amendments. Act Nov. 29, 1989, P. L. 101-189, Div A, Title XIV, § 1404(b)(3), 103 Stat. 1586; Nov. 5, 1990, P. L. 101-510, Div A, Title VI, Part D, § 631(1), 104 Stat. 1580, provides: "The amendments made by paragraphs (1) and (2) [amending subsec. (d) of this section and 38 USCS § 3101(c)(1)] shall take effect on April 1, 1992.".

CROSS REFERENCES

Computation of retired pay, 10 USCS § 1401.

Years of service, computation of, 10 USCS § 1405.

Cadets at Military, Air Force, and Naval Academies, appointment of children of members granted retired pay, 10 USCS §§ 4342, 6954, 9342.

This section is referred to in 10 USCS §§ 1331, 1370, 1405–1408, 1447, 1448, 1482, 6954, 9342, 12731a, 12732, 12738.

RESEARCH GUIDE

Am Jur:

53A Am Jur 2d, Military and Civil Defense § 176.

INTERPRETIVE NOTES AND DECISIONS

1. Generally
2. Nature of retired pay
3. Eligibility [10 USCS § 1331(a) (now § 12731(a))]
4. —Applicable service
5. Date of entitlement]10 USCS § 1331(e) (now § 12731(e))]
6. Estoppel
7. Judicial review

1. Generally

There is no vested or contractual right to retired military pay, which is dependent upon statutory rights rather than common law rules governing contracts; until passage of act of June 29, 1948, there was no law which provided for longevity retirement pay for members of reserves; therefore enactment of 10 USCS § 1331 (now § 12731) did not violate any vested right of plaintiff. Goodley v United States (1971) 194 Ct Cl 829, 441 F2d 1175.

Retirement status for military personnel and right to retirement pay are created and controlled by statute. Mayer v United States (1973) 201 Ct Cl 105.

Only statutory duty imposed on services under 10 USCS § 12731(d) is to notify member that he has completed twenty years of service required for non-regular retired pay eligibility, and there is nothing in that provision, or any other provision, that imposes similar duty regarding member compliance with wartime active duty requirement of 10 USCS § 12731(c); absent such statutory duty, years of service notification requirement cannot be extended to require notification of wartime active service. Master Sergeant Henry W. Schuchardt, USAR (Retired) (10/8/96) Comp. Gen. Dec. No. B-274195.

Provision in former 10 USCS § 1332 (now codified at 10 USCS § 12732) for computation of years of service to determine eligibility for retired pay under former 10 USCS § 1331 (now codified at 10 USCS § 12731), must be read together with concept of ''reserve'' of armed force in former § 1331(c); if member is credited under former § 1332 with years of service for service involved, either because he had federally recognized status before 6/15/33 or because his service was in federally recognized unit before 6/15/33, then he had to be ''reserve'' for former § 1331(c) purposes. DOHA Case No. 96121102 (8/22/97).

2. Nature of retired pay

Regular military retirement pay received under 10 USCS § 1331 (now § 12731) is not annuity, per se, and must be placed in such fund by earner or recipient in order to qualify as annuity. Moore v O'Cheskey (1974, App) 87 NM 66, 529 P2d 292, cert den (1974) 87 NM 48, 529 P2d 274.

3. Eligibility [10 USCS § 1331(a) (now § 12731(a))]

Exclusion for retirement pay purposes of persons who served in Armed Forces Reserves or National Guard prior to World War II is the product of a deliberate and rational choice within constitutional power of Congress. Alexander v Fioto (1977) 430 US 634, 51 L Ed 2d 694, 97 S Ct 1345.

Act of June 29, 1948, c. 708, 62 Stat. 1081 gave retired reserve officer who had reached age before its enactment and was otherwise qualified right to receive retirement pay commencing on date of its enactment once his application for retirement pay was approved by army regardless of when application was made, and portion of special army regulation imposing statute of limitation on that part of claim for retirement pay from June 29, 1948, to March 31, 1951, date his application was approved, was invalid as contrary to Act. Seagrave v United States (1955) 131 Ct Cl 790, 128 F Supp 400.

Plaintiff who had retired from active military service in 1950, under § 6 of Act of Feb. 21, 1946, 60 Stat. 26, 27 [10 USCS § 6323], was twice recalled to active duty in 1961, and upon his release in 1961 applied for retirement pay under 10 USCS § 1331 (now § 12731), which would have permitted him to credit concurrent periods of civilian and military service for military retired pay as well as civil service annuity [see 10 USCS § 1336 (now § 12736)], and was excluded by 10 USCS § 1331 (a)(4) (now § 12731(a)(4)), because he was still qualified in 1961 for retirement pay under 10 USCS § 6323. Merrill v United States (1964) 168 Ct Cl 1, 338 F2d 372.

Claimant's cause of action accrues and he becomes eligible for retired pay upon receiving notice of eligibility to receive retired pay benefits because of agency determination that at time of his discharge, he was credited with 20 years of qualifying service. Garcia v United States (1980) 223 Ct Cl 110, 617 F2d 218.

Disqualification for retirement pay set forth at 10 USCS § 1331(c) (now § 12731(c)) did not apply to individual who had served complete term of twenty years in regular military service following 1947. Fioto v United States Dep't of Army (1976, ED NY) 409 F Supp 831, revd on other grounds (1977) 430 US 634, 51 L Ed 2d 694, 97 S Ct 1345.

Claim for non-regular retired pay under 10 USCS

§ 1331 (now § 12731) is deemed to accrue only after service's determination that claimant has met required service; application filed almost 6 years after meeting age requirement is not barred by elapse of more than 6 years between meeting age requirement and determination that service member was eligible for retired pay. (1977) 62 Op Comp Gen 227.

Written notice required by 10 USCS § 1331 (now § 12731) need not be in any specific format, and notice from authorized activity of service advising member that he has completed requirements for retired pay is sufficient to satisfy § 1331 (now § 12731) and invoke 10 USCS § 1406 preventing denial of pay due to administrative error. (1979) 58 Op Comp Gen 390.

Retired officer who was entitled to retirement benefits under 10 USCS § 8911 was not entitled to retirement benefits under 10 USCS § 1331 (now § 12731); latter statute clearly precludes its application to those entitled to retirement benefits under any other provision of law, not merely those actually receiving other retirement benefits. Flurett v United States (1993) 28 Fed Cl 153.

4. —Applicable service

Provision of 10 USCS § 1331(c) (now § 12731(c)) excluding individuals who were in Armed Forces Reserves or National Guard prior to World War II from eligibility for retirement pay unless active duty was performed during designated or wartime periods describes persons who are not eligible for retirement pay, and does not describe periods of service which may or may not be counted towards eligibility for retirement pay. Alexander v Fioto (1977) 430 US 634, 51 L Ed 2d 694, 97 S Ct 1345.

Service of National Guard officer as United States property and disbursing officer, by appointment of governor and approval by Secretary of Army, could not be considered as active federal service. Hyde v United States (1956) 134 Ct Cl 690, 139 F Supp 752.

In determining requisite 20 years service for entitlement to retirement pay, former reserve officer who received honorable discharge on July 9, 1919, and was appointed reserve captain on January 28, 1920, period between above dates was not includable. Forester v United States (1961) 154 Ct Cl 270, 291 F2d 397.

Service as civilian operations analyst with Army Air Force, in part in Pacific Theater of War from January 14 through September 29, 1945, including assimilated rank of colonel and wearing of military uniform, cannot be counted as active duty of member of Armed Forces to satisfy requirement of 10 USCS § 1331(c) in determining eligibility to receive longevity retired pay, when read in light of 10 USCS § 101(22) and § 1332(b) (now § 12732(b)). Mayer v United States (1973) 201 Ct Cl 105.

Only statutory duty imposed on services under 10 USCS § 12731(d) is to notify member that he has completed twenty years of service required for non-regular retired pay eligibility, and there is nothing in that provision, or any other provision, that imposes similar duty regarding member compliance with wartime active duty requirement of 10 USCS § 12731(c); absent such statutory duty, years of service notification requirement cannot be extended to require notification of wartime active service. Master Sergeant Henry W. Schuchardt, USAR (Retired) (10/8/96) Comp. Gen. Dec. No. B-274195.

5. Date of entitlement]10 USCS § 1331(e) (now § 12731(e))]

Retired reserve officer who had reached age of 60 years and completed required military service upon enactment of retirement law, was entitled to retirement pay from June 29, 1948, date of its enactment, although upon his inquiry in 1948 he was informed that he did not have sufficient military service to qualify, and accordingly postponed making formal application until 1950. Hyde v United States (1956) 134 Ct Cl 690, 139 F Supp 752.

10 USCS § 1331(e) regarding date of entitlement to retirement pay is not applicable retroactively. Cooper v United States (1973) 203 Ct Cl 300.

6. Estoppel

Even though Air Force officials may have encouraged applicant to accept commission, furnished him with copy of Air Force Retirement Policy brochure, encouraged him to maintain high level of participation in order to earn points credible for retirement purposes, and kept applicant regularly informed of accrual of his points, such actions do not estop Government from denying applicant retirement pay if 10 USCS § 1331 (now § 12731) requirements so dictate. Mayer v United States (1973) 201 Ct Cl 105.

7. Judicial review

After full and fair consideration, decision of Air Force Board for Correction of Military Records that plaintiff was not entitled to longevity retired pay because he did not have qualifying service pursuant to 10 USCS § 1331(c) (now § 12731(c)), will not be disturbed by Court of Claims unless it is arbitrary, capricious, or contrary to law. Mayer v United States (1973) 201 Ct Cl 105.

§ 12731a. Temporary special retirement qualification authority

(a) Retirement with at least 15 years of service. For the purposes of section 12731 of this title, the Secretary concerned may—

(1) during the period described in subsection (b), determine to treat a member

of the Selected Reserve of a reserve component of the armed force under the jurisdiction of that Secretary as having met the service requirements of subsection (a)(2) of that section and provide the member with the notification required by subsection (d) of that section if the member—

(A) as of October 1, 1991, has completed at least 15, and less than 20, years of service computed under section 12732 of this title; or

(B) after that date and before October 1, 1999, completes 15 years of service computed under that section; and

(2) upon the request of the member submitted to the Secretary, transfer the member to the Retired Reserve.

(b) Period of authority. The period referred to in subsection (a)(1) is the period beginning on October 23, 1992, and ending on October 1, 1999.

(c) Applicability subject to needs of the service. (1) The Secretary concerned may limit the applicability of subsection (a) to any category of personnel defined by the Secretary in order to meet a need of the armed force under the jurisdiction of the Secretary to reduce the number of members in certain grades, the number of members who have completed a certain number of years of service, or the number of members who possess certain military skills or are serving in designated competitive categories.

(2) A limitation under paragraph (1) shall be consistent with the purpose set forth in section 4414(a) of the National Defense Authorization Act for Fiscal Year 1993 (Public Law 102-484; 106 Stat. 2713 [10 USCS § 1162 note]).

(3) Notwithstanding the provisions of section 4415(2) of the Defense Conversion, Reinvestment, and Transition Assistance Act of 1992 (division of Public Law 102-484; 106 Stat. 2714 [10 USCS § 1162 note]), the Secretary concerned may, consistent with the other provisions of this section, provide the notification required by section 12731(d) of this title to a member who no longer meets the qualifications for membership in the Selected Reserve solely because the member is unfit because of physical disability. Such notification may not be made if the disability is the result of the member's intentional misconduct, willful neglect, or willful failure to comply with standards and qualifications for retention established by the Secretary concerned or was incurred during a period of unauthorized absence.

(d) Exclusion. This section does not apply to persons referred to in section 12731(c) of this title.

(e) Regulations. The authority provided in this section shall be subject to regulations prescribed by the Secretary of Defense and by the Secretary of Transportation with respect to the Coast Guard.

(Added Oct. 23, 1992, P. L. 102-484, Div D, Title XLIV, Subtitle B, § 4417(a), 106 Stat. 2716; May 31, 1993, P. L. 103-35, Title II, § 201(f)(3), 107 Stat. 99; Nov. 30, 1993, P. L. 103-160, Div A, Title V, Subtitle F, §§ 561(f)(4), 564(c), 107 Stat. 1668, 1670; Oct. 5, 1994, P. L. 103-337, Div A, Title V, Subtitle B, § 517, Title XVI, Subtitle C, § 1662(j)(1), 108 Stat. 2754, 3000; Feb. 10, 1996, P. L. 104-106, Div A, Title XV, § 1501(b)(21), 110 Stat. 497.)

HISTORY; ANCILLARY LAWS AND DIRECTIVES

Amendments:

1993. Act May 31, 1993, in subsec. (b), substituted ''October 23, 1992,'' for ''the date of the enactment of the National Defense Authorization Act for Fiscal Year 1993''.

Act Nov. 30, 1993, in subsec. (a), in the introductory matter, substituted ''Secretary concerned'' for ''Secretary of a military department'', in para. (1)(B), substituted '' October 1, 1999'' for ''October 1, 1995'' and, in para. (2), deleted ''within one year after the date of the notification referred to in paragraph (1)'' following ''Secretary''; in subsec. (b), substituted ''October 1, 1999'' for ''October 1, 1995''; in subsec. (c)(1), deleted ''of the military department'' following ''The Secretary; and, in subsec. (e), substituted ''and by the Secretary of Transportation with respect to the Coast Guard.'' for a concluding period.

1994. Act Oct. 5, 1994, in subsec. (c), added para. (3).

Such Act further (effective 12/1/94 as provided by § 1691 of such Act, which appears as 10 USCS § 10001 note) transferred this section, enacted as part of Chapter 67, to Chapter 1223, and substituted the section heading and text for ones which read:

''§ 1331a. Temporary special retirement qualification authority

''(a) Retirement with at least 15 years of service. For the purposes of section 1331 of this title, the Secretary concerned may—

''(1) during the period described in subsection (b), determine to treat a member of the Selected Reserve of a reserve component of the armed force under the jurisdiction of that Secretary as having met the service requirements of subsection (a)(2) of that section and provide the member with the notification required by subsection (d) of that section if the member—

''(A) as of October 1, 1991, has completed at least 15, and less than 20, years of service computed under section 1332 of this title; or

''(B) after that date and before October 1, 1999, completes 15 years of service computed under that section; and

''(2) upon the request of the member submitted to the Secretary, transfer the member to the Retired Reserve.

''(b) Period of authority. The period referred to in subsection (a)(1) is the period beginning on October 23, 1992, and ending on October 1, 1999.

''(c) Applicability subject to needs of the service. (1) The Secretary concerned may limit the applicability of subsection (a) to any category of personnel defined by the Secretary in order to meet a need of the armed force under the jurisdiction of the Secretary to reduce the number of members in certain grades, the number of members who have completed a certain number of years of service, or the number of members who possess certain military skills or are serving in designated competitive categories.

''(2) A limitation under paragraph (1) shall be consistent with the purpose set forth in section 4414(a) of the National Defense Authorization Act for Fiscal Year 1993.

''(3) Notwithstanding the provisions of section 4415(2) of the Defense Conversion Reinvestment, and Transition Assistance Act of 1992 (division D of Public Law 102-484; 106 Stat. 2714), the Secretary concerned may, consistent with the other provisions of this section, provide the notification required by section 1331(d) of this title to a member who no longer meets the qualifications for membership in the Selected Reserve solely because the member is unfit because of physical disability. Such notification may not be made if the disability is the result of the member's intentional misconduct, willful neglect, or willful failure to comply with standards and qualifications for retention established by the Secretary concerned or was incurred during a period of unauthorized absence.

''(d) Exclusion. This section does not apply to persons referred to in section 1331(c) of this title.

''(e) Regulations. The authority provided in this section shall be subject to regulations prescribed by the Secretary of Defense and by the Secretary of Transportation with respect to the Coast Guard.''.

1996. Act Feb. 10, 1996 (effective as if included in Act Oct. 5, 1994, P. L. 103-337, as enacted on Oct. 5, 1994, as provided by § 1501(f)(3) of Act Feb. 10, 1996, which appears as 10 USCS § 113 note), in subsec. (c)(3), inserted a comma after ''Defense Conversion''.

CROSS REFERENCES

This section is referred to in 38 USCS §§ 1965, 1968.

RESEARCH GUIDE

Am Jur:

53A Am Jur 2d, Military and Civil Defense § 176.

§ 12732. Entitlement to retired pay: computation of years of service

(a) Except as provided in subsection (b), for the purpose of determining whether a person is entitled to retired pay under section 12731 of this title, the person's years of service are computed by adding the following:

(1) The person's years of service, before July 1, 1949, in the following:

(A) The armed forces.

(B) The federally recognized National Guard before June 15, 1933.

(C) A federally recognized status in the National Guard before June 15, 1933.

(D) The National Guard after June 14, 1933, if his service therein was continuous from the date of his enlistment in the National Guard, or his Federal recognition as an officer therein, to the date of his enlistment or appointment, as the case may be, in the National Guard of the United States, the Army National Guard of the United States, or the Air National Guard of the United States.

(E) The Naval Reserve Force.

(F) The Naval Militia that conformed to the standards prescribed by the Secretary of the Navy.

(G) The National Naval Volunteers.

(H) The Army Nurse Corps, the Navy Nurse Corps, the Nurse Corps Reserve of the Army, or the Nurse Corps Reserve of the Navy, as it existed at any time after February 2, 1901.

(I) The Army under an appointment under the Act of December 22, 1942 (ch. 805, 56 Stat. 1072).

(J) An active full-time status, except as a student or apprentice, with the Medical Department of the Army as a civilian employee—

(i) in the dietetic or physical therapy categories, if the service was performed after April 6, 1917, and before April 1, 1943; or

(ii) in the occupational therapy category, if the service was performed before appointment in the Army Nurse Corps or the Women's Medical Specialist Corps [Army Medical Specialist Corps] and before January 1, 1949, or before appointment in the Air Force before January 1, 1949, with a view to designation as an Air Force nurse or medical specialist.

(2) Each one-year period, after July 1, 1949, in which the person has been credited with at least 50 points on the following basis:

(A) One point for each day of—

(i) active service; or

(ii) full-time service under sections 316, 502, 503, 504, and 505 of title 32 while performing annual training duty or while attending a prescribed course of instruction at a school designated as a service school by law or by the Secretary concerned;

if that service conformed to required standards and qualifications.

(B) One point for each attendance at a drill or period of equivalent instruction that was prescribed for that year by the Secretary concerned and conformed to the requirements prescribed by law, including attendance under section 502 of title 32.

(C) Points at the rate of 15 a year for membership—

(i) in a reserve component of an armed force,

(ii) in the Army or the Air Force without component, or

(iii) in any other category covered by subsection (a)(1) except a regular component.

(D) Points credited for the year under section 2126(b) of this title.

For the purpose of clauses (A), (B), (C), and (D), service in the National Guard shall be treated as if it were service in a reserve component, if the person concerned was later appointed in the National Guard of the United States, the Army National Guard of the United States, the Air National Guard of the United States, or as a Reserve of the Army or the Air Force, and served continuously in the National Guard from the date of his Federal recognition to the date of that appointment.

(3) The person's years of active service in the Commissioned Corps of the Public Health Service.

(4) The person's years of active commissioned service in the National Oceanic and Atmospheric Administration (including active commissioned service in the Environmental Science Services Administration and in the Coast and Geodetic Survey).

(b) The following service may not be counted under subsection (a):

(1) Service (other than active service) in an inactive section of the Organized

Reserve Corps or of the Army Reserve, or in an inactive section of the officers' section of the Air Force Reserve.

(2) Service (other than active service) after June 30, 1949, while on the Honorary Retired List of the Naval Reserve or of the Marine Corps Reserve.

(3) Service in the inactive National Guard.

(4) Service in a non-federally recognized status in the National Guard.

(5) Service in the Fleet Reserve or the Fleet Marine Corps Reserve.

(6) Service as an inactive Reserve nurse of the Army Nurse Corps established by the Act of February 2, 1901 (ch. 192, 31 Stat. 753) [unclassified], as amended, and service before July 1, 1938, as an inactive Reserve nurse of the Navy Nurse Corps established by the Act of May 13, 1908 (ch. 166, 35 Stat. 146).

(7) Service in any status other than that as commissioned officer, warrant officer, nurse, flight officer, aviation midshipman, appointed aviation cadet, or enlisted member, and that described in clauses (I) and (J) of subsection (a)(1).

(Aug. 10, 1956, ch 1041, § 1, 70A Stat. 102; Sept. 2, 1958, P. L. 85-861, § 33(a)(9), 72 Stat. 1565; Aug. 25, 1959, P. L. 86-197, § 1(1)–(3), 73 Stat. 425; Oct. 8, 1964, P. L. 88-636, § 1, 78 Stat. 1034; Dec. 26, 1974, P. L. 93-545, § 1, 88 Stat. 1741; Dec. 12, 1980, P. L. 96-513, Title V, Part B, § 511(48), 94 Stat. 2924; Oct. 5, 1994, P. L. 103-337, Div A, Title XVI, Subtitle C, § 1662(j)(1), 108 Stat. 3000; Sept. 23, 1996, P. L. 104-201, Div A, Title V, Subtitle E, § 543(b)(1), 110 Stat. 2522.)

HISTORY; ANCILLARY LAWS AND DIRECTIVES

Prior law and revision:

1956 ACT

Revised Section	Source (USCS)	Source (Statutes at Large)
1332(a)	10:1036a(b). 10:1036a(c). 10:1036e(a). 10:1036e(b). 10:1036e(c) (less applicability to determination of retired pay). 10:1036e(d) (less applicability to determination of retired pay). 34:440i(b). 34:440i(c). 34:440m(a). 34:440m(b). 34:440m(c) (less applicability to determination of retired pay).	June 29, 1948, ch. 708, § 302(b), (c), 62 Stat. 1089; Sept. 7, 1949, ch. 547, §§ 1, 2, 63 Stat. 693. June 29, 1948, ch. 708, § 306 (less (c) and 9d), as applicable to determination of retired pay), 62 Stat. 1088.

Revised Section	Source (USCS)	Source (Statutes at Large)
	34:440m(d) (less applicability to determination of retired pay).	
1332(b)	10:1036e(e).	
	10:1036e(f).	
	34:440m(e).	
	34:440m(f).	

Subsection (a) consolidates the provisions of 10:1036a and 1036e(b)–(d), and 34:440i and 440m(b)–(d), relating to service that may be counted in determining eligibility for retired pay under this chapter. 10:1036e(a) and 34:440m(a) are omitted as covered by the enumeration of the service that may be counted for the purposes of the revised section.

In subsection (a)(1)(A)–(F), the requirement that the service must have been satisfactory is omitted as executed, since all service before July 1, 1949, has been found to have been satisfactory by the Secretaries concerned.

In subsection (a)(1)(A), the words ''the armed forces'' are substituted for clauses (1), (2), (5)–(7), (9), (10), and (13)–(16), of 10:1036e(c) and 34:440m(c), and so much of clause (8) of 10:1036e(c) and 34:440m(c) as relates to the Naval Reserve and the Naval Reserve Force as constituted after February 28, 1925, since the service covered by those clauses when added to service in the regular components, comprises all service in the armed forces.

In subsection (a)(1)(B)–(C), the words ''June 15'' are inserted to reflect the exact date of the change in National Guard status made by section 5 of the act of June 15, 1933, ch. 87, 48 Stat. 155, which established the National Guard of the United States as a reserve component of the Army.

In subsection (a)(1)(D), 10:1036e(c)(8) (last 25 words), 10:1036e(c)(9) (last 22 words), 34:440m(c)(8) (last 25 words), and 34:440m(c)(9) (last 22 words) are omitted as covered by subsection (b)(5).

In subsection (a)(2)(A), the words ''service that conformed to required standards and qualifications'' are substituted for 10:1036e(b) and 34:440m(d). In clause (a)(2)(A), 10:1036e(d) and 34:440m(d), which make it clear that ''active Federal service'', in the sense in which that term is used in 10:1036a–e and 34:440i–m, includes annual training duty and attendance at service schools, are omitted as covered by sections 101(22) and 101(24) of this title.

In subsection (a)(2)(A) and (B), specific reference is made to National Guard service to reflect the opinion of the Judge Advocate General of the Army (JAGA, 1956/1908, 13 Feb. 1956).

In subsection (a)(2)(C), the words ''other than active Federal service'' are omitted, since the points for membership are not reduced by active duty (see opinion of the Judge Advocate General of the Army (JAGA, 1953/2016, 3 March 1953)).

In subsections (a) and (b), the words ''active service'' are substituted for the words ''active Federal service'' for uniformity of expression. In clause (5), the words ''transferred thereto after completion of 16 or more years of active naval service'' are omitted, since other authorized fleet reserve categories have not been used and authority for them is omitted from this revised title as unnecessary.

Subsection (b)(1)–(4) is inserted because of 10:1036e(e) and (f) and 34:440m(e) and (f), which state that the service enumerated in those clauses may not be considered in determining eligibility for retired pay under this chapter. Clause (5) is based on the exclusions in 34:440m(c)(8)–(9).

Subsection (b)(6) is inserted for clarity since 10:1036a and 34:440i were limited in applicability to service in the status of a ''commissioned officer, warrant officer, flight officer, or enlisted person.''

1958 Act

The word ''full-time'' is inserted for clarity. The other change reflects the opinion of the Judge Advocate General of the Army (JAGA 1956/1908, Feb. 13, 1956) that duty performed under section 92 of the National Defense Act, the source statute for section 502 of title 32, was creditable in determining entitlement to retired pay under section 302 of the Army and Air Force Vitalization and Retirement Equalization Act of 1948 (62 Stat. 1087), the source statute for section 1332 of title 10.

References in text:

The ''Act of December 22, 1942 (ch. 805, 56 Stat. 1072)'', referred to in this section, is Act Dec. 22, 1942, ch 805, 56 Stat. 1072, which was classified to 10 U.S.C. § 164, 10 U.S.C. § 81 note, and 37 U.S.C. § 113 note, and which was repealed as executed by Act Aug. 10, 1956, ch 1941, § 53, 70A Stat. 641.

The ''Act of May 13, 1908 (ch. 166, 35 Stat. 146)'', referred to in this section, is Act May 13, 1908, ch 166, 35 Stat. 146, which formerly appeared as 5 U.S.C. §§ 442 and 443 and 34 U.S.C. §§ 1, 41, 42, 383, 385, 461, 867, 1102, 1103, and which was repealed by Act Aug. 10, 1956, ch 1041, § 53, 70A Stat. 654.

Explanatory notes:

The bracketed words ''Army Medical Specialist Corps'' are inserted in subsec. (a)(1)(J)(ii) of this section on the authority of Act Aug. 21, 1957, P. L. 85-155, 71 Stat. 375, which redesignated the Women's Medical Specialist Corps as the Army Medical Specialist Corps; see 10 USCS § 3070, and see also Act Aug. 9, 1955, ch 654, 69 Stat. 579.

Amendments:

1958. Act Sept. 2, 1958 (effective 8/10/56, for all purposes, as provided by § 33 (g) of such Act, which appears as 10 USCS § 101 note), in subsec. (a)(2)(A)(ii), inserted ''full-time'' and ''502,''.

1959. Act Aug. 25, 1959, in subsec. (a), substituted para. (1) for one which read:

''(1) his years of service, before July 1, 1949, in—

''(A) the armed forces;

''(B) the federally recognized National Guard before June 15, 1933;

''(C) a federally recognized status in the National Guard before June 15, 1933;

''(D) the Naval Reserve Force;

''(E) the Naval Militia that conformed to the standards prescribed by the Secretary of the Navy; and

''(F) the National Naval Volunteers; and'',

and, in para. (2), inserted the concluding matter; and, in subsec. (b), substituted paras. (6) and (7) for para. (6), which read: ''Service in any status other than that as a commissioned officer, warrant officer, flight officer, or enlisted member.''.

1964. Act Oct. 8, 1964 (effective as provided by § 2 of such Act, which appears as a note to this section), in subsec. (a), in para. (1)(J)(ii), deleted ''and'' after the semicolon, in para. (2), substituted a semicolon for the concluding period, and added paras. (3) and (4).

1974. Act Dec. 26, 1974, in subsec. (b)(7), inserted ''aviation midshipman,''.

1980. Act Dec. 12, 1980 (effective upon enactment on 12/12/80, as provided by § 701(b)(3) of such Act, which appears as 10 USCS § 101 note), in subsec. (a)(4), substituted ''National Oceanic and Atmospheric Administration (including active commissioned service in the Environmental Science Services Administration and in the Coast and Geodetic Survey)'' for ''Coast and Geodetic Survey'', and substituted ''under'' for ''pursuant to''.

1994. Act Oct. 5, 1994 (effective 12/1/94 as provided by § 1691 of such Act, which appears as 10 USCS § 10001 note) transferred this section, enacted as part of Chapter 67, to Chapter 1223, and substituted this section for one which read:

''§ 1332. Computation of years of service in determining entitlement to retired pay

''(a) Except as provided in subsection (b), for the purpose of determining whether a person is entitled to retired pay under section 1331 of this title, his years of service are computed by adding—

''(1) his years of service, before July 1, 1949, in—

''(A) the armed forces;

''(B) the federally recognized National Guard before June 15, 1933;

''(C) a federally recognized status in the National Guard before June 15, 1933;

''(D) the National Guard after June 14, 1933, if his service therein was continuous from the date of his enlistment in the National Guard, or his Federal recognition as an officer therein, to the date of his enlistment or appointment, as the case may be, in the National Guard of the United States, the Army National Guard of the United States, or the Air National Guard of the United States;

''(E) the Naval Reserve Force;

''(F) the Naval Militia that conformed to the standards prescribed by the Secretary of the Navy;

''(G) the National Naval Volunteers;

''(H) the Army Nurse Corps, the Navy Nurse Corps, the Nurse Corps Reserve of the Army, or the Nurse Corps Reserve of the Navy, as it existed at any time after February 2, 1901;

''(I) the Army under an appointment under the Act of December 22, 1942 (ch. 805, 56 Stat. 1072); and

''(J) an active full-time status, except as a student or apprentice, with the Medical Department of the Army as a civilian employee—

''(i) in the dietetic or physical therapy categories, if the service was performed after April 6, 1917, and before April 1, 1943; or ''(ii) in the occupational therapy category, if the service was performed before appointment in the Army Nurse Corps or the Women's Medical Specialist Corps and before January 1, 1949, or before appointment in the Air Force before January 1, 1949, with a view to designation as an Air Force nurse or medical specialist;

''(2) each one-year period, after July 1, 1949, in which he has been credited with at least 50 points on the following basis—

''(A) one point for each day of—

''(i) active service; or

''(ii) full-time service under sections 316, 502, 503, 504, and 505 of title 32 while performing annual training duty or while attending a prescribed course of instruction at a school designated as a service school by law or by the Secretary concerned;

if that service conformed to required standards and qualifications;

''(B) one point for each attendance at a drill or period of equivalent instruction that was prescribed for that year by the Secretary concerned and conformed to the requirements prescribed by law, including attendance under section 502 of title 32; and

''(C) points at the rate of 15 a year for membership in a reserve component of an armed force, in the Army or the Air Force without component, or in any other category covered by subsection (a)(1) except a regular component.

For the purpose of clauses (A), (B), and (C), service in the National Guard shall be treated as if it were service in a reserve component, if the person concerned was later appointed in the National Guard of the United States, the Army National Guard of the United States, the Air National Guard of the United States, or as a Reserve of the Army or the Air Force, and served continuously in the National Guard from the date of his Federal recognition to the date of that appointment;

''(3) his years of active service in the Commissioned Corps of the Public Health Service during such time as the Commissioned Corps was a military service pursuant to declaration made by the President under section 216 of the Public Health Service Act (42 U. S. C. 217); and

''(4) his years of active commissioned service in the National Oceanic and Atmospheric Administration (including active commissioned service in the Environmental Science Services Administration and in the Coast and Geodetic Survey) during such time as he was transferred to the service and jurisdiction of a military department under section 16 of the Act of May 22, 1917 (33 U.S.C. 855).

''(b) The following service may not be counted under subsection (a):

''(1) Service (other than active service) in an inactive section of the Organized Reserve Corps or of the Army Reserve, or in an inactive section of the officers' section of the Air Force Reserve.

''(2) Service (other than active service) after June 30, 1949, while on the Honorary Retired List of the Naval Reserve or of the Marine Corps Reserve.

''(3) Service in the inactive National Guard.

''(4) Service in a non-federally recognized status in the National Guard.

''(5) Service in the Fleet Reserve or the Fleet Marine Corps Reserve.

''(6) Service as an inactive Reserve nurse of the Army Nurse Corps established by the Act of February 2, 1901 (ch. 192, 31 Stat. 753), as amended, and service before July 1, 1938, as an inactive Reserve nurse of the Navy Nurse Corps established by the Act of May 13, 1908 (ch. 166, 35 Stat. 146).

"(7) Service in any status other than that as commissioned officer, warrant officer, nurse, flight officer, aviation midshipman, appointed aviation cadet, or enlisted member, and that described in clauses (I) and (J) of subsection (a)(1).".

1996. Act Sept. 23, 1996, in subsec. (a)(2), added subpara. (D) and, in the concluding matter, substituted "(C), and (D)" for "and (C)".

Transfer of functions:

All functions of the Public Health Service, of the Surgeon General of the Public Health Service, and of all other officers and employees of the Public Health Service, and all functions of all agencies of or in the Public Health Service were transferred to the Secretary of Health, Education, and Welfare by 1966 Reorg. Plan No. 3, 31 Fed. Reg. 8855, 80 Stat. 1610, effective June 25, 1966, which appears at 5 USCS § 903 note.

The Secretary of Health, Education, and Welfare was redesignated as the Secretary of Health and Human Services by Act Oct. 17, 1979, P. L. 96-88, Title V, § 509, 93 Stat. 695, which appears as 20 USCS § 3508, which also provided that any reference to the Secretary of Health, Education, and Welfare in any law in force on the effective date of such Act on Oct. 17, 1979, shall be deemed to refer and apply to the Secretary of Health and Human Services, except to the extent such reference is a function or office transferred to the Secretary of Education or the Department of Education under Act Oct. 17, 1979.

Other provisions:

Additional clerical service creditable under 10 USCS §§ 1331 et seq. Act Sept. 2, 1958, P. L. 85-861, § 15, 72 Stat. 1558, provided: "(a) Notwithstanding [former] section 1332(b)(6) of title 10, United States Code [subsec. (b)(7) of this section], a person is entitled to count his service as an Army field clerk or as a field clerk, Quartermaster Corps, as active service in determining his entitlement to retired pay under [former] chapter 67 of title 10, United States Code, and in computing his retired pay under that chapter.

"(b) Notwithstanding [former] section 1332(b)(6) of title 10, United States Code [subsec. (b)(7) of this section], a warrant officer is entitled to count classified service as an Army headquarters clerk or as a clerk of the Army Quartermaster Corps that he performed under any law in effect before August 29, 1916, as active service in determining his entitlement to retired pay under [former] chapter 67 of title 10, United States Code, and in computing his retired pay under that chapter.".

Act Aug. 25, 1959, P. L. 86-197; savings provision. Act Aug. 25, 1959, P. L. 86-197, § 3, 73 Stat. 426, provided: "This Act [amending this section, among other things; for full classification, consult USCS Tables volumes] does not deprive any person of any service credit to which he was entitled on the day before the effective date of this Act [enacted Aug. 25, 1959].".

Coast Guard Women's Reserve; constructive service. Act June 12, 1962, P. L. 87-482, 76 Stat. 95, provided:

"That any person who was a member of the Coast Guard Women's Reserve and who served on active duty therein for at least one year prior to July 25, 1947; who was separated therefrom under honorable conditions; and who also had membership therein for any period between November 1, 1949, and July 1, 1956, shall be deemed to have served on inactive duty with the Coast Guard Women's Reserve from July 25, 1947, to November 1, 1949, in the grade or rating satisfactorily held on active duty prior to July 25, 1947.

"Sec. 2. Creditable constructive service for a person qualified under section 1 hereof shall be applied when providing retirement benefits under the Army and Air Force Vitalization and Retirement Equalization Act of 1948, as amended [Act June 29, 1948, ch 708, 62 Stat. 1081; for classification, consult USCS Tables volumes], or any other Act under which the individual may be entitled to retirement from the Armed Forces.

"Sec. 3. Additional pay accruing to any person by virtue of increased creditable service resulting from the inclusion of constructive service creditable by application of section 1 hereof shall not be made for active or inactive duty for which pay is authorized by competent authority which is performed prior to the first day of the calendar quarter next succeeding the calendar quarter in which this Act becomes effective [enacted June 12, 1962].".

Application of Oct. 8, 1964 amendments. Act Oct. 8, 1964, P. L. 88-636, § 2, 78 Stat. 1034, provided: "The amendments made by this Act [amending subsecs. (a)(3) and (4) of this section] shall apply to any period before enactment of this Act during which the Commissioned Corps of the Public Health Service has had the status of a military service, and to any period before enactment of this Act during which commissioned personnel of the Coast and Geodetic Survey were transferred to the service and jurisdiction of a military department.".

Tracking system for award of retirement points; recommendations to Congress. Act Sept. 23, 1996, P. L. 104-201, Div A, Title V, Subtitle D, § 531(b), (c), 110 Stat. 2517, provides:

"(b) Tracking system for award of retirement points. To better enable the Secretary of Defense and Congress to assess the cost and the effect on readiness of the amendment made by subsection (a) and of other potential changes to the Reserve retirement system under chapter 1223 of title 10, United States Code [10 USCS §§ 12731 et seq.], the Secretary of Defense shall require the Secretary of each military department to implement a system to monitor the award of retirement points for purposes of that chapter by categories in accordance with the recommendation set forth in the August 1988 report of the Sixth Quadrennial Review of Military Compensation.

"(c) Recommendations to Congress. The Secretary shall submit to Congress, not later than one year after the date of the enactment of this Act, the recommendations of the Secretary with regard to the adoption of the following Reserve retirement initiatives recommended in the August 1988 report of the Sixth Quadrennial Review of Military Compensation:

"(1) Elimination of membership points under subparagraph (C) of section 12732(a)(2) of title 10, United States Code, in conjunction with a decrease from 50 to 35 in the number of points required for a satisfactory year under that section.

"(2) Limitation to 60 in any year on the number of points that may be credited under subparagraph (B) of section 12732(a)(2) of such title at two points per day.

"(3) Limitation to 360 in any year on the total number of retirement points countable for purposes of section 12733 of such title.".

CROSS REFERENCES

Transfer to inactive status list instead status list instead of separation, , 10 USCS § 1209.

Active duty, retention after becoming qualified for retired pay, 10 USCS § 12308.

Standards and qualification for reserve commissioned officer to be retained in active status, 10 USCS § 12642.

Uniform allowance, 37 USCS § 416.

This section is referred to in 5 USCS § 3329; 10 USCS §§ 1063, 1176, 1209, 1482, 2126, 3850, 6389, 6391, 8850, 12308, 12642, 12646, 12731, 12731a, 12733, 14704.

RESEARCH GUIDE

Am Jur:

53A Am Jur 2d, Military and Civil Defense § 176.

Auto-Cite®: Cases and annotations referred to herein can be further researched through the Auto-Cite® computer-assisted research service. Use Auto-Cite to check citations for form, parallel references, prior and later history, and annotation references.

INTERPRETIVE NOTES AND DECISIONS

1. Generally
2. Relationship with other law
3. Service in reserves, generally
4. —Active reserves
5. —Coast Guard
6. Service at academies
7. Service in National Guard
8. Miscellaneous

1. Generally

Plaintiff, claiming that he relied on a letter from the Army Reserves and that he relied upon the representations made by his superior indicating that he had fulfilled the required 20 years to qualify for retirement pay, was denied such benefits since he, in fact, had not complied with the required 20 years and since estoppel against the government was not applicable. Montilla v United States (1972) 198 Ct Cl 48, 457 F2d 978.

2. Relationship with other law

Provision in former 10 USCS § 1332 (now codified at 10 USCS § 12732) for computation of years of service to determine eligibility for retired pay under former 10 USCS § 1331 (now codified at 10 USCS § 12731), must be read together with concept of "reserve" of armed force in former § 1331(c); if member is credited under former § 1332 with years of service for service involved, either because he had federally recognized status before 6/15/33 or because his service was in federally recognized unit before 6/15/33, then he had to be "reserve" for former § 1331(c) purposes. DOHA Case No. 96121102 (8/22/97).

3. Service in reserves, generally

Reserve officer called to active duty in 1917, whose Reserve commission was converted to commission in United States Army and was thereafter discharged, was not only completely separated from military service, but his commission was terminated; accordingly, time between his discharge in 1919 and his later appointment in 1920 to Reserve unit could not be counted in computing in credible service time for eligibility for Reserve officer retired pay. Forester v United States (1961) 154 Ct Cl 270, 291 F2d 397.

Member of Reserve prior to August 16, 1945 is not eligible at age 60 for retired pay for non-regular service unless he performed active duty in World

War I, World War II, or Korean War, pursuant to 10 USCS § 1332 (now § 12732). Goodley v United States (1971) 194 Ct Cl 829, 441 F2d 1175.

4. —Active reserves

Time served in Active Reserves is creditable in computing time of service where Secretary of Army retains serviceman in Active Reserves, rather than transfer to Retired Reserves, where serviceman has reached maximum retirement age for grade and classification and retention on Active Reserve list is at serviceman's request. Fogg v United States (1967) 180 Ct Cl 605.

5. —Coast Guard

Service as temporary enrolled member of Coast Guard Reserve from January 5, 1944 to September 30, 1945 terminated by certificate of disenrollment under honorable circumstances, is not included in computing years of active service for longevity retirement pay purposes under 10 USCS § 1332 (now § 12732). Goodley v United States (1971) 194 Ct Cl 829, 441 F2d 1175.

6. Service at academies

Reserve colonel on honorary retired list of Army was not entitled to count his service as cadet in United States military academy, ending in 1910. Williams v United States (1953) 127 Ct Cl 167, 117 F Supp 189.

Service as cadet at United States military academy under appointment made prior to August 24, 1912, was active federal service and was included as basis for computation of retirement pay. Brand v United States (1955) 133 Ct Cl 115, 134 F Supp 669.

7. Service in National Guard

Major general, who retired in 1933, was entitled to retirement pay on basis of National Guard service rendered after 1903, since National Guard was federally recognized after 1903. Price v United States (1951) 121 Ct Cl 664, 100 F Supp 310, cert den (1953) 344 US 911, 97 L Ed 703, 73 S Ct 333.

Applicant could not base claim for credit for time spent as property and disbursing officer in Tennessee National Guard, as such officers were not subject to military orders or military disciplinary action, could quit at any time or be removed by Governor, could not be ordered out of his State by Army and he could not be court-martialed and was not subject to Federal annual leave laws. Hyde v United States (1956) 134 Ct Cl 690, 139 F Supp 752.

8. Miscellaneous

Suit for retirement pay is barred by laches where claimant was on notice as of 1960 that there was problem affecting reserve status and did nothing until 1976. Goodwyn v United States (1983) 2 Cl Ct 600.

Retirement pay applicant is entitled to compute double time for service rendered in Cuba and Philippine Islands prior to 1912 as prescribed in 10 USCS § 3914 note; applicant does not lose his right to claim double time because he subsequently became officer. Whitaker v United States (1956) 134 Ct Cl 245.

§ 12733. Computation of retired pay: computation of years of service

For the purpose of computing the retired pay of a person under this chapter [10 USCS §§ 12731 et seq.], the person's years of service and any fraction of such a year are computed by dividing 360 into the sum of the following:

(1) The person's days of active service.

(2) The person's days of full-time service under sections 316, 502, 503, 504, and 505 of title 32 while performing annual training duty or while attending a prescribed course of instruction at a school designated as a service school by law or by the Secretary concerned.

(3) One day for each point credited to the person under clause (B), (C), or (D) of section 12732(a)(2) of this title, but not more than 60 days in any one year of service before the year of service that includes September 23, 1996, and not more than 75 days in any subsequent year of service.

(4) 50 days for each year before July 1, 1949, and proportionately for each fraction of a year, of service (other than active service) in a reserve component of an armed force, in the Army or the Air Force without component, or in any other category covered by section 12732(a)(1) of this title, except a regular component.

(Aug. 10, 1956, ch 1041, § 1, 70A Stat. 103; Sept. 2, 1958, P. L. 85-861,

§ 33(a)(10), 72 Stat. 1565; Oct. 5, 1994, P. L. 103-337, Div A, Title XVI, Subtitle C, § 1662(j)(1), 108 Stat. 3002; Sept. 23, 1996, P. L. 104-201, Div A, Title V, Subtitle D, § 531(a), Subtitle E, § 543(b)(2), 110 Stat. 2517, 2522; Nov. 18, 1997, P. L. 105-85, Div A, Title X, Subtitle G, § 1073(a)(67), (c)(4), 111 Stat. 1904.)

HISTORY; ANCILLARY LAWS AND DIRECTIVES

Prior law and revision:

1956 ACT

Revised Section	Source (USCS)	Source (Statutes at Large)
1333	10:1036b (less 1st 91 words, and less 1st proviso). 10:1036e(c) (as applicable to determination of retired pay). 10:1036e(d) (as applicable to determination of retired pay). 34:440j (less 1st 91 words, and less 1st proviso). 34:440m(c) (as applicable to determination of retired pay). 34:440m(d) (as applicable to determination of retired pay).	June 29, 1948, ch. 708, §§ 303 (less 1st 91 words, and less 1st proviso), 306 ((c) and (d), as applicable to determination of retired pay), 62 Stat. 1088–1090; Sept. 7, 1949, ch. 547, § 3, 63 Stat. 693.

The revised section consolidates provisions of 10:1036b and 1036e, and 34:440j and 440m, relating to the years of service that may be counted in determining retired pay for persons entitled to that pay under this chapter. Clause (1) is substituted for 10:1036b(i). In clause (3), the words "and proportionately for each fraction of a year" are inserted to make clear that parts of years must be counted. 10:1036e(d) and 34:440m(d) are omitted as covered by sections 101(22) and 101(24) of this title.

1958 ACT

The change is necessary so that active service and service described in section 1332(a)(2)(A)(ii) that was performed on or before July 1, 1949, may be counted in computing retired pay, as provided by the source law, section 303(i) of the Army and Air Force Vitalization and Retirement Equalization Act of 1948 (62 Stat. 1088) and in accordance with the opinion of the Judge Advocate General of the Army (JAGA 1956/1908, Feb. 13, 1956).

Amendments:

1958. Act Sept. 2, 1958 (effective 8/10/56, for all purposes, as provided by § 33(g) of such Act) substituted para. (1) for one which read: "the days of service credited to him under section 1332(a)(2)(A) of this title;'', redesignated paras. (2) and (3) to be (3) and (4), respectively, and added new para. (2).

1994. Act Oct. 5, 1994 (effective 12/1/94 as provided by § 1691 of such Act, which appears as 10 USCS § 10001 note) transferred this section, enacted as part of Chapter 67, to Chapter 1223, and substituted this section for the transferred one, which read:

''§ 1333. Computation of years of service in computing retired pay

''For the purpose of computing the retired pay of a person under this chapter, his years of service and any fraction of such a year are computed by adding—

''(1) his days of active service;

''(2)his days of full-time service under sections 316, 502, 503, 504, and 505 of title 32 while performing annual training duty or while attending a prescribed course of instruction at a school designated as a service school by law or by the Secretary concerned;

''(3) one day for each point credited to him under clause (B) or (C) of section 1332(a)(2) of this title, but not more than 60 days in any one year; and

''(4) 50 days for each year before July 1, 1949, and proportionately for each fraction of a year, of service (other than active service) in a reserve component of an armed force, in the Army or the Air Force without component, or in any other category covered by section 1332(a)(1) of this title except a regular component;

and by dividing the sum of that addition by 360.''.

1996. Act Sept. 23, 1996, as amended by Act Nov. 18, 1997 (effective and applicable as provided by § 1073(c) and (i) of such Act, which appear as notes to 10 USCS §§ 2502 and 101, respectively), in para. (3), substituted ''(C), or (D)'' for ''or (C)'' and inserted ''of service before the year of service in which the date of the enactment of the National Defense Authorization Act for Fiscal Year 1997 occurs and not more than 75 days in any subsequent year of service''.

1997. Act Nov. 18, 1997 (applicable as provided by § 1073(i) of such Act, which appears as 10 USCS § 101 note), in para. (3), inserted a comma following ''(B)'', and substituted ''that includes September 23, 1996,'' for ''in which the date of the enactment of the National Defense Authorization Act for Fiscal Year 1997 occurs''.

Such Act further (effective and applicable as provided by § 1073(c) and (i) of such Act, which appear as notes to 10 USCS §§ 2502 and 101, respectively), amended the directory language of Act Sept. 23, 1996, without affecting the text of this section.

CROSS REFERENCES

Retirement or separation for physical disability, computation of service, 10 USCS § 1208.

Computation of years of service, 10 USCS § 1405.

This section is referred to in 10 USCS §§ 1208, 1209, 1405, 12731, 12739.

RESEARCH GUIDE

Am Jur:

53A Am Jur 2d, Military and Civil Defense § 176.

INTERPRETIVE NOTES AND DECISIONS

Major general, who retired in 1933, is entitled to retirement pay on basis of national guard service rendered after 1903, since national guard was federally recognized after 1903. Price v United States (1951) 121 Ct Cl 664, 100 F Supp 310, cert den (1953) 344 US 911, 97 L Ed 703, 73 S Ct 333.

Guard officer is not entitled to credit for attendance at drills and target practice prior to July 1, 1949. Price v United States (1952) 121 Ct Cl 681, 104 F Supp 99, cert den (1953) 344 US 911, 97 L Ed 703, 73 S Ct 333.

Reserve major generals who have not been retired prior to reaching age 60 pursuant to 10 USCS § 8852 (now repealed), and who are otherwise qualified for retirement upon reaching age 60 pursuant to 10 USCS §§ 1331 et seq. (now §§ 12731 et seq.), are not entitled to credit for service after reaching age 60 for purposes of computing retirement pay under 10 USCS § 1333 (now § 12733) unless they have been retained in service by order of Secretary pursuant to 10 USCS § 676 (now § 12308) or § 8852(b) (now repealed). (1979) 58 Op Comp Gen 674.

§ 12734. Time not creditable toward years of service

(a) Service in an inactive status may not be counted in any computation of years of service under this chapter [10 USCS §§ 12731 et seq.].

(b) Time spent after retirement (without pay) for failure to conform to standards and qualifications prescribed under section 12641 of this title may not be credited in a computation of years of service under this chapter [10 USCS §§ 12731 et seq.].

(Aug. 10, 1956, ch 1041, § 1, 70A Stat. 104; Sept. 7, 1962, P. L. 87-651, Title I, § 108, 76 Stat. 509; Oct. 5, 1994, P. L. 103-337, Div A, Title XVI, Subtitle C, § 1662(j)(1), 108 Stat. 3003.)

HISTORY; ANCILLARY LAWS AND DIRECTIVES

Prior law and revision:

1956 ACT

Revised Section	Source (USCS)	Source (Statutes at Large)
1334(a)	10:1036c (last sentence, as applicable to inactive status). 10:1036g (last 41 words of 2d sentence). 34:440k (last sentence, as applicable to to inactive status). 34:440*o* (last 41 words of 2d sentence). 50:931(b) (less 1st 16 words).	June 29, 1948, ch. 708, §§ 304, (last sentence), 308 (last 41 words of 2d sentence), 62 Stat. 1088, 1090. July 9, 1952, ch. 608, § 211(b) (less 1st 16 words), 66 Stat. 485.
1334(b)	10:1036c (last sentence, less applicability to inactive status).	

Revised Section	Source (USCS)	Source (Statutes at Large)
	34:440k (last sentence, less applicability to inactive status).	

Subsection (a) is substituted for 10:1036c (1st 17 words of last sentence, as applicable to inactive status), 10:1036g (last 41 words of 2d sentence), 34:440k (last 17 words of last sentence, as applicable to inactive status), and 34:440 *o* (last 41 words of 2d sentence). 10:1036c (proviso of last sentence, as applicable to inactive status) and 34:440k (proviso of last sentence, as applicable to inactive status) are omitted as executed. 10:1036c (last sentence, less 1st 17 words and less proviso, as applicable to inactive status) and 34:440k (last sentence, less 1st 17 words and less proviso, as applicable to inactive status) are omitted as surplusage.

In subsection (b), 10:1036c (proviso of last sentence, less applicability to inactive status) and 34:440k (proviso of last sentence, less applicability to inactive status) are omitted as executed. 10:1036c (last sentence, less 1st 17 words and less proviso, less applicability to inactive status) and 34:440k (last sentence, less 1st 17 words and less proviso, less applicability to inactive status) are omitted as surplusage.

1962 ACT

The change conforms section 1334(b) of title 10 to the source law, the last sentence of section 304 of the Army and Air Force Vitalization and Retirement Equalization Act of 1948 (62 Stat. 1089). Section 305 makes the change retroactive to August 10, 1956, the date of repeal of the source law by the original military codification act of that date.

Amendments:

1962. Act Sept. 7, 1962 (effective as of 8/10/56, for all purposes, as provided by § 305 of such Act, which appears as a note to this section), in subsec. (b), substituted "(without pay) for failure to conform to standards and qualifications prescribed under section 1001 of this title" for "or transfer to the Retired Reserve" and substituted "a computation" for "any computation".

1994. Act Oct. 5, 1994 (effective 12/1/94 as provided by § 1691 of such Act, which appears as 10 USCS § 10001 note) transferred this section, enacted as part of Chapter 67, to Chapter 1223, and substituted the section heading and text for ones which read:

"§ 1334. Time not creditable toward years of service

"(a) Service in an inactive status may not be counted in any computation of years of service under this chapter.

"(b) Time spent after retirement (without pay) for failure to conform to standards and qualifications prescribed under section 1001 of this title may not be credited in a computation of years of service under this chapter.".

Other provisions:

Act Sept. 7, 1962, P. L. 87-651, Title III, § 305, 76 Stat. 526, provided: "Section 108 of this Act [amending this section] is effective as of August 10, 1956, for all purposes. Section 304 of this Act is effective as of February 6, 1959.".

CROSS REFERENCES

This section is referred to in 10 USCS § 10153.

RESEARCH GUIDE

Am Jur:

53A Am Jur 2d, Military and Civil Defense § 176.

§ 12735. Inactive status list

(a) A member who would be eligible for retired pay under this chapter [10 USCS §§ 12731 et seq.] but for the fact that that member is under 60 years of age may be transferred, at his request and by direction of the Secretary concerned, to such inactive status list as may be established for members of his armed force, other than members of a regular component.

(b) While on an inactive status list under subsection (a), a member is not required to participate in any training or other program prescribed for his component.

(c) The Secretary may at any time recall to active status a member who is on an inactive status list under subsection (a).

(Aug. 10, 1956, ch 1041, § 1, 70A Stat. 104; Oct. 5, 1994, P. L. 103-337, Div A, Title XVI, Subtitle C, § 1662(j)(1), 108 Stat. 3003.)

HISTORY; ANCILLARY LAWS AND DIRECTIVES

Prior law and revision:

Revised Section	Source (USCS)	Source (Statutes at Large)
1335(a)	10:1036g (1st sentence). 34:440o (1st sentence).	June 29, 1948, ch. 708, § 308 (less last 41 words of 2d sentence), 62 Stat. 1090.
1335(b)	10:1036g (2d sentence, less last 41 words). 34:440*o* (2d sentence, less last 41 words).	
1335(c)	10:1036g (less 1st and 2d sentences). 34:440*o* (less 1st and 2d sentences).	

In subsection (a), the words ''would be eligible but for the fact that he is under 60 years of age'' are substituted for the words ''has not attained the age of sixty years but is eligible in all other respects''. The words ''for members of his armed force, other than members of a regular component'' are substituted for the words ''for the reserve components of the Army of the United States or Air Force of the United States'', since the source statute applied to all members except members of the regular components. The words ''as has been, or'' and ''by law or regulation'' are omitted as surplusage.

In subsection (b), the words ''after the effective date of such transfer'' are omitted as surplusage.

In subsection (c), 10:1036g (last 32 words of last sentence) and 34:440*o* (last 32 words of last sentence) are omitted as surplusage.

Amendments:

1994. Act Oct. 5, 1994 (effective 12/1/94 as provided by § 1691 of such Act, which appears as 10 USCS § 10001 note) transferred this section, enacted as part of Chapter 67, to Chapter 1223, and substituted the section heading and text for ones which read:

"§ 1335. Inactive status list

"(a) A person who would be eligible for retired pay under this chapter but for the fact that he is under 60 years of age may be transferred, at his request and by direction of the Secretary concerned, to such inactive status list as may be established for members of his armed force, other than members of a regular component.

"(b) While on an inactive status list under subsection (a), a person is not required to participate in any training or other program prescribed for his component.

"(c) The Secretary may at any time recall to active status a member who is on an inactive status list under subsection (a).".

CROSS REFERENCES

This section is referred to in 10 USCS § 1209.

RESEARCH GUIDE

Am Jur:

53A Am Jur 2d, Military and Civil Defense § 176.

§ 12736. Service credited for retired pay benefits not excluded for other benefits

No period of service included wholly or partly in determining a person's right to, or the amount of, retired pay under this chapter may be excluded in determining his eligibility for any annuity, pension, or old-age benefit, under any other law, on account of civilian employment by the United States or otherwise, or in determining the amount payable under that law, if that service is otherwise properly credited under it.

(Aug. 10, 1956, ch 1041, § 1, 70A Stat. 104; Oct. 5, 1994, P. L. 103-337, Div A, Title XVI, Subtitle C, § 1662(j)(1), 108 Stat. 3003.)

HISTORY; ANCILLARY LAWS AND DIRECTIVES

Prior law and revision:

Revised Section	Source (USCS)	Source (Statutes at Large)
1336	10:1036d (less 1st sentence). 34:440*l* (less 1st sentence).	June 29, 1948, ch. 708, § 305 (less 1st sentence), 62 Stat. 1089.

Amendments:

1994. Act Oct. 5, 1994 (effective 12/1/94 as provided by § 1691 of such Act, which appears as 10 USCS § 10001 note) transferred this section, enacted as part of Chapter 67, to Chapter 1223, and substituted the section heading and text for ones which read:

''§ 1336. Service credited for retired pay benefits not excluded for other benefits

''No period of service included wholly or partly in determining a person's right to, or the amount of, retired pay under this chapter may be excluded in determining his eligibility for any annuity, pension, or old-age benefit, under any other law, on account of civilian employment by the United States or otherwise, or in determining the amount payable under that law, if that service is otherwise properly credited under it.''.

RESEARCH GUIDE

Am Jur:

53A Am Jur 2d, Military and Civil Defense § 176.

INTERPRETIVE NOTES AND DECISIONS

1. Generally
2. Relationship with state laws

1. Generally

Congress intended, in enacting 10 USCS § 1336 (now § 12736), that periods of service used in computing retirement pay under 10 USCS §§ 1331 et seq (now §§ 12731 et seq.). for non-regular military service should not be excluded from retirement programs established by other laws solely because retiree would also receive military pension under §§ 1331 et seq (now §§ 12731 et seq.). Cantwell v County of San Mateo (1980, CA9 Cal) 631 F2d 631, cert den (1981) 450 US 998, 68 L Ed 2d 199, 101 S Ct 1703.

2. Relationship with state laws

Under Supremacy Clause of Federal Constitution (Art VI, cl 2), 10 USCS § 1336 (now § 12736) prevails over California statute which conflicts with it in that § 1336 (now § 12736) requires credit to be given for retired Reservist's active service in both military and county retirement plans and state statute denies such credit, thus interfering with Federal purpose; since Congressional power to enact § 1336 (now § 12736) is under Federal Constitution (Art I, § 8, cls 11, 12, 13) it infringes no Tenth Amendment rights of state. Cantwell v County of San Mateo (1980, CA9 Cal) 631 F2d 631, cert den (1981) 450 US 998, 68 L Ed 2d 199, 101 S Ct 1703.

§ 12737. Limitation on active duty

A member of the armed forces may not be ordered to active duty solely for the purpose of qualifying the member for retired pay under this chapter [10 USCS §§ 12831 et seq.].

(Aug. 10, 1956, ch 1041, § 1, 70A Stat. 104; Oct. 5, 1994, P. L. 103-337, Div A, Title XVI, Subtitle C, § 1662(j)(1), 108 Stat. 3003.)

HISTORY; ANCILLARY LAWS AND DIRECTIVES

Prior law and revision:

Revised Section	Source (USCS)	Source (Statutes at Large)
1337	10:1036h. 34:440p.	June 29, 1948, ch. 708, § 309, 62 Stat. 1090.

10:1036h (1st sentence) and 34:440p (1st sentence) are omitted as surplusage. The words ''member of the armed forces'' are substituted for the word ''person'', since only a member may be ''ordered to active duty''.

Amendments:

1994. Act Oct. 5, 1994 (effective 12/1/94 as provided by § 1691 of such Act, which appears as 10 USCS § 10001 note) transferred this section, enacted as part of Chapter 67, to Chapter 1223, and substituted the section heading and text for ones which read:

''§ 1337. Limitation on active duty

''No member of the armed forces may be ordered to active duty solely for the purpose of qualifying him for retired pay under this chapter.''.

RESEARCH GUIDE

Am Jur:

53A Am Jur 2d, Military and Civil Defense § 176.

§ 12738. Limitations on revocation of retired pay

(a) After a person is granted retired pay under this chapter [10 USCS §§ 12731 et seq.], or is notified in accordance with section 12731(d) of this title that the person has completed the years of service required for eligibility for retired pay under this chapter [10 USCS §§ 12731 et seq.], the person's eligibility for retired pay may not be denied or revoked on the basis of any error, miscalculation, misinformation, or administrative determination of years of service performed as required by section 12731(a)(2) of this title, unless it resulted directly from the fraud or misrepresentation of the person.

(b) The number of years of creditable service upon which retired pay is computed may be adjusted to correct any error, miscalculation, misinformation, or administrative determination and when such a correction is made the person is entitled to retired pay in accordance with the number of years of creditable service, as corrected, from the date the person is granted retired pay.

(Added Oct. 14, 1966, P. L. 89-652, § 2(1), 80 Stat. 902; July 1, 1986, P. L. 99-348, Title I, § 104(a), 100 Stat. 686; Oct. 5, 1994, P. L. 103-337, Div A, Title XVI, Subtitle C, § 1662(j)(1), 108 Stat. 3003.)

HISTORY; ANCILLARY LAWS AND DIRECTIVES

Amendments:

1986. Act July 1, 1986 redesignated this section, which formerly appeared as 10 USCS § 1406, as § 1338, and in this section, as so redesignated, designated the sentence beginning ''After a person . . .'' as subsec. (a), and in subsec. (a), as so designated, substituted ''this chapter'' for ''chapter 67 of this title'' in two places; and designated the sentence beginning ''The number of years . . .'' as subsec. (b).

1994. Act Oct. 5, 1994 (effective 12/1/94 as provided by § 1691 of such Act, which appears as 10 USCS § 10001 note) transferred this section, enacted as part of Chapter 67, to Chapter 1223, and substituted the section heading and text for ones which read:

''§ 1338. Limitations on revocation of retired pay

''(a) After a person has been granted retired pay under this chapter or has been notified in accordance with section 1331(d) of this title that he has completed the years of service required for eligibility for retired pay under this chapter, the person's eligibility for retired pay may not be denied or revoked on the basis of any error, miscalculation, misinformation, or administrative determination of years of service performed as required by section 1331(a)(2) of this title, unless it resulted directly from the fraud or misrepresentation of the person.

''(b) The number of years of creditable service upon which retired pay is computed may be adjusted to correct any error, miscalculation, misinformation, or administrative determination and when such a correction is made the person is entitled to retired pay in accordance with the number of years of creditable service, as corrected, from the date he is granted retired pay.''.

Other provisions:

Entitlement to retirement pay after October 14, 1966; conclusiveness. Act Oct. 14, 1966, P. L. 89-652, § 3, 80 Stat. 902, provides: ''Notwithstanding section 1406 [now 12738] of title 10, United States Code, as added by this Act—

''(1) the granting of retired pay to a person under chapter 67 [now 1223] of that title is conclusive as to that person's entitlement to such pay only if the payment of that retired pay is begun after the effective date of this Act; and

''(2) a notification that a person has completed the years of service required for eligibility for retired pay under chapter 67 [now 1223] of that title is conclusive as to the person's subsequent entitlement to such pay only if the notification is made after the effective date of this Act.''

RESEARCH GUIDE

Am Jur:

53A Am Jur 2d, Military and Civil Defense § 176.

§ 12739. Computation of retired pay

(a) The monthly retired pay of a person entitled to that pay under this chapter [10 USCS §§ 12731 et seq.] is the product of—

(1) the retired pay base for that person as computed under section 1406(b)(2) or 1407 of this title; and

(2) $2^1/_2$ percent of the years of service credited to that person under section 12733 of this title.

(b) The amount computed under subsection (a) may not exceed 75 percent of the retired pay base upon which the computation is based.

(c) Amounts computed under this section, if not a multiple of $1, shall be rounded down to the next lower multiple of $1.

(Added Oct. 5, 1994, P. L. 103-337, Div A, Title XVI, Subtitle C, § 1662(j)(1), 108 Stat. 3004.)

HISTORY; ANCILLARY LAWS AND DIRECTIVES

Effective date of section:

This section took effect on Dec. 1, 1994, pursuant to Act Oct. 5, 1994, P. L. 103-337, Div A, Title XVI, Subtitle F, § 1691, 108 Stat. 3026, which appears as 10 USCS 10001 note.

CROSS REFERENCES

This section is referred to in 10 USCS §§ 1209, 12731.

RESEARCH GUIDE

Am Jur:

53A Am Jur 2d, Military and Civil Defense § 176.

§ 12740. Eligibility: denial upon certain punitive discharges or dismissals

A person who—

(1) is convicted of an offense under the Uniform Code of Military Justice (chapter 47 of this title [10 USCS §§ 801 et seq.]) and whose sentence includes death; or

(2) is separated pursuant to sentence of a court-martial with a dishonorable discharge, a bad conduct discharge, or (in the case of an officer) a dismissal,

is not eligible for retired pay under this chapter [10 USCS §§ 12731 et seq.].

(Added Feb. 10, 1996, P. L. 104-106, Div A, Title VI, Subtitle D, § 632(a)(1), 110 Stat. 365.)

HISTORY; ANCILLARY LAWS AND DIRECTIVES

Other provisions:

Applicability of section. Act Feb. 10, 1996, P. L. 104-106, Div A, Title VI, Subtitle D, § 632(b), 110 Stat. 365, provides: ''Section 12740 of title 10, United States Code, as added by subsection (a), shall apply with respect to court-martial sentences adjudged after the date of the enactment of this Act.''.

CHAPTER 1225. RETIRED GRADE

HISTORY; ANCILLARY LAWS AND DIRECTIVES

Amendments:

1994. Act Oct. 5, 1994, P. L. 103-337, Div A, Title XVI, Subtitle C, § 1662(k)(1), 108 Stat. 3005 (effective 12/1/94 as provided by § 1691 of such Act, which appears as 10 USCS § 10001 note), added the chapter heading and analysis.

§ 12771. Reserve officers: grade on transfer to Retired Reserve

Unless entitled to a higher grade under another provision of law, a reserve commissioned officer, other than a commissioned warrant officer, who is transferred to the Retired Reserve is entitled to be placed on the retired list established by section 12774(a) of this title in the highest grade in which he served satisfactorily, as determined by the Secretary concerned and in accordance with section 1370(d), in the armed force in which he is serving on the date of transfer.

(Added Oct. 5, 1994, P. L. 103-337, Div A, Title XVI, Subtitle C, § 1662(k)(1), 108 Stat. 3005.)

HISTORY; ANCILLARY LAWS AND DIRECTIVES

Effective date of section:

This section took effect on Dec. 1, 1994, pursuant to Act Oct. 5, 1994, P. L. 103-337, Div A, Title XVI, Subtitle F, § 1691, 108 Stat. 3026, which appears as 10 USCS 10001 note.

CROSS REFERENCES

This section is referred to in 10 USCS § 12773.

INTERPRETIVE NOTES AND DECISIONS

Determination of what constitutes satisfactory service in highest grade, required to be made by Secretary of service involved before officer may be advanced on retired list to that rank, is matter left to discretion of Secretary who may validly decide to employ quantitative as well as qualitative factors in making such determination; once directive has been issued establishing criteria to be followed Secretary must abide by those criteria. O'Keefe v United States (1966) 174 Ct Cl 537.

Special Order providing that officer was to be retired in grade of major and that his reserve grade was that of lieutenant colonel could not be interpreted as promotion order evidencing that officer was promoted to higher grade while on active duty as basis for claim to entitlement to retirement pay of lieutenant colonel, as entitlement to pay in grade to which officer had been transferred under former 10 USCS § 1374(a) was precluded by provisions of former § 1374(d). Pfister v United States (1974) 203 Ct Cl 459.

§ 12772. Reserve commissioned officers who have served as Attending Physician to the Congress: grade on transfer to Retired Reserve

Unless entitled to a higher grade under another provision of law, a reserve commissioned officer who is transferred to the Retired Reserve after having served in the position of Attending Physician to the Congress is entitled to be placed on the retired list established by section 12774(a) of this title in the grade held by the officer while serving in that position.

(Added Oct. 5, 1994, P. L. 103-337, Div A, Title XVI, Subtitle C, § 1662(k)(1), 108 Stat. 3005.)

HISTORY; ANCILLARY LAWS AND DIRECTIVES

Effective date of section:

This section took effect on Dec. 1, 1994, pursuant to Act Oct. 5, 1994, P. L. 103-337, Div A, Title XVI, Subtitle F, § 1691, 108 Stat. 3026, which appears as 10 USCS 10001 note.

CROSS REFERENCES

This section is referred to in 10 USCS § 12773.

§ 12773. Limitation on accrual of increased pay or benefits

Unless otherwise provided by law, no person is entitled to increased pay or other benefits because of sections 12771 and 12772 of this title.

(Added Oct. 5, 1994, P. L. 103-337, Div A, Title XVI, Subtitle C, § 1662(k)(1), 108 Stat. 3005.)

HISTORY; ANCILLARY LAWS AND DIRECTIVES

Effective date of section:

This section took effect on Dec. 1, 1994, pursuant to Act Oct. 5, 1994, P. L. 103-337, Div A, Title XVI, Subtitle F, § 1691, 108 Stat. 3026, which appears as 10 USCS 10001 note.

§ 12774. Retired lists

(a) Under regulations prescribed by the Secretary concerned, there shall be maintained retired lists containing the names of the Reserves of the armed forces under the Secretary's jurisdiction who are in the Retired Reserve.

(b) The Secretary of the Navy shall maintain a United States Naval Reserve Retired List containing the names of members of the Naval Reserve and the Marine Corps Reserve entitled to retired pay.

(Added Oct. 5, 1994, P. L. 103-337, Div A, Title XVI, Subtitle C, § 1662(k)(1), 108 Stat. 3006.)

HISTORY; ANCILLARY LAWS AND DIRECTIVES

Effective date of section:

This section took effect on Dec. 1, 1994, pursuant to Act Oct. 5, 1994, P. L. 103-337, Div A, Title XVI, Subtitle F, § 1691, 108 Stat. 3026, which appears as 10 USCS 10001 note.

CROSS REFERENCES

Temporary disability retired lists, 10 USCS § 1376.

Army and Air Force retirement lists, 10 USCS §§ 3966, 8966.

Voluntary retirement after 30 years or 20 years of active service, retired pay, 10 USCS § 6327.

Grade of retired members recalled to active duty, 10 USCS § 6483.

Naval Reserve and Marine Corps Reserve; administration, 10 USCS §§ 10108, 10109.

This section is referred to in 10 USCS §§ 1431, 12771, 12772.

INTERPRETIVE NOTES AND DECISIONS

Naval reserve officer, who had been awarded Navy cross for combat service in World War I and was otherwise eligible, and who was transferred to United States naval reserve retired list pursuant to predecessor to former 10 USCS § 6017 with rank of captain but with retired pay based upon rank of commander, was entitled to three-fourths of his pay as commander. Yarnall v United States (1955) 131 Ct Cl 111, 129 F Supp 211.

PART III. PROMOTION AND RETENTION OF OFFICERS ON THE RESERVE ACTIVE-STATUS LIST

HISTORY; ANCILLARY LAWS AND DIRECTIVES

Amendments:

1994. Act Oct. 5, 1994, P. L. 103-337, Div A, Title XVI, Subtitle A, Part I, § 1611, 108 Stat. 2922 (effective as provided by § 1691 of such Act, which appears as 10 USCS § 10001 note), added the part heading and analysis.

CHAPTER 1401. APPLICABILITY AND RESERVE ACTIVE-STATUS LISTS

HISTORY; ANCILLARY LAWS AND DIRECTIVES

Amendments:

1994. Act Oct. 5, 1994, P. L. 103-337, Div A, Title XVI, Subtitle A, Part I, § 1611, 108 Stat. 2922 (effective as provided by § 1691 of such Act, which appears as 10 USCS § 10001 note), added the chapter heading and analysis.

§ 14001. Applicability of this part

This chapter and chapters 1403 through 1411 of this title [10 USCS §§ 14001 et seq. and §§ 14101 et seq.–14901 et seq.] apply, as appropriate, to all reserve officers of the Army, Navy, Air Force, and Marine Corps except warrant officers.

(Added Oct. 5, 1994, P. L. 103-337, Div A, Title XVI, Subtitle A, Part I, § 1611, 108 Stat. 2922.)

HISTORY; ANCILLARY LAWS AND DIRECTIVES

Effective date of section:

This section is effective Oct. 1, 1996, as provided by Act Oct. 5, 1994, P. L. 103-337, Div A, Title XVI, Subtitle F, § 1691(b)(1), 108 Stat. 3026, which appears as 10 USCS 10001 note.

Other provisions:

Effects of selection for promotion and failure of selection for Army and Air Force officers. Act Oct. 5, 1994, P. L. 103-337, Div A, Title XVI, Subtitle E, § 1682, 108 Stat. 3021, provides:

''(a) Promotions to fill vacancies. A reserve commissioned officer of the Army or Air Force (other than a commissioned warrant officer) who, on the day before the effective date of this title [effective Oct. 1, 1996, as provided by § 1691(b)(2) of Act Oct. 5, 1994, P. L. 103-337 (10 USCS § 10001 note)], is recommended for promotion to fill a vacancy in the Army Reserve or the Air Force Reserve under section 3383, 3384, 8372, or 8373 of title 10, United States Code, as in effect on the day before the effective date of this title [effective Oct. 1, 1996, as provided by § 1691(b)(2) of Act Oct. 5, 1994, P. L. 103-337 (10 USCS § 10001 note)], in the next higher reserve grade shall be considered to have been recommended for promotion to that grade by a vacancy promotion board under section 14101(a)(2) of title 10, United States Code, as added by this title.

''(b) Promotions other than to fill vacancies. A reserve officer of the Army or Air Force who, on the day before the effective date of this title [effective Oct. 1, 1996, as provided by § 1691(b)(2) of Act Oct. 5, 1994, P. L. 103-337 (10 USCS § 10001 note)], is recommended for promotion under section 3366, 3367, 3370, 3371, 8366, or 8371 of title 10, United States Code, as in effect on the day before the effective date of this title [effective Oct. 1, 1996, as provided by § 1691(b)(2) of Act Oct. 5, 1994, P. L. 103-337 (10 USCS § 10001 note)], to a reserve grade higher than the grade in which the officer is serving shall be considered to have been recommended for promotion by a mandatory promotion board convened under section 14101(a)(1) of title 10, United States Code, as added by this title.

''(c) Officers found qualified for promotion to first lieutenant. A reserve officer of the Army or Air Force who, on the effective date of this title [effective Oct. 1, 1996, as provided by § 1691(b)(2) of Act Oct. 5, 1994, P. L. 103-337 (10 USCS § 10001 note)], holds the grade of second lieutenant and has been found qualified for promotion to the grade of first lieutenant in accordance with section 3365, 3382, or 8365 of title 10, United States Code, as in effect on the day before the effective date of this title, shall be promoted to that grade on the date on which the officer would have been promoted under the provisions of chapter 337 or 837 of such title, as in effect on the day before the effective date of this title [effective Oct. 1, 1996, as provided by § 1691(b)(2) of Act Oct. 5, 1994, P. L. 103-337 (10 USCS § 10001 note)], unless sooner promoted under regulations prescribed by the Secretary of the Army or the Secretary of the Air Force under section 14308(b) of title 10, United States Code, as added by this title.

''(d) Officers once failed of selection. (1) A reserve officer of the Army in the grade of first lieutenant, captain, or major who, on the day before the effective date of this title [effective Oct. 1, 1996, as provided by § 1691(b)(2) of Act Oct. 5, 1994, P. L. 103-337 (10 USCS § 10001 note)], has been considered once but not recommended for promotion to the next higher reserve grade under section 3366 or 3367 of title 10, United States Code, or a reserve officer of the Air Force in the grade of first lieutenant, captain, or major who, on the day before the effective date of this title [effective Oct. 1, 1996, as provided by § 1691(b)(2) of Act Oct. 5, 1994, P. L. 103-337 (10 USCS § 10001 note)], is a deferred officer within the meaning of section 8368 of such title, shall be considered to have been considered once but not selected for promotion by a board convened under section 14101(a)(1) of title 10, United States Code, as added by this title. If the officer is later considered for promotion by a selection board convened under that section and is not selected for promotion (or is selected for promotion but declines to accept the promotion), the officer shall be considered for all purposes to have twice failed of selection for promotion.

''(2) In the case of a reserve officer of the Army or Air Force in an active status who, on the day before the effective date of this title [effective Oct. 1, 1996, as provided by § 1691(b)(2) of Act Oct. 5, 1994, P. L. 103-337 (10 USCS § 10001 note)], is in the grade of first lieutenant, captain, or major and whose name has been removed, under the provisions of section 3363(f) of title 10, United States Code, from a list of officers recommended for promotion or who has previously not been promoted because the President declined to appoint the officer in the next higher grade under section 8377 of such title as in effect on the day before the effective date of this title [effective Oct. 1, 1996, as provided by § 1691(b)(2) of Act Oct. 5, 1994, P. L. 103-337 (10 USCS § 10001 note)], or whose name was removed from a list of officers recommended for promotion to the next higher grade because the Senate did not consent to the officer's appointment, if the officer is later considered for promotion by a selection board convened by section 14101(a)(1) of title 10, United States Code, as added by this title, and (A) is not selected for promotion, (B) is selected for promotion but removed from the list of officers recommended or approved for promotion, or (C) is selected for promotion but declines to accept the promotion, the officer shall be considered for all purposes to have twice failed of selection for promotion.

''(e) Officers twice failed of selection. A reserve officer of the Army or Air Force in an active status who, on the day before the effective date of this title [effective Oct. 1, 1996, as provided by § 1691(b)(2) of Act Oct. 5, 1994, P. L. 103-337 (10 USCS § 10001 note)], is in the grade of first lieutenant, captain, or major and on that date is subject to be treated as prescribed in section 3846 or 8846 of title 10, United States Code, shall continue to be governed by that section as in effect on the day before the effective date of this title [effective Oct. 1, 1996, as provided by § 1691(b)(2) of Act Oct. 5, 1994, P. L. 103-337 (10 USCS § 10001 note)].

''(f) Officers with approved promotion declinations in effect. A reserve officer of the Army who, on the day before the effective date of this title [effective Oct. 1, 1996, as provided by § 1691(b)(2) of Act Oct. 5, 1994, P. L. 103-337 (10 USCS § 10001 note)], has declined a promotion under subsection (f) or (g) of section 3364 of title 10, United States Code, shall while carried on the reserve active status list be subject to the provisions of subsections (h), (i), and (j) of such section, as in effect on the day before the effective date of this title [effective Oct. 1, 1996, as provided by § 1691(b)(2) of Act Oct. 5, 1994, P. L. 103-337 (10 USCS § 10001 note)], except that the name of an officer to whom this section applies shall be placed on a promotion list under section 14308(a) of title 10, United States

Code (as added by this title), and, at the end of the approved period of declination, shall be considered to have failed of promotion if the officer again declines to accept the promotion.

''(g) Covered officers. This section applies to reserve officers of the Army and Air Force who—

''(1) on the day before the effective date of this title [effective Oct. 1, 1996, as provided by § 1691(b)(2) of Act Oct. 5, 1994, P. L. 103-337 (10 USCS § 10001 note)] are in an active status; and

''(2) on the effective date of this title [effective Oct. 1, 1996, as provided by § 1691(b)(2) of Act Oct. 5, 1994, P. L. 103-337 (10 USCS § 10001 note)] are subject to placement on the reserve active-status list of the Army or the Air Force.''.

Effects of selection for promotion and failure of selection for Navy and Marine Corps officers. Act Oct. 5, 1994, P. L. 103-337, Div A, Title XVI, Subtitle E, § 1683, 108 Stat. 3023, provides:

''(a) Recommendations for promotion. An officer covered by this section who, on the day before the effective date of this title [effective Oct. 1, 1996, as provided by § 1691(b)(2) of Act Oct. 5, 1994, P. L. 103-337 (10 USCS § 10001 note)], has been recommended for promotion to a reserve grade higher than the grade in which the officer is serving shall be considered to have been recommended for promotion to that grade under section 14101(a) of title 10, United States Code, as added by this title.

''(b) Failures of selection. An officer covered by this section who, on the day before the effective date of this title [effective Oct. 1, 1996, as provided by § 1691(b)(2) of Act Oct. 5, 1994, P. L. 103-337 (10 USCS § 10001 note)] is considered to have failed of selection for promotion one or more times under chapter 549 of title 10, United States Code, to a grade below captain, in the case of a reserve officer of the Navy, or to a grade below colonel, in the case of a reserve officer of the Marine Corps, shall be subject to chapters 1405 and 1407 of title 10, United States Code, as added by this title, as if such failure or failures had occurred under the provisions of those chapters.

''(c) Officers other than covered officers recommended for promotion. A reserve officer of the Navy or Marine Corps who on the day before the effective date of this title [effective Oct. 1, 1996, as provided by § 1691(b)(2) of Act Oct. 5, 1994, P. L. 103-337 (10 USCS § 10001 note)] (1) has been recommended for promotion in the approved report of a selection board convened under chapter 549 of title 10, United States Code, and (2) was on the active-duty list of the Navy or Marine Corps may be promoted under that chapter, as in effect on the day before the effective date of this title [effective Oct. 1, 1996, as provided by § 1691(b)(2) of Act Oct. 5, 1994, P. L. 103-337 (10 USCS § 10001 note)].

''(d) Officers found qualified for promotion to lieutenant (junior grade) or first lieutenant. A covered officer who, on the effective date of this title, holds the grade of second lieutenant and has been found qualified for promotion in accordance with section 5908 or 5910 of title 10, United States Code, as in effect on the day before the effective date of this title [effective Oct. 1, 1996, as provided by § 1691(b)(2) of Act Oct. 5, 1994, P. L. 103-337 (10 USCS § 10001 note)], shall be promoted on the date on which the officer would have been promoted under the provisions of chapter 549 of such title, as in effect on the day before the effective date of this title [effective Oct. 1, 1996, as provided by § 1691(b)(2) of Act Oct. 5, 1994, P. L. 103-337 (10 USCS § 10001 note)], unless sooner promoted under regulations prescribed by the Secretary of the Navy under section 14307(b) of such title, as added by this title.

"(e) Officers whose names have been omitted from a list furnished to a selection board. A covered officer whose name, as of the effective date of this title [effective Oct. 1, 1996, as provided by § 1691(b)(2) of Act Oct. 5, 1994, P. L. 103-337 (10 USCS § 10001 note)], had been omitted by administrative error from the list of officers furnished the most recent selection board to consider officers of the same grade and component, shall be considered by a special selection board established under section 14502 of title 10, United States Code, as added by this title. If the officer is selected for promotion by that board, the officer shall be promoted as specified in section 5904 of title 10, United States Code, as in effect on the day before the effective date of this title [effective Oct. 1, 1996, as provided by § 1691(b)(2) of Act Oct. 5, 1994, P. L. 103-337 (10 USCS § 10001 note)].

"(f) Covered officers. Except as provided in subsection (c), this section applies to any reserve officer of the Navy or Marine Corps who (1) before the effective date of this title [effective Oct. 1, 1996, as provided by § 1691(b)(2) of Act Oct. 5, 1994, P. L. 103-337 (10 USCS § 10001 note)] is in an active status, and (2) on the effective date of this title is subject to placement on the reserve active-status list of the Navy or Marine Corps.".

§ 14002. Reserve active-status lists: requirement for each armed force

(a) The Secretary of each military department shall maintain a single list, to be known as the reserve active-status list, for each armed force under the Secretary's jurisdiction. That list shall include the names of all reserve officers of that armed force who are in an active status other than those on an active-duty list described in section 620 of this title or warrant officers (including commissioned warrant officers).

(b) The reserve active-status list for the Army shall include officers in the Army Reserve and the Army National Guard of the United States. The reserve active-status list for the Air Force shall include officers in the Air Force Reserve and the Air National Guard of the United States. The Secretary of the Navy shall maintain separate lists for the Naval Reserve and the Marine Corps Reserve.

(Added Oct. 5, 1994, P. L. 103-337, Div A, Title XVI, Subtitle A, Part I, § 1611, 108 Stat. 2922.)

HISTORY; ANCILLARY LAWS AND DIRECTIVES

Effective date of section:

This section is effective Oct. 1, 1996, as provided by Act Oct. 5, 1994, P. L. 103-337, Div A, Title XVI, Subtitle F, § 1691(b)(1), 108 Stat. 3026, which appears as 10 USCS 10001 note.

Other provisions:

Establishment of reserve active-status list. Act Oct. 5, 1994, P. L. 103-337, Div A, Title XVI, Subtitle E, § 1686, 108 Stat. 3024, provides:

''(a) Six-month deadline. Not later than six months after the effective date of this title [effective Oct. 1, 1996, as provided by § 1691(b)(2) of Act Oct. 5, 1994, P. L. 103-337 (10 USCS § 10001 note)], the Secretary of the military department concerned shall ensure that—

''(1) all officers of the Army, Navy, Air Force, and Marine Corps who are required to be placed on the reserve active-status list of their Armed Force under section 14002 of title 10, United States Code, as added by this title, shall be placed on the list for their armed force and in their competitive category; and

''(2) the relative seniority of those officers on each such list shall be established.

''(b) Regulations. The Secretary concerned shall prescribe regulations for the establishment of relative seniority. The Secretary of the Army and the Secretary of the Air Force shall, in prescribing such regulations, provide for the consideration of both promotion service established under section 3360(b) or 8360(e) of title 10, United States Code, as in effect on the day before the effective date of this title [effective Oct. 1, 1996, as provided by § 1691(b)(2) of Act Oct. 5, 1994, P. L. 103-337 (10 USCS § 10001 note)], and total commissioned service established under section 3360(c) or 8366(e) of such title, as in effect on the day before the effective date of this title [effective Oct. 1, 1996, as provided by § 1691(b)(2) of Act Oct. 5, 1994, P. L. 103-337 (10 USCS § 10001 note)]. An officer placed on a reserve active-status list in accordance with this section shall be considered to have been on the list as of the effective date of this title [effective Oct. 1, 1996, as provided by § 1691(b)(2) of Act Oct. 5, 1994, P. L. 103-337 (10 USCS § 10001 note)].''.

Preservation of relative seniority under the initial establishment of the reserve active-status list. Act Oct. 5, 1994, P. L. 103-337, Div A, Title XVI, Subtitle E, § 1687, 108 Stat. 3025, provides: ''In order to maintain the relative seniority among reserve officers of the Army, Navy, Air Force, or Marine Corps as determined under section 1686 [note to this section], the Secretary of the military department concerned may, during the one-year period beginning on the effective date of this title [effective Oct. 1, 1996, as provided by § 1691(b)(2) of Act Oct. 5, 1994, P. L. 103-337 (10 USCS § 10001 note)], adjust the date of rank of any reserve officer of such Armed Force who was in an active status but not on the active-duty list on such effective date.''.

CROSS REFERENCES

This section is referred to in 10 USCS § 101.

§ 14003. Reserve active-status lists: position of officers on the list

(a) Position on list. Officers shall be carried on the reserve active-status list of the armed force of which they are members in the order of seniority of the grade in which they are serving in an active status. Officers serving in the same grade shall be carried in the order of their rank in that grade.

(b) Effect on position held by reason of temporary appointment or assignment. An officer whose position on the reserve active-status list results from service under a temporary appointment or in a grade held by reason of assignment to a position has, when that appointment or assignment ends, the grade and position on that list that the officer would have held if the officer had not received that appointment or assignment.

(Added Oct. 5, 1994, P. L. 103-337, Div A, Title XVI, Subtitle A, Part I, § 1611, 108 Stat. 2923; Feb. 10, 1996, P. L. 104-106, Div A, Title XV, § 1501(b)(22), 110 Stat. 497.)

HISTORY; ANCILLARY LAWS AND DIRECTIVES

Effective date of section:

This section is effective Oct. 1, 1996, as provided by Act Oct. 5, 1994, P. L. 103-337, Div A, Title XVI, Subtitle F, § 1691(b)(1), 108 Stat. 3026, which appears as 10 USCS 10001 note.

Amendments:

1996. Act Feb. 10, 1996 (effective as if included in Act Oct. 5, 1994, P. L. 103-337, as enacted on Oct. 5, 1994, as provided by § 1501(f)(3) of Act Feb. 10, 1996, which appears as 10 USCS § 113 note), in the section heading, inserted ''lists''.

§ 14004. Reserve active-status lists: eligibility for Reserve promotion

Except as otherwise provided by law, an officer must be on a reserve active-status list to be eligible under chapter 1405 of this title [10 USCS §§ 14301 et seq.] for consideration for selection for promotion or for promotion.

(Added Oct. 5, 1994, P. L. 103-337, Div A, Title XVI, Subtitle A, Part I, § 1611, 108 Stat. 2923.)

HISTORY; ANCILLARY LAWS AND DIRECTIVES

Effective date of section:

This section is effective Oct. 1, 1996, as provided by Act Oct. 5, 1994, P. L. 103-337, Div A, Title XVI, Subtitle F, § 1691(b)(1), 108 Stat. 3026, which appears as 10 USCS 10001 note.

§ 14005. Competitive categories

Each officer whose name appears on a reserve active-status list shall be placed in a competitive category. The competitive categories for each armed force shall be specified by the Secretary of the military department concerned under regulations prescribed by the Secretary of Defense. Officers in the same competitive category shall compete among themselves for promotion.

(Added Oct. 5, 1994, P. L. 103-337, Div A, Title XVI, Subtitle A, Part I, § 1611, 108 Stat. 2923.)

HISTORY; ANCILLARY LAWS AND DIRECTIVES

Effective date of section:

This section is effective Oct. 1, 1996, as provided by Act Oct. 5, 1994, P. L. 103-337, Div A, Title XVI, Subtitle F, § 1691(b)(1), 108 Stat. 3026, which appears as 10 USCS 10001 note.

§ 14006. Determination of years in grade

For the purpose of chapters 1403 through 1411 of this title [10 USCS §§ 14101 et seq.–14901 et seq.], an officer's years of service in a grade are computed from the officer's date of rank in grade as determined under section 741(d) of this title.

(Added Oct. 5, 1994, P. L. 103-337, Div A, Title XVI, Subtitle A, Part I, § 1611, 108 Stat. 2923.)

HISTORY; ANCILLARY LAWS AND DIRECTIVES

Effective date of section:

This section is effective Oct. 1, 1996, as provided by Act Oct. 5, 1994, P. L. 103-337, Div A, Title XVI, Subtitle F, § 1691(b)(1), 108 Stat. 3026, which appears as 10 USCS 10001 note.

CHAPTER 1403. SELECTION BOARDS

HISTORY; ANCILLARY LAWS AND DIRECTIVES

Amendments:

1994. Act Oct. 5, 1994, P. L. 103-337, Div A, Title XVI, Subtitle A, Part I, § 1611, 108 Stat. 2923 (effective as provided by § 1691, which appears as 10 USCS § 10001 note), added the chapter heading and analysis.

1996. Act Feb. 10, 1996, P. L. 104-106, Div A, Title XV, § 1501(b)(23), 110 Stat. 497 (effective as if included in Act Oct. 5, 1994, P. L. 103-337, as enacted on Oct. 5, 1994, as provided by § 1501(f)(3) of Act Feb. 10, 1996, which appears as 10 USCS § 113 note), amended the analysis of this chapter by substituting ''promotion board'' for ''selection board'' in item 14105.

§ 14101. Convening of selection boards

(a) Promotion boards. (1) Whenever the needs of the Army, Navy, Air Force, or Marine Corps require, the Secretary concerned shall convene a selection board to recommend for promotion to the next higher grade, under chapter 1405 of this title, officers on the reserve active-status list of that armed force in a permanent grade from first lieutenant through brigadier general or, in the case of the Naval Reserve, lieutenant (junior grade) through rear admiral (lower half). A selection board convened under this subsection shall be known as a ''promotion board''.

(2) A promotion board convened to recommend reserve officers of the Army or reserve officers of the Air Force for promotion (A) to fill a position vacancy under section 14315 of this title, or (B) to the grade of brigadier general or major general, shall be known as a ''vacancy promotion board''. Any other promotion board convened under this subsection shall be known as a ''mandatory promotion board''.

(b) Continuation boards. Whenever the needs of the Army, Navy, Air Force, or Marine Corps require, the Secretary concerned may convene a selection board to recommend officers of that armed force—

(1) for continuation on the reserve active-status list under section 14701 of this title;

(2) for selective early removal from the reserve active-status list under section 14704 of this title; or

(3) for selective early retirement under section 14705 of this title selection board convened under this subsection shall be known as a "continuation board".

(Added Oct. 5, 1994, P. L. 103-337, Div A, Title XVI, Subtitle A, Part I, § 1611, 108 Stat. 2924; Nov. 18, 1997, P. L. 105-85, Div A, Title V, Subtitle B, § 514(a), 111 Stat. 1732.)

HISTORY; ANCILLARY LAWS AND DIRECTIVES

Effective date of section:

This section became effective on Oct. 1, 1996, as provided by § 1691(b)(1) of Act Oct. 5, 1994, P. L. 103-337, which appears as 10 USCS § 10001 note.

Amendments:

1997. Act Nov. 18, 1997, in subsec. (a)(2), deleted "(except in the case of a board convened to consider officers as provided in section 14301(e) of this title)" following "general, shall".

CROSS REFERENCES

This section is referred to in 10 USCS §§ 14102–14110, 14301, 14304–14308, 14312, 14315–14317, 14501, 14502, 14701, 14704, 14705.

§ 14102. Selection boards: appointment and composition

(a) Appointment. Members of selection boards convened under section 14101 of this title shall be appointed by the Secretary of the military department concerned in accordance with this section. Promotion boards and special selection boards shall consist of five or more officers. Continuation boards shall consist of three or more officers. All of the officers of any such selection board shall be of the same armed force as the officers under consideration by the board.

(b) Composition. At least one-half of the members of such a selection board shall be reserve officers, to include at least one reserve officer from each reserve component from which officers are to be considered by the board. Each member of a selection board must hold a permanent grade higher than the grade of the officers under consideration by the board, and no member of a board may hold a grade below major or lieutenant commander.

(c) Representation of competitive categories. (1) Except as provided in paragraph (2), a selection board shall include at least one officer from each competitive category of officers to be considered by the board.

(2) A selection board need not include an officer from a competitive category to be considered by the board if there is no officer of that competitive category on the reserve active-status list or the active-duty list in a permanent grade higher than the grade of the officers to be considered by the board

and otherwise eligible to serve on the board. However, in such a case, the Secretary of the military department concerned, in his discretion, may appoint as a member of the board a retired officer of that competitive category who is in the same armed force as the officers under consideration by the board who holds a higher grade than the grade of the officers under consideration.

(d) Prohibition of service on consecutive promotion boards. No officer may be a member of two successive promotion boards convened under section 14101(a) of this title for the consideration of officers of the same competitive category and grade if the second of the two boards is to consider any officer who was considered and not recommended for promotion to the next higher grade by the first of the two boards.

(Added Oct. 5, 1994, P. L. 103-337, Div A, Title XVI, Subtitle A, Part I, § 1611, 108 Stat. 2924.)

HISTORY; ANCILLARY LAWS AND DIRECTIVES

Effective date of section:

This section is effective Oct. 1, 1996, as provided by Act Oct. 5, 1994, P. L. 103-337, Div A, Title XVI, Subtitle F, § 1691(b)(1), 108 Stat. 3026, which appears as 10 USCS 10001 note.

CROSS REFERENCES

This section is referred to in 10 USCS § 14502.

§ 14103. Oath of members

Each member of a selection board convened under section 14101 of this title shall take an oath to perform the duties of a member of the board without prejudice or partiality, having in view both the special fitness of officers and the efficiency of the member's armed force.

(Added Oct. 5, 1994, P. L. 103-337, Div A, Title XVI, Subtitle A, Part I, § 1611, 108 Stat. 2925.)

HISTORY; ANCILLARY LAWS AND DIRECTIVES

Effective date of section:

This section is effective Oct. 1, 1996, as provided by Act Oct. 5, 1994, P. L. 103-337, Div A, Title XVI, Subtitle F, § 1691(b)(1), 108 Stat. 3026, which appears as 10 USCS 10001 note.

CROSS REFERENCES

This section is referred to in 10 USCS § 14502.

§ 14104. Confidentiality of board proceedings

Except as otherwise authorized or required by law, the proceedings of a selection board convened under section 14101 of this title may not be disclosed to any person not a member of the board.

(Added Oct. 5, 1994, P. L. 103-337, Div A, Title XVI, Subtitle A, Part I, § 1611, 108 Stat. 2925.)

HISTORY; ANCILLARY LAWS AND DIRECTIVES

Effective date of section:

This section is effective Oct. 1, 1996, as provided by Act Oct. 5, 1994, P. L. 103-337, Div A, Title XVI, Subtitle F, § 1691(b)(1), 108 Stat. 3026, which appears as 10 USCS 10001 note.

CROSS REFERENCES

This section is referred to in 10 USCS § 14502.

§ 14105. Notice of convening of promotion board

(a) Required notice. At least 30 days before a promotion board is convened under section 14101(a) of this title to consider officers in a grade and competitive category for promotion to the next higher grade, the Secretary concerned shall either (1) notify in writing the officers eligible for consideration by the board for promotion regarding the convening of the board, or (2) issue a general written notice to the armed force concerned regarding the convening of the board.

(b) Content of notice. A notice under subsection (a) shall include the date on which the board is to convene and (except in the case of a vacancy promotion board) the name and date of rank of the junior officer, and of the senior officer, in the promotion zone as of the date of the notice.

(Added Oct. 5, 1994, P. L. 103-337, Div A, Title XVI, Subtitle A, Part I, § 1611, 108 Stat. 2925.)

HISTORY; ANCILLARY LAWS AND DIRECTIVES

Effective date of section:

This section is effective Oct. 1, 1996, as provided by Act Oct. 5, 1994, P. L. 103-337, Div A, Title XVI, Subtitle F, § 1691(b)(1), 108 Stat. 3026, which appears as 10 USCS 10001 note.

§ 14106. Communication with board by officers under consideration

Subject to regulations prescribed by the Secretary of the military department concerned, an officer eligible for consideration by a promotion board convened under section 14101(a) of this title who is in the promotion zone or above the promotion zone, or who is to be considered by a vacancy promotion board, may send a written communication to the board calling attention to any matter concerning the officer which the officer considers important to the officer's case. Any such communication shall be sent so as to arrive not later than the date on which the board convenes. The board shall give consideration to any timely communication under this section.

(Added Oct. 5, 1994, P. L. 103-337, Div A, Title XVI, Subtitle A, Part I, § 1611, 108 Stat. 2925.)

HISTORY; ANCILLARY LAWS AND DIRECTIVES

Effective date of section:

This section is effective Oct. 1, 1996, as provided by Act Oct. 5, 1994, P. L. 103-337, Div A, Title XVI, Subtitle F, § 1691(b)(1), 108 Stat. 3026, which appears as 10 USCS 10001 note.

CROSS REFERENCES

This section is referred to in 10 USCS § 14107.

§ 14107. Information furnished by the Secretary concerned to promotion boards

(a) Integrity of the promotion selection board process. (1) The Secretary of Defense shall prescribe regulations governing information furnished to selection boards convened under section 14101(a) of this title. Those regulations shall apply uniformly among the military departments. Any regulations prescribed by the Secretary of a military department to supplement those regulations may not take effect without the approval of the Secretary of Defense in writing.

(2) No information concerning a particular eligible officer may be furnished to a selection board except for the following:

(A) Information that is in the officer's official military personnel file and that is provided to the selection board in accordance with the regulations prescribed by the Secretary of Defense pursuant to paragraph (1).

(B) Other information that is determined by the Secretary of the military department concerned, after review by that Secretary in accordance with standards and procedures set out in the regulations prescribed by the Secretary of Defense pursuant to paragraph (1), to be substantiated, relevant information that could reasonably and materially affect the deliberations of the promotion board.

(C) Subject to such limitations as may be prescribed in those regulations, information communicated to the board by the officer in accordance with this section, section 14106 of this title (including any comment on information referred to in subparagraph (A) regarding that officer), or other applicable law.

(D) A factual summary of the information described in subparagraphs (A), (B), and (C) that, in accordance with the regulations prescribed pursuant to paragraph (1) is prepared by administrative personnel for the purpose of facilitating the work of the selection board.

(3) Information provided to a promotion board in accordance with paragraph (2) shall be made available to all members of the board and shall be made a part of the record of the board. Communication of such information shall be in a written form or in the form of an audio or video recording. If a communication is in the form of an audio or video recording, a written transcription of the recording shall also be made a part of the record of the promotion board.

(4) Paragraphs (2) and (3) do not apply to the furnishing of appropriate administrative processing information to the promotion board by an administrative staff designated to assist the board, but only to the extent that oral communications are necessary to facilitate the work of the board.

(5) Information furnished to a promotion board that is described in subparagraph (B), (C), or (D) of paragraph (2) may not be furnished to a later promotion board unless—

(A) the information has been properly placed in the official military personnel file of the officer concerned; or

(B) the information is provided to the later selection board in accordance with paragraph (2).

(6)(A) Before information described in paragraph (2)(B) regarding an eligible officer is furnished to a selection board, the Secretary of the military department concerned shall ensure—

(i) that such information is made available to such officer; and

(ii) that the officer is afforded a reasonable opportunity to submit comments on that information to the promotion board.

(B) If an officer cannot be given access to the information referred to in subparagraph (A) because of its classification status, the officer shall, to the maximum extent practicable, be furnished an appropriate summary of the information.

(b) Information to be furnished. The Secretary of the military department concerned shall furnish to a promotion board convened under section 14101(a) of this title the following:

(1) In the case of a mandatory promotion board, the maximum number (as determined in accordance with section 14307 of this title) of officers in each competitive category under consideration that the board is authorized to recommend for promotion to the next higher grade.

(2) The name of each officer in each competitive category under consideration who is to be considered by the board for promotion.

(3) The pertinent records (as determined by the Secretary) of each officer whose name is furnished to the board.

(4) Information or guidelines relating to the needs of the armed force concerned for officers having particular skills, including (except in the case of a vacancy promotion board) guidelines or information relating to either a minimum number or a maximum number of officers with particular skills within a competitive category.

(5) Such other information or guidelines as the Secretary concerned may determine to be necessary to enable the board to perform its functions.

(c) Limitation on modifying furnished information. Information or guidelines furnished to a selection board under subsection (a) may not be modified, withdrawn, or supplemented after the board submits its report to the Secretary of the military department concerned pursuant to section 14109(a) of this title. However, in the case of a report returned to a board pursuant to section 14110(a) of this title for further proceedings because of a determination by the Secretary of the military department concerned that the board acted contrary to law, regulation, or guidelines, the Secretary may modify, withdraw, or supplement such information or guidelines as part of a written explanation to the board as provided in that section.

(d) Officers in health-professions competitive categories. The Secretary of each military department, under uniform regulations prescribed by the Secretary of Defense, shall include in guidelines furnished to a promotion board convened under section 14101(a) of this title that is considering officers in a health-professions competitive category for promotion to a grade below colonel or, in the case of officers of the Naval Reserve, captain, a direction that the board give consideration to an officer's clinical proficiency and skill as a health professional to at least as great an extent as the board gives to the officer's administrative and management skills.

(Added Oct. 5, 1994, P. L. 103-337, Div A, Title XVI, Subtitle A, Part I, § 1611, 108 Stat. 2926.)

HISTORY; ANCILLARY LAWS AND DIRECTIVES

Effective date of section:

This section is effective Oct. 1, 1996, as provided by Act Oct. 5, 1994, P. L. 103-337, Div A, Title XVI, Subtitle F, § 1691(b)(1), 108 Stat. 3026, which appears as 10 USCS 10001 note.

CROSS REFERENCES

This section is referred to in 10 USCS §§ 14108, 14109, 14110.

§ 14108. Recommendations by promotion boards

(a) Recommendation of best qualified officers . A promotion board convened under section 14101(a) of this title shall recommend for promotion to the next higher grade those officers considered by the board whom the board considers best qualified for promotion within each competitive category considered by the board or, in the case of a vacancy promotion board, among those officers considered to fill a vacancy. In determining those officers who are best qualified for promotion, the board shall give due consideration to the needs of the armed force concerned for officers with particular skills (as noted in the guidelines or information furnished the board under section 14107 of this title).

(b) Majority required. A promotion board convened under section 14101(a) of this title may not recommend an officer for promotion unless—

(1) the officer receives the recommendation of a majority of the members of the board; and

(2) a majority of the members of the board finds that the officer is fully qualified for promotion.

(c) Board recommendation required for promotion. Except as otherwise provided by law, an officer on the reserve active-status list may not be promoted to a higher grade under chapter 1405 of this title [10 USCS §§ 14301 et seq.] unless the officer is considered and recommended for promotion to that grade by a promotion board convened under section 14101(a) of this title (or by a special selection board convened under section 14502 of this title).

(d) Disclosure of board recommendations. The recommendations of a promotion board may be disclosed only in accordance with regulations prescribed by the Secretary of Defense. Those recommendations may not be disclosed to a person not a member of the board (or a member of the administrative staff designated by the Secretary concerned to assist the board) until the written report of the recommendations of the board, required by section 14109 of this title, is signed by each member of the board.

(e) Prohibition of coercion and unauthorized influence of actions of board members. The Secretary convening a promotion board under section 14101(a) of this title, and an officer or other official exercising authority over any member of a selection board, may not—

(1) censure, reprimand, or admonish the selection board or any member of the board with respect to the recommendations of the board or the exercise of any lawful function within the authorized discretion of the board; or

(2) attempt to coerce or, by any unauthorized means, influence any action of a promotion board or any member of a promotion board in the formulation of the board's recommendations.

(Added Oct. 5, 1994, P. L. 103-337, Div A, Title XVI, Subtitle A, Part I, § 1611, 108 Stat. 2928.)

HISTORY; ANCILLARY LAWS AND DIRECTIVES

Effective date of section:

This section is effective Oct. 1, 1996, as provided by Act Oct. 5, 1994, P. L. 103-337, Div A, Title XVI, Subtitle F, § 1691(b)(1), 108 Stat. 3026, which appears as 10 USCS 10001 note.

§ 14109. Reports of promotion boards: in general

(a) Report of officers recommended for promotion. Each promotion board convened under section 14101(a) of this title shall submit to the Secretary of the military department concerned a report in writing containing a list of the names of the officers recommended by the board for promotion. The report shall be signed by each member of the board.

(b) Certification. Each report under subsection (a) shall include a certification—

(1) that the board has carefully considered the record of each officer whose name was furnished to the board; and

(2) that, in the case of a promotion board convened under section 14101(a) of this title, in the opinion of a majority of the members of the board, the officers recommended for promotion by the board are best qualified for promotion to meet the needs of the armed force concerned (as noted in the guidelines or information furnished the board under section 14107 of this title) among those officers whose names were furnished to the selection board.

(c) Show-cause recommendations. (1) A promotion board convened under section 14101(a) of this title shall include in its report to the Secretary concerned the name of any reserve officer before it for consideration for promotion whose record, in the opinion of a majority of the members of the board, indicates that the officer should be required to show cause for retention in an active status.

(2) If such a report names an officer as having a record which indicates that the officer should be required to show cause for retention, the Secretary concerned may provide for the review of the record of that officer as provided under regulations prescribed under section 14902 of this title.

(Added Oct. 5, 1994, P. L. 103-337, Div A, Title XVI, Subtitle A, Part I, § 1611, 108 Stat. 2928.)

HISTORY; ANCILLARY LAWS AND DIRECTIVES

Effective date of section:

This section is effective Oct. 1, 1996, as provided by Act Oct. 5, 1994, P. L. 103-337, Div A, Title XVI, Subtitle F, § 1691(b)(1), 108 Stat. 3026, which appears as 10 USCS 10001 note.

CROSS REFERENCES

This section is referred to in 10 USCS §§ 14107, 14108, 14110, 14502.

§ 14110. Reports of promotion boards: review by Secretary

(a) Review of report. Upon receipt of the report of a promotion board submitted under section 14109(a) of this title, the Secretary of the military department concerned shall review the report to determine whether the board has acted contrary to law or regulation or to guidelines furnished the board under section 14107(a) of this title. Following that review, unless the Secretary concerned makes a determination as described in subsection (b), the Secretary shall submit the report as required by section 14111 of this title.

(b) Return of report for further proceedings. If, on the basis of a review of the report under subsection (a), the Secretary of the military department concerned determines that the board acted contrary to law or regulation or to guidelines furnished the board under section 14107(a) of this title, the Secretary shall return the report, together with a written explanation of the basis for such determination, to the board for further proceedings. Upon receipt of a report returned by the Secretary concerned under this subsection, the selection board (or a subsequent selection board convened under section 14101(a) of this title for the same grade and competitive category) shall conduct such proceedings as may be necessary in order to revise the report to be consistent with law, regulation, and such guidelines and shall resubmit the report, as revised, to the Secretary in accordance with section 14109 of this title.

(Added Oct. 5, 1994, P. L. 103-337, Div A, Title XVI, Subtitle A, Part I, § 1611, 108 Stat. 2929.)

HISTORY; ANCILLARY LAWS AND DIRECTIVES

Effective date of section:

This section is effective Oct. 1, 1996, as provided by Act Oct. 5, 1994, P. L. 103-337, Div A, Title XVI, Subtitle F, § 1691(b)(1), 108 Stat. 3026, which appears as 10 USCS 10001 note.

CROSS REFERENCES

This section is referred to in 10 USCS §§ 14107, 14111, 14502.

§ 14111. Reports of selection boards: transmittal to President

(a) Transmittal to President. The Secretary concerned, after final review of the report of a selection board under section 14110 of this title, shall submit the report with the Secretary's recommendations, to the Secretary of Defense for transmittal by the Secretary to the President for approval or disapproval. If the authority of the President to approve or disapprove the report of a promotion board is delegated to the Secretary of Defense, that authority may not be redelegated except to an official in the Office of the Secretary of Defense.

(b) Removal of name from board report. The name of an officer recommended for promotion by a selection board may be removed from the report of the selection board only by the President.

(c) Recommendations for removal of selected officers from report. If the Secretary of a military department or the Secretary of Defense makes a recommendation under this section that the name of an officer be removed from the report of a promotion board and the recommendation is accompanied by information that was not presented to that promotion board, that information shall be made available to that officer. The officer shall then be afforded a reasonable opportunity to submit comments on that information to the officials making the recommendation and the officials reviewing the recommendation. If an eligible officer cannot be given access to such information because of its classification status, the officer shall, to the maximum extent practicable, be provided with an appropriate summary of the information.

(Added Oct. 5, 1994, P. L. 103-337, Div A, Title XVI, Subtitle A, Part I, § 1611, 108 Stat. 2929.)

HISTORY; ANCILLARY LAWS AND DIRECTIVES

Effective date of section:

This section is effective Oct. 1, 1996, as provided by Act Oct. 5, 1994, P. L. 103-337, Div A, Title XVI, Subtitle F, § 1691(b)(1), 108 Stat. 3026, which appears as 10 USCS 10001 note.

CROSS REFERENCES

This section is referred to in 10 USCS §§ 14110, 14501, 14502.

§ 14112. Dissemination of names of officers selected

Upon approval by the President of the report of a promotion board, the names of the officers recommended for promotion by the promotion board (other than any name removed by the President) may be disseminated to the armed force concerned. If those names have not been sooner disseminated, those names (other than the name of any officer whose promotion the Senate failed to confirm) shall be promptly disseminated to the armed force concerned upon confirmation by the Senate.

(Added Oct. 5, 1994, P. L. 103-337, Div A, Title XVI, Subtitle A, Part I, § 1611, 108 Stat. 2930.)

HISTORY; ANCILLARY LAWS AND DIRECTIVES

Effective date of section:

This section is effective Oct. 1, 1996, as provided by Act Oct. 5, 1994, P. L. 103-337, Div A, Title XVI, Subtitle F, § 1691(b)(1), 108 Stat. 3026, which appears as 10 USCS 10001 note.

CHAPTER 1405. PROMOTIONS

HISTORY; ANCILLARY LAWS AND DIRECTIVES

Amendments:

1994. Act Oct. 5, 1994, P. L. 103-337, Div A, Title XVI, Subtitle A, Part I, § 1611, 108 Stat. 2930 (effective as provided by § 1691 of such Act, which appears as 10 USCS § 10001 note), added the chapter heading and analysis.

1996. Act Feb. 10, 1996, P. L. 104-106, Div A, Title XV, § 1501(b)(24), 110 Stat. 497 (effective as if included in Act Oct. 5, 1994, P. L. 103-337, as enacted on Oct. 5, 1994, as provided by § 1501(f)(3) of Act Feb. 10, 1996, which appears as 10 USCS § 113 note), amended the analysis of this chapter by substituting ''Number'' for ''Numbers'' in item 14307, by substituting the semicolon for a colon in item 14309, and by capitalizing ''State'' in item 14314.

§ 14301. Eligibility for consideration for promotion: general rules

(a) One-year rule. An officer is eligible under this chapter [10 USCS §§ 14301 et seq.] for consideration for promotion by a promotion board convened under section 14101(a) of this title only if—

(1) the officer is on the reserve active-status list of the Army, Navy, Air Force, or Marine Corps; and

(2) during the one-year period ending on the date of the convening of the promotion board the officer has continuously performed service on either the reserve active-status list or the active-duty list (or on a combination of both lists).

(b) Requirement for consideration of all officers in and above the zone. Whenever a promotion board (other than a vacancy promotion board) is convened under section 14101(a) of this title for consideration of officers in a competitive category who are eligible under this chapter [10 USCS §§ 14301 et seq.] for consideration for promotion to the next higher grade, each officer in the promotion zone, and each officer above the promotion zone, for that grade and competitive category shall be considered for promotion.

(c) Previously selected officers not eligible to be considered. A promotion board convened under section 14101(a) of this title may not consider for promotion to the next higher grade any of the following officers:

(1) An officer whose name is on a promotion list for that grade as a result of recommendation for promotion to that grade by an earlier selection board convened under that section or section 14502 of this title or under chapter 36 of this title [10 USCS §§ 611 et seq.].

(2) An officer who is recommended for promotion to that grade in the report of an earlier selection board convened under a provision referred to in paragraph (1), in the case of such a report that has not yet been approved by the President.

(3) An officer who has been approved for Federal recognition by a board convened under section 307 of title 32 and nominated by the President for promotion to that grade as a reserve of the Army or of the Air Force as the case may be, if that nomination is pending before the Senate.

(4) An officer who has been nominated by the President for promotion to that grade under any other provision of law, if that nomination is pending before the Senate.

(d) Officers below the zone. The Secretary of the military department concerned may, by regulation, prescribe procedures to limit the officers to be considered by a selection board from below the promotion zone to those officers who are determined to be exceptionally well qualified for promotion. The regulations shall include criteria for determining which officers below the promotion zone are exceptionally well qualified for promotion.

(e) Certain reserve officers of the Air Force. A reserve officer of the Air Force who (1) is in the Air National Guard of the United States and holds the grade of lieutenant colonel, colonel, or brigadier general, or (2) is in the Air Force Reserve and holds the grade of colonel or brigadier general, is not eligible for consideration for promotion by a mandatory promotion board convened under section 14101(a) of this title.

(f) Nonconsideration of officers scheduled for removal from reserve active-status list. The Secretary of the military department concerned may, by regulation, provide for the exclusion from consideration for promotion by a promotion board of any officer otherwise eligible to be considered by the board who has an established date for removal from the reserve active-status list that is not more than 90 days after the date on which the selection board for which the officer would otherwise be eligible is to be convened.

(Added Oct. 5, 1994, P. L. 103-337, Div A, Title XVI, Subtitle A, Part I, § 1611, 108 Stat. 2931; Nov. 18, 1997, P. L. 105-85, Div A, Title V, Subtitle A, § 503(b), (c), Subtitle B, § 514(b), 111 Stat. 1725, 1732.)

HISTORY; ANCILLARY LAWS AND DIRECTIVES

Effective date of section:

This section became effective on Oct. 1, 1996, as provided by § 1691(b)(1) of Act Oct. 5, 1994, P. L. 103-337, which appears as 10 USCS 10001 note.

Amendments:

1997. Act Nov. 18, 1997 (effective and applicable as provided by § 503(d) of such Act, which appears as 10 USCS § 619 note), in subsec. (c), in the introductory matter, substituted ''grade any of the following officers:'' for ''grade—'', in para. (1), substituted ''An officer'' for ''an officer'' and substituted the concluding period for a semicolon, in para. (2), substituted ''An officer'' for ''an officer'' and substituted the concluding period for ''; or'' and, in para. (3), substituted ''An officer'' for ''an officer'', redesignated paras. (2) and (3) as paras. (3) and (4), respectively, added new para. (2), and, in paras. (3) and (4) as redesignated, substituted ''that grade'' for ''the next higher grade'' and inserted '', if that nomination is pending before the Senate,''.

Such Act further deleted subsec. (e), which read: ''(e) Reserve officers of the Army; consideration for brigadier general and major general. In the case of officers of the Army, if the Secretary of the Army determines that vacancies are authorized or anticipated in the reserve grades of major general or brigadier general for officers who are on the reserve active-status list and who are not assigned to units organized to serve as a unit and the Secretary convenes a mandatory promotion board under section 14101(a) of this title to consider officers for promotion to fill such vacancies, the Secretary may limit the officers to be considered by that board to those determined to be exceptionally well qualified for promotion under such criteria and procedures as the Secretary may by regulation prescribe.''; and redesignated subsecs. (f) and (g) as subsecs. (e) and (f), respectively.

CROSS REFERENCES

This section is referred to in 10 USCS §§ 14101, 14304.

§ 14302. Promotion zones

(a) Promotion zones generally. For purposes of this chapter [10 USCS §§ 14301 et seq.], a promotion zone is an eligibility category for the consideration of officers by a mandatory promotion board. A promotion zone consists of those officers on the reserve active-status list who are in the same grade and competitive category and who meet the requirements of both paragraphs (1) and (2) or the requirements of paragraph (3), as follows:

(1)(A) In the case of officers in grades below colonel, for reserve officers of the Army, Air Force, and Marine Corps, or captain, for officers of the Naval Reserve, those who have neither (i) failed of selection for promotion to the next higher grade, nor (ii) been removed from a list of officers recommended for promotion to that grade.

(B) In the case of officers in the grade of colonel or brigadier general, for reserve officers of the Army and Marine Corps, or in the grade of captain or rear admiral (lower half), for reserve officers of the Navy, those who have neither (i) been recommended for promotion to the next higher grade when considered in the promotion zone, nor (ii) been removed from a list of officers recommended for promotion to that grade.

(2) Those officers who are senior to the officer designated by the Secretary of the military department concerned to be the junior officer in the promotion zone eligible for consideration for promotion to the next higher grade and the officer so designated.

(3) Those officers who—

(A) have been selected from below the zone for promotion to the next higher grade or by a vacancy promotion board, but whose names were removed from the list of officers recommended for promotion to that next higher grade resulting from that selection;

(B) have not failed of selection for promotion to that next higher grade; and

(C) are senior to the officer designated by the Secretary of the military department concerned to be the junior officer in the promotion zone eligible for consideration for promotion to that next higher grade and the officer so designated.

(b) Officers above the zone. Officers on the reserve active-status list are considered to be above the promotion zone for a grade and competitive category if they—

(1) are eligible for consideration for promotion to the next higher grade;

(2) are in the same grade as those officers in the promotion zone for that competitive category; and

(3) are senior to the senior officer in the promotion zone for that competitive category.

(c) Officers below the zone. Officers on the reserve active-status list are considered to be below the promotion zone for a grade and competitive category if they—

(1) are eligible for consideration for promotion to the next higher grade;

(2) are in the same grade as those officers in the promotion zone for that competitive category; and

(3) are junior to the junior officer in the promotion zone for that competitive category.

(Added Oct. 5, 1994, P. L. 103-337, Div A, Title XVI, Subtitle A, Part I, § 1611, 108 Stat. 2932.)

HISTORY; ANCILLARY LAWS AND DIRECTIVES

Effective date of section:

This section is effective Oct. 1, 1996, as provided by Act Oct. 5, 1994, P. L. 103-337, Div A, Title XVI, Subtitle F, § 1691(b)(1), 108 Stat. 3026, which appears as 10 USCS 10001 note.

§ 14303. Eligibility for consideration for promotion: minimum years of service in grade

(a) Officers in pay grades O-1 and O-2. An officer who is on the reserve active-status list of the Army, Navy, Air Force, or Marine Corps and holds a permanent appointment in the grade of second lieutenant or first lieutenant as a reserve officer of the Army, Air Force, or Marine Corps, or in the grade of ensign or lieutenant (junior grade) as a reserve officer of the Navy, may not be promoted to the next higher grade, or granted Federal recognition in that grade, until the officer has completed the following years of service in grade:

(1) Eighteen months, in the case of an officer holding a permanent appointment in the grade of second lieutenant or ensign.

(2) Two years, in the case of an officer holding a permanent appointment in the grade of first lieutenant or lieutenant (junior grade).

(b) Officers in pay grades O-3 and above. Subject to subsection (d), an officer who is on the reserve active-status list of the Army, Air Force, or Marine Corps and holds a permanent appointment in a grade above first lieutenant, or who is on the reserve active-status list of the Navy in a grade above lieutenant (junior grade), may not be considered for selection for promotion to the next higher grade, or examined for Federal recognition in the next higher grade, until the officer has completed the following years of service in grade:

(1) Three years, in the case of an officer of the Army, Air Force, or Marine Corps holding a permanent appointment in the grade of captain, major, or lieutenant colonel or in the case of a reserve officer of the Navy holding a permanent appointment in the grade of lieutenant, lieutenant commander, or commander.

(2) One year, in the case of an officer of the Army, Air Force, or Marine Corps holding a permanent appointment in the grade of colonel or brigadier general or in the case of a reserve officer of the Navy holding a permanent appointment in the grade of captain or rear admiral (lower half).

This subsection does not apply to an adjutant general or assistant adjutant general of a State or to an appointment in a higher grade which is based upon a specific provision of law.

(c) Authority to lengthen minimum period in grade. The Secretary concerned may prescribe a period of service in grade for eligibility for promotion, in the case of officers to whom subsection (a) applies, or for eligibility for consideration for promotion, in the case of officers to whom subsection (b) applies, that is longer than the applicable period specified in that subsection.

(d) Waivers to ensure two below-the-zone considerations. Subject to section 14307(b) of this title, the Secretary of the military department concerned may waive subsection (b) to the extent necessary to ensure that officers described in paragraph (1) of that subsection have at least two opportunities for consideration for promotion to the next higher grade as officers below the promotion zone.

(Added Oct. 5, 1994, P. L. 103-337, Div A, Title XVI, Subtitle A, Part I, § 1611, 108 Stat. 2933.)

HISTORY; ANCILLARY LAWS AND DIRECTIVES

Effective date of section:

This section is effective Oct. 1, 1996, as provided by Act Oct. 5, 1994, P. L. 103-337, Div A, Title XVI, Subtitle F, § 1691(b)(1), 108 Stat. 3026, which appears as 10 USCS 10001 note.

CROSS REFERENCES

This section is referred to in 10 USCS §§ 14305, 14315; 32 USCS §§ 309, 310.

§ 14304. Eligibility for consideration for promotion: maximum years of service in grade

(a) Consideration for promotion within specified times. (1) Officers described in paragraph (3) shall be placed in the promotion zone for that officer's grade and competitive category, and shall be considered for promotion to the next higher grade by a promotion board convened under section 14101(a) of this title, far enough in advance of completing the years of service in grade specified in the following table so that, if the officer is recommended for promotion, the promotion may be effective on or before the date on which the officer will complete those years of service.

Current Grade	Maximum years of service in grade
First lieutenant or Lieutenant (junior grade)	5 years
Captain or Navy Lieutenant	7 years
Major or Lieutenant commander	7 years

(2) Paragraph (1) is subject to subsections (a), (b), and (c) of section 14301 of this title and applies without regard to vacancies.

(3) Paragraph (1) applies to an officer who is on the reserve active-status list of the Army, Navy, Air Force, or Marine Corps and who holds a permanent appointment in the grade of first lieutenant, captain, or major as a reserve of the Army, Air Force, or Marine Corps, or to an officer on the reserve active-status list of the Navy in the grade of lieutenant (junior grade), lieutenant, or lieutenant commander as a reserve of the Navy, and who, while holding that appointment, has not been considered by a selection board convened under section 14101(a) or 14502 of this title for promotion to the next higher grade.

(b) Promotion date. An officer holding a permanent grade specified in the table in subsection (a) who is recommended for promotion to the next higher grade by a selection board the first time the officer is considered for promotion while in or above the promotion zone and who is placed on an approved promotion list established under section 14308(a) of this title shall (if not promoted sooner or removed from that list by the President or by reason of declination) be promoted, without regard to the existence of a vacancy, on the date on which the officer completes the maximum years of service in grade specified in subsection (a). The preceding sentence is subject to the limitations of section 12011 of this title.

(c) Waiver authority for Navy and Marine Corps running mate system. If the Secretary of the Navy establishes promotion zones for officers on the reserve active-status list of the Navy or the Marine Corps Reserve in accordance with a running mate system under section 14306 of this title, the Secretary may waive the requirements of subsection (a) to the extent the Secretary considers necessary in any case in which the years of service for promotion, or for consideration for promotion, within those zones will exceed the maximum years of service in grade specified in subsection (a).

(Added Oct. 5, 1994, P. L. 103-337, Div A, Title XVI, Subtitle A, Part I, § 1611, 108 Stat. 2934.)

HISTORY; ANCILLARY LAWS AND DIRECTIVES

Effective date of section:

This section is effective Oct. 1, 1996, as provided by Act Oct. 5, 1994, P. L. 103-337, Div A, Title XVI, Subtitle F, § 1691(b)(1), 108 Stat. 3026, which appears as 10 USCS 10001 note.

Other provisions:

Minimum service qualifications for promotion. Act Oct. 5, 1994, P. L. 103-337, Div A, Title XVI, Subtitle E, § 1685, 108 Stat. 3024, provides: "During the five-year period beginning on the effective date of this title [effective Oct. 1, 1996, as provided by § 1691(b)(2) of Act Oct. 5, 1994, P. L. 103-337 (10 USCS § 10001 note)], the Secretary of the Army and the Secretary of the Air Force may waive the provisions of section 14304 of title 10, United States Code, as added by this title. The Secretary may, in addition, during any period in which such a waiver is in effect, establish minimum periods of total years of commissioned service an officer must have served to be eligible for consideration for promotion to the grade of captain, major, or lieutenant colonel by boards convened under section 14101(a) of title 10, United States Code, as added by this title.".

CROSS REFERENCES

This section is referred to in 10 USCS §§ 12009, 14305.

§ 14305. Establishment of promotion zones: mandatory consideration for promotion

(a) Establishment of zone. Before convening a mandatory promotion board under section 14101(a) of this title, the Secretary of the military department concerned shall establish a promotion zone for officers serving in each grade and competitive category to be considered by the board.

(b) Number in the zone. The Secretary concerned shall determine the number of officers in the promotion zone for officers serving in any grade and competitive category from among officers who are eligible for promotion in that grade and competitive category under the provisions of sections 14303 and 14304 of this title and who are otherwise eligible for promotion.

(c) Factors in determining number in the zone. The Secretary's determination under subsection (b) shall be made on the basis of an estimate of the fol lowing:

(1) The number of officers needed in that competitive category in the next higher grade in each of the next five years.

(2) In the case of a promotion zone for officers to be promoted to a grade to which the maximum years of in grade criteria established in section 14304 of this title apply, the number of officers in that competitive category who are required to be considered for selection for promotion to the next higher grade under that section.

(3) The number of officers that should be placed in the promotion zone in each of the next five years to provide to officers in those years relatively similar opportunities for promotion.

(Added Oct. 5, 1994, P. L. 103-337, Div A, Title XVI, Subtitle A, Part I, § 1611, 108 Stat. 2935.)

HISTORY; ANCILLARY LAWS AND DIRECTIVES

Effective date of section:

This section is effective Oct. 1, 1996, as provided by Act Oct. 5, 1994, P. L. 103-337, Div A, Title XVI, Subtitle F, § 1691(b)(1), 108 Stat. 3026, which appears as 10 USCS 10001 note.

CROSS REFERENCES

This section is referred to in 10 USCS § 14306.

§ 14306. Establishment of promotion zones: Naval Reserve and Marine Corps Reserve running mate system

(a) Authority of Secretary of the Navy. The Secretary of the Navy may by regulation implement section 14305 of this title by requiring that the promotion zone for consideration of officers on the reserve active-status list of the Navy or the Marine Corps for promotion to the next higher grade be determined in accordance with a running mate system as provided in subsection (b).

(b) Assignment of running mates. An officer to whom a running mate system applies shall be assigned as a running mate an officer of the same grade on the active-duty list of the same armed force. The officer on the reserve active-status list is in the promotion zone and is eligible for consideration for promotion to the next higher grade by a selection board convened under section 14101(a) of this title when that officer's running mate is in or above the promotion zone established for that officer's grade under chapter 36 of this title [10 USCS §§ 611 et seq.].

(c) Consideration of officers below the zone under a running mate system. If the Secretary of the Navy authorizes the selection of officers for promotion from below the promotion zone in accordance with section 14307 of this title, the number of officers to be considered from below the zone may be established through the application of the running mate system or otherwise as the Secretary determines to be appropriate to meet the needs of the Navy or Marine Corps.

(Added Oct. 5, 1994, P. L. 103-337, Div A, Title XVI, Subtitle A, Part I, § 1611, 108 Stat. 2935.)

HISTORY; ANCILLARY LAWS AND DIRECTIVES

Effective date of section:

This section is effective Oct. 1, 1996, as provided by Act Oct. 5, 1994, P. L. 103-337, Div A, Title XVI, Subtitle F, § 1691(b)(1), 108 Stat. 3026, which appears as 10 USCS 10001 note.

CROSS REFERENCES

This section is referred to in 10 USCS §§ 14304, 14308.

§ 14307. Number of officers to be recommended for promotion

(a) Determination of maximum number. Before convening a promotion board under section 14101(a) of this title for a grade and competitive category (other than a vacancy promotion board), the Secretary of the military department concerned, under regulations prescribed by the Secretary of Defense, shall determine the maximum number of officers in that grade and competitive category that the board may recommend for promotion. The Secretary shall make the determination under the preceding sentence of the maximum number that may be recommended with a view to having on the reserve active-status list a sufficient number of officers in each grade and competitive category to meet the needs of the armed force concerned for officers on that list. In order to make that determination, the Secretary shall determine (1) the number of positions needed to accomplish mission objectives which require officers of such competitive category in the grade to which the board will recommend officers for promotion, (2) the estimated number of officers needed to fill vacancies in such positions during the period in which it is anticipated that officers selected for promotion will be promoted, (3) the number of officers authorized by the Secretary of the military department concerned to serve on the reserve active-status list in the grade and competitive category under consideration, and (4) any statutory limitation on the number of officers in any grade or category (or combination thereof) authorized to be on the reserve active-status list.

(b) Below-the-zone selections. (1) The Secretary of the military department concerned may, when the needs of the armed force concerned require, authorize the consideration of officers in the grade of captain, major, or lieutenant colonel on the reserve active-status list of the Army or Air Force, in a grade above first lieutenant on the reserve active-status list of the Marine Corps, or in a grade above lieutenant (junior grade) on the reserve active-status list of the Navy, for promotion to the next higher grade from below the promotion zone.

(2) When selection from below the promotion zone is authorized, the Secretary shall establish the number of officers that may be recommended for promotion from below the promotion zone in each competitive category to be considered. That number may not exceed the number equal to 10 percent of the maximum number of officers that the board is authorized to recommend for promotion in such competitive category, except that the Secretary of Defense may authorize a greater number, not to exceed 15 percent of the total number of officers that the board is authorized to recommend for promotion, if the Secretary of Defense determines that the needs of the armed force concerned so require. If the maximum number determined under this paragraph is less than one, the board may recommend one officer for promotion from below the promotion zone.

(3) The number of officers recommended for promotion from below the promotion zone does not increase the maximum number of officers that the board is authorized to recommend for promotion under subsection (a).

(Added Oct. 5, 1994, P. L. 103-337, Div A, Title XVI, Subtitle A, Part I, § 1611, 108 Stat. 2936.)

HISTORY; ANCILLARY LAWS AND DIRECTIVES

Effective date of section:

This section is effective Oct. 1, 1996, as provided by Act Oct. 5, 1994, P. L. 103-337, Div A, Title XVI, Subtitle F, § 1691(b)(1), 108 Stat. 3026, which appears as 10 USCS 10001 note.

CROSS REFERENCES

This section is referred to in 10 USCS §§ 14107, 14303.

§ 14308. Promotions: how made

(a) Promotion list. When the report of a selection board convened under section 14101(a) or 14502 of this title is approved by the President, the Secretary of the military department concerned shall place the names of all officers selected for promotion within a competitive category on a single list for that competitive category, to be known as a promotion list, in the order of seniority of those officers on the reserve active-status list.

(b) Promotion; how made; order. (1) Officers on a promotion list for a competitive category shall be promoted in the manner specified in section 12203 of this title.

(2) Officers on a promotion list for a competitive category shall be promoted to the next higher grade in accordance with regulations prescribed by the Secretary of the military department concerned. Except as provided in section 14311, 14312, or 14502(e) of this title or in subsection (d) or (e), promotions shall be made in the order in which the names of officers appear on the promotion list and after officers previously selected for promotion in that competitive category have been promoted.

(3) Officers to be promoted to the grade of first lieutenant or lieutenant (junior grade) shall be promoted in accordance with regulations prescribed by the Secretary of the military department concerned.

(c) Date of rank. (1) The date of rank of an officer appointed to a higher grade under this section is determined under section 741(d)(2) of this title.

(2) Except as specifically authorized by law, a reserve officer is not entitled to additional pay or allowances if the effective date of the officer's promotion is adjusted to reflect a date earlier than the actual date of the officer's promotion.

(d) Officers with running mates. An officer to whom a running mate system applies under section 14306 of this title and who is selected for promotion is eligible for promotion to the grade for which selected when the officer who is that officer's running mate becomes eligible for promotion under chapter 36 of this title [10 USCS §§ 611 et seq.]. The effective date of the promotion of that officer shall be the same as that of the officer's running mate in the grade to which the running mate is promoted.

(e) Army Reserve and Air Force Reserve promotions to fill vacancies. Subject to this section and to section 14311(e) of this title, and under regulations prescribed by the Secretary of the military department concerned—

(1) an officer in the Army Reserve or the Air Force Reserve who is on a promotion list as a result of selection for promotion by a mandatory promotion board convened under section 14101(a) of this title or a board convened under section 14502 or chapter 36 of this title [10 USCS §§ 611 et seq.] may be promoted at any time to fill a vacancy in a position to which the officer is assigned; and

(2) an officer in a grade below colonel in the Army Reserve or the Air Force Reserve who is on a promotion list as a result of selection for promotion by a vacancy promotion board convened under section 14101(a) of this title may be promoted at any time to fill the vacancy for which the officer was selected.

(f) Effective date of promotion after Federal recognition. The effective date of a promotion of a reserve commissioned officer of the Army or the Air Force who is extended Federal recognition in the next higher grade in the Army National Guard or the Air National Guard under section 307 or 310 of title 32 shall be the date on which such Federal recognition in that grade is so extended.

(g) Army and Air Force general officer promotions. A reserve officer of the Army or the Air Force who is on a promotion list for promotion to the grade of brigadier general or major general as a result of selection by a vacancy promotion board may be promoted to that grade only to fill a vacancy in the Army Reserve or the Air Force Reserve, as the case may be, in that grade.

(Added Oct. 5, 1994, P. L. 103-337, Div A, Title XVI, Subtitle A, Part I, § 1611, 108 Stat. 2937; Nov. 18, 1997, P. L. 105-85, Div A, Title V, Subtitle B, § 514(c), 111 Stat. 1732.)

HISTORY; ANCILLARY LAWS AND DIRECTIVES

Effective date of section:

This section became effective on Oct. 1, 1996, as provided by § 1691(b)(1) of Act Oct. 5, 1994, P. L. 103-337, which appears as 10 USCS 10001 note.

Amendments:
1997. Act Nov. 18, 1997, in subsec. (e)(2), inserted "a grade below colonel in"; and, in subsec. (g), inserted "or the Air Force", substituted "in the Army Reserve or the Air Force Reserve, as the case may be, in that grade" for "in that grade in a unit of the Army Reserve that is organized to serve as a unit and that has attained the strength prescribed by the Secretary of the Army", and deleted "A reserve officer of the Air Force who is on a promotion list for promotion to the grade of brigadier general or major general as a result of selection by a vacancy promotion board may be promoted to that grade only to fill a vacancy in the Air Force Reserve in that grade." following "in that grade.".

§ 14309. Acceptance of promotion; oath of office

(a) Acceptance. An officer who is appointed to a higher grade under this chapter [10 USCS §§ 14301 et seq.] shall be considered to have accepted the appointment on the date on which the appointment is made unless the officer expressly declines the appointment or is granted a delay of promotion under section 14312 of this title.

(b) Oath. An officer who has served continuously since taking the oath of office prescribed in section 3331 of title 5 is not required to take a new oath upon appointment to a higher grade under this chapter [10 USCS §§ 14301 et seq.].
(Added Oct. 5, 1994, P. L. 103-337, Div A, Title XVI, Subtitle A, Part I, § 1611, 108 Stat. 2938.)

HISTORY; ANCILLARY LAWS AND DIRECTIVES

Effective date of section:
This section is effective Oct. 1, 1996, as provided by Act Oct. 5, 1994, P. L. 103-337, Div A, Title XVI, Subtitle F, § 1691(b)(1), 108 Stat. 3026, which appears as 10 USCS 10001 note.

§ 14310. Removal of officers from a list of officers recommended for promotion

(a) Removal by President. The President may remove the name of any officer from a promotion list at any time before the date on which the officer is promoted.

(b) Removal for withholding of Senate advice and consent. If the Senate does not give its advice and consent to the appointment to the next higher grade of an officer whose name is on a list of officers approved by the President for promotion (except in the case of promotions to a reserve grade to which appointments may be made by the President alone), the name of that officer shall be removed from the list.

(c) Continued eligibility for promotion. An officer whose name is removed from a list under subsection (a) or (b) continues to be eligible for consideration for promotion. If that officer is recommended for promotion by the next selection board convened for that officer's grade and competitive category and the officer is promoted, the Secretary of the military department concerned may, upon the promotion, grant the officer the same date of rank, the same effective date for the pay and allowances of the grade to which promoted, and the same position on the reserve active-status list, as the officer would have had if the officer's name had not been removed from the list.

(Added Oct. 5, 1994, P. L. 103-337, Div A, Title XVI, Subtitle A, Part I, § 1611, 108 Stat. 2938.)

HISTORY; ANCILLARY LAWS AND DIRECTIVES

Effective date of section:

This section is effective Oct. 1, 1996, as provided by Act Oct. 5, 1994, P. L. 103-337, Div A, Title XVI, Subtitle F, § 1691(b)(1), 108 Stat. 3026, which appears as 10 USCS 10001 note.

Other provisions:

Removals from promotion list. Act Oct. 5, 1994, P. L. 103-337, Div A, Title XVI, Subtitle E, § 1684(b), 108 Stat. 3024; Feb. 10, 1996, P. L. 104-106, Div A, Title XV, § 1501(a)(9), 110 Stat. 495 (effective as if included in Act Oct. 5, 1994, P. L. 103-337, as enacted on Oct. 5, 1994, as provided by § 1501(f)(3) of Act Feb. 10, 1996, which appears as 10 USCS § 113 note), provides: ''An action that was initiated before the effective date of this title [effective Oct. 1, 1996, as provided by § 1691(b) of Act Oct. 5, 1994, P. L. 103-337 (10 USCS § 10001 note)] under the laws and regulations in effect before that date to remove the name of an officer from a promotion list or from a list of officers recommended or approved for promotion shall continue on and after such date as if such action had been initiated under section 14111(c) or 14310, as appropriate, of title 10, United States Code, as added by this title.''.

CROSS REFERENCES

This section is referred to in 10 USCS § 14501.

§ 14311. Delay of promotion: involuntary

(a) Delay during investigations and proceedings. (1) Under regulations prescribed by the Secretary of the military department concerned, the appointment of an officer to a higher grade may be delayed if any of the following applies before the date on which the appointment would otherwise be made:

(A) Sworn charges against the officer have been received by an officer exercising general court-martial jurisdiction over the officer and the charges have not been disposed of.

(B) An investigation is being conducted to determine whether disciplinary action of any kind should be brought against the officer.

(C) A board of officers has been convened under section 14903 of this title to review the record of the officer.

(D) A criminal proceeding in a Federal or State court of competent jurisdiction is pending against the officer.

(2) If disciplinary action is not taken against the officer, if the charges against the officer are withdrawn or dismissed, if the officer is not separated by the

Secretary of the military department concerned as the result of having been required to show cause for retention, or if the officer is acquitted of the charges, as the case may be, then (unless action to delay the officer's appointment to the higher grade has been taken under subsection (b)) the officer shall be retained on the promotion list, list of officers found qualified for Federal recognition, or list of officers nominated by the President to the Senate for appointment in a higher reserve grade and shall, upon promotion to the next higher grade, have the same date of rank, the same effective date for the pay and allowances of the grade to which promoted, and the same position on the reserve active-status list as the officer would have had if no delay had intervened, unless the Secretary concerned determines that the officer was unqualified for promotion for any part of the delay. If the Secretary makes such a determination, the Secretary may adjust such date of rank, effective date of pay and allowances, and position on the reserve active-status list as the Secretary considers appropriate under the circumstances.

(b) Delay for lack of qualifications. Under regulations prescribed by the Secretary of the military department concerned, the appointment of an officer to a higher grade may also be delayed if there is cause to believe that the officer is mentally, physically, morally, or professionally unqualified to perform the duties of the grade to which selected. If the Secretary concerned later determines that the officer is qualified for promotion to the higher grade, the officer shall be retained on the promotion list, the list of officers found qualified for Federal recognition, or list of officers nominated by the President to the Senate for appointment in a higher reserve grade, and shall, upon promotion to that grade, have the same date of rank, the same effective date for pay and allowances of that grade, and the same position on the reserve active-status list as the officer would have had if no delay had intervened, unless the Secretary concerned determines that the officer was unqualified for promotion for any part of the delay. If the Secretary makes such a determination, the Secretary may adjust such date of rank, effective date of pay and allowances, and position on the reserve active-status list as the Secretary considers appropriate under the circumstances.

(c) Notice to officer. (1) The appointment of an officer to a higher grade may not be delayed under subsection (a) or (b) unless the officer is given written notice of the grounds for the delay. The preceding sentence does not apply if it is impracticable to give the officer written notice before the date on which the appointment to the higher grade would otherwise take effect, but in such a case the written notice shall be given as soon as practicable.

(2) An officer whose promotion is delayed under subsection (a) or (b) shall be given an opportunity to make a written statement to the Secretary of the military department concerned in response to the action taken. The Secretary shall give consideration to any such statement.

(d) Maximum length of delay in promotion. The appointment of an officer to a higher grade may not be delayed under subsection (a) or (b) for more than six months after the date on which the officer would otherwise have been promoted unless the Secretary concerned specifies a further period of delay. An officer's appointment may not be delayed more than 90 days after final action has been taken in any criminal case against the officer in a Federal or State court of competent jurisdiction or more than 90 days after final action has been taken in any court-martial case against the officer. Except for court action, a promotion may not be delayed more than 18 months after the date on which the officer would otherwise have been promoted.

(e) Delay because of limitations on officer strength in grade or duties to which assigned. (1) Under regulations prescribed by the Secretary of Defense, the promotion of a reserve officer on the reserve active-status list who is serving on active duty, or who is on full-time National Guard duty for administration of the reserves or the National Guard, to a grade to which the strength limitations of section 12011 of this title apply shall be delayed if necessary to ensure compliance with those strength limitations. The delay shall expire when the Secretary determines that the delay is no longer required to ensure such compliance.

(2) The promotion of an officer described in paragraph (1) shall also be delayed while the officer is on duty described in that paragraph unless the Secretary of the military department concerned, under regulations prescribed by the Secretary of Defense, determines that the duty assignment of the officer requires a higher grade than the grade currently held by the officer.

(3) The date of rank and position on the reserve active-status list of a reserve officer whose promotion to or Federal recognition in the next higher grade was delayed under paragraph (1) or (2) solely as the result of the limitations imposed under the regulations prescribed by the Secretary of Defense or contained in section 12011 of this title shall be the date on which the officer would have been promoted to or recognized in the higher grade had such limitations not existed.

(4) If an officer whose promotion is delayed under paragraph (1) or (2) completes the period of active duty or full-time National Guard duty that the officer is required by law or regulation to perform as a member of a reserve component, the officer may request release from active duty or full-time National Guard duty. If the request is granted, the officer's promotion shall be effective upon the officer's release from such duty. The date of rank and position on the reserve active-status list of the officer shall be the date the officer would have been promoted to or recognized in the higher grade had the limitations imposed under regulations prescribed by the Secretary of Defense contained in section 12011 of this title not existed. If an officer whose promotion is delayed under paragraph (1) or (2) has not completed the period of active duty or full-time National Guard duty that the officer is required by law or regulation to perform as a member of a reserve component, the officer may be retained on active duty or on full-time National Guard duty in the grade in which the officer was serving before the officer's being found qualified for Federal recognition or the officer's selection for the promotion until the officer completes that required period of duty.

(Added Oct. 5, 1994, P. L. 103-337, Div A, Title XVI, Subtitle A, Part I, § 1611, 108 Stat. 2939.)

HISTORY; ANCILLARY LAWS AND DIRECTIVES

Effective date of section:

This section is effective Oct. 1, 1996, as provided by Act Oct. 5, 1994, P. L. 103-337, Div A, Title XVI, Subtitle F, § 1691(b)(1), 108 Stat. 3026, which appears as 10 USCS 10001 note.

Other provisions:

Delays in promotions. Act Oct. 5, 1994, P. L. 103-337, Div A, Title XVI, Subtitle E, § 1684(a), 108 Stat. 3024, provides:

"(1) A delay in a promotion that is in effect on the day before the effective date of this title [effective Oct. 1, 1996, as provided by § 1691(b) of Act Oct. 5, 1994, P. L. 103-337 (10 USCS § 10001 note)] under the laws and regulations in effect on that date shall continue in effect on and after that date as if the promotion had been delayed under section 14311 of title 10, United States Code, as added by this title.

"(2) The delay of the promotion of a reserve officer of the Army or the Air Force which was in effect solely to achieve compliance with limitations set out in section 524 of title 10, United States Code, or with regulations prescribed by the Secretary of Defense with respect to sections 3380(c) and 8380(c) of title 10, United States Code, as in effect on the day before the effective date of this title [effective Oct. 1, 1996, as provided by § 1691(b) of Act Oct. 5, 1994, P. L. 103-337 (10 USCS § 10001 note)], shall continue in effect as if the promotion had been delayed under section 14311(e) of such title, as added by this title.".

CROSS REFERENCES

This section is referred to in 10 USCS §§ 14308, 14316.

§ 14312. Delay of promotion: voluntary

(a) Authority for voluntary delays. (1) The Secretary of the military department concerned may, by regulation, permit delays of a promotion of an officer who is recommended for promotion by a mandatory selection board convened under section 14101(a) or a special selection board convened under section 14502 of this title at the request of the officer concerned. Such delays, in the case of any promotion, may extend for any period not to exceed three years from the date on which the officer would otherwise be promoted.

(2) Regulations under this section shall provide that—

(A) a request for such a delay of promotion must be submitted by the officer concerned before the delay may be approved; and

(B) denial of such a request shall not be considered to be a failure of selection for promotion unless the officer declines to accept a promotion under circumstances set forth in subsection (c).

(b) Effect of approval of request. If a request for delay of a promotion under subsection (a) is approved, the officer's name shall remain on the promotion list during the authorized period of delay (unless removed under any other provision of law). Upon the end of the period of the authorized delay, or at any time during such period, the officer may accept the promotion, which shall be effective on the date of acceptance. Such an acceptance of a promotion shall be made in accordance with regulations prescribed under this section.

(c) Effect of declining a promotion. An officer's name shall be removed from the promotion list and, if the officer is serving in a grade below colonel or, in the case of the Navy, captain, the officer shall be considered to have failed of selection for promotion if any of the following applies:

(1) The Secretary concerned has not authorized voluntary delays of promotion under subsection (a) to the grade concerned and the officer declines to accept an appointment to a higher grade.

(2) The Secretary concerned has authorized voluntary delays of promotion under subsection (a), but has denied the request of the officer for a delay of promotion and the officer then declines to accept an appointment to a higher grade.

(3) The Secretary concerned has approved the request of an officer for a delay of promotion and, upon the end of the period of delay authorized in accordance with regulations prescribed under subsection (a), the officer then declines to accept an appointment to a higher grade.

(Added Oct. 5, 1994, P. L. 103-337, Div A, Title XVI, Subtitle A, Part I, § 1611, 108 Stat. 2941.)

HISTORY; ANCILLARY LAWS AND DIRECTIVES

Effective date of section:

This section is effective Oct. 1, 1996, as provided by Act Oct. 5, 1994, P. L. 103-337, Div A, Title XVI, Subtitle F, § 1691(b)(1), 108 Stat. 3026, which appears as 10 USCS 10001 note.

§ 14313. Authority to vacate promotions to grade of brigadier general or rear admiral (lower half)

(a) Authority. The President may vacate the appointment of a reserve officer to the grade of brigadier general or rear admiral (lower half) if the period of time during which the officer has served in that grade after promotion to that grade is less than 18 months.

(b) Effect of promotion being vacated. Except as provided in subsection (c), an officer whose promotion to the grade of brigadier general is vacated under this section holds the grade of colonel as a reserve of the armed force of which the officer is a member. An officer whose promotion to the grade of rear admiral (lower half) is vacated under this section holds the grade of captain in the Naval Reserve. Upon assuming the lower grade, the officer shall have the same position on the reserve active-status list as the officer would have had if the officer had not served in the higher grade.

(c) Special rule for officers serving as adjutant general. In the case of an officer serving as an adjutant general or assistant adjutant general whose promotion to the grade of brigadier general is vacated under this section, the officer then holds the reserve grade held by that officer immediately before the officer's appointment as adjutant general or assistant adjutant general.

(Added Oct. 5, 1994, P. L. 103-337, Div A, Title XVI, Subtitle A, Part I, § 1611, 108 Stat. 2942.)

HISTORY; ANCILLARY LAWS AND DIRECTIVES

Effective date of section:

This section is effective Oct. 1, 1996, as provided by Act Oct. 5, 1994, P. L. 103-337, Div A, Title XVI, Subtitle F, § 1691(b)(1), 108 Stat. 3026, which appears as 10 USCS 10001 note.

§ 14314. Army and Air Force commissioned officers: generals ceasing to occupy positions commensurate with grade; State adjutants general

(a) General officers. Within 30 days after a reserve officer of the Army or the Air Force on the reserve active-status list in a general officer grade ceases to occupy a position commensurate with that grade (or commensurate with a higher grade), the Secretary concerned shall transfer or discharge the officer in accordance with whichever of the following the officer elects:

(1) Transfer the officer in grade to the Retired Reserve, if the officer is qualified and applies for the transfer.

(2) Transfer the officer in grade to the inactive status list of the Standby Reserve, if the officer is qualified.

(3) Discharge the officer from the officer's reserve appointment and, if the officer is qualified and applies therefor, appoint the officer in the reserve grade held by the officer as a reserve officer before the officer's appointment in a general officer grade.

(4) Discharge the officer from the officer's reserve appointment.

(b) Adjutants general. If a reserve officer who is federally recognized in the Army National Guard or the Air National Guard solely because of the officer's appointment as adjutant general or assistant adjutant general of a State ceases to occupy that position, the Secretary concerned, not later than 30 days after the date on which the officer ceases to occupy that position, shall—

(1) withdraw that officer's Federal recognition; and

(2) require that the officer—

(A) be transferred in grade to the Retired Reserve, if the officer is qualified and applies for the transfer;

(B) be discharged from the officer's reserve appointment and appointed in the reserve grade held by the officer as a reserve officer immediately before the appointment of that officer as adjutant general or assistant adjutant general, if the officer is qualified and applies for that appointment; or

(C) be discharged from the officer's reserve appointment.

(c) Credit for service in grade. An officer who is appointed under subsection (a)(3) or (b)(2)(B) shall be credited with an amount of service in the grade in which appointed that is equal to the amount of prior service in an active status in that grade and in any higher grade.

(Added Oct. 5, 1994, P. L. 103-337, Div A, Title XVI, Subtitle A, Part I, § 1611, 108 Stat. 2942; Sept. 23, 1996, P. L. 104-201, Div A, Title V, Subtitle E, § 544(c), 110 Stat. 2523.)

HISTORY; ANCILLARY LAWS AND DIRECTIVES

Effective date of section:

This section is effective Oct. 1, 1996, as provided by Act Oct. 5, 1994, P. L. 103-337, Div A, Title XVI, Subtitle F, § 1691(b)(1), 108 Stat. 3026, which appears as 10 USCS 10001 note.

Amendments:

1996. Act Sept. 23, 1996, in subsec. (b)(2)(B), deleted ''of the Air Force'' following ''reserve officer''.

CROSS REFERENCES

This section is referred to in 10 USCS §§ 12009, 14317.

§ 14315. Position vacancy promotions: Army and Air Force officers

(a) Officers eligible for consideration for vacancy promotions below brigadier general. A reserve officer of the Army who is in the Army Reserve, or a reserve officer of the Air Force who is in the Air Force Reserve, who is on the reserve active-status list in the grade of first lieutenant, captain, major, or lieutenant colonel is eligible for consideration for promotion to the next higher grade under this section if each of the following applies:

(1) The officer is occupying or, as determined by the Secretary concerned, is available to occupy a position in the same competitive category as the officer and for which a grade higher than the one held by that officer is authorized.

(2) The officer is fully qualified to meet all requirements for the position as established by the Secretary of the military department concerned.

(3) The officer has held the officer's present grade for the minimum period of service prescribed in section 14303 of this title for eligibility for consideration for promotion to the higher grade.

(b) Consideration for vacancy promotion to brigadier general or major general. (1) A reserve officer of the Army who is in the Army Reserve and on the reserve active-status list in the grade of colonel or brigadier general may be considered for promotion to the next higher grade under this section if the officer (A) is assigned to the duties of a general officer of the next higher reserve grade in the Army Reserve, (B) has held the officer's present grade for the minimum period of service prescribed in section 14303 of this title for eligibility for consideration for promotion to the higher grade, and (C) meets the standards for consideration prescribed by the Secretary of the Army.

(2) A reserve officer of the Air Force who is in the Air Force Reserve and on the reserve active-status list in the grade of colonel or brigadier general may be considered for promotion to the next higher grade under this section if the officer (A) is assigned to the duties of a general officer of the next higher reserve grade, and (B) meets the standards for consideration prescribed by the Secretary of the Air Force.

(c) Vacancy promotion boards. Consideration for promotion under this section shall be by a vacancy promotion board convened under section 14101(a) of this title.

(d) Effect of nonselection. An officer who is considered for promotion under this section and is not selected shall not be considered to have failed of selection for promotion.

(e) Special rule for officers failed of selection. A reserve officer of the Army or the Air Force who is considered as failed of selection for promotion under section 14501 of this title to a grade may be considered for promotion under this section or, if selected, promoted to that grade only if the Secretary of the military department concerned finds that the officer is the only qualified officer available to fill the vacancy. The Secretary concerned may not delegate the authority under the preceding sentence.

(Added Oct. 5, 1994, P. L. 103-337, Div A, Title XVI, Subtitle A, Part I, § 1611, 108 Stat. 2943; Feb. 10, 1996, P. L. 104-106, Div A, Title XV, § 1501(b)(25), 110 Stat. 497; Nov. 18, 1997, P. L. 105-85, Div A, Title V, Subtitle B, § 514(d), 111 Stat. 1732.)

HISTORY; ANCILLARY LAWS AND DIRECTIVES

Effective date of section:

This section became effective Oct. 1, 1996, as provided by § 1691(b)(1) of Act Oct. 5, 1994, P. L. 103-337, which appears as 10 USCS 10001 note.

Amendments:

1996. Act Feb. 10, 1996 (effective as if included in Act Oct. 5, 1994, P. L. 103-337, as enacted on Oct. 5, 1994, as provided by § 1501(f)(3) of Act Feb. 10, 1996, which appears as 10 USCS § 113 note), in subsec. (a) in the introductory matter, substituted ''a reserve officer'' for ''a Reserve officer'' preceding ''of the Air Force''.

1997. Act Nov. 18, 1997, in subsec. (b)(1)(A), substituted ''duties of a general officer of the next higher reserve grade in the Army Reserve,'' for ''duties of a general officer of the next higher reserve grade in a unit of the Army Reserve organized to serve as a unit,''.

CROSS REFERENCES

This section is referred to in 10 USCS 14101.

§ 14316. Army National Guard and Air National Guard: appointment to and Federal recognition in a higher reserve grade after selection for promotion

(a) Opportunity for promotion to fill a vacancy in the guard. If an officer of the Army National Guard of the United States or the Air National Guard of the United States is recommended by a mandatory selection board convened under section 14101(a) or a special selection board convened under section 14502 of this title for promotion to the next higher grade, an opportunity shall be given to the appropriate authority of the State to promote that officer to fill a vacancy in the Army National Guard or the Air National Guard of that jurisdiction.

(b) Automatic Federal recognition. An officer of the Army National Guard of the United States or the Air National Guard of the United States who is on a promotion list for promotion to the next higher grade as a result of selection for promotion as described in subsection (a) and who before the date of promotion is appointed in that higher grade to fill a vacancy in the Army National Guard or Air National Guard shall—

(1) be extended Federal recognition in that grade, without the examination prescribed in section 307 of title 32; and

(2) subject to section 14311(e) of this title, be promoted to that reserve grade effective on the date of the officer's appointment in that grade in the Army National Guard or Air National Guard.

(c) National Guard officers failed of selection. An officer who is considered as failed of selection for promotion under section 14501 of this title to a grade may be extended Federal recognition in that grade only if the Secretary of the military department concerned finds that the officer is the only qualified officer available to fill a vacancy. The Secretary concerned may not delegate the authority under the preceding sentence.

(d) Transfer to Army Reserve or Air Force Reserve. If, on the date on which an officer of the Army National Guard of the United States or of the Air National Guard of the United States who is on a promotion list as described in subsection (a) is to be promoted, the officer has not been promoted to fill a vacancy in the higher grade in the Army National Guard or the Air National Guard, the officer's Federal recognition in the officer's reserve grade shall be withdrawn and the officer shall be promoted and transferred to the Army Reserve or the Air Force Reserve as appropriate.

(Added Oct. 5, 1994, P. L. 103-337, Div A, Title XVI, Subtitle A, Part I, § 1611, 108 Stat. 2944.)

HISTORY; ANCILLARY LAWS AND DIRECTIVES

Effective date of section:

This section is effective Oct. 1, 1996, as provided by Act Oct. 5, 1994, P. L. 103-337, Div A, Title XVI, Subtitle F, § 1691(b)(1), 108 Stat. 3026, which appears as 10 USCS 10001 note.

§ 14317. Officers in transition to and from the active-status list or active-duty list

(a) Effect of transfer to inactive status or retired status. If a reserve officer on the reserve active-status list is transferred to an inactive status or to a retired status after having been recommended for promotion to a higher grade under this chapter or chapter 36 of this title [10 USCS §§ 611 et seq.], or after having been found qualified for Federal recognition in the higher grade under title 32, but before being promoted, the officer—

(1) shall be treated as if the officer had not been considered and recommended for promotion by the selection board or examined and been found qualified for Federal recognition; and

(2) may not be placed on a promotion list or promoted to the higher grade after returning to an active status,

unless the officer is again recommended for promotion by a selection board convened under chapter 36 of this title [10 USCS §§ 611 et seq.] or section 14101(a) or 14502 of this title or examined for Federal recognition under title 32.

(b) Effect of placement on active-duty list. A reserve officer who is on a promotion list as a result of selection for promotion by a mandatory promotion board convened under section 14101(a) or a special selection board convened under section 14502 of this title and who before being promoted is placed on the active-duty list of the same armed force and placed in the same competitive category shall, under regulations prescribed by the Secretary of Defense, be placed on an appropriate promotion list for officers on the active-duty list established under chapter 36 of this title [10 USCS §§ 611 et seq.].

(c) Officers on a promotion list removed from active-duty list. An officer who is on the active-duty list and is on a promotion list as the result of selection for promotion by a selection board convened under chapter 36 of this title [10 USCS §§ 611 et seq.] and who before being promoted is removed from the active-duty list and placed on the reserve active-status list of the same armed force and in the same competitive category (including a regular officer who on removal from the active-duty list is appointed as a reserve officer and placed on the reserve active-status list) shall, under regulations prescribed by the Secretary of Defense, be placed on an appropriate promotion list established under this chapter [10 USCS §§ 14301 et seq.].

(d) Officers selected for position vacancies. If a reserve officer is ordered to active duty (other than active duty for training) or full-time National Guard duty (other than full-time National Guard duty for training only) after being recommended for promotion under section 14315 of this title to fill a position vacancy or examined for Federal recognition under title 32, and before being promoted to fill that vacancy, the officer shall not be promoted while serving such active duty or full-time National Guard duty unless the officer is ordered to active duty as a member of the unit in which the vacancy exists when that unit is ordered to active duty. If, under this subsection, the name of an officer is removed from a list of officers recommended for promotion, the officer shall be treated as if the officer had not been considered for promotion or examined for Federal recognition.

(e) Officers ordered to active duty in time of war or national emergency. Under regulations prescribed by the Secretary of the military department concerned, a reserve officer who is not on the active-duty list and who is ordered to active duty in time of war or national emergency may, if eligible, be considered for promotion by a mandatory promotion board convened under section 14101(a) or a special selection board convened under section 14502 of this title for not more than two years from the date the officer is ordered to active duty unless the President suspends the operation of this section under the provisions of section 123 or 10213 of this title.

(Added Oct. 5, 1994, P. L. 103-337, Div A, Title XVI, Subtitle A, Part I,

§ 1611, 108 Stat. 2945; Feb. 10, 1996, P. L. 104-106, Div A, Title XV, § 1501(b)(26), 110 Stat. 497; Nov. 18, 1997, P. L. 105-85, Div A, Title X, Subtitle G, § 1073(a)(68), 111 Stat. 1904.)

HISTORY; ANCILLARY LAWS AND DIRECTIVES

Effective date of section:

This section is effective Oct. 1, 1996, as provided by Act Oct. 5, 1994, P. L. 103-337, Div A, Title XVI, Subtitle F, § 1691(b)(1), 108 Stat. 3026, which appears as 10 USCS 10001 note.

Amendments:

1996. Act Feb. 10, 1996 (effective as if included in Act Oct. 5, 1995, P. L. 103-337, as enacted on Oct. 5, 1994, as provided by § 1501(f)(3) of Act Feb. 10, 1996, which appears as 10 USCS § 113 note), in subsec. (e), inserted the heading and substituted "section 123 or 10213" for "section 10213 or 644".

1997. Act Nov. 18, 1997 (applicable as provided by § 1073(i) of such Act, which appears as 10 USCS § 101 note), in subsec. (d), substituted "section 14315" for "section 14314".

CROSS REFERENCES

This section is referred to in 10 USCS §§ 741, 12009.

CHAPTER 1407. FAILURE OF SELECTION FOR PROMOTION AND INVOLUNTARY SEPARATION

HISTORY; ANCILLARY LAWS AND DIRECTIVES

Amendments:

1994. Act Oct. 5, 1994, P. L. 103-337, Div A, Title XVI, Subtitle A, Part I, § 1611, 108 Stat. 2946 (effective as provided by § 1691, which appears as 10 USCS § 10001 note) added the chapter heading and analysis.

1996. Act Feb. 10, 1996, P. L. 104-106, Div A, Title XV, § 1501(b)(27), 110 Stat. 497 (effective as if included in Act Oct. 5, 1994, P. L. 103-337, as enacted on Oct. 5, 1994, as provided by § 1501(f)(3) of Act Feb. 10, 1996, which appears as 10 USCS § 113 note), amended the analysis of this chapter by inserting ''reserve'' preceding ''lieutenant'' in item 14506, by inserting ''reserve'' preceding ''active-status'' in item 14507, and by inserting ''in grades'' in item 14509.

§ 14501. Failure of selection for promotion

(a) Officers below the grade of colonel or Navy captain. An officer on the reserve active-status list in a grade below the grade of colonel or, in the case of an officer in the Naval Reserve, captain who is in or above the promotion zone established for that officer's grade and competitive category and who (1) is considered but not recommended for promotion (other than by a vacancy promotion board), or (2) declines to accept a promotion for which selected (other than by a vacancy promotion board), shall be considered to have failed of selection for promotion.

(b) Officers twice failed of selection. An officer shall be considered for all purposes to have twice failed of selection for promotion if any of the following applies:

(1) The officer is considered but not recommended for promotion a second time by a mandatory promotion board convened under section 14101(a) or a special selection board convened under section 14502(a) of this title.

(2) The officer declines to accept a promotion for which recommended by a mandatory promotion board convened under section 14101(a) or a special selection board convened under section 14502(a) or 14502(b) of this title after previously failing of selection or after the officer's name was removed from the report of a selection board under section 14111(b) or from a promotion list under section 14310 of this title after recommendation for promotion by an earlier selection board described in subsection (a).

(3) The officer's name has been removed from the report of a selection board under section 14111(b) or from a promotion list under section 14310 of this title after recommendation by a mandatory promotion board convened under section 14101(a) or by a special selection board convened under section 14502(a) or 14502(b) of this title and—

(A) the officer is not recommended for promotion by the next mandatory promotion board convened under section 14101(a) or special selection board convened under section 14502(a) of this title for that officer's grade and competitive category; or

(B) the officer's name is again removed from the report of a selection board under section 14111(b) or from a promotion list under section 14310 of this title.

(Added Oct. 5, 1994, P. L. 103-337, Div A, Title XVI, Subtitle A, Part I, § 1611, 108 Stat. 2946; Feb. 10, 1996, P. L. 104-106, Div A, Title XV, § 1501(b)(28), 110 Stat. 498.)

HISTORY; ANCILLARY LAWS AND DIRECTIVES

Effective date of section:

This section is effective Oct. 1, 1996, as provided by Act Oct. 5, 1994, P. L. 103-337, Div A, Title XVI, Subtitle F, § 1691(b)(1), 108 Stat. 3026, which appears as 10 USCS 10001 note.

Amendments:

1996. Act Feb. 10, 1996 (effective as if included in Act Oct. 5, 1995, P. L. 103-337, as enacted on Oct. 5, 1994, as provided by § 1501(f)(3) of Act

Feb. 10, 1996, which appears as 10 USCS § 113 note), in subsec. (a), inserted the heading.

Other provisions:

Continuation on the reserve active-status list of certain reserve colonels of the Army and Air Force. Act Oct. 5, 1994, P. L. 103-337, Div A, Title XVI, Subtitle E, § 1681, 108 Stat. 3021, provides:

''(a) Continuation under old law. Except as provided in subsection (b), a reserve officer of the Army or the Air Force who, on the effective date of this title [effective Oct. 1, 1996, as provided by § 1691(b)(2) of Act Oct. 5, 1994, P. L. 103-337 (10 USCS § 10001 note)]—

''(1) is subject to placement on the reserve active-status list of the Army or the Air Force; and

''(2)(A) holds the reserve grade of colonel, (B) is on a list of officers recommended for promotion to the reserve grade of colonel, or (C) has been nominated by the President for appointment in the reserve grade of colonel,

shall continue to be subject to mandatory transfer to the Retired Reserve or discharge from the officer's reserve appointment under section 3851 or 8851 of title 10, United States Code, as in effect on the day before the effective date of this title [effective Oct. 1, 1996, as provided by § 1691(b)(2) of Act Oct. 5, 1994, P. L. 103-337 (10 USCS § 10001 note)].

''(b) Exemption. This section does not apply to an officer who is—

''(1) sooner transferred from an active status or discharged under some other provision of law;

''(2) promoted to a higher grade, unless the officer was on a list of officers recommended for promotion to the reserve grade of colonel before the effective date of this title [effective Oct. 1, 1996, as provided by § 1691(b)(2) of Act Oct. 5, 1994, P. L. 103-337 (10 USCS § 10001 note)]; or

''(3) continued on the reserve active-status list under section 14701 of title 10, United States Code, as added by this title.''.

Mandatory separation for age for certain reserve officers of the Navy and Marine Corps. Act Oct. 5, 1994, P. L. 103-337, Div A, Title XVI, Subtitle E, § 1690, 108 Stat. 3025, provides:

''(a) Savings provisions for required separation age. A reserve officer of the Navy or the Marine Corps—

''(1) who—

''(A) on the effective date of this title [effective Oct. 1, 1996, as provided by § 1691(b)(2) of Act Oct. 5, 1994, P. L. 103-337 (10 USCS § 10001 note)] is in an active status, and

''(B) on the day before the effective date of this title [effective Oct. 1, 1996, as provided by § 1691(b)(2) of Act Oct. 5, 1994, P. L. 103-337 (10 USCS § 10001 note)] was an officer described in section 6389(e), 6397(a), 6403(a), or 6403(b) of title 10, United States Code; and

''(2) who, on or after the effective date of this title [effective Oct. 1, 1996, as provided by § 1691(b)(2) of Act Oct. 5, 1994, P. L. 103-337 (10 USCS § 10001 note)] is subject to elimination from an active status under any provision of such title, is entitled to be treated as that officer would have been treated under section 6397 or 6403 as applicable, as in effect on the day before the effective date of this title [effective Oct. 1, 1996, as provided by § 1691(b)(2) of Act Oct. 5, 1994, P. L. 103-337 (10 USCS § 10001 note)], if that treatment would result in the date for the officer's separation from an active status being a later date than the date established under the law in effect on or after the effective date of this title [effective Oct. 1, 1996, as provided by § 1691(b)(2) of Act Oct. 5, 1994, P. L. 103-337 (10 USCS § 10001 note)].

"(b) Savings provisions for mandatory separation for age. An officer who was initially appointed in the Naval Reserve or the Marine Corps Reserve before January 1, 1953, and who cannot complete 20 years of service computed under section 12732 of this title before he becomes 62 years of age, but can complete this service by the time he becomes 64 years of age, may be retained in an active status not later than the date he becomes 64 years of age.

"(c) An officer who was initially appointed in the Naval Reserve or the Marine Corps Reserve before the effective date of this title [effective Oct. 1, 1996, as provided by § 1691(b)(2) of Act Oct. 5, 1994, P. L. 103-337 (10 USCS § 10001 note)], and who cannot complete 20 years of service computed under section 12732 of this title before he becomes 60 years of age, but can complete this service by the time he becomes 62 years of age, may be retained in an active status not later than the date he becomes 62 years of age.".

CROSS REFERENCES

This section is referred to in 10 USCS §§ 14315, 14316.

§ 14502. Special selection boards: correction of errors

(a) Officers not considered because of administrative error. (1) In the case of an officer or former officer who the Secretary of the military department concerned determines was not considered for selection for promotion from in or above the promotion zone by a mandatory promotion board convened under section 14101(a) of this title because of administrative error, the Secretary concerned shall convene a special selection board under this subsection to determine whether such officer or former officer should be recommended for promotion. Any such board shall be convened under regulations prescribed by the Secretary of Defense and shall be appointed and composed in accordance with section 14102 of this title and shall include the representation of competitive categories required by that section. The members of a board convened under this subsection shall be required to take an oath in the same manner as prescribed in section 14103 of this title.

(2) A special selection board convened under this subsection shall consider the record of the officer or former officer as that record would have appeared to the promotion board that should have considered the officer or former officer. That record shall be compared with a sampling of the records of those officers of the same grade and competitive category who were recommended for promotion and those officers of the same grade and competitive category who were not recommended for promotion by that board.

(3) If a special selection board convened under paragraph (1) does not rec-

ommend for promotion an officer or former officer in a grade below the grade of colonel or, in the case of an officer or former officer of the Navy, captain, whose name was referred to it for consideration, the officer or former officer shall be considered to have failed of selection for promotion.

(b) Officers considered but not selected; material error. (1) In the case of an officer or former officer who was eligible for promotion and was considered for selection for promotion from in or above the promotion zone under this chapter [10 USCS §§ 14501 et seq.] by a selection board but was not selected, the Secretary of the military department concerned may, under regulations prescribed by the Secretary of Defense, convene a special selection board under this subsection to determine whether the officer or former officer should be recommended for promotion, if the Secretary determines that—

(A) the action of the selection board that considered the officer or former officer was contrary to law or involved material error of fact or material administrative error; or

(B) the selection board did not have before it for its consideration material information.

(2) A special selection board convened under paragraph (1) shall be appointed and composed in accordance with section 14102 of this title (including the representation of competitive categories required by that section), and the members of such a board shall take an oath in the same manner as prescribed in section 14103 of this title.

(3) Such board shall consider the record of the officer or former officer as that record, if corrected, would have appeared to the selection board that considered the officer or former officer. That record shall be compared with a sampling of the records of those officers of the same grade and competitive category who were recommended for promotion and those officers of the same grade and competitive category who were not recommended for promotion by that board.

(4) If a special selection board convened under paragraph (1) does not recommend for promotion an officer or former officer in the grade of lieutenant colonel or commander or below whose name was referred to it for consideration, the officer or former officer shall be considered to have failed of selection for promotion by the board which did consider the officer but incurs no additional failure of selection for promotion from the action of the special selection board.

(c) Report. Each special selection board convened under this section shall submit to the Secretary of the military department concerned a written report, signed by each member of the board, containing the name of each officer it recommends for promotion and certifying that the board has considered carefully the record of each officer whose name was referred to it.

(d) Applicable provisions. The provisions of sections 14104, 14109, 14110, and 14111 of this title apply to the report and proceedings of a special selection board convened under this section in the same manner as they apply to the report and proceedings of a promotion board convened under section 14101(a) of this title.

(e) Appointment of officers recommended for promotion. (1) An officer whose name is placed on a promotion list as a result of recommendation for promotion by a special selection board convened under this section, shall, as soon as practicable, be appointed to the next higher grade in accordance with the law and policies which would have been applicable had he been recommended for promotion by the board which should have considered or which did consider him.

(2) An officer who is promoted to the next higher grade as the result of the recommendation of a special selection board convened under this section shall, upon such promotion, have the same date of rank, the same effective date for the pay and allowances of that grade, and the same position on the reserve active-status list as the officer would have had if the officer had been recommended for promotion to that grade by the selection board which should have considered, or which did consider, the officer.

(3) If the report of a special selection board convened under this section, as approved by the President, recommends for promotion to the next higher grade an officer not currently eligible for promotion or a former officer whose name was referred to it for consideration, the Secretary concerned may act under section 1552 of this title to correct the military record of the officer or former officer to correct an error or remove an injustice resulting from not being selected for promotion by the board which should have considered, or which did consider, the officer.

(f) Time limits for consideration. The Secretary of Defense may prescribe by regulation the circumstances under which consideration by a special selection board is contingent upon application for consideration by an officer or former officer and time limits within which an officer or former officer must make such application in order to be considered by a special selection board under this section.

(g) Limitation of other jurisdiction. No official or court of the United States shall have power or jurisdiction—

(1) over any claim based in any way on the failure of an officer or former officer of the armed forces to be selected for promotion by a selection board convened under chapter 1403 of this title [10 USCS §§ 14101 et seq.] until —

(A) the claim has been referred to a special selection board by the Secretary concerned and acted upon by that board; or

(B) the claim has been rejected by the Secretary without consideration by a special selection board; or

(2) to grant any relief on such a claim unless the officer or former officer has been selected for promotion by a special selection board convened under this section to consider the officer's claim.

(h) Judicial review. (1) A court of the United States may review a determination by the Secretary concerned under subsection (a)(1), (b)(1), or (e)(3) not to convene a special selection board. If a court finds the determination to be arbitrary or capricious, not based on substantial evidence, or otherwise contrary to law, it shall remand the case to the Secretary concerned, who shall provide for consideration of the officer or former officer by a special selection board under this section.

(2) If a court finds that the action of a special selection board which considers an officer or former officer was contrary to law or involved material error of fact or material administrative error, it shall remand the case to the Secretary concerned, who shall provide the officer or former officer reconsideration by a new special selection board.

(i) Designation of boards. The Secretary of the military department concerned may designate a promotion board convened under section 14101(a) of this title as a special selection board convened under this section. A board so designated may function in both capacities.

(Added Oct. 5, 1994, P. L. 103-337, Div A, Title XVI, Subtitle A, Part I, § 1611, 108 Stat. 2947.)

HISTORY; ANCILLARY LAWS AND DIRECTIVES

Effective date of section:

This section is effective Oct. 1, 1996, as provided by Act Oct. 5, 1994, P. L. 103-337, Div A, Title XVI, Subtitle F, § 1691(b)(1), 108 Stat. 3026, which appears as 10 USCS 10001 note.

CROSS REFERENCES

This section is referred to in 10 USCS §§ 14108, 14301, 14304, 14308, 14312, 14316, 14317, 14501.

§ 14503. Discharge of officers with less than five years of commissioned service or found not qualified for promotion to first lieutenant or lieutenant (junior grade)

(a) Authorized discharges. The Secretary of the military department concerned may discharge any reserve officer who—

(1) has less than five years of service in an active status as a commissioned officer; or

(2) is serving in the grade of second lieutenant or ensign and has been found not qualified for promotion to the grade of first lieutenant or lieutenant (junior grade).

(b) Time for discharge. (1) An officer described in subsection (a)(2)—

(A) may be discharged at any time after being found not qualified for promotion; and

(B) if not sooner discharged, shall be discharged at the end of the 18-month period beginning on the date on which the officer is first found not qualified for promotion.

(2) Paragraph (1) shall not apply if the officer is sooner promoted.

(c) Regulations. Discharges under this section shall be made under regulations prescribed by the Secretary of Defense and may be made without regard to section 12645 of this title.

(Added Oct. 5, 1994, P. L. 103-337, Div A, Title XVI, Subtitle A, Part I, § 1611, 108 Stat. 2949.)

HISTORY; ANCILLARY LAWS AND DIRECTIVES

Effective date of section:

This section is effective Oct. 1, 1996, as provided by Act Oct. 5, 1994, P. L. 103-337, Div A, Title XVI, Subtitle F, § 1691(b)(1), 108 Stat. 3026, which appears as 10 USCS 10001 note.

Other provisions:

Rights for officers with over three years service. Act Oct. 5, 1994, P. L. 103-337, Div A, Title XVI, Subtitle E, § 1689, 108 Stat. 3025, provides: ''A reserve officer of the Army, Navy, Air Force, or Marine Corps who was in an active status on the day before the effective date of this title [effective Oct. 1, 1996, as provided by § 1691(b)(2) of Act Oct. 5, 1994, P. L. 103-337 (10 USCS § 10001 note)] and who was subject to placement of the reserve active-status list on the effective date of this title [effective Oct. 1, 1996, as provided by § 1691(b)(2) of Act Oct. 5, 1994, P. L. 103-337 (10 USCS § 10001 note)] may not be discharged under section 14503 of title 10, United States Code, as added by this title, until on or after the day on which that officer completes three years of continuous service as a reserve commissioned officer.''.

CROSS REFERENCES

This section is referred to in 10 USCS § 14703.

§ 14504. Effect of failure of selection for promotion: reserve first lieutenants of the Army, Air Force, and Marine Corps and reserve lieutenants (junior grade) of the Navy

(a) General rule. A first lieutenant on the reserve active-status list of the Army, Air Force, or Marine Corps or a lieutenant (junior grade) on the reserve active-status list of the Navy who has failed of selection for promotion to the next higher grade for the second time and whose name is not on a list of officers recommended for promotion to the next higher grade shall be separated in accordance with section 14513 of this title not later than the first day of the seventh month after the month in which the President approves the report of the board which considered the officer for the second time.

(b) Exceptions. Subsection (a) does not apply (1) in the case of an officer retained as provided by regulation of the Secretary of the military department concerned in order to meet planned mobilization needs for a period not in excess of 24 months beginning with the date on which the President approves the report of the selection board which resulted in the second failure, or (2) as provided in section 12546 or 12686 of this title.

(Added Oct. 5, 1994, P. L. 103-337, Div A, Title XVI, Subtitle A, Part I, § 1611, 108 Stat. 2950.)

HISTORY; ANCILLARY LAWS AND DIRECTIVES

Effective date of section:

This section is effective Oct. 1, 1996, as provided by Act Oct. 5, 1994, P. L. 103-337, Div A, Title XVI, Subtitle F, § 1691(b)(1), 108 Stat. 3026, which appears as 10 USCS 10001 note.

CROSS REFERENCES

This section is referred to in 10 USCS §§ 14513, 14703.

§ 14505. Effect of failure of selection for promotion: reserve captains of the Army, Air Force, and Marine Corps and reserve lieutenants of the Navy

Unless retained as provided in section 12646 or 12686 of this title, a captain on the reserve active-status list of the Army, Air Force, or Marine Corps or a lieutenant on the reserve active-status list of the Navy who has failed of selection for promotion to the next higher grade for the second time and whose name is not on a list of officers recommended for promotion to the next higher grade and who has not been selected for continuation on the reserve active-status list under section 14701 of this title, shall be separated in accordance with section 14513 of this title not later than the first day of the seventh month after the month in which the President approves the report of the board which considered the officer for the second time.

(Added Oct. 5, 1994, P. L. 103-337, Div A, Title XVI, Subtitle A, Part I, § 1611, 108 Stat. 2950.)

HISTORY; ANCILLARY LAWS AND DIRECTIVES

Effective date of section:

This section is effective Oct. 1, 1996, as provided by Act Oct. 5, 1994, P. L. 103-337, Div A, Title XVI, Subtitle F, § 1691(b)(1), 108 Stat. 3026, which appears as 10 USCS 10001 note.

CROSS REFERENCES

This section is referred to in 10 USCS §§ 14513, 14701.

§ 14506. Effect of failure of selection for promotion: reserve majors of the Army, Air Force, and Marine Corps and reserve lieutenant commanders of the Navy

Unless retained as provided in section 12646, 12686, 14701, or 14702 of this title, each reserve officer of the Army, Navy, Air Force, or Marine Corps who holds the grade of major or lieutenant commander who has failed of selection to the next higher grade for the second time and whose name is not on a list of officers recommended for promotion to the next higher grade shall, if not earlier removed from the reserve active-status list, be removed from that list in accordance with section 14513 of this title on the first day of the month after the month in which the officer completes 20 years of commissioned service.

(Added Oct. 5, 1994, P. L. 103-337, Div A, Title XVI, Subtitle A, Part I, § 1611, 108 Stat. 2951; Feb. 10, 1996, P. L. 104-106, Div A, Title XV, § 1501(b)(29), 110 Stat. 498.)

HISTORY; ANCILLARY LAWS AND DIRECTIVES

Effective date of section:

This section is effective Oct. 1, 1996, as provided by Act Oct. 5, 1994, P. L. 103-337, Div A, Title XVI, Subtitle F, § 1691(b)(1), 108 Stat. 3026, which appears as 10 USCS 10001 note.

Amendments:

1996. Act Feb. 10, 1996 (effective as if included in Act Oct. 5, 1994, P. L. 103-337, as enacted on Oct. 5, 1994, as provided by § 1501(f)(3) of Act Feb. 10, 1996, which appears as 10 USCS § 113 note), in the section heading, inserted a comma following ''Air Force''.

CROSS REFERENCES

This section is referred to in 10 USCS §§ 14513, 14701–14703.

§ 14507. Removal from the reserve active-status list for years of service: reserve lieutenant colonels and colonels of the Army, Air Force, and Marine Corps and reserve commanders and captains of the Navy

(a) Lieutenant colonels and commanders. Unless continued on the reserve active-status list under section 14701 or 14702 of this title or retained as provided in section 12646 or 12686 of this title, each reserve officer of the Army, Navy, Air Force, or Marine Corps who holds the grade of lieutenant colonel or commander and who is not on a list of officers recommended for promotion to the next higher grade shall (if not earlier removed from the reserve active-status list) be removed from that list under section 14514 of this title on the first day of the month after the month in which the officer completes 28 years of commissioned service.

(b) Colonels and Navy captains. Unless continued on the reserve active-status list under section 14701 or 14702 of this title or retained as provided in section 12646 or 12686 of this title, each reserve officer of the Army, Air Force, or Marine Corps who holds the grade of colonel, and each reserve officer of the Navy who holds the grade of captain, and who is not on a list of officers recommended for promotion to the next higher grade shall (if not earlier removed from the reserve active-status list) be removed from that list under section 14514 of this title on the first day of the month after the month in which the officer completes 30 years of commissioned service. This subsection does not apply to the adjutant general or assistant adjutants general of a State.

(c) Temporary authority to retain certain officers designated as judge advocates. (1) Notwithstanding the provisions of subsections (a) and (b), the Secretary of the Air Force may retain on the reserve active-status list any reserve officer of the Air Force who is designated as a judge advocate and who obtained the first professional degree in law while on an educational delay program subsequent to being commissioned through the Reserve Officers' Training Corps.

(2) No more than 50 officers may be retained on the reserve active-status list under the authority of paragraph (1) at any time.

(3) No officer may be retained on the reserve active-status list under the authority of paragraph (1) for a period exceeding three years from the date

on which, but for that authority, that officer would have been removed from the reserve active-status list under subsection (a) or (b).

(4) The authority of the Secretary of the Air Force under paragraph (1) expires on September 30, 2003.

(Added Oct. 5, 1994, P. L. 103-337, Div A, Title XVI, Subtitle A, Part I, § 1611, 108 Stat. 2951; Sept. 23, 1996, P. L. 104-201, Div A, Title V, Subtitle A, § 508(a), 110 Stat. 2513.)

HISTORY; ANCILLARY LAWS AND DIRECTIVES

Effective date of section:

This section is effective Oct. 1, 1996, as provided by Act Oct. 5, 1994, P. L. 103-337, Div A, Title XVI, Subtitle F, § 1691(b)(1), 108 Stat. 3026, which appears as 10 USCS 10001 note.

Amendments:

1996. Act Sept. 23, 1996 (effective 10/1/96, as provided by § 508(b) of such Act, which appears as a note to this section) added subsec. (c).

Other provisions:

Effective date of subsec. (c). Act Sept. 23, 1996, P. L. 104-201, Div A, Title V, Subtitle A, § 508(b), 110 Stat. 2513, provides: "Subsection (c) of section 14507 of title 10, United States Code, as added by subsection (a), shall take effect on October 1, 1996.".

CROSS REFERENCES

Adjutants general and assistant adjutants general, references applicable to other officers of National Guard, 10 USCS § 10214.

This section is referred to in 10 USCS §§ 10214, 14514, 14701, 14702.

§ 14508. Removal from the reserve active-status list for years of service: reserve general and flag officers

(a) Thirty years service or five years in grade. Unless retired, transferred to the Retired Reserve, or discharged at an earlier date, each reserve officer of the Army, Air Force, or Marine Corps in the grade of brigadier general who has not been recommended for promotion to the grade of major general, and each reserve officer of the Navy in the grade of rear admiral (lower half) who has not been recommended for promotion to rear admiral shall, 30 days after completion of 30 years of commissioned service or on the fifth anniversary of the date of the officer's appointment in the grade of brigadier general or rear admiral (lower half), whichever is later, be separated in accordance with section 14514 of this title.

(b) Thirty-five years service or five years in grade. Unless retired, transferred to the Retired Reserve, or discharged at an earlier date, each reserve officer of the Army, Air Force, or Marine Corps in the grade of major general, and each reserve officer of the Navy in the grade of rear admiral, shall, 30 days after completion of 35 years of commissioned service or on the fifth anniversary of the date of the officer's appointment in the grade of major general or rear admiral, whichever is later, be separated in accordance with section 14514 of this title.

(c) Retention of brigadier generals. A reserve officer of the Army or Air Force in the grade of brigadier general who would otherwise be removed from an active status under subsection (a) may, in the discretion of the Secretary of the Army or the Secretary of the Air Force, as the case may be, be retained in an active status, but not later than the last day of the month in which the officer becomes 60 years of age. Not more than 10 officers of the Army and not more than 10 officers of the Air Force may be retained under this subsection at any one time.

(d) Retention of major generals. A reserve officer of the Army or Air Force in the grade of major general who would otherwise be removed from an active status under subsection (b) may, in the discretion of the Secretary of the Army or the Secretary of the Air Force, as the case may be, be retained in an active status, but not later than the date on which the officer becomes 62 years of age. Not more than 10 officers of the Army and not more than 10 officers of the Air Force may be retained under this subsection at any one time.

(e) Exception for State adjutants general and assistant adjutants general. This section does not apply to an officer who is the adjutant general or assistant adjutant general of a State.

(Added Oct. 5, 1994, P. L. 103-337, Div A, Title XVI, Subtitle A, Part I, § 1611, 108 Stat. 2951; Feb. 10, 1996, P. L. 104-106, Div A, Title XV, § 1501(b)(30), 110 Stat. 498; Nov. 18, 1997, P. L. 105-85, Div A, Title V, Subtitle C, § 521(b), 111 Stat. 1734.)

HISTORY; ANCILLARY LAWS AND DIRECTIVES

Effective date of section:

This section became effective on Oct. 1, 1996, as provided by § 1691(b)(1) of Act Oct. 5, 1994, P. L. 103-337, which appears as 10 USCS § 10001 note.

Amendments:

1996. Act Feb. 10, 1996 (effective as if included in Act Oct. 5, 1995, P. L. 103-337, as enacted on Oct. 5, 1994, as provided by § 1501(f)(3) of Act Feb. 10, 1996, which appears as 10 USCS § 113 note), in subsecs. (c) and (d), deleted "this" after "from an active status under".

1997. Act Nov. 18, 1997, in subsec. (c), substituted "not later than the last day of the month in which the officer becomes 60 years of age" for "not later than the date on which the officer becomes 60 years of age".

CROSS REFERENCES

Adjutants general and assistant adjutants general, references applicable to other officers of National Guard, 10 USCS § 10214.

This section is referred to in 10 USCS §§ 10214, 14514, 14701, 14702.

§ 14509. Separation at age 60: reserve officers in grades below brigadier general or rear admiral (lower half)

Each reserve officer of the Army, Navy, Air Force, or Marine Corps in a grade below brigadier general or rear admiral (lower half) who has not been recommended for promotion to the grade of brigadier general or rear admiral (lower half) and is not a member of the Retired Reserve shall, on the last day of the month in which that officer becomes 60 years of age, be separated in accordance with section 14515 of this title.

(Added Oct. 5, 1994, P. L. 103-337, Div A, Title XVI, Subtitle A, Part I, § 1611, 108 Stat. 2952.)

HISTORY; ANCILLARY LAWS AND DIRECTIVES

Effective date of section:

This section is effective Oct. 1, 1996, as provided by Act Oct. 5, 1994, P. L. 103-337, Div A, Title XVI, Subtitle F, § 1691(b)(1), 108 Stat. 3026, which appears as 10 USCS 10001 note.

CROSS REFERENCES

This section is referred to in 10 USCS §§ 14515, 14701.

§ 14510. Separation at age 60: reserve brigadier generals and rear admirals (lower half)

Unless retired, transferred to the Retired Reserve, or discharged at an earlier date, each reserve officer of the Army, Air Force, or Marine Corps in the grade of brigadier general who has not been recommended for promotion to the grade of major general, and each reserve rear admiral (lower half) of the Navy who has not been recommended for promotion to the grade of rear admiral, except an officer covered by section 14512 of this title, shall be separated in accordance with section 14515 of this title on the last day of the month in which the officer becomes 60 years of age.

(Added Oct. 5, 1994, P. L. 103-337, Div A, Title XVI, Subtitle A, Part I, § 1611, 108 Stat. 2952.)

HISTORY; ANCILLARY LAWS AND DIRECTIVES

Effective date of section:

This section is effective Oct. 1, 1996, as provided by Act Oct. 5, 1994, P. L. 103-337, Div A, Title XVI, Subtitle F, § 1691(b)(1), 108 Stat. 3026, which appears as 10 USCS 10001 note.

CROSS REFERENCES

This section is referred to in 10 USCS §§ 14512, 14515.

§ 14511. Separation at age 62: major generals and rear admirals

Unless retired, transferred to the Retired Reserve, or discharged at an earlier date, each reserve officer of the Army, Air Force, or Marine Corps in the grade of major general and each reserve officer of the Navy in the grade of rear admiral, except an officer covered by section 14512 of this title, shall be separated in accordance with section 14515 of this title on the last day of the month in which the officer becomes 62 years of age.

(Added Oct. 5, 1994, P. L. 103-337, Div A, Title XVI, Subtitle A, Part I, § 1611, 108 Stat. 2953.)

HISTORY; ANCILLARY LAWS AND DIRECTIVES

Effective date of section:

This section is effective Oct. 1, 1996, as provided by Act Oct. 5, 1994, P. L. 103-337, Div A, Title XVI, Subtitle F, § 1691(b)(1), 108 Stat. 3026, which appears as 10 USCS 10001 note.

CROSS REFERENCES

This section is referred to in 10 USCS §§ 14512, 14515.

§ 14512. Separation at age 64: officers holding certain offices

(a) Army and Air Force. Unless retired, transferred to the Retired Reserve, or discharged at an earlier date, a reserve officer of the Army or Air Force who is Chief of the National Guard Bureau, an adjutant general, or if a reserve officer of the Army, commanding general of the troops of a State, shall on the last day of the month in which the officer becomes 64 years of age, be separated in accordance with section 14515 of this title.

(b) Navy and Marine Corps. The Secretary of the Navy may defer the retirement under section 14510 or 14511 of a reserve officer of the Navy in a grade above captain or a reserve officer of the Marine Corps in a grade above colonel and retain the officer in an active status until the officer becomes 64 years of age. Not more than 10 officers may be so deferred at any one time, distributed between the Naval Reserve and the Marine Corps Reserve as the Secretary determines.

(Added Oct. 5, 1994, P. L. 103-337, Div A, Title XVI, Subtitle A, Part I, § 1611, 108 Stat. 2953.)

HISTORY; ANCILLARY LAWS AND DIRECTIVES

Effective date of section:

This section is effective Oct. 1, 1996, as provided by Act Oct. 5, 1994, P. L. 103-337, Div A, Title XVI, Subtitle F, § 1691(b)(1), 108 Stat. 3026, which appears as 10 USCS 10001 note.

CROSS REFERENCES

Adjutants general and assistant adjutants general, references applicable to other officers of National Guard, 10 USCS § 10214.

This section is referred to in 10 USCS §§ 10214, 14510, 14511, 14515.

§ 14513. Separation for failure of selection of promotion

Each reserve officer of the Army, Navy, Air Force, or Marine Corps who is in an active status and whose removal from an active status or from a reserve active-status list is required by section 14504, 14505, or 14506 of this title shall (unless the officer's separation is deferred or the officer is continued in an active status under another provision of law) not later than the date specified in those sections—

(1) be transferred to an inactive status if the Secretary concerned determines that the officer has skills which may be required to meet the mobilization needs of the officer's armed force;

(2) be transferred to the Retired Reserve, if the officer is qualified and applies for such transfer; or

(3) if the officer is not transferred to an inactive status or to the Retired Reserve, be discharged from the officer's reserve appointment.

(Added Oct. 5, 1994, P. L. 103-337, Div A, Title XVI, Subtitle A, Part I, § 1611, 108 Stat. 2953.)

HISTORY; ANCILLARY LAWS AND DIRECTIVES

Effective date of section:

This section is effective Oct. 1, 1996, as provided by Act Oct. 5, 1994, P. L. 103-337, Div A, Title XVI, Subtitle F, § 1691(b)(1), 108 Stat. 3026, which appears as 10 USCS 10001 note.

CROSS REFERENCES

This section is referred to in 10 USCS §§ 12646, 14504–14506, 14516, 14517, 14701.

§ 14514. Discharge or retirement for years of service or after selection for early removal

Each reserve officer of the Army, Navy, Air Force, or Marine Corps who is in an active status and who is required to be removed from an active status or from a reserve active-status list, as the case may be, under section 14507, 14508, 14704, or 14705 of this title (unless the officer is sooner separated or the officer's separation is deferred or the officer is continued in an active status under another provision of law), in accordance with those sections, shall—

(1) be transferred to the Retired Reserve, if the officer is qualified and applies for such transfer; or

(2) if the officer is not qualified or does not apply for such transfer, be discharged from the officer's reserve appointment.

(Added Oct. 5, 1994, P. L. 103-337, Div A, Title XVI, Subtitle A, Part I, § 1611, 108 Stat. 2953.)

HISTORY; ANCILLARY LAWS AND DIRECTIVES

Effective date of section:

This section is effective Oct. 1, 1996, as provided by Act Oct. 5, 1994, P. L. 103-337, Div A, Title XVI, Subtitle F, § 1691(b)(1), 108 Stat. 3026, which appears as 10 USCS 10001 note.

CROSS REFERENCES

Reserve components, limitations on separation inapplicable to discharges under this section, 10 USCS § 12683.

This section is referred to in 10 USCS §§ 12646, 12683, 14516, 14517, 14701, 14704, 14705.

§ 14515. Discharge or retirement for age

Each reserve officer of the Army, Navy, Air Force, or Marine Corps who is in an active status or on an inactive-status list and who reaches the maximum age specified in section 14509, 14510, 14511, or 14512 of this title for the officer's grade or position shall (unless the officer is sooner separated or the officer's separation is deferred or the officer is continued in an active status under another provision of law) not later than the last day of the month in which the officer reaches that maximum age—

(1) be transferred to the Retired Reserve, if the officer is qualified and applies for such transfer; or

(2) if the officer is not qualified or does not apply for transfer to the Retired Reserve, be discharged from the officer's reserve appointment.

(Added Oct. 5, 1994, P. L. 103-337, Div A, Title XVI, Subtitle A, Part I, § 1611, 108 Stat. 2954; Feb. 10, 1996, P. L. 104-106, Div A, Title XV, § 1501(b)(31), 110 Stat. 498.)

HISTORY; ANCILLARY LAWS AND DIRECTIVES

Effective date of section:

This section is effective Oct. 1, 1996, as provided by Act Oct. 5, 1994, P. L. 103-337, Div A, Title XVI, Subtitle F, § 1691(b)(1), 108 Stat. 3026, which appears as 10 USCS 10001 note.

Amendments:

1996. Act Feb. 10, 1996 (effective as if included in Act Oct. 5, 1994, P. L. 103-337, as enacted on Oct. 5, 1994, as provided by § 1501(f)(3) of Act Feb. 10, 1996, which appears as 10 USCS § 113 note) substituted ''inactive-status'' for ''inactive status''.

CROSS REFERENCES

Reserve components, limitations on separation inapplicable to discharges under this section, 10 USCS § 12683.

This section is referred to in 10 USCS §§ 12683, 14509–14512, 14516, 14517.

§ 14516. Separation to be considered involuntary

The separation of an officer pursuant to section 14513, 14514, or 14515 of this title shall be considered to be an involuntary separation for purposes of any other provision of law.

(Added Oct. 5, 1994, P. L. 103-337, Div A, Title XVI, Subtitle A, Part I, § 1611, 108 Stat. 2954.)

HISTORY; ANCILLARY LAWS AND DIRECTIVES

Effective date of section:

This section is effective Oct. 1, 1996, as provided by Act Oct. 5, 1994, P. L. 103-337, Div A, Title XVI, Subtitle F, § 1691(b)(1), 108 Stat. 3026, which appears as 10 USCS 10001 note.

§ 14517. Entitlement of officers discharged under this chapter to separation pay

An officer who is discharged under section 14513, 14514, or 14515 of this title is entitled to separation pay under section 1174 of this title if otherwise eligible under that section.

(Added Oct. 5, 1994, P. L. 103-337, Div A, Title XVI, Subtitle A, Part I, § 1611, 108 Stat. 2954.)

HISTORY; ANCILLARY LAWS AND DIRECTIVES

Effective date of section:

This section is effective Oct. 1, 1996, as provided by Act Oct. 5, 1994, P. L. 103-337, Div A, Title XVI, Subtitle F, § 1691(b)(1), 108 Stat. 3026, which appears as 10 USCS 10001 note.

CHAPTER 1409. CONTINUATION OF OFFICERS ON THE RESERVE ACTIVE-STATUS LIST AND SELECTIVE EARLY REMOVAL

Sec.

HISTORY; ANCILLARY LAWS AND DIRECTIVES

Amendments:

1994. Act Oct. 5, 1994, P. L. 103-337, Div A, Title XVI, Subtitle A, Part I, § 1611, 108 Stat. 2954 (effective as provided by § 1691 of such Act, which appears as 10 USCS § 10001 note), added the chapter heading and analysis.

§ 14701. Selection of officers for continuation on the reserve active-status list

(a) Consideration for continuation. (1) Upon application, a reserve officer of the Army, Navy, Air Force, or Marine Corps who is required to be removed from the reserve active-status list under section 14505, 14506, or 14507 of this title may, subject to the needs of the service and to section 14509 of this title, be considered for continuation on the reserve active-status list by a selection board convened under section 14101(b) of this title.

(2) A reserve officer who holds the grade of captain in the Army, Air Force, or Marine Corps or the grade of lieutenant in the Navy and who is subject to separation under section 14513 of this title may not be continued on the reserve active-status list under this subsection for a period which extends beyond the last day of the month in which the officer completes 20 years of commissioned service.

(3) A reserve officer who holds the grade of major or lieutenant commander and who is subject to separation under section 14513 of this title may not be continued on the reserve active-status list under this subsection for a period which extends beyond the last day of the month in which the officer completes 24 years of commissioned service.

(4) A reserve officer who holds the grade of lieutenant colonel or commander and who is subject to separation under section 14514 of this title may not be continued on the reserve active-status list under this subsection for a pe-

riod which extends beyond the last day of the month in which the officer completes 33 years of commissioned service.

(5) A reserve officer who holds the grade of colonel in the Army, Air Force, or Marine Corps or the grade of captain in the Navy and who is subject to separation under section 14514 of this title may not be continued on the reserve active-status list under this subsection for a period which extends beyond the last day of the month in which the officer completes 35 years of commissioned service.

(6) An officer who is selected for continuation on the reserve active-status list as a result of the convening of a selection board under section 14101(b) of this title but who declines to continue on that list shall be separated in accordance with section 14513 or 14514 of this title, as the case may be.

(7) Each officer who is continued on the reserve active-status list under this section, who is not subsequently promoted or continued on the active-status list, and whose name is not on a list of officers recommended for promotion to the next higher grade shall (unless sooner separated under another provision of law) be separated in accordance with section 14513 or 14514 of this title, as appropriate, upon the expiration of the period for which the officer was continued on the reserve active-status list.

(b) Approval of Secretary concerned. Continuation of an officer on the reserve active-status list under this section pursuant to action of a continuation board convened under section 14101(b) of this title is subject to the approval of the Secretary of the military department concerned.

(c) Instructions to continuation boards. A continuation board convened under section 14101(b) of this title to consider officers for continuation on the reserve active-status list under this section shall act in accordance with the instructions and directions provided to the board by the Secretary of the military department concerned.

(d) Regulations. The Secretary of Defense shall prescribe regulations for the administration of this section.

(Added Oct. 5, 1994, P. L. 103-337, Div A, Title XVI, Subtitle A, Part I, § 1611, 108 Stat. 2955.)

HISTORY; ANCILLARY LAWS AND DIRECTIVES

Effective date of section:

This section is effective Oct. 1, 1996, as provided by Act Oct. 5, 1994, P. L. 103-337, Div A, Title XVI, Subtitle F, § 1691(b)(1), 108 Stat. 3026, which appears as 10 USCS 10001 note.

CROSS REFERENCES

This section is referred to in 10 USCS §§ 14101, 14505–14507.

§ 14702. Retention on reserve active-status list of certain officers until age 60

(a) Retention. Notwithstanding the provisions of section 14506, 14507, or

14508 of this title, the Secretary of the military department concerned may, with the officer's consent, retain on the reserve active-status list an officer in the grade of major, lieutenant colonel, colonel, or brigadier general who is—

(1) an officer of the Army National Guard of the United States and assigned to a headquarters or headquarters detachment of a State; or

(2) a reserve officer of the Army or Air Force who, as a condition of continued employment as a National Guard or Reserve technician is required by the Secretary concerned to maintain membership in a Selected Reserve unit or organization.

(b) Separation at age 60. An officer may be retained under this section only so long as the officer continues to meet the conditions of subsection (a)(1) or (a)(2). An officer may not be retained under this section after the last day of the month in which the officer becomes 60 years of age.

(Added Oct. 5, 1994, P. L. 103-337, Div A, Title XVI, Subtitle A, Part I, § 1611, 108 Stat. 2955; Nov. 18, 1997, P. L. 105-85, Div A, Title V, Subtitle C, § 521(a), 111 Stat. 1734.)

HISTORY; ANCILLARY LAWS AND DIRECTIVES

Effective date of section:

This section became effective on Oct. 1, 1996, as provided by § 1691(b)(1) of Act Oct. 5, 1994, P. L. 103-337, which appears as 10 USCS 10001 note.

Amendments:

1997. Act Nov. 18, 1997, in subsec. (a), substituted "section 14506, 14507, or 14508" for "section 14506 or 14507" and substituted "colonel, or brigadier general" for "or colonel".

CROSS REFERENCES

This section is referred to in 10 USCS §§ 14506, 14507.

§ 14703. Authority to retain chaplains and officers in medical specialties until specified age

(a) Retention. Notwithstanding any provision of chapter 1407 of this title [10 USCS §§ 14501 et seq.] and except for officers referred to in sections 14503, 14504, 14505, and 14506 of this title and under regulations prescribed by the Secretary of Defense—

(1) the Secretary of the Army may, with the officer's consent, retain in an active status any reserve officer assigned to the Medical Corps, the Dental Corps, the Veterinary Corps, the Medical Services Corps (if the officer has been designated as allied health officer or biomedical sciences officer in that Corps), the Optometry Section of the Medical Services Corps, the Chaplains, the Army Nurse Corps, or the Army Medical Specialists Corps;

(2) the Secretary of the Navy may, with the officer's consent, retain in an active status any reserve officer appointed in the Medical Corps, Dental Corps, Nurse Corps, or Chaplain Corps or appointed in the Medical Services Corps and designated to perform as a veterinarian, optometrist, podiatrist, allied health officer, or biomedical sciences officer; and

(3) the Secretary of the Air Force may, with the officer's consent, retain in an active status any reserve officer who is designated as a medical officer, dental officer, veterinary officer, Air Force nurse, or chaplain or who is designated as a biomedical sciences officer and is qualified for service as a veterinarian, optometrist, or podiatrist.

(b) Separation at specified age. An officer may not be retained in active status under this section later than the date on which the officer becomes 67 years of age (or, in the case of a reserve officer of the Army in the Chaplains or a reserve officer of the Air Force designated as a chaplain, 60 years of age).

(Added Oct. 5, 1994, P. L. 103-337, Div A, Title XVI, Subtitle A, Part I, § 1611, 108 Stat. 2956.)

HISTORY; ANCILLARY LAWS AND DIRECTIVES

Effective date of section:

This section is effective Oct. 1, 1996, as provided by Act Oct. 5, 1994, P. L. 103-337, Div A, Title XVI, Subtitle F, § 1691(b)(1), 108 Stat. 3026, which appears as 10 USCS 10001 note.

§ 14704. Selective early removal from the reserve active-status list

(a) Boards to recommend officers for removal from reserve active-status list. Whenever the Secretary of the military department concerned determines that there are in any reserve component under the jurisdiction of the Secretary too many officers in any grade and competitive category who have at least 30 years of service computed under section 14706 of this title or at least 20 years of service computed under section 12732 of this title, the Secretary may convene a selection board under section 14101(b) of this title to consider all officers on that list who are in that grade and competitive category, and who have that amount of service, for the purpose of recommending officers by name for removal from the reserve active-status list, in the number specified by the Secretary by each grade and competitive category.

(b) Separation of officers selected. In the case of an officer recommended for separation in the report of a board under subsection (a), the Secretary may separate the officer in accordance with section 14514 of this title.

(c) Regulations. The Secretary of the military department concerned shall prescribe regulations for the administration of this section.

(Added Oct. 5, 1994, P. L. 103-337, Div A, Title XVI, Subtitle A, Part I, § 1611, 108 Stat. 2956.)

HISTORY; ANCILLARY LAWS AND DIRECTIVES

Effective date of section:

This section is effective Oct. 1, 1996, as provided by Act Oct. 5, 1994, P. L. 103-337, Div A, Title XVI, Subtitle F, § 1691(b)(1), 108 Stat. 3026, which appears as 10 USCS 10001 note.

CROSS REFERENCES

This section is referred to in 10 USCS §§ 14101, 14514.

§ 14705. Selective early retirement: reserve general and flag officers of the Navy and Marine Corps

(a) Authority to consider. An officer in the Naval Reserve in an active status serving in the grade of rear admiral (lower half) or rear admiral and an officer in the Marine Corps Reserve in an active status serving in the grade of brigadier general or major general may be considered for early retirement whenever the Secretary of the Navy determines that such action is necessary.

(b) Boards. If the Secretary of the Navy determines that consideration for early retirement under this section is necessary, the Secretary shall convene a board under section 14101(b) of this title to recommend an appropriate number of officers for early retirement.

(c) Separation under section 14514. An officer selected for early retirement under this section shall be separated in accordance with section 14514 of this title.

(Added Oct. 5, 1994, P. L. 103-337, Div A, Title XVI, Subtitle A, Part I, § 1611, 108 Stat. 2957.)

HISTORY; ANCILLARY LAWS AND DIRECTIVES

Effective date of section:

This section is effective Oct. 1, 1996, as provided by Act Oct. 5, 1994, P. L. 103-337, Div A, Title XVI, Subtitle F, § 1691(b)(1), 108 Stat. 3026, which appears as 10 USCS 10001 note.

CROSS REFERENCES

This section is referred to in 10 USCS § 14704.

§ 14706. Computation of total years of service

For the purpose of this chapter [10 USCS §§ 14701 et seq.] and chapter 1407 of this title [10 USCS §§ 14501 et seq.], a reserve officer's years of service include all service, other than constructive service, of the officer as a commissioned officer of any uniformed service (other than service as a warrant officer).

(Added Oct. 5, 1994, P. L. 103-337, Div A, Title XVI, Subtitle A, Part I, § 1611, 108 Stat. 2957.)

HISTORY; ANCILLARY LAWS AND DIRECTIVES

Effective date of section:

This section is effective Oct. 1, 1996, as provided by Act Oct. 5, 1994, P. L. 103-337, Div A, Title XVI, Subtitle F, § 1691(b)(1), 108 Stat. 3026, which appears as 10 USCS 10001 note.

CROSS REFERENCES

This section is referred to in 10 USCS § 14704.

CHAPTER 1411. ADDITIONAL PROVISIONS RELATING TO INVOLUNTARY SEPARATION

Sec.

HISTORY; ANCILLARY LAWS AND DIRECTIVES

Amendments:

1994. Act Oct. 5, 1994, P. L. 103-337, Div A, Title XVI, Subtitle A, Part I, § 1611, 108 Stat. 2957 (effective as provided by § 1691 of such Act, which appears as 10 USCS § 10001 note), added the chapter heading and analysis.

§ 14901. Separation of chaplains for loss of professional qualifications

(a) Separation. Under regulations prescribed by the Secretary of Defense, an officer on the reserve active-status list who is appointed or designated as a chaplain may, if the officer fails to maintain the qualifications needed to perform the professional function of a chaplain, be discharged. The authority under the preceding sentence applies without regard to the provisions of section 12645 of this title.

(b) Effect of separation. If an officer separated under this section is eligible for retirement, the officer may be retired. If the officer has completed the years of service required for eligibility for retired pay under chapter 1223 of this title [10 USCS §§ 12731 et seq.], the officer may be transferred to the Retired Reserve.

(Added Oct. 5, 1994, P. L. 103-337, Div A, Title XVI, Subtitle A, Part I, § 1611, 108 Stat. 2922.)

HISTORY; ANCILLARY LAWS AND DIRECTIVES

Effective date of section:

This section became effective on Oct. 1, 1996, as provided by Act Oct. 5, 1994, P. L. 103-337, Div A, Title XVI, Subtitle F, § 1691(b)(1), 108 Stat. 3026, which appears as 10 USCS 10001 note.

CROSS REFERENCES

Reserve components, limitations on separation inapplicable to separation under this section, 10 USCS § 12683.

This section is referred to in 10 USCS § 12683.

§ 14902. Separation for substandard performance and for certain other reasons

(a) Substandard performance of duty. The Secretary of the military department concerned shall prescribe, by regulation, procedures for the review at any time of the record of any reserve officer to determine whether that officer should be required, because that officer's performance has fallen below standards prescribed by the Secretary concerned, to show cause for retention in an active status.

(b) Misconduct, etc. The Secretary of the military department concerned shall prescribe, by regulation, procedures for the review at any time of the record of any reserve officer to determine whether that officer should be required, because of misconduct, because of moral or professional dereliction, or because the officer's retention is not clearly consistent with the interests of national security, to show cause for retention in an active status.

(c) Regulations. The authority of the Secretary of a military department under this section shall be carried out subject to such limitations as the Secretary of Defense may prescribe by regulation.

(Added Oct. 5, 1994, P. L. 103-337, Div A, Title XVI, Subtitle A, Part I, § 1611, 108 Stat. 2958.)

HISTORY; ANCILLARY LAWS AND DIRECTIVES

Effective date of section:

This section became effective on Oct. 1, 1996, as provided by Act Oct. 5, 1994, P. L. 103-337, Div A, Title XVI, Subtitle F, § 1691(b)(1), 108 Stat. 3026, which appears as 10 USCS 10001 note.

CROSS REFERENCES

This section is referred to in 10 USCS §§ 14109, 14903–14905.

§ 14903. Boards of inquiry

(a) Convening of boards. The Secretary of the military department concerned shall convene a board of inquiry at such time and place as the Secretary may prescribe to receive evidence and review the case of any officer who has been required to show cause for retention in an active status under section 14902 of this title. Each board of inquiry shall be composed of not less than three officers who have the qualifications prescribed in section 14906 of this title.

(b) Right to fair hearing. A board of inquiry shall give a fair and impartial hearing to each officer required under section 14902 of this title to show cause for retention in an active status.

(c) Recommendations to Secretary. If a board of inquiry determines that the officer has failed to establish that the officer should be retained in an active status, the board shall recommend to the Secretary concerned that the officer not be retained in an active status.

(d) Action by Secretary. After review of the recommendation of the board of inquiry, the Secretary may—

(1) remove the officer from an active status; or

(2) determine that the case be closed.

(e) Action in cases where cause for retention is established. (1) If a board of inquiry determines that an officer has established that the officer should be retained in an active status or if the Secretary determines that the case be closed, the officer's case is closed.

(2) An officer who is required to show cause for retention under section 14902(a) of this title and whose case is closed under paragraph (1) may not again be required to show cause for retention under such subsection during the one-year period beginning on the date of that determination.

(3)(A) Subject to subparagraph (B), an officer who is required to show cause for retention under section 14902(b) of this title and whose case is closed under paragraph (1) may again be required to show cause for retention at any time.

(B) An officer who has been required to show cause for retention under section 14902(b) of this title and who is thereafter retained in an active status may not again be required to show cause for retention under such section solely because of conduct which was the subject of the previous proceeding, unless the recommendations of the board of inquiry that considered the officer's case are determined to have been obtained by fraud or collusion.

(Added Oct. 5, 1994, P. L. 103-337, Div A, Title XVI, Subtitle A, Part I, § 1611, 108 Stat. 2958; Feb. 10, 1996, P. L. 104-106, Div A, Title XV, § 1501(b)(32), 110 Stat. 498.)

HISTORY; ANCILLARY LAWS AND DIRECTIVES

Effective date of section:

This section became effective on Oct. 1, 1996, as provided by Act Oct. 5, 1994, P. L. 103-337, Div A, Title XVI, Subtitle F, § 1691(b)(1), 108 Stat. 3026, which appears as 10 USCS 10001 note.

Amendments:

1996. Act Feb. 10, 1996 (effective as if included in Act Oct. 5, 1994, P. L. 103-337, as enacted on Oct. 5, 1994, as provided by § 1501(f)(3) of Act Feb. 10, 1996, which appears as 10 USCS § 113 note), in subsec. (b), substituted "title" for "chapter".

CROSS REFERENCES

This section is referred to in 10 USCS §§ 14311, 14905.

§ 14904. Rights and procedures

(a) Procedural rights. Under regulations prescribed by the Secretary of Defense, an officer required under section 14902 of this title to show cause for retention in an active status—

(1) shall be notified in writing, at least 30 days before the hearing of the of-

ficer's case by a board of inquiry, of the reasons for which the officer is being required to show cause for retention in an active status;

(2) shall be allowed a reasonable time, as determined by the board of inquiry, to prepare for showing of cause for retention in an active status;

(3) shall be allowed to appear in person and to be represented by counsel at proceedings before the board of inquiry; and

(4) shall be allowed full access to, and shall be furnished copies of, records relevant to the case, except that the board of inquiry shall withhold any record that the Secretary concerned determines should be withheld in the interest of national security.

(b) Summary of records withheld. When a record is withheld under subsection (a)(4), the officer whose case is under consideration shall, to the extent that the interest of national security permits, be furnished a summary of the record so withheld.

(Added Oct. 5, 1994, P. L. 103-337, Div A, Title XVI, Subtitle A, Part I, § 1611, 108 Stat. 2959.)

HISTORY; ANCILLARY LAWS AND DIRECTIVES

Effective date of section:

This section became effective on Oct. 1, 1996, as provided by Act Oct. 5, 1994, P. L. 103-337, Div A, Title XVI, Subtitle F, § 1691(b)(1), 108 Stat. 3026, which appears as 10 USCS 10001 note.

§ 14905. Officer considered for removal: retirement or discharge

(a) Voluntary retirement or discharge. At any time during proceedings under this chapter with respect to the removal of an officer from an active status, the Secretary of the military department concerned may grant a request by the officer—

(1) for voluntary retirement, if the officer is qualified for retirement;

(2) for transfer to the Retired Reserve if the officer has completed the years of service required for eligibility for retired pay under chapter 1223 of this title [10 USCS §§ 12731 et seq.] and is otherwise eligible for transfer to the Retired Reserve; or

(3) for discharge in accordance with subsection (b)(3).

(b) Required retirement or discharge. An officer removed from an active status under section 14903 of this title shall—

(1) if eligible for voluntary retirement under any provision of law on the date of such removal, be retired in the grade and with the retired pay for which he would be eligible if retired under that provision;

(2) if eligible for transfer to the Retired Reserve and has completed the years of service required for retired pay under chapter 1223 of this title [10 USCS §§ 12731 et seq.], be transferred to the Retired Reserve; and

(3) if ineligible for retirement or transfer to the Retired Reserve under paragraph (1) or (2) on the date of such removal—

(A) be honorably discharged in the grade then held, in the case of an officer whose case was brought under subsection (a) of section 14902 of this title; or

(B) be discharged in the grade then held, in the case of an officer whose case was brought under subsection (b) of section 14902 of this title.

(c) Separation pay. An officer who is discharged under subsection (b)(3) is entitled, if eligible therefor, to separation pay under section 1174(c) of this title.

(Added Oct. 5, 1994, P. L. 103-337, Div A, Title XVI, Subtitle A, Part I, § 1611, 108 Stat. 2959.)

HISTORY; ANCILLARY LAWS AND DIRECTIVES

Effective date of section:

This section became effective on Oct. 1, 1996, as provided by Act Oct. 5, 1994, P. L. 103-337, Div A, Title XVI, Subtitle F, § 1691(b)(1), 108 Stat. 3026, which appears as 10 USCS 10001 note.

§ 14906. Officers eligible to serve on boards

(a) Composition of boards. (1) Each officer who serves on a board convened under this chapter shall be an officer of the same armed force as the officer being required to show cause for retention in an active status.

(2) An officer may not serve on a board under this chapter unless the officer holds a grade above lieutenant colonel or commander and is senior in grade and rank to any officer considered by the board.

(b) Limitation. A person may not be a member of more than one board convened under this chapter [10 USCS §§ 14901 et seq.] to consider the same officer.

(Added Oct. 5, 1994, P. L. 103-337, Div A, Title XVI, Subtitle A, Part I, § 1611, 108 Stat. 2960.)

HISTORY; ANCILLARY LAWS AND DIRECTIVES

Effective date of section:

This section became effective on Oct. 1, 1996, as provided by Act Oct. 5, 1994, P. L. 103-337, Div A, Title XVI, Subtitle F, § 1691(b)(1), 108 Stat. 3026, which appears as 10 USCS 10001 note.

CROSS REFERENCES

This section is referred to in 10 USCS § 14903.

§ 14907. Army National Guard of the United States and Air National Guard of the United States: discharge and withdrawal of Federal recognition of officers absent without leave

(a) Authority to withdraw Federal recognition. If an officer of the Army National Guard of the United States or the Air National Guard of the United States has been absent without leave for three months, the Secretary of the Army or the Secretary of the Air Force, as appropriate, may—

(1) terminate the reserve appointment of the officer; and

(2) withdraw the officer's Federal recognition as an officer of the National Guard.

(b) Discharge from Reserve appointment. An officer of the Army National Guard of the United States or the Air National Guard of the United States whose Federal recognition as an officer of the National Guard is withdrawn under section 323(b) of title 32 shall be discharged from the officer's appointment as a reserve officer of the Army or the Air Force, as the case may be.

(Added Oct. 5, 1994, P. L. 103-337, Div A, Title XVI, Subtitle A, Part I, § 1611, 108 Stat. 2960.)

HISTORY; ANCILLARY LAWS AND DIRECTIVES

Effective date of section:

This section became effective on Oct. 1, 1996, as provided by Act Oct. 5, 1994, P. L. 103-337, Div A, Title XVI, Subtitle F, § 1691(b)(1), 108 Stat. 3026, which appears as 10 USCS 10001 note.

CROSS REFERENCES

Reserve components, limitations on separation inapplicable to discharges under this section, 10 USCS § 12683.

This section is referred to in 10 USCS § 12683.

PART IV. TRAINING FOR RESERVE COMPONENTS AND EDUCATIONAL ASSISTANCE PROGRAMS

HISTORY; ANCILLARY LAWS AND DIRECTIVES

Amendments:

1994. Act Oct. 5, 1994, P. L. 103-337, Div A, Title XVI, Subtitle C, § 1663(a), 108 Stat. 3006 (effective 12/1/94 as provided by § 1691 of such Act, which appears as 10 USCS § 10001 note), added the part heading and analysis.

1996. Act Feb. 10, 1996, P. L. 104-106, Div A, Title XV, § 1501(b)(1), 110 Stat. 495 (effective as if included in Act Oct. 5, 1994, P. L. 103-337, as enacted on Oct. 5, 1994, as provided by § 1501(f)(3) of Act Feb. 10, 1996, which appears as 10 USCS § 113 note), amended the analysis of this part by substituting ''Repayment Programs'' for ''Repayments'' in item 1609.

CHAPTER 1601. TRAINING GENERALLY [No present sections]

HISTORY; ANCILLARY LAWS AND DIRECTIVES

Amendments:

1994. Act Oct. 5, 1994, P. L. 103-337, Div A, Title XVI, Subtitle C, § 1663(a), 108 Stat. 3006 (effective 12/1/94 as provided by § 1691 of such Act, which appears as 10 USCS § 10001 note), added the chapter heading.

CHAPTER 1606. EDUCATIONAL ASSISTANCE FOR MEMBERS OF THE SELECTED RESERVE

Sec.

HISTORY; ANCILLARY LAWS AND DIRECTIVES

Amendments:

1994. Act Oct. 5, 1994, P. L. 103-337, Div A, Title XVI, Subtitle C, § 1663(b)(1), 108 Stat. 3006 (effective 12/1/94 as provided by § 1691 of such Act, which appears as 10 USCS § 10001 note), added the chapter heading and analysis.

1996. Act Feb. 10, 1996, P. L. 104-106, Div A, Title XV, § 1501(b)(33), 110 Stat. 498 (effective as if included in Act Oct. 5, 1994, P. L. 103-337, as enacted on Oct. 5, 1994, as provided by § 1501(f)(3) of Act Feb. 10, 1996, which appears as 10 USCS § 113 note), amended the analysis of this chapter by substituting ''limitation'' for ''limitations'' in item 16133.

§ 16131. Educational assistance program: establishment; amount

(a) To encourage membership in units of the Selected Reserve of the Ready Reserve, the Secretary of each military department, under regulations prescribed by the Secretary of Defense, and the Secretary of Transportation, under regulations prescribed by the Secretary with respect to the Coast Guard when it is not operating as a service in the Navy, shall establish and maintain a program to provide educational assistance to members of the Selected Reserve of the Ready Reserve of the armed forces under the jurisdiction of the Secretary concerned who agree to remain members of the Selected Reserve for a period of not less than six years.

(b)(1) Except as provided [in] subsections (d) through (f), each educational assistance program established under subsection (a) shall provide for payment by the Secretary concerned, through the Secretary of Veterans Affairs, to each person entitled to educational assistance under this chapter [10 USCS §§ 16131 et seq.] who is pursuing a program of education of an educational assistance allowance at the following rates:

(A) $251 (as increased from time to time under paragraph (2)) per month for each month of full-time pursuit of a program of education;

(B) $188 (as increased from time to time under paragraph (2)) per month for each month of three-quarter-time pursuit of a program of education;

(C) $125 (as increased from time to time under paragraph (2)) per month for each month of half-time pursuit of a program of education; and

(D) an appropriately reduced rate, as determined under regulations which the Secretary of Veterans Affairs shall prescribe, for each month of less than half-time pursuit of a program of education, except that no payment may be made to a person for less than half-time pursuit if tuition assistance is otherwise available to the person for such pursuit from the military department concerned.

(2) With respect to any fiscal year, the Secretary shall provide a percentage increase (rounded to the nearest dollar) in the rates payable under subparagraphs (A), (B), and (C) of paragraph (1) equal to the percentage by which—

(A) the Consumer Price Index (all items, United States city average) for the 12-month period ending on the June 30 preceding the beginning of the fiscal year for which the increase is made, exceeds

(B) such Consumer Price Index for the 12-month period preceding the 12-month period described in subparagraph (A).

(c)(1) Educational assistance may be provided under this chapter [10 USCS §§ 16131 et seq.] for pursuit of any program of education that is an approved program of education for purposes of chapter 30 of title 38 [38 USCS §§ 3001 et seq.].

(2) Subject to section 3695 of title 38, the maximum number of months of educational assistance that may be provided to any person under this chapter [10 USCS §§ 16131 et seq.] is 36 (or the equivalent thereof in part-time educational assistance);

(3)(A) Notwithstanding any other provision of this chapter [10 USCS §§ 16131 et seq.] or chapter 36 of title 38 [38 USCS §§ 3670 et seq.], any payment of an educational assistance allowance described in subparagraph (B) of this paragraph shall not—

(i) be charged against the entitlement of any individual under this chapter [10 USCS §§ 16131 et seq.]; or

(ii) be counted toward the aggregate period for which section 3695 of title 38 limits an individual's receipt of assistance.

(B) The payment of the educational assistance allowance referred to in subparagraph (A) of this paragraph is the payment of such an allowance to the individual for pursuit of a course or courses under this chapter [10 USCS §§ 16131 et seq.] if the Secretary of Veterans Affairs finds that the individual—

(i) had to discontinue such course pursuit as a result of being ordered to serve on active duty under section 12301(a), 12301(d), 12301(g), 12302, or 12304 of this title; and

(ii) failed to receive credit or training time toward completion of the individual's approved educational, professional, or vocational objective as a result of having to discontinue, as described in clause (i), the individual's course pursuit.

(C) The period for which, by reason of this subsection, an educational assistance allowance is not charged against entitlement or counted toward the applicable aggregate period under section 3695 of title 38 shall not exceed the portion of the period of enrollment in the course or courses for which the individual failed to receive credit or with respect to which the individual lost training time, as determined under subparagraph (B)(ii).

(d)(1) Except as provided in paragraph (2), the amount of the monthly educational assistance allowance payable to a person pursuing a full-time program of apprenticeship or other on-the-job training under this chapter [10 USCS §§ 16131 et seq.] is—

(A) for each of the first six months of the person's pursuit of such program, 75 percent of the monthly educational assistance allowance otherwise payable to such person under this chapter [10 USCS §§ 16131 et seq.];

(B) for each of the second six months of the person's pursuit of such program, 55 percent of such monthly educational assistance allowance; and

(C) for each of the months following the first 12 months of the person's pursuit of such program, 35 percent of such monthly educational assistance allowance.

(2) In any month in which any person pursuing a program of education consisting of a program of apprenticeship or other on-the-job training fails to complete 120 hours of training, the amount of the monthly educational assistance allowance payable under this chapter [10 USCS §§ 16131 et seq.] to the person shall be limited to the same proportion of the applicable full-time rate as the number of hours worked during such month, rounded to the nearest 8 hours, bears to 120 hours.

(3)(A) Except as provided in subparagraph (B), for each month that such person is paid a monthly educational assistance allowance under this chapter [10 USCS §§ 16131 et seq.], the person's entitlement under this chapter [10 USCS §§ 16131 et seq.] shall be charged at the rate of—

(i) 75 percent of a month in the case of payments made in accordance with paragraph (1)(A);

(ii) 55 percent of a month in the case of payments made in accordance with paragraph (1)(B); and

(iii) 35 percent of a month in the case of payments made in accordance with paragraph (1)(C).

(B) Any such charge to the entitlement shall be reduced proportionately in accordance with the reduction in payment under paragraph (2).

(e)(1)(A) The amount of the educational assistance allowance payable under this chapter [10 USCS §§ 16131 et seq.] to a person who enters into an agreement to pursue, and is pursuing, a program of education exclusively by correspondence is an amount equal to 55 percent of the established charge which the institution requires nonveterans to pay for the course or courses pursued by such person.

(B) For purposes of subparagraph (A), the term "established charge" means the lesser of—

(i) the charge for the course or courses determined on the basis of the lowest extended time payment plan offered by the institution and approved by the appropriate State approving agency; or

(ii) the actual charge to the person for such course or courses.

(C) Such allowance shall be paid quarterly on a pro rata basis for the lessons completed by the person and serviced by the institution.

(2) In each case in which the amount of educational assistance is determined under paragraph (1), the period of entitlement of the person concerned shall be charged with one month for each amount equal to the amount of the monthly rate payable under subsection (b)(1)(A) for the fiscal year concerned which is paid to the individual as an educational assistance allowance.

(f)(1) Each individual who is pursuing a program of education consisting exclusively of flight training approved as meeting the requirements of section 16136(c) of this title shall be paid an educational assistance allowance under this chapter [10 USCS §§ 16131 et seq.] in the amount equal to 60 percent of the established charges for tuition and fees which similarly circumstanced nonveterans enrolled in the same flight course are required to pay.

(2) No educational assistance allowance may be paid under this chapter [10 USCS §§ 16131 et seq.] to an individual for any month during which such individual is pursuing a program of education consisting exclusively of flight training until the Secretary has received from that individual and the institution providing such training a certification of the flight training received by the individual during that month and the tuition and other fees charged for that training.

(3) The period of entitlement of an individual pursuing a program of education described in paragraph (1) shall be charged with one month for each amount equal to the amount of the monthly rate payable under subsection (b)(1)(A) for the fiscal year concerned which is paid to that individual as an educational assistance allowance for such program.

(4) The number of solo flying hours for which an individual may be paid an educational assistance allowance under this subsection may not exceed the minimum number of solo flying hours required by the Federal Aviation Administration for the flight rating or certification which is the goal of the individual's flight training.

(g)(1)(A) Subject to subparagraph (B), the Secretary of Veterans Affairs shall approve individualized tutorial assistance for any person entitled to educational assistance under this chapter [10 USCS §§ 16131 et seq.] who—

(i) is enrolled in and pursuing a postsecondary course of education on a half-time or more basis at an educational institution; and

(ii) has a deficiency in a subject required as a part of, or which is prerequisite to, or which is indispensable to the satisfactory pursuit of, the program of education.

(B) The Secretary of Veterans Affairs shall not approve individualized tutorial assistance for a person pursuing a program of education under this paragraph unless such assistance is necessary for the person to successfully complete the program of education.

(2)(A) Subject to subparagraph (B), the Secretary concerned, through the

Secretary of Veterans Affairs, shall pay to a person receiving individualized tutorial assistance pursuant to paragraph (1) a tutorial assistance allowance. The amount of the allowance payable under this paragraph may not exceed $100 for any month, nor aggregate more than $1,200. The amount of the allowance paid under this paragraph shall be in addition to the amount of educational assistance allowance payable to a person under this chapter [10 USCS §§ 16131 et seq.].

(B) A tutorial assistance allowance may not be paid to a person under this paragraph until the educational institution at which the person is enrolled certifies that—

(i) the individualized tutorial assistance is essential to correct a deficiency of the person in a subject required as a part of, or which is prerequisite to, or which is indispensable to the satisfactory pursuit of, an approved program of education;

(ii) the tutor chosen to perform such assistance is qualified to provide such assistance and is not the person's parent, spouse, child (whether or not married or over eighteen years of age), brother, or sister; and

(iii) the charges for such assistance do not exceed the customary charges for such tutorial assistance.

(3)(A) A person's period of entitlement to educational assistance under this chapter [10 USCS §§ 16131 et seq.] shall be charged only with respect to the amount of tutorial assistance paid to the person under this subsection in excess of $600.

(B) A person's period of entitlement to educational assistance under this chapter [10 USCS §§ 16131 et seq.] shall be charged at the rate of one month for each amount of assistance paid to the individual under this section in excess of $600 that is equal to the amount of the monthly educational assistance allowance which the person is otherwise eligible to receive for full-time pursuit of an institutional course under this chapter [10 USCS §§ 16131 et seq.].

(h) A program of education in a course of instruction beyond the baccalaureate degree level shall be provided under this chapter [10 USCS §§ 16131 et seq.], subject to the availability of appropriations.

(i)(1) In the case of a person who has a skill or specialty designated by the Secretary concerned as a skill or specialty in which there is a critical shortage of personnel or for which it is difficult to recruit or, in the case of critical units, retain personnel, the Secretary concerned may increase the rate of the educational assistance allowance applicable to that person to such rate in excess of the rate prescribed under subparagraphs (A) through (D) of subsection (b)(1) as the Secretary of Defense considers appropriate, but the amount of any such increase may not exceed $350 per month.

(2) In the case of a person who has a skill or specialty designated by the Secretary concerned as a skill or specialty in which there is a critical shortage of personnel or for which it is difficult to recruit or, in the case of critical units, retain personnel, who is eligible for educational benefits under chapter 30 (other than section 3012) of title 38 [38 USCS §§ 3001 et seq.

(other than § 3012)] and who meets the eligibility criteria specified in subparagraphs (A) and (B) of section 16132(a)(1) of this title, the Secretary concerned may increase the rate of the educational assistance allowance applicable to that person to such rate in excess of the rate prescribed under section 3015 of title 38 as the Secretary of Defense considers appropriate, but the amount of any such increase may not exceed $350 per month.

(3) The authority provided by paragraphs (1) and (2) shall be exercised by the Secretaries concerned under regulations prescribed by the Secretary of Defense.

(Added July 30, 1977, P. L. 95-79, Title IV, § 402(a), 91 Stat. 328; Nov. 9, 1979, P. L. 96-107, Title IV, § 402(a), 93 Stat. 808; Sept. 8, 1980, P. L. 96-342, Title IX, § 906(a)(1), 94 Stat. 1117; Dec. 12, 1980, P. L. 96-513, Title V, Part B, § 511(68), 94 Stat. 2926; Oct. 19, 1984, P. L. 98-525, Title VII, § 705(a)(1) in part, 98 Stat. 2565; Nov. 18, 1988, P. L. 100-689, Title I, Part A, §§ 110(a), 111(b)(1), 102 Stat. 4170; Nov. 29, 1989, P. L. 101-189, Div A, Title VI, Part E, §§ 642(b), 645(a), (b)(1), 103 Stat. 1456, 1458; Dec. 18, 1989, P. L. 101-237, Title IV, § 422(b)(2), 103 Stat. 2089; April 6, 1991, P. L. 102-25, Title III, Part C, § 337(b), 105 Stat. 90; Oct. 10, 1991, P. L. 102-127, § 2(d), 105 Stat. 621; Oct. 29, 1992, P. L. 102-568, Title III, §§ 301(b), (d), 310(b), 318, 320(a)(1), 106 Stat. 4326, 4330, 4334, 4335; Aug. 10, 1993, P. L. 103-66, Title XII, § 12009(b), 107 Stat. 416; Nov. 30, 1993, P. L. 103-160, Div A, Title V, Subtitle B, § 518, 107 Stat. 1651; Oct. 5, 1994, P. L. 103-337, Div A, Title XVI, Subtitle C, § 1663(b)(2), (3), 108 Stat. 3006, 3007; Feb. 10, 1996, P. L. 104-106, Div A, Title X, Subtitle G, § 1076, 110 Stat. 450; Oct. 9, 1996, P. L. 104-275, Title I, § 105(d), 110 Stat. 3327; Nov. 18, 1997, P. L. 105-85, Div A, Title V, Subtitle E, Part II, § 553(a), 111 Stat. 1748; June 9, 1998, P. L. 105-178, Title VIII, Subtitle B, § 8203(b)(1)–(3), 112 Stat. 493.)

HISTORY; ANCILLARY LAWS AND DIRECTIVES

Explanatory notes:

The word "in" has been inserted in brackets in subsec. (b)(1) to indicate the probable intent of Congress to include such word.

Amendments:

1979. Act Nov. 9, 1979, in subsec. (b)(1), substituted "100 per cent" for "50 per cent".

1980. Act Sept. 8, 1980 (effective 10/1/80, as provided by § 906(a)(2) of such Act, which appears as a note to this section), in subsec. (c), substituted "$1,000" for "$500", and substituted "$4,000" for "$2,000".

Act Dec. 12, 1980 (effective upon enactment on 12/12/80, as provided by § 701(b)(3) of such Act, which appears as 10 USCS § 101 note), in subsec. (a), substituted "armed forces" for "armed force"; in subsec. (b)(2), inserted "of this title"; and, in subsec. (d), substituted "Secretary of Education" for "Commissioner of Education, Department of Health, Education, and Welfare".

1984. Act Oct. 19, 1984 (effective 7/1/85 as provided by § 705(b) of such Act, which appears as a note to this section) substituted this section for one which read:

''§ 2131. Educational assistance program: establishment; amount

''(a) To encourage enlistments in units of the Selected Reserve of the Ready Reserve, the Secretary of each military department, under regulations prescribed by the Secretary of Defense, and the Secretary of Transportation, under regulations prescribed by him with respect to the Coast Guard when it is not operating as a service in the Navy, may establish and maintain a program to provide educational assistance to enlisted members of the Selected Reserve of the Ready Reserve of the armed forces under his jurisdiction.

''(b)(1) An educational assistance program established under subsection (a) shall provide for payment by the Secretary concerned of 100 percent of the educational expenses incurred by a member for instruction at an accredited institution. Expenses for which payment may be made under this section include tuition, fees, books, laboratory fees, and shop fees for consumable materials used as part of classroom or shop instruction. Payments under this section shall be limited to those educational expenses normally incurred by students at the institution involved.

''(2) To receive assistance under this section, a member must be eligible for such assistance under section 2132 of this title and must submit an application for such assistance in such form and manner as the Secretary concerned shall prescribe and be approved for such assistance by the Secretary concerned.

''(c) Educational assistance may be provided to a member under this section until the member completes a course of instruction required for the award of a baccalaureate degree, or the equivalent evidence of completion of study, by an accredited institution, but the amount of educational assistance provided a member under this section may not exceed $1,000 in any twelve-month period, nor a total of $4,000.

''(d) For purposes of this section, the term 'accredited institution' means a civilian college, university, or trade, technical, or vocational school in the United States (including the District of Columbia, Puerto Rico, Guam, and the Virgin Islands) that provides education at the postsecondary level and that is accredited by a nationally recognized accrediting agency or association or by an accrediting agency or association recognized by the Secretary of Education.''.

1988. Act Nov. 18, 1988, in subsec. (b), in para. (2), deleted ''and'' following the semicolon, in para. (3), substituted ''; and'' for a period, and added para. (4); and in subsec. (c), in para. (2), inserted ''(or the equivalent thereof in part-time educational assistance)''.

1989. Act Nov. 29, 1989 (applicable as provided by § 642(d) of such Act, which appears as a note to this section), in subsec. (b), in the introductory matter, substituted ''Except as provided in subsections (d) through (f), each'' for ''Each'' and inserted '', through the Secretary of Veterans Affairs,''; and substituted subsec. (c) for one which read:

''(1) Educational assistance may only be provided under this chapter for pursuit of a program of education at an institution of higher learning and may not be provided to a person after the person has completed a course of instruction required for the award of a baccalaureate degree or the equivalent evidence of completion of study.

''(2) Subject to section 1795 of title 38, the maximum number of months of educational assistance that may be provided to any person under this chapter is 36 (or the equivalent thereof in part-time educational assistance);'';

and added subsecs. (d)–(f).

Such Act further, in subsec. (b), in the introductory matter, substituted ''of an educational'' for ''and educational'' and, in para. (4), substituted ''Secretary of Veterans Affairs'' for ''Administrator of Veterans' Affairs''.

Act Dec. 18, 1989 (effective 9/30/90, as provided by § 422(d) of such Act, which appears as a note to this section), in subsec. (b), substituted ''(g)'' for ''(f)''; and added subsec. (g).

1991. Act April 6, 1991, in subsec. (b), substituted ''(b)(1) Except as provided in paragraph (2) and'' for ''(b) Except as provided in'', redesignated former paras. (1)-(4) as subparas. (A)–(D), respectively, and added new para. (2); and, in subsecs. (f)(2) and (g)(3), substituted ''amount equal to the amount of the monthly rate payable under subsection (b)(1)(A) for the fiscal year concerned'' for ''$140''.

Act Oct. 10, 1991, in subsec. (c), added para. (3).

1992. Act Oct. 29, 1992 (effective 4/1/93 as provided by § 301(e) of such Act, which appears as a note to this section), in subsec. (b), in para. (1), in subpara. (A), substituted ''$190'' for ''$140'', in subpara. (B), substituted ''$143'' for ''$105'' and, in subpara. (C), substituted ''$95'' for ''$70'', in para. (2), deleted subpara. (A) which read'' ''During the period beginning on October 1, 1991, and ending on September 30, 1993, the monthly rates payable under subparagraphs (A), (B), and (C) of paragraph (1) shall be $170, $128, and $85, respectively.'', redesignated subpara. (B) as subpara. (A), and in such subparagraph as so redesignated, substituted ''shall provide a percentage increase in the monthly rates payable under subparagraphs (A), (B), and (C) of paragraph (1)'' for ''may continue to pay, in lieu of the rates payable under subparagraphs (A), (B), and (C) of paragraph (1), the monthly rates payable under subparagraph (A) of this paragraph and may provide a percentage increase in such rates'', redesignated subpara. (C) as subpara. (B), and in such subparagraph as so redesignated, substituted ''shall'' for ''may'' wherever appearing.

Such Act further (applicable as provided by § 310(d) of such Act, which appears as a note to this section), in subsec. (g), in para. (1), deleted ''(other than tuition and fees charged for or attributable to solo flying hours)'' following ''for tuition and fees'', and added para. (4).

Such Act further, in subsec. (c), in para. (2), substituted ''section 3695 of title 38'' for ''section 1795 of title 38'', in para. (3), in subpara. (B)(ii), substituted '', the individual's'' for ''of this subparagraph, his or her'' and, in subpara. (C), substituted the concluding period for ''of this paragraph.''; and added subsec. (h).

1993. Act Aug. 10, 1993, in subsec. (b)(2), substituted ''With respect to'' for

''(A) With respect to the fiscal year beginning on October 1, 1993, the Secretary shall provide a percentage increase in the monthly rates payable under subparagraphs (A), (B), and (C) of paragraph (1) equal to the percentage by which the Consumer Price Index (all items, United States city average, published by the Bureau of Labor Statistics) for the 12-month period ending June 30, 1993, exceeds such Consumer Price Index for the 12-month period ending June 30, 1992.

''(B) With respect to'',

redesignated cls. (i) and (ii) as subparas. (A) and (B), respectively, and, in subpara. (B) as so redesignated, substituted ''subparagraph (A)'' for ''clause (i)''.

Act Nov. 30, 1993, in subsec. (c)(1), substituted a period for ''other than a program of education in a course of instruction beyond the baccalaureate degree level.''; and added subsec. (i).

1994. Act Oct. 5, 1994 (effective 12/1/94 as provided by § 1691 of such Act, which appears as 10 USCS § 10001 note) transferred this section, enacted as 10 USCS § 2131, to Chapter 1606 and redesignated it as 10 USCS § 16131; in subsec. (c)(3)(B)(i), substituted ''section 12301(a), 12301(d), 12301(g), 12302, or 12304'' for ''section 672 (a), (d), or (g), 673, or 673b''; and, in subsec. (g)(1), substituted ''section 16136(c)'' for ''section 2136(c)''.

1996. Act Feb. 10, 1996 added subsec. (j).

Act Oct. 9, 1996, in subsec. (b)(1), substituted ''(f)'' for ''(g)''; deleted subsec. (e), which read:

''(e)(1) The amount of the monthly educational assistance allowance payable to a person pursuing a cooperative program under this chapter shall be 80 percent of the monthly allowance otherwise payable to such person under this chapter.

''(2) For each month that a person is paid a monthly educational assistance allowance for pursuit of a cooperative program under this chapter, the person's entitlement under this chapter shall be charged at the rate of 80 percent of a month.'';

and redesignated subsecs. (f)–(j) as subsecs. (e)–(i), respectively.

1997. Act Nov. 18, 1997, in subsec. (c)(3)(B)(i), deleted '', in connection with the Persian Gulf War,'' following ''ordered''.

1998. Act June 9, 1998 (effective on 10/1/98 as provided by § 8203(b)(4) of such Act, which appears as a note to this section), in subsec. (b), in para. (1), in the introductory matter, deleted ''in paragraph (2) and'' following ''Except as provided''. in subpara. (A), substituted ''$251 (as increased from time to time under paragraph (2))'' for ''$190'', in subpara. (B), substituted ''$188 (as increased from time to time under paragraph (2))'' for ''$143'' and, in subpara. (C), substituted ''$125 (as increased from time to time under paragraph (2))'' for ''$95'', and, in para. (2), substituted '', the Secretary shall provide a percentage increase (rounded to the nearest dollar) in the rates payable under subparagraphs (A), (B), and (C) of paragraph (1)'' for ''beginning on or after October 1, 1994, the Secretary shall continue to pay, in lieu of the rates payable under subparagraphs (A), (B), and (C) of paragraph (1), the monthly rates payable under this paragraph for the previous fiscal year and shall provide, for any such fiscal year, a percentage increase in such rates''.

Other provisions:

Application of Nov. 9, 1979 amendments. Act Nov. 9, 1979, P. L. 96-107, Title IV, § 402(c), 93 Stat. 808, provided: ''The amendments made by this section [amending this section and former 10 USCS § 2133] shall apply only to individuals enlisting in the Reserves after September 30, 1979.''.

Effective date of 1980 amendment. Act Sept. 8, 1980, P. L. 96-342, Title IX, § 906(a)(2), 94 Stat. 1117, provided ''The amendments amde by paragraph (1) [amending this section] shall take effect on October 1, 1980.''.

Effective date and application of Oct. 19, 1984 amendments. Act Oct. 19, 1984, P. L. 98-525, Title VII, § 705(b), 98 Stat. 2567, provided: ''The amendments made by this section [amending this section and former 10 USCS §§ 2132 et seq.] shall take effect on July 1, 1985, and shall apply only to members of the Armed Forces who qualify for educational assistance under chapter 106 of title 10, United States Code [10 USCS §§ 2131 et seq.], as amended by subsection (a), on or after such date.''.

Application of Nov. 29, 1989 amendments. Act Nov. 29, 1989, P. L. 101-189, Div A, Title VI, Part E, § 642(d), 103 Stat. 1458, provides: ''The amendments made by this section [amending this section and former 10 USCS § 2136(b)] shall apply with respect to any person who after September 30, 1990, meets the requirements set forth in subparagraph (A) or (B) of [former] section 2132(a)(1) of title 10, United States Code.''.

Effective date of Dec. 18, 1989 amendments. Act Dec. 18, 1989, P. L. 101-237, Title IV, § 422(d), 103 Stat. 2090, provides: ''The amendments made by this section [amending subsec. (g) of this section, former 10 USCS § 2136, and 38 USCS §§ 1432, 1434] shall take effect on September 30, 1990.''.

Effective date of amendments made by § 301 of Act Oct. 29, 1992; rule of construction. Act Oct. 29, 1992, P. L. 102-568, Title III, § 301(e), 106 Stat. 4326, provides:

''(1) The amendments made by this section [amending subsec. (b) of this section and subsecs. (a), (b) and (g) (formerly (f)) of 38 USCS § 3015] shall take effect on April 1, 1993.

''(2) The amendments made by this section [amending subsec. (b) of this section and subsecs. (a), (b) and (g) (formerly (f)) of 38 USCS § 3015] shall not be construed to change the account from which payment is made for that portion of a payment under chapter 30 of title 38, United States Code [38 USCS §§ 3001 et seq.], or chapter 106 of title 10, United States Code [10 USCS §§ 2131 et seq.], which is a Montgomery GI bill rate increase and a title III benefit is paid. For the purposes of this subsection, the terms 'Montgomery GI bill rate increase' and 'title III benefit' have the meanings provided in section 393 of the Persian Gulf Conflict Supplemental Authorization and Personnel Benefits Act of 1991 (105 Stat. 99) [unclassified].''.

Applicability of amendments made by § 310 of Act Oct. 29, 1992. Act Oct. 29, 1992, P. L. 102-568, Title III, § 310(d), 106 Stat. 4330, provides: ''The amendments made by this section [amending subsec. (g) of this section and 38 USCS §§ 3032(f) and 3231(f)] shall apply to flight training received under chapters 30 and 32 of title 38, United States Code [38 USCS §§ 3001 et seq. and 3201 et seq.], and chapter 106 of title 10, United States Code [10 USCS §§ 2131 et seq.], after September 30, 1992.''.

Limitation of cost-of-living adjustments for Montgomery GI Bill benefits. Act Aug. 10, 1993, P. L. 103-66, Title XII, § 12009(c), 107 Stat. 416, provides: ''The fiscal year 1995 cost-of-living adjustments in the rates of educational assistance payable under chapter 30 of title 38, United States Code [38 USCS §§ 3001 et seq.], and under chapter 106 of title 10, United States Code [10 USCS §§ 2131 et seq.], shall be the percentage equal to 50 percent of the percentage by which such assistance would be increased under section 3015(g) of title 38, and under [former] section 2131(b)(2) of title 10, United States Code, respectively, but for this section.''.

Effective date and application of June 9, 1998 amendments. Act June 9, 1998, P. L. 105-178, Title VIII, Subtitle B, § 8203(b)(4), 112 Stat. 494, provides: ''The amendments made by this subsection [amending this section] shall take effect on October 1, 1998, and shall apply with respect to educational assistance allowances paid for months after September 1998. However, no adjustment in rates of educational assistance shall be made under paragraph (2) of section 16131(b) of title 10, United States Code, as amended by paragraph (2), for fiscal year 1999.''.

CODE OF FEDERAL REGULATIONS

Department of Veterans Affairs—Loan guaranty and vocational rehabilitation and counseling programs, 48 CFR Part 871.

CROSS REFERENCES

This section is referred to in 10 USCS §§ 2131, 16132, 16135.

§ 16132. Eligibility for educational assistance

(a) A person who—

(1) after June 30, 1985—

(A) enlists, reenlists, or extends an enlistment as a Reserve for service in the Selected Reserve for a period of not less than six years; or

(B) is appointed as, or is serving as, a reserve officer and agrees to serve in the Selected Reserve for a period of not less than six years in addition to any other period of obligated service in the Selected Reserve to which the person may be subject; and

(2) before completing initial active duty for training has completed the requirements of a secondary school diploma (or an equivalency certificate), or in the case of an individual who reenlists or extends an enlistment as described in paragraph (1)(A) of this subsection, has completed such requirements at any time before such reenlistment or extension,

is entitled to educational assistance under section 16131 of this title.

(b) Educational assistance may not be provided to a member under this chapter [10 USCS §§ 16131 et seq.] until the member has completed the initial period of active duty for training required of the member.

(c) Each person who becomes entitled to educational assistance under subsection (a) shall at the time the person becomes so entitled be given a statement in writing summarizing the provisions of this chapter [10 USCS §§ 16131 et seq.] and stating clearly and prominently the substance of sections 16134 and 16135 of this title as such sections may apply to the person. At the request of the Secretary of Veterans Affairs, the Secretary of Defense shall transmit a notice of entitlement for each such person to that Secretary.

(d) A person who serves in the Selected Reserve may not receive credit for such service under both the program established by chapter 30 of title 38 [38 USCS §§ 3001 et seq.] and the program established by this chapter [10 USCS

§§ 16131 et seq.] but shall elect (in such form and manner as the Secretary of Veterans Affairs may prescribe) the program to which such service is to be credited. However, a person may not receive credit under the program established by this chapter [10 USCS §§ 16131 et seq.] for service (in any grade) on full-time active duty or full-time National Guard duty for the purpose of organizing, administering, recruiting, instructing, or training the reserve components in a position which is included in the end strength required to be authorized each year by section 115(a)(1)(B) of this title.

(Added July 30, 1977, P. L. 95-79, Title IV, § 402(a), 91 Stat. 329; Oct. 20, 1978, P. L. 95-485, Title IV, § 402(a), 92 Stat. 1613; Dec. 12, 1980, P. L. 96-513, Title V, Part B, § 511(69), 94 Stat. 2926; Oct. 19, 1984, P. L. 98-525, Title VII, § 705(a)(1) in part, 98 Stat. 2565; June 1, 1987, P. L. 100-48, § 4, 101 Stat. 331; Nov. 18, 1988, P. L. 100-689, Title I, Part A, §§ 110(b), 111(b)(2)–(4), 102 Stat. 4170, 4173; Nov. 29, 1989, P. L. 101-189, Div A, Title VI, Part E, §§ 643(a), 645(a), (b)(2), 103 Stat. 1458; April 6, 1991, P. L. 102-25, Title VII, § 701(f)(6), 105 Stat. 115; Oct. 5, 1994, P. L. 103-337, Div A, Title XVI, Subtitle C, § 1663(b)(2), (4), 108 Stat. 3006, 3007; Feb. 10, 1996, P. L. 104-106, Div A, Title XV, § 1501(b)(34), 110 Stat. 498.)

HISTORY; ANCILLARY LAWS AND DIRECTIVES

Amendments:

1978. Act Oct. 20, 1978, in subsec. (b)(1), substituted "not less than six years" for "automatically extended by two years" and substituted "last day of the term" for "eighth anniversary".

1980. Act Dec. 12, 1980 (effective upon enactment as provided by § 701(b)(3) of such Act, which appears as 10 USCS § 101 note), in subsec. (a), in the introductory matter, in subsecs. (b)(1) and (2), and in subsec. (c), in the introductory matter, inserted "of this title".

1984. Act Oct. 19, 1984 (effective 7/1/85 as provided by § 705(b) of such Act, which appears as 10 USCS § 16131 note) substituted this section and catchline for ones which read:

"§ 2132. Eligibility for educational assistance

"(a) To be eligible for educational assistance under section 2131 of this title, a member must not be serving on active duty for more than thirty days and must—

"(1) be an enlisted member of the Selected Reserve of the Ready Reserve of an armed force;

"(2) have initially enlisted as a Reserve for service in a unit of the Selected Reserve of a reserve component after September 30, 1977;

"(3) never have served in an armed force before such enlistment;

"(4) At the time of such enlistment have executed an agreement as prescribed by subsection (b);

"(5) be a graduate from secondary school;

"(6) have completed the initial period of active duty for training required of such member;

"(7) if the member is assigned to a unit, be participating satisfactorily in training with such unit; and

"(8) have served less than eight years as a Reserve.

"(b)(1) An agreement referred to in subsection (a)(4) shall be in writing and shall provide that if the member accepts educational assistance under section 2131 of this title, the period of enlistment of such member shall be not less than six years and if the member is discharged for the purpose of accepting an appointment as an officer, the member shall remain a member of the Ready Reserve until the last day of the term of such enlistment.

"(2) A member who enlists after September 30, 1977, but before regulations to carry out this chapter are promulgated shall be eligible for educational assistance under section 2131 of this title if he is otherwise eligible for such assistance under subsection (a) and if he executes an agreement as described in paragraph (1) not later than one year after the date on which regulations to carry out this chapter are first promulgated.

"(c) Educational assistance being provided a member under section 2131 of this title may be continued to a member who otherwise continues to qualify for such assistance if such member—

"(1) is discharged in order to accept an immediate appointment as an officer in the Ready Reserve; or

"(2) is no longer a member of the Selected Reserve, if such member is a member of the Ready Reserve and has served at least six years in the Selected Reserve of the Ready Reserve.".

1987. Act June 1, 1987, in subsec. (a)(1), substituted "after June 30, 1985" for "during the period beginning on July 1, 1985, and ending on June 30, 1988".

1988. Act Nov. 18, 1988, in subsec. (a), in para. (2), substituted "completed the requirements of" for "received", and inserted ", or in the case of an individual who reenlists or extends an enlistment as described in paragraph (1)(A) of this subsection, has completed such requirements at any time before such reenlistment or extension"; substituted subsec. (b) for one which read:

"(b) Educational assistance may not be provided to a member under this chapter until the member—

"(1) has completed the initial period of active duty for training required of the member; and

"(2) has completed 180 days of service in the Selected Reserve.";

in subsec. (c), inserted the sentence beginning "At the request of the Administrator . . ."; and substituted subsec. (d) for one which read: "(d) A person who is entitled to educational assistance under chapter 30 of title 38 based on section 1412 of that title may not also be provided educational assistance under this chapter.".

1989. Act Nov. 29, 1989, in subsec. (c), substituted "Secretary of Veterans Affairs" for "Administrator of Veterans' Affairs" and substituted "to that Secretary" for "to the Administrator"; and, in subsec. (d), substituted "A person" for "An individual", and "Secretary of Veterans Affairs" for "Administrator of Veterans' Affairs", and added the sentence beginning "However, a person may not . . .".

1991. Act April 6, 1991, in subsec. (d), substituted "section 115(a)(1)(B)" for "section 115(b)(1)(A)(ii)".

1994. Act Oct. 5, 1994 (effective 12/1/94 as provided by § 1691 of such Act, which appears as 10 USCS § 10001 note) transferred this section, enacted as 10 USCS § 2132, to Chapter 1606 and redesignated it as 10 USCS § 16132; in subsec. (a), substituted ''section 161231'' for ''section 2131''; and, in subsec. (c), substituted ''section 16134 and 16135'' for ''sections 2134 and 2135''.

1996. Act Feb. 10, 1996 (effective as if included in Act Oct. 5, 1994, P. L. 103-337, as enacted on Oct. 5, 1994, as provided by § 1501(f)(3) of Act Feb. 10, 1996, which appears as 10 USCS § 113 note), in subsec. (c), substituted ''sections'' for ''section'' before ''16134''.

Other provisions:

Act Nov. 29, 1989, P. L. 101-189; savings provision. Act Nov. 29, 1989, P. L. 101-189, Div A, Title VI, Part E, § 643(b), 103 Stat. 1458, provides: ''The amendment made by subsection (a) [amending subsec. (d) of this section] shall not affect the eligibility for educational assistance of any person who before the date of the enactment of this Act is entitled to educational assistance under [former] section 2131(a) of title 10, United States Code.''.

CROSS REFERENCES

This section is referred to in 10 USCS § 16135.

§ 16133. Time limitation for use of entitlement

(a) Except as provided in subsection (b), the period during which a person entitled to educational assistance under this chapter [10 USCS §§ 16131 et seq.] may use such person's entitlement expires (1) at the end of the 10-year period beginning on the date on which such person becomes entitled to such assistance, or (2) on the date the person is separated from the Selected Reserve, whichever occurs first.

(b)(1) In the case of a person—

(A) who is separated from the Selected Reserve because of a disability which was not the result of the individual's own willful misconduct incurred on or after the date on which such person became entitled to educational assistance under this chapter [10 USCS §§ 16131 et seq.]; or

(B) who, on or after the date on which such person became entitled to educational assistance under this chapter [10 USCS §§ 16131 et seq.] ceases to be a member of the Selected Reserve during the period beginning on October 1, 1991, and ending on September 30, 1999, by reason of the inactivation of the person's unit of assignment or by reason of involuntarily ceasing to be designated as a member of the Selected Reserve pursuant to section 10143(a)) of this title,

the period for using entitlement prescribed by subsection (a) shall be determined without regard to clause (2) of such subsection.

(2) The provisions of section 3031(f) of title 38 shall apply to the period of entitlement prescribed by subsection (a).

(3) The provisions of section 3031(d) of title 38 apply to the period of entitlement prescribed by subsection (a) in the case of a disability incurred in or aggravated by service in the Selected Reserve.

(4) In the case of a member of the Selected Reserve of the Ready Reserve

who serves on active duty pursuant to an order to active duty issued under section 12301(a), 12301(d), 12301(g), 12302, or 12304 of this title—

(A) the period of such active duty service plus four months shall not be considered in determining the expiration date applicable to such member under subsection (a); and

(B) the member may not be considered to have been separated from the Selected Reserve for the purposes of clause (2) of such subsection by reason of the commencement of such active duty service.

(Added July 30, 1977, P. L. 95-79, Title IV, § 402(a), 91 Stat. 329; Nov. 9, 1979, P.L. 96-107, Title IV, § 402(b), 93 Stat. 808; Dec. 12, 1980, P. L. 96-513, Title V, Part B, § 511(70), 94 Stat. 2926; Oct. 19, 1984, P. L. 98-525, Title VII, § 705(a)(1) in part, 98 Stat. 2566; Sept. 29, 1988, P. L. 100-456, Div A, Title XII, Part D, § 1233(g)(2), 102 Stat. 2058; Nov. 18, 1988, P. L. 100-689, Title I, Part A, § 111(b)(5), 102 Stat. 4173; Oct. 10, 1991, P. L. 102-127, § 3, 105 Stat. 622; Oct. 23, 1992, P. L. 102-484, Div D, Title XLIV, Subtitle B, § 4419(a), 106 Stat. 2717; Oct. 29, 1992, P. L. 102-568, Title III, § 320(a)(2), 106 Stat. 4335; Nov. 30, 1993, P. L. 103-160, Div A, Title V, Subtitle F, § 561(m), 107 Stat. 1668; Oct. 5, 1994, P. L. 103-337, Div A, Title XVI, Subtitle C, § 1663(b)(2), (5), 108 Stat. 3006, 3007; Nov. 18, 1997, P. L. 105-85, Div A, Title V, Subtitle E, Part II, § 553(b), 111 Stat. 1748.)

HISTORY; ANCILLARY LAWS AND DIRECTIVES

Amendments:

1979. Act Nov. 9, 1979 (applicable as provided by § 402(c), which appears as 10 USCS § 16131 note) substituted subsec. (b) for one which read: ''A member who fails to participate satisfactorily in training with his unit, if he is a member of a unit, shall refund the amount of all educational assistance received by such member under section 2131 unless the failure to participate in training was due to reasons beyond the control of the member. Any refund made by a member under this subsection shall not affect the period of obligation of such member to serve as a Reserve.''.

1980. Act Dec. 12, 1980 (effective upon enactment as provided by § 701(b)(3) of such Act, which appears as 10 USCS § 101 note), in subsec. (a), in the introductory matter, and in para. (4), inserted ''of this title''.

1984. Act Oct. 19, 1984 (effective 7/1/85 as provided by § 705(b) of such Act, which appears as 10 USCS § 16131 note) substituted this section for one which read:

''§ 2133. Termination of assistance; refund by member

''(a) Educational assistance being provided a member under section 2131 of this title shall be terminated if—

''(1) the member fails to participate satisfactorily in training with his unit, if he is a member of a unit;

''(2) the member is separated from his armed force, unless he is separated in order to accept an immediate appointment as an officer in the Ready Reserve;

''(3) the member completes eight years of service; or

''(4) the member receives financial assistance under section 2107 of this title as a member of the Senior Reserve Officers' Training Corps.

"(b)(1) A member who fails to participate satisfactorily in training with his unit, if he is a member of a unit, during a term of enlistment for which the member entered into an agreement under section 2132(a)(4) of this title shall refund an amount computed under paragraph (2) unless the failure to participate in training was due to reasons beyond the control of the member. Any refund by a member under this section shall not affect the period of obligation of such member to serve as a Reserve.

"(2) The amount of any refund under paragraph (1) shall be the amount equal to the product of—

"(A) the number of months of obligated service remaining during that term of enlistment divided by the total number of months of obligated service of that term of enlistment; and

"(B) the total amount of educational assistance provided to the member under section 2131 of this title.".

1988. Act Sept. 29, 1988, in subsec. (b)(1), substituted "section 1431(f)" for "section 1431(e)".

Act Nov. 18, 1988, in subsec. (a), substituted "chapter" for "section"; in subsec. (b), redesignated former paras. (1) and (2) as paras. (2) and (3), respectively added a new para. (1), and in para. (2) as redesignated purported to substitute "1413(f)" for "1413(e)", but such amendment had already been effectuated by Act Sept. 29, 1988.

1991. Act Oct. 10, 1991 added subsec. (b)(4).

1992. Act Oct. 23, 1992 substituted subsec. (b)(1) for one which read: "In the case of a person separated from the Selected Reserve because of a disability which was not the result of the individual's own willful misconduct incurred on or after the date on which such person became entitled to educational assistance under this chapter, the period for using entitlement prescribed by subsection (a) shall be determined without regard to clause (2) of such subsection.".

Act Oct. 29, 1992, in subsec. (b), in para. (2), substituted "section 3031(f) of title 38" for "section 1431(f) of title 38" and, in para. (3), substituted "section 3031(d) of title 38" for "section 1431(d) of title 38".

1993. Act Nov. 30, 1993, in subsec. (b)(1)(B), substituted "September 30, 1999," for "September 30, 1995,".

1994. Act Oct. 5, 1994 (effective 12/1/94 as provided by § 1691 of such Act, which appears as 10 USCS § 10001 note) transferred this section, enacted as 10 USCS § 2133, to Chapter 1606 and redesignated it as 10 USCS § 16133; in subsec. (b), in para. (1)(B), substituted "section 10143(a)" for "section 268(b)" and, in para. (4)(A), substituted "section 12301(a), 12301(d), 12301(g), 12302, or 12304" for "section 672 (a), (d), or (g), 673, or 673b".

1997. Act Nov. 18, 1997, in subsec. (b)(4), deleted "(A)" preceding "In the case", deleted ", during the Persian Gulf War," following "Reserve who", redesignated cls. (i) and (ii) as subparas. (A) and (B), respectively, and deleted former subpara. (B), which read: "(B) For the purpose of this paragraph, the term 'Persian Gulf War' shall have the meaning given such term in section 101(33) of title 38.".

§ 16134. Termination of assistance

Educational assistance may not be provided under this chapter [10 USCS §§ 16131 et seq.]—

(1) to a member receiving financial assistance under section 2107 of this title as a member of the Senior Reserve Officers' Training Corps program; or

(2) to a member who fails to participate satisfactorily in required training as a member of the Selected Reserve.

(Added July 30, 1977, P. L. 95-79, Title IV, § 402(a), 91 Stat. 330; Sept. 24, 1983, P. L. 98-94, Title XII, Part D, § 1268(14), 97 Stat. 707; Oct. 19, 1984, P. L. 98-525, Title VII, § 705(a)(1) in part, 98 Stat. 2566; Oct. 5, 1994, P. L. 103-337, Div A, Title XVI, Subtitle C, § 1663(b)(2), 108 Stat. 3006.)

HISTORY; ANCILLARY LAWS AND DIRECTIVES

Amendments:

1983. Act Sept. 24, 1983 deleted a sentence which read: ''The first such report shall be submitted not later than December 31, 1977.'', following ''at the time of such report.''.

1984. Act Oct. 19, 1984 (effective 7/1/85 as provided by § 705(b) of such Act, which appears as 10 USCS § 16131 note) substituted this section and catchline for ones which read:

''§ 2134. Reports to Congress

''The Secretary of Defense shall submit a report to the Congress every three months stating the number of members of the Selected Reserve of the Ready Reserve receiving educational assistance under this chapter at the time of such report and listing each unit of the Selected Reserve of the Ready Reserve to which any such member is assigned at the time of such report.''.

1994. Act Oct. 5, 1994 (effective 12/1/94 as provided by § 1691 of such Act, which appears as 10 USCS § 10001 note) transferred this section, enacted as 10 USCS § 2134, to Chapter 1606 and redesignated it as 10 USCS § 16134.

CROSS REFERENCES

This section is referred to in 10 USCS §§ 16131, 16132.

§ 16135. Failure to participate satisfactorily; penalties

(a)(1) A member of the Selected Reserve of the Ready Reserve of an armed force who fails to participate satisfactorily in required training as a member of the Selected Reserve during a term of enlistment or other period of obligated service that created entitlement of the member to educational assistance under this chapter [10 USCS §§ 16131 et seq.], and during which the member has received such assistance, shall, at the option of the Secretary concerned—

(A) be ordered to active duty for a period of two years or the period of obligated service the person has remaining under section 16132 of this title, whichever is less; or

(B) be required to refund to the United States an amount determined under subsection (b).

(2) The Secretary concerned may waive the requirements of paragraph (1), or may reduce the amount of any refund under clause (B) of such paragraph,

in the case of any individual member when the Secretary determines that the failure to participate satisfactorily was due to reasons beyond the control of the member.

(3) Any refund by a member under this section shall not affect the period of obligation of such member to serve as a Reserve in the Selected Reserve.

(b)(1) The amount of a refund under subsection (a) shall be the amount equal to the product of—

(A) the number of months of obligated service the person has remaining under the agreement entered into under section 16131(a) of this title divided by the original number of months of such obligation; and

(B) the total amount of educational assistance provided to the member under this chapter [10 USCS §§ 16131 et seq.],

as increased by interest determined under paragraph (2).

(2) The amount computed under paragraph (1) shall bear interest at the rate equal to the highest rate being paid by the United States on the day on which the refund is determined to be due for securities having maturities of 90 days or less and shall accrue from the day on which the member is first notified of the amount due to the United States as a refund under this section.

(Added July 30, 1977, P. L. 95-79, Title IV, § 402(a), 91 Stat. 330; Oct. 20, 1978, P. L. 95-485, Title IV, § 402(b), 92 Stat. 1613; Sept. 8, 1980, P. L. 96-342, Title IX, § 906(b), 94 Stat. 1117; Oct. 19, 1984, P. L. 98-525, Title VII, § 705(a)(1) in part, 98 Stat. 2566; Nov. 18, 1988, P. L. 100-689, Title I, Part A, § 111(b)(6), 102 Stat. 4173; Oct. 5, 1994, P. L. 103-337, Div A, Title XVI, Subtitle C, § 1663(b)(2), (6), 108 Stat. 3006, 3007; Feb. 10, 1996, P. L. 104-106, Div A, Title XV, § 1501(b)(35), 110 Stat. 498.)

HISTORY; ANCILLARY LAWS AND DIRECTIVES

Amendments:

1978. Act Oct. 20, 1978 substituted "1980" for "1978".

1980. Act Sept. 8, 1980 substituted "1985" for "1980".

1984. Act Oct. 19, 1984 (effective 7/1/85 as provided by § 705(b) of such Act, which appears as 10 USCS § 16131 note) substituted this section and catchline for ones which read:

"§ 2135. Termination of program

"No educational assistance may be provided under this chapter to any person enlisting as a Reserve after September 30, 1985.".

1988. Act Nov. 18, 1988, in subsec. (a)(1), inserted ", and during which the member has received such assistance,"; and, in subsec. (b)(1), substituted subpara. (A) for one which read: "(A) the number of months of obligated service remaining under the agreement entered into under section 2132(a)(3) divided by the original number of months of such obligation; and".

1994. Act Oct. 5, 1994 (effective 12/1/94 as provided by § 1691 of such Act, which appears as 10 USCS § 10001 note) transferred this section, enacted as 10 USCS § 2135, to Chapter 1606 and redesignated it as 10 USCS § 16135; and, in subsec. (a)(1)(A), substituted "section 16132" for "section 2132".

Such Act further (effective as above) purported to amend subsec. (b)(1)(A) by striking out "2132(a)" and by inserting in lieu thereof "16132(a)"; however, the amendment could not be executed because the matter to be stricken did not appear in such subsection.

1996. Act Feb. 10, 1996 (effective as if included in Act Oct. 5, 1994, P. L. 103-337, as enacted on Oct. 5, 1994, as provided by § 1501(f)(3) of Act Feb. 10, 1996, which appears as 10 USCS § 113 note), in subsec. (b)(1)(A), substituted "section 16131(a)" for "section 2131(a)".

CROSS REFERENCES

This section is referred to in 10 USCS § 16132; 38 USCS § 3485.

§ 16136. Administration of program

(a) Educational assistance under this chapter shall be provided through the Department of Veterans Affairs, under agreements to be entered into by the Secretary of Defense, and by the Secretary of Transportation, with the Secretary of Veterans Affairs. Such agreements shall include administrative procedures to ensure the prompt and timely transfer of funds from the Secretary concerned to the Department of Veterans Affairs for the making of payments under this chapter.

(b) Except as otherwise provided in this chapter, the provisions of sections 3470, 3471, 3474, 3476, 3482(g), 3483, and 3485 of title 38 and the provisions of subchapters I and II of chapter 36 of such title [38 USCS §§ 3670 et seq. and 3680 et seq.] (with the exception of sections 3686(a), 3687, and 3692) shall be applicable to the provision of educational assistance under this chapter. The term "eligible veteran" and the term "a person", as used in those provisions, shall be deemed for the purpose of the application of those provisions to this chapter to refer to a person eligible for educational assistance under this chapter.

(c) The Secretary of Veterans Affairs may approve the pursuit of flight training (in addition to a course of flight training that may be approved under section 3680A(b) of title 38) by an individual entitled to educational assistance under this chapter [10 USCS §§ 16131 et seq.] if—

(1) such training is generally accepted as necessary for the attainment of a recognized vocational objective in the field of aviation;

(2) the individual possesses a valid private pilot's license and meets the medical requirements necessary for a commercial pilot's license; and

(3) the flight school courses meet Federal Aviation Administration standards for such courses and are approved by the Federal Aviation Administration and the State approving agency.

(Added Oct. 19, 1984, P. L. 98-525, Title VII, § 705(a)(1) in part, 98 Stat. 2567; Nov. 29, 1989, P. L. 101-189, Div A, Title VI, Part E, §§ 642(c), 645, 103 Stat. 1457, 1458; Dec. 18, 1989, P. L. 101-237, Title IV, §§ 405(d)(3), 422(b)(1), 103 Stat. 2081, 2089; Nov. 5, 1990, P. L. 101-510, Div A, Title XIV, Part H, § 1484(j)(3), 104 Stat. 1718; March 22, 1991, P. L. 102-16, § 10(b), 105 Stat. 56; Oct. 29, 1992, P. L. 102-568, Title III, §§ 313(a)(6), 319, 320(a)(3), 106 Stat. 4333, 4335, 4336; Oct. 5, 1994, P. L. 103-337, Div A, Title

XVI, Subtitle C, § 1663(b)(2), 108 Stat. 3006; Nov. 2, 1994, P. L. 103-446, Title VI, § 601(c), 108 Stat. 4670.)

HISTORY; ANCILLARY LAWS AND DIRECTIVES

Effective date of section:

Act Oct. 19, 1984, P. L. 98-525, Title VII, § 705(b), 98 Stat. 2567, which appears as 10 USCS § 2131 note, provided that this section shall take effect July 1, 1985.

Amendments:

1989. Act Nov. 29, 1989 (applicable as provided by § 642(d) of such Act, which appears as 10 USCS § 16131 note), in subsec. (b), substituted the sentence beginning ''Except as otherwise provided . . .'' for ''Except as otherwise provided in this chapter, the provisions of sections 1663, 1670, 1671, 1673, 1674, 1676, 1682(g), and 1683 of chapter 34 of title 38 and the provisions of subchapters I and II of chapter 36 of such title (with the exception of sections 1780(a)(5), 1780(b), 1786, 1787(b)(1), and 1792) shall be applicable to the provision of educational assistance under this chapter.'' and substituted ''and the term 'a person', as used'' for '', as used''.

Such Act further, in subsec. (a), substituted ''Secretary of Veterans Affairs'' for ''Administrator of Veterans' Affairs''.

Act Dec. 18, 1989 (effective 5/1/90 and applicable as provided by § 405(e) of such Act, which appears as a note to this section), substituted ''1683, and 1685'' for ''and 1683''.

Such Act further (effective 9/30/90, as provided by § 422(d) of such Act, which appears as 10 USCS § 16131 note) added subsec. (c).

1990. Act Nov. 5, 1990, in subsec. (a), substituted ''Department of Veterans Affairs'' for ''Veterans'' Administration'' before '', under agreements'' and before ''for the making''.

1991. Act March 22, 1991, in subsec. (b), deleted ''1434(b), 1663,'' following ''sections'' and ''1780(g),'' following ''1780(c),''.

1992. Act Oct. 29, 1992, in subsec. (b), deleted ''1780(c),'' following ''exception of sections'' and, in such subsection as so amended, substituted ''sections 3470, 3471, 3474, 3476, 3482(g), 3483, and 3485 of title 38 and the provisions of subchapters I and II of chapter 36 of such title (with the exception of sections 3686(a), 3687, and 3692)'' for ''sections 1670, 1671, 1673, 1674, 1676, 1682(g), 1683, and 1685 of title 38 and the provisions of subchapters I and II of chapter 36 of such title (with the exception of sections 1786(a), 1787, and 1792)''.

Such Act further (applicable as provided by § 313(b) of such Act, which appears as a note to this section), in subsec. (c), in para. (1), substituted ''3680A(b)'' for ''1673(b)''.

1994. Act Oct. 5, 1994 (effective 12/1/94 as provided by § 1691 of such Act, which appears as 10 USCS § 10001 note) transferred this section, enacted as 10 USCS § 2136, to Chapter 1606 and redesignated it as 10 USCS § 16136.

Act Nov. 2, 1994 (effective 10/1/94, as provided by § 601(d) of such Act, which appears as 38 USCS § 3034 note), in subsec. (c), deleted para. (2), which read: ''This subsection shall not apply to a course of flight training that commences on or after October 1, 1994.'', deleted the designation for para. (1), and redesignated subparas. (A), (B), and (C), as paras. (1), (2), and (3).

Other provisions:

Effective date and application of Dec. 18, 1989 amendments. Act Dec. 18, 1989, P. L. 101-237, Title IV, § 405(e), 103 Stat. 2082, provides: ''The amendments made by this section [amending this section and 38 USCS prec § 1651, § 1685] shall take effect on May 1, 1990, and shall apply to services performed on or after that date.''.

Applicability of amendments made by § 313(a) of Act Oct. 29, 1992. Act Oct. 29, 1992, P. L. 102-568, Title III, § 313(b), 106 Stat. 4333, provides: ''The amendments made by paragraphs (2) through (6) of subsection (a) of this section [amending subsec. (c)(1) of this section, 38 USCS §§ 3034(a)(1) and (d)(1), and 3241(a)(1), (b)(1), and (c), and the chapter analysis preceding 38 USCS § 3451; adding 38 USCS § 3680A; and repealing 38 USCS § 3473] shall not apply to any person receiving educational assistance for pursuit of an independent study program in which the person was enrolled on the date of enactment of this section for as long as such person is continuously thereafter so enrolled and meets the requirements of eligibility for such assistance for the pursuit of such program under title 38, United States Code, or title 10, United States Code, in effect on that date.''.

CROSS REFERENCES

This section is referred to in 10 USCS § 16131.

§ 16137. Reports to Congress

The Secretary of Defense shall submit to the Congress a report not later than March 1 of each year concerning the operation of the educational assistance program established by this chapter [10 USCS §§ 16131 et seq.] during the preceding fiscal year. Each such report shall include the number of members of the Selected Reserve of the Ready Reserve of each armed force receiving, and the number entitled to receive, educational assistance under this chapter [10 USCS §§ 16131 et seq.] during the preceding fiscal year.

(Added Oct. 19, 1984, P. L. 98-525, Title VII, § 705(a)(1), 98 Stat. 2567; Oct. 5, 1994, P. L. 103-337, Div A, Title XVI, Subtitle C, § 1663(b)(2), 108 Stat. 3006; Feb. 10, 1996, P. L. 104-106, Div A, Title X, Subtitle G, § 1077, 110 Stat. 451.)

HISTORY; ANCILLARY LAWS AND DIRECTIVES

Effective date of section:

Act Oct. 19, 1984, P. L. 98-525, Title VII, § 705(b), 98 Stat. 2567, which appears as 10 USCS § 2131 note, provided that this section shall take effect July 1, 1985.

Amendments:

1994. Act Oct. 5, 1994 (effective 12/1/94 as provided by § 1691 of such Act, which appears as 10 USCS § 10001 note) transferred this section, enacted as 10 USCS § 2137, to Chapter 1606 and redesignated it as 10 USCS § 16137.

1996. Act Feb. 10, 1996 substituted "March 1 of each year" for "December 15 of each year".

CHAPTER 1608. HEALTH PROFESSIONS STIPEND PROGRAM

HISTORY; ANCILLARY LAWS AND DIRECTIVES

Amendments:

1994. Act Oct. 5, 1994, P. L. 103-337, Div A, Title XVI, Subtitle C, § 1663(c)(1), 108 Stat. 3007 (effective 12/1/94 as provided by § 1691 of such Act, which appears as 10 USCS § 10001 note), added the chapter heading and analysis.

§ 16201. Financial assistance: health-care professionals in reserve components

(a) Establishment of program. For the purpose of obtaining adequate numbers of commissioned officers in the reserve components who are qualified in health professions specialties critically needed in wartime, the Secretary of each military department may establish and maintain a program to provide financial assistance under this chapter [10 USCS §§ 16201 et seq.] to persons engaged in training in such specialties. Under such a program, the Secretary concerned may agree to pay a financial stipend to persons engaged in training in certain health care specialties in return for a commitment to subsequent service in the Ready Reserve.

(b) Physicians and dentists in critical specialties. (1) Under the stipend program under this chapter [10 USCS §§ 16201 et seq.], the Secretary of the military department concerned may enter into an agreement with a person who—

(A) is a graduate of a medical school and dental school;

(B) is eligible for appointment, designation, or assignment as a medical officer or dental officer in the Reserve of the armed force concerned; and

(C) is enrolled or has been accepted for enrollment in a residency program for physicians or dentists in a medical or dental specialty designated by the Secretary concerned as a specialty critically needed by that military department in wartime.

(2) Under the agreement—

(A) the Secretary shall agree to pay the participant a stipend, in an amount determined under subsection (e), for the period or the remainder of the period of the residency program in which the participant enrolls or is enrolled;

(B) the participant shall not be eligible to receive such stipend before appointment, designation, or assignment as a medical officer or dental officer for service in the Ready Reserve;

(C) the participant shall be subject to such active duty requirements as may be specified in the agreement and to active duty in time of war or national emergency as provided by law for members of the Ready Reserve; and

(D) the participant shall agree to serve, upon successful completion of the program, two years in the Ready Reserve for each year, or part thereof, for which the stipend is provided, to be served in the Selected Reserve or in the Individual Ready Reserve as specified in the agreement.

(c) Registered nurses in critical specialties. (1) Under the stipend program under this chapter [10 USCS §§ 16201 et seq.], the Secretary of the military department concerned may enter into an agreement with a person who—

(A) is a registered nurse;

(B) is eligible for appointment as—

(i) a Reserve officer for service in the Army Reserve in the Army Nurse Corps;

(ii) a Reserve officer for service in the Naval Reserve in the Navy Nurse Corps; or

(iii) a Reserve officer for service in the Air Force Reserve with a view to designation as an Air Force nurse under section 8067(e) of this title; and

(C) is enrolled or has been accepted for enrollment in an accredited program in nursing in a specialty designated by the Secretary concerned as a specialty critically needed by that military department in wartime.

(2) Under the agreement—

(A) the Secretary shall agree to pay the participant a stipend, in an amount determined under subsection (e), for the period or the remainder of the period of the nursing program in which the participant enrolls or is enrolled;

(B) the participant shall not be eligible to receive such stipend before being appointed as a Reserve officer for service in the Ready Reserve—

(i) in the Nurse Corps of the Army or Navy; or

(ii) as an Air Force nurse of the Air Force;

(C) the participant shall be subject to such active duty requirements as may be specified in the agreement and to active duty in time of war or national emergency as provided by law for members of the Ready Reserve; and

(D) the participant shall agree to serve, upon successful completion of the program, two years in the Ready Reserve for each year, or part thereof, for which the stipend is provided, to be served in the Selected Reserve or in the Individual Ready Reserve as specified in the agreement.

(d) Baccalaureate students in nursing or other health professions. (1) Under the stipend program under this chapter [10 USCS §§ 16201 et seq.], the Secretary of the military department concerned may enter into an agreement with a person who—

(A) will, upon completion of the program, be eligible to be appointed, designated, or assigned as a Reserve officer for duty as a nurse or other health professional; and

(B) is enrolled, or has been accepted for enrollment in the third or fourth year of—

(i) an accredited baccalaureate nursing program; or

(ii) any other accredited baccalaureate program leading to a degree in a health-care profession designated by the Secretary concerned as a profession critically needed by that military department in wartime.

(2) Under the agreement—

(A) the Secretary shall agree to pay the participant a stipend of $100 per month for the period or the remainder of the period of the baccalaureate program in which the participant enrolls or is enrolled;

(B) the participant shall not be eligible to receive such stipend before enlistment in the Ready Reserve;

(C) the participant shall be subject to such active duty requirements as may be specified in the agreement and to active duty in time of war or national emergency as provided by law for members of the Ready Reserve; and

(D) the participant shall agree to serve, upon graduation from the baccalaureate program, one year in the Ready Reserve for each year, or part thereof, for which the stipend is paid.

(e) Amount of stipend. The amount of a stipend under an agreement under subsection (b) or (c) shall be—

(1) the stipend rate in effect for participants in the Armed Forces Health Professions Scholarship Program under section 2121(d) of this title, if the participant has agreed to serve in the Selected Reserve; or

(2) one-half of that rate, if the participant has agreed to serve in the Individual Ready Reserve.

(Added Dec. 4, 1987, P. L. 100-180, Div A, Title VII, Part A, § 711(a)(3), 101 Stat. 1108; Oct. 5, 1994, P. L. 103-337, Div A, Title XVI, Subtitle C, § 1663(c)(2), (5), 108 Stat. 3007, 3008; Feb. 10, 1996, P. L. 104-106, Div A, Title VII, Subtitle D, § 736, 110 Stat. 383.)

HISTORY; ANCILLARY LAWS AND DIRECTIVES

Amendments:

1994. Act Oct. 5, 1994 (effective 12/1/94 as provided by § 1691 of such Act, which appears as 10 USCS § 10001 note) transferred this section, enacted as 10 USCS § 2128, to Chapter 1606 and redesignated it as 10 USCS § 16201; in subsecs. (a), (b)(1), (c)(1), and (d)(1), substituted "chapter" for "subchapter"; and deleted subsec. (f), which read: "(f) Individual Ready Reserve defined. In this subchapter, the term "Individual Ready Reserve" means that element of the Ready Reserve of an armed force other than the Selected Reserve.".

1996. Act Feb. 10, 1996, in subsec. (b), in the heading, inserted "and dentists", in para. (1), in subpara. (A), inserted "or dental school", in subpara. (B), inserted "or dental officer" and, in subpara. (C), substituted "physicians or dentists in a medical or dental specialty" for "physicians in a medical specialty" and, in para. (2)(B), inserted "or dental officer".

Other provisions:

Stipulation on financial assistance agreement. Act Dec. 4, 1987, P. L. 100-180, Div A, Title VII, Part A, § 711(e)(2), 101 Stat. 1111, provides: "An agreement entered into by the Secretary of a military department under section 2128 [16201] of title 10, United States Code, as added by subsection (a), may not obligate the United States to make a payment for any period before the date of the enactment of this Act.".

CROSS REFERENCES

This section is referred to in 10 USCS § 16202.

§ 16202. Reserve service: required active duty for training

(a) Selected Reserve. A person who is required under an agreement under section 16201 of this title to serve in the Selected Reserve shall serve not less than 12 days of active duty for training each year during the period of service required by the agreement.

(b) IRR service. A person who is required under an agreement under section 16201 of this title to serve in the Individual Ready Reserve shall serve—

(1) not less than 30 days of initial active duty for training; and

(2) not less than five days of active duty for training each year during the period of service required by the agreement.

(Added Dec. 4, 1987, P. L. 100-180, Div A, Title VII Part A, § 711(a)(3), 101 Stat. 1111; Oct. 5, 1994, P. L. 103-337, Div A, Title XVI, Subtitle C, § 1663(c)(3), (6), 108 Stat. 3007, 3008.)

HISTORY; ANCILLARY LAWS AND DIRECTIVES

Amendments:

1994. Act Oct. 5, 1994 (effective 12/1/94 as provided by § 1691 of such Act, which appears as 10 USCS § 10001 note) transferred this section, enacted as 10 USCS § 2129, to Chapter 1608 and redesignated it as 10 USCS § 16202; and substituted "section 16201" for "section 2128" in two places.

§ 16203. Penalties and limitations

(a) Failure to complete program of training. (1) A member of the program who, under regulations prescribed by the Secretary of Defense, is dropped from the program for deficiency in training, or for other reasons, shall be required, at the discretion of the Secretary concerned—

(A) to perform one year of active duty for each year (or part thereof) for which such person was provided financial assistance under this section; or

(B) to repay the United States an amount equal to the total amount paid to such person under the program.

(2) The Secretary of a military department, under regulations prescribed by the Secretary of Defense, may relieve a member participating in the program

who is dropped from the program from any requirement that may be imposed under paragraph (1), but such relief shall not relieve him from any military obligation imposed by any other law.

(b) Prohibitions of duplicate benefits. Financial assistance may not be provided under this section to a member receiving financial assistance under section 2107 of this title.

(Added Dec. 4, 1987, P. L. 100-180, Div A, Title VII, Part A, § 711(a)(3), 101 Stat. 1111; Oct. 5, 1994, P. L. 103-337, Div A, Title XVI, Subtitle C, § 1663(c)(4), 108 Stat. 3008.)

HISTORY; ANCILLARY LAWS AND DIRECTIVES

Amendments:

1994. Act Oct. 5, 1994 (effective 12/1/94 as provided by § 1691 of such Act, which appears as 10 USCS § 10001 note) transferred this section, enacted as 10 USCS § 2130, to Chapter 1608 and redesignated it as 10 USCS § 16203; substituted the heading for one which read: ''Penalties, limitations, and other administrative provisions''; and deleted subsec. (c), which read: ''(c) Regulations. This subchapter shall be administered under regulations prescribed by the Secretary of Defense.''.

§ 16204. Regulations

This chapter [10 USCS §§ 16201 et seq.] shall be administered under regulations prescribed by the Secretary of Defense.

(Added Oct. 5, 1994, P. L. 103-337, Div A, Title XVI, Subtitle C, § 1663(c)(1), 108 Stat. 3007.)

HISTORY; ANCILLARY LAWS AND DIRECTIVES

Effective date of section:

This section took effect on Dec. 1, 1994, pursuant to Act Oct. 5, 1994, P. L. 103-337, Div A, Title XVI, Subtitle F, § 1691, 108 Stat. 3026, which appears as 10 USCS 10001 note.

CHAPTER 1609. EDUCATION LOAN REPAYMENT PROGRAMS

HISTORY; ANCILLARY LAWS AND DIRECTIVES

Amendments:

1994. Act Oct. 5, 1994, P. L. 103-337, Div A, Title XVI, Subtitle C, § 1663(d)(1), 108 Stat. 3008 (effective 12/1/94 as provided by § 1691 of such Act, which appears as 10 USCS § 10001 note), added the chapter heading and analysis.

§ 16301. Education loan repayment program: enlisted members of Selected Reserve with critical specialties

(a)(1) Subject to the provisions of this section, the Secretary of Defense may repay—

(A) any loan made, insured, or guaranteed under part B of title IV of the Higher Education Act of 1965 (20 U.S.C. 1071 et seq.);

(B) any loan made under part D of such title (the William D. Ford Federal Direct Loan Program, 20 U.S.C. 1087a et seq.); or

(C) any loan made under part E of such title (20 U.S.C. 1087aa et seq.).

Repayment of any such loan shall be made on the basis of each complete year of service performed by the borrower.

(2) The Secretary may repay loans described in paragraph (1) in the case of any person for service performed as an enlisted member of the Selected Reserve of the Ready Reserve of an armed force in a reserve component and military specialty specified by the Secretary of Defense. The Secretary may repay such a loan only if the person to whom the loan was made performed such service after the loan was made.

(b) The portion or amount of a loan that may be repaid under subsection (a) is 15 percent or $500, whichever is greater, for each year of service.

(c) If a portion of a loan is repaid under this section for any year, interest on the remainder of the loan shall accrue and be paid in the same manner as is otherwise required.

(d) Nothing in this section shall be construed to authorize refunding any repayment of a loan.

(e) A person who transfers from service making the person eligible for repayment of loans under this section (as described in subsection (a)(2)) to service making the person eligible for repayment of loans under section 2171 of this title (as described in subsection (a)(2) of that section) during a year shall be eligible to have repaid a portion of such loan determined by giving appropriate fractional credit for each portion of the year so served, in accordance with regulations of the Secretary concerned.

(f) The Secretary of Defense shall, by regulation, prescribe a schedule for the allocation of funds made available to carry out the provisions of this section and section 2171 of this title during any year for which funds are not sufficient to pay the sum of the amounts eligible for repayment under subsection (a) and section 2171(a) of this title.

(Added Oct. 5, 1994, P. L. 103-337, Div A, Title XVI, Subtitle C, § 1663(d)(1), 108 Stat. 3008; Feb. 10, 1996, P. L. 104-106, Div A, Title X, Subtitle G, § 1079(b), 110 Stat. 451.)

HISTORY; ANCILLARY LAWS AND DIRECTIVES

Effective date of section:

This section took effect on Dec. 1, 1994, pursuant to Act Oct. 5, 1994, P. L. 103-337, Div A, Title XVI, Subtitle F, § 1691, 108 Stat. 3026, which appears as 10 USCS 10001 note.

Amendments:

1996. Act Feb. 10, 1996, in subsec. (a)(1), in subpara. (A), deleted ''or'' after the concluding semicolon, redesignated subpara. (B) as subpara. (C), and added new subpara. (B).

§ 16302. Education loan repayment program: health professions officers serving in Selected Reserve with wartime critical medical skill shortages

(a) Under regulations prescribed by the Secretary of Defense and subject to the other provisions of this section, the Secretary concerned may repay—

(1) a loan made, insured, or guaranteed under part B of title IV of the Higher Education Act of 1965 (20 U.S.C. 1071 et seq.);

(2) any loan made under part D of such title (the William D. Ford Federal Direct Loan Program, 20 U.S.C. 1087a et seq.); or

(3) a loan made under part E of such title (20 U.S.C. 1087aa et seq.) after October 1, 1975;

(4) a health professions education loan made or insured under part A of title VII of the Public Health Service Act (42 U.S.C. 292 et seq.) or under part B of title VIII of such Act (42 U.S.C. 297 et seq.); and

(5) a loan made, insured, or guaranteed through a recognized financial or educational institution if that loan was used to finance education regarding a health profession that the Secretary of Defense determines to be critically needed in order to meet identified wartime combat medical skill shortages.

(b) The Secretary concerned may repay loans described in subsection (a) only in the case of a person who—

(1) performs satisfactory service as an officer in the Selected Reserve of an armed force; and

(2) possesses professional qualifications in a health profession that the Sec-

retary of Defense has determined to be needed critically in order to meet identified wartime combat medical skill shortages.

(c)(1) The amount of any repayment of a loan made under this section on behalf of any person shall be determined on the basis of each complete year of service that is described in subsection (b)(1) and performed by the person after the date on which the loan was made.

(2) Subject to paragraph (3), the amount of a loan that may be repaid under this section on behalf of any person may not exceed $3,000 for each year of service described in paragraph (1).

(3) The total amount that may be repaid on behalf of any person under this section may not exceed $20,000.

(d) The authority provided in this section shall apply only in the case of a person first appointed as a commissioned officer before October 1, 1999.

(Added Nov. 8, 1985, P. L. 99-145, Title VI, Part F, § 671(a)(1) in part, 99 Stat. 662; Dec. 4, 1987, P. L. 100-180, Div A, Title VII, Part A, § 713, 101 Stat. 1112; Nov. 29, 1989, P. L. 101-189, Div A, Title VII, Part A, § 701(a)–(c), 103 Stat. 1467; Oct. 23, 1992, P. L. 102-484, Div A, Title VI, Subtitle B, § 612(f), 106 Stat. 2421; Nov. 30, 1993, P. L. 103-160, Div A, Title VI, Subtitle B, § 613(f), 107 Stat. 1681; Oct. 5, 1994, P. L. 103-337, Div A, Title VI, Subtitle B, § 613(e), Title X, Subtitle G, § 1070(a)(9), Title XVI, Subtitle C, § 1663(d)(2), 108 Stat. 2783, 2855, 3009; Feb. 10, 1996, P. L. 104-106, Div A, Title VI, Subtitle B, § 613(h), Title X, Subtitle G, § 1079(c), 110 Stat. 360, 452; Sept. 23, 1996, P. L. 104-201, Div A, Title VI, Subtitle B, § 613(g), 110 Stat. 2544; Nov. 18, 1997, P. L. 105-85, Div A, Title VI, Subtitle B, § 611(h), 111 Stat. 1785.)

HISTORY; ANCILLARY LAWS AND DIRECTIVES

Amendments:

1987. Act Dec. 4, 1987, in subsec. (a)(3), inserted "or under part B of title VIII of such Act (42 U.S.C. 297 et seq.)"; and in subsec. (d), substituted "October 1, 1990" for "October 1, 1988".

1989. Act Nov. 29, 1989, in subsec. (a), in para. (1), deleted "a portion of" preceding "a loan made", in para. (2), deleted "and" following the concluding semicolon, in para. (3), substituted "; and" for the concluding period, and added para. (4); in subsec. (c)(2), substituted "amount of" for "portion of"; and, in subsec. (d), substituted "October 1, 1992" for "October 1, 1990".

1992. Act Oct. 23, 1992, in subsec. (d), substituted "October 1, 1993" for "Octrober 1, 1992".

1993. Act Nov. 30, 1993, in subsec. (d), substituted "October 1, 1995" for "October 1, 1993".

1994. Act Oct. 5, 1994, in subsec. (a)(3), substituted "health professions education loan" for "health education assistance loan", substituted "part A" for "part C", and substituted "42 U.S.C. 292" for "42 U.S.C. 294"; and, in subsec. (d), substituted "October 1, 1996" for "October 1, 1995". Such Act further (effective 12/1/94, as provided by § 1691 of such Act, which appears as 10 USCS § 10001 note) transferred this section, enacted as 10 USCS § 2172, to Chapter 1609 and redesignated it as 10 USCS § 16302; and substituted the heading for one which read: ''Education loans for certain health professionals who serve in the Selected Reserve''.

1996. Act Feb. 10, 1996, in subsec. (a), redesignated paras. (2)–(4) as paras. (3)–(5), respectively, and added new para. (2); and, in subsec. (d), substituted ''October 1, 1997'' for ''October 1, 1996''.

Act Sept. 23, 1996, in subsec. (d), substituted ''October 1, 1998'' for ''October 1, 1997''.

1997. Act Nov. 18, 1997, in subsec. (d), substituted ''October 1, 1999'' for ''October 1, 1998''.

Other provisions:

Persons to whom applicable. Act Nov. 8, 1985, P. L. 99-145, Title VI, Part F, § 671(b)(2), 99 Stat. 663, provides: ''The authority provided under section 2172 [now § 16302] of title 10, United States Code, as added by subsection (a), shall apply only—

''(A) in the case of a person who is first appointed as a commissioned officer of an Armed Force after September 30, 1985; and

''(B) with respect to service performed after that date.''.

CROSS REFERENCES

This section is referred to in 20 USCS § 1087cc-1.

PART V. SERVICE, SUPPLY, AND PROCUREMENT

HISTORY; ANCILLARY LAWS AND DIRECTIVES

Amendments:

1994. Act Oct. 5, 1994, P. L. 103-337, Div A, Title XVI, Subtitle C, § 1664(a)(1), 108 Stat. 3010 (effective 12/1/94 as provided by § 1691 of such Act, which appears as 10 USCS § 10001 note), added the part heading and analysis.

CHAPTER 1801. ISSUE OF SERVICEABLE MATERIAL TO RESERVE COMPONENTS [No present sections]

HISTORY; ANCILLARY LAWS AND DIRECTIVES

Amendments:

1994. Act Oct. 5, 1994, P. L. 103-337, Div A, Title XVI, Subtitle C, § 1664(a)(1), 108 Stat. 3010 (effective 12/1/94 as provided by § 1691 of such Act, which appears as 10 USCS § 10001 note), added the chapter heading.

CHAPTER 1803. FACILITIES FOR RESERVE COMPONENTS

HISTORY; ANCILLARY LAWS AND DIRECTIVES

Amendments:

1958. Act Aug. 20, 1958, P. L. 85-685, Title VI, § 601(4), 72 Stat. 664, amended the analysis of this chapter by adding item 2233a.

Act Sept. 2, 1958, P. L. 85-861, § 1(42), 72 Stat. 1457, amended the analysis of this chapter by substituting item 2237 for one which read: ''Supervision of construction''.

1982. Act July 12, 1982, P.L. 97-214, § 3(b)(2), (c)(2), 96 Stat. 169, 170 (effective 10/1/82, as provided by § 12(a) of such Act, which appears as 10 USCS § 2801 note), amended the analysis of this chapter by substituting item 2233a for one which read: ''2233a. Limitations''; and by adding item 2239.

1994. Act Oct. 5, 1994, P. L. 103-337, Div A, Title XVI, Subtitle C, § 1664(b)(1), (3), 108 Stat. 3010 (effective 12/1/94 as provided by § 1691 of such Act, which appears as 10 USCS § 10001 note), transferred this chapter, formerly Chapter 133, to the end of Part V of Subtitle E, redesignated it as Chapter 1803 and, in the analysis, redesignated items 2231–2239 as items 18231–18239, respectively.

§ 18231. Purpose

The purpose of this chapter [10 USCS §§ 18231 et seq.] is to provide for—

(1) the acquisition, by purchase, lease, transfer, construction, expansion, rehabilitation, or conversion, of facilities necessary for the proper development, training, operation, and maintenance of the reserve components of the armed forces, including troop housing and messing facilities;

(2) the joint use of those facilities by units of two or more of those reserve components, to the greatest practicable extent for efficiency and economy;

(3) the use of those facilities, in time of war or national emergency, by those units and other units of the armed forces, to the greatest practicable extent for efficiency and economy; and

(4) any other use of those facilities by the United States, in time of war or national emergency, to the greatest practicable extent for efficiency and economy.

(Aug. 10, 1956, ch 1041, § 1, 70A Stat. 120; Aug. 29, 1957, P. L. 85-215, § 1, 71 Stat. 489; Oct. 5, 1994, P. L. 103-337, Div A, Title XVI, Subtitle C, § 1664(b)(2), 108 Stat. 3010.)

HISTORY; ANCILLARY LAWS AND DIRECTIVES

Prior law and revision:

Revised Section	Source (USCS)	Source (Statutes at Large)
2231	50:881.	Sept. 11, 1950, ch. 945, § 2, 64 Stat. 829.

In clause (1), the words "units of" are omitted as surplusage.

In clause (4), the words "United States" are substituted for the words "Federal Government".

Amendments:

1957. Act Aug. 29, 1957, in cl. (1), added ", including troop housing and messing facilities".

1994. Act Oct. 5, 1994 (effective 12/1/94 as provided by § 1691 of such Act, which appears as 10 USCS § 10001 note) transferred Chapter 133, including this section, to Part V of Subtitle E of Title 10, USCS; redesignated such Chapter as Chapter 1803; and redesignated this section, formerly 10 USCS § 2231, as 10 USCS § 18231.

§ 18232. Definitions

In this chapter [10 USCS §§ 18231 et seq.];

(1) The term "State" means any of the States of the United States, the District of Columbia, the Commonwealth of Puerto Rico, and each territory and possession of the United States and includes political subdivisions and military units thereof and tax-supported agencies therein.

(2) The term "facility" includes any (A) interest in land, (B) armory or other structure, and (C) storage or other facility normally needed for the administration and training of any unit of the reserve components of the armed forces.

(3) The term "armory" means a structure that houses one or more units of a reserve component and is used for training and administering those units. It includes a structure that is appurtenant to such a structure and houses equipment used for that training and administration.

(Aug. 10, 1956, ch 1041, § 1, 70A Stat. 121; Sept. 2, 1958, P. L. 85-861, § 1(36), 72 Stat. 1456; July 12, 1982, P.L. 97-214, § 3(d)(1), 96 Stat. 170; April 21, 1987, P. L. 100-26, § 7(k)(2), 101 Stat. 284; Oct. 5, 1994, P. L. 103-337, Div A, Title XVI, Subtitle C, § 1664(b)(2), 108 Stat. 3010.)

HISTORY; ANCILLARY LAWS AND DIRECTIVES

Prior law and revision:

1956 ACT

Revised Section	Source (USCS)	Source (Statutes at Large)
2232	50:886.	Sept. 11, 1950, ch. 945, § 7, 64 Stat. 831.

Clause (1) is substituted for 50:886(b). The words "(2) Puerto Rico; and (3) the District of Columbia" are omitted, since they are specifically included, where applicable, in the revised chapter. The words "together with any improvement thereto" and "of the United States" are omitted as surplusage. 50:886(c) is omitted, since the reserve components of the armed forces are named in section 261 of this title. 50:886(d) is omitted, since its subject matter is covered by other relevant sections of the revised chapter.

1958 ACT

Revised Section	Source (USCS)	Source (Statutes at Large)
2232	50:886.	Aug. 9, 1955, ch. 662, § 1(g), (h), 69 Stat. 594.

The last sentence of 50:886(b) is omitted as surplusage.

Amendments:

1958. Act Sept. 2, 1958 added cl. (3).

1982. Act July 12, 1982 (effective 10/1/82, as provided by § 12(a) of such Act, which appears as 10 USCS § 2801 note), substituted para. (1) for one which read: " 'State' and 'Territory' include political subdivisions and military units thereof and tax-supported agencies therein.".

1987. Act Apr. 21, 1987, in paras. (1)–(3), inserted "The term" and, in paras. (2) and (3), revised the first quoted word in each para. so that the initial letter of such word is lower case.

1994. Act Oct. 5, 1994 (effective 12/1/94 as provided by § 1691 of such Act, which appears as 10 USCS § 10001 note) transferred Chapter 133, including this section, to Part V of Subtitle E of Title 10, USCS; redesignated such Chapter as Chapter 1803; and redesignated this section, formerly 10 USCS § 2232, as 10 USCS § 18232.

§ 18233. Acquisition

(a) Subject to sections 18233a, 18234, 18235, 18236, and 18238 of this title and to subsection (c), the Secretary of Defense may—

(1) acquire by purchase, lease, or transfer, and construct, expand, rehabilitate, or convert and equip, such facilities as he determines to be necessary to carry out the purposes of this chapter [10 USCS §§ 18231 et seq.];

(2) contribute to any State such amounts as he determines to be necessary to expand, rehabilitate, or convert facilities owned by it or by the United States for use jointly by units of two or more reserve components of the armed forces or to acquire or construct facilities for such use;

(3) contribute to any State such amounts as he determines to be necessary

to expand, rehabilitate, or convert facilities owned by it (or to acquire, construct, expand, rehabilitate, or convert additional facilities) made necessary by the conversion, redesignation, or reorganization of units of the Army National Guard of the United States or the Air National Guard of the United States authorized by the Secretary of the military department concerned;

(4) contribute to any State such amounts for the acquisition, construction, expansion, rehabilitation, or conversion by it of additional facilities as he determines to be required by any increase in the strength of the Army National Guard of the United States or the Air National Guard of the United States;

(5) contribute to any State amounts for the acquisition, construction, expansion, rehabilitation, and conversion by such State of such additional facilities as the Secretary determines to be required because of the failure of existing facilities to meet the purposes of this chapter [10 USCS §§ 18231 et seq.]; and

(6) contribute to any State such amounts for the construction, alteration, or rehabilitation of critical portions of facilities as the Secretary determines to be required to meet a change in Department of Defense construction criteria or standards related to the execution of the Federal military mission assigned to the unit using the facility.

(b) Title to property acquired by the United States under subsection (a)(1) vests in the United States. Such property may be transferred to any State incident to the expansion, rehabilitation, or conversion of such property under subsection (a)(2) so long as the transfer of such property does not result in the creation of an enclave owned by a State within a Federal installation.

(c) The Secretary of Defense may delegate any of his authority or functions under this chapter [10 USCS §§ 18231 et seq.] to any department, agency, or officer of the Department of Defense.

(d) The expenses of leasing property under subsection (a)(1) may be paid from appropriations available for the payment of rent.

(e) The Secretary of Defense may procure, or contribute to any State such amounts as the Secretary determines to be necessary to procure, architectural and engineering services and construction design in connection with facilities to be established or developed under this chapter [10 USCS §§ 18231 et seq.] which are not otherwise authorized by law.

(f)(1) Authority provided by law to construct, expand, rehabilitate, convert, or equip any facility under this section includes authority to expend funds for surveys, administration, overhead, planning, and supervision incident to any such activity.

(2) Authority to acquire real property under this section includes authority to make surveys and to acquire interests in land (including temporary interests) by purchase, gift, exchange of Government-owned land, or otherwise.

(Aug. 10, 1956, ch 1041, § 1, 70A Stat. 121; Aug. 20, 1958, P. L. 85-685, Title VI, § 601(1), (2), 72 Stat. 664; Sept. 2, 1958, P. L. 85-861, § 1(37)–(39), 72

Stat. 1456; Nov. 26, 1979, P. L. 96-125, Title VII, § 703, 92 Stat. 947; Dec. 23, 1981, P. L. 97-99, Title VIII, §§ 803, 804, 95 Stat. 1380, 1381; July 12, 1982, P. L. 97-214, § 3(a), (d)(2) in part, (e)(1), 10(a)(2), 96 Stat. 169, 170, 175; Aug. 28, 1984, P. L. 98-407, Title VII, § 703(a), 98 Stat. 1517; Oct. 19, 1984, P. L. 98-525, Title XIV, § 1405(34), 98 Stat. 2624; Dec. 3, 1985, P. L. 99-167, Title VII, § 702(a), 99 Stat. 985; Dec. 5, 1991, P. L. 102-190, Div B, Title XXVIII, Part A, § 2801, 105 Stat. 1537; Oct. 5, 1994, P. L. 103-337, Div A, Title XVI, Subtitle C, § 1664(b)(2), (4), 108 Stat. 3010.)

HISTORY; ANCILLARY LAWS AND DIRECTIVES

Prior law and revision:

1956 ACT

Revised Section	Source (USCS)	Source (Statutes at Large)
2233(a)	50:882.	Sept. 11, 1950, ch. 945,
2233(b)	50:883(c)(1st sentence).	§§ 3, 4(c) (1st sentence),
2233(c)	50:884.	5, 64 Stat. 830, 831.

In subsection (a), the 16th through the 31st words are omitted as executed on July 1, 1955, the end of the 5-year period.

In subsection (a)(2), the words "to the extent required" are omitted as covered by the word "necessary". The words "use jointly by units of two or more of the reserve components of the armed forces" are substituted for the words "joint utilization of such facilities" to reflect 50:886(d).

In subsections (a)(2) and (3), the words "Territory, Puerto Rico, or the District of Columbia" are inserted to reflect 50:886(b).

In subsection (a)(3), the words "to be required" are substituted for the words "to have been made essential".

In subsection (b), the words "real or personal" are omitted as surplusage.

In subsection (c), the words "all or . . . part", "conferred", "imposed", "without relieving himself of the responsibility therefor", "or officers", and "as he may designate from time to time" are omitted as surplusage.

1958 ACT

Revised Section	Source (USCS)	Source (Statutes at Large)
2233(a)	50:882 (less 16th through 36th words and (a)).	Aug. 9, 1955, ch. 662, § 1(b), (d), 69 Stat. 593.
2233(b)	50:883(c) (2d sentence).	
2233(d)	50:882(a) (less last 12 words).	Aug. 3, 1956, ch. 939, § 414 (less last 12 words), 70 Stat. 1018.

In subsections (a)(2), (3), and (4), the words "Territory, Puerto Rico, or the District of Columbia" are inserted to reflect 50:886(c).

In subsection (d), 50:882(a) (1st 28 words) is omitted as covered by section 2233(a)(1) of this title.

Explanatory notes:

Subsequent to enactment of this section, Act Sept. 11, 1950 (cited in the Prior Law and Revision notes) was amended by Act Aug. 9, 1955, ch 662, 69 Stat. 593; Aug. 3, 1956, ch 939, Title IV, § 414, 70 Stat. 1018; Aug. 29, 1957, P. L. 85-215, § 2, 71 Stat. 490. The amendments were later repealed and reenacted in former 10 USCS §§ 2233, 2236–2238 by Act Aug. 20, 1958, P. L. 85-685, Title IV, § 602, 72 Stat. 665, and Act Sept. 2, 1958, P. L. 85-861, §§ 1(37)–(39), 16, 36, 72 Stat. 1456, 1558, 1568.

Amendments:

1958. Act Aug. 20, 1958, in the preliminary matter of subsec. (a), inserted "2233a," and deleted "and after consulting the Committees on Armed Services of the Senate and the House of Representatives," after "section,"; and added subsecs. (e) and (f).

Act Sept. 2, 1958, in subsec. (a), in para. (2), substituted "two or more reserve components" for "two or more of the reserve components", and deleted "and" after the semicolon at the end, redesignated para. (3) as para. (4), and added new para. (3); in subsec. (b), added "by the United States"; and added subsec. (d).

1979. Act Nov. 26, 1979, in subsec. (a), para. (3), deleted "and" following the semicolon, in para. (4), substituted "; and" for a period; and added para. (5).

1981. Act Dec. 23, 1981, in subsec. (a), in para. (2), inserted "or by the United States", in para. (4), deleted "and" following "States;", in para. (5), substituted "; and" for the concluding period, and added para. (6); and in subsec. (b), added the sentence beginning "Such property may be . . .".

1982. Act July 12, 1982 (effective 10/1/82, as provided by § 12(a) of such Act, which appears as 10 USCS § 2801 note), in subsec. (a), in paras. (2)–(4), deleted "or Territory, Puerto Rico, or the District of Columbia" following "any State", substituted para. (5) for one which read: "contribute to any State or Territory, Puerto Rico, or the District of Columbia, such amounts for the acquisition, construction, expansion, rehabilitation, or conversion by the failure of existing facilities to meet the purposes of this chapter. A contribution made for an armory may not be more than 75 percent of the cost of construction of which it is applied; and ", and, in para. (6), deleted "or Territory, Puerto Rico, or the District of Columbia" following "any State; in subsec. (e), substituted "architectural and engineering services and construction design" for "advance planning, construction design, and architectural services"; and substituted subsec. (f) for one which read: "Facilities authorized by subsection (a) shall not be considered 'military public works' under the provisions of the military construction authorization acts that repeal prior authorizations for military public works.".

1984. Act Aug. 28, 1984 (effective 10/1/84, as provided by § 703(b) of such Act, which appears as anote to this section), in subsec. (a)(6), substituted "critical portions of facilities" for "arms storage rooms" and substituted "construction criteria or standards related to the execution of the Federal military mission assigned to the unit using the facility" for "standards related to the safekeeping of arms".

Act Oct, 19, 1984, in subsec. (a), in the introductory matter, substituted "to subsection (c)" for "subsection (c) of this section"; and, in subsec. (b), deleted ''or Territory, Puerto Rico, or the District of Columbia'' following ''State'' wherever appearing.

1985. Act Dec. 3, 1985 substituted subsec. (e) for one which read: ''The Secretary of Defense may procure architectural and engineering services and construction design in connection with facilities to be established or developed under this chapter which are not otherwise authorized by law.''.

1991. Act Dec. 5, 1991, in subsec. (a)(2), inserted ''or to acquire or construct facilities for such use''.

1994. Act Oct. 5, 1994 (effective 12/1/94 as provided by § 1691 of such Act, which appears as 10 USCS § 10001 note) transferred Chapter 133, including this section, to Part V of Subtitle E of Title 10, USCS; redesignated such Chapter as Chapter 1803; and redesignated this section, formerly 10 USCS § 2233, as 10 USCS § 18233

Such Act further (effective as above), in subsec. (a), substituted ''sections 18233a, 18234, 18235, 18236, and 18238'' for ''sections 2233a, 2234, 2235, 2236, and 2238''.

Other provisions:

Obligation of funds before July 1, 1958. Act Sept. 2, 1958, P. L. 85-861, § 16, 72 Stat. 1558, provided that not more than $580,000,000 could be obligated for the purposes of this section before July 1, 1958, but with such limitation not applicable to the expenses for the leasing of property under subsec. (a)(1) of this section.

CROSS REFERENCES

This section is referred to in 10 USCS §§ 18233a–18237, 18239.

§ 18233a. Limitation on certain projects; authority to carry out small projects with operation and maintenance funds

(a)(1) Except as provided in paragraph (2), an expenditure or contribution in an amount in excess of $1,500,000 may not be made under section 18233 of this title for any facility until the Secretary of Defense has notified the Committee on Armed Services and the Committee on Appropriations of the Senate and the Committee on National Security and the Committee on Appropriations of the House of Representatives of the location, nature, and estimated cost of the facility and a period of 21 days has passed after receipt of such notification.

(2) Paragraph (1) does not apply to expenditures or contributions for the following:

(A) Facilities acquired by lease.

(B) A project for a facility that has been authorized by Congress, if the location and purpose of the facility are the same as when authorized and if, based upon bids received—

(i) the scope of work of the project, as approved by Congress, is not proposed to be reduced by more than 25 percent; and

(ii) the current working estimate of the cost of the project does not exceed the amount approved for the project by more than (I) 25 percent, or (II) 200 percent of the amount specified by section 2805(a)(2) of this title as the maximum amount for a minor military construction project, whichever is lesser.

(b) Under such regulations as the Secretary of Defense may prescribe, a project authorized under section 18233(a) of this title that costs $500,000 or less may be carried out with funds available for operations and maintenance.

(Added Aug. 20, 1958, P. L. 85-685, Title VI, § 601(3), 72 Stat. 665; July 27, 1962, P. L. 87-554, Title VII, § 701, 76 Stat. 243; Dec. 27, 1974, P. L. 93-552, Title VII, § 703, 88 Stat. 1770; Oct. 7, 1975, P. L. 94-107, Title VII, § 703, 89 Stat. 569; Nov. 26, 1979, P. L. 96-125, Title VII § 704, 93 Stat. 947; July 12, 1982, P. L. 97-214, § 3(c)(1), 96 Stat 169; Oct. 11, 1983, P. L. 98-115, Title VII, § 702 in part, 97 Stat. 782; Aug. 28, 1984, P. L. 98-407, Title VII, § 702 in part, 98 Stat. 1517; April 21, 1987, P. L. 100-26, § 7(f)(1), 101 Stat. 281; Dec. 4, 1987, P. L. 100-180, Div B, Subdiv 3, Title I, § 2304(a), 101 Stat. 1215; Dec. 5, 1991, P. L. 102-190, Div B, Title XXVIII, Part A, § 2804, 105 Stat. 1537; Oct. 5, 1994, P. L. 103-337, Div A, Title XVI, Subtitle C, § 1664(b)(2), (5), 108 Stat. 3010; Feb. 10, 1996, P. L. 104-106, Div A, Title XV, § 1502(a)(10), 110 Stat. 503.; Sept. 23, 1996, P. L. 104-201, Div B, Title XXVIII, Subtitle A, § 2801(b), (c), 110 Stat. 2787.)

HISTORY; ANCILLARY LAWS AND DIRECTIVES

Amendments:

1962. Act July 27, 1962 designated existing provisions as para. (1) and in para. (1) as so designated, substituted ''until after the expiration of thirty days from the date upon which the Secretary of Defense or his designee notifies the Senate and the House of Representatives of the location, nature, and estimated cost of such facility'' for ''that has not been authorized by a law authorizing appropriations for specific facilities for reserve forces'', and added para. (2).

1974. Act Dec. 27, 1974, in para. (1), substituted ''$100,000'' for ''$50,000''.

1975. Act Oct. 7, 1975, in para. (2), substituted ''$50,000'' for ''$25,000''.

1979. Act Nov. 26, 1979, in para. (1), substituted ''$175,000'' for ''$100,000''.

1982. Act July 12, 1982 (effective 10/1/82, as provided by § 12(a) of such Act, which appears as 10 USCS § 2801 note), substituted this section for one which read:

''§ 2233a. Limitation

''(1) No expenditure or contribution that is more than $175,000 may be made under section 2233 of this title for any facility until after the expiration of thirty days from the date upon which the Secretary of Defense or his designee notifies the Senate and the House of Representatives of the location, nature, and estimated cost of such facility. This requirement does not apply to the following:

''(a) Facilities acquired by lease.

''(b) Facilities acquired, constructed, expanded, rehabilitated, converted, or equipped to restore or replace facilities damaged or destroyed, where the Senate and the House of Representatives have been notified of that action.

"(2) Under such regulations as the Secretary of Defense may prescribe, any project authorized pursuant to section 2233(a) which does not cost more than $50,000 may be accomplished from appropriations available for maintenance and operations.".

1983. Act Oct. 11, 1983 (effective 10/1/83, as provided by § 702 of such Act), in subsec. (a)(1), substituted "$400,000 for "$200,000".

1984. Act Aug 28, 1984 (effective 10/1/84, as provided by § 702 of such Act), in subsec. (b), substituted "$100,000" for "$50,000".

1987. Act Apr. 21, 1987 purported to amend subsec. (a)(2)(B)(ii)(II) of this section by substituting "specified by section 2805(a)(2) of this title" for "specified by law"; however, there being no subcl. (II), the amendment was executed to subsec. (a)(2)(B)(ii) in order to effectuate the probable intention of Congress.

Act Dec. 4, 1987 (applicable as provided by § 2304(b) of such Act, which appears as a note to this section), in subsec. (b), substituted "$200,000" for "$100,000".

1991. Act Dec. 5, 1991, in subsec. (b), substituted "$300,000" for "$200,000".

1994. Act Oct. 5, 1994 (effective 12/1/94 as provided by § 1691 of such Act, which appears as 10 USCS § 10001 note) transferred Chapter 133, including this section, to Part V of Subtitle E of Title 10, USCS; redesignated such Chapter as Chapter 1803; and redesignated this section, formerly 10 USCS § 2233a, as 10 USCS § 18233a.

Such Act further (effective as above), in subsec. (a), substituted "section 18233" for "section 2233"; and, in subsec. (b), substituted "section 18233(a)" for "section 2233(a)".

1996. Act Feb. 10, 1996, in subsec. (a)(1), substituted "the Committee on Armed Services and the Committee on Appropriations of the Senate and the Committee on National Security and the Committee on Appropriations of the" for "the Committees on Armed Services and on Appropriations of the Senate and".

Act Sept. 23, 1996, in subsec. (a)(1), substituted "$1,500,000" for "$400,000"; and, in subsec. (b), substituted "$500,000" for "$300,000".

Other provisions:

Application of Dec. 4, 1987 amendment. Act Dec. 4, 1987, P. L. 100-180, Div B, Subdiv 3, Title I, § 2304(b), 101 Stat. 1215, provides: "The amendment made by subsection (a) [amending subsec. (b) of this section] shall apply to projects authorized under section 2233(a) [now § 18233(a)] of title 10, United States Code, for which contracts are entered into on or after the date of the enactment of this Act.".

CROSS REFERENCES

This section is referred to in 10 USCS § 18233.

INTERPRETIVE NOTES AND DECISIONS

Trial judge erroneously held, in inverse condemnation suit, that Air Force practice of acquiring successive one-year leaseholds on plaintiff's land adjoining air base amounted to compensable taking of fee or perpetual easement, since Air Force lacks authority, absent Congressional sanction in annual Military Construction Appropriation Act, to take fee or perpetual easement exceeding value limitation fixed in 10 USCS § 2233a(1) (now § 18233a(1)); court would thwart Congressional intent by finding that permanent or indefinite interest had been taken despite absence of Congressional consent. Southern California Financial Corp. v United States (1980) 225 Ct Cl 104, 634 F2d 521, cert den (1981) 451 US 937, 68 L Ed 2d 324, 101 S Ct 2016.

§ 18234. Location and use

No expenditures or contribution may be made for a facility under section 18233 of this title, unless the Secretary of Defense determines that—

(1) the number of units of the reserve components of the armed forces located or to be located in the area within which the facility is to be provided is not and will not be larger than the number that can reasonably be expected to be maintained at authorized strength, considering the number of persons living in the area who are qualified for membership in those reserve units; and

(2) the plan under which the facility is to be provided makes provision for the greatest practicable use of the facility jointly by units of two or more of those components.

(Aug. 10, 1956, ch 1041, § 1, 70A Stat. 121; Oct. 5, 1994, P. L. 103-337, Div A, Title XVI, Subtitle C, § 1664(b)(2), (6), 108 Stat. 3010.)

HISTORY; ANCILLARY LAWS AND DIRECTIVES

Prior law and revision:

Revised Section	Source (USCS)	Source (Statutes at Large)
2234	50:883(a).	Sept. 11, ch. 945, § 4(a), 64 Stat. 830.

The word ''community'' is omitted as covered by the word ''area''. The word ''program'' is omitted as covered by the word ''plan''. The words ''use . . . jointly by units of two or more of those components'' are substituted for the words ''joint utilization'' to reflect 50:886(d). The words ''is not and will not be larger than'' are substituted for the words ''does not exceed''. The word ''considering'' is substituted for the words ''taking into account''.

Amendments:

1994. Act Oct. 5, 1994 (effective 12/1/94 as provided by § 1691 of such Act, which appears as 10 USCS § 10001 note) transferred Chapter 133, including this section, to Part V of Subtitle E of Title 10, USCS; redesignated such Chapter as Chapter 1803; and redesignated this section, formerly 10 USCS § 2234, as 10 USCS § 18234.

Such Act further (effective as above) substituted ''section 18233'' for ''section 2233''.

CROSS REFERENCES

Authorized strength—Definition, 10 USCS § 101.

Authorized strength—Ready Reserve, 10 USCS §§ 10141 et seq.

Authorized strength—Naval Reserve and Marine Corps Reserve, 10 USCS § 12001.

Authorized strength—Army and Air Force Reserves, 10 USCS § 12002.

Authorized strength—Coast Guard Reserve, 14 USCS § 702.
This section is referred to in 20 USCS § 18233.

§ 18235. Administration; other use permitted by Secretary

(a) The Secretary of Defense, after consulting the Committee on Armed Services of the Senate and the Committee on National Security of the House of Representatives on matters of policy, may—

(1) administer, operate, maintain, and equip facilities constructed, expanded, rehabilitated, or converted under section 18233 of this title or otherwise acquired and used for the purposes of this chapter [10 USCS §§ 18231 et seq.];

(2) permit persons or organizations other than members and units of the armed forces to use those facilities under such leases or other agreements as he considers appropriate; and

(3) cover the payments received under those leases or agreements into the Treasury to the credit of the appropriation from which the cost of maintaining the facility, including its utilities and services, is paid.

(b) The Secretary may not permit any use or disposition to be made of a facility covered by subsection (a) that would interfere with its use—

(1) for administering and training the reserve components of the armed forces; or

(2) in time of war or national emergency, by other units of the armed forces or by the United States for any other purpose.

(Aug. 10, 1956, ch 1041, § 1, 70A Stat. 122; Oct. 5, 1994, P. L. 103-337, Div A, Title XVI, Subtitle C, § 1664(b)(2), (7), 108 Stat. 3010; Feb. 10, 1996, P. L. 104-106, Div A, Title XV, § 1502(a)(2), 110 Stat. 502.)

HISTORY; ANCILLARY LAWS AND DIRECTIVES

Prior law and revision:

Revised Section	Source (USCS)	Source (Statutes at Large)
2235(a)	50:883(c) (less 1st sentence, and less last 70 words of last sentence).	Sept. 11, 1950, ch. 945, § 4(c) (less 1st sentence), 64 Stat. 830.
2235(b)	50:883(c) (last 70 words of last sentence).	

In subsection (a), the words "from time to time" and "or appropriations" are omitted as surplusage.

In subsection (b), the words "United States" are substituted for the words "Federal Government". The words "units of" are omitted as surplusage. The words "may not" are substituted for the words "shall at no time".

Amendments:

1994. Act Oct. 5, 1994 (effective 12/1/94 as provided by § 1691 of such

Act, which appears as 10 USCS § 10001 note) transferred Chapter 133, including this section, to Part V of Subtitle E of Title 10, USCS; redesignated such Chapter as Chapter 1803; and redesignated this section, formerly 10 USCS § 2235, as 10 USCS § 18235.

Such Act further (effective as above), in subsec. (a)(1), substituted ''section 18233'' for ''section 2233(a)(1)''.

1996. Act Feb. 10, 1996, in subsec. (a), substituted ''Committee on Armed Services of the Senate and the Committee on National Security of the House of Representatives'' for ''Committees on Armed Services of the Senate and the House of Representatives''.

CROSS REFERENCES

This section is referred to in 10 USCS § 18233.

§ 18236. Contributions to States; other use permitted by States

(a) Contributions under section 18233 of this title are subject to such terms as the Secretary of Defense, after consulting the Committee on Armed Services of the Senate and the Committee on National Security of the House of Representatives, considers necessary for the purposes of this chapter [10 USCS §§ 18231 et seq.]. Except as otherwise agreed when the contribution is made, a facility provided by a contribution under paragraph (3) or (4) of section 18233(a) of this title may be used jointly by units of two or more reserve components of the armed forces only to the extent that the State considers practicable.

(b) A contribution made for an armory under paragraph (4) or (5) of section 18233(a) of this title may not exceed the sum of—

(1) 100 percent of the cost of architectural, engineering and design services (including advance architectural, engineering and design services under section 18233(e) of this title); and

(2) a percentage of the cost of construction (exclusive of the cost of architectural, engineering and design services) calculated so that upon completion of construction the total contribution (including the contribution for architectural, engineering and design services) equals 75 percent of the total cost of construction (including the cost of architectural, engineering and design services).

For the purpose of computing the cost of construction under this subsection, the amount contributed by a State may not include the cost or market value of any real property that it has contributed.

(c) If a State acquires, constructs, expands, rehabilitates, or converts a facility with amounts contributed under section 18233 of this title, it may—

(1) permit persons or organizations other than members and units of the armed forces to use the facility under such leases or other agreements as it considers appropriate; and

(2) apply amounts received under those leases or agreements to the cost of maintaining the facility.

(d) Except as otherwise agreed when the contribution is made, and except as the agreement is later changed, a State, may not permit any use or disposition of the facility that would interfere with its use—

(1) for administering and training the reserve components of the armed forces; or

(2) in time of war or national emergency, by other units of the armed forces or by the United States for any other purpose.

(Aug. 10, 1956, ch 1041, § 1, 70A Stat. 122; Sept. 2, 1958, P. L. 85-861, § 1(40), 72 Stat. 1456; July 12, 1982, P. L. 97-214, § 3(d)(2), (3), (e)(2), 96 Stat. 170; Dec. 3, 1985, P. L. 99-167, Title VII, § 702(b), 99 Stat. 985; Nov. 14, 1986, P. L. 99-661, Div A, Title XIII, Part E, § 1343(a)(11), 100 Stat. 3993; Oct. 5, 1994, P. L. 103-337, Div A, Title XVI, Subtitle C, § 1664(b)(2), (8), 108 Stat. 3010; Feb. 10, 1996, P. L. 104-106, Div A, Title XV, §§ 1501(b)(36), 1502(a)(2), 110 Stat. 498, 502.)

HISTORY; ANCILLARY LAWS AND DIRECTIVES

Prior law and revision:

1956 ACT

Revised Section	Source (USCS)	Source (Statutes at Large)
2236(a)	50:883(d) (1st sentence).	Sept. 11, 1950, ch. 945, § 4(d), (e), 64 Stat. 830.
2236(b)	50:883(d) (less 1st sentence).	
2236(c)	50:883(e) (less last 87 words).	
2236(d)	50:883(e) (last 87 words).	

Appropriate references to the Territories, Puerto Rico, and the District of Columbia are inserted throughout the revised section to reflect 50:886(b).

In subsection (a), the words "and conditions" are omitted as covered by the word "terms". The words "considers necessary for" are substituted for the words "shall deem necessary to accomplish". The words "used jointly by units of two or more reserve components of the armed forces" are substituted for the words "joint utilization", to reflect 50:886(d).

In subsection (b), the words "the construction to which it is to be applied" are substituted for the words "the additional or improved facilities to be constructed", since, under section 2233 of this title, contributions may be made for other purposes as well as additions and improvements. The words "may not include" are substituted for the words "shall be exclusive of".

In subsection (c)(1), the words "from time to time" are omitted as surplusage.

In subsection (c)(2), the words "defray in whole or in part" are omitted as surplusage.

In subsection (d), the words "except as the agreement is later changed" are substituted for the words "by subsequent modifications of the agreement." The words "units of" and "at no time" are omitted as surplusage. The words "United States" are substituted for the words "Federal Government".

1958 Act

Revised Section	Source (USCS)	Source (Statutes at Large)
2236(a)	50:883(d) (1st sentence).	Aug. 9, 1955, ch. 662,
2236(b)	50:883(d) (less 1st sentence).	§ 1(e), 69 Stat. 593.

In subsection (a), the words "may be used jointly" are substituted for the words "shall be subject to joint utilization". The words "and conditions" are omitted as surplusage.

Amendments:

1958. Act Sept. 2, 1958, in subsec. (a), added "or (4)"; and, in subsec. (b), substituted "A" for "No", substituted "an armory" for "a facility", substituted "(4)" for "(3)", and deleted "to be " before "applied".

1982. Act July 12, 1982 (effective 10/1/82, as provided by § 12(a) of such Act, which appears as 10 USCS § 2801 note), in subsec. (a), deleted "or Territory, Puerto Rico, or the District of Columbia, whichever is concerned," following "the State"; in subsec. (b), inserted "or (5)", and deleted "or Territory, Puerto Rico or the District of Columbia, whichever is concerned," following "the State"; and, in subsecs. (c) and (d), in the introductory matter, deleted "or Territory, Puerto Rico, or the District of Columbia" following "a State".

1985. Act Dec. 3, 1985 substituted subsec. (b) for one which read: "A contribution made for an armory under section 2233(a)(4) or (5) of this title may not be more than 75 percent of the cost of the construction to which it is applied. For the purpose of computing the cost of construction under this subsection, the amount contributed by the State may not include the cost or market value of any real property that it has contributed.".

1986. Act Nov. 14, 1986, in subsec. (b), in the concluding matter, deleted ", territory, the Commonwealth of Puerto Rico, or the District of Columbia, as the case may be," following "State".

1994. Act Oct. 5, 1994 (effective 12/1/94 as provided by § 1691 of such Act, which appears as 10 USCS § 10001 note) transferred Chapter 133, including this section, to Part V of Subtitle E of Title 10, USCS; redesignated such Chapter as Chapter 1803; and redesignated this section, formerly 10 USCS § 2236, as 10 USCS § 18236.

Such Act further (effective as above), in subsec. (a), substituted "section 18233" for "section 2233" and substituted "paragraph (3) or (4) of section 18233(a)" for "section 2233(a)(3) or (4)"; in subsec. (b), in the introductory matter, substituted "paragraph (4) or (5) of section 18233(a)" for "clause (4) or (5) of section 2233(a)"; and, in subsec. (c), substituted "section 18233" for "section 2233".

Such Act further (effective as above) purported to amend subsec. (b)(2) by substituting "section 18233(e)" for "section 2233(e)"; however, the amendment could not be executed because "section 2233(e)" did not appear in such subsection.

1996. Act Feb. 10, 1996, in subsec. (a), substituted "Committee on Armed

Services of the Senate and the Committee on National Security of the House of Representatives'' for ''Committees on Armed Services of the Senate and the House of Representatives''.

Such Act further (effective as if included in Act Oct. 5, 1994, P. L. 103-337, as enacted on Oct. 5, 1994, as provided by § 1501(f)(3) of Act Feb. 10, 1996, which appears as 10 USCS § 113 note), in subsec. (b)(1), substituted ''section 18233(e)'' for ''section 2233(e)''.

CROSS REFERENCES

This section is referred to in 10 USCS § 18233.

§ 18237. Supervision of construction: compliance with State law

(a) Any construction, expansion, rehabilitation, or conversion under section 18233(a)(1) of this title may be performed under the supervision of the Chief of Engineers of the Army or the head of such office or agency in the Department of the Navy as the Secretary of the Navy may designate.

(b) The construction, expansion, rehabilitation, or conversion of facilities in a State under paragraph (2), (3), (4), (5), or (6) of section 18233(a) of this title shall be done according to the laws of that jurisdiction and under the supervision of its officials, subject to the inspection and approval of the Secretary of Defense.

(Aug. 10, 1956, ch 1041, § 1, 70A Stat. 123; Sept. 2, 1958, P. L. 85-861, § 1(41), 72 Stat. 1457; Nov. 2, 1966, P. L. 89-718, § 19, 80 Stat. 1118; July 12, 1982, P. L. 97-214, § 3(d)(2), 96 Stat. 170; Oct. 5, 1994, P. L. 103-337, Div A, Title XVI, Subtitle C, § 1664(b)(2), (9), Title XXVIII, Subtitle E, § 2852, 108 Stat. 3010, 3011, 3072; Feb. 10, 1996, P. L. 104-106, Div A, Title XV, § 1501(b)(37), 110 Stat. 498.)

HISTORY; ANCILLARY LAWS AND DIRECTIVES

Prior law and revision:

1956 ACT

Revised Section	Source (USCS)	Source (Statutes at Large)
2237	50:885.	Sept. 11, 1950, ch. 945, § 6, 64 Stat. 831.

The words ''of facilities'' are omitted as surplusage. The words ''Chief of Engineers'' are substituted for the words ''Chief, Corps of Engineers'' to conform to section 3036(a)(1) of this title. The words ''of the Army'' and ''of the Navy'' are inserted for clarity.

1958 ACT

Revised Section	Source (USCS)	Source (Statutes at Large)
2237(a)	50:885(a).	Aug. 9, 1955, ch. 662,

Revised Section	Source (USCS)	Source (Statutes at Large)
2237(b)	50:885 (less (a)).	§ 1(f), 69 Stat. 594.

In subsection (b), the words "Territory, Puerto Rico, or the District of Columbia" are inserted to reflect 50:886(c).

Amendments:

1958. Act Sept. 2, 1958, in the section catchline, inserted ": compliance with State law"; designated existing provisions as subsec. (a), and therein substituted "under any provision of this chapter except section 2233(a)(2), (3), and (4) of this title" for "under this chapter"; and added subsec. (b).

1966. Act Nov. 2, 1966, in subsec. (a), substituted "the head of such office or agency in the Department of the Navy as the Secretary of the Navy may designate" for "the Chief of the Bureau of Yards and Docks of the Navy".

1982. Act July 12, 1982 (effective 10/1/82, as provided by § 12(a) of such Act, which appears as 10 USCS § 2801 note), in subsec. (b), deleted "or Territory, Puerto Rico, or the District of Columbia" following "a State".

1994. Act Oct. 5, 1994 (effective 12/1/94 as provided by § 1691 of such Act, which appears as 10 USCS § 10001 note) transferred Chapter 133, including this section, to Part V of Subtitle E of Title 10, USCS; redesignated such Chapter as Chapter 1803; and redesignated this section, formerly 10 USCS § 2237, as 10 USCS § 18237.

Such Act further (effective as above), in subsec. (a), substituted "paragraph (2), (3), or (4) of section 18233(a)" for "section 2233(a)(2), (3), and (4)"; and, in subsec. (b), substituted "paragraph (2), (3), or (4) of section 18233(a)" for "section 2233(a)(2), (3), or (4)".

Such Act further purported to amend subsec. (a) of 10 USCS § 2237 by striking out "under any provision" and all that follows through "and (4)" and inserting in lieu thereof "under section 2233(a)(1)"; however, because of prior amendments, the amendment was executed to subsec. (a) of this section (formerly 10 USCS § 2237) by substituting "under section 2233(a)(1)" for "under any provision of this chapter except paragraph (2), (3), or (4) of section 18233(a)" in order to effectuate the probable intent of Congress.

Such Act further purported to amend subsec. (b) of 10 USCS § 2237 by striking out "section 2233(a)(2), (3), or (4)" and inserting in lieu thereof "paragraph (2), (3), (4), (5), or (6) of section 2233(a)"; however, because of prior amendments, this amendment was executed to subsec. (b) of this section (formerly 10 USCS § 2237) by substituting "paragraph (2), (3), (4), (5), or (6) of section 2233(a)" for "paragraph (2), (3), or (4) of section 18233(a)" in order to effectuate the probable intent of Congress.

1996. Act Feb. 10, 1996 (effective as if included in Act Oct. 5, 1994, P. L. 103-337, as enacted on Oct. 5, 1994, as provided by § 1501(f)(3) of Act Feb. 10, 1996, which appears as 10 USCS § 113 note), in subsec. (a), substituted "section 18233(a)(1)" for "section 2233(a)(1)"; and, in subsec. (b), substituted "section 18233(a)" for "section 2233(a)".

§ 18238. Army National Guard of United States; Air National Guard of United States: limitation on relocation of units

A unit of the Army National Guard of the United States or the Air National

Guard of the United States may not be relocated or withdrawn under this chapter [10 USCS §§ 18231 et seq.] without the consent of the governor of the State or, in the case of the District of Columbia, the commanding general of the National Guard of the District of Columbia.

(Aug. 10, 1956, ch 1041, § 1, 70A Stat. 123; Sept. 2, 1958, P. L. 85-861, § 1(43), 72 Stat. 1457; July 12, 1982, P. L. 97-214, § 3(d)(4), 96 Stat. 170; Oct. 5, 1994, P. L. 103-337, Div A, Title XVI, Subtitle C, § 1664(b)(2), 108 Stat. 3010.)

HISTORY; ANCILLARY LAWS AND DIRECTIVES

Prior law and revision:

1956 ACT

Revised Section	Source (USCS)	Source (Statutes at Large)
2238	50:883(b).	Sept. 11, 1950, ch. 945, § 4(b), 64 Stat. 830.

The words ''from any community or area'' are omitted as surplusage. The word ''relocated'' is substituted for the words ''location . . . be changed''. The words ''Territory, or Puerto Rico, or the commanding general of the National Guard of the District of Columbia'' are inserted to reflect 50:886(b), since the source statute applied to the District of Columbia and there is no ''governor'' of the District of Columbia. The words ''as the case may be'' are substituted for the words ''within which such unit is situated''. The words ''with regard to such withdrawal or change of location'' are omitted as surplusage.

1958 ACT

Revised Section	Source (USCS)	Source (Statutes at Large)
2238	50:883(b).	Aug. 9, 1955, ch. 662, § 1(c), 69 Stat. 593.

The words ''shall have been consulted'' and ''such withdrawal or change of location'' are omitted as surplusage.

Amendments:

1958. Act Sept. 2, 1958 substituted the text of this section for text which read: ''No unit of the Army National Guard of the United States or the Air National Guard of the United States may be relocated or withdrawn under this chapter until the governor of the State or Territory, or Puerto Rico, or the commanding general of the National Guard of the District of Columbia, as the case may be, has been consulted.''.

1982. Act July 12, 1982 (effective 10/1/82, as provided by § 12(a) of such Act, which appears as 10 USCS § 2801 note), substituted ''or, in the case of the District of Columbia, the commanding general of the National Guard of the District of Columbia.'' for ''or Territory, or Puerto Rico, or the commanding general of the National Guard of the District of Columbia, as the case may be.''.

1994. Act Oct. 5, 1994 (effective 12/1/94 as provided by § 1691 of such Act, which appears as 10 USCS § 10001 note) transferred Chapter 133, including this section, to Part V of Subtitle E of Title 10, USCS; redesignated such Chapter as Chapter 1803; and redesignated this section, formerly 10 USCS § 2238, as 10 USCS § 18238.

CROSS REFERENCES

This section is referred to in 10 USCS § 18233.

§ 18239. Waiver of certain restrictions

(a) The Secretary of Defense and the Secretary of each military department may make expenditures and contributions under section 18233 of this title without regard to section 3324(a) and (b) of title 31.

(b) Authority provided by law to place permanent or temporary improvements on land under section 18233 of this title may be exercised on land not owned by the United States—

(1) before title to the land on which the improvement is located (or is to be located) is approved under section 355 of the Revised Statutes (40 U.S.C. 255); and

(2) even though the land will be held in other than a fee simple interest in a case in which the Secretary of the military department concerned determines that the interest to be acquired in the land is sufficient for the purposes of the project.

(Added July 12, 1982, P.L. 97-214, § 3(b)(1), 96 Stat. 169; Oct. 12, 1982, P. L. 97-295, § 1(23), 96 Stat. 1290; Oct. 15, 1982, P. L. 97-321, Title VIII, § 805(a)(2), 96 Stat. 1573; Oct. 5, 1994, P. L. 103-337, Div A, Title XVI, Subtitle C, § 1664(b)(2), (10), 108 Stat. 3010, 3011.)

HISTORY; ANCILLARY LAWS AND DIRECTIVES

Effective date of section:

This section became effective Oct. 1, 1982, as provided by Act July 12, 1982, P. L. 97-214, § 12(a), 96 Stat. 176, which appears as 10 USCS § 2801 note.

Amendments:

1982. Act Oct. 12, 1982 substituted ''section 3324(a) and (b) of title 31'' for ''section 3648 of the Revised Statutes (31 U.S.C. 529)''.

Act Oct. 15, 1982 substituted subsec. (b) for one which read: ''Authority provided by law to place permanent or temporary improvements on lands under section 2233 of this title may be exercised (1) before title to the land on which the improvement is located (or is to be located) is approved under section 355 of the Revised Statutes (40 U.S.C. 255), and (2) even though the land is held temporarily.''.

1994. Act Oct. 5, 1994 (effective 12/1/94 as provided by § 1691 of such Act, which appears as 10 USCS § 10001 note) transferred Chapter 133, including this section, to Part V of Subtitle E of Title 10, USCS; redesignated such Chapter as Chapter 1803; and redesignated this section, formerly 10 USCS § 2239, as 10 USCS § 18239.

Such Act further (effective as above) substituted ''section 18233'' for ''section 2233'' in two places.

CHAPTER 1805. MISCELLANEOUS PROVISIONS

HISTORY; ANCILLARY LAWS AND DIRECTIVES

1994. Act Oct. 5, 1994, P. L. 103-337, Div A, Title XVI, Subtitle C, § 1664(c)(1), 108 Stat. 3011 (effective 12/1/94 as provided by § 1691 of such Act, which appears as 10 USCS § 10001 note), added the chapter heading and analysis.

§ 18501. Reserve components: personnel and logistic support by military departments

The Secretary concerned is responsible for providing the personnel, equipment, facilities, and other general logistic support necessary to enable units and Reserves in the Ready Reserve of the reserve components under his jurisdiction to satisfy the training requirements and mobilization readiness requirements for those units and Reserves as recommended by the Secretary concerned and by the Chairman of the Joint Chiefs of Staff and approved by the Secretary of Defense, and as recommended by the Commandant of the Coast Guard and approved by the Secretary of Transportation when the Coast Guard is not operated as a service of the Navy.
(Added Oct. 5, 1994, P. L. 103-337, Div A, Title XVI, Subtitle C, § 1664(c)(1), 108 Stat. 3011.)

HISTORY; ANCILLARY LAWS AND DIRECTIVES

Effective date of section:

This section took effect on Dec. 1, 1994, pursuant to Act Oct. 5, 1994, P. L. 103-337, Div A, Title XVI, Subtitle F, § 1691, 108 Stat. 3026, which appears as 10 USCS 10001 note.

§ 18502. Reserve components: supplies, services, and facilities

(a) The Secretary concerned shall make available to the reserve components under his jurisdiction the supplies, services, and facilities of the armed forces under his jurisdiction that he considers necessary to support and develop those components.

(b) Whenever he finds it to be in the best interest of the United States, the Secretary concerned may issue supplies of the armed forces under his jurisdiction to the reserve components under his jurisdiction, without charge to the appropriations for those components for the cost or value of the supplies or for any related expense.

(c) Whenever he finds it to be in the best interest of the United States, the Secretary of the Army or the Secretary of the Air Force may issue to the Army

National Guard or the Air National Guard, as the case may be, supplies of the armed forces under his jurisdiction that are in addition to supplies issued to that National Guard under section 702 of title 32 or charged against its appropriations under section 106 or 107 of title 32, without charge to the appropriations for those components for the cost or value of the supplies or for any related expense.

(d) Supplies issued under subsection (b) or (c) may be repossessed or redistributed as prescribed by the Secretary concerned.

(Added Oct. 5, 1994, P. L. 103-337, Div A, Title XVI, Subtitle C, § 1664(c)(1), 108 Stat. 3012.)

HISTORY; ANCILLARY LAWS AND DIRECTIVES

Effective date of section:

This section took effect on Dec. 1, 1994, pursuant to Act Oct. 5, 1994, P. L. 103-337, Div A, Title XVI, Subtitle F, § 1691, 108 Stat. 3026, which appears as 10 USCS 10001 note.

INDEX

B

I

K

L

O

P

PUBLIC HEALTH SERVICE —Cont'd
Retirement.
Members on retired lists or receiving retainer pay, amount and computation of pay, 10 § 564 note.
Rules and regulations.
Fellowships, scholarships, or grants, acceptance by commissioned officers, 10 § 2603 note.
Scholarship program of National Health Service Corps.
Regulations for, 10 § 2603 note.
Warrant officers, pay and allowances, members on retired lists or receiving retainer pay, amount and computation of retired, retirement, retainer, or equivalent pay, 10 § 564 note.
Widows of retired officers, special annuity for, in lieu of VA pension, 10 § 1448 note.

PUBLIC LANDS.
Armed forces,
Appropriations available to Department of Defense for land acquisition, 10 § 138 note.
Depots.
Air Force and Air Force Department, acquisition of depots, 10 § 9773.
Armed forces, depot maintenance workload competitions, 10 § 2466.
Defense Department.
Appropriations available for land acquisition, 10 § 138 note.
Depots.
Air Force and Air Force Department, acquisition of depots, 10 § 9773.

PUBLIC OFFICERS AND EMPLOYEES.
Citizens and citizenship.
Defense Department, employment of noncitizens, 10 § 1584 note.

PUBLIC PROPERTY.
Use by armed forces, 10 § 4779.

PUERTO RICO.
Armed Forces.
Access of recruiting personnel to secondary educational institutions, release of data, etc., 10 § 503 note.
Procurement, restriction or contracting out commercial and industrial type function, 10 § 2304 note.
Education.
Secondary educational institutions, access of Armed Forces recruiting personnel to, release of data, etc., 10 § 503 note.

PUNITIVE ARTICLES.
Military justice code, 10 § 877 et seq.

Q

QUARTERMASTER.
Armed Forces.
See ARMED FORCES.

QUARTERMASTER GENERAL.
Armed forces.
Abolition, transfer of functions to Secretary of Army, 10 § 3036 note.

QUORUM.
Armed Forces.
Commission on Assignment of Women in Armed Forces, 10 § 113.
Commission on Roles and Missions, 10 § 111 note.

R

RACE.
Defense Department, biennial report on racial and ethnic issues, 10 § 451.

RADIO AND TELEVISION.
Navy.
Acquisition of land for radio stations, Secretary of Navy, 10 § 7223.
Secretary of Navy, 10 § 7223.
Secretary of Navy, 10 § 7223.

RAILROADS.
Federal Possession and Control Act (railroads in war), 10 § 4742.

RANK.
Air Force and Air Force Department.
See AIR FORCE AND AIR FORCE DEPARTMENT.
Definitions, 10 § 101.
Joint chiefs of staff, 10 § 152.
Navy and Navy Department.
See NAVY AND NAVY DEPARTMENT.

RAPE.
Military Justice Code, 10 § 920.

RATE OF EXCHANGE.
Armed forces, fluctuations in exchange rates of foreign countries, 10 § 2779.

RATES AND CHARGES.
Navy and Navy Department, payment or reimbursement, 10 § 7523.

RATINGS.
Air Force and Air Force Department, aeronautical rating as pilot, 10 § 2003.
Marine Corps ratings, authority to establish, 10 § 6013.
Navy and Navy Department, administration, 10 § 6013.

W